The Government and Politics of the European Union

Sixth Edition

Neill Nugent

First published 2006 by
PALGRAVE MACMILLAN
Houndmills, Basingstoke, Hampshire RG21 2XS and
175 Fifth Avenue, New York, N.Y. 10010
Companies and representatives throughout the world

PALGRAVE MACMILLAN is the global academic imprint of the Palgrave Macmillan division of St. Martin's Press, LLC and of Palgrave Macmillan Ltd. Macmillan® is a registered trademark in the United States, United Kingdom and other countries. Palgrave is a registered trademark in the European Union and other countries.

ISBN-13: 978–0–230–00001–5   hardback
ISBN-10: 0–230–00001–0   hardback
ISBN-13: 978–0–230–00002–5   paperback
ISBN-10: 0–230–00002–9   paperback

This book is printed on paper suitable for recycling and made from fully managed and sustained forest sources. Logging, pulping and manufacturing processes are expected to conform to the environmental regulations of the country of origin.

A catalogue record for this book is available from the British Library.

10   9   8   7   6   5   4   3   2
15   14   13   12   11   10   09   08   07

Printed and bound in China

THE EUROPEAN UNION SERIES

General Editors: Neill Nugent, William E. Paterson

The European Union series provides an authoritative library on the European Union, ranging from general introductory texts to definitive assessments of key institutions and actors, issues, policies and policy processes, and the role of member states.

Books in the series are written by leading scholars in their fields and reflect the most up-to-date research and debate. Particular attention is paid to accessibility and clear presentation for a wide audience of students, practitioners, and interested general readers.

The series editors are **Neill Nugent,** Professor of Politics and Jean Monnet Professor of European Integration, Manchester Metropolitan University, and **William E. Paterson,** Founding Director of the Institute of German Studies, University of Birmingham and Chairman of the German British Forum. Their co-editor until his death in July 1999, **Vincent Wright,** was a Fellow of Nuffield College, Oxford University.

Feedback on the series and book proposals are always welcome and should be sent to Steven Kennedy, Palgrave Macmillan, Houndmills, Basingstoke, Hampshire RG21 6XS, UK, or by e-mail to s.kennedy@palgrave.com

---

General textbooks

Published

Desmond Dinan **Encyclopedia of the European Union** [Rights: Europe only]

Desmond Dinan **Europe Recast: A History of European Union** [Rights: Europe only]

Desmond Dinan **Ever Closer Union: An Introduction to European Integration** (3rd edn) [Rights: Europe only]

Simon Hix **The Political System of the European Union (2nd edn)**

Paul Magnette **What is the European Union? Nature and Prospects**

John McCormick **Understanding the European Union: A Concise Introduction** (3rd edn)

Brent F. Nelsen and Alexander Stubb **The European Union: Readings on the Theory and Practice of European Integration** (3rd edn) [Rights: Europe only]

Neill Nugent (ed.) **European Union Enlargement**

Neill Nugent **The Government and Politics of the European Union (6th edn)** [Rights: World excluding USA and dependencies and Canada]

John Peterson and Elizabeth Bomberg **Decision-Making in the European Union**

Ben Rosamond **Theories of European Integration**

Forthcoming

Laurie Buonanno and Neill Nugent **Policies and Policy Processes of the European Union**

Mette Eilstrup Sangiovanni (ed.) **Debates on European Integration: A Reader**

Philippa Sherrington **Understanding European Union Governance**

Also planned

The Political Economy of the European Union

Series Standing Order (outside North America only)
ISBN 0–333–71695–7 hardcover
ISBN 0–333–69352–3 paperback
Full details from www.palgrave.com

Visit Palgrave Macmillan's
EU Resource area at
www.palgrave.com/politics/eu/

Summary of Contents

Contents

PART 4   POLICIES AND POLICY PROCESSES OF THE EUROPEAN UNION

List of Tables, Figures and Documents

Tables

Figures

Documents

Preface to the Sixth Edition

Many major developments have occurred in the European Union since the fifth edition of this book was completed in July 2002. Two of these developments have been especially important. First, in May 2004 the EU increased in size from fifteen member states to twenty-five. With this historic enlargement the EU was no longer a West European organisation but rather became a Europe-wide organisation. Second, in June 2004 national leaders reached agreement on the contents of the long discussed and exhaustively negotiated Constitutional Treaty, but then in 2005 saw the fruits of their labours rejected by voters in France and the Netherlands. The 'story' and significance of these two developments is taken up in this latest edition of *The Government and Politics of the European Union*, with new chapters on the 2004 enlargement and the Constitutional Treaty.

These two major developments have, however, been but the most obvious manifestations of a European integration process that has remained in constant evolution. This evolution is taken up throughout the book. As has been the case with previous new editions, no chapters have been left untouched. All contain extensive updating and rewriting, and some have been restructured.

To help keep readers up to date with the EU's evolution, Palgrave Macmillan maintain a web page where key facts – such as the composition of groups in the European Parliament – are updated as necessary. The web page also provides links to other useful and relevant websites. The address is < http://www.palgrave.com/politics/eu >

Tables 12.1, 13.1, 13.2, 13.3, 13.4, 13.5, 13.6, 13.7 and 17.1 are European Union copyright. The map on page xxiv is reproduced from *European Union Enlargement* edited by myself, by permission of Palgrave Macmillan with slight changes.

Thanks must be given to a number of people who have assisted me. Those readers who have kindly said they like and use the book have been a source of encouragement and have played a major part in prompting me to keep the book up to date. Clive Archer and Wyn Grant read individual chapters and provided valuable advice. As always, Steven Kennedy, my publisher, moved me along with good humour, and did not over-press when I fell behind schedule. Ann Edmondson was very helpful on the production side. Helen, Rachael, and Maureen provided willing support.

February 2006   NEILL NUGENT

List of Abbreviations

ABB	activity based budgeting
ACEA	Association of European Automobile Constructors
ACP	African, Caribbean and Pacific countries
ALDE	Group of the Alliance of Liberals and Democrats for Europe
AMCHAM-EU	EU Committee of the American Chamber of Commerce
APPE	Association of Petrochemical Producers in Europe
ASEAN	Association of South-East Asian Nations
BEUC	European Bureau of Consumers' Associations
BRITE	Basic Research in Industrial Technologies for Europe
CAP	Common Agricultural Policy
CCP	Common Commercial Policy
CCT	Common Customs Tariff
CDU/CSU	German Christian Democratic Union/Christian Social Union
CEA	European Insurance Committee
CEEC	Central and Eastern European country
CEEP	European Centre of Enterprises with Public Participation
CEFIC	European Chemical Industry Council
CEN	European Committee for Standardisation
CENELEC	European Committee for Electrotechnical Standardisation
CET	Common External Tariff
CFI	Court of First Instance
CFP	Common Fisheries Policy
CFSP	Common Foreign and Security Policy
COGECA	General Confederation of Agricultural Co-operatives in the European Union
COM	common organisation of the market
COPA	Committee of Agricultural Organisations in the European Union
COPS	Political and Security Committee
CoR	Committee of the Regions
COREPER	Committee of Permanent Representatives
CSCE	Conference on Security and Cooperation in Europe
CT	Constitutional Treaty
DG	Directorate General
EAFRD	European Agricultural Fund for Rural Development
EAGF	European Agricultural Guarantee Fund
EAGGF	European Agricultural Guidance and Guarantee Fund

EC	European Community
ECB	European Central Bank
ECJ	European Court of Justice
Ecofin	Council of Economic and Finance Ministers
ECSC	European Coal and Steel Community
ecu	European currency unit
ED	European Democratic Group
EDA	European Defence Agency
EDC	European Defence Community
EDF	European Development Fund
EEA	European Economic Area
EEB	European Environmental Bureau
EEC	European Economic Community
EES	European Employment Strategy
EESC	European Economic and Social Committee
EFPIA	European Federation of Pharmaceutical Industry Associations
EFTA	European Free Trade Association
EIB	European Investment Bank
EIF	European Investment Fund
ELDR	Federation of European Liberal, Democratic and Reform Parties
EMS	European Monetary System
EMU	European Monetary Union
ENP	European Neighbourhood Policy
EP	European Parliament
EPA	Economic Partnership Agreement
EPC	European Political Cooperation
EPF	European Passengers' Federation
EPP	European People's Party
EPP-ED	European People's Party/European Democrats
ERDF	European Regional Development Fund
ERM	Exchange Rate Mechanism
ERRF	European Rapid Reaction Force
ESBG	European Savings Bank Group
ESC	Economic and Social Committee
ESCB	European System of Central Banks
ESDI	European Security and Defence Identity
ESDP	European Security and Defence Policy
ESF	European Social Fund
ESPRIT	European Strategic Programme for Research and Development in Information Technology
ETUC	European Trade Union Confederation
EU	European Union
EUL	European United Left
EUMC	European Union Military Committee
EUMS	European Union Military Staff

Euratom	European Atomic Energy Community
EUREKA	European Research Coordinating Agency
EUROBIT	European Association of Manufacturers of Business Machines and Information Technology
EUROFER	European Confederation of Iron and Steel Industries
EUR-OP	Office for Official Publications of the European Communities
Europol	European Police Office
FCO	Foreign and Commonwealth Office
FRG	Federal Republic of Germany
FRY	Former Republic of Yugoslavia
FTA	Free Trade Area
G8	Group of Eight
GAERC	General Affairs and External Relations Council
GATT	General Agreement on Tariffs and Trade
GDP	gross domestic product
GDR	German Democratic Republic
GNI	gross national income
GNP	gross national product
IGC	Intergovernmental Conference
IGO	intergovernmental organisation
IMF	International Monetary Fund
JHA	Justice and Home Affairs
JRC	Joint Research Centre
LDC	least developed country
MEP	Member of the European Parliament
NATO	North Atlantic Treaty Organisation
NCB	National Central Bank
NGO	non-governmental organisation
NPAA	national programme for the adoption of the *acquis*
NTB	non-tariff barrier (to trade)
OECD	Organisation for Economic Cooperation and Development
OEEC	Organisation for European Economic Cooperation
OJ	*Official Journal of the European Union*
OLAF	European Anti-Fraud Office
OMC	open method of coordination
OSCE	Organisation for Security and Cooperation in Europe
PDB	Preliminary Draft Budget
PES	Party of European Socialists
PHARE	Programme of Community Aid for Central and Eastern European Countries
PLO	Palestine Liberation Organisation
QMV	qualified majority voting
RACE	Research and Development in Advanced Communications Technologies for Europe
R&TD	Research and Technological Development

SCA	Special Committee on Agriculture
SEA	Single European Act
SEM	Single European Market
SGP	Stability and Growth Pact
SME	small and medium-sized enterprise
TAC	total allowable catch (fish stocks)
TACIS	Programme for Technical Assistance to the Independent States of the Former Soviet Union and Mongolia
TEC	Treaty Establishing the European Community
TEU	Treaty on European Union
UEN	Union for Europe of the Nations Group
UK	United Kingdom
UKREP	United Kingdom Permanent Representation to the European Union
UN	United Nations
UNCTAD	United Nations Conference on Trade and Development
UNICE	Union of Industrial and Employers' Confederations of Europe
USA	United States of America
VAT	value added tax
WEU	Western European Union
WTO	World Trade Organisation

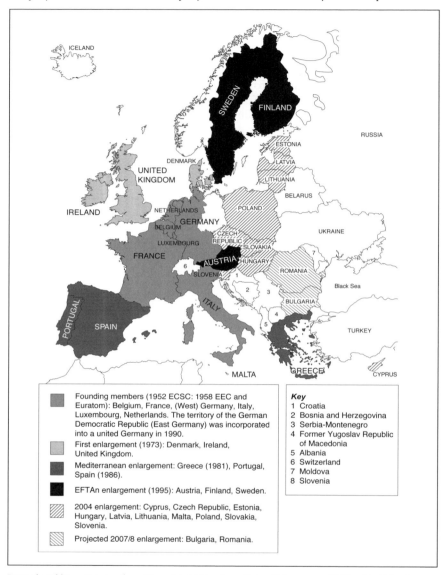

Founding members (1952 ECSC: 1958 EEC and Euratom): Belgium, France, (West) Germany, Italy, Luxembourg, Netherlands. The territory of the German Democratic Republic (East Germany) was incorporated into a united Germany in 1990.

First enlargement (1973): Denmark, Ireland, United Kingdom.

Mediterranean enlargement: Greece (1981), Portugal, Spain (1986).

EFTAn enlargement (1995): Austria, Finland, Sweden.

2004 enlargement: Cyprus, Czech Republic, Estonia, Hungary, Latvia, Lithuania, Malta, Poland, Slovakia, Slovenia.

Projected 2007/8 enlargement: Bulgaria, Romania.

Key
1 Croatia
2 Bosnia and Herzegovina
3 Serbia-Montenegro
4 Former Yugoslav Republic of Macedonia
5 Albania
6 Switzerland
7 Moldova
8 Slovenia

Reproduced by permission from Nugent (ed.) *European Union Enlargement* (2004) with slight changes.

Part 1

The Historical Evolution

No political system or organisation can properly be understood unless it is set in its historical and operational contexts. The structure and functioning of government institutions, the nature and dynamics of political forces, and the concerns and conduct of those who exercise power do not happen as a matter of chance. They are shaped, and are constantly being remoulded, by evolving forces and events.

Though a relatively new organisation, the European Union (EU) is no less subject to these dictates than are long established nation states, and like them its nature cannot be appreciated without reference to its historical sources or to the world in which it functions. Thus, the EU is often criticised for being weak in structure and quarrelsome in nature, with far too much bickering over matters such as the price of butter and not enough visionary thinking and united action to tackle unemployment, regional imbalances and other major problems. Unquestionably there is much in these criticisms, but that the EU should find harmonious collective policy-making difficult is not surprising to anyone with a historical perspective. For before they joined the European Community (EC)/ European Union member states made decisions for themselves on most matters. It is not easy, especially for large states or for states that believe themselves to have special interests, to have to cede sovereignty by transferring decision-making responsibilities to a multinational organisation in which other voices may prevail. Any explanation and understanding of what the EU is, and what it has and has not achieved, must recognise this. The EU must, in other words, be seen in the context of the forces that have made it and are still making it. Some of these forces have served to push the states together. Others have resulted in progress towards cooperation and integration sometimes being slow, difficult and contested.

The sovereignty issue may be used to illustrate the importance of both historical background and contemporary operational context in explaining and evaluating the European Union. Many of the EU's opponents and critics subscribe to the view that the nation state, not an international organisation, is the 'natural' supreme political unit. They argue that insofar as transferences of power to Brussels, Luxembourg and Strasbourg – the three main seats of the EU's institutions – undermine national sovereignty, they should be resisted. But what proponents of this view all too often fail to recognise is that national sovereignties were being steadily eroded long before the EC/EU was established, and since it was established sovereignties have been further eroded by forces that are not a consequence of EU membership. Whether it has been because of movements in financial markets, transfers of capital within multinational corporations, changing trade patterns, or United States military dominance, EU states have become increasingly affected by, and at the mercy of, international developments they cannot control. This loss of power may not have involved legal transfers of sovereignty as has been the case within the EU, but it has had a very similar effect. The fact is that in an ever expanding range of policy sectors, states have not been able to act in isolation but have had to adjust and adapt so as to fit in with an array of external influences. The EU should not, therefore, be viewed as constituting a unique threat to the sovereignties of its member states. On the contrary, it is in some ways an attempt to meet this threat by providing a means by which member states, if not able to regain their sovereignty, can at least re-assert control over aspects of decision-making by cooperating together at levels and in ways that match post-war internationalism.

The purpose of Part 1 is thus to provide a base for understanding the EU by tracing its evolution and placing it in its historical and operational settings.

There is always a problem in knowing quite where to start with the history of a subject in a chronological sense. How far back is it necessary to go to be able to properly describe and explain a subject – the subject in this case being the process of European integration. Chapter 1 begins with an outline of some of the major divisions that characterised Europe before the Second World War, so as to emphasise how momentous the post-war transformations that have occurred in Europe as part of the European integration process have been. The European integration process was, however, essentially confined until the 1990s to Western Europe, with the consequence that although the EU now includes amongst its membership states from across the continent, it was constructed by Western European states. Chapter 1 therefore focuses on the nature of, and the factors that explain, what developed into a transformation in the relations between the states of Western Europe after the Second World War. Particular attention is paid to the differing needs and positions of the Western European states and the consequences these had, and still do have, for the integration process.

Chapter 2 analyses the creation of the three European Communities: the European Coal and Steel Community (ECSC), which was founded by the Treaty of Paris in 1951, and the European Atomic Energy Community

(Euratom) and the European Economic Community (EEC), which were both established in March 1957 with the signing of the Treaties of Rome.

Chapter 3 describes the major features of the evolution of the European integration process since the Rome Treaties.

Chapter 4 looks at the broadening-out from the early 1990s of the *Western* European integration process, as Central and Eastern European countries, newly liberated from communism, applied to, and in 2004 became members of, the EU.

Chapter 1

The Transformation of Western Europe

The European integration process was initiated and developed in Western Europe. It was extended to Central and Eastern Europe only after the key features of the European Union (EU) as they are today had been created and become established. Until the collapse of communism in Central and Eastern Europe in 1989–90, countries such as Estonia, Latvia Hungary, and Poland – which became EU members in May 2004 – were either part of the Soviet Union or were located within the Soviet bloc. As such, they were quite outside the processes that were drawing Western European states increasingly close to one another in terms of their political and economic relationships.

An understanding and analysis of the European integration process must therefore begin by focusing on Western Europe.

Historical Divisions

Throughout its history Europe has been characterised much more by divisions, tensions and conflicts than it has by any common purpose or harmony of spirit. This applies to Western Europe as much as it does to the European continent as whole.

Language has been perhaps the most obvious divisive force. Linguists may identify structural similarities between European languages, but the fact is that most peoples of Western Europe have not been able to, and still cannot, directly converse with one another. (Today, 24 per cent of the citizens of the pre-May 2004 fifteen EU states speak German as their first language, 17 per cent English, 17 per cent French, and 16 per cent Italian. In total 53 per cent of EU-15 citizens claim to be able to speak at least one European language in addition to their mother tongue, with 41 per cent claiming to know English (Eurobarometer, 2001: 4).) Religion has been

5

another source of division, with the northern countries of Western Europe (except Ireland) being mainly Protestant, and the southern countries (including France but excluding Orthodox Greece) being predominantly Catholic. Contrasting cultural traditions and historical experiences have further served to develop distinct identifications – and feelings of 'us' and 'them' – across the map of Europe.

Along with the legacies of power struggles and wars, such differences help to explain why Western Europe has been divided into so many states, each with its own identity and loyalties. Some of these states – France, Spain and the United Kingdom for example – have existed in much their present geographical form for centuries. Others – including Germany, Italy and Ireland – were constituted only comparatively recently, mostly in the nineteenth and early twentieth centuries as nationalism flourished and as force was used to bring nation and state into closer alignment.

Until at least the Second World War, and in some cases well beyond, linguistic, religious and cultural divisions between the West European states were exacerbated by political and economic divisions.

Political divisions took the form of varying systems of government and competing ideological orientations. In the nineteenth and early twentieth centuries autocracies existed alongside emerging, and more liberal, parliamentary democracies. Between the two world wars parliamentary democracy found itself under attack and in some cases was overthrown: in Italy in 1922 by Fascism, in Germany in 1933 by Nazism, and in Spain after the 1936–9 civil war by conservative authoritarianism. It was not until the mid-1970s – following the collapse of the dictatorships of the Iberian peninsula and the overthrow of the military regime in Greece – that parliamentary democracy finally became general throughout Western Europe.

Economic divisions were no less marked. From the beginning of the Industrial Revolution until the middle of the nineteenth century Britain was industrially and commercially dominant. Gradually it was challenged – particularly by Germany, but also by Belgium, France and others – so that by the early years of the twentieth century competition between these countries for overseas markets was fierce. At the same time, the economies of the northern countries were increasingly differentiated from those of the south, with the former mostly having substantial industrial bases while the latter remained predominantly agricultural and underdeveloped.

Western Europe was thus long divided and many of its divisions were sources of tension, hostility and war. Finding their expression in economic and ideological competition, drives for national power and prestige, and territorial disputes, and compounded by dangerous mixtures of assertive/weak/incompetent leaderships, the divisions ensured that until after the Second World War rivalry and distrust governed the relationships between most of the states most of the time.

In the twentieth century alone two devastatingly destructive world wars, both of which began as European wars, were fought. The First (1914–18) saw the countries of the triple entente – Britain, France and Russia – plus Italy from 1915, fighting against Germany and Austria-Hungary. The Second (1939–45) saw Germany, assisted from 1940 by Italy, attempting to impose itself by force on virtually the whole of Europe outside the Iberian peninsula.

The background to the Second World War is worth outlining briefly because it puts in perspective how dramatically different, and how suddenly found, were the more cooperative relationships between the West European states in the post-1945 era. In short, the period between the wars was characterised by particularly sharp and fluid inter-state relations. There was no stable alliance system and no clear balance of power. For the most part, European states, including West European states, regarded one another with, at best, suspicion. Though multilateral and bilateral treaties, agreements, and pacts abounded, there was little overall pattern to them and few had any lasting effect. States came together in varying combinations on different issues in a manner that, far from indicating mutual confidence, was increasingly suggestive of fear.

From time to time in the inter-war period proposals for greater cooperation between European states were advanced but little came of them. The international climate – characterised by national rivalries and clashing interests – was not favourable, and most of the leading advocates of closer linkages were seen as having, as indeed they did have, specific national purposes in mind. Aristide Briand, for example, who was French Foreign Minister from 1925 to 1932, supported European cooperation but clearly had as his prime aim a stable European political system that would preserve the peace settlement that had been imposed on Germany by the 1919 Versailles Treaty. Gustav Stresemann, by contrast, who was the German Foreign Minister from 1923 to 1929, saw European cooperation as a way in which Germany could loosen the grip of Versailles and regain its position as a major power.

The lack of any real interest in European cooperation before the Second World War is revealed in the functioning of the League of Nations. Established in 1919 to provide for international collective security, in practice it was dominated by the Europeans and had some potential as a forum for developing understandings and improving relationships between the European states. It failed, and did so for three main reasons. First, its aims were vague and were interpreted in different ways. Second, it was intergovernmental in its structure and therefore dependent on the agreement of all member states before any action could be taken. Third, and crucially, the states wanted different things from it: some – notably France, most of the medium-sized central European countries that had been constituted in 1918–19 out of the collapsed Austria-Hungarian Empire, and to some extent Britain – saw it as a means of preserving the Versailles *status quo*; others – particularly Germany and Italy – wanted to use it to change the 1919 settlement and were prepared to leave or ignore it if it did not serve that purpose.

Inter-war Europe thus experienced rising tensions as national rivalries remained unharnessed and, above all, as German territorial and power ambitions could not be satisfied. When war finally did break out, the Axis Powers (Germany and Italy) gained control for a while over virtually the whole of the continent from the Atlantic to deep inside the Soviet Union. In Western Europe only Britain and those countries which remained neutral (Ireland, Portugal, Spain, Sweden and Switzerland) were not occupied. By May 1945, when German government representatives agreed to unconditional surrender, Nazism and Fascism had been defeated, but economies and political systems throughout Europe had been severely shaken, cities and towns had been destroyed and millions had been killed.

The Post-War Transformation

Since the Second World War the relations between the states of Western Europe have been transformed. There are three principal aspects of this.

Unbroken peace

Western European states have lived peacefully with one another since 1945 and armed confrontation between any two does not now appear to be even remotely possible. As Altiero Spinelli, one of the great advocates and architects of European integration, observed in 1985 shortly before his death:

> [a] major transformation ... has occurred in the political consciousness of Europeans, something which is completely new in their history. For centuries, neighbouring countries were seen as potential enemies against whom it was necessary to be on one's guard and ready to fight. Now, after the end of the most terrible of wars in Europe, these neighbours are perceived as friendly nations sharing a common destiny (Spinelli, 1986: xiii).

Spinelli's view of a common destiny is questionable, but the reality and importance of the transformation from hostile to friendly relations is not. Certainly the states have continued to compete against one another in many areas, and this has sometimes led to strains and tensions, but these disagreements have been mostly on issues where military conflict has not been relevant to the resolution of differences.

Indeed, not only has military conflict been irrelevant to the resolution of differences, but such friction as has occurred has been within a context in which West European states have usually shared similar views on who can be seen as friends and who are real or potential enemies. Until the revolutions and upheavals in Eastern Europe and the Soviet Union in the late 1980s/early 1990s, communism was the most obvious common threat and this led most significant Western European states to become full or part members of the same military alliance: the North Atlantic Treaty Organisation (NATO). With the communist danger now removed, Western security arrangements have been revamped to adjust to a situation in which Central and Eastern European countries (CEECs) are now partners in both NATO and the EU and in which the main potential security concerns are seen as lying in the Balkans, in bubbling national and ethnic tensions in parts of the former Soviet Empire, in the turbulence of the Middle East, and in the threat of international terrorism.

A transformed agenda

Throughout the international system the subject matter of discussions and negotiations between states has become much more varied. Whilst, as regional conflicts show, the case should not be overstated, international agendas have clearly become less focused on traditional 'high policy' issues and more on 'low policy' issues. That is, policies concerned with the existence and preservation of the state (such as territorial issues, defence policy and balance of power manoeuvrings) have been joined by policies that are more concerned with the wealth and welfare of populations (such as policies on trade, monetary stability, environmental protection, and airline safety).

This change in the content of agendas has been particularly marked throughout the Western industrialised world, but above all in Europe where, initially in Western Europe and now across much of the continent, a transformation can be said to have occurred. Classic 'power politics' have not of course disappeared, but they are not as dominant or as prominent as they were. When representatives of the EU states meet it is normally to consider topics that a generation or two ago would not even have been regarded as proper subjects for international negotiations, such as what constitutes 'fair' economic competition, how might research information be pooled to the general advantage, to what extent and by what means should sheep farmers be subsidised, and what should be the maximum weight of lorries permitted on roads?

New channels and processes

Paralleling, and partly occasioned by, the increasingly diverse international agenda, there has been a transformation in the ways in which states interrelate with one another. The traditional diplomatic means of inter-state communications via Ministries of Foreign Affairs and embassies have declined in importance as new channels and processes have become established.

As with changing agendas, changing forms of inter-state communication have been taken further in the Western industrialised world, and particularly in the EU, than anywhere else. There are now few significant parts of any Western state's political and administrative systems that do not have some involvement in the management of external relations. Written communications, telephone conversations, electronically transmitted messages, and bilateral and multilateral meetings between states increase by the year. Contacts range from the *ad hoc* and informal to the regularised and highly structured.

In the EU, representatives of the governments of the member states meet every working day for such purposes as taking binding decisions (decisions that in many circumstances may be taken by majority vote), exploring possibly advantageous policy coordination, and exchanging views and information. At the lower end of the seniority scale, junior and middle-ranking officials, often working from tightly drawn negotiating briefs and with their actions subject to later approval from national capitals, convene in committees to try to hammer out detailed agreements on proposed legislation. At the top end of the scale, Heads of Government regularly meet, for what are often wide-ranging deliberations, in forums such as: the European Council, which meets at least four times a year and where all EU states are represented; in bilateral meetings, which in the case of the British Prime Minister, the French President, the German Chancellor and the Italian Prime Minister take place at least once a year; and in the broader setting of the annual Group of Eight (G8) summits, which bring together the political leaders of Britain, France, Germany, Italy, Canada, Japan, Russia and the United States, plus the President of the European Commission and the Head of Government of the member state that is currently chairing the EU's Council of Ministers if she or he is not already present.

Explaining the Transformation, and its Nature

As has been noted above, until recently the European integration process was essentially a *Western* European integration process. The countries of Central and Eastern Europe that have become members of the EU have joined an organisation made by countries of Western Europe.

In seeking to explain post-war Western European cooperation and integration different commentators have often highlighted different factors, and sometimes indeed have looked in rather different directions. Four explanatory approaches will be outlined here: explanations that emphasise the deep roots of European integration, the importance of the changed post-1945 circumstances, the role of international influences, and the differing positions of Western European states. For analytical purposes these approaches will be considered here separately, but it should be recognised that, in practice, they are by no means mutually exclusive but rather complement, overlap and reinforce one another. It should be recognised, too, that their usefulness as explanations is not constant, but varies over time. So, for example, whilst political ideals and utopian visions of a united Europe may have had at least some part to play in the early post-war years, they increasingly counted for less as hard-headed national calculations of economic and political advantages and disadvantages loomed increasingly large as the principal determinants of the nature and pace of the integration process.

The deep roots of integration?

Some commentators and practitioners have found the roots of post-war developments in the distant past. Supporters and advocates of European integration have been especially prominent in this regard. They have suggested that Europe is, and has long been, a unique and identifiable entity. As evidence of this it is often argued that Europe was the cradle of modern civilisation and from this there developed European values and a European culture, art and literature. Walter Hallstein, the first President of the Commission of the EEC, typifies this sort of view:

> Europe is no creation. It is a rediscovery. The main difference between the formation of the United States of Europe and that of the United States of America is not that America did not have to merge a number of firmly established nation states, but that for more than a thousand years the idea of a unified Europe was never quite forgotten ...
>
> [The advocates of a European federation] know that Europe shares a sense of values: of what is good and bad; of what a man's rights should be and what are his duties; of how society should be ordered; of what is happiness and what disaster. Europe shares many things: its memories that we call history; achievements it can take pride in and events that are shameful; its joys and its sufferings; and not least its tomorrows (Hallstein, 1972: 15 and 16).

Clearly there is much idealism in this. People such as Hallstein are suggesting that transcending the differences, divergences and conflicts between peoples and states there has long been a certain commonality and identity of interest in Europe based on interrelationships between geography and historical, political, economic, social and cultural developments. It is a contentious view and certainly not one to which many historians would attach much importance. Divisions and dissension, they would contend, have been more prominent than identity of interest or shared values and experiences. Such limited commonality as has existed has largely been a consequence of geographical proximity.

But if the 'idealistic' interpretation no longer finds much favour, there are still those who stress the importance of the historical dimension of European integration. Inter-state relations in the nineteenth century are sometimes seen as foreshadowing post-1945 developments insofar as peace endured for much of the century and did so, in part at least, as a result of understandings and agreements between the major powers. However, a problem with this view is that it overstates the extent to which the nineteenth century was a century of peace, and it also exaggerates the extent to which the states did cooperate. Arguably, the so-called Concert of Nations was an embryonic attempt to exercise strategic control through diplomacy and summitry, but that was at a time when conservative autocracies ruled much of Europe and many of today's states did not even exist in their present form. And in any event, the system lasted at best only from 1815 to the Crimean War. It then gave way to the wars of the mid-nineteenth century and later to the balance of power – which was hardly based on European trust and cooperation – as the means of seeking to preserve the peace.

It is perhaps in the field of economic history that the most fertile ground for identifying long-term influences and explanations is to be found. From the late eighteenth century *national* economic integration began to occur, as barriers to economic activity *within* states were dismantled. This helped to promote, and in turn was encouraged by, national political integration, which manifested itself in nationalism and in the elevation of the sovereign state to the status of the supreme collective unit. From the middle of the nineteenth century the achievement and successes of this internal economic and political integration, allied with an increasing interconnectedness in Europe that followed from technological change and economic advance, resulted in increasing inter-state cooperation to promote trade, competition and growth. For some economic historians an embryonic European economy was being established. Pollard, for example, has written of the mid-nineteenth century:

> Europe's industrialisation proceeded relatively smoothly, among other reasons, precisely because it took place within what was in many essentials a single integrated economy, with a fair amount of movement

for labour, a greater amount of freedom for the movement of goods, and the greatest freedom of all for the movement of technology, know-how and capital (Pollard, 1981: 38–9).

But unlike the customary pattern within nation states, there was nothing inevitable about European economic integration. Nor was there a clear and developing relationship between it and political integration. On the contrary, from the last quarter of the nineteenth century, states, for a variety of reasons, moved increasingly in the direction of economic protectionism and at the same time developed national identities and consciousness such as had not been seen before. In the first part of the twentieth century, and especially between the wars, the European free trading system virtually disappeared, as states sought to protect themselves at the expense of others and national economies were increasingly re-shaped along autarkic lines. Alongside these increasingly closed economic systems developed the ever sharper political tensions and rivalries between the states that were noted earlier.

The European historical experience thus emphasises the extremely important, but often overlooked, fact that although industrialisation and economic liberalisation provide potential bases for the furtherance of interconnections, agreements, and harmonious relations between states, they do not ensure or guarantee them. The powers of Europe went to war with their principal trading partners in 1914. Furthermore, between the wars economic linkages did little to bring the nations together or to act as a restraint on governments when divergences developed in their aims and strategies. This must be borne in mind when, later in this chapter, attention is turned to modernisation and interdependence as explanations for post-war political and economic integration. Doubtless they have both been extremely important, but as pre-1939 European history shows, they do not have an inevitable integrationist logic attached to them. Much depends on their relationship to the circumstances of the time and, as will now be shown, these were very different in the post-1945 world from what they had been before the Second World War.

The impact of the Second World War

The Second World War unquestionably marked a turning point in the West European state system. Just a few years after the end of the war states were cooperating, and in some instances and in some respects were even integrating, in a manner that would have been inconceivable before the war. Fundamental to this transformation were a number of factors resultant upon the war that combined to bring about a radical change in both the climate of opinion and perceptions of requirements. These factors were political and economic in nature.

Political factors

These may be subdivided into four broad areas.

(1) Combating nationalism.   The Second World War produced a greater realisation than had existed ever before that unfettered and uninhibited nationalism was a recipe for war, which in the post-1945 world was increasingly seen as meaning mass destruction. At the international level this thinking was reflected in calls for a larger and more powerful body than the pre-war League of Nations, and it played an important part in the establishment of the United Nations in 1944. But the fact that the two world wars had begun as European wars, and that Germany was generally considered to be responsible for those wars, also brought forth demands and moves for specifically European arrangements. Amongst the strongest advocates of the creation of European arrangements were many of those who had been associated with the Resistance movements of Continental Europe which, from 1943 onwards, had come to be linked via liaising networks and from which ideas and proposals had been generated looking forward to a post-war world that would be based more on cooperation and less on confrontation.

There was thus a widely shared optimism at the end of the Second World War that if the European states could work together in joint schemes and organisations, barriers of mistrust could be broken down. On this basis, over 750 prominent Europeans came together in The Hague in May 1948 and from their Congress issued a call to the nations of Europe to create a political and economic union. This stimulated discussions at governmental levels, and in May 1949 the Statute of the Council of Europe was signed by representatives of ten states. Article 1 of the Statute includes the following:

> (a) The aim of the Council of Europe is to achieve a greater unity between its Members for the purpose of safeguarding and realising the ideals and principles which are their common heritage and facilitating their economic and social progress.
> (b) This aim shall be pursued through the organs of the Council by discussions of questions of common concern and by agreements and common action in economic, social, cultural, scientific, legal and administrative matters and in the maintenance and further realisation of human rights and fundamental freedoms (Robertson, 1961, Appendix – the Statute).

Despite these grandiose ambitions, however, the Council of Europe proved to be a disappointment to those who had hoped it might serve as the basis for a new West European state system. In part the problem was that its aims were too vague, in part that its decision-making structure was essentially intergovernmental and therefore weak, but the main problem was that some of its members, notably the UK, were not very interested in anything that went beyond limited and voluntary cooperation. (Ernest Bevin, British Foreign Secretary, commented on proposals for a really effective Council of Europe thus: 'Once you open that Pandora's box, you'll find it full of Trojan horses.') But the weaknesses of the Council should not be overstated. It was to perform, and continues to perform, certain useful functions – notably in the sphere of human rights through its European Convention of Human Rights, and as a forum for the discussion of matters of common interest to its member states. (The value of this latter function long lay in the fact that, unlike other Western European regional groups, virtually all West European states were members of the Council. In the 1990s, as CEECs became members, an additional value was acting as a forum for establishing links and building understanding between Western and Eastern Europe.)

(2) The new political map of Europe.   Although it was not immediately apparent when hostilities ceased in 1945, the Second World War was to result in a fundamental redrawing of the political map of Europe. By the late 1940s it was clear that the legacy of war had left the Continent, and with it Germany, divided in two. In Winston Churchill's phrase, an 'Iron Curtain' now divided East from West. In the East, a swathe of states were either incorporated into the Soviet Union or became part of the Soviet communist zone, which resulted in them being forcibly cut off from developments in Western Europe and being obliged to focus their political and economic ambitions and activities in accordance with Moscow's will.

In the West there was no question of the victorious powers – Britain and the United States – seeking or being able to impose anything like a Soviet-style straitjacket on the liberated countries. Nonetheless, if Western Europe did not quite take on the form of a bloc, liberal democratic systems were soon established and somewhat similar political ideas were prevailing in most of the states. Inevitably this facilitated intergovernmental relations.

Perhaps the most important idea shared by the governments stemmed directly from the East–West division of the continent: there was a determination to preserve Western Europe from communism. Not only had the Soviet Union extended its influence far into the European heartland, but in France and Italy domestic communist parties were commanding considerable support and from 1947 were engaging in what looked to many like revolutionary activities. The United States shared this anti-communist concern, and the encouragement and assistance which it gave to the West European states after the war to cooperate was partly driven by a belief that such cooperation could play a major part in helping to halt the communist advance. In March 1947 President Truman, concerned with events in Greece – where communists were trying to overthrow the government – outlined what became known as the Truman doctrine, which amounted to a political guarantee of support to 'free peoples who are resisting attempted subjugation by armed minorities or by outside pressures'. This political commitment was quickly followed up in 1948 by economic assistance in the form of Marshall Aid (see p. 18), and in 1949 by military protection with the foundation of NATO and a guarantee to the then ten NATO West European states (Canada and the United States brought the founding membership to twelve) of US military protection against a Soviet attack.

A role for the United States in Western Europe at this time should not be seen as having been unwelcome, for contrary to the impression that is sometimes given, US aid was not insidiously imposed on unwilling states but was actively sought. At the same time, the extent of US influence on Western European inter-state relations should not be exaggerated. By its political, economic and military interventions and assistance the United States did exert integrationist pressures and did help to make a number of developments possible, but the US government wanted much more West European inter-state integration than was actually achieved.

(3) The new international power balance.   With the post-war division of Europe, the moving of the international power balance from inter-European state relations to US–Soviet relations, and the onset of the Cold War from 1947–8 producing the possibility of Europe becoming a battleground between East and West, there was a sense from the late 1940s that Western Europe was beginning to look like an identifiable political entity in a way that it had not done before. Not all states or politicians shared this perspective, but from many of those who did there emerged a desire that the voice of Western Europe should be heard on the world stage and a belief that this could be achieved only through unity and by speaking with one voice. For some of the smaller European states, which had rarely exercised much international influence and whose very existence had periodically been threatened by larger neighbours, the prospects of such cooperation were particularly attractive.

(4) The German problem. The future of Germany naturally loomed large in the minds of those who had to deal with post-war reconstruction. Three times in seventy years, and twice in the twentieth century, Germany had occupied much of Europe. Rightly or wrongly it had come to be seen as innately aggressive. As a consequence, the initial inclination of most governments after the war was to try to contain Germany in some way.

Just how this should be done, however, divided the wartime allies, with the result that matters drifted until what was initially intended as an interim division of Germany into zones gave way, as the Cold War developed, into *a de jure* division: the Federal Republic of Germany (West Germany) and the German Democratic Republic (East Germany) were both formally constituted in 1949.

By this time, the Soviet Union was replacing Germany as the perceived principal threat to democracy and stability in Western Europe. As this occurred, those who were already arguing that a conciliatory approach towards Germany ought to be tried – since a policy of punitive containment had demonstrably failed between the wars – saw their hands strengthened by a growing feeling that attempts must be made to avoid the development of a political vacuum in West Germany that the communists might attempt to exploit. Furthermore, and the US government played an important role in pressing this view from the early 1950s, use of West Germany's power and wealth could help to reduce the contributions that other countries were making to the defence of Europe. The perceived desirability and need to incorporate the Federal Republic into the Western European mainstream thus further stimulated the pressure for inter-state cooperation and integration.

Economic factors

Just as pre-war and wartime experiences helped to produce the United Nations, so they also stimulated an interest in the creation of new international economic and financial arrangements. The first fruits of this were realised at the Bretton Woods Conference in 1944, where the representatives of forty-four countries, with the United Kingdom and the United States playing the leading roles, agreed to the establishment of two new bodies. The first was the International Monetary Fund (IMF), which was to alleviate currency instability by creating facilities for countries with temporary balance of payments difficulties to have access to short-term credit facilities. The second was the International Bank for Reconstruction and Development (the World Bank), which was to provide long-term loans for schemes that required major investment. In 1947, at much the same time as the IMF and the World Bank became operative, international economic cooperation was taken a stage further when twenty-three countries negotiated the General Agreement on Tariffs and Trade (GATT), whose purpose was to facilitate trade through the lowering of international trade barriers.

Although West European governments (or, more usually, national representatives, since governments on the continent were not properly restored until 1945–6) played their part in creating the new international economic arrangements, it was felt in many quarters that there should also be specifically West European-based economic initiatives and organisations. In 1947–8 this feeling was given a focus, an impetus and an urgency when the rapid post-war economic recovery that most states were able to engineer by the adoption of expansionist policies created massive balance of payments deficits, and dollar shortages in particular. Governments were faced with major currency problems, with not being able to pay for their imports and with the prospect of their economic recovery coming to a sudden and premature end. In these circumstances, and for reasons that were not altogether altruistic – a strong Western Europe was in its political, security and economic interests – the United States stepped in with economic aid in the form of the European Recovery Programme, or Marshall Aid as it came to be known after the US Secretary of State, George Marshall, who championed it. But there was a condition attached to the aid: the recipient states must endeavour to promote greater economic cooperation among themselves. As a result, the first major post-war Western European organisation, the Organisation for European Economic Cooperation (OEEC), was established, with sixteen founding member states, in April 1948. Its short-term task was to manage the US aid, encourage joint economic policies, and discourage barriers to trade; in the longer term, its stated aim was to build 'a sound European economy through the cooperation of its members'. In the event, although the OEEC did some valuable work – the most notable perhaps being to establish payments schemes which in the 1940s and 1950s did much to further trade between the member countries – it never made much progress towards its grander ambitions. Rather like the Council of Europe, its large and somewhat heterogeneous membership, coupled with the strictly intergovernmental nature of its decision-making structure, meant that ambitious proposals were always successfully opposed. Partly as a result of this, and partly in recognition of growing interdependence among all industrialised countries, in 1961 the OEEC gave way to the Organisation for Economic Cooperation and Development (OECD), whose membership was made open to non-European countries and which was to have broader objectives reflecting wider and changing interests.

The OEEC thus stemmed from post-war circumstances that mixed the general with the particular. That is to say, attitudes coming out of the war that favoured economic cooperation between West European states were given a direction by particular requirements that were related to the war and its immediate aftermath. Only three years later, as will be described in Chapter 2, a similar mixture of general underlying and specific triggering factors combined to produce the first of the European Communities: the European Coal and Steel Community (ECSC).

*   *   *

The most dramatic effect of the Second World War in Europe was, of course, the division of the continent. The War precluded the possibility of Central and Eastern European states participating in the new cooperation and integration schemes that were launched in the West of the continent in the post-war years.

In Western Europe, the effects of some of the political and economic factors associated with the Second World War, such as the presence of Resistance leaders in governments, were essentially short-term. Furthermore, some of the factors, such as the increased need and willingness of the Western European states to cooperate with one another to promote economic growth, were not so much caused by the war as given a push by it. Nonetheless, taken together the factors produced a set of circumstances that enabled Western European cooperation and integration to get off the ground in the 1940s and 1950s.

Western European states naturally differed in the particulars and perceptions of their post-war situations. As a result, there was no general agreement on precisely what the new spirit of cooperation should attempt to achieve. Many different schemes were advanced and many different organisations were established to tackle particular issues, problems and requirements. Thus the war did not produce anything remotely like a united West European movement between the states. But it did produce new realities and changed attitudes that enabled, or forced, virtually all the states to recognise at least some commonalities and shared interests. As a consequence, it became possible for new inter-state European organisations to be established. Of these organisations, those that were able to offer clear advantages and benefits to members were able to act as a base for further developments. As the ECSC in particular was to quickly demonstrate, cooperation and integration can breed more of the same

International, and European, interdependence

It has become customary to suggest that whilst both political and economic factors were crucial in promoting cooperation and integration in the formative post-war years, the former have now declined in relation to the latter. The impact of modernisation is generally agreed to be a key reason for this. It has broadened the international agenda from its traditional power and security concerns to embrace a range of economic and social issues, and at the same time it has produced an interconnectedness and interrelatedness between states, especially in the economic and monetary spheres, that amounts to an interdependence.

Economic interdependence has arisen particularly from three features of the post-1945 world: the enormously increased volume of world trade; the internationalisation of production, in which multinational corporations have played a prominent part; and – especially since the early 1970s – the fluctuations and uncertainties associated with currency exchange rates and international monetary arrangements. Within Western Europe there have been many regional dimensions to this development of interdependence, two of which have been especially important in promoting the integration process. First, since the Second World War the external trade of all significant Western European countries has become increasingly West European focused. The EC/EU has played an important role in encouraging this trend, and all EU-15 member states (that is, pre-May 2004 members) now conduct at least 60 per cent of their trade inside the EU. Second, from the 1960s monetary power within Western Europe increasingly came to be held by those who made the monetary decisions for the strongest economy: Germany. Changes in German interest rates or exchange rates had immense and potentially very destabilising implications elsewhere in Western Europe.

As a result of interdependence a wide variety of economic and financial issues can thus no longer be limited to, and indeed in some respects do not even bear much relationship to, national boundaries. States are increasingly vulnerable to outside events and are increasingly unable to act in isolation. They must consult, cooperate and, some would argue, integrate with one another in the interests of international and national economic stability and growth. In consequence, when a problem has been seen to require a truly international economic effort most West European states have been prepared to try to find solutions at this level: in the IMF, in GATT and its successor the World Trade Organisation (WTO), in the Bank for International Settlements, and elsewhere. When a regional response has seemed more appropriate or more practical, West European-based arrangements have been sought. The most obvious examples of such arrangements are EU-based. For instance: the creation of the Single European Market (SEM) is rooted in the belief that the dismantlement of trade barriers will further economic efficiency and prosperity in the participating states; the creation of Economic and Monetary Union (EMU) is based on the assumption that the coordination and the convergence of national economic and monetary policies and the establishment of a centrally managed single currency is necessary for the completion of the SEM programme and will serve to promote further trade, growth and prosperity; and the development at the EU level of advanced research programmes is a response to the growing belief that European states must pool their scientific and technological resources and knowledge if they are to compete successfully in world markets against the Americans, the Japanese and other competitors.

Economic interdependence is not the only feature of modern interdependence. Advances in communications and travel have placed on the international and European agendas issues that a generation or two ago either did not exist or were seen as being of purely domestic concern. Now it is commonly accepted that if these issues are to be properly managed they must be dealt with at the inter-state level. Governments thus discuss, and in Europe have adopted understandings and made decisions on, matters as diverse as transfrontier television arrangements, data protection, action against drug traffickers and football hooliganism.

But despite all the attention that is now given to interdependence as the motor of European integration, and despite the associated assertion that economic factors now far outweigh political factors in shaping relations between the EU states, the case should not be overstated. One reason for this is that modern interdependence does not necessarily produce an inescapable and wholly unavoidable set of integrationist processes and developments. There is certainly an integrationist logic attached to modern interdependence, but for much of integration to actually proceed political choices and decisions have to be made. As the history of negotiations on European integration since the Second World War demonstrate – from the negotiations in the late 1940s to establish the Council of Europe to the negotiations in the early 2000s on the Constitutional Treaty – politicians, and indeed publics, are capable of adopting an array of often sharply conflicting views of what is necessary and what is desirable when they are faced with particular choices and decisions. A second reason for exercising some caution when evaluating the impact on integration of economic interdependence is that political factors continue to be important in shaping the nature and pace of integration processes. This was clearly illustrated in the wake of the 1990 reunification of Germany, when a powerful stimulus to a new round of integrationist negotiations was the growing conviction among decision-making elites, most particularly in France, that if Germany was to be prevented from dominating the EU it must be tied more tightly to its neighbours. A third reason for not overemphasising the importance of modern interdependence to the neglect of other factors is that interdependence of a quite different kind – different in that it has arisen not from modernisation but rather from the relatively diminished significance of the European states in the post-1945 period – continues to play a part in encouraging cooperation and integration between states. So, for example, with respect to the external political role of the EU, the fact that European states have relatively limited power and weight when acting individually has provided a powerful inducement for them to try to speak as one if they wish to exert a significant influence on world political events. Most of the EU states do wish to exert such an influence and consequently, since the early 1970s, they have gradually strengthened their mechanisms for inter-state foreign policy cooperation so as to enable them to engage in extensive consultations, and increasingly to adopt joint positions, on foreign policy issues. Similar processes have been under way also in respect of security considerations, with the perception, until the collapse of communism, of the Soviet Union as Western Europe's main political enemy, allied with the inability of any single Western Europe state to offer by itself a wholly credible defence capability, encouraging close military cooperation between the states in the context of both the Western alliance and associated Western Europe defence groupings. The Soviet threat has now disappeared, but potential security dangers of many kinds still abound and these have played an important part in ensuring that not only civil security but also military security is now on the EU's agenda.

National considerations

Although most Western European states since 1945 have paid at least lip service to the idea of a united Western Europe, and more recently to a united Europe, there has never been any consensus between them on what this should mean in practice. The rhetoric has often been grand, but discussions on specific proposals have usually revealed considerable variations in ambitions, motives, intentions and perceptions. Most crucially of all, states have differed in their assessments of the consequences for them, in terms of gains and losses, of forging closer relations with their neighbours. As a result, some states have been prepared and able to go further than others, or have been prepared to do so at an earlier time. The advancement therefore of cooperation and integration between Western European states has been far from coherent or ordered. In the late 1940s and the 1950s most states were willing to be associated with intergovernmental organisations that made few demands on them – and hence joined the OEEC and the Council of Europe – but they were less enthusiastic when organisations were proposed that went beyond intergovernmental cooperation into supranational integration. Consequently, the more ambitious post-war schemes – for the ECSC, for a European Defence Community (EDC – which in the event was never established), and for the EEC and Euratom – initially involved only a restricted membership. It was not until circumstances and attitudes in other states changed, and until an obstacle that emerged amongst the founding states themselves – in the form of President de Gaulle's opposition to UK membership – was removed, that the EC gradually expanded in the 1970s, 1980s and 1990s to include eventually virtually all of Western Europe's larger and medium-sized states.

So while all West European states have long been touched by at least some of the factors that have been examined on the last few pages, the differences between them have resulted in their interest in, and their capacity and enthusiasm for, cooperation and integration varying in terms of both nature and timing. Much of the explanation for the nature and pace of the development of the European integration process since the Second World War is thus to be found in factors at the national level. In particular, it is to be found in the different circumstances and needs of the states of Western Europe and in the different attitudes that their governments have taken towards integration. These circumstances, needs and attitudes, and the consequent different types of influence West European states have had on the integration process, will now be examined. For the purposes of the examination, a useful way of grouping the states is according to when, if at all, they assumed EC/EU membership.

The founding members of the European Community: Belgium, France, West Germany, Italy, Luxembourg and the Netherlands

These six states, which in 1951 signed the Treaty of Paris to found the ECSC and in 1957 signed the Treaties of Rome to found the EEC and Euratom, were the first to show a willingness to go beyond the cooperative intergovernmental ventures that were established in Western Europe in the late 1940s. Cautiously, tentatively, and not without reservations, each took the view that the benefits of integration, as opposed to just cooperation, would outweigh what appeared to be the major disadvantage – a loss of sovereignty. Some of the perceived advantages that supranational organisations could offer were shared by all of the six, but there were also more nationally-based hopes and ambitions.

For the three Benelux countries, their experience of the Second World War had reemphasised their vulnerability to hostile and more powerful neighbours and the need to be on good terms with West Germany and France. Related to this, their size – Belgium and the Netherlands were only middle-ranking European powers whilst Luxembourg was a very small state – meant that their only real prospect of exercising any sort of influence in Europe, let alone the world, was through a more unified inter-state system. As for economic considerations, they were used to the idea of integration since Benelux economic agreements and arrangements pre-dated the war, and negotiations to re-launch and deepen these had been under way well before the war ended. There was also the fact that not one of the Benelux states was in a strong enough position to ignore Franco-German initiatives for economic integration.

Italy too had a number of reasons for welcoming close relations with other West European states. First, after more than twenty years of Fascist rule followed by military defeat, European integration offered the prospect of a new start, and from a basis of respectability. Second, in May 1947 (as also occurred in France) the Communist Party left government and for some years thereafter seemed to be intent on fermenting internal revolution. The clear anti-communist tenor of other West European governments looked comforting, and a possible source of assistance, to Italy's nervous Christian Democratic-led governments. Third, Italy faced economic difficulties on all fronts: with unemployment, inflation, balance of payments imbalances, currency instability and – especially in the south – poverty. Almost any scheme that offered the possibility of finding new markets and generating economic growth was to be welcomed.

Integration was seen as helping France to deal with two of its key post-war policy goals: the containment of Germany and economic growth. In the early 1950s the ECSC was especially important in this regard, offering the opportunity to break down age-old barriers and hostilities on the one hand and giving France access to vital German raw materials and markets on the other. Later in the 1950s, when 'the German problem' was seen as less pressing but German economic competition seemed to be posing an increasing threat, France took steps in the negotiations that produced the EEC to ensure that as part of the price of continued integration certain French interests – including economic protection for its farmers – would be given special treatment.

Konrad Adenauer, the West German Chancellor from 1949 to 1963, saw West European unification as the means by which the Federal Republic could establish itself in the international mainstream and German self-respect could be regained. Western Europe would also, along with the Atlantic Alliance, provide a much-needed buttress against the perceived threat from the East. More specifically, the ECSC would enable West Germany to rid itself of Allied restrictions and interference, and the more open markets of the EEC would offer immense opportunities for what, in the 1950s, quickly became the fastest growing economy in Western Europe.

✳   ✳   ✳

Since helping to create the EC in the 1950s, four of the founding states – Belgium, Luxembourg, the Netherlands and Italy – have remained firm and consistent supporters of the integration process. They have almost invariably backed, and sometimes have been prominent in the initiation of, the many proposals put forward over the years for further integrationist advance. The only significant exception to this has been the rejection by the Dutch people in a referendum in June 2005 of the proposed Constitutional Treaty. The reasons for, and the significance of, this vote are considered in Chapter 7.

Germany – or to be strictly accurate West Germany up to 1990 and united Germany since – has also been a reasonably dependable member of the integrationist camp. (German unification took the form of the German Democratic Republic – East Germany – integrating into the Federal Republic of Germany, so there was no question of a new state joining the Community and therefore no question of normal enlargement procedures applying.) However, in recent years the enthusiasm for integration has wobbled a little, with a reluctance to continue acting as the EU's main 'paymaster' being displayed and with reservations about continuing enlargements of the EU being expressed.

In the early years of the EC France assumed a very wary attitude towards the integration process. This was a consequence of President de Gaulle's hostility to any international organisation that assumed supranational characteristics and, thereby, undermined French national sovereignty. The economic benefits which the Community was bringing to France were recognised and welcomed, but they were not to be paid for with a transfer of national sovereignty to the likes of the Commission, the European Parliament or a Council of Ministers taking its decisions by majority vote. Since de Gaulle's resignation in 1969, France's concerns about loss of sovereignty have been less to the fore, though concerns about sovereignty have never quite disappeared and even today France still tends to take a more intergovernmentalist stance than the other five founding states with respect to the powers of the EU institutions. Notwithstanding this tendency, however, French presidents have sought to be prominent in moving integration ahead and have linked up with others, especially German Chancellors, for this purpose. It thus came as a considerable set-back to President Chirac when the French people rejected the Constitutional Treaty in a referendum held in May 2005 – a matter which, like the Dutch referendum on the Constitutional Treaty, will be considered in Chapter 7.

The 1973 enlargement: The United Kingdom, Denmark and Ireland

Three factors were especially important in governing the UK's attitude towards European integration in the post-war years. First, the UK saw itself as operating within what Winston Churchill described as three overlapping and interlocking relationships: the Empire and Commonwealth; the Atlantic Alliance and the 'special relationship' with the United States; and Western Europe. Until the early 1960s Western Europe was seen as being the least important of these relationships. Second, successive British governments were not prepared to accept the loss of sovereignty that integration implied. There were several reasons for this, of which the most important were: Britain's long established parliamentary tradition; the record, in which there was considerable pride, of not having been invaded or controlled by foreign powers in modern times; a generally held view that cessation of sovereignty was neither desirable nor necessary, since Britain was still a world power of the first rank; and a certain distaste with the idea of being dependent on the not altogether highly regarded governments and countries of 'the Continent'. Third, Britain's circumstances were such that three of the four main integrationist organisations to be proposed in the 1950s had few attractions in terms of their specific areas of concern: the restrictions on national decision-making powers entailed in the ECSC looked very unappealing to a country whose coal and steel capacity far exceeded that of any of the six; the EDC would have limited governmental manoeuvrability and options at a time when Britain's defences were already stretched by the attempt to maintain a world role; and Euratom looked as though it would involve sharing secrets with less advanced nuclear powers. Only the EEC seemed to have much to offer, but amongst the problems it carried with it was its proposed supranationalism. Attempts were made to persuade the six not to be so ambitious and to direct their attention to the construction of a West European free trade area, but with no success. As a result, and with a view to increasing its bargaining power with the six, Britain looked to other non-signatories of the Treaty of Rome. This led, in January 1960, to the Stockholm Convention, which established the European Free Trade Association (EFTA). The founding members of EFTA were Austria, Denmark, Norway, Portugal, Sweden, Switzerland and the UK.

Shortly after the EEC began functioning in 1958 the attitude of the UK government began to change and membership came to be sought. The first enlargement of the Community could, in fact, have occurred much earlier than it did had President de Gaulle not opposed UK applications in 1961 and 1967. He did so for a mixture of reasons: he feared the UK would rival and attempt to thwart his desire to place France at the centre of the European stage; he believed UK membership would unsettle the developing Franco–German alliance – an alliance that was given symbolic force with the signing in 1963 of a Friendship Treaty between the two countries; and he was suspicious of the UK's close links with the United States, thinking they would pave the way for American penetration and domination of Europe if the UK joined the Community. So the UK was barred from Community membership until de Gaulle was replaced as French President by Georges Pompidou in 1969. A different view was then taken in Paris: the UK might serve as a useful counterweight to the increasingly strong and self-confident Germany; UK governments would lend support to France's opposition to pressures from within the Community for increased supranationalism; and France would probably gain economically by virtue of having better access to UK markets and as a result of the UK being a net contributor to the Community budget.

The reasons for the UK's changed position on Europe were a mixture of the political and the economic. Politically, it was increasingly clear that the UK was no longer a world power of the first rank. Paralleling this decline, the nature and status of the 'special relationship' with the USA weakened and became increasingly questionable. Furthermore, the British Empire was giving way to the Commonwealth, a very loose organisation and not one that was capable of providing the UK with much international political support. Economically, indicators on growth in trade, investment, gross national product and income clearly showed that by the early 1960s the member states of the EC were outperforming the UK. Quite simply the figures appeared to show that in economic terms the Community was a success; all this at a time when the UK's pattern of trade, even when not a Community member, was turning away from the Commonwealth and towards Europe. Moreover, the growing economic strength of the EC seemed to be linked with growing political status.

Thus when Pompidou opened the EC door, the UK government entered willingly. However, since joining the Community Britain has been something of an awkward partner and has played an important role in slowing aspects of the integration process. This was especially so during the Conservative Party's term of office between 1979 and 1997, for it took a largely minimalist view of what the EC/EU should be doing and what organisational shape it should take. The strong preference was for the EC/EU to be concerned primarily with market-related matters, and more particularly for it to direct most of its efforts towards creating an integrated and largely deregulated European market. The proper and efficient operation of this market was not seen to require common economic, financial, and social policies, let alone a single currency. As for the political dimensions of Community/Union membership, the governments led by Margaret Thatcher and John Major were willing to support the development of intergovernmental cooperation when that seemed useful – as, for example, in the field of foreign policy and aspects of internal security policy – but they almost invariably sought to resist supranational developments and any loss of national sovereignty.

Since the election of a Labour government in 1997, the British stance in the EU has been much more cooperative, as exemplified by the willingness of the government led by Tony Blair to incorporate extensions to supranational decision-making in the Amsterdam and Nice Treaties, to provide a lead in the development of EU defence policy, and by the positive tone displayed by British ministers towards Europe. However, overall, Britain is still in the slow integration stream, as demonstrated by Labour's insistence that Britain be given an opt-out from certain treaty provisions that strengthen the EU's justice and home affairs policies and also by the decision not to join the single currency system.

✳   ✳   ✳

Denmark and Ireland were not interested in joining the Communities that were founded in the 1950s. Both of their economies were heavily dependent on agriculture, so the ECSC had little to offer them. As for the EEC, there were several reasons to doubt that it would be to their benefit, the most important of which was that both countries had strong economic and historical links elsewhere: in Denmark's case with the other Scandinavian countries and with the UK; in Ireland's case with the UK. These links with the UK resulted in both of them tying their willingness to join the EC with the outcome of the UK's attempts to gain membership, so they both applied and then withdrew their applications on two occasions in the 1960s and then became members in 1973.

Denmark's record since joining the Community has been not wholly dissimilar from that of the UK in that, aware of domestic scepticism about the supposed benefits of EC/EU membership, Danish governments have tended to be cautious in their approach to integration. The most dramatic manifestation of Danish concern with the integration process occurred in 1992, when in a national referendum the Danish people rejected Denmark's ratification of the Maastricht Treaty. This rejection, which was reversed in a second referendum in 1993, upset the schedule for applying the Treaty, took much wind out of the sails of those who wished to press ahead quickly with further integration, and resulted in Denmark distancing itself from certain future integrationist projects. As part of this distancing, Denmark, like the UK, did not become a member of the common currency system when it was launched in 1999, and then, in a referendum held in September 2000, the Danish people rejected a proposal to join.

Apart from one exceptional circumstance, Ireland has created no particular difficulties for the EC/EU since its accession. From time to time Irish governments have intimated that their support for further integration is conditional on Ireland continuing to be afforded generous treatment under the Common Agricultural Policy (CAP) and the Structural Funds, but there has been no significant resistance to developments aimed at deepening the integration process. The exceptional circumstance was the decision of the Irish people in a referendum held in June 2001 to reject ratification of the Nice Treaty. Unlike, however, the two 'No' referendum votes in Denmark, the Irish rejection was explained primarily not in terms of anti-EU sentiments but rather a variety of domestic political circumstances. The vote put the implementation of the Nice Treaty on hold until the Irish people approved the Treaty in a second referendum held in October 2002.

The 1981 and 1986 enlargements: Greece, Spain and Portugal

If the 1973 enlargement round resulted in a tilting of the balance of the Community to the north, the two enlargements of the 1980s brought about a counterbalancing to the south and the Mediterranean.

In the 1950s the Greek economy had been unsuitable for ECSC or EEC membership, being predominantly peasant-based. Additionally, Greece's history, culture and geographical position put it outside the West European mainstream. But just as the countries that joined the Community in 1973 would have liked to have become members earlier, so was the accession of Greece delayed longer than Greek governments would have liked. The initial problem, recognised on both sides when Greece made its first approaches to Brussels soon after the EEC came into being, was the underdeveloped nature of the Greek economy. A transitional period prior to membership was deemed to be necessary and this was negotiated in the form of an Association Agreement that came into force in 1962. Full incorporation into the Community would, it was understood, follow when the Greek economy was capable of sustaining the obligations imposed by membership. However, between April 1967, when there was a military coup in Greece, and June 1974, when civilian government was re-established, the Association Agreement was virtually suspended. It might be thought that this would have further delayed full membership, but in fact it had the opposite effect. After elections in Greece in November 1974 the new government immediately made clear its wish for Greece to become a full member of the Community. The Commission issued a formal opinion that Greece was still not economically ready and proposed a pre-accession period of unlimited duration, during which economic reforms could be implemented. In response, the Greek government restated its wish for full membership, and particularly emphasised how membership could help both to underpin Greek democracy and to consolidate Greece's West European and Western Alliance bonds. The Council of Ministers was sympathetic to these arguments and rejected the Commission's proposal. Membership negotiations were opened in July 1976 and Greece entered the Community in 1981.

Since becoming a member, Greece has generally supported the advancement of the integration process. That said, particular Greek policies, concerns, and special needs have sometimes created difficulties: Greece's relative poverty (it is the poorest EU-15 state) has contributed to pressures on the EU's redistributive policies and funds; the (until recently) somewhat unstable nature of the Greek economy has meant that it has sometimes had to seek special economic assistance from its partners; although it wished to join the single currency from its launch, it was the only EU member state that was unable to meet the qualifying convergence criteria for entry into the first wave; Greece's long-standing hostility towards Turkey – now fading, but not gone – and its complicated web of friendships and hostilities with parts of the former Yugoslavia have presented difficulties in the way of EU attempts to develop united and effective policies in South-East Europe; and Greece's special links with Cyprus led to it making threatening noises about EU enlargement to CEECs should Cyprus's application be blocked.

For many years both political and economic circumstances counted against Spanish and Portuguese EC membership. Politically, both countries were authoritarian dictatorships to which the democratic governments of the founding six states did not wish to be too closely attached. Economically, both were predominantly agricultural and underdeveloped, and both pursued essentially autarkic economic policies until the end of the 1950s: factors that hardly made them suitable candidates for the ECSC, and that had the knock-on effect of excluding them from the EEC negotiations, which were opened up only to the UK.

As with Greece, political considerations were extremely important in the relations between the two Iberian states and the Community prior to their accession. Initially the influence was a negative one: if Spain and Portugal had not had dictatorial political systems until the mid-1970s, in all probability they would have been allowed to join much sooner. Not that there was anything in the treaties to specify that members must be liberal democracies: Article 237 of the EEC Treaty simply stated 'Any European State may apply to become a member of the Community'. The assumption was, however – as it explicitly is today – that a democratic political system was a necessary qualification for entry.

So although both Spain and Portugal requested negotiations on association with the Community as early as 1962, and Spain made it quite clear that its request was with a view to full membership at some future date, both countries were treated with caution by the Community. Eventually they were granted preferential trade agreements, but it was only with the overthrow of the Caetano regime in Portugal in 1974 and the death of General Franco in 1975 that full membership became a real possibility. Portugal applied in March 1977 and Spain in July 1977. The negotiations were protracted and difficult, covering, amongst many problems, the threat posed to other Mediterranean countries by Spanish agriculture, the size of the Spanish fishing fleet, and the implications of cheap Spanish and Portuguese labour moving north. As with the Greek negotiations, political factors helped to overcome these difficulties: the member states wished to encourage political stability in southern Europe; there was the opportunity to widen and strengthen the political and economic base of the Community; and, by helping to link southern Europe to the north, there were seen to be strategic advantages for both Western Europe and NATO.

Since their accession both Spain and Portugal have broadly gone along with integrationist developments, with the former perhaps being a little more integrationist than the latter. The fear expressed in some quarters before their accession that they would come to constitute a disruptive Iberian bloc has not been realised. As would be expected, they do frequently adopt similar positions on issues of common concern but, as with other member states, their preferences on specific policy matters often diverge. The single greatest difficulty they, and more especially Spain, have created for the EU is the tough position they have (understandably) adopted in seeking to protect themselves when – most notably in the context of enlargement to CEECs – it has been suggested that the support they receive from the Structural Funds should be reduced.

The 1995 enlargement: Austria, Finland and Sweden

In 1992 the EC formally opened accession negotiations with Austria, Finland and Sweden, and in 1993 it opened negotiations with Norway. These negotiations were concluded successfully in March 1994, with a view to each of the countries becoming members of the EU after the terms of accession had been ratified at national level. However, in Norway the terms were rejected when the people voted against membership in a national referendum. In consequence, there were three rather than four new members of the EU in January 1995.

Two sets of factors stimulated the four countries (and Switzerland too – of which more in the next section) to seek membership of the EU. First, what previously had been regarded as virtually insuperable obstacles to EC membership came in the late 1980s and early 1990s to be seen as less of a problem. For Austria and Sweden (and also Switzerland) the end of the Cold War reduced the importance of their traditional attachment to neutrality. For Finland, the difficulties posed by the country's relative geographical isolation and special position in relation to the Soviet Union disappeared. Second, there were the relationships of these countries to the EC. Austria, Finland, Sweden and Norway, plus Switzerland, Iceland and the micro state of Liechtenstein, made up the membership of EFTA. When EFTA was constituted in 1960 – with, as noted above, Denmark, Portugal and the UK then also as members, but not, at that stage, Finland, Iceland or Liechtenstein – it had two principal objectives: the establishment of a free trade area in industrial products between the member countries, and the creation of a base for making the whole of Western Europe a free trade area for industrial goods. The first of these objectives was established in 1966 with the removal of virtually all customs duties and quantitative restrictions on trade in industrial products between EFTA countries, and the second was achieved in 1977 with the creation of an industrial free trade area between the EC and EFTA. Over time, however, despite relations between the EC and EFTA being friendly, and being indeed further developed via cooperation in such areas as environmental protection, scientific and technical research, and transport policy, the EFTA states increasingly came to view key aspects of the EC–EFTA relationship as unsatisfactory. One reason for their dissatisfaction was that the EC was collectively much stronger than EFTA. Another, and related, reason was that the EC was prone to present EFTA with *de facto* situations to which the EFTA countries had little option but to adjust – as, for example, when the Community laid down product specifications. This latter problem, of having to accept trading rules they had played no part in helping to formulate, became of increasing concern to EFTA countries as the EC's programme to complete the internal market by 1992 – the Single European Market (SEM) programme – gathered pace in the late 1980s and early 1990s. This concern played an important part in encouraging the EFTA countries to reconsider the attractions of EC membership. It also led the EC – concerned that a widening of its membership might threaten its own deepening – to suggest that EC–EFTA relations be strengthened by the creation of a European Economic Area (EEA) which would, in effect, extend the SEM programme to the EFTA states but would stop short of EC membership. The EEA was duly negotiated, and after a series of delays during the ratification process – occasioned by Switzerland withdrawing from the agreement (see p. 33) – came into effect in January 1994. However, by that stage it had come to be accepted by most interested parties – including the governments of the EC, which in the meantime had succeeded in moving Community deepening forward via the Maastricht Treaty – that the ambitions of the governments of Austria, Finland, Sweden and Norway would be satisfied only by full EU membership.

The negotiation of accession terms with the EFTAns (as the applicants were collectively called) was much easier and quicker than in previous negotiating rounds. This was partly because each of the applicants was already well adjusted to EU membership – being prosperous (and hence not posing potential problems for the EU budget), having already incorporated much of the Community's *acquis* into national law, and having a well established democratic political system. It was partly also because many of the matters that normally have to be covered in accession negotiations had already been sorted out in the EEA negotiations and agreement.

Since their accession, none of the 1995 entrants has created any major problems for the EU, although there was disappointment in 'integrationist quarters' when the Swedish people decided in a referendum held in September 2003 not to join the single currency system – by 56.1 per cent to 41.8 per cent on a 81.2 per cent turnout. Perhaps the most distinctive contribution that the three states have made to the EU has been to oblige the other member states to pay more attention than they might otherwise have done to the issues of openness, transparency and EU democracy.

Non-EU West European countries: Norway, Switzerland and Iceland

There are now only three significant Western European countries that are not members of the EU: Norway, Switzerland and Iceland.

Like Denmark and Ireland, Norway paralleled the UK in applying for EC membership in the 1960s (twice) and early 1970s. On the third occasion terms of entry were agreed by the Norwegian government, but were then rejected by the Norwegian people in a referendum in 1972 following a campaign in which suspicions about the implications for Norwegian agriculture, fishing, and national sovereignty featured prominently. Another application for membership was made in 1992, partly for the reasons set out above in relation to the unsatisfactory nature of EC–EFTA decision-making relations, partly because the government felt that Norway could not afford to ignore the applications of its neighbours and be the only Scandinavian country not to become an EU member, and partly because there were grounds (although by no means overwhelming grounds) for believing that the long-standing public opposition to membership was no longer as strong as it had been. Accession terms were quickly negotiated, but in the ensuing referendum in 1994 the issues raised echoed those of 1972, though with the additional argument being made by the opponents of membership that Norway had no need to join the EU since it was a prosperous country that, thanks to the EEA, already had the trading ties with the EU that it required. The people again voted against membership.

Until December 1992 Switzerland was in much the same position as Austria and Sweden. That is to say, it had long been a member of EFTA, the end of the Cold War had removed the main obstacle to it becoming a member of the EC/EU, an application for accession had been made, and it anticipated entry some time in the mid-1990s. However, in December 1992, in a referendum on whether to ratify the EEA, the Swiss people narrowly voted – by 50.3 per cent to 49.7 per cent – against ratification. As a consequence, the timetable for bringing the EEA into effect was delayed, and the Swiss application to join the EU necessarily had to be put aside.

Iceland considered the possibility of EC membership at the time of the 1973 enlargement but concluded that there were too many policy difficulties in the way, especially with regard to fishing. This continues to be the case and explains why Iceland did not join the other EFTA states in the 1990s when they sought EU accession.

As Switzerland and Norway did not become EU members in the EFTAn enlargement round, EFTA continues to exist, with Iceland and Liechtenstein as its other members. The EEA also continues, although Switzerland, of course, is not a member. Iceland, Norway and Switzerland are each linked in to many EU programmes and activities.

Concluding Remarks: The Ragged Nature of the Integration Process in Western Europe

After the Second World War the way in which West European governments related to and communicated with one another was gradually transformed. A key role in this transformation was played by new international governmental organisations. Some of these were global in their composition, others were regionally-based; some had sweeping but vaguely defined responsibilities, others had specific sectoral briefs; some were purely intergovernmental in structure, others were overlain with supranational powers. At a minimum, all provided frameworks in which national representatives met with one another to discuss matters of mutual interest.

The best known, most developed and most important of these West European-wide organisations has been what we now know as the EU. But the EU was never the only significant West Europe-wide organisation, and it was not the first such organisation to be established. On the contrary, after the Second World War numerous proposals were advanced and many arrangements were set in place for organised cooperation and integration among the states. The more ambitious of these sought to bring the whole of Western Europe together in some sort of federal union. The more cautious were limited to the pursuit of restricted aims for just some of the states.

So although the logic of circumstances and of political and economic changes brought the states much more closely together, there can hardly be said to have been a common and coherent integrationist force at work in Western Europe in the post-war years. Far from the states being bound together in the pursuit of a shared visionary mission, relations between them have frequently been extremely uncomfortable and uneasy, based as they have been on a host of different national needs and perceptions of what is possible and necessary. In consequence, the processes of cooperation and integration have operated in many different forums, at many different levels, in many different ways, and at many different speeds. Even in the EC/EU, which has been at the integrationist core, the course of the integration process has varied considerably with, for example, the mid-1970s until the early 1980s being years of relatively slow integrationist advance and the mid-1980s until the early 1990s being years of rapid progress.

It is, of course, the conflicting nature of many of the factors which affect the integration process that has resulted in the process being so rocky, uncertain and unpredictable. Moreover, the factors themselves have been subject to considerable and unforeseeable change, no more so than since the early 1990s with the context in which the pressures which affect the furtherance of integration being transformed by the ending of the Cold War and the break-up of the Soviet Union. After four decades of Europe having been politically divided in two, decades in which Western Europe tended to think of itself as *being* Europe, fundamental issues concerning the nature of the continent as a whole came onto the agenda. In these circumstances, new links, contacts and forms of cooperation were rapidly established between the countries of Western and Eastern Europe, advanced not least by many of the latter seeking EU membership within five years of having been released from Soviet domination. The manner in which the developments in the former communist bloc transformed what had been a *Western European integration* process into a *European integration* process are explored in Chapter 4.

Chapter 2

The Creation of the European Community

The European Coal and Steel Community
From the ECSC to the EEC
The EEC and Euratom Treaties
Concluding Remarks

The European Coal and Steel Community

Much of the early impetus behind the first of the European Communities, the ECSC, was provided by two Frenchmen. Jean Monnet, who had pioneered France's successful post-war experiment with indicative economic planning, provided much of the technical and administrative initiative and behind-the-scenes drive. Robert Schuman, the French Foreign Minister from 1948 to early 1953, acted as the political advocate. Both were ardent supporters of European unity, both believed that the OEEC and the Council of Europe – where anyone could be exempted from a decision – could not provide the necessary impetus, and both came to the conclusion that, in Monnet's words, 'A start would have to be made by doing something both more practical and more ambitious. National sovereignty would have to be tackled more boldly and on a narrower front' (Monnet, 1978: 274).

Many of those who were attracted to the ECSC saw it in very restrictive terms: as an organisation that might further certain limited and carefully defined purposes. Certainly it would not have been established had it not offered to potential member states – in particular its two main pillars, France and West Germany – the possibility that it might serve to satisfy specific and pressing national interests and needs. But for some, including Monnet and Schuman, the project was much more ambitious and long-term. When announcing the plan in May 1950, Schuman – in what subsequently became known as the Schuman Declaration – was quite explicit that the proposals were intended to be but the first step in the realisation of a vision of a united Europe that would have Franco–German reconciliation at its heart. But, he warned, 'Europe will not be made all at once, or according to a single plan. It will be built through concrete achievements which first create a *de facto* solidarity' (the Schuman Declaration is reproduced in Salmon and Nicoll, 1997: 44–6). In similar vein, Monnet informed governments during the negotiations:

> The Schuman proposals provide a basis for the building of a new Europe through the concrete achievement of a supranational regime within a limited but controlling area of economic effort. ... The indispensable first principle of these proposals is the abnegation of sovereignty in a limited but decisive field (Monnet, 1978: 316).

The German Chancellor, Konrad Adenauer, agreed with this. Addressing the Bundestag in June 1950 he stated:

> Let me make a point of declaring in so many words and in full agreement, not only with the French Government but also with M. Jean Monnet, that the importance of this project is above all political and not economic (quoted in ibid.: 319–20).

Schuman made it clear in his Declaration that whilst he hoped other countries would also participate, France and West Germany would proceed with the plan in any event (West Germany having already agreed privately in principle). Italy, Belgium, Luxembourg and the Netherlands took up the invitation, and in April 1951 the six countries signed the Treaty of Paris, which established the ECSC for a period of fifty years from the entry into force of the ECSC Treaty. The ECSC duly came into operation in July 1952 and lasted until the expiry of the Treaty in July 2002, when ECSC responsibilities and activities were transferred to the European Community.

The ECSC Treaty broke new ground in two principal ways. First, its policy aims were extremely ambitious, entailing not just the creation of a free trade area, but also laying the foundations for a common market in what at the time were some of the basic materials of any industrialised society: coal, coke, iron ore, steel and scrap. This, it was hoped, would ensure orderly supplies to all member states, produce a rational expansion and modernisation of production, and improve the conditions and life-styles of those working in the industries in question. Second, it was the first of the European inter-state organisations to possess significant suprana-tional characteristics. These could be found in the new central institutions, which had the power, amongst other things, to: see to the abolition and prohibition of internal tariff barriers, state subsidies and special charges, and restrictive practices; fix prices under certain conditions; harmonise external commercial policy, for example by setting minimum and max-imum customs duties on coal and steel imports from third countries; and impose levies on coal and steel production to finance the ECSC's activities. Four main institutions were created.

(1) *The High Authority* was set up 'To ensure that the objectives set out in this Treaty are attained in accordance with the provisions thereof' (Article 8 ECSC Treaty). To enable it to perform its tasks the High Authority could issue, either on its own initiative or after receiving the assent of the Council of Ministers: decisions (which were to be binding in all respects in the member states); recommendations (which were to be binding in their objectives); and opinions (which were not to have binding force). Matters upon which the High Authority was granted decision-making autonomy included the prohibition of subsidies and aids, decisions on whether or not agreements between undertakings were permissible, action against restrictive practices, the promotion of research, and the control of prices under certain conditions. It could impose fines on those who disregarded its decisions.

The High Authority thus had a formidable array of powers at its disposal and this, when taken in conjunction with its membership, gave it a clear supranational character. There were to be nine members, including at least one from each member state, and, crucially, all were to be 'completely independent in the performance of their duties'. In other words, no one would be, or should regard themselves as being, a national delegate or representative.

In a number of respects the High Authority's powers were stronger than those which were to be given to the High Authority's equivalent, the Commission, under the Treaties of Rome. This meant that after the institutions of the three Communities were merged in 1967, the Commission – which assumed the High Authority's powers – had rather more room for independent manoeuvre when acting under the Treaty of Paris than when acting under the Treaties of Rome. In practice, however, it was not always possible for these greater powers to be used to the full: from the earliest days of the ECSC, political realities dictated that the High Authority/Commission must be sensitive to governmental opinions and policies.

(2) *The Council of Ministers* was set up mainly as a result of the Benelux countries' concern that if the High Authority had too much power and there was no forum through which the states could exercise some control, the ECSC might be too Franco-German dominated. Ministers from the national governments were to constitute the membership of the Council, with each state having one representative.

According to Article 26 of the ECSC Treaty, 'The Council shall exercise its powers in the cases provided for and in the manner set out in this Treaty, in particular in order to harmonise the actions of the High Authority and that of the Governments, which are responsible for the general economic policies of their countries'. More specifically, the Treaty gave the Council formal control over some, but far from all, of the High Authority's actions: the Council had, for instance, to give its assent to the declaration of a manifest crisis which opened the door to production quotas. Decision-making procedures in the Council were to depend on the matter under consideration: sometimes a unanimous vote would be required, sometimes a qualified majority, sometimes a simple majority.

Practice subsequently showed the Council to be not altogether consistent in the manner in which it exercised its role under the ECSC Treaty. On the one hand, a general reluctance of the states to lose too much power over their domestic industries normally resulted in the Council seeking to take most major decisions itself. Since decision-making in the Council customarily proceeded on the basis of consensus, and since the states were often unable to agree when difficult decisions were called for, this frequently led to very weak, or indeed even to an absence of, decision-making. On the other hand, when practicalities and political convenience combined to suggest a less Council-centred decision-making approach, as they did with steel from the late 1970s, then the Council was prepared to allow the High Authority/Commission a considerable measure of independence.

(3) *The Common Assembly's* role was to provide a democratic input into ECSC decision-making. In practice it can hardly be said to have done so in the early years: members were not elected but were chosen by national parliaments, and the Assembly's powers – notwithstanding an ability to pass a motion of censure on the High Authority – were essentially only advisory. However, the expansion of the Assembly's remit under the Rome Treaties to cover all three Communities, plus developments from the 1970s such as the introduction of direct elections and more streamlined procedures, increasingly made for a more effective Assembly (or European Parliament as it was now called).

(4) *The Court of Justice* was created to settle conflicts between the states, between the organs of the Community, and between the states and the organs. Its judgements were to be enforceable within the territory of the member states. In similar fashion to the Assembly, but not the High Authority or Council of Ministers which remained separate until 1967, the Court assumed responsibility for all three Communities when the EEC and Euratom Treaties entered into force in 1958.

In addition to these four main institutions a Consultative Committee, made up of producers, workers and other interested parties, was also created by the ECSC Treaty. The role of the Committee was to be purely advisory.

* * *

In its early years the ECSC was judged to be an economic success. Customs tariffs and quotas were abolished, progress was made on the removal of non-tariff barriers to trade, the restructuring of the industries was assisted, politicians and civil servants from the member states became accustomed to working with one another and, above all, output and inter-state trade rapidly increased (although many economists would now query whether the increases were *because* of the ECSC). As a result, the ECSC helped to pave the way for further integration.

However, the success of the early years was soon checked. In 1958–9, when cheap oil imports and a fall in energy consumption combined to produce an overcapacity in coal production, the ECSC was faced with its first major crisis – and failed the test. The member states rejected the High Authority's proposals for a Community-wide solution and sought their own, uncoordinated, protective measures. The coal crisis thus revealed that the High Authority was not as powerful as many had believed and was not in a position to impose a general policy on the states if they were determined to resist.

This relative weakness of the High Authority/Commission to press policies right through is one of the principal reasons why truly integrated West European coal and steel industries, in which prices and distributive decisions are a consequence of an open and free market, have not fully emerged. Many barriers to intra-EU trade still remain. Some of these, such as restrictive practices and national subsidies, the High Authority and then the Commission have tried to remove, but with only limited success. Others, particularly in the steel sector, have been formulated and utilised by the Commission itself as its task has switched from encouraging expansion to managing contraction.

But arguably the major problem with the ECSC was that as coal and steel declined in importance in relation to other energy sources, what increasingly was required was not so much policies for coal and steel in isolation, but a coordinated and effective Community energy policy. National differences have prevented such a policy being developed, although there has been progress in recent years.

From the ECSC to the EEC

The perceived success of the ECSC in its early years provided an impetus for further integration. Another institutional development of the 1950s also played an important role in paving the way for the creation of the two additional European Communities that were to be created in 1957. This was the projected European Defence Community (EDC).

In the early 1950s, against the background of the Cold War and the outbreak of the Korean War, many Western politicians and military strategists saw the need for greater Western European cooperation in defence matters. This would involve the integration of West Germany – which was not a member of NATO – into the Western Alliance. The problem was that some European countries, especially France, were not yet ready for German rearmament, whilst West Germany itself, though willing to re-arm, was not willing to do so on the basis of the tightly controlled and restricted conditions that other countries appeared to have in mind for it. In these circumstances the French Prime Minister, René Pleven, launched proposals in October 1950 which offered a possible way forward. In announcing his plan to the National Assembly he stated that the French government 'proposes the creation, for our common defence, of a European Army under the political institutions of a united Europe' (Pleven's statement is reproduced in Harryvan and van der Harst, 1997: 65–9). By the end of 1951 the six governments involved in the establishment of the ECSC had agreed to establish an EDC. Its institutional structure was to be similar to the ECSC: a Joint Defence Commission, a Council of Ministers, an advisory Assembly and a Court of Justice.

In May 1952 a draft EDC Treaty was signed, but in the event the EDC and the European Political Community, which increasingly came to be associated with it, were not established. Ratification problems arose in France and Italy, and in August 1954 the French National Assembly rejected the EDC by 319 votes to 264 with 43 abstentions. There were a number of reasons for this: continuing unease about German rearmament; concern that the French government would not have sole control of its military forces; doubts about the efficiency of an integrated force; disquiet that the strongest European military power (the United Kingdom) was not participating; and a feeling that, with the end of the Korean War and the death of Stalin, the EDC was not as necessary as it had seemed when it was first proposed.

Following the collapse of the EDC project, an alternative and altogether less demanding approach was taken to the still outstanding question of West Germany's contribution to the defence of the West. This took the form of a revival and extension of the Brussels Treaty 'for collaboration in economic, social and cultural matters and for collective defence' that had been signed in 1948 by the three Benelux countries, France and the UK. At a conference in London in the autumn of 1954 West Germany and Italy agreed to accede to the Brussels Treaty and all seven countries agreed that the new arrangements should be incorporated into a Western European Union (WEU). The WEU came into effect in May 1955 as a loosely structured, essentially consultative, primarily defence-orientated organisation that, amongst other things, permitted West German rearmament subject to various constraints. It also enabled West Germany to become a member of NATO.

The failure of the EDC, especially when set alongside the 'success' of the WEU, highlighted the difficulties involved in pressing ahead too quickly with integrationist proposals. In particular, it showed that quasi-federalist approaches in politically sensitive areas would meet with resistance. But, at the same time, the fact that such an ambitious scheme as the EDC had come so close to adoption demonstrated that alternative initiatives, especially if they were based on the original Schuman view that political union could be best achieved through economic integration, might well be successful. It was partly with this in mind that the Foreign Ministers of the ECSC six met at Messina in Sicily in June 1955 to discuss proposals by the three Benelux countries for further economic integration. At Messina the Ministers agreed on a resolution that included the following:

> The governments . . . believe the moment has come to go a step further towards the construction of Europe. In their opinion this step should first of all be taken in the economic field.
>
> They consider that the further progress must be towards the setting up of a united Europe by the development of common institutions, the gradual merging of national economies, the creation of a common market, and the gradual harmonization of their social policies.
>
> Such a policy appears to them to be indispensable if Europe's position in the world is to be maintained, her influence restored, and the standard of living of her population progressively raised (the Resolution is reproduced in Salmon and Nicoll, 1997: 59–61).

To give effect to the Messina Resolution, a committee of governmental representatives and experts was established under the chairmanship of the Belgian Foreign Minister, Paul-Henri Spaak. The UK was invited to participate and did so until November 1955, but then withdrew when it became apparent that its hopes of limiting developments to the establishment of a loose free trade area were not acceptable to the six. In April 1956 the Foreign Ministers accepted the report of the Spaak Committee and used it as the basis for negotiations that in 1957 produced the two Treaties of Rome: the more important of these treaties established the European Economic Community (EEC) and the other the European Atomic Energy Community (Euratom).

Both before and after April 1956 the negotiations between the six governments were extensive and intense. At the end of the negotiations it can be said that, in broad terms, provisions were made in the treaties for those areas upon which the governments were able to reach agreement, but where there were divisions matters were largely left aside for further negotiations and were either omitted from the treaties altogether or were referred to only in a general way. So the EEC Treaty set out fairly clear rules on trade, but only guiding principles were laid down for social and agricultural policy.

The inclusion in the EEC Treaty of topics such as social and agricultural policy reflected a series of compromises among the six countries, especially between the two strongest ones – France and West Germany. France feared that Germany was likely to become the main beneficiary of the more open markets of the proposed customs union and so looked for compensation elsewhere. This took a number of forms, most notably: insisting on special protection for agriculture – French farmers had historically been well protected from foreign competition and around one-fifth of the French population still earned a living from the land; pressing the case of an atomic energy Community, which would help guarantee France greater independence in energy; and seeking privileged relations with the six for France's overseas dependencies.

Eventually the negotiations were completed, and on 25 March 1957 the two treaties were signed. Only in France and Italy were there any problems with ratification: the French Chamber of Deputies voted 342 for and 239 against, and the Italian Chamber of Deputies voted 311 for and 144 against. In both countries the largest opposition bloc comprised the communists. The treaties came into effect on 1 January 1958.

The EEC and Euratom Treaties

The policy concerns of the EEC Treaty

Of the two Rome Treaties the EEC Treaty was by far the most important. Article 2 of the Treaty laid down the following broad objectives:

> The Community shall have as its task, by establishing a common market and progressively approximating the economic policies of Member States, to promote throughout the Community a harmonious develop-ment of economic activities, a continuous and balanced expansion, an increase in stability, an accelerated raising of the standard of living and closer relations between the states belonging to it.

Many of the subsequent Treaty articles were concerned with following up these broad objectives with fuller, though still often rather general, guidelines for policy development. These policy guidelines can be grouped under two broad headings.

Policy guidelines concerned with the establishment of a common market

The common market was to be based on the following:

(1)   The removal of all tariffs and quantitative restrictions on internal trade. This would make the Community a free trade area.
(2)   The erection of a Common External Tariff (CET). This would mean that goods entering the Community would do so on the same basis no matter what their point of entry. No member state would therefore be in a position to gain a competitive advantage by, say, reducing the external tariffs on vital raw materials. The CET would take the Community beyond a mere free trade area and make it a customs union. It would also serve as the basis for the development of a Common Commercial Policy (CCP).
(3)   The prohibition of a range of practices having as their effect the distortion or prevention of competition between the member states.
(4)   Measures to promote not only the free movement of goods between the member states but also the free movement of persons, services and capital.

Policy guidelines concerned with making the Community more than just a common market

Making it exactly what, however, was left unclear, as it had to be given the uncertainties, disagreements and compromises that formed the background to the signing of the Treaty. There was certainly the implication of a movement towards some sort of general economic integration and references were made to the 'coordination' of economic and monetary policies, but they were vague and implicitly long-term. Such references as there were to specific sectoral policies – as, for example, with the provisions for 'the adoption of a common policy in the sphere of agriculture', and the statement that the objectives of the Treaty 'shall ... be pursued by Member States within the framework of a common transport policy' – were couched in somewhat general terms.

*   *   *

The EEC Treaty was thus very different in character from the constitutions of nation states. Whereas the latter have little, if anything, to say about policy, the EEC Treaty had policy as its main concern. The nature of that concern was such that many have suggested that the policy framework indicated and outlined in the Treaty was guided by a clear philosophy or ideology: that of free-market, liberal, non-interventionist capitalism. Unquestionably there is much in this view: on the one hand the market mechanism and the need to prevent abuses to competition were accorded a high priority; on the other hand there were few references to ways in which joint activities and interventions should be promoted for non-market-based purposes. But the case should not be overstated. First, because competition itself was seen as requiring considerable intervention and management from the centre. Second, because there were some provisions for non-market policies: in the proposed common policy for agriculture, for example, which was given a special place in the Treaty precisely because of (mainly French) fears of what would happen should agriculture be exposed to a totally free market; in the proposed social policy, which was intended to help soften unacceptable market consequences; and in the proposed common transport policy where specific allowance was to be made for aids 'if they meet the needs of coordination of transport or if they represent reimbursement for the discharge of certain obligations inherent in the concept of a pubic service'. Third, because the Treaty was highly dependent on the future cooperation of the member states for successful policy development, there was never any question – given the Christian Democratic and Social Democratic principles of most EC governments – of an immediate abandonment of national economic controls and a remorseless and inevitable drive towards uninhibited free market capitalism.

The policy concerns of the Euratom Treaty

The policy concerns of the Euratom Treaty were naturally confined to the atomic energy field. Chapters of the Treaty covered such areas of activity as promotion of research, dissemination of information, health and safety, supplies, and a nuclear common market. However, and even more than with the EEC Treaty, differences between the states on key points resulted in the force of many of the provisions of these chapters being watered down by exceptions and loopholes. For example, under Article 52 an agency was established with 'exclusive right to conclude contracts relating to the supply of ores, scarce materials and special fissile materials coming from inside the Community or from outside'. Article 66, however, set out circumstances in which states could buy on the world markets provided Commission approval was obtained. Similarly, Treaty provisions aimed at a pooling and sharing of technical information and knowledge were greatly weakened – largely at French insistence – by provisions allowing for secrecy where national security was involved.

The institutional provisions of the treaties

The ECSC Treaty served as the institutional model for the EEC and Euratom Treaties, but with modifications which had as their effect a tilting away from supranationalism towards intergovernmentalism. As with the ECSC, both the EEC and Euratom were to have four principal institutions:

(1) An appointed *Commission* would assume the role exercised by the High Authority under the ECSC. That is, it would be the principal policy initiator, it would have some decision-making powers of its own, and it would carry certain responsibilities for policy implementation. But it would have less power than the High Authority to impose decisions on member states.

(2) A *Council of Ministers,* with greater powers than its equivalent under the ECSC, would be the principal decision-making body. Circumstances in which it must take its decisions unanimously, and circumstances in which majority and qualified majority votes were permissible, were specified.

(3) An *Assembly* would exercise advisory and (limited) supervisory powers. Initially it would be composed of delegates from national parliaments, but after appropriate arrangements were made it was to be elected 'by direct universal suffrage in accordance with a uniform procedure in all Member States'.

(4) A *Court of Justice* was charged with the duty of ensuring that 'in the interpretation and application of this Treaty the law is observed'.

A Convention, which was also signed on 25 March 1957, specified that the Assembly and the Court of Justice should be common to all three Communities.

✻   ✻   ✻

These institutional arrangements were rather more intergovernmental in character than those who dreamed of political integration would have liked. In particular, the Council of Ministers was judged to have been given too much power and there was also disappointment that most of the key decisions in the Council would have to be made unanimously. However, there was hope for the future in that there were grounds for believing that the system could, and probably would, serve as a launching pad for a creeping supranationalism. One of these grounds was provision in the EEC Treaty for increased use of majority voting in the Council as the Community became established. Another was the expectation that the Assembly would soon be elected by direct suffrage and that its authority would thereby be increased. And a third was the seemingly reasonable assumption that if the Community proved to be a success the member states would become less concerned about their national rights and would increasingly cede greater powers to the central institutions.

Concluding Remarks

The Treaty of Paris and the two Treaties of Rome are thus the Founding Treaties of the three European Communities. At the time of their signings they marked major steps forward in the development of post-war inter-state relations. They did so by laying the bases for signatory states to integrate specific and core areas of their economic activities and by embodying a degree of supranationalism in the decision-making arrangements they established for the new Communities.

Insofar as it was the first treaty, the Treaty of Paris holds a special place in the history of European integration. In terms of long-term impact, however, the EEC Treaty has been the most important in that it has been on its wide policy base that much of European integration since 1958 has been constructed.

Though they laid down reasonably clear guidelines on, and requirements for, certain matters, the Founding Treaties were not intended to act as straitjackets with respect to the future shape and development of the Communities. Rather, they provided frameworks within which certain things would be expected to happen and other things could happen if decision-makers so chose.

Attention is, therefore, now turned to the development of European integration since the Rome Treaties came into force in January 1958.

Chapter 3

The Evolution of the European Community and Union

Treaty Development
Enlargement
Development of Policy Processes
Development of Policies
Concluding Remarks

Since the European Communities were created, European integration has advanced in many ways. This chapter outlines the most important of these ways.

The examination does not take the form of a detailed account of the unfolding of the integration process. For those who want such an account, the best starting point is Dinan, 2004. Nor does the chapter provide a chronological history – a Chronology of Main Events is included at the end of the book. Rather, the chapter provides an overview of the main features of the integration process.

Four main features are considered: treaty development; enlargement; the development of policy processes; and the development of policies. Since each of these features is explored further in other chapters of the book, attention in this chapter is restricted to the identification of key points associated with the features and to showing how they have impacted on one another.

Treaty Development

As was shown in Chapter 2, the Treaty of Paris and the two Treaties of Rome constitute the Founding Treaties of the European Communities. Over the years, in response to pressures for the EC/EU treaty framework to be extended, strengthened, and made more democratic, the Founding Treaties – especially the EEC Treaty – have been amended and supplemented by subsequent treaties. In 2002 the fifty-year life of the ECSC Treaty expired and responsibility for coal and steel was transferred to the European Community (as the EEC was re-named at Maastricht).

The EU's treaty framework today is thus radically different from the framework that was laid down in the 1950s.

The first major set of revisions to the Founding Treaties were incorporated in the 1986 Single European Act (SEA), which was something of a mixed bag, containing tidying up provisions, provisions designed to give the Community a broader policy remit, and provisions altering aspects of Community decision-making. There were two main aspects to these last provisions. On the one hand, the capacity of the Council of Ministers to take decisions by qualified majority vote (QMV) was strengthened, with the purpose of enabling the Community to pass the laws that would be necessary to give effect to the aim that was agreed at the June 1985 Milan European Council meeting of 'completing' the internal market by December 1992. On the other hand, with a view to be seen to be doing something about the so-called 'democratic deficit', the influence of the European Parliament (EP) (the Assembly started calling itself the European Parliament from 1962) was strengthened via the creation of a two stage legislative procedure – 'the cooperation procedure' – for some legislative proposals. Taken together, the Milan summit and the SEA are often described as heralding the 're-launch' of European integration in that they provided the foundations for a considerable increase in the pace of integration after some years of, if not sclerosis as is sometimes claimed, slow integrationist advance.

The 1992 Maastricht Treaty built on the momentum that the SEA provided for the integration process and advanced it significantly further. It did so in two main ways. First, it created the new organisation of the European Union, which was based on three pillars: the European Communities, a Common Foreign and Security Policy (CFSP), and Cooperation in the Fields of Justice and Home Affairs (JHA). Second, like the SEA, it furthered policy and institutional deepening: the former, most notably, by laying down a procedure and a timetable for moving to Economic and Monetary Union (EMU) with a single currency; the latter, most notably, by further extending provision for QMV in the Council and by creating a new legislative procedure – co-decision – which, for the first time, gave the EP the power of veto over some legislative proposals.

The 1997 Amsterdam Treaty was neither as far-reaching nor as ambitious as either the SEA or the Maastricht Treaty. Indeed, for Euroenthusiasts it was something of a disappointment in that it did not complete what had been intended to be its main job, namely adjusting the composition of the EU's institutions in preparation for enlargement. Nonetheless, it was significant for the integration process in that, like the SEA and the Maastricht Treaty, it too carried policy and institutional deepening forward, albeit more modestly. In respect of policy deepening, its main contribution was to strengthen the EU's decision-making capacity in certain justice and home affairs spheres. In respect of institutional deepening, its most important changes were to extend the co-decision procedure to more policy spheres and to virtually abolish the cooperation procedure.

The 2001 Nice Treaty was always intended to be limited in scope in that its remit was largely restricted to dealing with the 'Amsterdam leftovers'. That is to say, its main task was to make changes in the composition of the EU's institutions and in the voting strengths and voting procedures in the Council so as to enable the EU to absorb applicant states, whilst at the same time not undermining the capacity of the EU to function in a tolerably efficient manner. This, as Chapter 6 shows, the Treaty did.

The most recent of the EU's major treaties – the 2004 Treaty Establishing a Constitution for Europe – continued the pattern of all the treaties since the SEA in that it provided for advances in both policy and institutional integration. But it was also in important respects different from earlier treaties. One way in which it was so was by being much more extensively prepared – most notably in the forum of a Constitutional Convention – before being formally negotiated by governmental representatives. (All EC/EU treaties have been negotiated between governments in what are known as Intergovernmental Conferences – IGCs.) Another way in which the 2004 Treaty was different was in its use of the word 'Constitution', which was widely seen as having great symbolic significance for the developing character of the EU. And a third way in which the Constitutional Treaty – as the 2004 Treaty came to be widely called – was different, was that it ran into major ratification difficulties. There had been some difficulties in ratifying earlier treaties, as is shown in Chapters 5 and 6, but these difficulties had not been seen at the time as being insuperable, and in the event they proved not to be so. But the difficulties with ratifying the Constitutional Treaty were of quite a different order, with two founding member states – the Netherlands and France – rejecting it in referendums held in mid-2005. The consequences of these referendums was initially disputed, with many 'pro-integrationists' arguing for a continuation of the ratification process in the hope that somehow the Constitution could be rescued and with many others concluding that the Constitution could never come into force. Over time, however, 'realities' increasingly favoured the latter position and the prospects of the whole of the Treaty eventually entering into force became extremely bleak.

Enlargement

From an original EC membership of six, the EU at the time of writing (early 2006) numbers twenty five member states. As is explained in

Chapters 2 and 4, this enlargement has taken place in five stages: in 1973 (when Denmark, Ireland and the UK joined), in 1981 (when Greece joined), in 1986 (when Portugal and Spain joined), in 1995 (when Austria, Finland and Sweden joined), and in 2004 (when Cyprus, the Czech Republic, Estonia, Hungary, Latvia, Lithuania, Malta, Poland, Slovakia, and Slovenia joined). The twenty five will soon increase to twenty seven, probably in 2007 when Bulgaria and Romania are scheduled to join.

All five enlargements have inevitably affected and changed the Union in important ways. First, and most obviously, the Union has, simply by becoming bigger, become a more important international organisation. It now contains a population of over 450 million; its membership includes all the larger, and traditionally more influential, West European states, and all the similar states of Central and Eastern Europe outside the Balkans and the former Soviet Union; and it is the world's principal commercial power, accounting for around one-fifth of world imports and exports (not counting commerce between the member states themselves).

Second, the EU's institutions have grown in size to accommodate representatives of acceding states, and internal decision-making has become more complex because of the wider range of national and political interests that have to be satisfied. Given the inevitably increased difficulty of obtaining unanimity in the expanded Council, enlargement has been an important driving factor behind the increases in QMV that have been provided for in the rounds of treaty reform since the SEA.

Third, the Franco–German axis, though still highly influential in helping to set the pace of the integration process, is not as dominant as it was when there were only six member states. More generally, as the number of smaller states has increased, it has not been as easy for the larger states to push through their preferences.

Fourth, policy debates, concerns and priorities have been affected by new members bringing with them their own requirements, preferences and problems. For example, the growing influence, as a result of the second and third enlargements, of southern, less industrialised and poorer countries quickly led to calls both for a re-orientation of the Common Agricultural Policy (CAP) away from northern temperate products to-wards Mediterranean products, and for redistributive policies that directly assist economic development in the south. The 1995 enlargement to the EFTAns has played a part in increasing the attention that is now being given by the EU to such matters as openness and accountability in decision-making and efficiency and sound financial management in decision implementation. And the 2004 enlargement has produced pressures for the EU's budget to be focused more towards assisting with economic development in the CEECs.

Development of Policy Processes

The Founding Treaties indicated a pattern of policy-making and decision-making in which the Commission would propose, the Parliament would advise, the Council would decide, and – when law was made – the Court of Justice would interpret. For many years this is how inter-institutional relationships and processes generally worked in practice, and indeed in a few decision-making areas they still do so. But since the re-launch of the integration process in the mid-1980s there have been many additions and amendments to the pattern. Four of these additions and amendments are particularly worth noting.

First, the relationships between the four institutions themselves have altered in a number of ways. As integration has evolved, all of the institutions have extended their interests and simultaneously become increasingly less compartmentalised and less self-contained within the EU system. This has led not only to a certain blurring of responsibilities as the dividing lines between who does what have become less clear, but also to changes in the powers of, and balance between, institutions as there has emerged a more general sharing of powers. So, for example, the Council of Ministers has usurped some of the Commission's proposing responsibilities by becoming progressively more involved in helping to initiate and set the policy agenda; the Court has significantly affected the direction and pace of the integration process by issuing many judgements with considerable policy and institutional implications; and the EP, greatly assisted by treaty changes, has steadily extended its influence, especially its legislative influence. Indeed, such has been the increase in the EP's legislative role that the former Commission–Council axis on which EU legislative processes were based has been replaced by a Council–Commission–EP triangle.

Second, an increasing range of participants not associated with the four main institutions have become involved in policy-making and decision-making. The most important of these participants are the Heads of Government who, in regular summits – known as European Council meetings – have come to assume key agenda-setting and decision taking responsibilities that have had the effect of reducing the power and manoeuvrability of both the Council of Ministers and the Commission. Prominent amongst other actors who have inserted or attempted to insert themselves into decision-making processes are the many national and transnational sectoral interests and pressures that have come to cluster around the main institutions in order to monitor developments and, when possible, to advise or pressurise decision-makers.

Third, policy processes have become more varied and complex as they have come to function in many different ways at many different levels.

In addition to what occurs in the structured settings of Council and Commission meetings, Parliamentary plenaries and committees, and Court sittings, there is a mosaic of less formal channels in which representatives of the institutions, the states, and interests, meet and interact to discuss and produce policies and decisions. Which processes and channels operate in particular cases, and what types of interactions occur therein, varies considerably from sector to sector, and can even do so from decision to decision.

Fourth, policy processes have become, in some respects at least, more efficient and democratic. They have become more efficient insofar as treaty reforms have made it possible for an increasing number of Council decisions to be taken by QMV rather than requiring unanimity. Decision-making has thus been less hampered by having to wait for the slowest. Policy processes have become more democratic insofar as the EP – the only EU institution to be directly elected – has become more influential.

Development of Policies

The EU's policy portfolio has expanded steadily over the years, stimulated and encouraged by factors such as treaty provisions, the increasing internationalisation and competitiveness of economic forces, a growing recognition of the benefits of working together, integrationist pressures emanating from central institutions (notably the Commission and the EP), and the stimulus that policy development in one sphere has given to developments in other spheres.

The policies that lie closest to the heart of the EU's policy framework are those related to what used to be called 'the Common Market' and which is now known as 'the internal market' or 'the Single European Market' (SEM). In essence, these policies are designed to promote the free movement of goods, services, capital and people between the member states, and to enable the EU to act jointly and present a common front in its economic and trading relations with third countries. Since the mid-1980s – when the creation of the SEM was given priority via the '1992 programme' and the SEA – there has been considerable development of these market-based policies. This has resulted in a great increase in the range and extent of the EU's regulatory presence, which is somewhat ironic given that a key aim of the SEM programme has been to liberalise and deregulate the functioning of the market. It has, however, been generally recognised and conceded by EU decision-makers that the market can operate on a reasonably fair and open basis only if key features of it are properly managed and controlled from the centre.

The EU has thus developed many policies with direct implications for the operation of the market. Amongst the regulatory activities in which EU decision-makers have been much concerned are: the establishment of essential conditions for product standards and for their testing and certification (the details are usually worked out by European standards organisations); the liberalisation of national economies, including opening up national monopolies and protected industries in such spheres as energy, transport and telecommunications to competition; the laying down of criteria that companies must satisfy if they wish to trade in the EU market (this has been very important, for example, in the sphere of financial services); and controlling the circumstances in which governments can or cannot subsidise domestic industries.

In addition to these 'pure' market policies, several policy areas in the social sphere that have market implications have also become increasingly subject to EU regulatory control. This has usually been a consequence of some mix of genuine social concern coupled with a recognition that divergences of national approaches and standards create – whatever their intended purpose – trade barriers. Examples of policy areas that have become subject to such social regulation are the environment, consumer protection, and working conditions.

Another, and crucial, policy aspect of the SEM momentum has been its role in respect of Economic and Monetary Union (EMU). Having long been identified as a Community goal, real progress towards EMU only began in the late 1980s when most of the member states – strongly encouraged by the President of the Commission, Jacques Delors – came to the view that harmonised macroeconomic and financial policies and a single currency were necessary if the SEM was to realise its full potential. Accordingly, a strategy for creating a single currency-based EMU gradually developed. This was put into specific form – with the laying down of procedures and a timetable – in the Maastricht Treaty.

Central to the Maastricht provisions on EMU were conditions – called convergence criteria – that countries would have to meet if they were to become members of the single currency system. The qualifying conditions – low rates of inflation, low interest rates, the avoidance of excessive budgetary and national debt deficits, and currency stability – were designed to ensure that the single currency zone would be based on sound economic and monetary foundations. The conditions were subsequently used as a basis for the development of a Stability and Growth Pact, which is a framework for national economic and monetary policies within the single currency zone designed to ensure that stability is not threatened by national imbalances or 'irresponsible' national policies.

The Maastricht Treaty offered the possibility of the single currency system being launched in 1997, but that proved to be premature. However, the system did come into operation on 1 January 1999, with eleven of the EU's fifteen member states fixing their exchange rates and the common currency – the euro – coming into existence. Of the four non-participating states, Denmark, Sweden and the UK chose not to join, whilst Greece was unable to meet the convergence criteria. Greece's position was, however, quickly deemed to be in order and it too became a member of the system on 1 January 2001. National banknotes and coins were phased out in early 2002 and were replaced by euro notes and coins. As a consequence of the creation of EMU, it is thus now the position that twelve EU states have the same currency and, in consequence, also have the same interest rates and external exchange rates – which are determined by the European Central Bank that was created as part of the EMU system.

A striking feature of the EU's policy portfolio has always been its limited involvement with policy areas which account for the bulk of public expenditure – such as social welfare, education, health and defence. The main exception to this lack of involvement with heavy expenditure policy areas has been agriculture, where the CAP has imposed heavy burdens on the EU's annual budget. Since the early 1980s a series of measures have been adopted that have had the effect of bringing at least some aspects of the CAP's problems – including heavy overproduction – under control, but agriculture still accounts for over forty per cent of EU expenditure.

Paralleling the attempts to bring the CAP under control has been increased attention to other policy areas that also impose budgetary demands. Regional and social policies have received particular attention, especially via the development and growth of the EU's two main cohesion funds – the European Regional Development Fund (ERDF) and the European Social Fund (ESF). However, even with the growth of these two areas, and with more funding being channelled to the likes of research policy and energy policy, the EU budget still only accounts for just over one per cent of total EU gross domestic product (GDP) and less than three per cent of total EU public expenditure.

Beyond economic and economic-related policies, the EU has also moved into other policy areas over the years. The most significant of these areas – significant in that they involve highly sensitive policy areas that are far removed from the original EEC policy focus on the construction of a common market – are the Common Foreign and Security Policy (CFSP) and the associated European Security and Defence Policy (ESDP), and Justice and Home Affairs (JHA) policies. These policy areas are still very much in the course of development, but they nonetheless have advanced considerably in both institutional and policy terms. This advancement is seen in the treaties, with the *de facto* growing role of foreign policy from the early 1970s first being given treaty acknowledgement by the SEA, and with both foreign and security and justice and home affairs policies being important components of, and being considerably strengthened by, the Maastricht, Amsterdam and Nice treaties.

So extensive and diverse has policy development been since the Community was established that there are now policies of at least some sort in place in virtually every sphere of public policy. No other combination of states has arrangements even remotely like those that apply in the EU, where cooperation and integration are consciously practised across such a wide range of policy sectors and where so many policy responsibilities have been transferred from individual states to collective institutions.

The nature of the EU's policy interests and responsibilities are examined at length in Part 4.

Concluding Remarks

The EU is still recognisably based on the three European Communities that were founded in the 1950s. The most obvious ways in which it is so are in its institutional structure and in the continuance of the common market/ internal market as the 'core' of policy activity.

However, in many fundamental ways European integration has clearly advanced considerably since it was given its initial organisational expression by the Founding Treaties. This advancement has taken two broad forms. On the one hand, there has been a deepening, with the development of institutional and policy integration in numerous and far-reaching respects. On the other hand, there has been a widening, with the EU expanding in the 1970s, 1980s and 1990s to embrace virtually the whole of Western Europe, and then – dramatically and momentously – expanding further in 2004 to incorporate much of Central and Eastern Europe. This latter enlargement, which has transformed what had been a process of Western European integration into a process of near Europe-wide integration, is explored in the next chapter.

Chapter 4

From Western to Pan-European Integration

The Movement Towards a Europe-wide EU
The Challenges of Enlargement for the EU
Why Has the EU Been Willing to Enlarge?
Dealing With the Challenges: EU Preparations for Enlargement
The New EU

The collapse of communist regimes in Central and Eastern Europe in 1989–90, followed by the collapse of the Soviet Union in 1991, transformed the nature of the European integration process. It did so in two interrelated ways. First, the door was opened to what became by far the largest enlargement round in the EU's history, with states that previously had no prospect of membership suddenly having a case and applying for admission. Second, what had been a process of *Western* European integration moved to a near Europe-*wide* process of integration.

This chapter examines the movement towards, and the consequences of, this transformation in the integration process. The chapter begins by describing the unfolding of events in the 1990s, with particular reference to the aspirations of the applicant states and the EU's response to the pressures on it to greatly increase the size of its membership. The challenges to the EU of admitting the applicants are then considered. Having established that the challenges were – and indeed still are – considerable, consideration is next given to why the EU, a highly successful organisation, granted membership to states whose accession was widely seen as posing major problems for the EU whilst offering it – at least in the short term – seemingly few benefits. The adjustments made by the EU to accommodate the new members are then examined. Finally, the chapter looks at the impact of the new member states on the EU since their accession.

The Movement Towards a Europe-wide EU

The enlargement of the EU that saw ten countries become EU members on 1 May 2004 and is likely to see two more become members in 2007–08, is commonly referred to as the Eastern European, or Central and Eastern

European, enlargement round. Though convenient, this description is, however, misleading as in addition to ten Central and Eastern European countries (CEECs) the round also included two countries that are located in neither Central nor Eastern Europe, namely the two small Mediterranean islands of Cyprus and Malta. The round is, therefore, referred to here as the 10 + 2 enlargement round.

The unfolding of the round is best told by taking the two groups of states in the round – the CEECs and the Mediterranean islands – separately.

The Central and Eastern European countries

The 10 + 2 enlargement round may be said to have formally begun with the applications of Cyprus and Malta in 1990, but it took on its main thrust with applications from CEECs in the early to mid-1990s.

After gaining their independence in 1989–90 following the collapse of communism, most CEECs were soon openly expressing the hope that, as they established liberal democratic and market-based systems and as East–West relations were transformed, the way would be eased for their accession to the EU. Whilst the circumstances of individual CEECs varied, they were all driven by a broadly similar mixture of overlapping and interconnected political, security and economic motivations. Politically, there was a widespread desire to become (re)integrated into the European, and more broadly the Western, world. This resulted in CEEC governments necessarily seeking membership of the EU – the organisation which both symbolised 'the new' Europe and embodied much of its drive. In security terms, EU membership was seen as offering a measure of 'soft' security protection – to bolster the 'hard' protection of NATO, which most CEECs also were seeking to join – especially against any communist revival or nationalist surge. And economically, the EU market was clearly crucial for trade, whilst the EU as an entity offered a framework and policies to assist with and to underpin economic liberalisation, re-structuring, regeneration and growth.

In the early 1990s the (then) EU-12, prompted and guided by the Commission, were quick to assist CEECs as they set out about economic and political reconstruction. The assistance, which took various forms, was given on the assumption that it was but the first step in what was likely to be a long transitional process of building EU–CEEC relations. Certainly, EU membership for CEECs was generally regarded by EU decision-makers not to be a realistic prospect for many years. After all, the CEECs were still in the very early stages of post-communist reconstruction and were nowhere near being ready to meet the demands and disciplines of EU membership. Furthermore, from the very early 1990s the

EU was itself preoccupied with other matters, including the EFTAn enlargement round and negotiating and then applying the Maastricht Treaty.

However, notwithstanding the reservations of most of the member states about moving too quickly, an incremental process of 'rhetorical ratcheting-up' soon began to unfold, in which increasingly specific promises about membership were made to CEECs. A key step in the process occurred at the June 1993 Copenhagen European Council where, in the knowledge that applications from CEECs were likely in the near future, EU leaders declared in the Conclusions of the Presidency (in effect, the official communiqué of summit meetings) that 'the associated countries in Central and Eastern Europe that so desire shall become members of the European Union. Accession will take place as soon as an associated country is able to assume the obligations of membership by satisfying the economic and political conditions required' (European Council, 1993: 12).

So as to ensure that the enlargement to CEECs would not threaten the functioning or continuing development of the EU, the Copenhagen summit also laid down – for the first time in the Community's history – conditions that countries aspiring to membership would have to meet. All that had existed hitherto was the very open Article 237 of the EEC Treaty which stated 'Any European State may apply to become a member of the Community. ... The conditions of admission and the adjustment to the Treaty necessitated thereby shall be the subject of an agreement between the Member States and the applicant State'. The Copenhagen conditions – or criteria as they came to be known – were designed so that there would be a convergence between existing and new member states in respect of their political and economic systems and also that new member states would be able to adopt and implement Union laws and policies (these laws and policies being generally referred to as the *acquis*). The key paragraph setting out the Copenhagen criteria stated:

> Membership requires that the candidate country has achieved stability of institutions guaranteeing democracy, the rule of law, human rights and respect for and protection of minorities, the existence of a functioning market economy as well as the capacity to cope with competitive pressure and market forces within the Union. Membership presupposes the candidate's ability to take on the obligations of membership including adherence to the aims of political, economic and monetary union (European Council, 1993: 12).

Between March 1994, when Hungary applied, and January 1996, when the Czech Republic applied, ten CEECs formally applied for EU membership (see Chronology). The December 1995 Madrid European Council formally reacted to these applications by requesting the Commission to investigate the implications for the EU of enlargement to these countries and to produce opinions on each of the CEEC applicants. This led to the issuing in July 1997 of the Commission's influential communication *Agenda 2000: For a Stronger and Wider Union* (European Commission, 1997a), which claimed that enlargement could be achieved with little extra cost to the Union provided significant reforms were made to the existing main spending areas – agriculture and structural policies. As for the requested opinions on the applicants, the Commission recommended that negotiations should be opened with five of the ten CEECs – the Czech Republic, Estonia, Hungary, Poland and Slovenia – plus Cyprus, but should be delayed with the other five – Bulgaria, Latvia, Lithuania, Romania, and Slovakia until their economic (and in the case of Slovakia, political) transitions were further advanced. (Malta had suspended its application at this time.) The European Council accepted the Commission's recommendations at its December 1997 Luxembourg meeting and negotiations with what came to be referred to as the '5 + 1 first wave' states duly began in March 1998.

Before long, however, the Luxembourg decision came to be viewed as having been mistaken. One reason for this was that the link that had long been recognised between enlargement and European security was put into sharper focus with continuing turbulence in the Balkans. In particular, the NATO campaign in Kosovo in early 1999 highlighted the continuing dangers in South-East Europe and the broader dangers inherent in letting 'second wave' countries believe they were being left on one side. A second reason was that some of the second wave countries began to narrow the gap between them and first wave countries. And a third reason was that the Luxembourg summit had not only differentiated between first and second wave countries, but had also decided that Turkey – which had applied for membership as long back as 1987 – was not yet eligible to be even considered. Strong expressions of dissatisfaction by the Turkish government about how Turkey was being treated, coupled with suggestions that it might be forced to look elsewhere for friends, resulted in the EU having to re-consider its position on Turkey.

Accordingly, the enlargement strategy was revised at the 1999 Helsinki summit where it was decided that: negotiations with the second wave 5 + 1 states would be opened in early 2000 (the 1 being Malta – see below); decisions on the preparedness for membership of all 10 + 2 states to become EU members would be made solely on the basis of their progress in negotiations, not on when the negotiations with them were opened; and Turkey would be given the status of being a 'candidate country'.

Such was the progress in the accession negotiations with the second wave states, which opened in February 2000, that it soon became apparent to both participants and observers that far from enlargement proceeding in a series of stages, as had been assumed, there was likely to a 'big bang' enlargement round some time before the June 2004 EP elections – with perhaps all negotiating states other than Bulgaria and Romania joining the EU. In November 2000 the Commission set out a revised enlargement strategy, incorporating a more flexible framework and a 'roadmap' allowing for negotiations with the more prepared states to be completed by December 2002. The Commission's strategy and targets were welcomed by the December 2000 Nice summit and the June 2001 Gothenburg summit confirmed that EU-15 leaders hoped negotiations with applicants that were ready could be concluded by December 2002. This hope was realised at the December 2002 Copenhagen summit when the European Council, on the basis of reports and recommendations from the Commission, decided that an accession treaty could be signed in April 2003 with all negotiating states apart from Bulgaria and Romania, with a view to them becoming members in May 2004 – that is, in time for them to be able to participate fully in the June 2004 EP elections. It was further decided that if Bulgaria and Romania made satisfactory progress in complying with the membership criteria, they could anticipate membership in 2007 (European Council, 2002b).

An Accession Treaty with the ten states – eight CEECs, plus Malta and Cyprus – was duly signed in April 2003. By September 2003, all eight CEECs had held successful ratification referendums (see Chronology) and, as scheduled, the eight, along with Cyprus and Malta, became EU members on 1 May 2004.

Cyprus and Malta

Although they are geographically distant from the West European heartland, the two small Mediterranean states of Cyprus and Malta are usually thought of – and have largely thought of themselves – as being part of the west European tradition. Both countries applied for EC membership in July 1990, but their applications were received unenthusiastically. This was partly because of a reluctance by the EC to tackle the institutional questions that would be raised by the accession of very small states. In the case of Cyprus it was also because it was the view of most EC decision-makers that problems arising from the division of the island and Turkey's occupation of North Cyprus – over 30 000 Turkish troops had been based there since a Turkish invasion in 1974 occasioned by a right-wing Greek coup on the island – must be resolved before the accession of Cyprus could be contemplated. However, the prospects for both countries improved in June 1993 when the Commission issued its official opinions on the two applications. Whilst recognising that there were many difficulties ahead, the Commission generally supported the applications and, in a significant break with the past, indicated that it did not favour allowing the partition of Cyprus to be a reason for permanently excluding the accession of Greek Cyprus. The European Council moved the process further forward when it decided at its June 1994 Corfu meeting that 'the next phase of enlargement of the Union will involve Cyprus and Malta' (European Council, 1994). In March 1995 the Council of Ministers was even more specific when it announced that negotiations with Cyprus and Malta would open six months after the conclusion of the Intergovernmental Conference (IGC) that was scheduled to begin in 1996. An election in Malta in 1996 then delayed Malta's plans, by bringing to power a government that put the EU application on hold. Nonetheless, the Cyprus application continued to be advanced and accession negotiations opened in March 1998 in parallel with the opening of accession negotiations with the five first wave CEECs. In September 1998 a further change of government in Malta resulted in the country's membership application being revived and the EU opened accession negotiations with it, alongside negotiations with the second wave CEECs, in February 2000.

Cyprus's situation within the $10 + 2$ round was always extremely difficult and sensitive. On the one hand, the Greek Cypriot government, acting in accordance with its established position in international law and in the name of the Republic of Cyprus, insisted from the very outset of its attempt to join the EU that it represented the whole island and would be conducting accession negotiations on that basis, even though in practice its writ ran only in the south. On the other hand, the Turkish Cypriot leadership in the north, strongly supported by Turkey, totally rejected the right of the Greek Cypriots to claim to be negotiating on behalf of all of Cyprus. EU leaders hoped that a solution to this situation – which is commonly referred to as 'the Cyprus Problem' – would be found before the end of the accession negotiations, but there were never solid grounds for these hopes. Delaying Cyprus's accession until the Cyprus Problem was resolved remained a possibility throughout the accession negotiations, but not a very realistic one because Greece threatened to veto all of the EU aspirants if Cyprus's accession was postponed. At the same time, however, accepting a divided Cyprus as an EU member risked damaging the EU's relations with Turkey.

At the December 1999 Helsinki European Council meeting, the EU-15 leaders agreed on how they would manage the conflicting pressures associated with the Cyprus application. On the one hand, they declared that whilst a settlement was much desired, it would not in itself be a precondition for Cyprus's accession. On the other hand, they sought to mollify Turkey by stating that 'Turkey is a candidate state destined to join the Union on the basis of the same criteria as applied to the other candidate States' (European Council, 1999d: 3). Hopes that the Cyprus Problem would still be resolved prior to accession were raised in 2002 when talks – they did not amount to negotiations – were conducted under United Nations auspices between the leaders of the Greek and Turkish Cypriot sides. However, with no solution reached by the time of the key December 2002 Copenhagen summit – the summit that took final decisions on which of the $10+2$ applicant states had completed accession negotiations and the target date for their accession – the EU-15 leaders acted on the basis of their Helsinki decision and decided Cyprus could join the EU in May 2004, along with the eight CEECs and Malta. A consequence of this decision was that if no settlement could be reached before Cyprus's accession, then because in legal, though not practical, terms the whole of the island of Cyprus would be joining the EU, a foreign power – Turkey – would be occupying EU 'territory'.

Subsequent to the 2002 Copenhagen summit, a ratification referendum on its accession treaty was held successfully in Malta in April 2003. In Cyprus the government decided that a referendum would be not be held unless it could be tied in with a resolution of the Cyprus Problem. With no such resolution seemingly pending, Cyprus's membership was ratified by the Cyprus parliament in July 2003 – thus resulting in Cyprus being the only one of the ten acceding states not to directly seek the approval of the national electorate.

In the autumn of 2003 the UN, which had made various attempts over the years to broker a Cyprus peace settlement, sought to take advantage of Cyprus's scheduled EU membership to launch another round of peace negotiations. The hope was that with the question of Cyprus's EU membership 'resolved', both sides would display increased flexibility. A highly detailed settlement plan – known as the Annan Plan, after the UN's Secretary General – was issued, but despite being revised several times to meet objections it was rejected by the Greek Cypriot government on the grounds that it was too favourable to the Turkish Cypriots. Both sides did, however, agree to put the Plan to binding referendums to be held on the same day in April 2004 in both parts of the island. In the referendums, the Turkish Cypriots voted to accept the Plan by 64.9 per cent to 35.1 per cent on a 87 per cent turnout, but the Greek Cypriots, encouraged by their government, voted to reject it by 75.8 per cent to 24.2 per cent on a 89 per cent turnout. The fact that in the south of the island there was no penalty of exclusion from the EU for voting for rejection was a major factor in determining the outcome. Accordingly, on 1 May 2004 the whole of Cyprus legally joined the EU, but the part of the island that had voted to accept the Plan was, in practice, excluded.

The Challenges of Enlargement for the EU

The 10 + 2 enlargement round posed, and still poses, many challenges for the EU. Most of these challenges were dealt with before enlargement occurred, but it may be many years before some are deemed to have been satisfactorily resolved.

The principal challenges can be grouped under four broad headings.

The identity problem

There has long been a debate in the academic literature about whether the EU can be said to be based on a collective identity and what the implications of the existence or absence of such an identity are for the stability and effectiveness of the EU as a political system (see, for example, Smith, 1992; Howe, 1995).

Prior to the 2004 enlargement it was not difficult to make out a case that no collective identity existed and that this was a key reason why the EU system so often creaked. There were, after all, many divisions and differences between the peoples and governments of the EU-15 states: divisions and differences based on language, religious background, political ideology and – above all – national and cultural histories, values, and interests. Did not these divisions and differences, especially those stemming from nationhood, make it hard for EU citizens to identify with one another and with the EU polity? Insofar as any sort of collective identity could be said to exist, was it based on anything more than the loosest of generally shared attachments and values, related perhaps to notions of the desirability of democracy and individual liberty? And did this absence of a firm common identity not make it extremely difficult to construct and maintain a strong and fully effective political system?

The 10 + 2 enlargement has clearly further diluted such (weak) identity as the EU could claim to have. The CEECs were and are in important respects very different from the EU-15 'norm'. Has admitting them ended any prospect of a genuine EU identity being forged – be it through such symbols as the flag and the anthem or through policy effectiveness? For those who aspire to the creation of a federal Europe, this is a major concern. For those who have no such aspirations, it may make it easier to slow the pace of integrationist advance.

The identity issue is raised in even sharper focus in the case of Turkey. It is so partly because most of Turkey is not geographically located in Europe and partly – and for many of those who are opposed to Turkish membership, mainly – because it is an Islamic country.

Institutions and decision-making processes

A major political challenge posed for the EU by the 10 + 2 enlargement was adapting its institutions to accommodate so many new member states. In the past, acceding states were accommodated largely just by making institutional allocations to them in approximate proportion to their population size. So, new member states were allocated a voting weight in the Council, a number of MEPs, a Commissioner (except in the cases of the UK and Spain which, because they are large states, were allocated two), a judge in each of the courts and so on. This approach was, however, not so easy to use in the 10 + 2 enlargement round, partly because some institutions – notably the Commission and the EP – were seen as already becoming too large and partly because of the sheer number of applicants.

Closely related to the challenge of institutional adaptation was a perceived requirement to adapt decision-making processes. As was the case at the time of the Spanish and Portuguese accessions of the mid-1980s and the EFTAn accessions of the mid-1990s, it was recognised that bringing in new member states would make quick and efficient decision-making more difficult unless decision-making processes were streamlined. Calls were made for a thorough overhaul of the processes but, as in previous enlargement rounds, the debate in practice focused primarily on further reducing the national veto in the Council of Ministers by extending QMV.

The solutions that were agreed to deal with the challenges of institutional and decision-making adaptation are outlined later in this chapter and in Chapter 6.

Economic difficulties

Though the 10 + 2 states created potential market opportunities for the EU-15, they also created considerable economic difficulties. They did so for three main reasons.

First, though the 10 + 2 enlargement round increases the size of the EU's population by around 30 per cent, the size of the EU's GDP increases by only about 5 per cent. With the exceptions of Cyprus and Slovenia, all 10 + 2 states in 2004 had a GDP per head lower than that of the EU-15's poorest member state, Greece. Moreover, all 10 + 2 states were below the EU average, with eight (Bulgaria, Estonia, Latvia, Lithuania, Poland, Romania, Slovakia and Slovenia) at less than 50 per cent of the average and two (the prospective 2007 accession states of Bulgaria and Romania) at less than 30 per cent. Enlargement, in other words, would, and now has, brought less prosperous states into the EU, which, amongst other things, has led to demands for more generous redistributive policies.

Second, most 10 + 2 states have relatively large, but very inefficient, agricultural sectors. So, for example, as compared with agriculture accounting for less than 5 per cent of EU-15 employment, it accounts for around 25 per cent in Poland and 21 per cent in Bulgaria. When Bulgaria and Romania become EU members, enlargement will have approximately doubled the size of the EU's agricultural labour force and increased its agricultural area by about half. Inevitably, therefore, the 10 + 2 enlargement has greatly increased pressures on the CAP and the already existing pressures for its further reform.

Third, there is still a heavy reliance in the CEECs on outdated and inefficient industries that have only been able to survive through state support of various kinds. This situation is changing as the CEEC economies modernise and liberalise, helped in no small part by the stimulus and guidance of the accession process, but there remains far to go. If CEEC economies do not become competitive quickly – and in most instances this will necessitate attracting increased levels of inward investment – they clearly could face very difficult economic times, and the aspirations of all of them for single currency system membership may have to be put on hold. More broadly, slow economic adaptation in CEECs could be damaging also for the wider EU internal market economy.

External relations and policies

The EU's foreign and security policies have not been developed as far or as rapidly as many policy practitioners would have liked. The central reason they have not been so is the number and the depth of the differences between member states over both the general nature and bases of the policies and over specific policy issues. By increasing the heterogeneity of EU membership, enlargement makes it even more difficult than in the past for the EU to be able to develop united stances on the bases of shared identities and interests.

Furthermore, some of the new member states have particular external policy interests and orientations that were always likely to create specific difficulties. Cyprus is the most obvious such member state, with its continuing dispute with Turkey over the Cyprus Problem resulting in it taking a hard line in respect of Turkey's attempts to become an EU member. In the future, the close physical proximity of some CEECs to western former Soviet states could result in them pressing, against the wishes of 'old' EU states, for EU membership for the likes of Georgia, Moldova, and the Ukraine.

Why Has the EU Been Willing to Enlarge?

Given the challenges posed by post-EFTAn applicants, why has the EU – a highly successful organisation in most respects – been willing to risk enlargement? Why has it allowed major potential difficulties to be created for itself, and indeed permitted the very nature of the EU to be significantly changed, by allowing ten states to become members in 2004, two more to be scheduled for membership in 2007, and yet two more – Croatia and Turkey – to have opened accession negotiations in 2005? Would not a more sensible approach have been to have established very close relations with all the applicant states that have created major challenges for the EU but to have stopped short of offering them a membership perspective? Two types of explanation for why the EU has proceeded with enlargement will be considered here.

Rationalist explanations

For many EU policy practitioners the challenges and negativities of enlarging the EU to 'difficult' applicants have been, and still are, at least partly offset by positive considerations. Two considerations are especially important:

- *Economic advantages*. A larger internal market creates considerable market and business opportunities for existing EU states. This is all the more so when acceding states have relatively inefficient and under-invested economies, as has been the case since the EFTAn round with all would-be EU states to the east and south of the EU's (shifting) borders. The accession of the ten states in 2004 added some 75 million people to the EU's population, and therefore also its internal market, the accession of Bulgaria and Romania will add another 31 million, and should Turkey ever become a member there could be approaching another 100 million.
- *Political and security advantages*. It is very much in the EU's interests that neighbouring states – and especially those with which it shares borders – should have solid and stable liberal democratic political systems. More broadly, the promotion of liberal democracy and of respect for human rights have increasingly become central features of EU foreign policy, and enlargement policy has virtually become a part of foreign policy. With the CEECs, it came to be accepted by the EU's member states in the early to mid-1990s that early EU membership for CEECs would assist them to consolidate their newly-based democratic

systems – both by bringing them inside 'the democratic fold' and by subsequently opening them up to the possibility of sanctions in the event of any democratic 'slippage' (under Articles 6 and 7 TEU, which provide for suspension of EU rights if a member state is in serious and persistent breach of the Union's founding principles of liberty, democracy, respect for human rights and fundamental freedoms, and the rule of law).

Beyond promoting the consolidation of liberal democracy, enlargement has also been seen to provide other possible political and security advantages. One of these is that an enlarged EU clearly carries more weight in its external relations and dealings. And in the particular case of Turkey, its accession could provide valuable bridges between Europe and the Middle East and Asia and between the West and the Islamic world.

The extent to which, and the intensity with which, such motivations in favour of enlargement have been felt in member states has varied, both at a general level and in terms of attitudes towards particular applicants. Germany was clearly the EU-15 state with most to gain from admitting the CEECs, primarily because of its geographical position and the market opportunities enlargement to the east offered to it. Another EU-15 state with potentially much to gain, though for quite different reasons, was the UK, which saw, as it still sees with Turkey, a larger and more heterogeneous EU being less disposed to, and capable of, moving the EU in the supranational direction that some member states support but UK governments mostly oppose. The EU-15 states with least to gain from CEEC accessions were those less prosperous states on the EU's western side – Spain and Portugal – which would not only be unlikely to gain much from the larger market but would be threatened with reductions in their Structural Fund support as much poorer countries than themselves joined.

As for attitudes towards particular 10 + 2 applicants, there was always more general support for the early membership of countries such as Hungary and the Czech Republic which were relatively more advanced politically and economically than for Bulgaria or Romania which are the least advanced of the CEEC 10. Beyond this general support, some applicants virtually had patrons amongst EU-15 states. For example: Germany was a very strong supporter of Poland, and just a little less so of Hungary and the Czech Republic, partly because their membership would promote the interests and identity of 'MittelEuropa' in the EU; the Scandinavian member states promoted the applications of the three Baltic states, largely for a mixture of cultural and strategic reasons; and Greece sponsored Cyprus, for reasons of ethnic identity and historical linkage.

Constructivist explanations

Sociologists, and more particularly constructivists, take as their starting point for explaining EU enlargement processes and developments post the EFTANs the fact that whilst enlargement has certainly offered opportunities to existing member states it also has presented them with stiff challenges and unwanted consequences. From this, it is concluded that the actions of the existing member states cannot be wholly explained in rational or instrumental terms. If they had acted purely on the basis of their own national interests and preferences regarding the future nature of the EU some member states should have voted to reject the applications of at least some of the applicants. That they did not do so means that these member states have not been driven, or at least not completely driven, by 'objective' national political and economic situations and needs. Rather, their positions have been socially constructed, which is to say they have been shaped largely by social identities, norms and values.

As applied to the admission of the CEECs, Schimmelfennig (2001, 2002) has emphasised the collective identity and obligations that can exist between liberal democratic states and argues that once the case for a rapid enlargement to CEECs began to be pressed – by the European Commission and some EU-15 states – states that were reluctant became swept up in an unfolding 'rhetorical commitment' to fledgling and neighbouring democratic states that led to a 'rhetorical entrapment'. 'By argumentatively entrapping the opponents of a firm commitment to Eastern enlargement, they [the supporters of enlargement] brought about a collective outcome that would not have been expected given the constellation of powers and interests' (2001: 77).

Sjursen (2002) argues in similar vein, though for her the key driving factor was kinship-based duty rather than a sense of obligation to fellow liberal democracies. She argues that the 2004 enlargement is to be understood, in part at least, in terms of the existence of a community-based European identity, even though it is not a fully understood or defined identity. The decision to admit CEECs 'against' many self interests demonstrates she argues, 'that in order to trigger a decision to enlarge, something more than instrumental calculations and something less than a selfless concern for human rights has been at play' (p. 509).

Taking Sjursen's argument a little further, it certainly is the case that EU politicians generally have felt that the uniting of most of the continent within the EU framework is a good thing in itself, quite apart from the specific advantages it can bring. In the case of the CEECs, these feelings amounted in the 1990s almost to a moral duty. Having seen the CEECs rid themselves of the communist system that Western Europe so opposed for the forty-plus years of the Cold War, it was seen as an obligation in many

EU governmental circles to help CEECs to realise their ambitions to become prosperous and democratic states within 'the European family' of nations. Would it, it was argued, be not only irresponsible and churlish but forgetful and unprincipled not to accommodate such CEEC needs and desires? As Sedelmeier has put it, 'The discourse of a collective EU identify, characterised by a responsibility towards the CEECs, became a central aspect of EU policy' (Sedelmeier, 2000: 269).

Constructivist explanations may also be applied to the Turkish application. They can help explain why in the second half of the 1990s and the early 2000s the EU moved from its preferred policy of being close to Turkey but stopping short of holding out the possibility of membership to giving Turkey a foreseeable membership perspective. The gradually evolving 'upgrading' of language – which can be traced through European Council Conclusions – produced a situation that made it progressively difficult for doubters and opponents to backtrack. Notions of collective identity and kinship-based duty are by no means as strong in respect of Turkey than they were in respect of CEECs, which helps explain why the upgrading of the language has been much more hesitant and drawn out in the Turkish case than it was in the case of the CEECs. But some such notions – emanating in part from shared membership of European and Western organisations, in part too from empathy with Turkey's liberalising and democratising reform programmes, and in part from a sense of responsibility towards an Islamic state that is looking to Europe and the West – appears to exist amongst many European governing elites.

Dealing With the Challenges: EU Preparations for Enlargement

Given the enormity of the challenges posed by the 10 + 2 enlargement round, it was not possible for the round to proceed according to the 'classical method' (Preston, 1995) in which the focus was on the willingness and ability of applicants to accept the *acquis communautaire* and negotiations were largely taken up with the extent and length of transition periods. Rather it had to be an 'adaptive' enlargement round, in which the EU had to do much more than in previous enlargement rounds to assist applicant countries to meet the conditions of EU membership and in which also the EU had to change and adapt more than in previous rounds.

The EU prepared for the 10 + 2 enlargement by, on the one hand, working with the applicants to enable them to meet the requirements of membership and, on the other hand, adjusting itself so that applicants could be accommodated without causing too much disruption or threatening the functioning of the EU system.

Working with the applicants

Soon after the collapse of communism the EU began working closely with CEECs as they sought to transform their economies and consolidate their new democratic political systems. Initially the EU focused on providing financial aid and technical assistance, but soon broadened its approach into a wide range of activities. By the late 1990s there were two principal frameworks in place:

- *Association Agreements* or, as they became more generally known, *Europe Agreements*. These formed the legal bases for association between applicant countries and the EU and had as their objective the provision of frameworks enabling applicants to integrate gradually into the Union. They mostly covered the establishment of free trade areas, the liberalisation of economic activity, technical and legal assistance, and political dialogue. Association agreements were contracted with all of the applicants. The agreements with Cyprus, Malta and Turkey were signed in the early 1970s, though they did not promise EU accession and their liberalisation of trade provisions were scheduled to be introduced only over a long period. The association agreements with the CEECs were signed between 1993 and 1997 and these did explicitly offer the prospect of EU accession.
- *Accession partnerships*. Launched for the CEECs in 1998, and later for Cyprus, Malta and Turkey, these provided a single framework for activity involved in the transition to membership. In particular, they identified priority areas in which the *acquis* was to be adopted, established coordinating mechanisms for the various financial assistance programmes, and monitored progress in meeting the accession conditions. An important element of the partnerships was national programmes for the adoption of the *acquis* (NPAAs), which involved applicants specifying the laws, the institutional and administrative reforms, and the human and budgetary resources they intended to deploy in the priority areas identified in the partnerships.

Accession negotiations with all of the applicants except Turkey proceeded alongside the development and progressive strengthening of these arrangements. Or, perhaps it is more accurate to say that an accession process proceeded, for there can hardly be said to have been negotiations in the commonly understood sense of the word. The applicants were given very little room for manoeuvre. They had no choice but to incorporate the 80 000 or so pages of the *acquis* into national law, to have unfavourable terms imposed in respect of financial support from the CAP and Structural Funds, to accept being granted relatively few transitional measures, and to have to make significant changes to national administrative structures and practices. In other words, before becoming members the ten states that joined in 2004 had, as those states that are currently negotiating have, to adopt the EU model.

Adjusting the EU for enlargement

In previous enlargement rounds the burden of adaptation fell largely on the applicants. However, in the 10 + 2 round the EU had to make considerable adjustments itself, both to its institutional and decision-making systems and to some of its policies.

Institutional adjustments

The Amsterdam Treaty was supposed to deal with the adjustments to the institutional and decision-making systems by thoroughly overhauling the arrangements that were still recognisably based on those that had been created for 'the Founding Six' in the 1950s. However, as is shown in Chapter 5, in the 1996–7 IGC the member states were unable to agree on all the changes that would be necessary and it was only with the Nice Treaty that the job was completed – or, at least, that sufficient changes were made to permit enlargement to proceed.

The changes made at Amsterdam and Nice are described in Chapters 5 and 6, so they will be only briefly outlined here. The most important institutional changes arising from enlargement covered in the treaties were:

– upper limits were set on the size of the Commission, the EP, the ESC, and the CoR (an upper limit of 700 on the EP that was set at Amsterdam was changed at Nice);
– from 2005 and until such time as the EU has 27 members each member state will have one Commissioner (Nice);
– national representations in the EU's institutions were set (Nice);
– allocations of votes in the Council and QMV majorities were set (Nice);
– QMV was extended to more treaty articles (mainly Amsterdam, but with some minor extensions at Nice);
– provision was made for enhanced, or flexible, cooperation (established at Amsterdam and made easier to apply at Nice).

These various institutional changes incorporated a set of reforms that enabled enlargement to go ahead, but they hardly amounted to the more comprehensive reform of the EU that many believed was necessary for an EU of 15-plus, and even more so one of 25-plus, member states. Aware of this, the national leaders agreed at Nice to open up a debate on the future of the EU and to convene another IGC in 2004. This led to the 2004 Constitutional Treaty, which is considered in Chapter 7.

Policy adjustments

The changes to policies in preparation for the 10 + 2 enlargement mainly concerned the two policy areas that account for most of the EU's budgetary expenditure, agriculture and the Structural Funds.

Details of these changes are given in Part 4 of this book, so as with institutional changes only a brief outline will be given here. The Commission did much to set the reform agenda with the publication in 1997 of its communication *Agenda 2000: For a Stronger and Wider Union* (European Commission, 1997a). Key recommendations in the communication were: a continuing movement of CAP away from price support to direct income support; targeting Structural Funds more tightly so as to deal with economic and social deprivation; and keeping EU budgetary expenditure within its existing limit of 1.27 per cent of total EU GDP. The Commission's recommendations were, after the customary horse-trading between member states on particular matters – which resulted in some watering down of the CAP proposals – subsequently broadly accepted by the Heads of Government at their March 1999 Berlin summit, and were later translated into legislation.

Whether, however, the post-*Agenda 2000* arrangements were adequate to permit enlargement to proceed without creating major difficulties was always doubtful. Certainly the Commission's view consistently was that more radical reform of both the CAP and the Structural Funds was necessary, given that most applicants would be beneficiaries – and some would be major beneficiaries – of both policy areas in their existing form. Significantly, when in February 2002 the Commission produced proposals for the application of the two policies to the prospective new member states, the most striking feature of the proposals was long transition periods – of up to ten years – before new member states would be treated on the same basis as existing member states. Hardly surprisingly, the proposals were received with dismay in most CEECs, but the Council (of the then EU-15) supported them so the applicant states were obliged to accept them.

The New EU

As was shown in Chapter 1, each enlargement round prior to the 10 + 2 round has had implications for the nature and operation of the EU. The 10 + 2 round has naturally had particularly significant implications, given the number and nature of the states becoming EU members.

One of these implications has stemmed from the logistics of conducting EU processes. Policy process forums are now attended by far more people than in the EU-15, which means meeting rooms need to be larger, there is less time for those who wish to speak to be able to do so, and exchanges tend to be more formal. At senior decision-making levels, most particularly at ministerial level in the Council, meetings may consist of little more than participants presenting pre-prepared positions rather than engaging in real negotiations.

Problems associated with the number of EU languages have increased. The 2004 enlargement added nine new official languages to the existing eleven, making for a possible 380 language combinations as opposed to the previous 110. In practice, as in the past, much of the day-to-day work of the EU administration continues to be undertaken in English or French, but this is not always possible where documents need to be translated. Moreover, it has never been possible at the 'political' level of EU institutions, where there is less language proficiency and where national representatives who can speak English or French often choose not to do so. Various devices are being used to tackle these linguistic problems, including more use of language relays and pressures being placed on officials to produce shorter documents, but difficulties of many sorts remain – including delays in the translation of documents and MEPs from small states not always having access to translation facilities in their own language.

Since becoming EU members the new states have naturally been inputting into policy and decision-making processes. In a few instances a new member state has had a considerable impact on an individual basis. So, for example, even before it officially joined the EU, Poland allied with Spain at the December 2003 European Council meeting to block agreement on the Constitutional Treaty (see Chapter 7). And Cyprus has ensured that 'the Cyprus Problem' issue has remained to the fore, not least by using it to extract 'recognition' (of Cyprus) concessions from Turkey and by vetoing EU aid and trade legislation designed to assist northern Cyprus.

However, a concern expressed in some quarters prior to the 2004 enlargement that the accession of CEECs would result in a new line of division opening in the EU between 'old' and 'new' member states has proved to be unfounded. There are two main reasons for this. The first is that enlargement has not disturbed the preference amongst EU states for decisions to be made wherever possible by compromise and consensus. Except on core and deeply felt issues, the predisposition of member states has continued to be conciliatory and to avoid division. The second reason is that the new member states just do not have the same needs or views on all issues. To be sure there is a similarity of needs and views on a few issues amongst CEECs – mostly stemming from their geographical locations in the east of the continent and their lower levels of GDP per capita (the latter of which makes them strongly supportive of increased redistributive spending via the EU budget). But even on issues stemming from these factors, CEECs are not a wholly cohesive bloc inside the EU. Moreover, such cohesion as there is at present is likely to decline as CEECs become 'Europeanised' by membership and as some CEECs grow economically faster than others.

The fact is, as has always been the case, that cleavages in the EU continue to be cross-cutting more than they are cumulative. So, whilst CEECs may generally align with one another on a few issues where there are internal EU divisions, so do some EU-15 states: most publicly and notably France and Germany. Such CEEC shared interests as there are on the likes of the size and use of the EU's cohesion funds and on relations with western former Soviet states are not part of an overall and stable alliance pattern in which CEECs also act together on CAP reform, the Lisbon Agenda, and other disputatious EU issues.

The Evolving Treaty Framework

From 1957 to the mid-1980s there was only modest treaty development within the EC. However, since the mid-1980s rounds of treaty reform have been carried out every few years. Four major new treaties have been concluded and brought into force – the 1986 Single European Act, the 1992 Maastricht Treaty, the 1997 Amsterdam Treaty, and the 2001 Nice Treaty. In addition, another major treaty – the Treaty Establishing a Constitution for Europe – has been agreed by the governments of the member states, but it has not taken effect because of ratification problems.

Part 2 examines all five of these and shows how they have been central to the evolution of the European integration process. The treaties are examined individually in Chapters 5, 6 and 7, and collectively in Chapter 8.

Chapter 5

From Rome to Amsterdam

Up to the Single European Act
The Single European Act
The Maastricht Treaty
The Treaty of Amsterdam
Concluding Remarks

As was noted in Chapter 3, the Founding Treaties of the 1950s that created the European Communities have been supplemented and amended in various ways by subsequent treaties. This chapter examines these treaties up to the 1997 Treaty of Amsterdam.

Up to the Single European Act

In addition to accession treaties providing for the enlargements of the Community in 1973, 1981 and 1986, a number of other treaties were also concluded in the period between the signing of the Treaties of Rome in 1957 and the Single European Act in 1986. Four of these treaties were of particular significance.

The Treaty Establishing a Single Council and a Single Commission of the European Communities

Signed in 1965, coming into force in 1967, and generally known as the Merger Treaty, this treaty established a single Council of Ministers for all three Communities (though different individuals would attend different meetings) and merged the High Authority of the ECSC, the Commission of Euratom, and the EEC Commission into one Commission. The powers exercised by these merged bodies were still to be based on the Founding Treaties: in other words, the Treaties and the Communities themselves were not merged. To clarify and simplify the existing texts relating to the single Community institutions, this treaty was repealed by the 1997 Amsterdam Treaty and its relevant parts were incorporated as appropriate into the Community Treaties.

The Treaty Amending Certain Budgetary Provisions of the Treaties and the Treaty Amending Certain Financial Provisions of the Treaties

The first of these treaties was signed in 1970 and the second in 1975. Together, they laid down a budgetary procedure and allocated budgetary powers between the EC institutions. Of particular importance, given its relative weakness in most policy areas, were powers allocated to the European Parliament. The 1975 Treaty also established a Court of Auditors to examine the accounts of all revenue and expenditure of the Community.

The Act Concerning the Election of the Representatives of the Assembly by Direct Universal Suffrage

Signed in 1976, but not ratified by all the member states until 1978, this Act provided the legal base for direct elections to the EP and laid down certain rules for their conduct. The Act did not in any direct way increase the Parliament's powers.

The Single European Act (SEA)

It was recognised at the June 1985 Milan European Council meeting that the legislative measures that would be required to give effect to the priority SEM programme (see Chapter 3) would have little chance of being passed unless Community decision-making procedures were changed. Accordingly, and because too it was thought certain other treaty-related matters required addressing, it was decided to establish an Intergovernmental Conference (IGC) to negotiate and prepare treaty reforms. (See Chapter 3 for an account of how IGCs operate.) The IGC duly undertook its work in the second half of 1985 and culminated at the December 1985 Luxembourg summit when the national leaders agreed to what they called the Single European Act (SEA). After legal and translation work had been undertaken on the political deal reached at the summit, the SEA was formally signed in February 1986, but it did not come into force until mid-1987 because of ratification difficulties in Ireland. The SEA contained a wide range of measures, of which the most important were as follows:

(1)   Completion of the internal market by 1992 was identified as a specific goal and was incorporated into the EEC Treaty. A programme for completing the internal market had already been agreed at the Milan summit, but according the goal treaty status enhanced its prospect of

success (as did the introduction of QMV for most internal market decisions – see the third point below).

(2)   A number of new policy areas – most of which were already being developed – were formally incorporated into the EEC Treaty, so the capacity for decision-making in these areas was increased. The new policy areas included environment, research and technological development, and 'economic and social cohesion'.

(3)   A new legislative procedure – the cooperation procedure – was established with a view to improving the efficiency of decision-making in the Council of Ministers and increasing, though not by too much, the powers of the EP. Regarding the first of these aims, the Council's ability to take decisions by QMV was extended to most decisions subject to the procedure, whilst regarding the second aim the single reading of legislative proposals under the established consultation procedure was extended to two readings. Several legislative areas were covered by the new procedure including, crucially, most of the measures 'which have as their object the establishment and functioning of the internal market'.

(4)   The EP's role and potential influence in the Community was further increased by the establishment of a new 'assent procedure'. Under the procedure, the EP's assent, by an absolute majority of members, became necessary both for the accession of new members to the Community and for association agreements between the Community and third countries.

(5)   European Political Cooperation (EPC, the then official Community term for foreign policy cooperation), which had increasingly been practised since the early 1970s, but outside the treaty framework, was put on a legal basis (but not by treaty incorporation).

(6)   Meetings between the twelve Heads of Government in the framework of the European Council, which had been taking place since 1975, were given legal recognition (but not by treaty incorporation).

(7)   The capacity of the Court of Justice, which had been becoming very overstretched, was extended by a provision for the establishment of a new Court of First Instance.

The SEA thus provided a major boost to the European integration process. It did so on the one hand by strengthening the treaty base for policy activity, most particularly in respect of the completion of the internal market where a deadline was set. It did so on the other hand by strengthening the Community's institutional system, especially in respect of the increased capacity of the Council of Ministers to take decisions by QMV and the increased legislative powers given to the EP.

The Maastricht Treaty

The origins of the Treaty

Many of the Community's decision-making elites – both in Community institutions and in member states – were disappointed with the SEA. It did not, they believed, sufficiently advance the process of integration, so even before the SEA was ratified the view was being expressed in many influential quarters that further integration would soon be necessary. In the second half of the 1980s a number of factors combined to give weight and force to this body of opinion. These factors were both internal and external in nature.

The internal factors were mostly associated with the stimulus to further integration provided by the 're-launching' of the Community in the mid-1980s. This re-launching, which was embodied in the SEM programme and in the SEA, contained its own integrationist logic in that it gave greater urgency to some long-standing but unresolved issues facing the Community and it also served to bring new issues onto the Community's agenda. Four factors were of particular importance in this respect. First, many member states increasingly came to the view that the full benefits of the SEM would only be realised if action was taken to bring about Economic and Monetary Union (EMU). More particularly, a single currency was increasingly seen as being necessary to eliminate the distortions to trade occasioned by changes in the value of currencies. This would provide more stable conditions for business planning and remove the cost of currency conversion. Second, there was growing acceptance of the need for a 'social dimension' that would soften and offset some of the liberal market/deregulatory implications of the SEM. In addition to equity arguments for a social dimension, member states with high levels of social provision were anxious that there should not be 'social dumping' in the form of businesses being attracted to countries where the level of social provision was low and where, in consequence, business overheads were also likely to be low. Third, the dismantling of border controls in the internal market created pressure for new and greatly improved mechanisms at Community level to deal with such problems as cross-border crime, drug trafficking, international terrorism, and the movement of peoples (the latter included growing concern about the 'threat' of mass migration from Eastern Europe and North Africa to Western Europe). Fourth, the long-standing problem of a 'democratic deficit', which had been only partially addressed in the SEA, was increasingly seen as needing attention as the Community exercised ever more power over a broad range of policy areas but in a political context where its decision-makers were not democratically accountable.

The external factors arose largely from the break-up of the communist bloc and the Soviet Union. As with internal factors, there were four main aspects to this. First, the collapse of communism in Central and Eastern Europe from the autumn of 1989, and the emergence in its place of would-be liberal democratic states with market-based economies, produced the like-lihood that the Community would increasingly be dealing not just with West European but with Europe-wide issues and problems. In such circumstances – and with the EFTA countries also contributing to the emergence of a wider Europe via the projected EEA and the prospect of EC membership applications – it seemed to many that the Community should consolidate and strengthen itself so as to be better able to meet the challenges of the rapidly transforming Europe. Second, the unification of Germany, which formally took place in October 1990, increased the potential for German domination of the Community and led many to conclude that it was necessary to advance the integration process in order to ensure the consolidation of a European Germany rather than a German Europe. Greater integration would also, it was argued, ensure that the new Germany would not be tempted to start detaching itself from aspects of Community affairs in order to take advantage of the new opportunities to its east. Third, the break-up of the Soviet Union in 1991 added to the sense of uncertainty about the future nature and stability of the European continent. More broadly, it also raised questions about the shape and direction of the international system. In this situation, the existing pressure to strengthen the Community's policy and institutional capacities was inevitably height-ened. Fourth, the ending of the Cold War had to be addressed since it heralded the disappearance of the framework that had provided much of the rationale, focus and setting for the foreign and defence policies of most West European countries for over forty years. Questions now inevitably arose about the suitability of existing arrangements in the post-Cold War era. Was it not time for the Community to develop and strengthen its foreign and security policy roles and mechanisms?

From the mid-1980s several factors thus combined to build up a head of steam for another round of Community deepening: that is, for further integration between the member states. There were, of course, those who sought to resist the rising pressures – notably the UK government, which had little desire to go much beyond a common market with various forms of intergovernmental cooperation tacked on – but most of the Commu-nity's key decision-making elites accepted the need for further integration. Their motives varied considerably: for some, long-held adherence to the federalist cause was a source of inspiration; for many, there was a fear that if deepening was not pursued the Community could be seriously threa-tened by dilution when the anticipated widening of the Community in the form of accession by EFTA states took place in the mid-1990s; and for virtually all, there was a perceived need to press ahead with, and enhance the Community's competence and authority with regard to, at least some of the issues and matters that had become problematical since the mid-1980s – EMU, the social dimension, foreign and security policy, and the efficiency and accountability of the Community's institutions. As the 1980s gave way to the 1990s there was therefore a widely-held belief in most Community circles that further fundamental reforms were necessary.

The making of the Treaty

At a series of European Council meetings between 1988 and 1990 steps were taken that led to the convening of IGCs on Political Union and on Economic and Monetary Union (for details, see the fourth edition of this book, pp. 62–3).

The IGCs met throughout 1991. Certain generalisations can be made about the positions adopted by their key participants – representatives of the member states. The Netherlands, Luxembourg, Belgium and Italy were the most consistent in taking a highly integrationist – federalist, some would call it – outlook. Spain, Ireland, Portugal, Greece and, to a lesser extent, Denmark were willing to support significant integrationist advances but had reservations on a number of specific issues. Spain, Ireland, Portugal and Greece also made it clear that – as the least prosperous member states of the Community – they wished to see a considerable strengthening of policies dealing with economic and social cohesion included in any final agreement. France was very supportive of EMU but tended towards an intergovernmental stance in the Political Union IGC – by arguing, for example, for a stronger European Council and only very limited increases in the powers of the EP. Germany, by contrast with France, was a firm advocate of further political integration, and especially of greater powers for the EP, but was very cautious on EMU. Finally, the United Kingdom adopted a minimalist position on virtually all proposals that implied integration with supranational implications.

But generalisations tell only part of the story, for on particular subjects in the IGCs there was often a complex mosaic of views, reflecting different national interests. This can be illustrated by the reactions to a proposal put forward by the Dutch Presidency in early November to apply the proposed co-decision-making procedure (which would greatly enhance the powers of the EP) to a wide span of Community policies: Spain and Portugal opposed the application of the procedure to the research framework programme and to the environment; Luxembourg, with some support from the Commission, opposed its application to internal market harmonisation; France and Spain opposed its application to the objectives of the Community's Structural Funds, and France also opposed its application to development cooperation programmes; and the UK opposed its application to just about anything.

Despite all these differences, however, progress was gradually made and, as scheduled, both IGCs presented their reports to the December 1991 meeting of the European Council in Maastricht. The IGC on EMU was able to reach agreement on virtually all issues within its remit and to present clear recommendations on treaty reform to the summit. The IGC on Political Union – which had had to deal with a much wider range of institutional and policy issues – was not so successful, in that a number of particularly contentious matters had to be referred to the summit for final resolution.

At the Maastricht meeting the matters that had proved impossible to resolve during the IGCs were tackled. The most difficult of these were the UK's opposition to any significant extension of the Community's social dimension and its desire not to participate in the projected single currency. After extremely difficult, tense and exhausting negotiations all the outstanding issues were resolved. Concessions were made on all sides and a new treaty – the Treaty on European Union (TEU) – was agreed.

After careful examination by a working party of legal and linguistic experts, the TEU was formally signed by Foreign and Finance Ministers in Maastricht in February 1992.

The contents of the Treaty

The Maastricht Treaty created a new organisation, the European Union, which was to be based on three pillars: the European Communities; a Common Foreign and Security Policy (CFSP); and Cooperation in the Fields of Justice and Home Affairs (JHA).

Much time and effort was expended in the IGC on Political Union haggling over how the Treaty should describe the European Union, both in terms of its current character and the stage of its evolutionary progress. Most states wanted the word 'federal' included, and would have settled for a phrase that appeared in drafts where the Treaty was described as marking 'a new stage in the process leading gradually to a Union with a federal goal'. The UK government, however, was unwilling to see 'the F word' appear in any form at all and in the political trading that occurred at the Maastricht summit this point was conceded to the UK and the reference to federalism was replaced by 'This Treaty marks a new stage in the process of creating an ever closer union among the peoples of Europe, in which decisions are taken as closely as possible to the citizen'. To most continental Europeans the phrase 'ever closer union' sounded more centralist than the word 'federal', but the UK delegation was satisfied.

The EU was assigned a range of objectives, would be based on a set of guiding principles – including subsidiarity and respect for democracy and human rights – and would be governed by an institutional structure presided over by the European Council.

Most of the provisions of the Treaty were concerned with the three pillars, which in the case of pillar one meant amending the Treaties of the three European Communities, and in the cases of pillars two and three meant laying down guiding principles and operating rules.

Pillar one: the European Communities

This was by far the most important pillar since it incorporated most of the EU's policy responsibilities. Under the Treaty, the *acquis* of the existing three Communities was preserved and in several important respects was extended and strengthened by revisions of the EEC, ECSC and Euratom Treaties. The revisions of the EEC Treaty were naturally the most significant and it is upon these that attention will focus here.

Article 1 of the revised EEC Treaty stated the following: 'By this Treaty, the High Contracting Parties establish among themselves a European Community'. This meant that the European Economic Community – the EEC – was renamed the European Community. A rather confusing situation was thereby produced, in which the European Community became part of the European Communities, which in turn became part of the European Union.

Two important new principles were introduced into what now became the Treaty Establishing the European Community (TEC). First, the much discussed principle of subsidiarity was formally incorporated by a new, and rather vaguely worded, Article 3b (Article 5 in the post-Amsterdam Consolidated Treaty):

> The Community shall act within the limits of the powers conferred upon it by this Treaty and of the objectives assigned to it therein.
>
> In areas which do not fall within its exclusive competence, the Community shall take action, in accordance with the principle of subsidiarity, only if and in so far as the objectives of the proposed action cannot be sufficiently achieved by the Member States and can therefore, by reason of the scale or effects of the proposed action, be better achieved by the Community.
>
> Any action by the Community shall not go beyond what is necessary to achieve the objectives of this Treaty.

Since the Treaty was negotiated, European Council meetings have developed guidelines designed to assist with the application of the subsidiarity principle. In general, what has happened in practice is that subsidiarity has been taken to mean that policies should be decided at the national level, and perhaps even at regional or local levels, whenever possible.

Second, the TEC established Union citizenship, with every national of a member state becoming a citizen of the Union. Though symbolically significant, the practical effect of this was limited since citizens of the Union would only 'enjoy the rights conferred by this Treaty'. One of these rights was the right to live and work anywhere in the territory of the member states, subject to certain limitations. Union citizens were also given the right to vote and stand as candidates in EP and local elections, again subject to certain limitations.

Because the principles of subsidiarity and Union citizenship were incorporated into the TEC, and not just confined to the Common Provisions of the TEU, they were subject to the jurisdiction of the ECJ.

Other revisions made by the Maastricht Treaty to the TEC can be grouped under two broad headings.

(1) *Institutional changes.* The revisions falling under this heading were mostly designed to improve the efficiency and democratic nature of the Community's institutional structures and decision-making processes. Overall, the greatest impact was on the Council of Ministers, which was empowered to take a greater range of decisions on the basis of QMV, and on the EP, which was given increased powers and influence in several areas – notably in terms of legislation. The following list includes the most significant institutional changes:

- A new legislative procedure – the co-decision procedure – was established. In effect the co-decision procedure extended the cooperation procedure established by the SEA, by allowing – if the Council and the EP could not agree at second reading – for the convening of a conciliation committee and for a third reading of legislation by both the Council and the EP. Unlike the cooperation procedure, however, which enabled a determined Council to ignore the EP's expressed views, the co-decision procedure would allow the EP, for the first time, to veto legislative proposals it did not wish to accept.
- The policy areas subject to the cooperation procedure were revised, with some areas previously covered by the procedure being 'transferred out' to the co-decision procedure, and some new policy areas previously subject to the consultation procedure (which only allows for one reading of legislation) being 'transferred in'.
- The scope of the assent procedure, by which EP approval is necessary for certain EC actions, was extended.

- From January 1995 the term of office of Commissioners was extended from four to five years so as to bring the lifespan of a Commission closely into line with the lifespan of a Parliament. The national governments were to nominate by common accord, after consulting the EP, the person they intended to appoint as the President of the Commission. Other members of the Commission were to be nominated by the national governments in the established manner, but now in consultation with the nominee for Commission President. The entire prospective Commission was to be subject to a vote of approval by the EP before being formally appointed by common accord of the national governments.

- A Committee of the Regions was established to provide the Council and the Commission with advice on matters of major importance for the regions. The Committee was to be of the same size and to have the same distribution of national representatives as the Economic and Social Committee, but its members were to be representatives of regional and local authorities.

- The ECJ was given the power to impose fines on member states that failed to comply with its judgements or failed to implement Community law.

- The EP was to appoint an Ombudsman to receive complaints from citizens 'covering instances of maladministration in the activities of the Community institutions or bodies, with the exception of the Court of Justice and the Court of First Instance acting in their judicial role'.

(2) *Policy changes.* The EC's policy competence was extended and strengthened. It was so in four main ways.

- The main features of Economic and Monetary Union (EMU) were defined and a timetable for establishing it was specified. Regarding the features, EMU was to include the irrevocable fixing of exchange rates leading to the introduction of a single currency and to the establishment of a European Central Bank (ECB) which would operate within the framework of a European System of Central Banks (ESCB). The main objective of the ESCB would be to maintain price stability. Under EMU, member states were to regard their economic policies as a matter of common concern and were to coordinate them within the Council. Regarding the timetable, EMU was to be established in three stages, with stage three beginning no later than 1 January 1999 for those states which could meet the specified convergence criteria. In a protocol attached to the Treaty it was recognised that the United Kingdom 'shall not be obliged or committed to move to the third stage of Economic and Monetary Union without a separate decision to do so by its government and Parliament'. In another protocol the Danish government reserved the right to hold a national referendum before participating in the third stage of EMU.

- Some policy areas in which the Community had not been previously involved, or in which its involvement had not had an explicit Treaty base, were brought into the TEC for the first time. For example, a new chapter of the Treaty confirmed the Community's commitment to help developing countries and to do so by providing multi-annual programmes. Beyond development policy, most of the other policy areas newly introduced into the TEC were brought in only in a rather tentative manner, in the sense that the Community's responsibilities were carefully restricted. Policy areas thus identified included education, public health, consumer protection, trans-European networks and competitiveness of industry.

- Community responsibilities in some policy areas that were first given treaty recognition in the SEA were further developed. This applied particularly to research and technological development, the environment, and economic and social cohesion. As part of the strengthening of economic and social cohesion, a new fund – the Cohesion Fund – was established to provide financial assistance for environmental programmes and trans-European transport infrastructures.

- A policy area that created particular difficulties during the negotiations both before and at Maastricht was social policy. Eleven member states wished to build on and give a firm treaty base to the Social Charter, which had been adopted (by eleven votes to one) by the European Council in 1989, whilst the UK government wished to see no extension to the Community's existing responsibilities in this area – either by way of itemising specific social policies that the Community would develop, or by relaxing unanimity requirements and increasing the circumstances in which decisions could be taken by QMV. After almost bringing the Maastricht summit to the point of collapse, the impasse was resolved by the eleven contracting a separate protocol and agreement on social policy.

Pillar two: a Common Foreign and Security Policy

The SEA stated that the member states 'shall endeavour jointly to formulate and implement a European foreign policy'. The TEU greatly stiffened this aim by specifying that the EU and its member states 'shall define and implement a common foreign and security policy ... covering all areas of foreign and security policy', and by further specifying that the common policy 'shall include all questions related to the security of the Union, including the eventual framing of a common defence policy, which might in time lead to a common defence'.

The objectives of the Common Foreign and Security Policy (CFSP) were defined only in general terms: for example, 'to safeguard the common values, fundamental interests and independence of the Union', and 'to develop and consolidate democracy and the rule of law, and respect for human rights and fundamental freedoms'. More specific definition and elaboration of the principles and general guidelines of the CFSP were to be the responsibility of the European Council.

There were to be three principal ways in which the objectives of the CFSP were to be pursued:

- Systematic cooperation was to be established between the member states on any matter of foreign and security policy that was of general interest. Whenever it deemed it necessary the Council should, on the basis of unanimity, define common positions. Member states should ensure that their national policies conformed to such common positions. On the basis of general guidelines from the European Council, the Council could decide that a matter was to be the subject of joint action.
- In deciding on joint action, or at any stage during the development of a joint action, the Council could determine that implementation decisions should be taken by QMV.
- The Western European Union (WEU), which 'is an integral part of the development of the Union', was requested 'to elaborate and implement decisions and actions of the Union which had defence implications. The Council shall, in agreement with the institutions of the WEU, adopt the necessary practical arrangements'. In a Declaration annexed to the Treaty, the Community members of the WEU stated that the WEU 'will be developed as the defence component of the European Union and as the means to strengthen the European pillar of the Atlantic Alliance'.

This second pillar of the TEU thus put European Political Cooperation (EPC), which had been well established for some time, within the broader framework of a Common Foreign and Security Policy. The pillar was also extremely significant in that it introduced two important new elements into the West European integration process. First, although foreign policy remained essentially intergovernmental in character, it nonetheless became potentially subject to some QMV, if only for 'second-order' decisions. Second, defence made its first formal appearance on the policy agenda, albeit somewhat tentatively.

Pillar three: Cooperation in the Spheres of Justice and Home Affairs

The member states were to regard the following areas as matters of common interest: asylum policy; rules governing, and controls on, the crossing by persons of the external borders of the member states;

immigration policy and residence rights of third-country nationals; combating drug addiction; combating international fraud; judicial cooperation in civil matters; judicial cooperation in criminal matters; customs cooperation; and police cooperation to combat terrorism, drug trafficking and other serious crime through an EU-wide police intelligence office (Europol). Any measures taken in regard to these matters was to be in compliance with the European Convention of Human Rights.

In the nine areas of common interest the Council could: adopt joint positions and promote any suitable form of cooperation, with decisions to be taken by unanimity; adopt joint actions, with the possibility of deciding, by unanimity, that measures implementing joint actions could be adopted by a qualified majority; draw up conventions to be recommended to the member states for adoption in accordance with their respective constitutional requirements, with – unless otherwise provided by the conventions – implementing measures to be adopted within the Council by a majority of two-thirds of the member states.

To facilitate cooperation in the areas of common interest, the member states were obliged by the Treaty to establish coordinating mechanisms between the relevant departments of their administrations. At the political level these mechanisms were to be headed by the Council of Ministers (Justice and Home Affairs), and at the administrative level by the Article K.4 Coordinating Committee (the Committee being established under Article K.4 of the Treaty).

As with the CFSP pillar of the TEU, the significance of the Justice and Home Affairs (JHA) pillar lay not only in the substantive content of its provisions but also in the broader contribution it would make to the integration process in Europe. There were, as there were with the CFSP pillar, policy and institutional aspects to this. Regarding the policy aspects, a legal base was given to cooperation in areas of activity that in the past had either been dealt with purely on a national basis or had been the subject of only rather loose and informal cooperation between the member states. Regarding the institutional aspects, whilst intergovernmentalism continued to prevail, a small element of supranationalism appeared with the possibility of qualified majority decisions on certain aspects of policy implementation, and a somewhat larger element appeared in this same policy area with provision in the TEC for a common visa policy and for decisions on visas to be determined by QMV from 1996.

Ratification of the Treaty

In accordance with established procedures for Community treaties and treaty amendments, Article R of the TEU stated that ratification by the member states should be 'in accordance with their respective constitutional requirements'. In ten of the member states this meant that ratification would be by parliamentary approval only, whilst in the other two – Ireland and Denmark – it also meant the holding of national referendums.

It was hoped that all ratifications could proceed relatively smoothly and quickly so as to enable the Treaty to enter into force on 1 January 1993. In eight member states – including Ireland – these hopes were realised, but in four they were not:

- In Denmark, in June 1992 the Danish people voted, by 50.7 per cent to 49.3 per cent, against ratification. Naturally this threw the ratification schedule off course, but more importantly it also had considerable implications for the interpretation of the Treaty because it was subsequently decided at European Council meetings that a twin-track approach would be needed to persuade the Danes to give their approval in a second referendum. At the general level, integrationist rhetoric would be toned down and the decentralising subsidiarity principle, which was only briefly referred to in the Treaty, would be given greater precision and a greatly enhanced status. At the level of dealing with specific Danish concerns, Denmark would be given special guarantees, notably in the form of clear opt-outs from the Treaty provisions for a single currency and for a possible future EU defence policy. These 'concessions' to the Danes produced approval of the Treaty, by 56.8 per cent to 43.2 per cent, when the second referendum was held in May 1993.
- Shortly after the Danish vote was announced, President Mitterrand decided that France too would hold a referendum on the Treaty. The main reason for his decision was that he anticipated that the Treaty would be comfortably endorsed and that this would serve to boost his domestic authority. In the event, however, the referendum campaign was bitterly and closely fought, but ratification just squeezed through in September 1992 by 51.05 per cent to 48.95 per cent.
- In the United Kingdom, a combination of several factors – notably the government's narrow majority in the House of Commons, considerable Parliamentary scepticism on the claimed beneficial consequences of the Treaty, and opposition by the Labour Party to the opt-out which had been granted to the UK from the Treaty's Social Chapter – combined to create a protracted ratification process in Parliament which was not completed until July 1993.
- Problems in Germany arose not from the people (there was no referendum) nor from the politicians (both the Bundestag and the Bundesrat ratified the Treaty with huge majorities in December 1992), but rather from claims that ratification would infringe the country's

constitution. It was not until October 1993 that the German Constitutional Court ruled that there was no infringement, though it laid down conditions that would have to be met if there were to be significant changes or additions to the Treaty in the future.

German ratification cleared the way for the implementation of the Treaty, which took effect on 1 November 1993 – ten months later than originally planned.

The Treaty of Amsterdam

The making of the Treaty

Article N of the TEU specified that another IGC should be convened in 1996 to examine the operation of the Treaty. This specification was included mainly at the behest of those member states which were dissatisfied at what they saw to be the insufficient integrationist progress of the Maastricht Treaty. The advance notice given in the TEU of the convening of another IGC in 1996 allowed the Amsterdam Treaty to be considered and prepared over a much longer period than any other treaty in the EC/EU's history.

As part of the preparation the European Council decided at its June 1994 Corfu meeting to establish a 'Reflection Group', charged with clearing some of the ground for the IGC by examining and elaborating ideas for Treaty revisions. The Reflection Group was composed of 18 members: one representative from each member state (mainly junior ministers from Ministries of Foreign/External Affairs, or very senior diplomats); two representatives from the EP (one Socialist and one Christian Democrat); and one representative from the Commission (the Commissioner with responsibility for the IGC). It was not intended that the Group would engage in negotiations or attempt to make final decisions. The main thrust of the Group's report when it was issued in December 1995 was to recommend that the IGC should focus on trying to achieve results in three main areas: making Europe more relevant to its citizens; enabling the EU to work better and prepare for enlargement; and giving the EU greater capacity for external action. However, beyond agreement on these questions and on a few broad principles and specific issues, it was clear that there were deep divisions in the Group on the traditionally difficult topics. The positions taken by the national representatives were not identified, but the report was studded with such phrases as 'one of us believes that', 'one of us is opposed to', and 'a broad majority of members of the Group favours'. Given the already well-known position of most governments on most EU issues, and especially the UK's continuing opposition to further integration, most of these phrases could be interpreted without too much difficulty.

The experience of the Reflection Group did not thus augur well for the IGC, which was formally launched at a special Heads of Government meeting in Turin in March 1996. Little was achieved in 1996 or early 1997 on the more controversial questions: should there be extensions to QMV in the Council, should the balance of votes in the Council be weighted more towards the larger member states, should the powers of the EP be extended, and should parts of the CFSP and JHA pillars be transferred to the first pillar and/or be placed on a more supranational basis? Few IGC participants were, however, overly concerned about the lack of progress. There were two reasons for this. First, EU negotiations on constitutional/institutional issues – and indeed on most major contested issues – customarily begin slowly and then speed up as deadlines approach. Second, there were strong grounds for believing that the main obstacle to achieving progress – the UK government's opposition to further integration – would be at least partly removed by the likely outcome of the general election which had to be held before the scheduled conclusion of the IGC at the June 1997 Amsterdam summit.

The UK obstacle was indeed duly removed when, in the May 1997 election, the Conservatives were defeated after 18 years in government and replaced by Labour. Tony Blair, the new Prime Minister, declared that his government would pursue a policy of 'constructive engagement' with the EU, and this was immediately reflected in the closing weeks of the IGC when the UK's approach became much more positive than it had been under the Conservatives. There was not a complete policy about-turn, but on most issues the UK's previous 'awkwardness' and isolationism largely disappeared.

The UK's changed stance helped to make the Amsterdam summit, which marked the last stage of the IGC, somewhat smoother than the Maastricht summit. But there were still differences to be resolved at Amsterdam and not a few tensions in the air, some of which stemmed from the newly elected French Socialist government attempting to use the summit to renegotiate the terms of the EMU Stability Pact and some of which were a consequence of the German Chancellor, Helmut Kohl, adopting an unexpectedly cautious attitude to some proposed reforms as a result of domestic political difficulties. Notwithstanding these problems, however, the summit was not marked by the ill-temper, brinkmanship and threat of breakdown that had characterised the Maastricht summit. Political agreement on the contents of the Treaty was reached at the summit and, after the necessary legal and translation work had been undertaken, the Treaty was formally signed in October 1997.

At the time of the signing of the Treaty it was generally anticipated that there would be no major difficulties with its ratification. The contents of the Treaty were, after all, more modest than those of the TEU, and the Danish government had taken steps to try to ensure that there would be no repeat of the 1992 referendum defeat – notably by securing an opt-out for Denmark from sensitive aspects of the Treaty dealing with the free movement of persons. But though ratification was never seriously endangered, it was considerably delayed. The problem this time was not a referendum result: only two referendums were held – in Ireland and Denmark – and the Treaty was approved by a comfortable majority in each country. Rather, the problem was that some of the member states were slow to set the ratification process in motion, and some had to deal with domestic political and legal difficulties before ratification could be effected. In France, for example, the ratification process could not even begin until the national constitution had been amended to take account of some of the Treaty's justice and home affairs provisions.

France was the last member state to ratify, in March 1999, and the Treaty eventually came into force in May 1999.

The contents of the Treaty

It was always likely that the Amsterdam Treaty would not be as innovative or as important as either the SEA or the TEU. The intention from the outset was that it would essentially be a revising rather than a pioneering treaty. Moreover, even in respect of revisions, the great issue of internal EU debate in the mid- to late 1990s – EMU – was not on the IGC's agenda.

Events in the EU do not, of course, always work out as originally intended or anticipated. But there was no great push in the period immediately before or during the IGC to upgrade the Amsterdam Treaty from a modernising and consolidating exercise into a transforming one. Most national leaders had, after all, adopted a somewhat cautious attitude towards integration since the ratification difficulties with the TEU in 1992 had shown the danger of attempting to press ahead too fast. The assertion by Jacques Santer when he became Commission President in 1995 that the aim must be to 'do less, but do it better', captured much of the post-Maastricht mood.

In consequence, the Amsterdam Treaty had no great *projet* to guide and drive it, in the manner that the SEA had the SEM and the TEU had EMU. There was a major new EU *projet* in hand at the time of the negotiations on the Treaty – preparing for the anticipated accession of Central and Eastern European countries (CEECs) – but although this issue featured prominently in the IGC's deliberations it was not placed centre stage in the Treaty itself. This was partly because many of the more important internal

EU changes needed to accommodate the CEECs – notably reform of the CAP and of the Structural Funds – did not require Treaty amendment. It was partly also because enlargement was still some way off, so the amendments that would be necessary to enable the EU to accommodate an additional ten to twelve members – amendments focusing primarily on institutional issues – were not seen as being over-urgent.

This is not to say that institutional reform was not examined at length in the IGC. Moreover, some progress was made in that it was agreed to cap the size of the EP at 700 (a decision later rescinded by the Nice IGC), and modest extensions were made to the legal base of QMV in the first (EC) pillar and considerable extensions were made to it in the second (CFSP) pillar. However, no agreement could be reached on two key institutional issues, namely the size of the Commission and Council voting rules after enlargement, though a basis for an agreement on these matters in a future IGC (which, it was decided, would have to be called at least one year before EU membership exceeded twenty) was identified. This agreement anticipated a trade-off between those states with two Commissioners having only one Commissioner in exchange for a compensatory re-weighting of votes to their advantage in the Council.

But modest though the Treaty was as compared with the SEA and the TEU, it did nonetheless contain changes of some significance for the governance of the EU. The most significant of these changes – grouped into the six sections of the Treaty – are now outlined.

Section I: Freedom, Security and Justice

This rather mixed section covered some of the principles and values of the Union, strengthened the bases for the establishment of an area in which there could be free movement of persons 'behind' common entry rules, and developed a framework for police and judicial cooperation in criminal matters. The main contents of the section were as follows:

- The common provisions of the TEU were amended to give greater emphasis to the general principles underlying the Union: 'The Union is founded on the principles of liberty, democracy, respect for human rights and fundamental freedoms, and the rule of law' (Article 6). It was specified that applicant states must respect these principles, and for the first time a procedure was laid down for suspending some of the membership rights of any member state that failed to respect the principles.
- The EU became empowered to 'take appropriate action to combat discrimination based on sex, racial or ethnic origin, religion or belief, disability, age or sexual orientation' (Article 12 TEC). However, the

consultation legislative procedure would apply (thus giving the EP only a rather weak role) and unanimity would be required in the Council.

- A number of JHA and JHA-related policy areas were transferred to the EC, and the ways in which and the means by which they should be developed were set out in some detail. The main purpose of this was to facilitate, within a period of five years after the entry into force of the Treaty, the adoption of measures that would result in the progressive establishment of 'an area of freedom, security and justice' (Article 61 TEC) in which there would be free movement of persons behind a common external border. Policy issues to be covered by the TEC were now to include visas, asylum, immigration, refugees and displaced persons, and judicial cooperation in civil matters. Apart from visas, where the consultation procedure with QMV was to apply for five years and the co-decision procedure thereafter, decision-making in all of these policy areas was to be by the consultation procedure and unanimity in the Council. However, provision was made for the Council to be able to decide after five years to change decision-making in any or all of the areas to co-decision with QMV. The UK insisted that its special island status meant that it could not be party to this free movement of persons title, so in a special protocol it and Ireland – which wanted to maintain its Common Travel Area with the UK – were given opt-outs. Denmark also was not to be fully associated with the title because of its 'special position'.

- Underpinning the free movement of persons title, the Schengen *acquis* was integrated into the EU framework through a protocol annexed to the TEU and the TEC. Based on agreements signed by some member states in 1985 and 1990, the *acquis* consisted of rules and supporting measures dealing with the abolition of checks at internal borders. It would be up to the Council, acting unanimously, to determine where each of the provisions and decisions constituting the *acquis* should be located in the EU framework. By the time of the Amsterdam Treaty, all EU member states apart from Ireland and the UK were Schengen members so, as with the free movement of persons title of the TEC, Ireland and the UK were allowed to opt out from the Schengen Protocol.

- The transfer of so many JHA policy issues to the EC inevitably meant that pillar three of the TEU changed in character. Under its new title, 'Provisions on Police and Judicial Cooperation in Criminal Matters', it now focused on providing citizens 'with a high level of safety within an area of freedom, security and justice by developing common action among the Member States in the fields of police and judicial cooperation in criminal matters and by preventing and combating racism and xenophobia' (Article 29 TEU). A feature of the new pillar three was that the ECJ was given greater jurisdictional power than it had had under the former JHA pillar. However, this was subject to considerable limitations, not least in that it did not extend to reviewing the validity or proportionality of law and order enforcement measures and operations in the member states.

Section II: The Union and its Citizens

This section was also rather mixed, but in broad terms it dealt with policies and issues that directly affect EU citizens. Amongst the provisions of the section were the following:

- A new title on employment was inserted into the TEC, emphasising the importance the EU attaches to promoting employment and creating procedures to assist it in achieving this aim.
- The Social Chapter of the TEC, which existed only as a protocol attached to the Treaty because of the opt-out the UK government had negotiated at Maastricht, was fully incorporated into the TEC.
- The importance of the principles of subsidiarity and proportionality was re-emphasised, and the nature of the principles themselves was given a little more clarification in a protocol annexed to the TEC.
- The importance attached to environmental, public health and consumer protection policies in the TEC was upgraded and strengthened.
- Provisions for enhancing openness and transparency in EU decision-making were set down in the TEU and the TEC.

Section III: An Effective and Coherent External Policy

The objectives of the CFSP pillar were left largely unchanged, but operational and management mechanisms were strengthened with a view to improving the EU's effectiveness and efficiency:

- The main CFSP policy instruments were left much as before, but they were set out in a clearer and more streamlined manner. There were to be five instruments: definition of the CFSP's principles and general guidelines; common strategies; joint actions; common positions; and strengthened cooperation between the member states.
- The first two policy instruments were to be intergovernmental in character in that decisions would be taken by the European Council acting unanimously. Abstentions would not prevent the taking of a vote. The fifth instrument would also be intergovernmental in that it did not extend beyond inter-state cooperation.
- QMV was established as the norm for adopting and implementing joint actions and common positions, thus making these policy instruments

essentially supranational. However, if 'for important and stated reasons of national policy' a state declared it proposed to oppose the adoption of a decision by QMV, a vote would not be taken. In such a circumstance the Council, acting by QMV, could decide to refer the matter to the European Council for decision by unanimity. For the first time – 30 years after the Luxembourg Compromise – a vital national interest veto was thus given formal treaty status in a policy area where QMV could be used.

- A new device, 'constructive abstention', was introduced whereby a state abstaining in a vote could issue a declaration that would result in it not being obliged to apply the decision taken, whilst recognising that the decision did commit the EU.
- A CFSP High Representative was to assist the Council, and especially the Council Presidency, in all CFSP matters, including external representation.
- Under a declaration attached to the Treaty, a policy planning and early warning unit – consisting of personnel drawn from the Council Secretariat, the member states, the Commission, and the WEU – was to be established in the Council Secretariat under the responsibility of the High Representative.
- Specific security issues were identified for the first time as falling within the remit of the EU, with the incorporation of the so-called Petersberg tasks of 'humanitarian and rescue tasks, peacekeeping tasks and tasks of combat forces in crisis management, including peacekeeping' (Article 17 TEU).
- Though the Treaty did not give the EU explicit legal personality, it came close to doing so by giving it the power to enter into CFSP-related agreements with third countries.
- The much disputed issue of CFSP financing was settled, with most expenditure, other than that on operations with military or defence implications, being charged to the EC budget. The budgetary process thus become an arena in which the EP – whose formal powers in relation to the CFSP remained weak – could exert a significant policy influence.

In the EU's EC pillar, the powers of the Commission and the Council under Article 113 of the TEC (dealing with external trade) had been disputed since the early 1990s, with the Commission pressing for its sole negotiating power with third countries in respect of goods to be extended to services and intellectual property, and the Council resisting this. A 1994 ECJ ruling on the issue did little to resolve matters. The Amsterdam Treaty contained a supplement to Article 133 (the renumbered Article 113) enabling the Council, 'acting unanimously on a proposal from the

Commission and after consulting the European Parliament' to extend the application of the Article to services and intellectual property.

Section IV: The Union's Institutions

This section addressed decision-making and the functioning of the EU institutions. As noted above, some of the more difficult outstanding issues were postponed to a further IGC which would be held when EU enlargement was imminent. Disappointing, however, though this was for those who wished to see decision-making and institutional arrangements put in place in preparation for enlargement, the following significant reforms were nonetheless agreed:

- Major revisions were made in the TEC to the application of the EU's legislative procedures. Most importantly: the cooperation procedure was virtually abandoned, being now restricted to a handful of EMU decisions (it was left for these because the IGC negotiators did not wish to risk opening the highly sensitive EMU 'box'); and the remit of the co-decision procedure was extended to 23 new cases, making it the 'normal' procedure for most policy legislation in that it would apply to most areas apart from agriculture and justice and home affairs matters (where the consultation procedure would continue to apply).
- The co-decision procedure was streamlined and the EP's position under the procedure was strengthened (see Chapter 16).
- There was increased provision for the use of QMV in the Council, though not by as much as had been anticipated following Chancellor Kohl's unexpected caution on the matter (see p. 94) and problems that a number of governments had with particular proposed extensions. Within the EC pillar, areas to which QMV was extended included employment guidelines, social exclusion, equal opportunities and treatment for men and women, and various aspects of research decision-making. Within the CFSP pillar, QMV became, as was shown in Section III, the norm for implementing CFSP joint actions and common positions. Within the third pillar there was little change, with unanimity being required except for some implementing decisions.
- A number of changes were made to the TEC in respect of the appointment of the President and other members of the Commission, and the position of the President was strengthened: what had become established in 1994 as a *de facto* right of the EP to approve the European Council's nominee for Commission President was given treaty status; the nominations of the national governments to the College must now be made 'by common accord' with the President-designate; the Commission would now be required to work 'under the political

guidance of its President'; and in a Declaration attached to the Treaty it was stated that 'the President of the Commission must enjoy broad discretion in the allocation of the tasks within the College, as well as in any reshuffling of those tasks during a Commission's term of office'.

The main themes of the institutional changes contained in the Amsterdam Treaty were thus, as with the comparable changes of the SEA and the Maastricht Treaty, aimed at increasing the efficiency and extending the democratic base of decision-making.

Section V: Closer Cooperation – 'Flexibility'

Since the Exchange Rate Mechanism (ERM) of the European Monetary System (EMS) was created in the late 1970s, the European integration process has involved some flexibility in the sense that not all member states have participated in all activities. This type of flexibility was increased in the 1980s, notably with the establishment of the Schengen system on a partial membership basis, and was given treaty status in the Maastricht Treaty with the UK's Social Chapter opt-out and special arrangements for the UK and Denmark on EMU.

Discussions on flexibility intensified after Maastricht, with the more pro-integrationist member states expressing dissatisfaction at being 'held back' by the less integrationist states – especially the UK. This dissatisfaction led to the Amsterdam Treaty incorporating new provisions into the first and third pillars of the TEU to allow a less than full complement of member states – but constituting 'at least a majority' – to establish closer cooperation between themselves, and for this purpose to be able to make use of the EU's institutions, procedures and mechanisms. Flexibility of this kind was to be used only as a last resort and was made subject to various restrictions – it should not, for example, affect the *acquis communautaire* and it should be open to all member states. The authorisation to establish closer cooperation was granted to the Council acting by QMV, but if 'a member of the Council declares that, for important and stated reasons of national policy, it intends to oppose the granting of an authorisation by a qualified majority, a vote shall not be taken. The Council may, acting by a qualified majority, request that the matter be referred to the Council, meeting in the composition of the Heads of State or Government, for decision by unanimity' (Article 11 TEC; much the same formulation was written into Article 40 of the TEU in reference to pillar three issues).

The rules on closer cooperation thus struck a balance between, as Niels Ersbøll – former Secretary General of the Council and the personal representative of the Danish Foreign Minister in the 1996–7 IGC – put it, 'an unavoidable need for greater flexibility, as the Union progresses into new and nationally sensitive areas ... and the common interest in maintaining the basic principle of equal rights and obligations, characteristic of European integration from the outset' (Ersbøll, 1997: 10).

Section VI: Simplification and Consolidation of the Treaties

As part of the attempt to make Europe more relevant and accessible to its citizens, a number of redundant articles were repealed from the Treaties establishing the three European Communities, and in a declaration annexed to the Amsterdam Treaty it was stated that there should be 'a consolidation of all the relevant Treaties, including the Treaty on European Union'. Consolidation was deemed necessary because the setting and numbering of the existing treaties was already, and after the Amsterdam Treaty would be even more so, extremely confusing to all but the most informed practitioners and experts. In particular, the repeal of many TEC articles had left numerous gaps in the Treaty's numbering system; the many new articles that had been added to the TEC over the years, notably by the SEA, the TEU, and now the Amsterdam Treaty, had been 'squeezed' in, with the consequence that several articles contained many sub-articles covering significantly different topics – Article 130, for example, extended from Article 130 (industry) to Article 130y (cooperation with third countries and with international organisations); and the TEU articles had not been numbered at all, but had been lettered – so, for example, CFSP articles ran from J to J11 and JHA articles from K to K9.

Renumbering resulted in the TEU articles being numbered from 1–53, rather than from A–S (see Document 8.1, p. 130). The TEC became numbered from 1–314, rather than from 1–248 (see Document 8.2, pp. 130–2). The ECSC and Euratom treaties were not renumbered, and a full consolidation of all the EU treaties into one treaty was not attempted.

Concluding Remarks

The EC/EU's treaty framework evolved considerably in the period from the Treaties of Rome to the Treaty of Amsterdam. All of the treaties negotiated in this forty-year period advanced the integrationist process in at least some way.

The SEA and the Maastricht and Amsterdam treaties were particularly important. They were so most obviously because of the wide range of policy and institutional measures they contained. But they were so partly too because each did something for the integrationist spirit over and above the specific treaty additions and amendments they contained. So, the SEA, along with the SEM programme, heralded the re-launch of the integration process after years of relative stagnation and provided a major stimulus to the integrationist momentum. The Maastricht Treaty laid the foundations for EMU and also created a symbolically important new organisational form – the European Union – based on three pillars. And the Amsterdam Treaty, though disappointing to those who looked for major reforms, did help to pick up integrationist advance after the caution that had followed upon the 1992 Danish referendum, and did signal also the wish of the UK government to enter the EU mainstream.

Chapter 6

The Treaty of Nice

The Background to the Treaty
The Contents of the Treaty
The Charter of Fundamental Rights of the European Union
The Significance of the Treaty

The Background to the Treaty

Though the Treaty of Amsterdam incorporated many changes to the EU's treaties, it did not succeed in what was supposed to be its central purpose: preparing the EU's institutions for enlargement. With enlargement still some way off, the national governments were just not subject to enough pressure to find the political will to reach agreement on key issues.

Accordingly, the governments attached to the TEC a 'Protocol on the institutions with the prospect of enlargement of the European Union' in which provision was made for another IGC to be convened 'at least one year before the membership exceeds twenty'. Its task would be to carry out 'a comprehensive review of the provisions of the Treaties on the composition and functioning of the institutions'. Significantly, the bases on which an agreement could be reached on two of the most difficult institutional issues – the size of the Commission and voting weights in the Council – were identified in the Protocol with a statement that at the time of the next enlargement of the Union 'the Commission shall comprise one national of each of the Member States, provided that, by that date, the weighting of the votes in the Council has been modified, whether by re-weighting of the votes or by dual majority, in a manner acceptable to all member states, taking into account all relevant elements, notably compensating those Member States which give up the possibility of nominating a second member of the Commission'.

With enlargement negotiations opening in 1998 with six candidate countries and negotiations with another six likely to open in the near future, the Heads of Government of the member states decided at their June 1999 Cologne summit that the IGC should be convened in early 2000 and concluded by the year's end. Accordingly, the IGC opened in February 2000 and closed at the December 2000 Nice European Council. (The way in which the IGC was conducted is outlined in Chapter 8 and is described in detail in Galloway, 2001.)

The remit of the IGC was initially limited to the so-called 'Amsterdam leftovers', that is to the composition of the Commission, the weighting of votes among the members of the Council, and the further extension of QMV to new areas. From the beginning of the IGC, however, the Commission and some of the member states lobbied for an additional item to be placed on the agenda, namely the strengthening and simplification of the enhanced cooperation procedure that had been created under the Amsterdam Treaty. Eventually, this item did become part of the agenda, as did a number of other issues as the IGC progressed.

The Contents of the Treaty

The composition and functioning of the institutions

The Commission

The IGC did not, as many thought it should, take a decision on the maximum size of the College of Commissioners. Rather, it agreed that from 2005 the College would consist of one national per member state, thus resulting in the five largest states losing their right to have two Commissioners. It was further agreed that once the EU numbered 27 members a decision would be taken on the exact size of the College and on arrangements for a fair rotation system between the member states.

Arrangements for the appointment of the College were changed, most notably with the replacement of unanimity by QMV in the European Council and Council of Ministers for key decisions. Henceforth, under Article 214 TEC:

- The President will be nominated by the European Council acting by QMV, and – as before – with this appointment requiring the approval of the EP.
- The Council will adopt the list of other persons it intends to nominate to the College by QMV and – as before – in agreement with the appointed President.
- The whole College will be appointed by the Council by QMV after – as before – approval by the EP.

The powers of the Commission President were also strengthened, primarily by giving full treaty status in Article 217 TEC to powers he had been given in a Declaration attached to the Amsterdam Treaty. In addition to the Commission working under the 'political guidance' of the President (which was provided for under the Amsterdam Treaty), the President would now: decide on the Commission's 'internal organisation';

allocate the responsibilities of Commissioners and if necessary reshuffle them during a Commission's term of office; appoint Vice Presidents after receiving the approval of the College; and require a Commissioner to resign after obtaining the approval of the College.

The Council of Ministers

A central feature of the IGC was a determination by the EU's large member states to protect their position in the Council as enlargement brought in many small states. Various options were explored on this, with the following mixed solution – to apply from 1 January 2005 – eventually being agreed:

(1)   The voting weights of the member states under QMV were changed. Overall, small states continue to be over-represented, but there was some tilting of the balance towards large member states. As can be seen in Table 6.1, amongst the large states Germany remains particularly under-represented in terms of voting weight in relation to population size. This is largely because France was especially resistant to Germany having more votes than the other large states.

A related decision assisting large states was that the threshold for a qualified majority was raised. The EU-15 requirement – 62 votes out of 87, or 71.26 per cent – would be replaced in a transitional process in which the QMV threshold would move according to the pace of accessions up to a maximum of 73.4 per cent. When the EU eventually reached 27 members the threshold would be 255 out of 345, or 73.91 per cent. (For an account and full analysis of the QMV debate and decisions of Nice, see Galloway, 2001: 76–93.)

(2)   Provision was made for any member state to request verification that a qualified majority represents at least 62 per cent of the total population of the Union. If it does not, no decision can be taken. This stipulation clearly advantages the more populous states.

Slightly offsetting these two provisions that are to the advantage of large states, it was, on the insistence of smaller states, also agreed at Nice that decisions taken by QMV must be approved by a majority of states. This was inserted into the Treaty because, though it was not mathematically possible in the EU-15 for QMV majorities to be attained by a minority of states, it would be in the enlarged EU.

* * *

As in all IGCs since the SEA, much attention was given to further extensions of QMV However, of the 70 or so treaty provisions still subject to unanimity, only 45 were discussed. The remainder – including such areas as common defence, revision of the treaties, and comitology – were left aside because they were deemed to be constitutional or too sensitive in nature.

Extensions of QMV on entry into force of the Nice Treaty were agreed for 37 Treaty provisions: 4 in the TEU and 33 in the TEC. Extensions were also agreed for a further 8 TEC provisions for various dates subsequent to the entry into force of the Treaty, though with some of these dependent on a Council decision by unanimity. (These figures are taken from Galloway, 2001: 199–201. Commentaries vary in the figures they give on the number of QMV extensions depending on whether: conditional extensions are counted; extensions with time-lags are counted; more than one change in a single Treaty article is counted more than once. See, for example: European Commission, 2001; Bond and Feus, 2001; European Parliament, 2001.)

Many of the extensions covered relatively uncontentious and, for the most part, not very politically significant matters. They included: 'incentive measures to combat discrimination' (Article 13(2) TEC); 'minimum standards for giving temporary protection to refugees' (63(2)(a) TEC); approval of the Rules of Procedure of the ECJ (233 TEC) and of the CFI (224 TEC); and appointments of members of the Economic and Social Committee (259(1) TEC) and of the Committee of Regions (263 TEC). Amongst more controversial and politically important matters to move to QMV on the entry into force of the Treaty were: measures to facilitate freedom of movement of the citizen (18 TEC); measures assisting judicial cooperation in civil matters, except aspects relating to family law (65 TEC); the conclusion of international agreements in the area of trade in services and the commercial aspects of property, though with exemptions (133(5) TEC); actions in the field of industrial policy (157(3) TEC); and the nomination and appointment of the President and members of the Commission (214 TEC). A partial and deferred – until 2004 – switch to QMV was agreed for provisions of Title IV of the TEC covering visas, asylum, immigration and other policies related to free movement of persons. QMV was also provided for the reform of the Structural and Cohesion Funds (161 TEC) and for the adoption of the EU's Financial Regulations (279(1) TEC) but not until 2007 – that is, until after the multi-annual financial perspective setting out spending plans for the years 2007–13 had been negotiated. (For a full list of QMV extensions, see European Commission, 2001; Bond and Feus, 2001; Galloway, 2001.)

The European Parliament

One of the few institutional provisions agreed in the Amsterdam IGC to help prepare the EU for enlargement was the setting of a ceiling of 700 on

Table 6.1 Populations and institutional representations of EU member states

	Population (millions)	Percentage of EU-27	Weighted votes in Council					EP seats			Members of Economic and Social Committee and Committee of the Regions	
			Pre-Nice		Post-Nice			Pre-Nice	Post-Nice*	Percentage EU-27	Pre-Nice	Post-Nice
			Number of votes	Percentage of votes	Number of votes	Percentage of votes EU-15	Percentage of votes EU-27					
Germany	82.5	17.05	10	11.5	29	12.2	8.41	99	99	13.52	24	24
UK	59.7	12.31	10	11.5	29	12.2	8.41	87	72	9.84	24	24
France	58.9	12.25	10	11.5	29	12.2	8.41	87	72	9.84	24	24
Italy	57.9	11.97	10	11.5	29	12.2	8.41	87	72	9.84	24	24
Spain	42.3	8.19	8	9.2	27	11.4	7.83	64	50	6.83	21	21
Netherlands	16.3	3.28	5	5.7	13	5.5	3.77	31	25	3.42	12	12
Greece	11.0	2.19	5	5.7	12	5.1	3.48	25	22	3.01	12	12
Portugal	10.5	2.14	5	5.7	12	5.1	3.48	25	22	3.01	12	12
Belgium	10.4	2.10	5	5.7	12	5.1	3.48	25	22	3.01	12	12
Sweden	9.0	1.84	4	4.6	10	4.2	2.90	22	18	2.46	12	12
Austria	8.1	1.68	4	4.6	10	4.2	2.90	21	17	2.32	12	12
Denmark	5.4	1.10	3	3.4	7	2.9	2.03	16	13	1.78	9	9
Finland	5.2	1.07	3	3.4	7	2.9	2.03	16	13	1.78	9	9

Ireland	4.0	0.78	3	3.4	7	2.9	2.03	15	12	1.64	9	9
Luxembourg	0.5	0.09	2	2.3	4	1.7	1.16	6	6	0.82	6	6
Total EU-15	381.7	77.99	87	100.0	237	100.0		626	535	73.12	222	222
Poland	38.2	8.04	–	–	27	–	7.83	–	50	6.83	–	21
Romania	22.5	4.67	–	–	14	–	4.06	–	33	4.51	–	15
Czech Republic	10.2	2.14	–	–	12	–	3.48	–	20	2.73	–	12
Hungary	10.1	2.10	–	–	12	–	3.48	–	20	2.73	–	12
Bulgaria	8.2	1.71	–	–	10	–	2.90	–	17	2.32	–	12
Slovakia	5.4	1.12	–	–	7	–	2.03	–	13	1.78	–	9
Lithuania	3.4	0.77	–	–	7	–	2.03	–	12	1.64	–	9
Latvia	2.3	0.51	–	–	4	–	1.16	–	8	1.09	–	7
Slovenia	2.0	0.41	–	–	4	–	1.16	–	7	0.96	–	7
Estonia	1.4	0.30	–	–	4	–	1.16	–	6	0.82	–	7
Cyprus	0.7	0.16	–	–	4	–	1.16	–	6	0.82	–	6
Malta	0.4	0.08	–	–	3	–	0.87	–	5	0.68	–	5
Total EU-27	486.5	100	–	100.0	345	–	100	–	732	100	–	344

Sources: data from European Commission, 2001; European Commission, 2005g; European Parliament, 2001; Wessels, 2001.

*In the 2004–09 Parliament most states have a larger number of MEPs than provided for under the Nice agreement. This is because it was decided – partly to satisfy those states that were 'under-represented' by the Nice agreement – to redistribute, for the 2004–09 Parliament only, the 'surplus' Bulgarian and Romanian allocations.

the size of the EP. Under pressure not to reduce the size of national representations by too much, this ceiling was raised by the Nice IGC to 732.

The raised ceiling still required cuts in the numbers of seats allocated to EU-15 states. It was agreed that a reduction of 91 – from 626 to 535 – would be made, but this would not fully apply until 2009. In the meantime, the total number of MEPs in the 2004–09 Parliament would vary according to the pace of accessions of new states.

As for the distribution of seats between states, there was extensive bargaining in the IGC over both the distribution between EU-15 states and the allocations to be made to the prospective member states. Concerning EU-15 states, only the largest and smallest states – Germany and Luxembourg – did not have a reduction in their number of MEPs. Concerning the prospective member states, some blatantly discriminatory decisions were made with, for example, Hungary and the Czech Republic being allocated fewer seats than Belgium or Portugal even though they had very similar populations. This situation was later rectified when the seats provisionally allocated to Bulgaria and Romania were re-assigned for the purposes of the 2004 EP elections.

The courts

A number of changes were made to the Treaty articles covering the EU's two courts with a view to preparing them for enlargement, improving their functioning, and amending and clarifying their responsibilities.

The size of the Court of Justice (ECJ) remained unchanged at 'one judge per Member State', but that of the Court of First Instance (CFI) – which hitherto had not been specified in the Treaty – was now specified as being 'at least one judge per Member State'.

ECJ cases previously dealt with in full plenary session would now normally be dealt with in a Grand Chamber – comprised, though this was not specified in the Treaty itself, of eleven judges.

To lighten the workload of the ECJ, the types of cases coming before the CFI was widened to include most direct actions and, for the first time, preliminary rulings in specific areas. So as to allow the CFI to take on its new responsibilities, the Council, acting unanimously, was given the power to establish judicial panels to hear and determine certain classes of cases that hitherto have been handled by the CFI. Decisions taken by judicial panels would be subject to a right of appeal to the CFI 'where there is a serious risk of the unity or consistency of Community law being affected' (Article 225 TEC).

The Rules of Procedure of the two courts were made easier to determine, in that they would now require only qualified majority rather than unanimous approval by the Council.

Decision-making procedures

The Nice Treaty was much more restrained than had been the SEA and the Maastricht and Amsterdam treaties in making changes to the form and application of the EU's decision-making procedures.

The most striking changes to *form* were to the Amsterdam-created enhanced cooperation procedure (flexible cooperation as it is often called) which had provided a base for states which are ready and willing to engage in an activity within the EU framework when not all states wish to proceed. The Amsterdam arrangements had been widely criticised for being too restrictive and almost unworkable. Two changes were made to those arrangements to make enhanced cooperation, whilst still a procedure of last resort, more flexible and potentially more usable. First, the minimum number of member states required for enhanced cooperation was set at eight, as compared with the Amsterdam stipulation that a majority of states was required. This means that the minimum proportion of states needed for enhanced cooperation will fall as the size of the EU grows. Second, in the first and third pillars, the possibility of any single state vetoing enhanced cooperation was removed and replaced by the possibility of an appeal to the European Council, which will be able to act by QMV.

Less striking changes to form were mainly to the benefit of the EP. Under Article 7 TEU, it would now join the Commission and member states in being able to launch an initiative to charge a member state with a breach of fundamental rights. Under Article 20 TEC, it would join the Commission, Council and member states in being able to challenge the legality of an act in the Court of Justice. And under Article 300 TEC it was given equal status with the Council, Commission and member states in being able to obtain an opinion from the ECJ on the validity of international agreements.

As for changes to the *application* of decision-making procedures, enhanced cooperation was affected here too in that the Treaty provided for the possibility of it to be used in the second (CFSP) pillar for the implementation of joint actions and common positions that do not have military or defence implications. It would, however, be more difficult to use than under the first (EC) and third (Police and Judicial Cooperation) pillars since the Council would decide on its possible usage on a two-thirds vote and any member state could ask that the matter be referred to the European Council for a unanimous decision.

The co-decision procedure, which gives the EP a veto over proposals, was also extended in its application, but only to seven treaty articles. New articles to be covered by the procedure included certain anti-discrimination measures, judicial cooperation in civil matters (except family law), and specific industrial policy support measures. The EP's hopes and request that the procedure should apply to all decisions where QMV applies was resisted, with the consequence that in some important policy areas – including agriculture and competition – the consultation procedure, which only gives the EP consultative and advisory powers, would still apply.

The assent procedure – under which decisions require the assent of the EP – was extended in its application. First, it would now apply when enhanced cooperation concerns an area that falls under the co-decision procedure. Second, responding to recent electoral successes and participation in government of Jörg Haider's right-wing Freedom Party (FPÖ) in Austria, it was decided that the assent procedure would apply in determining whether 'there is a clear risk of a serious breach by a Member State' of the principles on which the EU is founded (Article 7 TEC). (The Amsterdam Treaty had established the use of the assent procedure for breaches of EU principles, but had restricted its application to determining whether 'a serious and persistent breach' already existed.) The principles themselves would remain those specified in Article 6 TEU as being 'liberty, democracy, respect for human rights and fundamental freedoms, and the rule of law'. If a breach was held to be at risk or to exist, the Council could determine appropriate action, including – a new Nice provision – making recommendations where a risk existed, or – an Amsterdam-established provision – suspending EU voting rights.

New competences

The IGC's focus on institutional issues meant that not as much attention was given as had been in previous IGCs to extending the EU's policy competences. Only two significant extensions were made.

First, following on from the 1999 Tampere summit which focused on justice and home affairs matters, new forms of cooperation in the fight against organised crime were identified. Following on also from Tampere, the means of operationalising such cooperation were strengthened by giving treaty recognition and support to the European Judicial Cooperation Unit (Eurojust) which the Tampere Council had decided to establish for the purposes of facilitating coordination and action between national prosecuting authorities in respect of serious cross-border crime.

Second, the objectives of social policy were widened with the addition to the list of social policy objectives set out in Article 137 TEC of two new objectives: combating social exclusion and the modernisation (but specifically not the harmonisation) of social protection systems.

The Charter of Fundamental Rights of the European Union

At its Cologne meeting in June 1999, the European Council declared that 'the fundamental rights applicable at Union level should be consolidated in a Charter and thereby made more evident' (European Council, 1999b: 18). The European Council further declared that a draft document should be prepared in advance of the December 2000 European Council meeting, when it would then be considered 'whether and, if so, how the Charter should be integrated into the treaties' (ibid.: Annex iv).

The composition of the body – called a Convention – charged with drawing up the Charter was broadly outlined at Cologne and then specified at the October 1999 Tampere summit. It had 62 members, drawn from four sources: fifteen representatives of the heads of state and government; a representative of the President of the Commission; sixteen members of the EP; and thirty members of national parliaments. There were also four observers: two representatives from the Court of Justice and two from the Council of Europe, one of whom represented the European Court of Human Rights. This membership was quite unique in that for the first time EU representatives were meeting with national representatives to draft a Union text. A much broader, and arguably more democratic, base was thus being used than in IGCs (which are composed of governmental representatives).

The Charter was agreed by the Convention in October 2000. Its high tone and ambitions may be seen by quoting from its Preamble:

> Conscious of its spiritual and moral heritage, the Union is founded on the indivisible, universal values of human dignity, freedom, equality and solidarity; it is based on the principles of democracy and the rule of law. It places the individual at the heart of its activities, by establishing the citizenship of the Union and by creating an area of freedom, security and justice.
>
> The Union contributes to the preservation and to the development of these common values while respecting the diversity of the cultures and traditions of the peoples of Europe as well as the national identities of the Member States and the organisation of their public authorities at national, regional and local levels; it seeks to promote balanced and sustainable development and ensures free movement of persons, goods, services and capital, and the freedom of establishment (*Official Journal*, C364: 43, 18 December 2000).

Following the Preamble, the Charter is organised into six chapters:

I (Articles 1–5): dignity. Rights covered under this chapter include: the right to life, including the prohibition of the death penalty; the integrity of the person including prohibition of the reproductive cloning of human beings; and the prohibition of torture or inhumane treatment.

II (Articles 6–19): freedoms. Included here are the right to liberty and security; respect for private and family life; protection of personal data; freedom of thought, conscience and religion; freedom of expression; freedom to conduct business; and the right to property.

III (Articles 20–26): equality. Amongst the rights recognised in this chapter are equality before the law, non-discrimination, equality between men and women, and the rights of the child.

IV (Articles 27–38): solidarity. This chapter includes workers' rights to information and consultation within undertakings, the right of collective bargaining and action, fair and just working conditions, health care rights, and consumer protection.

V (Articles 39–46): citizens' rights. Rights listed here include the right of a citizen to vote and stand as a candidate at EP and municipal elections in the member states in which he or she resides, the right to good administration, the right of movement and residence within the Union, and the right of diplomatic or consular protection by the authorities of any member state in a third country in which the member state of which he or she is a national is not represented.

VI (Articles 47–50): justice. This chapter includes the right to an effective remedy and to a fair trial, the presumption of innocence and right of defence, and adherence to the principles of legality and proportionality of criminal offences and penalties.

* * *

Some governments wanted to take advantage of the 2000 IGC to give treaty status to the Charter. However, resistance from the UK government, with some support from four other states, resulted in it not being mentioned at all in the Nice Treaty, though it was 'solemnly proclaimed' at Nice by the Council, EP and Commission. Quite where this left the Charter in legal terms was initially uncertain, though it was clear it would have at least some legal impact for it did, in effect, come close to 'communautarising' a series of rights that hitherto had become recognised in the Community's legal system but in a somewhat tangential manner.

Practice has subsequently come to show that the Charter does indeed contribute to the strengthening and certainty of the EU's legal system in that citizens, institutions, national governments and judges are better informed as to just what is meant by fundamental rights in the Union.

Legal submissions before the EU's courts have referred to the Charter. And the Commission has assessed the compatibility of proposed legislation with the Charter and, where appropriate, has referred to the Charter in the preamble of legislative proposals.

The status of the Charter was subsequently one of the issues considered in the IGC on the Constitutional Treaty. As will be seen in the next chapter, under the Constitutional Treaty it is given full legal force, but for that to take effect the Treaty must be ratified.

The Significance of the Treaty

The narrow focus of the Nice Treaty helped to make its ratification relatively straightforward, except in Ireland where, as was explained on p. 28, domestic political circumstances resulted in the Irish people rejecting ratification in a referendum held in June 2001. The Treaty therefore had to be put on hold until, in a second referendum held in October 2002, the Irish people gave it their approval. The Treaty came into force in February 2003.

The Treaty was narrower than its predecessors in that it was concerned almost exclusively with institutional matters. The IGC that produced it was, as Galloway (2001: 21) has observed, driven largely by concerns about the relative power and influence of member states in the Union. Criticism of the IGC for not having addressed wider issues of EU's governance – concerning, for example, the power balance between the Union and the member states or the 'constitutionalisation' and simplification of the treaties – misunderstand what the IGC was established to do.

It achieved what it was intended to do: take decisions about EU institutions that created the necessary bases for the planned expansion of the EU to incorporate Central, Eastern and Southern European countries. Beyond providing for this widening of the EU, the Treaty also provided for some deepening by further edging forward the integration process through, for example, the increased powers given to the EP and the wider legal base of QMV in the Council.

The broader issues that critics of the Treaty would have liked to have seen explored in the 2000 IGC were scheduled for another IGC that a declaration attached to the Nice Treaty programmed to be convened in 2004.

Chapter 7

The Constitutional Treaty

The Making of the Treaty
The Contents of the Treaty
Ratification
Concluding Remarks

The Making of the Treaty

As was noted at the end of Chapter 6, it was recognised at the time agreement was reached on the Nice Treaty that it contained little more than the bare minimum in preparing the EU for enlargement. The Treaty made provision for fitting the new member states into the Commission, the Council, the EP and the other EU institutions, but it did little to tackle wider matters relating to how the much larger and more heterogeneous EU could function with reasonable efficiency and effectiveness.

Thus recognising the limitations of the treaty they had contracted, the national leaders agreed at Nice to open up a debate on the future of the EU and to convene another IGC in 2004. To facilitate the debate and help prepare the IGC, the December 2001 European Council meeting issued the *Laeken Declaration on the Future of the European Union* which provided for the establishment of a Convention on the Future of Europe (European Council, 2001).

The Constitutional Convention

The Laeken Declaration declared that the soon-to-be enlarged European Union needed to become 'more democratic, more transparent and more efficient' (European Council, 2001: 21). The Union also needed to resolve three basic challenges: 'how to bring citizens, and primarily the young, closer to the European design and the European institutions'; 'how to organise politics and the European political area in an enlarged Union'; and 'how to develop the Union into a stabilising factor and a model in the new, multipolar world' (European Council, ibid.).

These general aims and challenges resulted in the Convention being asked to examine a number of key issues. These included establishing a better division and definition of EU competences, simplifying the Union's instruments, increasing democracy, transparency and efficiency, and simplifying and reorganising the treaties – with this to include the option of leading 'in the long run to the adoption of a constitutional text in the Union' (European Council, 2001: 24).

The Convention was composed of 105 members:

- a chairman, the former French President, Valéry Giscard D'Estaing, and two vice chairmen: Guiliano Amato, a former Italian Prime Minister, and Jean-Luc Dehaene, a former Belgian Prime Minister;
- representatives of the Heads of State or Government of the member states (15);
- representatives of the Heads of State or Government of the candidate states (13);
- representatives of the national parliaments of the member states (30);
- representatives of the national parliaments of the candidate states (26);
- representatives of the European Commission (2);
- representatives of the European Parliament (16).

Representatives of the (then) soon-to-be acceding states were to be able to play a full part in the proceedings of the Convention, but were not to be able to prevent any consensus emerging between (the then 15) member states.

Alternatives were appointed for all representatives. In addition, observer status was given to: the European Economic and Social Committee (3 representatives); the Committee of the Regions (6); the social partners (3); and the European Ombudsman.

The dominant presence in the Convention was thus parliamentarians rather than governmental representatives: deliberately so since the Convention was not intended to replicate an IGC.

The Convention opened its proceedings on 28 February 2002. Its work was undertaken in four forums:

- *The Office of the President.* Giscard D'Estaing did much to set the focus and pace and to shape the outcomes of the Convention. He had clear ideas on a number of issues, including strengthening the European Council, moving the Commission to a more collegial model, and simplifying procedures in the interests of efficiency and democracy. In the closing period, when disagreements between Convention members were creating difficulties, he was highly proactive in ensuring progress was made.
- *The Praesidium.* This was composed of 13 Convention members, including the Chairman and two Vice-Chairmen. Its job was to provide direction and impetus, most particularly by ensuring the work of the Convention was being properly organised and tasks were being completed.

- *Working Groups.* Eleven of these were established to examine particular issues in depth.
- *Plenary Sessions.* Normally held over a two-day period at least once each month, plenaries held general debates, deliberated on working group reports, and gradually moved towards the adoption of a final text.

The work of the four forums was supported by a well organised and flexible secretariat. The Laeken Declaration had stated that the Convention's 'final document will provide a starting point for discussions in the Intergovernmental Conference, which will take the ultimate decisions' (European Council, 2001: 25). As, however, the work of the Convention proceeded, it became increasingly clear from statements by governmental leaders that the final document would be likely not just to provide a 'starting point' for IGC discussions but in many respects would determine them. It also quickly became clear that the Convention was not going to restrict itself to a minimalist interpretation of its remit but was going to draw up a full draft constitution for the Union. These developments resulted in the work of the Convention attracting growing attention, not least from national governments – some of which replaced sitting Convention representatives with more senior figures.

The Convention's draft had been scheduled to be presented to the June 2003 Thessaloniki European Council, but in the event only Parts I and II of what was a four-part text were ready. Parts III and IV were considered and approved at a final Convention plenary in July. On the insistence of Giscard D'Estaing, who feared open divisions would weaken the weight of the Convention's position, texts were adopted by consensus rather than by voting. The final text was formally presented to the Italian presidency on 18 July 2003.

This final text took the form of a draft Treaty Establishing a Constitution for Europe. The nature of its contents will be considered later in this chapter, since most of them were incorporated by the ensuing IGC. Suffice it to note here that the recommendations were, for the most part, relatively modest and essentially incrementalist in manner. This is precisely the reason most of them were acceptable to the IGC: they were set within the general thinking frameworks of national governments. (For a detailed history and account of the Constitutional Convention, see Norman, 2003.)

The Intergovernmental Conference

The IGC opened on 4 October 2003. In terms of its composition it was similar to previous IGCs, with Heads of State or Government formally at the apex, Foreign Ministers meeting regularly to review and prod progress, and most of the detailed work being undertaken by senior national officials. However, in terms of its functioning it was very different in two respects from earlier IGCs. First, its agenda was largely set by the Treaty Establishing a Constitution for Europe that had been agreed by the Constitutional Convention. Second, it was scheduled to be very short in duration, with the intention being that final agreement on the new treaty would be reached at the December 2003 European Council meeting.

As always, governments approached the IGC with a mixture of views. On particular issues individual governments were decidedly in favour of some measures being adopted, decidedly opposed to others, and open on some. So, for example, nine states – the Czech Republic, Ireland, Italy, Lithuania, Malta, Poland, Portugal, Slovakia, and Spain – wanted the inclusion of a reference to Europe's Christian inheritance and values. Seven (smaller) states – Austria, Denmark, Estonia, Ireland, the Netherlands, Portugal and Slovenia – wanted to retain the system of a rotating Council presidency. And eight (including all former 'non-aligned') states – Austria, Denmark, Estonia, Finland, Ireland, Poland, Sweden and the UK – were opposed to the inclusion of a collective defence clause.

To try and ensure such differences between states were not given too much of an airing, which would have slowed progress, the approach of the Italian presidency was to stick as closely as possible to the Convention's draft. Attempts by governments to re-open particular matters that had been agreed in the Convention were generally discouraged. However, two issues proved to be highly troublesome, and could not be resolved when the European Council met in Brussels on 12–13 December. The first concerned the size of the College of Commissioners. The Convention had recommended that from 2009 the size be reduced to fifteen, but with non-voting Commissioners also to be appointed. Most member states had concerns about this, but small states particularly did so because the Commission traditionally has been seen as helping to protect the interests of smaller states against larger ones. The second, and at the summit more heated, issue concerned voting arrangements in the Council of Ministers. The Convention had recommended that QMV voting weights be abandoned in favour of a double majority system in which majorities would be deemed to exist for proposals that were supported by a majority of states representing at least 60 per cent of the EU's total population. Germany was especially anxious to accept this recommendation since the Nice arrangements had assigned to it a proportionately small voting weight – only 29 votes for its population of just over 80 million, as compared with the 27 votes assigned to each of Poland and Spain despite both countries having populations of just under 40 million.

At the December summit, agreement could not be reached on these two issues. If the Council voting system issues had been resolved then a deal probably could have been found on the size of the College issue, but Poland and Spain refused to abandon the system that had given them such over-generous treatment. Accordingly, and amidst whispered accusations from some participants that the Italian presidency had not handled proceedings well, the summit failed to finalise the text of the Constitutional Treaty.

It was thus left to the succeeding Council Presidency – Ireland – to pick up the pieces and try to find a consensus. In so doing it was greatly assisted by a general election in Spain in March, which saw the incumbent conservative government replaced with a socialist government that was – partly because it was keen to establish close relations with France and Germany – more flexible on the Council voting issue. This left Poland isolated: a position that, as both a new member state and a member state that knew it faced political battles ahead on the likes of CAP and the cohesion funds, it did not wish to be in.

Accordingly, the Irish presidency was authorised by the European Council in late March to reconvene the IGC. An agreement was subsequently brokered on the Commission and Council issues: on the former, the size of the College was capped, but on the basis of a formula that was different to that proposed by the Convention, and from 2014 rather than 2009; on the latter, Council voting weights were dropped, but the thresholds for majorities was raised from what the Convention had advocated both in respect of the number of member states and the proportion of the EU population they represented (see below for the details on both issues). The IGC was concluded at the European Council meeting in Brussels on 17–18 June 2004. After the customary work by lawyers and translators, the Constitutional Treaty was formally signed in Rome on 29 October 2004.

The Contents of the Treaty

The Constitutional Treaty (CT) is a single text that replaces the existing treaties on which the EU is based – that is, the Treaty on European Union (TEU) and the Treaty Establishing the European Community (TEC) in their post-Nice forms. Far from being the relatively short document that many – especially Euro-enthusiasts – had hoped it would be, the CT is extremely long. It consists of a preamble, four parts that run to a total of 448 articles, 36 protocols, 2 annexes, and 50 declarations (Treaty Establishing a Constitution for Europe, 2004).

The four parts of the CT are organised as follows:

Part I (articles 1–60) lays down the general rules and principles underlying the Union. The EU's objectives, powers, institutions, and decision-making procedures are all identified.

Part II (articles 61–114) incorporates the Charter of Fundamental Rights, which had been 'solemnly proclaimed' at Nice, into the Treaty.

Part III (articles 115–436) covers the Union's policies and functioning. Most of this part incorporates provisions of existing treaties.

Part IV (articles 437–448) consists of general and final provisions, including procedures for adopting and revising the Treaty.

Table 7.1 overleaf provides a summary of the key changes included in the CT. (For longer accounts, see Church and Phinnemore, 2005; Phinnemore, 2004.) Taking the text as a whole, what are its main features?

First, despite the use of the symbolically important word 'constitution', the hope of Euro-enthusiasts that a reasonably simple document would be produced that would be widely recognised as being a 'proper' constitution was not realised. It partly would have been so had the CT been confined to Part I and the Charter of Fundamental Rights, for they cover much of the sort of ground that is found in national constitutions. However, such is the nature of the EU that the governments of member states generally wish to codify many detailed matters concerning the Union's functioning, and hence wished the long and detailed Part III – in essence the TEC, which covers many technical matters of little interest to the ordinary citizen – to be part of the CT. But, in any event, Parts I and II are weak on some traditionally core constitutional matters: there is no enunciation of a clear philosophy of government; there is no robust underpinning of EU citizenship (which remains weak); there is no provision for an EU budget that is capable of financing significant spending policies; and the instruments given to the EU to protect and promote the interests of its citizens via foreign and defence policies remain relatively weak.

Second, most of the CT's contents are taken from the treaties it is designed to replace – namely, the TEU and the TEC as they have been amended over the years – plus the Charter of Fundamental Rights. In consequence, most of the Treaty confirms the existing treaty *acquis*.

Third, the new content is largely of the type that has featured in all of the treaties since the SEA. That is, it consists, for the most part, of relatively modest changes designed to make the EU more efficient and more democratic. To give just one example: much publicity was given to the new post of Union Minister for Foreign Affairs, but this is really just a merging of two existing positions – the Council's High Representative for the CFSP and the Commission's External Relations Commissioner.

Fourth, an important theme running through some of the changes is to give the EU greater coherence and identity. This is seen in the abolition of the pillar structure, the assignment of legal personality to the EU, the creation of the semi-permanent President of the European Council, and the above mentioned merging of the existing separate Council and

Table 7.1   *Key changes included in the Constitutional Treaty*

Treaty Structure

- The existing EU treaties are replaced with a single treaty.
- The three pillar structure is abolished. However, the essentially intergovernmental arrangements of the CFSP and parts of JHA are retained via restricted powers for the Commission, exclusion from ECJ jurisdiction, and limited provision for QMV in the Council.
- The Charter of Fundamental Rights is incorporated into the Treaty and is thus given full legal status and becomes legally binding.

The Nature and Competences of the Union

- Removal of the existing treaty article referring to 'creating an ever closer union among the peoples of Europe'.
- The Treaty's opening articles set out the values and objectives on which the Union is based. The values include respect for human dignity, freedom, democracy, equality, the role of law and respect for human rights. The objectives include the promotion of peace, offering Union citizens an area of freedom, security and justice without internal frontiers, an internal market where competition is free and undistorted, and the combating of social exclusion and discrimination.
- The Union is given legal personality.
- The competences of the Union – both exclusive and shared – are set out. The main exclusive competences are the common commercial policy and customs union, competition rules necessary for the functioning of the internal market, and monetary policy for euro members.

Legal Acts and Procedures

- Legal acts of the Union are to consist of:

  laws (equivalent to current regulations)
  framework laws (equivalent to current directives)
  regulations
  decisions

  Laws and framework laws are normally to be adopted jointly by the EP and the Council. Regulations and decisions are normally implementing laws adopted by the Commission, though in some areas they are adopted either by the European Council or the European Central Bank.
- The remit of the co-decision procedure is extended. The procedure is re-named the 'ordinary legislative procedure'.

The Institutions

The Commission

- Until 2014 the College to continue to be composed of one member per member state. From 2014 the size of the College to correspond to two-thirds of the number of member states, with nationalities assigned on a basis of equal rotation amongst the states.
- An enhanced role for the Commission President, including in the selection of the other Commissioners.

The European Council

- Established as a separate institution distinct from the Council of Ministers.
- To elect its own President, by QMV, for a 2½ year term which may be renewable once.
- The responsibilities of the President to be confined to European Council business.

The Council of Ministers

- From November 2009, QMV to change from the Nice triple majority formula to a double majority formula in which a majority must contain at least 55% of the member states comprising at least 65% of the EU population. The majority must also include at least 15 member states (making the 55% rule redundant until the EU numbers 28 members). A blocking minority must include at least four Council members.
- Some extensions to QMV. However, areas where unanimity – and hence the national veto – remain include the CFSP (except implementing measures), the ESDP, enhanced cooperation, treaty reform, taxation, EU budgetary matters, aspects of social policy, and allocation of the structural funds.
- The Presidency of the Council to be held by groups of three members for a period of eighteen months, with each member of the group chairing for six months.
- The Foreign Affairs Council to be chaired by the Union Minister for Foreign Affairs.

Union Minister for Foreign Affairs

- To be appointed by the European Council acting by QMV, with the agreement of the President of the Commission.
- He/she to conduct the Union's common foreign and security policy. In this, he/she is to be assisted by a newly created European External Action Service.
- He/she to be a Vice President of the Commission.

Table 7.1 continued overleaf

Table 7.1 *continued*

European Parliament

- Its maximum size is increased from 732 to 750, with no state to have either more than 96 members or less than 6.
- Its powers are strengthened by extensions to the remit of the co-decision procedure and increased powers over trade policy and the budget.

Other

- The roles of national parliaments are increased by: 1) requiring the Commission to reconsider a proposal if one-third of national parliaments claim it may breach the subsidiarity principle; 2) empowering all national parliaments to veto a European Council decision to change Council decision-making in a given area or case from unanimity to QMV (itself a new power for the European Council).
- A number of Treaty articles provide for greater transparency and citizen participation. For example, the proceedings of the Council are to be open when it is exercising its legislative functions; citizens have the right to invite the Commission to submit a legislative proposal by collecting one million signatures in a 'significant number' of member states.
- Provision is made for the suspension of certain membership rights, including voting rights, in the event of there being a risk of a breach of the values of the Union in a member state.
- General arrangements for withdrawing from the Union are set out.

Commission foreign policy posts into a single Union Minister for Foreign Affairs.

Fifth, changes in institutional provisions and decision-making arrangements do not have much overall effect on the intergovernmental/supranational balance within the Union. A small tilting in a supranational direction may be seen in the increased capacity of the Council to take decisions by QMV. But this increased capacity applies mostly to relatively low-key and technical areas. In highly sensitive areas – including treaty reform, enlargement, financial matters, social policy, and most areas of CFSP and all of ESDP – unanimity continues to prevail. Moreover, intergovernmentalism may be said to be given a boost by the strengthening of the capacity of the EU's most intergovernmental institution – the European Council – through the creation of a new post of European Council President.

*   *   *

In summary, whilst the contents of the CT disappointed those who wished to see it provide for major integrationist advance, the Treaty is more than the tidying-up exercise it has been portrayed by some as being. It is true that it does not contain anything comparable to the SEA's internal market mission or the Maastricht Treaty's arrangements for creating EMU. But it does contain significant changes and additions to the structure and contents of the existing treaties. These changes and additions are mostly with a view to simplifying and clarifying the nature, enhancing the operation, and strengthening the democratic character of the enlarged EU.

But the significance of the CT lies not only in its specific provisions for EU structures, institutions, decision-making processes, and policies. It also has great significance with its use of the word 'constitution', which suggests to many Europeans – both of Euro-integrationist and Eurosceptic persuasions – a highly symbolic advance in the process of 'building Europe'. Largely because of this symbolic importance, the Treaty attracted much more political attention during the treaty-making process than had earlier amending treaties, which resulted in major problems when the process moved to ratification.

Ratification

As with all of the EU's treaties, the CT could not enter into force until it had been ratified by all of the member states. Aware that ratification by all 25 member states was by no means a formality, it was specified in Part IV of the Treaty that if by two years after the signing of the Treaty four-fifths of the member states had completed ratification but one or more states 'have encountered difficulties in proceeding with ratification', the matter would be referred to the European Council – for unspecified action. With the Treaty being formally signed in October 2004, all member states were thus obliged to try and ratify by October 2006 at the latest.

In the past, member states have almost invariably ratified post-accession treaties by a parliamentary vote. The exceptions have been those occasional instances when referendums have been used: in Ireland for all four treaties from the SEA; in Denmark for the SEA, Maastricht and Amsterdam treaties; and in France for the Maastricht Treaty. With the Constitutional Treaty more widespread use of referendums was always likely: partly because of the perceived highly symbolic importance of the treaty, and partly because of the much larger number of member states in the enlarged EU. Quite how widespread promises of referendums were to become, however – amounting ultimately to almost half of the member states – was not anticipated. The major factor bringing about the increase was domestic political pressures. In the UK, for example, Prime Minister

Blair, anticipating the next general election, responded to a Conservative Party promise that it would call a referendum on the Constitutional Treaty by promising one himself. This in turn heightened pressures in France on President Chirac to hold a referendum.

A referendum is, of course, much more difficult for a government to control than a parliamentary vote. Citizens can 'cause problems' in two ways: by taking a contrary view to the government on the issue at stake, or by expressing a view on an issue or issues other than the one that features in the referendum question. Both of these problems arose when ratification referendums were held in France on 29 May 2005 and three days later in the Netherlands on 1 June.

By the time the French and Dutch referendums were held, ten member states plus the European Parliament had, in fact, already ratified the Treaty. The first state to ratify was Lithuania, whose parliament set the tone for other national parliaments when, just two weeks after the Treaty was signed, it voted for ratification by an overwhelming majority. However, in the one state of the ten where a referendum was held – Spain – ratification was not so straightforward: 76.7 per cent of those who voted were in favour of ratification, but there was only a very low – 42.3 per cent – turnout.

In France and the Netherlands the possibility of *No* votes increased over the course of the referendum campaigns. One reason for this was growing opposition to the form of the Treaty, which was seen by many as embracing elite rather than popular wishes. Another reason was concerns about the supposed 'Anglo-American' social and economic values contained in the Treaty: although, in reality, the CT contained no significant changes in values from previous treaties, opponents of the Treaty presented it as doing so – to the background of concerns about whether existing welfare systems could be sustained. And a third reason was that various 'non-Treaty' matters featured in the campaigns – including political opposition to the governments in power, insecurities arising from the May 2004 enlargement and projected Turkish accession, and resentment in the Netherlands over the country being the largest per capita contributor to the EU budget.

The outcomes of the two referendums were clear rejections of the CT. In France, 54.9 per cent voted against ratification on a 69.7 per cent turnout, whilst in the Netherlands 61.7 per cent voted against on a 63 per cent turnout.

The question then became 'what now?'. European leaders quickly divided on this. Should the ratification process continue, on the basis that all citizens were entitled to express their view and with the CT's own 'four-fifths' provision (see above) suggesting the Treaty was not necessarily lost because a couple of states had failed to ratify. Prominent amongst those advocating continuation were the Luxembourg President of the Council, Jean-Claude Junker, President Chirac, and Chancellor Schröder. Foremost amongst those taking a contrary view was Prime Minister Blair, who hinted the ratification process should at least be put on hold because the Treaty could not enter into force unless it was ratified by all member states and that no longer looked to be possible. In the days immediately following the referendums Blair was, however, very careful not to openly pronounce the Treaty as dead – for fear of being accused of taking the lead on this.

As it happened, a European Council meeting was already scheduled for the week after the referendums. With realities beginning to be absorbed, and with governments that had promised referendums increasingly realising that roll-on effects from France and the Netherlands would likely now make the referendums in their own countries much more difficult to win, the summit decided on caution. In a Declaration it was stated that the matter would be set aside until the first half of 2006 so as to allow for a 'period of reflection [which] will be used to enable a broad debate to take place in each of our countries ...' (European Council, 2005b). Those states that had not yet conducted their ratification processes were given discretion as to what to do. In the event, this resulted in all of those states that were committed to holding referendums postponing them, except Luxembourg where the arch Euro-integrationist, Prime Minister Junker, proceeded with the referendum that was already scheduled for early July: in this most integrationist of states, 56.52 per cent voted yes and 43.48 voted no, on a 90.5 per cent turnout.

But the Luxembourg result naturally was not enough to re-stimulate the ratification process, and in the ensuing months the member state governments made little progress in deciding what to do.

Concluding Remarks

The Constitutional Treaty was made in a different manner to the EU's preceding treaties. The processes leading to its finalisation involved, due largely to the key role played by the Constitutional Convention, a more open process and a process in which political actors independent of national governments had a significant role to play.

But though the treaty-making process was different, the outcome of the process was strikingly similar to predecessors. For the Constitutional Treaty is a consolidating rather than a radical document. It contains measures designed to improve the nature and functioning of the EU, but none that would transform them. There is, for example, no fundamental upheaval in the EU's institutional structures nor any great extension in its policy competences. As such, the CT is in the tradition of earlier amending treaties: adjusting, and in some respects advancing, the integrationist process in an incrementalist manner. Arguably, the adjustments and the advances provided for in the CT are of a lesser order than those contained in the SEA and the Maastricht Treaty, where bases were laid for significant policy extensions and for new decision-making procedures.

Where the CT is most different, and has been so since it was first mooted, is in the high profile attached to it. Much of this profile has stemmed from the use of the symbolically important word 'constitution', which has led to exchanges between Treaty supporters and opponents that often have had little relation to the Treaty's real contents.

In the aftermath of the French and Dutch referendums there was much debate amongst interested parties over how to proceed. In broad terms, three possibilities were advanced. First, continue with the ratification process, hope that other states would ratify, and think about ways of overcoming the French and Dutch *Nos*. In other words, try to revive the whole Treaty. Second, at the other extreme, recognise that the referendum results meant the end of the Treaty and continue operating on the basis of the Nice Treaty. Third – a middle way – accept that the whole Treaty could not be retained, but explore ways of salvaging its most important parts.

Neither the first nor second of these options ever had much prospects of success: the first because the two *No* votes were too decisive and because also they increased the likelihood of *Nos* elsewhere; the second because most EU practitioners regretted the loss of the Treaty and wanted to recover much of it. Accordingly, by early 2006 it seemed likely that some sort of partial recovery operation would be launched. Making changes that do not require treaty authorisation is one route that is likely to be taken. Such changes could include giving more powers to national parliaments, opening up the legislative part of Council meetings, and even creating the European Council President – though this change would likely create political difficulties given that it is one of the more prominent features of the CT. Another possible route is the negotiation of a lower profile, more 'conventional', treaty that will not attract the need for so many referendums.

Of course, making changes in these ways will take time. But the fact that the contents of the CT are not so radical as opponents have usually claimed means the EU can survive the consequences of non-ratification better than Europhiles have usually suggested.

Chapter 8

Treaties and the Integration Process

The Making of Treaties
Treaties and the Nature of European Integration
Concluding Remarks: An Ongoing Process

Since the SEA it has become customary for rounds of treaty reform to occur every four to five years. One reason for this is that the logic and momentum of the integration process has come to require periodic revision of the treaties so as both to 'catch up' with evolving realities and to enable desired developments to occur. Another reason is that because all treaties are a consequence of intergovernmental bargaining, some governments are inevitably disappointed with the outcomes of treaties and so start pressing for another round of treaty reform almost before a negotiated treaty has been ratified and applied. And a third reason is that the last three treaties to have been ratified – those of Maastricht, Amsterdam and Nice – have explicitly provided for further rounds of treaty reform: in the Maastricht case in response to pressures from dissatisfied governments at the Treaty's outcome, and in the Amsterdam and Nice cases in consequence of a general recognition that the Treaties were leaving unfinished business.

This chapter builds on the earlier chapters that have examined specific treaties in detail by stepping back and examining how rounds of treaty reform fit into and contribute to the integration process.

Documents 8.1 and 8.2 are included to help set the examination in context, by showing the overall framework of the two main treaties – the TEU and TEC – as they are post-Nice. (The Nice Treaty added only one new title – Title XXI TEC – and no new chapters to the post-Amsterdam Treaties.)

The Making of Treaties

Treaty-making is very much an intergovernmental process, as the name of the forum for deciding on the contents of treaties – Intergovernmental Conferences (IGCs) – makes clear. The key actors in IGCs are representatives of the governments of the member states, and unanimity amongst them is necessary for treaty provisions to be agreed.

Document 8.1   The Treaty on European Union: contents

I   TEXT OF THE TREATY
Preamble   *Articles*

Title I	Common provisions	1–7
Title II	Provisions amending the Treaty establishing the European Economic Community with a view to establishing the European Community	8
Title III	Provisions amending the Treaty establishing the European Coal and Steel Community*	9
Title IV	Provisions amending the Treaty establishing the European Atomic Energy Community	10
Title V	Provisions on a common foreign and security policy	11–28
Title VI	Provisions on police and judicial cooperation in criminal matters	29–42
Title VII	Provisions on closer cooperation	43–45
Title VIII	Final provisions	46–53

II   PROTOCOLS (9)

---

* The ECSC Treaty expired in July 2002, at which point special treatment for coal and steel ceased to exit and they were fully integrated in the TEC.

Document 8.2   The Treaty Establishing the European Community: contents*

I   TEXT OF THE TREATY
Preamble   *Articles*

Part One	Principles	1–16
Part Two	Citizenship of the Union	17–22
Part Three	Community policies	23–181
TITLE I	Free movement of goods	23–31
Chapter 1	The Customs Union	25–27
Chapter 2	Prohibition of quantitative restrictions between member states	28–31
TITLE II	Agriculture	32–38
TITLE III	Free movement of persons, services and capital	39–60
Chapter 1	Workers	39–42
Chapter 2	Right of establishment	43–48
Chapter 3	Services	49–55
Chapter 4	Capital and payments	56–60

→

→

Document 8.2 continued

*Post-Nice. The only change made at Nice to the setting out of the contents agreed at Amsterdam was the addition of Title XXI.

As was explained in Chapter 7, the Constitutional Treaty IGC was unique. One way in which it was so was that most of the contents of the CT were set out and agreed before the IGC ever met – in the Constitutional Convention. Unlike in IGCs where all voting participants are governmental representatives, most of the members of the Constitutional Convention were parliamentarians. A second way in which the CT IGC was unique was in the very short time period scheduled for it: just two months, from October to December 2003. And a third way in which it was unique is that agreement on the contents of the Treaty could not be reached at the European Council meeting that was supposed to conclude the IGC, which was chaired by the Italian presidency. This meant that the IGC had to be suspended until the succeeding, Irish, presidency identified the path to a solution, which was reached at the June 2004 meeting of the European Council.

Apart, however, from the special circumstances of the CT IGC, all other IGCs have conformed to a similar pattern. Deliberations have occurred at four levels, which in ascending order have been as follows:

- Working parties of national experts have been established and convened to examine particular issues as and when they have been deemed to be necessary. They have identified relevant points and tried to establish a consensus wherever possible, but they have not normally engaged in negotiations in the sense of trading points on matters that have a contentious or political dimension. An example of a highly influential expert group is that which was established – under the name 'Friends of the Presidency' – in the lead-up to the Nice Treaty to deal with ways of improving the functioning of the EU's legal system, and in particular speeding up decision-making in the EU's two courts, the Court of Justice and the Court of First Instance.

- A group known as the 'personal representatives of the minister' or the 'preparatory group' has undertaken most of the detailed negotiations. The members of the group have been mainly very senior national officials – mostly the Permanent Representatives of the member states to the EU (see Chapter 10). The group in the 2000 IGC consisted of ten Permanent Representatives, three senior officials from foreign ministries, and two junior ministers. The frequency of group meetings has depended on progress and on the overall IGC timetable, but fortnightly meetings have been the norm.

- Foreign Ministers have supposedly overseen the process and provided political guidance and impetus. However, as Galloway (2001: 34) has shown in his work on the 2000 IGC, it has been difficult for Foreign Ministers to exercise this role in a manner that has enabled them to assert authority over the Conference: many of the issues on the agenda have been highly specialised and outside the normal departmental remits of participants, so there often has been a lack of enthusiasm and willingness to resolve matters being discussed; some Foreign Ministers have bad attendance records, and their representatives often have not had, or have not felt they have had, authority to agree deals on contested matters; the multiple subject inter-linkages have made partial deals difficult to reach; and there are relatively few meetings – IGC business normally has been dealt with as an additional item on the Foreign Minister's regular monthly meeting. (The EMU provisions of the Maastricht Treaty were an exception to this arrangement. Two IGCs prepared the Treaty: a Political IGC that operated as described here, and a parallel but separate IGC that prepared the EMU provisions of the Treaty and which was overseen by Finance Ministers.)

- IGCs have culminated at a European Council meeting, where all outstanding issues have been negotiated and traded. Almost invariably, the main players – Heads of Government – have been subject to information overload as a battery of information on issues that need to be resolved has been directed at them. Much of the business has been conducted in an almost feverish atmosphere, with deadlines postponed, much of the business conducted in informal bilaterals and huddled groups, and often with at least one delegation threatening to return home if it is not given further satisfaction or if a deal is not made. The Nice European Council broke the record for all European summits – being spread over four days.

With this extensive structure, IGCs have inevitably taken up many working hours. Leaving aside expert group work, the 2000 IGC took up 370 hours, involving thirty meetings of the personal representatives, ten of the Foreign Affairs Ministers, and three of the European Council (Wessels, 2001).

The main responsibility for pulling everything together and setting the pace in IGCs falls to the Council Presidency. As Galloway (2001: 33) says, the Presidency acts as 'the engine driving the Conference'. It exercises this role by convening and chairing all meetings at all levels, tabling discussion and proposal papers that act as the basis for negotiations (other states, the Commission and the EP also produce papers but they are more for information purposes), and generally trying to identify and mediate compromises. A problem in the 2000 IGC was that the French Presidency, which was responsible for the second half of the IGC, was in some respects badly organised and was seen by several member states – especially some of the smaller states – as being too robust in pressing its own views on certain issues and insufficiently focused on trying to broker agreements that would be generally acceptable (Ross, 2001). The Italian Presidency under which the CT IGC was scheduled to be concluded was similarly seen by many participants and observers to be deficient. In its case the principal charge was that it was too casual and under-prepared for the supposedly closing IGC in December 2003.

Because IGCs are intergovernmental in character, the EU's two main non-governmental institutions – the Commission and the EP – struggle to exert much influence. The Commission is a participant in IGCs at all three levels and does its utmost – not least via the submission of position papers – to influence outcomes. However, because it does not enjoy the same negotiating status as the member states, and is certainly in no position to attempt to veto agreements, its negotiating hand is weak and its influence on eventual outcomes is usually marginal.

The EP is even more disadvantaged than the Commission in that it does not fully participate in all IGC meetings. This is precisely why it so favoured the Constitutional Convention that laid the foundations for the CT IGC. Indeed the EP used to not participate in IGCs at all, but was given two sets of opportunities to do so in the 1996–7 IGC: the President of the EP addressed and had an exchange of views with the Foreign Ministers at their monthly meeting; and the EP appointed two representatives to engage in monthly detailed exchanges of view with the preparatory group. In addition, the two EP representatives were briefed after each IGC meeting and the EP was sent copies of all working documents and position papers. The Nice IGC advanced the EP's position in that, though it continued to be excluded from ministerial and Heads of Government meetings (apart from the President of the EP continuing to have an exchange of views with Foreign Ministers before their formal sessions began), two 'observers' from the EP were permitted to participate in preparatory group meetings. Like the Commission, the EP makes submissions to IGCs and, again like the Commission, it has usually been disappointed by IGC outcomes. Its position is not helped by not having assent power over treaties, though it does vote on resolutions on treaty outcomes. Overall, such influence as it has exercised has been mostly in relation to expansions of its own powers, where it has kept up constant pressure.

Treaties and the Nature of European Integration

In terms of understanding the foundations, development and essential nature of the EU, the 'stories' of the Treaties are extremely revealing. They are so because they highlight and confirm the following long-established characteristics and features of the integration process.

Economics before politics

The major advances in integration have tended to take the form of agreeing to integrate aspects of economic activity and then, at times seemingly as an afterthought, realising that this requires political integration too if there is to be political direction and control. In practice there has naturally been considerable overlap and blurring between the economic and the political, but from 1950–1, when the ECSC was created, the economic has usually preceded the political.

In terms of the treaties, the strengthening of the EU institutions that has been provided for in all of the treaties since the SEA has been largely a consequence of this being seen to be necessary if (mainly economic) policy development is to be achieved. Most specifically, the first post-foundation treaty extension to QMV that was contained in the SEA was seen as being a prerequisite for the passage of the SEM programme, whilst the decision in 1991 to establish the IGC on Political Union was in considerable measure a follow-on from the earlier decision to establish the IGC on EMU.

Flexibility

When the member states, or a sufficient number of them, have wished to act together in a policy area and the established mechanisms have been judged to be not suitable for the purpose, then alternative ways of proceeding have usually been found. This was, for example, the case with the establishment and development of EPC from the early 1970s, the EMS from the late 1970s, and the Schengen System (designed to assist free movement of persons) from the mid-1980s.

The Maastricht, Amsterdam and Nice Treaties built on and greatly extended this tradition of being adaptable and innovative in respect of policy development. The Maastricht Treaty did so via the construction of two non-Community pillars (some states regarded it as premature to bring the policy areas covered by the pillars into the EC) and also via, for the first time, the non-inclusion of member states in policy areas specifically identified in the Treaties (the UK and Danish opt-outs). The Amsterdam Treaty incorporated new opt-outs (for Denmark, Ireland, and the UK), and further 'constitutionalised' flexibility by the enhanced cooperation provisions that were added to the TEC and the third pillar and the constructive abstention provision that was added to the second pillar. The Nice Treaty streamlined the Amsterdam enhanced cooperation arrangements, primarily by making them easier to apply.

Incrementalism

The integration process has been characterised by an almost constant edging forward, with 'advances' followed by pressures for more advances. Phases and forms of integration have frequently followed almost inevitably and logically from earlier – and often less significant – phases and forms. In a pattern well understood by those who are persuaded by historical institutionalist interpretations of the evolution of the integration process (see, for example, Pierson, 1998), and especially by the importance of 'path dependence' in shaping the nature of the evolution, the treaty architects have, as Wessels (2001: 212–14) has shown, developed an almost ideal three-step type of integration cascade. In the first phase, governments realise the advantages of cooperating with other EU countries in a particular policy area and attempt to do so on a very loose intergovern-mental basis, often on the margins of, or even outside, the EU framework. When this form of cooperation proves to be insufficient, the governments move to the second phase, which sees the policy area given clear treaty recognition and moved firmly into the organisational framework of the Union, but still on an essentially intergovernmental basis in that the role of the Commission is limited, the EP is at best given only consultative rights, Council decisions are by unanimity, and the Court has few – if any – powers. In the third phase, governments realise they must permit stronger decision-making processes if aims are to be achieved, so the supranational route is taken with more effective powers and roles assigned to the Commission, EP and Court and, most importantly, QMV permitted in the Council.

Table 8.1 demonstrates how the treaties have advanced the integrationist cause in this incrementalist manner by, on the one hand, expanding the EU's policy remit and potential and, on the other hand, strengthening the supranationalist character of EU decision-making. These two aspects of increasing integration are, of course, intertwined with, for example, the EP's steadily increasing powers having resulted in large part from policy transfers to the EC/EU producing growing demands for decision-makers to be made more accountable. (The CT is not included in Table 8.1 since its future is unclear at the time of writing.)

The precise way in which the integrationist logic works does, of course, vary according to an array of circumstances. The justice and home affairs policy area, however, may be taken as an example of how it can work. From modest beginnings in the mid-1970s when, quite outside the framework of the treaties, governments began to cooperate with one another on such matters as cross-border crime and the fight against terrorism, the policy area has steadily developed: cooperation was stepped up in the 1980s through what became known as the Trevi process; justice and home affairs (JHA) was given treaty status in pillar three of the Maastricht Treaty, though very much on an intergovernmental basis; much of pillar three was transferred into pillar one by the Amsterdam Treaty, some provision was made for QMV, and new justice and home affairs issues – including provisions for tighter and stronger police cooperation – were added to pillar three; and the Nice Treaty further extended QMV in the policy area.

The incrementalist logic of the treaties in an integrationist direction is perhaps most starkly witnessed by the difficulty in identifying a single clear example of a treaty provision that has reversed an aspect of European integration to any significant degree. Perhaps the greater emphasis given in the EEC Treaty than in the ECSC Treaty to unanimity in the Council may be thought of as such an example, but that was as the European Community was being established, and the EEC Treaty as a whole did, of course, mark a major step forward in the process. The attention given to subsidiarity in the Maastricht Treaty may perhaps be thought of as another example, but its inclusion was partly for symbolic reasons and the way in which it was described in the Treaty did not give it great bite. And a third example may be thought to be the attempted strengthening of the institutional capacity of the essentially intergovernmental European Council in the CT through the creation of a semi-permanent president. But, of course. the CT has not been ratified. The fact is that there have been no 'hard' and accomplished treaty reversals, such as a change from QMV to unanimity in Council voting procedures or of a policy sphere being removed from an EU treaty because it is deemed to be an exclusively national responsibility.

Table 8.1 *Summary of the contents of the main EU treaties, showing principal institutional and policy provisions*

Name of Treaty	Date signed	Date came into effect	Institutional provisions	Policy provisions
Treaty of Paris	April 1951	July 1952	Creates: High Authority, Council of Ministers (with some QMV), Common Assembly, Court of Justice	Lays foundations for a common market in coal, steel, coke, iron ore, and scrap.
Treaty of Rome Establishing the European Economic Community	March 1957	January 1958	Creates: Commission, Council of Ministers (QMV more restricted than under Treaty of Paris), Assembly, Court of Justice } to serve all three communities	Lays foundations and timetable for a customs union with removal of internal barriers to trade and the establishment of a common external tariff; foundations also laid for deeper economic integration through the creation of a common market and some common policies – including agriculture and transport.
Treaty of Rome Establishing the European Atomic Energy Community	March 1957	January 1958	Creates: Commission, Council of Ministers, Assembly, Court of Justice } to serve all three communities	Provides for the possibility of a common market in nuclear materials, but with safeguards built in. Other activities in the nuclear field to be promoted.

Single European Act	February 1986	– European Council is given legal recognition. – The legal capacity of the Council to take decisions by QMV is extended – notably to internal market measures. – A new legislative procedure – the cooperation procedure – is created, which gives the EP more powers. – An assent procedure is also created which results in the assent of the EP being required.	– The aim of completing the internal market by 1992 is given treaty status. – New policy areas are added to the EEC Treaty, notably environment, economic and social cohesion, and research and development. – European Political Cooperation (foreign policy) is given legal recognition.
Treaty on European Union (the Maastricht Treaty)	February 1992	– Creates the European Union as a three pillar structure. – Extends legal base of QMV. – Creates co-decision legislative procedure, which increases the power of the EP.	– A framework and timetable for creating Economic and Monetary Union is incorporated in the EC Treaty. – Pillars two and three create the treaty foundations for a Common Foreign and Security Policy (CFSP) and Cooperation in the Fields of Justice and Home Affairs (JHA). – Several new policy areas are added to the EC Treaty, including development, public health, and consumer protection.

Table continued overleaf

Table 8.1 *continued*

Name of Treaty	Date signed	Date came into effect	Institutional provisions	Policy provisions
Treaty of Amsterdam	October 1997	May 1999	– Extends legal base of QMV. – Extends the co-decision procedure to more policy spheres, and amends aspects of the procedure to the EP's advantage. – Creates enhanced cooperation procedure.	– CFSP provisions are strengthened. – Much of JHA pillar is transferred to EC pillar. – New policy areas are added to EC pillar, including anti-discrimination, promoting employment, and consumer protection.
Treaty of Nice	February 2001		– Changes national representations in EU institutions in preparation for enlargement. – Changes QMV weightings – Extends legal base of QMV. – Small extensions to application of co-decision procedure. – Makes enhanced cooperation procedure easier to apply.	Only marginal extensions of existing policy areas, mainly in the JHA and social policy fields in the Council.

Increased complexity

The treaties are the outcomes of negotiations between national governments. In the negotiations, the governments attempt to make the EU more
effective and efficient, but they also seek to promote and defend national
interests. These objectives are not always easily compatible, with the
consequence that complex formulas and arrangements often have to be put
in place to reach agreements.

Treaty complexity is no more clearly demonstrated than with the TEU.
In some respects the TEU is a framework treaty, laying down general
principles and a structure for the EU. The Community treaties are
component parts of the EU framework (see Document 8.1). In other
respects, however, the TEU is a substantive treaty, specifying in Titles V
and VI quite detailed provisions in policy areas the member states prefer
not to have 'communautarised' – primarily because they want the policy
areas covered by pillars two and three, foreign and security policy and
police and judicial cooperation policy, to be intergovernmental in
character.

As for the main Community treaty, the TEC, it has become considerably
more complex over the years. The original 1957 EEC Treaty was
complicated enough, with 240 articles, many of them covering detailed
policy points. But as the text has been amended in rounds of Treaty reform
that have added new policy competences and decision-making arrangements, so has it become ever more impenetrable for all but subject
specialists. The Treaty – re-named at Maastricht the European Community Treaty – was tidied up a little as part of the Amsterdam revisions, but
not in such a way as to make it accessible to 'the general reader': the TEC
has had 314 articles since Amsterdam, most of which include sub-articles
and many of which cover the sort of subject matter that would normally be
expected to be found in policy legislation rather than a document which –
in the absence of the CT or anything else – serves as a key part of the EU's
'constitution'. (See Document 8.2 for the TEC's contents.)

At a more specific level, the sphere in which treaty negotiations
have produced the most complex outcomes is in respect of decision-
making processes, which have become ever more numerous with every
succeeding treaty. Following the Nice Treaty, there are no less than
38 combinations of possible voting modalities in the Council and participation opportunities for the EP. Of the 38 combinations, 22 are legislative
in nature (Wessels, 2001: 201). When the positions of other EU institutions
are added, the number of decision-making processes increases even
further. Significantly, the CT IGC made little progress in simplifying this
mosaic.

Not only have the treaties produced a steady increase in the number of decision-making processes, but they have also produced some extremely complicated processes. The prize for complexity should, perhaps, be awarded to Article 7 TEU as amended by the Nice Treaty, which includes the following:

1. On a reasoned proposal by one-third of the Member States, by the European Parliament or by the Commission, the Council, acting by a majority of four-fifths of its members after obtaining the assent of the European Parliament, may determine that there is a clear threat of a serious breach by a Member State of principles mentioned in Article 6(1) [which states the Union is founded on such principles as liberty, democracy and respect for human rights], and address appropriate recommendations to that State ...
2. The Council, meeting in the composition of the Heads of State or Government and acting by unanimity on a proposal by one-third of the Member States or by the Commission and after obtaining the assent of the European Parliament may determine the existence of a serious and persistent breach by a Member State of principles mentioned in Article 6(1), after inviting the government of the Member State in question to submit its observations ...
6. For the purpose of paragraphs 1 and 2, the European Parliament shall act by a two-thirds majority of the votes cast, representing a majority of its Members.

A quite different example of how the treaties have produced complex outcomes is in the many protocols and declarations that customarily have been attached to them. Protocols have the same binding legal effect as treaty articles, but declarations are essentially political statements. Designed for a variety of purposes – such as providing clarification on treaty articles and laying down bases for extra-treaty policy activity – protocols and declarations can, in practice, make the understanding of treaties even more difficult for all but the trained expert. To illustrate how widespread the use of protocols and declarations has become, the Maastricht Treaty was widely criticised for containing far too many protocols (17) and declarations (35), but the Amsterdam Treaty actually exceeded this: one protocol was annexed to the TEU only; four protocols were annexed to the TEU and the TEC; five protocols were annexed to the TEC only; three protocols were annexed to the TEU and to all three Community Treaties; 51 declarations were 'adopted by the Conference'; and there were eight declarations 'of which the Conference took note'. Four protocols and 24 declarations were attached to the Nice Treaty, and there were three declarations of which the Conference 'took note'.

Variable pace

The pace of the integration process has varied considerably since the Community was founded in the 1950s with, in general terms, the period up to the mid-1960s and from the mid-1980s to the early 1990s being times of rapid integration, and the late 1960s to the early 1980s and the period since the early 1990s being more sluggish. The Maastricht and Amsterdam Treaties illustrate this variable pace. The Maastricht Treaty was negotiated at a time when the governments of most member states were generally optimistic and ebullient in their attitudes to European integration, with the consequence that they wanted to see, and made sure that they did see, major integrationist advances incorporated into the Treaty. By contrast, when the Amsterdam Treaty was being negotiated the mood was less upbeat – not least because the 1992 Danish referendum had obliged supporters of further integration to become more cautious – and so less was sought from, and less was put into, the Treaty.

Interplay between supranational and national actors

Some analysts of European integration have made much of the role played in the integration process by supranational actors, most particularly the Commission, the EP, and the Court of Justice. Other analysts have played down the role of these actors and have argued that whilst they may have exercised some influence on the course of events, the EU's key actors have been representatives of the governments of the member states meeting in the European Council and the Council of Ministers. (There is a review of these different interpretations of the integration process in Chapter 21.)

At first sight, the decision-making processes associated with the making of the EU's treaties would appear to provide support only for the second of these analytical interpretations: the membership of IGCs consists of national governmental representatives, with the Commission present but having no vote; decision-making in the IGCs is based on bargaining between the national governmental representatives, with agreements on some particularly difficult issues being reached only after hard direct negotiations between Heads of Government; and the supranational EU institutions – especially the Commission and the EP – have been generally disappointed with the outcomes of the IGCs, with both having pressed in recent IGCs for greater extensions to QMV and to their own powers than have been incorporated in the treaties.

However, although the making of the EU's treaties may appear to provide strong support for an intergovernmental interpretation of the integration process, the case should not be overstated. First, treaty-making processes are not typical EU decision-making processes since they lead to what Peterson (1995) has called 'history-making' decisions, and are therefore the very processes in which the role of national governments is likely to be most prominent. Second, although it does not have voting powers, the Commission is an active participant in IGCs and the EP was allowed to make a direct input into the 1996–7 and 2000 IGCs. Finally, there is evidence – provided, for example by Beach (2005) – to indicate that the Commission and the EP have been able to exercise influence in IGCs. The influence is, however, 'contingent upon the negotiating context and whether they [supranational EU institutions] use appropriate leadership strategies' (Beach, 2005: 245).

Benefits for everybody

The integrationist advances achieved in the treaties have been made possible by the member states judging it to be in their interests to promote integration. Certainly in all of the treaty-making negotiations there have been disagreements between the states as to just how much, and what kind of, integration they have wanted. But it has nonetheless been recognised that there are benefits for all to be gained from the integration process – with the furtherance of economic growth and the promotion of harmonious relations between the states of Europe being the most obvious benefits.

However, because of their own distinctive needs and preferences, states have sometimes argued that in addition to taking a share of general benefits they should also be awarded special benefits. The award of special benefits in treaties has usually taken the form of providing a base for some sort of policy development that will be especially helpful to a particular state or group of states. So, for example, the SEA provided such a policy base when, largely at the behest of the poorer member states, it included provisions for the development of redistributive policies. The Maastricht Treaty did much the same thing, with the creation of a Cohesion Fund that would be directed at the four poorest member states (Greece, Ireland, Portugal and Spain).

An elite-driven process

Insofar as political and administrative elites tend to set the policy agenda, and insofar as they usually take decisions without consulting their electorates, political activity in all nation states – in Europe and beyond – may be said to be elite-driven. But this is particularly the case in the EU because there are no direct lines of accountability between decision-makers and the citizenry. There is no opportunity to elect a European government or parliament with full decision-making powers. Arguably this would not matter too much if there were grounds for believing that most citizens were strongly supportive of the integration process, or were happy to leave decisions about integration to the appropriate elites. However, public opinion polls have suggested that in some member states considerable reservations and doubts have existed at various times.

The extent to which the integration process is elite-driven, and the extent to which elites do not always reflect popular concerns, has been demonstrated by difficulties in ratifying the treaties. Problems began with the ratification of the Maastricht Treaty, when not only did the Danes vote 'No' in their first referendum and the French almost vote 'No', but opinion polls indicated that German and UK voters too might have rejected the Treaty if they had been given the opportunity to do so. The increased caution shown by national representatives in the 1996–7 IGC can perhaps be seen as partly reflecting greater sensitivity to the popular concerns that the Maastricht ratification process had highlighted. However, the extent of this sensitivity should not be overstated, as is demonstrated by the fact that despite all the post-Maastricht talk about promoting openness and democracy in the EU, there was no movement towards opening up the treaty-making process to popular participation. On the contrary, only the Danish and Irish governments – which, as with the SEA and the TEU, were virtually compelled to do so – included referendums as part of their national ratification procedures. And only the Irish government consulted the people on the ratification of the Nice Treaty – and they duly rejected it at the first time of asking, though more for domestic political reasons than because they opposed the treaty.

The most dramatic, and in its consequences most important, demonstration of the elite-driven nature of the integration process occurred when, for reasons that were set out in Chapter 7, several member states moved to hold referendums on the Constitutional Treaty. In two of the EU's founding states – France and the Netherlands – the Treaty was rejected by the people. This was not so much because voters objected to specific Treaty provisions, but rather for a range of 'non-Treaty' reasons including concerns about such aspects of the integration process as the 2004 enlargement, possible Turkish accession, the perceived increasing influence of liberal market principles, and – in the Netherlands – the financing of the EU budget. The French and Dutch referendums showed, as other planned national referendums may have shown if they had proceeded, that aspects of the integration process are not so strongly supported by citizens as they are by elites.

Concluding Remarks: An Ongoing Process

However the EU's political nature is to be described – and this matter is examined in Chapter 21 – all of the EC/EU ratified treaties have contributed significantly to development of the European integration process. None of the treaties has, however, in any sense marked the end of the process or even identified where that end may be. The discussions and negotiations that have taken place before and at all the major IGCs have been characterised by considerable differences between the participants on the nature and pace of integration. What has emerged from the processes that have produced the treaties have been compromises: compromises that have included aspects of different visions of the future of Europe, and compromises that, while failing to advance integration as much as some governments had hoped, have advanced it further than others would have liked. There has therefore, as was noted at the beginning of this chapter, been no shortage of important political actors wanting to return to treaty-making, and there has been no shortage of good reasons for periodically re-examining the treaties.

Such now has become the regularity of IGCs that an expectation has become established that the treaties will be changed at regular intervals. But it is unlikely in the foreseeable future that they will be changed in the manner that was attempted by the Constitutional Treaty process. In all probability there will be a turning away from the grandiose and highly symbolised approach of the CT and a return to steady and under-stated incrementalism.

Part 3

The Institutions and Political Actors of the European Union

There are five main EU institutions: the Commission, the Council of Ministers, the European Council, the European Parliament, and the Court of Justice. Chapters 9–13 consider each of these institutions and the political actors that are associated with them. Chapter 13 has also been taken as the most appropriate place to examine the nature and status of EU law.

Chapter 14 looks at those institutions and actors which, though not given a chapter in their own right, nonetheless also exercise a significant influence in the EU: the European Economic and Social Committee, the Committee of the Regions, the European Investment Bank, the European System of Central Banks, the Court of Auditors, and interests.

Chapter 9

The Commission

Appointment and Composition
Organisation
Responsibilities and Powers
Concluding Remarks

Frequently portrayed as the civil service of the EU, in reality the Commission is rather more and rather less than that: rather more in the sense that the treaties and political practice have assigned to it much greater policy-initiating and decision-making powers than those enjoyed, in theory at least, by national civil services; rather less in that its role in policy implementation is greatly limited by the fact that agencies in the member states are charged with most of the EU's day-to-day administrative responsibilities.

The Commission is centrally involved in EU decision-making at all levels and on all fronts. With an array of power resources and policy instruments at its disposal, and strengthened by the frequent unwillingness or inability of other EU institutions to provide clear leadership, the Commission is at the very heart of the EU system.

Appointment and Composition

The College of Commissioners

Seated at the summit of the Commission are the individual Commissioners, who are each in charge of particular policy areas and who meet collectively as the College of Commissioners. Originally they numbered nine, but with enlargements their size has grown: to thirteen, to fourteen, to seventeen, to twenty, and to twenty five following the 2004 enlargement. The reason for the lack of symmetry between the number of Commissioners and the number of member states prior to 2004 is that each of the larger states (France, Germany, Italy, Spain and the UK) used to have two Commissioners. However, so as to avoid the size of the College becoming too big after enlargement it was agreed at the 2000 Nice summit that:

- from January 2005 all member states would have just one Commissioner;
- when the EU numbered 27 member states 'the number of Members of the Commission shall be less than the number of Member States ...

149

> Members of the Commission shall be chosen according to a rotation system based on the principle of equality, the implementing arrangements for which shall be adopted by the Council, acting unanimously . . . The number of Members of the Commission shall be set by the Council, acting unanimously' (Treaty of Nice, Protocol A, Article 4).

In the IGC that produced the Constitutional Treaty it was resolved that the College scheduled to assume office in 2009 would continue to be composed of one Commissioner per member state. However, from 2014, the size of the College would be equivalent to two-thirds of the number of member states. This principle may still ultimately be applied, even if the full CT itself is not.

Appointment procedure

Prior to the College that took office in January 1993, Colleges were appointed every four years by common accord of the governments of the member states. The Maastricht Treaty changed this procedure, primarily in order to strengthen the links between the Commission and the EP. This strengthening was achieved in two ways. The first was by formalising and somewhat stiffening practices that developed in the 1980s regarding the appointment of the Commission and its President: the member state governments now became obliged to consult the EP on who should be President, and the College-designate became obliged to present itself before the EP for a vote of confidence. The second was by bringing the terms of office of the EP and the Commission into close alignment: Colleges would now serve a five-year term and would take up office six months after EP elections, which are held on a fixed basis in the June of years ending in four and nine. (So as to bring about the alignment, a transitional two-year College served from January 1993 to January 1995.)

On the occasion of the first application of the new appointments procedure – in respect of the College that assumed office in January 1995 – the EP pressed its new powers to the full. When Jacques Santer, the Luxembourg Prime Minister, was nominated as President-designate in mid-1994 (at short notice and as a compromise candidate following the UK government's refusal to support the Belgian Prime Minister, Jean-Luc Dehaene), the EP was in fact barely consulted. However the EP made it quite clear to the European Council (the forum in which the nominee of the national governments is agreed) that whoever was nominated would be required to appear before the Parliament and a vote on confirmation would be held. The assumption would be that if the nominee was not confirmed his candidature would be withdrawn. Chancellor Kohl, acting in his capacity as Council President, confirmed that the EP would indeed have a *de facto* veto over the nomination. In the event Santer was confirmed, but only by a narrow majority: there were 260 votes in favour, 238 against, and 23 abstentions. As for the vote of approval on the whole College, the EP held 'hearings', with each of the Commissioners-designate being required to appear before the appropriate EP committee before the plenary vote was held. There was strong criticism of five of the Commissioners-designate, but given that there was no provision for singling them out in a vote, the EP, after being given certain reassurances by Santer, gave a vote of confidence to the new College by 417 votes to 104.

The Amsterdam Treaty confirmed the *de facto* confirmatory power the EP had assigned to itself on the appointment of the Commission President. The Treaty also gave the President a potential veto over the national nominees for appointment to the College. (Under the Maastricht Treaty he was supposed to be consulted on the national nominees to the College, but in practice this amounted to little in 1994.) The Nice Treaty further altered the procedure by specifying that the decisions in the European Council on the nomination of the President and on the other Commissioners plus the decision on the appointment of the whole College, could henceforth be made by qualified majority vote rather than by consensus.

Accordingly, the relevant Treaty provisions on the appointment of the President and the College are, post-Nice, as follows:

> The Council, meeting in the composition of Heads of State or Government and acting by a qualified majority, shall nominate the person it intends to appoint as President of the Commission; the nomination shall be approved by the European Parliament.

> The Council, acting by a qualified majority and by common accord with the nominee for President, shall adopt the list of the other persons whom it intends to appoint as Members of the Commission, drawn up in accordance with the proposals made by each Member State.

> The President and the other Members of the Commission thus nominated shall be subject as a body to a vote of approval by the European Parliament. After approval by the European Parliament, the President and the other Members of the Commission shall be appointed by the Council, acting by a qualified majority (Article 214.2 TEC).

The 1999 resignation of the Santer College and the appointment of the Prodi College

At the time the Amsterdam Treaty was negotiated it was assumed that its provisions on the appointment of the College would be given their first use for the College that was due to assume office in January 2000. However, in March 1999 the Santer College was pressurised – most particularly by the EP, which was threatening to dismiss it by passing a motion of censure – into resigning, nine months before the scheduled end of its term of office. (Although formally the EP can only dismiss the Commission by passing a motion of censure by a two-thirds majority of the votes cast that includes a majority of all Parliament's members, it is likely that in practice a nominal majority vote would so undermine the College's credibility that it would have little option but to resign.)

The circumstances that produced deep dissatisfaction with the Santer College and led to its resignation are described on p. 252. Essentially, they centred on indications in a report drawn up by a committee of independent experts that there was some substance to long-held suspicions that at least one Commissioner (Edith Cresson) had shown favouritism in issuing contracts, that Santer had been insufficiently vigilant in the exercise of some of his responsibilities, that there were problems of financial mismanagement in certain parts of the Commission, and that the College as a whole had displayed a general lack of responsibility for the Commission's actions (Committee of Independent Experts, 1999a).

Almost immediately after resigning the Santer College announced that it would stay in office in a caretaker capacity until a replacement College was appointed. This gave the governments of the member states breathing space, both to decide on a collective basis how they should proceed and to consider on an individual basis who they wished to nominate to the replacement College. There were two collective decisions to be made. First, who should replace Jacques Santer as Commission President? Santer initially considered trying to stay on himself, but MEPs quickly made it clear that they would not support him – which forced him to recognise that he could not return. Second, should the replacement College be appointed on an interim basis to see out the remaining months of the Santer College's term or should the process of appointing a new full-term College be brought forward?

A special summit to consider these questions did not have to be called, since one was already timetabled for ten days after the College's resignation. This was the March 1999 Berlin summit, which had been arranged by the German Council Presidency to enable final decisions to be taken on the Commission's *Agenda 2000* package of budgetary and policy reforms. At the summit, the national leaders decided to nominate the former Italian Prime Minister, Romano Prodi, to be the new Commission President. They further decided that they wanted a full-term rather than an interim College.

Prodi's nomination was endorsed by the EP in May by 392 votes to 72, with 41 abstentions. It soon became apparent, however, that it would take some time for the other Commissioners to be nominated and then approved by the EP, so it was decided to ask the Santer College (minus Santer himself, who resigned to run in the EP election) to stay in office until a new College could be appointed in the autumn. The nominations for the other Commissioners were then duly made, though seemingly with only limited influence exercised by Prodi. EP committees held 'hearings' on each Commissioner-designate in late August/early September and then, after a plenary debate on the new College, the Parliament voted to endorse the Prodi Commission by 414 votes to 142, with 35 abstentions. It was agreed that the EP's endorsement covered a full five-year term as well as the three and a half months that would have remained of the Santer Commission's term.

The appointment of the Barroso College

The events leading to the appointment of the College that in 2004 succeeded Prodi's College illustrate just how politicised the appointments process is, both in terms of the keen interest taken by EU actors in the political composition of the incoming College and in terms of inter-institutional relations.

In the months leading up to the June 2004 European Council meeting which was due to agree on who should be nominated to be the new Commission President, the names of many prominent EU figures were mentioned as 'strong possibilities'. Eventually, however, especially after the June 2004 EP elections produced a centre-right majority, two very experienced and moderate right of centre figures emerged as strong favourites: the Belgian Prime Minister, Guy Verhofstadt, and the British External Relations Commissioner, Chris Patten. In all probability either would have received the qualified majority support that would have sufficed under the Nice Treaty to be appointed. However, no vote was ever put at the June summit. It was not so because the British Prime Minister, Tony Blair, was resolutely opposed to Verhofstadt (who had 'led' the opposition in the EU to the invasion of Iraq, and who also was perhaps seen as being too integrationist) and the French President, Jacques Chirac, was opposed to Patten (because he was British). Since a President-designate who was known not to have the support of a large member state clearly would be greatly handicapped politically, the summit broke up with no name put forward. Intense informal exchanges then ensued between EU politicians, which resulted in agreement being reached on the Portuguese Prime Minister, José Manuel Barroso. A special summit was convened to formally endorse him and shortly afterwards he was approved by the EP – by 413 votes to 251 – after formally addressing the Parliament in plenary session.

Agreement had barely been reached on Barroso before some governments were announcing the name of their Commissioner-designate, which
was hardly indicative of Barroso having had much input into the selection
process. In the case of the new member states quick announcements were
reasonable enough since most of them chose to re-nominate the people
who had only been Commissioners since May 2004. In the case of the
EU-15, however, the spirit of nominating 'in common accord' with the
President-designate appears to have applied in little more than a formal
sense. Insofar as Barroso did have views which had an effect, it was
towards the end of the process when he expressed open concern that his
College might contain a smaller proportion of women than its predecessor.
In the event it did not.

As, in the autumn of 2004, the EP moved towards, and then held, its
now customary committee 'hearings', criticisms were made of five of the
Commissioners-designate. In two cases this was because of a suspicion of a
possible conflict of interest with the portfolio they had been assigned: the
Dutch Commissioner-designate Neelie Kroes who had been assigned
competition policy and the Danish Commissioner-designate Mariann
Fischer-Boel who had been assigned agriculture policy. In one case it
was because the Commissioner-designate was seen as not being up to the
job: the Hungarian, László Kovács, who had been assigned energy
policy. In another, and more serious, case it was because the Latvian
Commissioner-designate, Ingrida Udre, was believed to be associated with
funding irregularities in her national political party. And in the most
serious case of all, the Italian Commissioner-designate, Rocco Buttiglione,
was deemed to be wholly inappropriate for the justice and home affairs
portfolio he had been assigned following comments he made in his hearing
about homosexuality and the role of women that were judged by many
MEPs to be prejudiced and unacceptable.

As the plenary confirmation vote approached, Barroso refused to make
changes, save for transferring certain anti-discrimination and civil liberties
dimensions of the JHA portfolio from Buttiglione to himself. This proved
not enough to satisfy MEPs so, with the prospect of a defeat looming,
Barroso withdrew his College-designate on the very morning of the day the
vote was scheduled to be held. Over subsequent days, Buttiglione and Udre
stood down and Kovács was transferred to the taxation portfolio. This
was acceptable to the EP, which then duly approved the revamped College
by 449 votes to 149, with 82 abstentions. The Barroso College was thus
eventually able to assume office – three weeks later than had been intended
– on 22 November 2004.

The EP's ability to force changes to the composition of, and allocation
of portfolios in, the Barroso College provides a particularly graphic

illustration of how it has become increasingly important for the Commission to be highly sensitive to the views of MEPs. Formally, the EP in 2004 only had the power to approve or disapprove the College as a whole; it could not identify individual Commissioners who it would refuse to endorse. But Buttiglione was, in effect, singled out and rejected. In forcing Barroso to react to their views on this matter the EP damaged the standing of the new President even before he assumed office.

Impartiality and independence

Although individual Commissioners frequently are referred to as 'the Finnish Commissioner', 'the Hungarian Commissioner', and so on, Commissioners are in fact not supposed to be national representatives. Rather, they should 'in the general interest of the Community, be completely independent in the performance of their duties'. Much the same sentiments pertain to the requirement that Commissioners should 'neither seek nor take instructions from any government or from any other body' (Article 213 TEC).

In practice, full impartiality is neither achieved nor attempted. Although Commissioners are formally appointed by the Council with the agreement of the President-designate and the EP, in reality all but the President are national nominees. It would therefore be quite unrealistic to expect Commissioners, upon assuming office, suddenly to detach themselves from previous loyalties and concern themselves solely with 'the wider European interest' – not least since a factor in their appointment is likely to have been an expectation that they would keep an eye on the national interest. The Treaty's insistence on the complete independence of Commissioners is therefore interpreted flexibly. Indeed, total neutrality is not even desirable since the work of the Commission is likely to be facilitated by Commissioners maintaining their links with sources of influence throughout the EU, and they can most easily do this in their own member states. But the requirements of the system and the necessities of the EU's institutional make-up are such that real problems arise if Commissioners try to push their own states' interests too hard. It is both legitimate and helpful to bring favoured national interests onto the agenda, to help clear national obstacles from the path, to explain to other Commissioners what is likely to be acceptable in 'my' national capital. But to go further and act consistently and blatantly as a national spokesman, or even to be seen as being over-chauvinistic, as a few Commissioners occasionally have, is to risk losing credibility with other Commissioners. It also makes it difficult for the Commission to function properly since it clearly cannot fulfil its set tasks if its divisions match those of the Council of Ministers.

Characteristics of Commissioners

There are no rules or understandings as to what sort of people, with what sort of experience and background, member state governments should nominate to be Commissioners. It used to be the case that most Commissioners tended to be former national politicians just short of the top rank. However, as the EU, and the Commission with it, has become increasingly important, so has the political weight of the College's membership increased, and now most Commissioners are former ministers, and some of them very senior ministers.

Given the diverse political compositions of the EU's national governments there is naturally a range of political opinion represented in the Commission. Crucially, all governments have made it their custom to nominate people who are broadly pro-European and have not been associated with any extremist party or any extreme wing of a mainstream party. So whilst Colleges certainly contain party political differences, these are usually within a range that permits at least reasonable working relationships. (For a detailed analysis of the characteristics of Commissioners, see Macmullen, 2000.)

The President

The most prestigious and potentially influential College post is the Presidency. Although most important Commission decisions must be taken collectively by the College, the President:

- is the most prominent, and usually the best known, of the Commissioners.
- is the principal representative of the Commission in its dealings with other EU institutions and with outside bodies.
- is generally expected to give a sense of direction to his fellow Commissioners and, more broadly, to the Commission as a whole. This latter role was strengthened by the Amsterdam Treaty, which added the following to the TEC: 'The Commission shall work under the political guidance of its President' (Article 217).
- allocates Commissioners' portfolios (see next section).
- may require fellow Commissioners to resign, after obtaining the approval of the College. This provision, which was added to Article 217 TEC by the Nice Treaty, was inserted because of Edith Cresson's refusal to resign in the dying days of the Santer Commission even though she was generally seen to have become tainted by accusations of inappropriate conduct.

- is directly responsible for overseeing some of the Commission's most important administrative services – notably the Secretariat General which, amongst other functions, is responsible for the coordination of Commission activities and for relations with the Council and the EP.
- may take on specific policy responsibilities of his own, usually in harness with other Commissioners.

Inevitably, given the importance of the office, the European Council is very careful about who is nominated to be Commission President. It has come to be generally accepted that only the most prominent of national politicians will be considered, as is witnessed by the last four Presidents: Jacques Delors was a former French Finance Minister, Jacques Santer and Romano Prodi were former Prime Ministers – Santer of Luxembourg and Prodi of Italy – whilst José Manuel Barroso was the serving Prime Minister of Portugal.

Portfolios

All Commissioners apart from the President are assigned a portfolio: that is, a particular area of responsibility. Some portfolios, such as Budget, Competition, and Environment are more or less fixed but others, especially those of a broader and less specific nature, can be varied, or even created, depending on how a new President sees the role and tasks of the Commission and depending too sometimes on the pressures to which he is subject from Commissioners-designate.

Prior to the implementation of the Amsterdam Treaty, the distribution of portfolios among the Commissioners was largely a matter of negotiation and political balance. The President's will was the most important factor, but he could not allocate posts simply in accordance with his own preferences. He was intensively lobbied – by the incoming Commissioners themselves, and sometimes by governments trying to get 'their' Commissioners into positions that were especially important from the national point of view. Furthermore, the President was made aware that re-nominated Commissioners – of which there were usually nine or ten – might well be looking for advancement to more important portfolios, and that the five states with two Commissioners expected at least one of 'their' nominees to be allocated a senior post. Bearing in mind all these difficulties, it is not surprising that unless a resignation, death or enlargement enforced it, reshuffles did not usually occur during the lifetime of a Commission.

Clearly this situation meant that Commissioners were not necessarily assigned to the most appropriate posts, and also that not much could be done if a Commissioner was not performing satisfactorily. The situation was partly addressed in a declaration attached to the Amsterdam Treaty (Declaration 32), which provided the President with broad discretion in the allocation of tasks within the College and allowed him to effect a re-shuffling of the tasks during a College's term of office. The contents of the Declaration were upgraded to Article 217 of the TEC by the Nice Treaty.

Up to the time of writing, no significant re-shuffling of portfolios has occurred once a College has assumed office. There is, however, no question but that Prodi and Barroso acted much more autonomously than had their predecessors when making the original portfolio allocations between Commissioners-designate.

Cabinets

To assist them in the performance of their duties, Commissioners have personal *cabinets*. These consist of small teams of officials numbering, under rules introduced by Prodi designed to ensure *cabinets* are not too large or too powerful, six officials plus support staff, except for the President's *cabinet* which has nine officials. Members of *cabinets* used to be mostly fellow nationals of the Commissioner, but Prodi made it clear shortly after being nominated as Commission President that he wished to see *cabinets* acquire a more markedly multinational character. To give effect to this, new rules were introduced requiring that each *cabinet* should include at least three nationalities and indicating that the *chef de cabinet* or the *deputy chef de cabinet* should preferably be of a different nationality to the Commissioner.

Typically, a *cabinet* member is a dynamic, extremely hard-working, 30–40-year-old, who has been seconded or recruited from some part of the EU administration, from the civil service of a member state, or from a political party or sectional interest with which the Commissioner has links.

Cabinets undertake a number of tasks: they gather information and seek to keep their Commissioner informed of developments within and outside his or her allocated policy area; they liaise with other parts of the Commission, including other *cabinets,* for purposes such as clearing up routine matters, building support for their Commissioner's policy priorities, and generally trying to shape policy proposals as they come up the Commission system; and they act as a sort of unofficial advocate/protector in the Commission of the interests of their Commissioner's country. Over and above these tasks, the President's *cabinet* is centrally involved in brokering the many different views and interests that exist amongst Commissioners and in the Commission as a whole to ensure that, as an institution, the Commission is clear, coherent, cohesive and efficient (see pp. 163–6 for further discussion of the roles of Commissioners' *cabinets*).

The Commission bureaucracy

Below the Commissioners lies the Commission bureaucracy. This is by far the biggest element of the whole EU administrative framework, though it is tiny compared with the size of administrations in the member states. In 2004 the Commission's staffing establishment numbered only 23 320 – fewer than in many national ministries and, indeed, many large city councils (EU member states average around 300 civil servants per 10 000 inhabitants, as against 0.8 per 10 000 for all EU institutions). Of these 23 320, 17 388 were employed in administration – including just over 6000 at senior policy-making levels – and 3672 were engaged in research and technological development. The 17 388 includes just over 2000 engaged in the translation and interpretation work necessitated by the EU's twenty working languages: the twenty languages produce 380 possible language combinations, although most of the Commission's internal business is conducted in French or English. (Figures on authorised staffing in the EU's institutions are set out each year in the EU's budget, which is published in the *Official Journal*, and also in the annual *General Report on the Activities of the European Union*, which is compiled by the Commission. The figures given here are from the 2004 *General Report*.) The Commission also makes use of temporary staff of various kinds, including national officials on secondment and experts contracted for specific purposes.

Permanent staff are recruited on the basis of open competitive procedures, which for the senior levels are highly competitive. An internal career structure exists and most of the top jobs are filled via internal promotion. However, pure meritocratic principles are disturbed by a policy that tries to provide for a reasonable national balance amongst staff. All governments have watched this closely and have sought to ensure that their own nationals are well represented throughout the EU administrative framework, especially in the upper reaches. For the most senior posts something akin to an informal national quota system has operated, though this is now – in theory at least – being phased out as part of a broad programme that has been under way since the Prodi College assumed office to modernise Commission personnel, management and administrative policies. This multinational staffing policy of the Commission, and indeed of the other EU institutions, has both advantages and disadvantages. The main advantages are:

(1) The staff have a wide range of experience and knowledge drawn from across all the member states.

(2) The confidence of national governments and administrations in EU decision-making is helped by the knowledge that compatriots are involved in policy preparation and administration.

(3) Those who have to deal with the EU, be they senior national civil servants or paid lobbyists, can often more easily do so by using their fellow nationals as access points. A two-way flow of information between the EU and the member states is thus facilitated.

The main disadvantages are:

(1) Insofar as some senior personnel decisions are not made on the basis of pure meritocratic principles but result in part at least from a wish for there to be a reasonable distribution of nationals from all member states in the upper reaches of the Commission, two damaging consequences can follow. First, the best available people do not necessarily fill all posts. Second, the morale and commitment of some staff can be damaged.

(2) Senior officials can occasionally be less than wholly and completely EU-minded. For however impartial and even-handed they are supposed to be, they cannot, and usually do not wish to, completely divest themselves of their national identifications and loyalties.

(3) There are differing policy styles in the Commission, reflecting different national styles. These differences are gradually being flattened out as the Commission matures as a bureaucracy and develops its own norms and procedures, but the differences can still create difficulties when officials from different nationalities are used to working in different ways.

Organisation

The Directorates General and other services

The Commission is divided into organisational units in much the same way as national governments are divided into ministries and departments. In total there were thirty eight such organisational units in late 2005. Collectively the organisational units are referred to as the services. Most of the organisational units carry the title Directorates General (DG) whilst those that do not are known as specialised services. A list of the DGs and specialised services is given in Table 9.1.

The size and internal organisation of DGs and specialised services varies. Most commonly, they have a staff of between 200 and 500, divided into four to six directorates, which in turn are each divided into three or four units. However, policy importance, workloads and specialisations within DGs produce many departures from this norm. Thus in terms of size, DG Agriculture employs almost 1000 staff whilst DG Education and Culture employs around 150. As for organisational structure, DG Agriculture has eleven directorates and 48 units, whilst DG Taxation and Customs Union has five directorates and 19 units.

Table 9.1 *Directorates General and specialised services of the Commission*

POLICIES	EXTERNAL RELATIONS
Agriculture and Rural Development	Development
Competition	Enlargement
Economic and Financial Affairs	EuropeAid – Co-operation Office
Education and Culture	External Relations
Employment, Social Affairs and Equal Opportunities	Humanitarian Aid Office – ECHO
Enterprise and Industry	Trade
Environment	**GENERAL SERVICES**
Fisheries and Maritime Affairs	European Anti-Fraud Office*
Health and Consumer Protection	Eurostat*
Information Society and Media	Press and Communication
Internal Market and Services	Publications Office*
Joint Research Centre	Secretariat General*
Justice, Freedom and Security	**INTERNAL SERVICES**
Regional Policy	Budget
Research	Bureau of European Policy Advisers*
Taxation and Customs Union	Informatics
Transport and Energy	Infrastructures and Logistics – Brussels*
	Infrastructures and Logistics – Luxembourg*
	Internal Audit Service
	Interpretation
	Legal Service*
	Personnel and Administration
	Translation

* Not a Directorate General

There is no hard and fast reason as to why some services have DG status and others do not. It is true that the eight non-DG services tend to be more concerned with providing support for policies than directly handling policies, but in practice these two activities intertwine and overlap. Certainly non-DG services should not be thought of as being junior to DGs, not least since some of them – most notably the Secretariat General, which has a general responsibility for ensuring the Commission as a whole functions effectively and efficiently, and the Legal Service – are amongst the most prestigious locations within the services.

The hierarchical structure

The hierarchical structure of the Commission is as follows:

- All important matters are channelled through the weekly meetings of the College of Commissioners. At these meetings decisions are taken unanimously if possible, but by majority vote if need be.
- In particular policy areas the Commissioner holding the portfolio in question carries the main leadership responsibility.
- DGs are formally headed by Directors General, who are responsible to the appropriate Commissioner.
- Directorates are headed by Directors, who report to the Director General or, in the case of large DGs, to a Deputy Director General.
- Units are headed by Heads of Unit, who report to the Director responsible.

The structure thus appears to be quite clear, but in practice it is not completely so. At the topmost echelons in particular the lines of authority and accountability are sometimes blurred. One reason for this is that an imperfect match sometimes exists between Commissioners' portfolios and the responsibilities of services. EC/EU enlargements and the consequent increases in the size of the Commission over the years, plus a streamlining of portfolios initiated by Prodi, have allowed for greater specialisation on the part of individual Commissioners and a better alignment with the responsibilities of services. However, even now, with more services than there are Commissioners, some Commissioners have to carry responsibilities that touch on the work of several services.

Another structural problem concerning Commissioners is the curious halfway position in which they are placed. To use the British parallel, they are more than permanent secretaries but less than ministers. For whilst they are the principal Commission spokesmen in their assigned policy areas, they are not members of the Council of Ministers – the body that, often in association with the EP, takes most final decisions on important policy matters.

These structural arrangements mean that any notion of individual responsibility, such as exists in most member states in relation to ministers – albeit usually only weakly and subject to prevailing political currents – is difficult to apply to Commissioners. It might even be questioned whether it is reasonable that the Commission should be subject to collective responsibility – as it is by virtue of Article 201 of the TEC which, as was noted above, obliges it to resign if a motion of censure on its activities is passed in the EP by a two-thirds majority of the votes cast, representing a majority of all members. Collective responsibility may be thought to be reasonable insofar as all Commission proposals and decisions are made collectively and not in the name of individual Commissioners, but at the same time it may be thought to be unreasonable insofar as the ability of the Commission to undertake its various tasks successfully is highly dependent on other EU actors. In practice no censure motion has been passed although, as was shown above and as is discussed in Chapter 12, one came close to being so in January 1999 and it was the near certainty of one being passed that prompted the Santer College's resignation in March 1999.

Decision-making mechanisms

The hierarchical structure that has just been described produces a 'model' route via which proposals for decisions make their way through the Commission machinery:

- An initial draft is drawn up at middle-ranking policy grade level in the appropriate DG. Outside assistance – from consultants, academics, national officials and experts, and sectional interests – is sought, and if necessary contracted, as appropriate. The parameters of the draft are likely to be determined by a combination of existing EU policy commitments, the Commission's annual work programme, and guidelines that have been laid down at senior Commission and/or Council levels.
- The draft is passed upwards – through superiors within the DG, through the *cabinet* of the Commissioner responsible, and through the weekly meeting of the *chefs de cabinet* – until the College of Commissioners is reached. During its passage the draft may be extensively revised.
- The College of Commissioners can do virtually what it likes with the proposal. It may accept it, reject it, refer it back to the DG for redrafting, or defer taking a decision.

From this 'model' route all sorts of variations are possible, and in practice are commonplace. For example, if draft proposals are relatively uncontroversial or there is some urgency involved, procedures and devices can be employed to prevent logjams at the top and expedite the business in hand. One such procedure enables the College of Commissioners to authorise the most appropriate amongst their number to take decisions on their behalf. Another procedure is the so-called 'written procedure', by which proposals that seem to be straightforward are circulated amongst all Commissioners and are officially adopted if no objection is lodged within a specified time, usually a week. Urgent proposals can be adopted even more quickly by 'accelerated written procedure'.

Another set of circumstances producing departures from the 'model' route is when policy issues cut across the Commission's administrative divisions – a very common occurrence given the sectoral specialisations of the DGs. For example, a draft directive aimed at providing a framework in which alternative sources of energy might be researched and developed would probably originate in DG Transport and Energy, but would have direct implications for DG Research, DG Budget, and perhaps DG Enterprise and Industry. Sometimes policy and legislative proposals do not just touch on the work of other DGs but give rise to sharp conflicts, the sources of which may be traced back to the conflicting 'missions' of DGs: for example, there are sometimes disputes between DG Competition and DG Regional Policy, with the latter tending to be much less concerned than the former about rigidly applying EU competition rules if European industry is thereby assisted and advantaged. Provision for liaison and coordination is thus essential if the Commission is to be effective and efficient. There are various procedures and mechanisms aimed at providing this necessary coordination. Four of these are particularly worth noting.

First, at the level of the DGs, various management practices and devices have been developed to try to rectify the increasingly recognised problem of horizontal coordination. In many policy areas this results in important coordinating functions being performed by a host of standing and *ad hoc* arrangements: inter-service groups and meetings are the most important of these arrangements, but there are also task forces, project groups, and numerous informal and one-off exchanges from Director General level downwards.

Second, the main institutional agency for promoting coordination is the Secretariat General of the Commission, which is specifically charged with ensuring that proper coordination and communication takes place across the Commission. In exercising this duty the Secretariat satisfies itself that all Commission interests have been consulted before a proposal is submitted to the College of Commissioners.

Third, the President of the Commission has an ill-defined, but generally expected, coordinating responsibility. A forceful personality may be able to achieve a great deal in forging a measure of collective identity out of the varied collection of people from quite different national and political backgrounds who sit around the Commission table. But it can only be done tactfully and with adroit use of social skills. Jacques Delors, who presided over three Commissions between 1985 and 1995, unquestionably had a forceful personality, but he also displayed traits and acted in ways that had the effect of undermining team spirit amongst his colleagues. For example, he indicated clear policy preferences and interests of his own; he occasionally made important policy pronouncements before fully consulting the other Commissioners; he criticised Commissioners during Commission meetings and sometimes, usually by implication rather than directly, did so in public too; and he frequently appeared to give more weight to the counsel of personal advisers and to people who reported directly to him –

drawn principally from his *cabinet* and from the Commission's Forward Studies Unit (since reconstituted and now known as the Bureau of European Policy Advisers) – than to the views of his fellow Commissioners.

Fourth, the College of Commissioners, in theory at least, is in a strong position to coordinate activity and take a broad view of Commission affairs. Everything of importance is referred to the Commissioners' weekly meeting and at that meeting the whole sweep of Commission interests is represented by the portfolios of those gathered around the table.

Commissioners' meetings are always preceded by other meetings designed to ease the way to decision-making:

- Informal and *ad hoc* consultations may occur between Commissioners who are particularly affected by a proposal.
- Groups of Commissioners in related and overlapping policy areas exist for the purpose of facilitating liaison and cooperation and enabling discussions at College meetings to be well prepared and efficient. Amongst Groups of Commissioners in the Barroso College are ones on the Lisbon Strategy, External Relations, and Competitiveness.
- The Commissioners' agenda is always considered at a weekly meeting of the heads of the Commissioners' *cabinets*. These *chefs de cabinet* meetings are chaired by the Commission's Secretary General and are usually held two days before the meetings of the Commission itself. Their main purpose is to reduce the agenda for Commission meetings by reaching agreements on as many items as possible and referring only controversial/difficult/major/politically sensitive matters to the Commissioners.
- Feeding into *chefs de cabinet* meetings are the outcomes of meetings between the *cabinet* members responsible for particular policy areas. As part of his stated aim to reduce the role of *cabinets* in the Commission system, under Prodi there were not so many of these meetings as there used to be. However, they could not be entirely eliminated because they are very important in facilitating the flow of information at College level and allowing policy proposals to be evaluated in the context of the Commission's overall objectives.
- Officials from the different *cabinets,* who are generally well known to one another, often exchange views on an informal basis if a proposal looks as though it may create difficulties. (Officially *cabinets* do not become involved until a proposal has been formally launched by a DG, but earlier consultation is common. If this consultation is seen by DGs to amount to interference, tensions and hostilities can arise – not least because *cabinet* officials are usually junior in career terms to officials in the upper reaches of DGs.)

However, despite these various coordinating arrangements, a feeling persists in many quarters that the Commission continues to function in too compartmentalised a manner, with insufficient attention being paid to overall EU policy coherence. Amongst the problems are the following.

(1) The Commission has a rather rigid organisational framework. Despite the development of horizontal links of the kind that have just been noted, structural relationships, both between and within DGs, remain essentially vertical. Although encouragement has been given, principally via the President's office, to the creation of agencies and teams that can plan on a broad front, these are not fully developed, and in any event they have found it difficult to assert their authority in relation to the DGs, especially the larger and traditionally more independent DGs. As for the President himself, he has only limited powers to direct the actions of DGs.

(2) Departmental and policy loyalties sometimes tend to discourage new and integrated approaches to problems and the pooling of ideas. Demarcation lines between spheres of responsibility are fairly tightly drawn and policy competences can be too jealously guarded.

(3) Sheer workload makes it difficult for many Commissioners and senior officials to look much beyond their own immediate tasks. One of the duties of a Commissioner's *cabinet* is to keep him or her abreast of general policy developments, but it remains the case that the Commissioner holding the portfolio on, say, research, can hardly be blamed if she or he has little to contribute to a Commission discussion on the milk market regime.

Responsibilities and Powers

Some of the Commission's responsibilities and powers are prescribed in the treaties and in EU legislation. Others are not formally laid down but have developed from practical necessity and the requirements of the EU system.

Whilst recognising that there is some overlap between the categories, the responsibilities and associated powers of the Commission may be grouped under six major headings: proposer and developer of policies and legislation, executive functions, guardian of the legal framework, external representative and negotiator, mediator and conciliator, and promoter of the general interest.

Proposer and developer of policies and legislation

Article 211 TEC includes the provision that the Commission 'shall formulate recommendations or deliver opinions on matters dealt with in this Treaty, if it expressly so provides or if the Commission considers it necessary'.

What this means in practice is that the Commission is charged with the responsibility of proposing measures that are likely to advance the development of the EU. Where legislation is envisaged, this power to propose is exclusive to the Commission. The Commission also has proposing and initiating powers under pillars two and three of the EU (in the latter case, only since the Amsterdam Treaty), but these are shared with the member states: there is no exclusive power of proposal since legislation is not made under these pillars.

In addition to its formal treaty powers, political realities arising from the institutional structure of the EU also dictate that the Commission should be centrally involved in formulating and developing policy. The most important of these realities is that there is nothing like an EU Prime Minister or government capable of providing the EU with clear and consistent policy direction, let alone a coherent legislative programme. Senior Commission officials who have transferred from national civil services are often greatly surprised by the lack of political direction from above and the amount of room for policy and legislative initiation that is available to them. Their duties are often only broadly defined and there can be considerable potential, especially for more senior officials, to stimulate development in specific and, if they wish, new and innovative policy areas. An indication of the scale of this activity is seen in the fact that in an average year the Commission presents around 400 proposals, recommendations and draft instruments for adoption by the Council or by the EP and the Council, about 40 directives, 150 regulations and 200 decisions. Additionally, it presents 300 or so communications and reports, plus a handful of White and Green Papers.

Although in practice they greatly overlap, it will be useful here, for analytical purposes, to look separately at policy initiation and development on the one hand, and legislative initiation and development on the other.

* * *

Policy initiation and development takes place at several levels in that it ranges from sweeping 'macro' policies to detailed policies for particular sectors. Whatever the level, however, the Commission – important though it is – does not have a totally free hand in what it does. As is shown at various points elsewhere in this book, all sorts of other actors – including the Council of Ministers, the EP, the member states, sectional groups, regional and local authorities, and private firms – also attempt to play a part in the policy process. They do so by engaging in such activities as producing policy papers, issuing exhortations and recommendations, and lobbying. Such activities are frequently designed to exert direct policy pressure on the Commission. From its earliest deliberations on a possible policy initiation the Commission has to take note of many of these outside voices if its proposals are to find broad support and be effective in the sectors to which they are directed. The Commission must concern itself not only with what it believes to be desirable but also with what is possible. The policy preferences of others must be recognised and, where necessary and appropriate, be accommodated.

Of the many pressures and influences to which the Commission is subject in the exercise of its policy initiation functions, the most important are those which emanate from the Council of Ministers. When the Council indicates that it wishes to see certain sorts of proposal laid before it, the Commission is obliged to respond. However, important though the Council has become as a policy-initiating body, the extent to which this has produced a decline in the initiating responsibilities and powers of the Commission ought not to be exaggerated. For the Council often finds it difficult to be bold and imaginative, and tends to be better at responding than at originating and proposing. Further to this, there has been an increasing tendency since the early 1980s for major policy initiatives to be sanctioned at European Council rather than Council of Ministers level, and the Commission has adjusted itself quite well to this shift by not only taking instructions from the European Council but also using it to legitimise its own policy preferences. EU enlargement illustrates this mutual interdependence of the Commission and the European Council in terms of policy initiation and development, with there barely having been a European Council meeting since the early 1990s that has either not received a report of some kind from the Commission on an aspect of enlargement or has not asked that such a report be prepared.

The Commission's policy-initiating activities cover both major and cross-sectoral policies and policy programmes such as enlargement and the functioning of the internal market and also specific policy areas. Examples of the latter include: attempting to generate a more integrated approach to a policy area – as with the 2001 White Paper *European Transport Policy for 2010: Time to Decide*, or the 2005 Green Paper on energy efficiency *Doing More With Less*; attempting to strengthen existing policy frameworks – as with the 1997 Communication *Consumer Health and Food Safety* and the associated Green Paper *The General Principles of Food Law in the European Union*; and attempting to promote ideas, discussion and interest as a possible preliminary to getting a new policy area or initiative off the ground – as with the 2005 discussion document *A European Institute of Technology?* that was issued as part of the mid-term review of the Lisbon Process. But whatever their particular focus, most – though not all – policy initiatives need to be followed up with legislation if they are to have bite and be effective.

*   *   *

If the Commission is well placed with regard to policy initiation and development, it is even better placed with regard to *legislative initiation and development*, for it alone has the power to initiate and draft legislative proposals. The other two main institutions involved in the legislative process, the Council and the EP, can request the Commission to produce proposals (the Council under Article 208 of the TEC and the EP under Article 192), but they cannot do the initiating or drafting themselves. Moreover, after a legislative proposal has been formally tabled the Commission still retains a considerable measure of control, for it is difficult for the Council or the EP to amend it without the Commission's agreement: the Council can only do so by acting unanimously and the EP can only do so in specified circumstances and then only with the support of an absolute majority of its component members (see Chapter 16 for details on this).

As with the preparation of policy proposals, the Commission makes considerable use of outside sources, and is often subject to considerable outside pressures, when preparing legislative proposals. The preparation of legislative proposals is thus often accompanied by an extensive sounding and listening process, especially at the pre-proposal stage – that is, before the Commission has formally presented a proposal to the Council and the EP. In this process an important role is played by a vast network of advisory committees that have been established over the years.

The Commission's advisory committee network

The committees are of two main types.

(1) *Expert committees*. These consist of national officials, experts and specialists of various sorts. Although nominated by national governments the committee members are not normally viewed as official governmental spokesmen in the way that members of Council working groups are (see Chapter 10), so it is usually possible for them to conduct their affairs on a reasonably informal basis. Many of these committees are well-established, meet on a fairly regular basis, and have a more or less fixed membership; others are *ad hoc* – set up, very frequently, to discuss an early draft of a Commission legislative proposal – and can hardly be even described as committees in that they may only ever meet once or twice. In terms of their interests and concerns, some of the committees are wide-ranging, such as the Advisory Committee on Restrictive Practices and Dominant Positions and the Advisory Committee on Community Actions for the Elderly, while others are more specialised and technical, such as the Advisory Committee on Unfair Pricing Practices in Maritime Transport and the Committee of Experts on International Road Tariffs.

(2) *Consultative committees*. These are composed of representatives of sectional interests and are organised and funded by the Commission without reference to the national governments. Members are normally appointed by the Commission from nominations made by representative EU-level organisations: either umbrella groups such as the Union of Industrial and Employers' Confederations of Europe (UNICE), the European Trade Union Confederation (ETUC), and the Committee of Agricultural Organisations in the European Union (COPA), or more specialised sectoral organisations and liaison groups such as the European Tour Operators' Association (ETOA) or the European Association of Manufacturers of Business Machines and Information Technology (EUROBIT). The effect of this appointments policy is that the consultative committees are overwhelmingly composed of full-time employees of associations and groups. Agriculture is a policy sector where there are many consultative committees, with over twenty committees for products covered by a market regime plus half a dozen or so more general committees. Most of the agricultural advisory committees have a membership of around fifty, but there are a few exceptions: the largest are those dealing with cereals, milk and dairy products, and sugar, whilst the smallest are the veterinary committee and the committee on hops.

In addition to these two types of committees there are many hybrids with mixed forms of membership.

Most of the advisory committees are chaired and serviced by the Commission. A few are serviced by the Council and technically are Council committees, but the Commission has observer status on these so the distinction between the two types of committee is of little significance in terms of their ability to advise the Commission.

The extent to which policy sectors are covered by advisory committees varies. One factor making for variation is the degree of importance of the policy within the EU's policy framework – it is hardly surprising, for example, that there should be many more agricultural advisory committees than there are educational advisory committees. Another factor is the dependence of the Commission in particular policy areas on outside expertise and technical knowledge. A third factor is the preferences of DGs – some incline towards the establishment of committees to provide them with advice, while others prefer to do their listening in less structured ways.

The influence exercised by advisory committees varies enormously. In general, the committees of national experts are better placed than the consultative committees. There are a number of reasons for this. First, Commission consultation with the expert committees is usually compulsory in the procedure for drafting legislation, whereas it is usually optional with the consultative committees. Second, the expert committees can often go beyond offering the Commission technical advice and alert it to probable governmental reactions to a proposal, and therefore to possible problems that may arise at a future decision-making stage if certain views are not incorporated. Third, expert committees also have the advantage over consultative committees of tending to meet more regularly – often convening as necessary when something important is in the offing, whereas consultative committees tend to gather on average no more than two or three times a year. Usually, consultative committees are at their most influential when they have high-ranking figures amongst their membership, when they are given the opportunity to discuss policy at an early stage of development, when the timetable for the enactment of a proposal is flexible, and when the matter under consideration is not too constrained by existing legislation.

Executive functions

The Commission exercises wide executive responsibilities. That is, it is closely involved in the management, supervision and implementation of EU policies. Just how involved varies considerably across the policy spectrum, but as a general rule the Commission's executive functions tend to be more concerned with monitoring and coordinating developments, laying down the ground rules, carrying out investigations and giving rulings on significant matters (such as proposed company mergers, state aid, and applications for derogations from EU law) than they are with detailed 'ground level' policy implementation.

Three aspects of the Commission's executive functions are worth special emphasis.

Rule-making powers

It is not possible for the treaties, or for legislation made in the name of the Council or the European Parliament and the Council, to cover every possible area and eventuality in which a rule may be required. In circumstances and under conditions that are defined by the treaties and/or EU legislation the Commission is therefore delegated rule-making powers. This puts the Commission in a similar position to national executives: because of the frequent need for quick decisions in that grey area where policy overlaps with administration, and because too of the need to relieve the normal legislative process of over-involvement with highly detailed and specialised matters, it is desirable to have truncated and special rule-making arrangements for administrative and technical law.

The Commission used to issue at least 4000 legislative instruments per year in the form of directives, regulations, and decisions (see Chapter 13 for an examination of the different types of EU legislative instrument). In recent years, however, with most of the SEM programme in place and with the Commission conscious of the expectation arising from the subsidiarity principle that it should issue laws only when they are absolutely necessary, the number has been much lower. In 2004 the Commission issued 672 regulations, 408 decisions and 59 directives. The Commission also issues recommendations and opinions, but these do not have full legislative force.

Most Commission legislation is confined to the filling in of details, or to the taking of decisions, that follow automatically from Council or European Parliament and Council legislation. So the greatest proportion of Commission legislation is made up of regulations dealing with price adjustments and market support measures under the Common Agricultural Policy. But not quite all of the Commission's rule-making powers are confined to the routine and the straightforward. In several policy areas opportunities exist to make not just 'administrative' law but what verges on 'policy' law. For example, in managing EU trade policy the Commission has considerable discretion in deciding whether to apply preventive measures in order to protect the EU market from dumping by third countries. And in implementing the EU's competition policy, the Commission has taken advantage of the rather generally phrased Article 81 of the TEC to clarify and develop the position on restrictive practices through the issuing of regulations and decisions.

As will be shown below, the Commission works closely with committees of governmental representatives when exercising its rule-making powers.

Management of EU finances

On the revenue side of the budget, EU income is subject to tight constraints (see Chapter 17 for an explanation of budgetary revenue). In overseeing the collection of this income the Commission has two main duties: to see that the correct rates are applied within certain categories of revenue, and to ensure that the proper payments are made to the EU by those national authorities which act as the EU's collecting agents.

On the expenditure side, the administrative arrangements vary according to the type of expenditure concerned. The Commission must, however, always operate within the approved annual budget (the EU is not legally permitted to run a budget deficit) and on the basis of the guidelines for expenditure headings that are laid down in EU law. Of the various ways in which the EU spends its money two are especially important in that together they account for around 80 per cent of total budgetary expenditure.

First, there is Common Agricultural Policy (CAP) spending, which accounts for around 45 per cent of the annual budget and is used for agricultural support and rural development purposes. Up to 2006 this had been based on the European Agricultural Guidance and Guarantee Fund (EAGGF), but in June 2005 the Agriculture Ministers agreed to change CAP funding arrangements from 2007 to coincide with the application of a new financial perspective for the years 2007–13 (financial perspectives are multi-annual planning instruments on which all EU annual budgets are based: see Chapter 17). The decision taken by the Ministers was to replace the EAGGF with two new funds that would be better tailored to the 'new CAP': the European Agricultural Guarantee Fund (EAGF) and the European Agricultural Fund for Rural Development (EAFRD).

General management decisions on the use of CAP funds – such as whether, and on what conditions, to dispose of product surpluses – are taken by the Commission, usually via an appropriate management committee (see pp. 178–80). As is shown in Chapter 18, the practical application of agricultural policy and management decisions occurs at national levels through appropriate agencies.

Second, there is cohesion policy spending, which accounts for over 35 per cent of total EU expenditure. The EU's cohesion policy is aimed at reducing economic and social disparities in the Union, at both national and regional levels. As with CAP spending, cohesion policy funding arrangements have been changed under the 2007–13 financial perspective, with financial instruments reduced from a previous six to three: the European Regional Development Fund (ERDF), the European Social Fund (ESF), and the Cohesion Fund (see Chapter 15 for details).

Programming, partnership, co-financing and evaluation are key principles of cohesion policy. The practical effect of this in management terms is that cohesion policy is based on a tiered system in which the roles and responsibilities of actors, including the Commission, vary at different levels. The post-2007 system differs in details from, but is similar in spirit to, its predecessor. The key features of the system are: overall strategic decisions are taken by the Council, on the basis of Commission proposals; broad programming decisions for member states and regions are developed jointly between the Commission and member states (with it being left to member states as to who participates on their side, but with regional and local authority involvement expected); implementation decisions are monitored by the Commission but are undertaken through institutional arrangements of the member states involving national, regional and local authorities, and also social partners and representatives of civil society.

* * *

Moving beyond the specific aspects of the Commission's financial management functions to look at the overall picture, it is clear that the Commission's ability to manage EU finances effectively is greatly weakened by the fact that the Council and the EP (especially the former) control the upper limits of the revenue base and take framework spending decisions. In the past this sometimes caused considerable difficulties because it meant that if it became obvious during the course of a financial year that expenditure was exceeding income the Commission could not step in at an early stage and take appropriate action by, for example, increasing the value added tax (VAT) ceiling on revenue or reducing agricultural price guarantees. All the Commission could do, and regularly did, was to make out a case as to what should be done. This dependence on the Council and EP remains, but the general situation is not as fraught as it was, because since 1988 there have been clearer controls on the growth of both income and expenditure, via medium-term financial planning instruments known as financial perspectives. There also are mechanisms available to the Commission to enable it to act quickly if expenditure expands beyond targets in the main 'problem' area of agriculture.

Another, quite different, factor in weakening the Commission's financial management capability is that it does not itself directly undertake much of the front-line implementation of EU spending programmes and schemes. Rather, it mostly works through external – mainly national and subnational – agencies which, acting on its behalf, execute some 80 per cent of the EU budget. This point about the reliance of the Commission on external agencies is explored in the next section, but it is worth emphasising here too, not least since a major thrust of criticisms often made of the Commission is that it is too lax in its monitoring and control mechanisms in respect of many of these agencies. Under a programme of financial management reforms that was drawn up in the early months of the Prodi Commission and which was set out in a 2000 White Paper (European Commission, 2000) many changes to procedures and practices have been introduced. They include: the adoption of activity-based management and budgeting, to provide for improved financial planning and the better alignment of political priorities and the allocation of resources; the enhancement of accountability procedures within the Commission; a sharper separation between the approval and the auditing of expenditure functions; and less contracting out of implementing functions to private sector agencies (such contracting out had become increasingly common in the 1990s, largely as part of an attempt to deal with Commission understaffing).

*   *   *

Before leaving the Commission's responsibilities for financial management, it should also be noted that the Commission has some responsibilities for coordinating and managing finances that are not drawn exclusively from EU sources. These responsibilities mostly cover environmental programmes, scientific and technological research programmes, and educational programmes in which the member states are joined by non-member states. A particularly important programme area in which the Commission has assumed coordination and management responsibilities has been the provision of Western assistance to states of the former Soviet bloc and Soviet Union.

Supervision of 'front-line' policy implementation

The Commission's role with regard to the implementation of EU policies is primarily that of supervisor and overseer. It does undertake some direct policy implementation, most notably in connection with competition policy – which is considered below in the section on the guardian of the legal framework. However, the bulk of the practical/routine/day-by-day/front-line implementation of EU policies is not undertaken by the Commission itself but is delegated to appropriate agencies within the member states. Examples of such national agencies are: Customs and Excise Authorities, which deal with most matters pertaining to movements across the EU's external and internal borders; veterinary inspection teams, which check quality standards on foodstuffs; and Ministries of Agriculture and Agricultural Intervention Boards, which are responsible for controlling the volume of agricultural produce on domestic markets and which deal directly with farmers and traders about payments and charges. To ensure that policies are applied in a reasonably uniform manner throughout the member states the Commission attempts to supervise, or at least hold a watching brief on, the national agencies and the way they perform their EU duties. It is a task that carries with it many difficulties, four of which are especially important.

First, in general the Commission is not sufficiently resourced for the job. There just are not enough officials in the DGs, and not enough money to contract the required help from outside agencies, to see that the agriculture, fishing, regional and other policies are properly implemented. The Commission is therefore heavily dependent on the good faith and willing cooperation of the member states. However, even in those policy spheres where it is in almost constant communication with national officials, the Commission cannot be aware of everything that is going on, and with respect to those areas where contacts and flows of communication between Brussels and national agencies are irregular and not well ordered it is almost impossible for Commission officials to have an accurate idea as to what is happening 'at the front'. Even if the Commission comes to suspect that something is amiss with an aspect of policy implementation, lack of resources can mean that it is not possible for the matter to be fully investigated. In respect of fraud, for example, in 2004 there were only 329 officials in the European Anti-Fraud Office (OLAF) which is attached to the Commission (European Commission, 2005b).

The second difficulty is that even when they are willing to cooperate fully, national agencies are not always as capable of implementing policies as the Commission would wish. One reason for this is that some EU policies are, by their very nature, very difficult to administer. For example, the Common Fisheries Policy is extremely difficult to police, with the provisions on fishing zones, total allowable catches and conservation requiring surveillance measures such as obligatory and properly kept logbooks, port inspections and aerial patrols. Another reason why national agencies are not always capable of effective policy implementation is that national officials are often poorly trained and/or are overburdened by the complexities of EU rules. The jumble of rules that officials have to apply is illustrated by the import levy on biscuits, which varies according to cereal, milk, fat and sugar content, while the export refund varies also according to egg content. Another example of rule complexity is seen in respect of the export of beef, which is subject to numerous separate regulations, which themselves are subject to an array of permanent and temporary amendments.

The third difficulty is that agencies in the member states do not always wish to see EU law applied. Competition policy, for example, is rich in such examples, but sometimes there is little action the Commission can take against a deliberately recalcitrant state given the range of policy instruments available to governments that wish to assist domestic industries and the secretiveness with which these can often be arranged.

The fourth and final difficulty is that EU law can be genuinely open to different interpretations. Sometimes indeed it is deliberately flexible so as to allow for adjustments to national circumstances.

Comitology

As is clear from the above discussion, a number of different procedures apply with regard to how the Commission exercises its executive functions. Many of the procedures involve the use of different types of implementing committees, which has resulted in the word 'comitology' being used to describe the arrangements associated with the procedures.

Because the procedures were becoming ever more confusing and complex, and because the projected completion of the internal market by 1992 would entail a host of implementing decisions, comitology arrangements were clarified by the SEA and by a Council decision of 13 July 1987. While no new procedures were introduced, it was established what the possible procedures were and guidelines were laid down as to which of the procedures should be used in particular cases. In 1999 the Council replaced the 1987 decision with *Council Decision of 28 June 1999 Laying Down the Procedures for the Exercise of Implementing Powers Conferred on the Commission* (1999/468/EC, *Official Journal*, L184, 17 July 1999). This 1999 decision left the procedures that had been laid down in 1987 in place, but in streamlined form.

Prior to the 1999 decision there had been frequent disputes between the Council on the one hand and the Commission and EP on the other over the nature and application of the procedures. Indeed, the 1999 Decision stemmed in large part from an attempt on the part of the Council to allay at least some of the concerns of the other two institutions. Disputes arose from the fact that, as can be seen in Table 9.2, the powers of the institutions vary considerably according to which procedure is used: advisory committees can only *advise* the Commission; management committees can *block* Commission decisions by a qualified majority vote (QMV); regulatory committees must give their *approval* for Commission decisions by QMV; and under safeguard measure the Council has a variety of consultative, confirming, amending and revoking powers.

The main bones of contention between the institutions were, and since the 1999 Decision still are, focused on:

- Complaints by the Commission and the EP that the Council has made too much use of the regulatory committee procedure and insufficient use of the advisory committee procedure. In 2004, there were 31 committees in existence that used just the advisory procedure, 64 that used just the management procedure, 95 that used just the regulatory procedure, 3 that used just the safeguard procedure, and 55 that used more than one procedure (European Commission, 2005a: 9–10).
- Complaints by the EP that it is provided with insufficient information about deliberations in comitology committees and that it has only very limited scrutiny powers over the committees, even though much of the implementing legislation that is channelled through them is based on EP and Council legislation. Under the 1999 Council Decision and an EP–Commission agreement of February 2000 on the procedures for implementing the Decision, the EP does receive more information than it used to do. Furthermore, the EP is in certain circumstances able to request the re-examination of decisions. Overall, however, it is still largely on the outside and often in a position of reacting to matters that have moved on by the time it considers them.

Table 9.2   *Procedures to be used in respect of the Commission's implementing powers* *

Advisory Procedure	The Commission submits a draft of the measures to be taken to the committee. The committee delivers an opinion on the draft, by a simple majority if necessary. The Commission takes 'the utmost account' of the opinion delivered by the committee.
Management Procedure	The Commission submits a draft of the measures to be taken to the committee. If the Commission's measures are opposed by a qualified majority in the committee then the Commission may defer application of its decision for a period which shall not exceed three months. Within the three-month period the Council may take a different decision by a qualified majority vote.
Regulatory Procedure	The Commission submits a draft of the measures to be taken by the committee. If the Commission's measures are not supported by a qualified majority in the committee, or if no opinion is delivered, the matter is referred to the Council. The Council may, within a period not exceeding three months, take a decision on the Commission's proposal by a qualified majority. If the decision is to oppose the proposal, the Commission must re-examine it and may then resubmit its proposal, submit an amended proposal, or present a legislative proposal. If the Council does not act within the three-month period the proposal shall be adopted by the Commission.

Safeguard Procedure	No committee is appointed, but the Commission must notify, and in some cases must consult with, the member states in respect of a measure to be taken.
	
	    Any member state may refer the Commission's decision to the Council, within a time limit to be determined.
	
	    The Council may take a different decision by a qualified majority within a time limit to be determined. Alternatively, it may be stipulated in the enabling legislation that the Council, acting by a qualified majority, may confirm, amend, or revoke the Commission's decision and that if the Council takes no decision within a time limit to be determined the Commission's decision is revoked.

* Which procedure applies is specified in the enabling legislation.

In 2004 there were a total of 248 comitology committees, with the most numerous found in the spheres of Transport/Energy/Trans-European networks (40), Environment (35), Enterprise (30), and Agriculture (30) (European Commission, 2005a: 8). The scope and range of activities covered by comitology committees varies enormously. Some, such as the Insurance Committee (a regulatory committee), the Standing Committee on Medicinal Products for Home Use (regulatory), and the Committee of the European Social Fund (advisory) have fairly broad briefs. Others, including most of the many committees charged with assisting with the adaptation to technical and scientific progress of existing legislation, are highly specialised. Examples of specialised committees include the Management Committee for Bananas (management), the Committee for Implementation of the Directive on Packaging and Packaging Waste (regulatory) and the Committee on Directives related to Textile Names and Labelling (advisory).

* * *

Looking at management and regulatory committees a little more closely – advisory committees having been discussed earlier in the chapter – both types of committee are chaired and serviced by the Commission. The committee members are governmental representatives with, in an average-sized committee, two or three middle-ranking officials from appropriate ministries attending on behalf of each member state. There is no hard and fast distinction of either principle or policy responsibility between the two types of committee. In the past, management committees were mostly concerned with agriculture, with most having a specific sectoral responsibility for the CAP'S product regimes, but there are now an increasing number in other areas too. Regulatory committees tend to be concerned with harmonisation and vary greatly in their sectoral interests.

Management and regulatory committees do similar things with variations occurring not so much between management and regulatory comittees as such but rather between individual committees according to their terms of reference, the nature of the subject matter with which they are concerned, and how they are regarded by the Commission. In addition to considering proposed Commission decisions, agenda items for committee meetings could include analysing the significance of data of various kinds, looking at how existing legislation is working, considering how existing legislation may be modified to take account of technical developments (the particular responsibility of the technical progress committees) and assessing market situations (a prime task for the agricultural committees). Committees meet as appropriate, which means almost weekly in the case of agricultural products that require frequent market adjustments, such as cereals, sugar and wines, and in other cases means hardly at all.

* * *

Those who criticise the EU on the ground that it is undermining national sovereignties sometimes cite comitology committees as part of their case. They point to the rarity of adverse opinions, the low number of no opinions, the frequency with which measures go through without unanimous support, and the ability of the Commission – especially under the advisory and management procedures – to ignore or circumvent unfavourable votes. There is, however, another side to this; a side which suggests that the power of the Commission to control the committees and impose its will on the states ought not to be exaggerated. Five points in particular ought to be noted. First, although some of the committees do exercise important powers, for the most part they tend to work within fairly narrowly defined limits. Anything very controversial can be referred to a Council meeting, although in practice less than one per cent of the 2500–3000 legal instruments passing through comitology committees in an average year are so referred. (The committees also pass a similar number of opinions.) Second, many negative votes by states are cast tactically rather than as part of a real attempt to stop a proposal. That is, a national delegation might well recognise that a measure is going to be approved but will vote against it or abstain in order to satisfy a political interest at home. Third, as with all aspects of its activity, it is just not in the Commission's long-term interests to abuse its powers by forcing unwelcome or unpopular measures through a committee. It wants and needs cooperation, and if a proposal meets serious opposition in a committee a good chairperson will, unless special circumstances apply, suggest revisions rather than press for a vote that may have divisive consequences. Fourth, the Council tends to be jealous of its powers and would move quickly against the Commission if it thought comitology committees were being used to undermine Council power. Finally, where particularly important policy matters are concerned, or when the member states have been unable to agree on what sort of committee to establish, the Council sometimes reserves implementing powers for itself.

Taking a broad view, comitology committees are therefore to be seen as a means by which the member states seek to ensure the Commission does not become too independent of them. In conceptual terms, the committees are one of a number of mechanisms and devices found throughout the EU system used by the EU's principals – the member states – to maintain control over their agents – especially the Commission – where control is desired.

The guardian of the legal framework

In association with the Court of Justice, the Commission is charged with ensuring that the treaties and EU legislation are respected. This role links closely with the Commission's supervisory and implementing responsibilities. Indeed the lack of a full EU-wide policy-implementing framework means that its legal watchdog role serves, to some extent, as a substitute for the detailed day-to-day application of policies that at national level involves such routine activities as inspecting premises, checking employee lists, and auditing returns. It is a role that is extremely difficult to exercise: transgressors of EU law do not normally wish to advertise their illegal actions, and they are often protected by, or may even be, national authorities.

The Commission may become aware of possible illegalities in one of a number of ways. In the case of non-transposition or incorrect transposition of a directive into national law this is obvious enough, since directives normally specify a time by which the Commission must be supplied with full details of national transposition measures. A second way is through self-notification. For example, states are obliged to notify the Commission about all national draft regulations and standards concerning technical specifications so that the Commission may satisfy itself that they will not cause barriers to trade. Similarly, under Article 88 TEC, state aid must be referred to the Commission for its inspection. Self-notifications also come forward under Article 81 TEC which deals with restrictive business practices because although parties are not obliged to notify the Commission of such practices, they frequently do so, either because they wish for clarification on whether or not a practice is in legal violation or because they wish to seek an exemption (if a notification is not made within a specified time limit exemption is not permissible). A third way in which illegalities may come to the Commission's attention is from the many representations that are made by individuals, organisations, firms or member states who believe that their interests are being damaged by the alleged illegal actions of another party. For example, Germany has frequently complained about the amount of subsidies that many national governments give to their steel industries. And a fourth way is through the Commission's own efforts. Such efforts may take one of several forms: investigations by one of its small monitoring/investigatory/fraud teams; careful analysis of the information that is supplied by outside agencies; or simply a Commission official reading a newspaper report that suggests a government or a firm is doing, or is not doing, something that looks suspicious under EU law.

Infringement proceedings are initiated against member states for not notifying the Commission of measures taken to transpose directives into national law, for non-transposition or incorrect transposition of directives, and for non-application or incorrect application of EU law – most commonly in connection with the internal market, industrial affairs, indirect taxation, agriculture, and environmental and consumer protection. Before any formal action is taken against a state it is informed by the Commission that it is in possible breach of its legal obligations. If, after the Commission has carried out an investigation, the breach is confirmed and continues, a procedure comes into force under Article 226 TEC whereby the Commission

> shall deliver a reasoned opinion on the matter after giving the State concerned the opportunity to submit its observations. If the State concerned does not comply with the opinion within the period laid down by the Commission, the latter may bring the matter before the Court of Justice.

Since most infringements have implications for the functioning of the market, the Commission usually seeks to ensure that these procedures operate according to a tight timetable: normally a state is given about two months to present its observations and a similar period to comply with the reasoned opinion.

Most cases, it must be emphasised, are settled at an early stage. So in an average year the Commission issues around 1000 letters of formal notice, 500 reasoned opinions, and makes 150 references to the Court of Justice. One reason for so many early settlements is that most infringements occur not as a result of wilful avoidance of EU law but rather from genuine differences over interpretation, or from national administrative and legislative procedures that have occasioned delay.

Although there are differences between member states in their enthusiasm for aspects of EU law, most wish to avoid open confrontation with EU institutions. If states do not wish to submit to an EU law it is therefore more customary for them to drag their feet rather than be openly obstructive. Delay can, however, be a form of obstruction, in that states know it could be years before the Commission, and even more the Court of Justice, brings them to heel. Environmental legislation illustrates this, with most states not having fully incorporated and/or implemented only parts of long-standing EU legislation – on matters such as air pollution, bathing water and drinking water.

With regard to what action the Commission can take if it discovers breaches or prospective breaches of EU law, that depends very much on the circumstances. Four different sorts of circumstance will be taken as illustrations of this point:

- *Non-compliance by a member state.* Until the entry into force of the Maastricht Treaty in 1993, the Commission was not empowered to impose sanctions against member states that were in breach of their legal obligations. Respect for Commission decisions was dependent on the goodwill and political judgement of the states themselves, backed up by the ability of the Commission to make a referral to the Court of Justice – though the Court too could not impose sanctions. However, the Maastricht Treaty gave the Commission power, when a member state refuses to comply with a judgement of the Court, to bring the state back before the Court and in so doing to specify a financial penalty that should be imposed. The size of the penalty must reflect the seriousness of the legal infringement, the duration of the infringement, and the state's ability to pay (using GDP as an indicator). The Court takes the final decision. The first state to be fined by the Court was Greece, which in 2000 was held to have failed to fulfil its obligations on waste directives and was ordered to pay €20 000 per day until it complied with the Court's judgement. On a much bigger scale, in May 2002 the Commission asked the Court to fine France €242 650 per day for being in breach of EU insurance laws.

- *Firms breaching EU law on restrictive practices and abuse of dominant market positions.* Treaty provisions (notably Articles 81 and 82 of the TEC), secondary legislation and Court judgements have established a considerable volume of EU law in the sphere of restrictive practices and abuse of dominant market positions. If at all possible, the Commission avoids resorting to law and taking formal action against firms. This is partly because of the ill-feeling that can be generated by open confrontation and partly because the use of law and formal action involves cumbersome and protracted procedures to establish a case. Offending parties are therefore encouraged to fall into line or to reach an agreement with the Commission during the extensive informal processes, which can last several years, that always precede formal proceedings. If, however, informal processes fail, fines and required actions can result. Such was the case with Microsoft in 2004, when the Commission ruled that it had abused its dominant position in the group server operating systems and media player markets. A €497 million fine was imposed and it also was required to introduce a modified version of its Windows operating system and to reveal details of its Windows software codes so as to enable competitors to produce compatible products.
- *Firms breaching EU rules on state aid.* Articles 87–9 of the TEC provide the Commission with the power to take action against what is deemed to be unacceptable state subsidisation of business and industry. This power can take the form of requiring that the state aid in question be repaid, as was the case in January 2002 when the French bank Crédit Mutuel was instructed to repay €164 million to the French government. The Commission decided that the aid, which had been granted to help pay for special reduced tax bank accounts, gave Crédit Mutuel an unfair advantage over its competitors. Generally, however, indeed in about

95 per cent of the cases it investigates, state aid applications and allegations result in the aid being authorised.

- *Potential breaches of EU rules on company mergers.* Council Regulation 4064/89 (the so-called Merger Control Regulation), which came into effect in September 1990, specifies the Commission's powers in some detail. Information regarding proposed mergers and takeovers above certain limits has to be notified to the Commission. On receipt of the information the Commission must decide within one month whether it proposes either to let the deal go ahead because competition would not be harmed, or to open proceedings. If it decides on the latter it has four months to carry out an investigation, in the course of which it is entitled to enter the premises of firms and seize documents. Any firm that supplies false information during the course of a Commission inquiry, or conducts a merger or takeover without gaining clearance from the Commission, is liable to be fined up to 10 per cent of its annual sales. In practice the Commission normally authorises the proposed mergers that are referred to it, though conditions are often laid down requiring, for example, some of the assets of the merging firms to be sold off. The best known prohibition is the Commission's decision in 2001 not to authorise the proposed €42 billion merger between the US companies General Electric and Honeywell, even though the US authorities had cleared the merger subject only to minor divestment. Explaining the decision, the Competition Commissioner said the companies made too few concessions, too late, and that 'The merger ... would have severely reduced competition in the aerospace industry and resulted ultimately in higher prices for customers, particularly airlines' (*The Guardian*, 4 July 2001).

As with most of its other activities, the Commission's ability to exercise its legal guardianship function is blunted by a number of constraints and restrictions. Three are especially important:

- The problem of limited resources means that choices have to be made about which cases are worth pursuing, and with how much vigour. For example only about seventy officials – in a specially created task force located in DG Competition – undertake the detailed and highly complex work that is necessary to give effect to the 1989 Merger Control Regulation.
- Relevant and sufficiently detailed information can be difficult to obtain – either because it is deliberately hidden from prying Commission officials or because, as is the case with many aspects of market conditions, reliable figures are just not available. An example of an EU law that is difficult to apply because of lack of information is the 1979

Council Directive on the Conservation of Wild Birds (79/409/EEC). Amongst other things, the Directive provides protection for most species of migrant birds and forbids killing for trade and by indiscriminate methods. Because the shooting of birds is popular in some countries, several governments were slow to transpose the Directive into national law and have been reluctant to do much about applying the law since it has been transposed. On the first of these implementing problems – transposition – the Commission can acquire the information it needs since states are obliged to inform it of the measures they have taken. On the second of the implementation problems, however – application of the law by national authorities against transgressors – the Commission has been much less able to make judgements about whether states are fulfilling their responsibilities: it is very difficult to know what efforts are really being made by national authorities to catch shooters and hunters.

- Political considerations can inhibit the Commission from acting as vigorously as it might in certain problem areas and in particular cases. An important reason for this is that the Commission does not normally wish to upset or politically embarrass the governments of member states if it is at all avoidable: the Commission does, after all, have to work closely and continuously with the national governments both on an individual and – in the Council of Ministers – on a collective basis. An example of political pressures inhibiting the Commission in this way is provided by the above-cited Conservation of Wild Birds Directive: in addition to the practical problem of acquiring information on the killing of birds, the Commission's sensitive political antennae serve to hold it in check in that it is well aware of the unpopularity and political difficulties that would be created for some governments if action were taken against the thousands who break this law. Another example of the inhibiting role of political pressures is the cautious line that the Commission has often adopted towards multinational corporations that appear to be in breach of EU competition law: to take action against multinationals is to risk generating political opposition from the member states in which the companies are based, and also risks being self-defeating in that it may cause companies to transfer their activities outside the EU. (There are also, of course, practical problems of the sort noted in the previous point when seeking to act against multinationals: it is very difficult to follow investigations through when dealing with organisations that are located in several countries, some of which may be outside Europe.) In exercising the role of guardian of the legal framework, the Commission thus attempts to operate in a flexible and politically sensitive manner. It would not be in its or the EU's interests to use an overly heavy hand.

External representative and negotiator

The Commission's roles in respect of the EU's external relations are considered in some detail in Chapter 19, so attention here will be limited simply to identifying those roles. There are, essentially, six.

First, the Commission is centrally involved in determining and conducting the EU's external trade relations. On the basis of Article 133 TEC, and with its actions always subject to Council approval, the Commission represents and acts on behalf of the EU both in formal negotiations, such as those that are conducted under the auspices of the World Trade Organisation (WTO), and in the more informal and exploratory exchanges that are common between, for example, the EU and the USA over world agricultural trade, and between the EU and Japan over access to each other's markets.

Second, the Commission has important negotiating and managing responsibilities in respect of the various special external agreements that the EU has with many countries and groups of countries. These agreements take many forms but the more advanced include not only privileged trading conditions but also financial aid and political dialogue.

Third, the Commission represents the EU at, and participates in the work of, a number of important international organisations. Three of these are specifically mentioned in the TEC: the United Nations and its specialised agencies (Article 302); the Council of Europe (Article 303); and the Organisation for Economic Cooperation and Development (Article 304).

Fourth, the Commission has responsibilities for acting as a key point of contact between the EU and non-member states. Over 160 countries have diplomatic missions accredited to the EU and the Commission is expected to keep them informed about EU affairs, either through the circulation of documents or by making its officials available for information briefings and lobbying. The EU, for its part, maintains an extensive network of diplomatic missions abroad, numbering over 130 delegations and offices, and these are staffed by Commission employees.

Fifth, as was shown in Chapters 3 and 4, the Commission is entrusted with important responsibilities with regard to applications for EU membership. Upon receipt of an application the Council normally asks the Commission to carry out a detailed investigation of the implications and to submit an opinion. If and when negotiations begin, the Commission, operating within Council-approved guidelines, acts as the EU's main negotiator, except on showpiece ministerial occasions or when particularly sensitive or difficult matters call for an inter-ministerial resolution of differences. When negotiations are completed the Commission makes a recommendation to the Council – in practice to the European Council –

as to whether an applicant should be accepted for membership. The whole process – from the lodging of an application to accession – can take years.

Finally, the Commission is 'fully associated' with the work carried out under the CFSP pillar of the TEU. The intergovernmental and non-EC nature of the CFSP pillar naturally means that the Commission's role is essentially supportive and secondary to that of the Council, and not in any way comparable to the role it undertakes with regard to external trade. That said, however, the Commission's CFSP inputs can be important, especially when the Council Presidency is under-resourced or overstretched and when EC instruments – usually associated with trade or development aid – are utilised in support of CFSP activities.

Mediator and conciliator

Much of EU decision-making, especially in the Council of Ministers, is based on searches for agreements between competing interests. The Commission is very much involved in trying to bring about these agreements, and a great deal of its time is taken up looking for common ground that amounts to more than the lowest common denominator. This mediating and conciliating role obliges the Commission to be sometimes guarded and cautious with its proposals. Radical initiatives, perhaps involving what it really believes needs to be done, are almost certain to meet with fierce opposition. More moderate proposals on the other hand, perhaps taking the form of adjustments and extensions to existing policy, and preferably presented in a technocratic rather than an ideological manner, are more likely to be acceptable. Hence the Commission must often subject itself to a somewhat grudging incrementalism.

The Commission is not the only EU body that consciously seeks to oil the wheels of decision-making. As is shown in Chapter 10, the Council itself has mediating mechanisms, notably via its Presidency. But the Commission is particularly well placed to act as mediator and conciliator. One reason for this is that it is normally seen as being non-partisan: its proposals may therefore be viewed less suspiciously than any which come from, say, the chairperson of a Council working group. Another reason is that in many instances the Commission is simply in the best position to judge which proposals are likely to command support, both inside and outside the Council. This is because of the continuous and extensive discussions which the Commission has with interested parties from the earliest considerations of a policy proposal through to its enactment. Unlike the other institutions, the Commission is represented at virtually every stage and in virtually every forum of the EU's decision-making system.

Although there are naturally limitations on what can be achieved, the effectiveness with which the Commission exercises this mediating role can be considerably influenced by the competence of its officials. While, for example, one Commission official may play a crucial role in driving a proposal through a Council working group, another may so misjudge a situation as not only to prejudice the Commission's own position but also to threaten the progress of the whole proposal. Many questions must be handled with care and political sensitivity. When should a proposal be brought forward, and in what form? At what point will an adjustment in the Commission's position open the way to progress in the Council? Is there anything to be gained from informal discussions with 'awkward delegations'? These, and questions such as these, call for highly developed political skills.

Promoter of the general interest

In performing each of the above tasks the Commission is supposed to stand apart from sectional and national interests. While others might look to the particular, it should look to the general; while others might look to the benefits to be gained from the next deal, it should keep at least one eye on the horizon. As many have described it, the Commission should be the 'conscience' of the Union.

In looking to the general interest, the expectation is that the Commission should not only avoid partisanship but also should look to the overall good functioning and cohesion of the Union. This is seen to require acting in ways that strike a balance, and if necessary reconciles differences, between different actors and interests: for example, in terms of the member states, between the large and small, between northern and southern, between old and new, and between net contributors to and net beneficiaries from the EU budget.

Worthy, however, though it may be in theory, this is a role that is difficult to operationalise. One reason why it is so is that it is highly questionable whether such a thing as the 'general interest' exists: there are few initiatives that do not threaten the interests of at least one member state – were this not to be the case there would not be so many disagreements in the Council.

In practice, therefore, the Commission tends not to be so detached, so far-seeing or so enthusiastic in pressing the *esprit communautaire* as some would like. This is not to say that it does not attempt to map out the future or attempt to press for developments that it believes will be generally beneficial. On the contrary, it is precisely because the Commission does seek to act and mobilise in the general interest that the smaller EU states tend to see it as something of a protector and hence are normally supportive of the Commission being given greater powers. Nor is it to deny that the Commission is sometimes ambitious in its approach and long-term in its perspective. But the fact is that the Commission operates in the real EU world, and often that necessitates looking to the short rather than to the long term, and to what is possible rather than what is ideally desirable.

Concluding Remarks

In recent years the Commission appears to have been a less effective institution than it was from the mid-1980s to the early 1990s, when it was leading the march to complete the internal market and was championing such initiatives as EMU and the social dimension. Commentators have suggested that there has been a diminution in the Commission's initiating role and a corresponding weakening of its ability to offer real vision and leadership. It has become, it is claimed, too reactive in exercising its responsibilities: reactive to the pressures of the many interests to which it is subject; reactive to the immediacy of events; and above all reactive to the increasing number of 'instructions' it receives from the Council of Ministers and the European Council.

Unquestionably, there is something in this view. The explanation for why it has happened is to be sought in a number of factors that have combined to weaken the Commission's institutional position:

- The rather rigid vertical lines within the Commission's own organisational structure sometimes make it difficult for a broad vision to emerge.
- The tensions that are seemingly present between the politically creative elements of the Commission's responsibilities and the bureaucratic roles of administering and implementing have perhaps never been properly resolved.
- The frequent appearance on the EU agenda of politically sensitive matters coupled with the desire of politicians not to cede too much power to others if they can avoid it have resulted in at least some member states being reluctant to grant too much further autonomy to the Commission.
- The fact that so many policy responsibilities are now exercised at the EU level means that the room for further Commission-led grand initiatives is not so great as formerly it was.
- Like national administrations, the Commission has been affected and infected by prevailing notions of rolling back the responsibilities of public sector organisations and of concentrating on making them more efficient in what they do, not more powerful in what they could do.

- The increasing use of 'new modes of governance' – based on flexible and non-legislative policy instruments, notably via the open method of coordination (see Chapter 15) – has weakened the Commission's influence in that it does not have exclusive initiating rights nor strong implementing powers in policy area where such an approach is being practised.
- The 'humiliations' of 1999 and 2004 – when the Santer College was forced to resign and Barroso was obliged to change the composition of his College – have clearly damaged the Commission's standing.

But notwithstanding these problems, the extent to which there has been a decline in the position of the Commission should not be exaggerated. Certainly it has had to trim more than it would like, and it has suffered its share of political defeats – not least in its wish for stronger treaty-based powers. But in some respects its powers have actually increased as it has adapted itself to the ever-changing nature of and demands upon the EU. As has been shown, the Commission exercises, either by itself or in association with other bodies, a number of crucially important functions. Moreover, it has been at the heart of pressing the case for, and putting forward specific proposals in relation to, many of the major issues that have been at the heart of the EU agenda in recent years: consolidating and further extending the SEM; ensuring the success of EMU; driving forward the enlargement process; promoting the strategy for increasing employment; and shifting the CAP from a price support system to an income support system.

The Commission's position in the EU system and its ability to affect the integration process is unquestionably stronger when favourable circumstances prevail. Amongst the circumstances that favour it are the existence of QMV in the Council (because it is then less subject to member state control), the absence of strong conflicts in the Council and the EP (because there is less likelihood of a body of opinion being resistant to its proposals), and uncertainty amongst decision-makers about optimum policies (because they are more likely to be susceptible to Commission leadership). But even when such circumstances do not exist the Commission still usually provides a key institutional presence, and not only for policy implementation purposes. The Commission is, in short, central and vital to the whole EU system.

Chapter 10

The Council of Ministers

Responsibilities and Functions
Composition
The Operation of the Council
Concluding Remarks

The Council of Ministers is the principal meeting place of the national governments.

When the Community was founded in the 1950s many expected that in time, as joint policies were seen to work and as the states came to trust one another more, the role of the Council would gradually decline, especially in relation to the Commission. This has not happened. On the contrary, by guarding and building on the responsibilities that are accorded to it in the treaties, and by adapting its internal mechanisms to enable it to cope more easily with the increasing volume of business that has come its way, the Council not only has defended, but in some respects has extended, its power and influence. This has naturally produced some frustration in the Commission, and also in the EP. It has also ensured, especially when set alongside the now very important position of the European Council in the EU's institutional system, that national governments have remained centrally placed to shape and influence most aspects of EU business.

Responsibilities and Functions

The functions undertaken by the Council can be classified in various ways. Hayes-Renshaw and Wallace (2006) identify four main functions: legislative – developing and making legislation; executive – taking direct responsibility in some policy areas for exercising executive power; steering – 'devising the big bargains that orient the future work of the Union' (p. 325); and forum – 'providing an arena through which the member governments attempt to develop convergent national approaches to one or other policy challenges in fields where the Union does not have clear collective policy powers' (ibid.).

A three-fold classification is used here. As compared with the Hayes-Renshaw and Wallace classification, their legislative function is broadened, their executive function is retained, a different category – mediator – is added, and their steering and forum functions are subsumed – within the

191

first and third categories. The steering function is, however, revisited in Chapter 11, for much of what the Council does in this regard takes the form of preparing European Council decisions and declarations.

Policy and law maker

The principal responsibility of the Council is to take policy and legislative decisions. As is shown in other chapters, other EU institutions – especially the Commission and the EP – also have such powers, but they are not comparable to those of the Council.

The extent to which the Council must work with, and is dependent upon the cooperation of, the Commission and the EP in respect of policy and decision-making varies between policy areas and according to what type of decisions are being made. In broad terms, the Council has most room for independent manoeuvre when it is not acting within 'the Community method' for then it is not restricted to taking decisions only on the basis of Commission proposals and the EP is largely limited to, at best, consultative and information-sharing roles. Such is the case in respect of the policy areas covered by pillars two and three, both of which have increased enormously in importance in recent years. The increased importance of the CFSP (pillar two) owes much to the creation by the Amsterdam Treaty of the position of High Representative for the CFSP which is based in the Council and also to the development since the late 1990s of the fledgling European Security and Defence Policy (ESDP) to sit alongside the CFSP. An indication of the importance of the CFSP is seen in the fact that in an average year the Council issues around 150 declarations on foreign policy matters and oversees a number of foreign policy actions. The increased importance of the JHA (pillar three) area stems, on the one hand, from the intensified need to combat terrorism that has so dominated the international agenda since the September 11th atrocity and, on the other hand, from issues associated with EU enlargement – notably those related to movement of people.

The Council is least independent under pillar one, especially where legislation is concerned. There are two main reasons for this. First, when making legislation the Council can only act on the basis of proposals that are made to it by the Commission. Second, treaty reforms have resulted in the EP becoming a very important actor in the legislative process. Prior to the TEU the Council was formally the EC's sole legislature, but under the co-decision procedure created by the Maastricht Treaty the EP became co-legislator with the Council in those policy areas where the procedure applies. As a result of treaty reforms, the procedure now applies to most directives – the most important legislative measures (see Chapter 13).

An indication of the Council's legislative role is seen in the volume of legislation it approves, either by itself or jointly with the EP. In 2004 the Council adopted 17 directives, 146 regulations and 40 decisions in its own name, and under co-decision with the EP adopted 31 directives, 40 regulations and 4 decisions (see Table 13.1, p. 288).

It should not be thought that because the TEC states that the Council can only develop legislation on the basis of Commission proposals, the Council is thereby deprived of all powers of initiation. In practice, ways have been found if not to circumvent the Commission entirely, at least to allow the Council a significant policy-initiating role. Article 208 TEC is especially useful: 'The Council may request the Commission to undertake any studies the Council considers desirable for the attainment of the common objectives, and to submit to it any appropriate proposals.' In the view of many observers the use that has been made of this article, and the very specific instructions that have sometimes been issued to the Commission under its aegis, are against its intended spirit. Be that as it may, the political weight of the Council is such that the Commission is bound to pay close attention to the ministers' wishes.

In addition to Article 208, three other factors have been useful in facilitating the Council's policy-initiating role under pillar one.

(1) The adoption by the Council of opinions, resolutions, agreements and recommendations. These are not legal texts but they carry political weight and it is difficult for the Commission to ignore them. Sometimes they are explicitly designed to pressurise the Commission to come up with proposals for legislation.

(2) The increasingly developed Council machinery. There are now many places in the Council's network where ideas can be generated. One of these places is the Council Presidency, which is often to the fore in prompting the Council to consider new policy directions and priorities.

(3) The increasing willingness of the states to found aspects of their cooperation not on EU law but on non-binding agreements and under-standings. Such non-legal arrangements, which do not have to be initiated by the Commission, are increasingly found also in policy spheres where national differences make it very difficult for law to be agreed. Such, for example, is the case with the non monetary dimensions of EMU and also with the Lisbon Process – much of which is built not on legislation but on the much looser open method of coordination (OMC) (see Chapter 15).

Executive

The Commission is the principal EU institution responsible for the implementation of EU policies and laws. It is the Commission that undertakes the limited amount of direct EU-level implementation of pillar one policies, and it is the Commission that liaises with and oversees the work of the agencies in the member states that undertake most 'front-line' pillar one implementation.

However, as was shown in Chapter 9, in undertaking many of its pillar one implementation functions the Commission is obliged to work with and through comitology committees composed of national governmental officials. These committees are not formally part of the Council machinery or system, but they do give the Council indirect executive powers as a result of their membership and more direct powers in that in some circumstances challenges to the Commission by a committee are referred to the ministers for final resolution.

Pillars two and three provide for very direct Council executive activity. Under pillar two, many of the declarations issued by the Council on foreign policy matters are, in effect, executive decisions in that they are operationalising principled positions developed and pronounced earlier by the European Council and by the Council of Ministers itself. CFSP executive activity also involves taking operational decisions in respect of the EU's increasing number of 'special representatives', 'peace missions', and 'observers' in various international trouble spots. Under pillar three, executive activity involves an array of operational management matters, much of it in relation to Schengen (see Chapter 15) and movement of people issues.

Mediator

The Council exercises important responsibilities in the key activities of mediation and consensus building. Of course, as the forum in which the national representatives meet, the Council has always served the function of developing mutual understanding between the member states both on prospective and established and on general and specific EU matters. Moreover, a necessary prerequisite for successful policy development has always been that Council participants display an ability to compromise in negotiations. But as the EU has grown in size, as more difficult policy areas have come onto the agenda, and as political and economic change has broken down some of the pioneering spirit of the early days, so has positive and active mediation come to be ever more necessary: mediation primarily between the different national and ideological interests represented in the Council, but also between the Council and the Commission, the Council and the EP, and the Council and non-institutional interests. The Commission has taken on much of this task, but so too have agencies of the Council itself – most notably the Presidency and the Secretariat.

* * *

The Council has both gained and lost responsibilities over the years. The most obvious gain has been the extended scope of its policy interests. As is noted at several points in this book, the EU's policy remit is now such that there are very few spheres of public policy in which the EU is not involved to at least some extent. This in turn means that there are few policy spheres in which the Council is not seeking to launch or shape initiatives and to take decisions of some sort.

There are two principal respects in which the Council may be said to have lost responsibilities, or at least to have become obliged to share them. First, the European Council – the body that brings together the Heads of Government – has assumed increasingly greater responsibility for taking the final political decisions on such 'history-making' issues as new accessions, institutional reform, the launching of broad policy initiatives, and the strategic direction of external relations (see Chapter 11). Second, as noted above, the legislative powers of the EP have increased, to such an extent that most politically significant Commission proposals for legislation now need its approval as well as that of the Council.

Composition

The ministers

Ministerial meetings are at the apex of the Council machinery. Legally there is only one Council of Ministers, but in practice there are more in the sense that the Council meets in different formations or configurations to deal with different policy areas.

The Council used to meet in over twenty formations but a concern that this was too many led to the European Council deciding at its December 1999 Helsinki meeting to reduce the number in an attempt to improve the consistency and coherence of the Council's work. The number of formations was capped at sixteen. However, it was decided at the June 2002 Seville summit that sixteen was still too high and the number was further reduced to nine (see Table 10.1).

The General Affairs and External Relations Council (GAERC) – known just as the General Affairs Council until it was re-named at the Seville summit – which is composed of Foreign Ministers, has the widest brief. It has always handled foreign policy and external trade and has had a loosely understood responsibility for dealing with horizontal issues relating to policy initiation and coordination and for tackling particularly politically sensitive matters. At Seville, however, both its external and horizontal responsibilities were extended and it was also specifically charged with responsibilities in relation to the operation of the European Council. In the words of the Seville summit's official conclusions, the GAERC would now deal with:

(a) preparation for and follow-up to the European Council (including the coordinating activities necessary to that end), institutional and administrative questions, horizontal dossiers which affect several of the Union's policies and any dossier entrusted to it by the European Council, having regard to EMU operating rules;

(b) the whole of the Union's external action, namely common foreign and security policy, European security and defence policy, foreign trade, development cooperation and humanitarian aid (European Council, 2002b: Annex II: Measures Concerning the Structure and Functioning of the Council).

To enable the GAERC to deal with these two aspects of its work, it was further agreed at Seville that the two aspects would henceforth be dealt with in separate meetings, with separate agendas and possibly on different dates. In practice, the two sets of meetings are almost invariably scheduled to follow on from one another.

The Economic and Finance Council (Ecofin) also has a broad remit in that, especially since the development of EMU, few economic and financial issues are excluded from its portfolio. Its meetings often are preceded by meetings of the Eurogroup, which brings together the Economic or Finance Ministers of the states that are members of the eurozone. Non-Eurogroup ministers have sometimes complained of the Eurogroup trying to set the agenda and frame the decisions of Ecofin on monetary questions – as the Eurogroup certainly did, for example, in 2005 in respect of the changes that were made to the rules of the Stability and Growth Pact.

Beyond the General Affairs and Ecofin Councils, more sectoral matters are dealt with, as can be seen from Table 10.1, by sectoral or technical

Table 10.1 *Council formations since Seville*

General Affairs and External Relations
Economic and Financial Affairs
Cooperation in the Fields of Justice and Home Affairs
Employment, Social Policy, Health and Consumer Affairs
Competitiveness
Transport, Telecommunications and Energy
Agriculture and Fisheries
Environment
Education, Youth and Culture

Source: information from Council homepage on Europa website.

Councils, which are composed of Ministers of Agriculture, Transport, Environment and so on. The reduction in the number of Council formations and the corresponding broadening of the policy portfolios of each formation means that member states often send more than one minister to the same Council meeting.

The national representatives who attend ministerial meetings can differ in terms of their status and/or policy responsibilities. This can inhibit efficient decision-making. The problem arises because the states themselves decide by whom they wish to be represented, and their decisions may vary in one of two ways:

(1) *Level of seniority*. Normally, by prior arrangement, Council meetings are attended by ministers of a similar standing, but circumstances do arise when the various delegations are headed by people at different levels of seniority. This may be because a relevant minister has pressing domestic business or because it is judged that an agenda does not warrant his or her attendance. Occasionally she or he may be 'unavoidably delayed' if a meeting is unwanted and/or has a politically awkward issue on the agenda. Whatever the reason, a reduction in the status and political weight of a delegation may make it difficult for binding decisions to be agreed.

(2) *Sectoral responsibility*. Usually it is obvious which government departments should be represented at Council meetings, but not always. Doubts may arise because agenda items straddle policy divisions, or because member states organise their central government departments in different ways. As a result, it is possible for ministers from rather different national ministries, with different responsibilities and interests, to be present. The difficulties this creates are sometimes compounded, especially in broad policy areas, by the minister attending not feeling able to speak on behalf of other ministers with a direct interest and therefore insisting on the matter being referred back to national capitals.

States are not, therefore, always comparably represented at ministerial meetings. But whether a country's representative is a senior minister, a junior minister or, as occasionally is the case, the Permanent Representative or even a senior diplomat, care is always taken to ensure that national interests are defended. The main way this is done is by the attendance at all meetings of not only the national representative but also small national delegations. These delegations comprise national officials and experts plus, at important meetings or meetings where there is a wide-ranging agenda, junior ministers to assist the senior minister. So, for example, Trade Ministers usually accompany Foreign Ministers to meetings of the GAERC when trade issues are to be considered. Similarly, Budget Ministers – who had their own separate Council pre-Seville – usually accompany Economic and Finance Ministers to the Ecofin Council when the EU's budget is on the agenda. Normally four or five officials and experts support the 'inner table team' (that is, the most senior national representatives who actually sit at the negotiating table), but this number can vary according to the policy area concerned, the importance of the items on the agenda, and the size of the meeting room. The task of the supporting teams is to ensure that the head of the delegation is properly briefed, fully understands the implications of what is being discussed, and does not make negotiating mistakes. Sometimes, when very confidential matters are being discussed or when a meeting is deadlocked, the size of delegations may, on a proposal from the President, be reduced to 'Ministers plus two', 'Ministers plus one' or, exceptionally, 'Ministers and Commission'.

Altogether there are usually between 70 and 80 Council meetings in an average year, with many held towards the end of a country's six-month Presidency. Meetings are normally held in Brussels, but the April, June, and October meetings are held in Luxembourg.

The regularity with which meetings of individual formations of the Council are held reflects their importance in the Council system and the extent to which there is EU policy interest and activity in their area. So, the GAERC Council meets the most frequently with, on average, two meetings per month. The Ecofin, Agriculture and JHA Councils meet most months, whilst the other Councils do not normally meet more than twice during each Council Presidency.

Unless there are particularly difficult matters to be resolved, meetings do not normally last more than a day. A typical meeting begins about 10.00 a.m. and finishes around 6.00 p.m. or 7.00 p.m. Foreign Ministers and Ecofin Ministers are the most likely to meet over two days, and when they do it is common to start with lunch on day 1 and finish around lunchtime on day 2.

Outside the formal Council framework, ministers, particularly Foreign Ministers and Ecofin Ministers, have periodic weekend gatherings, usually in the country of the Presidency, to discuss matters on an informal basis without the pressure of having to take decisions. Informal ministerial gatherings are especially common in the opening weeks of Council Presidencies, when Presidencies are keen to discuss their priorities with colleagues and to gain feedback on what colleagues want.

The Committee of Permanent Representatives

Each of the member states has a national delegation – or Permanent Representation as they are formally known – in Brussels, which acts as a kind of embassy to the EU. The Permanent Representations are headed by a Permanent Representative, who is normally a diplomat of very senior rank, and are staffed, in the case of the larger states, by about fifty officials plus back-up support. About half of the officials are drawn from the diplomatic services of the member states, the others being seconded from appropriate national ministries such as Agriculture, Trade and Finance.

Of the many forums in which governments meet 'in Council' below ministerial level, the most important is the Committee of Permanent Representatives (COREPER). Although no provision was made for such a body under the Treaty of Paris, ministers established a coordinating committee of senior officials as early as 1953, and under the Treaties of Rome the Council was permitted to create a similar committee under its Rules of Procedure. Under Article 4 of the 1965 Merger Treaty these committees were merged and were formally incorporated into the Community system: 'A committee consisting of the Permanent Representatives of the Member States shall be responsible for preparing the work of the Council and for carrying out the tasks assigned to it by the Council.'

There are in fact two COREPERs: COREPER II and COREPER I. Each normally meets once a week. COREPER II is the more senior. At its meetings the member state delegations are headed by the Permanent Representatives and its agendas are the more 'political' of the two COREPERs. It works mainly for the GAERC (and through it for the European Council), the Ecofin, and the JHA Councils. It also often deals with issues for other Council meetings that are particularly sensitive or controversial. COREPER II is assisted in its tasks by the Antici Group, which is made up of senior officials from the Permanent Representations and which, in addition to assisting COREPER II, acts as a key information-gathering and mediating forum between the member states.

At COREPER I meetings, national delegations are headed by the Deputy Permanent Representatives. COREPER I works mainly for the Councils not covered by COREPER II. Because of the nature of the business covered by these Councils, COREPER I tends to deal with more specific and technical policy and legislative matters than does COREPER II.

In addition to preparing Council meetings, COREPER also exercises a number of more general functions on behalf of the ministers in the Council and EU systems. As Bostock (2002: 215) has put it. COREPER 'should be thought of as a co-ordinator of Council business, partly as a fixer and trouble-shooter'. It is able to exercise such roles because, again to quote Bostock (p. 226), it 'is a body composed of officials with the seniority and proximity to ministers to take a politically informed view, but with the diplomat's and bureaucrat's obligation to master the technicalities of the dossier before him'. Such qualities make COREPER members ideal when – as COREPER I members usually do – they represent the Council in conciliation meetings with the EP under the co-decision procedure (on the procedure, see Chapters 12 and 16).

But whilst not querying COREPER's central role in the Council system, it has to be recognised that there has been a marginal decline in COREPER's position and effectiveness in recent years. One reason for this is that, as will be shown below, in the increasingly important and busy foreign and security and economic and finance policy areas, very senior Council committees have come to act almost on a comparable level to COREPER and to have a considerable measure of discretion in how they operate. Another reason is that COREPER has inevitably become less 'clubbable' as the EU has grown in size, which has reduced COREPER's ability to 'get things done' through informal means.

Committees and working groups

A complicated network of committees and working groups assists and prepares the work of the Council of Ministers and COREPER.

Council committees are composed of national officials, are serviced by Council administrators, and have as their task providing advice to the Council and the Commission as appropriate, and in some instances as directed. The most important Council committees are:

- The Special Committee on Agriculture (SCA). Because of the volume and complexity of EU activity in the agricultural sector, most of the 'routine' and 'non political' pre-ministerial-level work on agriculture is undertaken not in COREPER but in the SCA. The SCA, which is staffed by senior officials from the Permanent Representations and national Ministries of Agriculture, usually meets at least weekly.
- The Article 133 Committee deals with trade policy. Any significant action undertaken by the EU in international trade negotiations is preceded by internal coordination via this Committee. It normally meets once a week: the full members – who are very senior officials in national Ministries of Trade or the equivalent – meet monthly, and the deputies – who are middle-ranking officials from the Ministries, or sometimes from the Permanent Representations – meet three times a month. The Committee performs two main functions: it drafts the briefs that the Commission negotiates on behalf of the EU with third countries (the Committee's draft is referred, via COREPER, to the Ministers for their approval); and it acts as a consultative committee to the Council and the Commission – by, for example, indicating to the Commission what it should do when problems arise during the course of a set of trade negotiations.
- The Economic and Financial Committee, which was established at the start of the third stage of EMU in January 1999, focuses on economic

and financial policy, capital movements, and international monetary relations. The members of the Committee – of which there are two from each member state (one from the administration and one from the national Central Bank), plus two from the Commission, and two from the European Central Bank – are senior and influential economic and financial experts: they are, in other words, people who can normally communicate directly with whomsoever they wish, and who are customarily listened to.

- The Political and Security Committee (COPS) is the main Council committee under the EU's CFSP pillar (see Chapter 19 for details). It is composed of senior officials from the Permanent Representations, though sometimes it also meets at the level of Political Directors of the member states.

- Two committees of senior national officials deal with JHA matters: the Article 36 Committee (CATS – *Comité Article Trente Six*) deals with pillar three business whilst the Strategic Committee on Immigration, Frontiers, and Asylum (SCIFA) handles pillar one JHA issues.

- The Standing Committee on Employment is unusual in two respects. First, it is composed not only of governmental representatives but also of sectional interest representatives – the latter being drawn from both sides of industry. Second, the governmental representations are headed by the ministers themselves, or, if they are unable to attend, their personal representatives. The Committee meets twice a year to discuss matters of interest and, where possible, to make recommendations to the Employment, Social Policy, and Health and Consumer Affairs Council. The nature of the membership of the Committee, with ministerial representation, means that when general agreement can be reached, the matter is likely to be taken up by the Council.

In addition to the just listed committees, many other committees also assist the work of the Council. Among them are the Committee on Scientific and Technical Research, the Employment Committee, and the Economic Policy Committee. There also are various groupings that are not always referred to as committees, but sometimes as working parties or simply meetings, that are found especially in emerging policy areas. In addition, there has been an increasing tendency in recent years for *ad hoc* committees of senior national officials – sometimes referred to as 'High-Level Groups' – to be established for the purpose of developing initiatives and policies (though not of course for the purpose of drafting legislation) in new and sensitive areas.

The role of *Council working groups* (also known as working parties) is more specific than that of most of the committees in that their main job is to carry out detailed analyses of formally tabled Commission proposals for legislation. The number of working groups in existence at any one time varies according to the overall nature of the EU's workload and the preferences of the Presidency in office, but in recent years there have usually been over 150. (It is impossible to give a precise figure because many working groups are *ad hoc* in nature.) Members of working groups, of whom there are usually two or three per member state, are almost invariably national officials and experts based either in the Permanent Representations or in appropriate national ministries. Occasionally governments appoint non-civil servants to a working group delegation when highly technical or complex issues are under consideration.

Working groups meet as and when required, usually with an interval of at least three weeks between meetings so as to allow the Council's Secretariat time to circulate minutes and agendas – in all of the languages of the member states. For permanent working groups with a heavy workload meetings may be regular, whilst for others, where nothing much comes up within their terms of reference, there may be very few meetings. Up to fifteen or so different working groups are in session in Brussels on most working days. On completion of their analyses of Commission proposals, working groups report to COREPER or to one of the Council's senior committees.

The General Secretariat

The main administrative support for the work of the Council is provided by the General Secretariat. This is headed by the Council's Secretary-General, who also acts as the EU's High Representative for the Common Foreign and Security Policy. The day-to-day responsibility for overseeing the running of the Secretariat falls to the Deputy Secretary-General.

The Secretariat has a staff of just over 2500, most of whom are located in Directorates General dealing with different policy areas. Of the 2500, around 300 are at diplomatic level. The Secretariat's base, which also houses Council meetings, is located near to the main Commission and EP buildings in Brussels.

The Secretariat's main responsibility is to service the Council machinery – from ministerial to working group levels. This involves activities such as preparing draft agendas, keeping records, providing legal advice, processing and circulating decisions and documentation, translating, and generally monitoring policy developments so as to provide an element of continuity and coordination in Council proceedings. This last task includes seeking to ensure a smooth transition between Presidencies by performing a liaising role with officials from the preceding, the incumbent and the incoming Presidential states.

In exercising many of its responsibilities, the Secretariat works closely with representatives from the member state of the President-in-office (see below). This is essential because key decisions about such matters as priorities, meetings and agendas are primarily in the hands of the Presidency. Before all Council meetings at all levels Secretariat officials give the Presidency a full briefing about subject content, the current state of play on the agenda items, and possible tactics – 'the Poles are isolated', 'there is strong resistance to this in Spain and Portugal, so caution is advised', 'a possible vote has been signalled in the agenda papers and, if taken, will find the necessary majority', and so on.

The extent to which Presidencies rely on the Secretariat varies considerably, with smaller countries, because of their more limited administrative resources, tending to be most reliant. Even the larger countries, however, have much to gain by making use of the Secretariat's resources and its knowledge of what approaches are most likely to be effective in particular situations.

The main reason why Presidencies are sometimes a little reluctant to make too much use of the Secretariat is that there is a natural tendency for them to rely heavily on their own national officials as they seek to achieve a successful six-month period of office by getting measures through. It is largely for this reason that the staff of a state's Permanent Representation increases in size during a Presidential tenureship. Something approaching a dual servicing of the Presidency is apparent in the way at Council meetings, at all levels, the President sits with officials from the General Secretariat on one side and national advisers on the other.

The Operation of the Council

The Council Presidency

The Council Presidency rotates between the states on a six-monthly basis: January until June, July until December. The rotation used to be in alphabetical order, but is now arranged in groupings of three states. Table 10.2 lists the Presidency rotation from 2007–20.

The main tasks of the Presidency are as follows.

(1) Arranging (in close association with the General Secretariat) and chairing most Council meetings from ministerial level downwards. Prior to the Seville summit the Presidency chaired virtually all Council meetings apart from a few committees and working groups that have a permanent chairman. However, as part of the Seville summit's streamlining of the Council structures it was decided that where it was clear that dossiers

Table 10.2   *Rotation of Council Presidencies 2007–20*

Germany	Jan–June	2007
Portugal	July–Dec	2007
Slovenia	Jan–June	2008
France	July–Dec	2008
Czech Republic	Jan–June	2009
Sweden	July–Dec	2009
Spain	Jan–June	2010
Belgium	July–Dec	2010
Hungary	Jan–June	2011
Poland	July–Dec	2011
Denmark	Jan–June	2012
Cyprus	July–Dec	2012
Ireland	Jan–June	2013
Lithuania	July–Dec	2013
Greece	Jan–June	2014
Italy	July–Dec	2014
Latvia	Jan–June	2015
Luxembourg	July–Dec	2015
Netherlands	Jan–June	2016
Slovakia	July–Dec	2016
Malta	Jan–June	2017
UK	July–Dec	2017
Estonia	Jan–June	2018
Bulgaria	July–Dec	2018
Austria	Jan–June	2019
Romania	July–Dec	2019
Finland	Jan–June	2020

Source: information from Council homepage on Europa website.

would be dealt with mainly during the next Presidency or where issues would be dealt with at ministerial level during the next Presidency, then some of the Council's sub-ministerial meetings – though not COREPER – should be chaired by the country holding the next Presidency. In the same spirit of trying to ensure that a single member state assumes responsibility for taking issues through the Council machinery, it was decided in the specific case of the examination of the EU's annual budget that all meetings would be chaired by the country holding the Presidency during the second six-month period of the year.

In an unprecedented move in 2002, Denmark, which held the Presidency in the second half of the year, did not chair meetings dealing with the ESDP because of domestic sensitivities about the policy area. By agreement, Greece, which occupied the Presidency in the first half of 2003, chaired ESDP meetings in place of Denmark.

As the chair of meetings, the Presidency has considerable – though not complete – control over how often Council bodies meet, over agendas, and over what happens during the course of meetings.

(2) Launching and building a consensus for initiatives. A successful Presidency is normally regarded as one that gets things done. This can usually only be achieved by extensive negotiating, persuading, manoeuvring, cajoling, mediating and bargaining with and between the member states, and with the Commission and the EP.

(3) Ensuring some continuity and consistency of policy development. An important mechanism used for this purpose has long been the troika, made up of the preceding, current and succeeding Presidencies. However, the Seville summit decided that more weight should be given to an annual operating programme of Council activities that would be proposed by the two next presidencies and finalised by the GAERC every December. The programme would be set within the framework of three-year multi-annual strategic programmes adopted by the European Council and would include the political priorities for the year and a list of indicative agendas for the various formation of the Council.

(4) Representing the Council in dealings with outside bodies. This task is exercised most frequently with regard to other EU institutions (such as regular appearances before the EP), and with non-member countries in connection with external EU policies, especially the CFSP.

Holding the Presidency has advantages and disadvantages. One advantage is the prestige and status that is associated with the office: during the six-month term of office the Presidential state is at the very heart of EU affairs; its ministers – especially its Head of Government and its Foreign Minister – meet with prominent international statesmen and dignitaries on behalf of the EU; and media focus and interest is considerable. Another advantage is that during its term of office a Presidency can do more than it can as an ordinary member state to help shape and set the pace of EU policy priorities. The extent of the potential of the Presidency in terms of policy development should not, however, be exaggerated. Though Presidencies set out their priorities when they enter office, they do not start with a clean sheet but have to deal with uncompleted business from previous Presidencies and with rolling work programmes. Furthermore, six months is just not long enough for the full working through of policy initiatives – especially if legislation is required.

As for the disadvantages of holding the Presidency, one is the heavy administrative burdens that are attached to the job – burdens that some of the smaller states find difficult to carry. A second disadvantage is that the Presidency is expected to adopt a broadly consensual position on disputed issues, which can limit its ability to defend its own national interests. Such was the case in the first half of 1999, when the German Presidency felt inhibited about over-pressing its dissatisfaction with the deal that emerged on the financial perspective which set the framework for EU budgetary income and expenditure over the 2000–6 period. And a third disadvantage is the blow to esteem and standing that is incurred when a state is judged to have run a poor Presidency. For example, French prestige was certainly undermined by the many criticisms made of its Presidency in the second half of 2000. Amongst the criticisms were that the Presidency was too heavy handed, was weakened and complicated by the Presidential–Governmental cohabitation arrangements, and departed from neutrality by favouring the institutional interests of the EU's large member states in the Intergovernmental Conference that produced the Nice Treaty (Ross, 2001).

The hierarchical structure

As indicated above, a hierarchy exists in the Council. It consists of: ministers – with the GAERC and to an extent also the Ecofin Council informally recognised as being the most senior Councils; COREPER and other specialised high level committees such as the SCA and COPS; and the working groups. The European Council is also sometimes thought of as being part of this hierarchy, but in fact it is not properly part of the Council system, even though it does have the political capability of issuing what amount to instructions to the ministers.

The Council's hierarchical structure is neither tight nor rigidly applied. The GAERC's seniority over the sectoral Councils is, for example, even post-Seville, only partially developed, whilst important committees and working groups can sometimes communicate directly with ministers. Nonetheless, the hierarchy does, for the most part, work. This is best illustrated by looking at the Council's procedures for dealing with a Commission proposal for Council, or EP and Council, legislation.

The *first stage* is initial examination of the Commission's text. This is normally undertaken by a working group or, if it is of very broad application, several working groups. If no appropriate permanent working group exists, an *ad hoc* one is established.

As can be seen from Table 10.3, several factors can affect the progress of the proposal. A factor that has greatly increased in importance over the years is whether the proposal is subject to qualified majority voting

Table 10.3 *Principal factors determining the progress of a proposal through the Council machinery*

- The urgency of the proposal
- The controversiality of the proposal and support/opposition amongst the states
- The extent to which the Commission has tailored its text to accommodate national objections/reservations voiced at the pre-proposal stage
- The complexity of the proposal's provisions
- The ability of the Commission to allay doubts by the way it gives clarifications and answers questions
- The judgements made by the Commission on whether, or when, it should accept modifications to its proposals
- The competence of the Presidency
- The agility and flexibility of the participants to devise (usually through the Presidency and the Commission) and accept compromise formulae
- The availability of, and willingness of the states to use, majority voting

(QMV) rules (see pp. 211–12) when it appears before the ministers (formal votes are not taken below ministerial level). If it is not, and unanimity is required, then working group deliberations may take as long as is necessary to reach an agreement – which can mean months or even years. If it is, then delegations that find themselves isolated in the working group are obliged to anticipate the possibility of their country being outvoted when the ministers consider the proposal, and therefore engage in damage limitation. This usually involves adopting some combination of three strategies. First, if the proposal is judged to be important to national interests, then this is stressed during the working group's deliberations, in the hope that other delegations will take a sympathetic view and will either make concessions or not seek to press ahead too fast. Second, if the proposal is judged to be not too damaging or unacceptable, then attempts will be made to amend it, but it is unlikely that too much of a fuss will be made. Third, an attempt may be made to 'do a deal' or 'come to an understanding' with other delegations so that a blocking minority of states is created.

The General Secretariat of the Council is always pressing for progress and tries to ensure that a working group does not need to meet more than three times to discuss any one proposal. The first working group meeting normally consists of a general discussion of key points. Subsequent meetings are then taken up with line-by-line examination of the Commission's text. If all goes well, a document is eventually produced indicating points of agreement and disagreement, and quite possibly having attached to it reservations that states have entered to indicate that they are not yet in a position formally to commit themselves to the text or a part of it. (States may enter reservations at any stage of the Council process. These can vary from an indication that a particular clause of a draft text is not yet in an acceptable form, to a general withholding of approval until the text has been cleared by the appropriate national authorities.)

The *second stage* is the reference of the working group's document to COREPER, perhaps via one of the Council's high level committees. Placed between the working groups and the ministers, COREPER acts as a sort of filtering agency for ministerial meetings. It attempts to clear as much of the ground as possible to ensure that only the most difficult and sensitive of matters detain the ministers in discussion. So when the conditions for the adoption of a measure have been met in a working group, COREPER is likely to confirm the group's opinion and advance it to the ministers for formal enactment. If, however, agreement has not been reached by a working group, COREPER can do one of three things: try itself to resolve the issue (which its greater political status might permit); refer it back to the working group, perhaps with accompanying indications of where an agreement might be found; or pass it upwards to the ministers.

Most matters requiring a Council decision are resolved at working group or COREPER level. Hayes-Renshaw and Wallace (2006: 53) estimate that on average about 70 per cent of Council business is agreed at working group level and a further 15–20 per cent at COREPER level. Kuasmanen (1998), an official in the General Secretariat of the Council, gives similar figures, estimating that between 75–85 per cent of matters are resolved at committee and working group level, most of the remaining matters at COREPER level, leaving only about 5 per cent of issues requiring substantial discussion and decision at ministerial level.

Whatever progress proposals have made at working group and COR-EPER levels, formal adoption is only possible at ministerial level. Ministerial meetings thus constitute *the third and final stage* of the Council's procedure. Items on ministerial meeting agendas are grouped under two headings: 'A points' and 'B points'. Matters that have been agreed at COREPER level, and on which it is thought Council approval will be given without discussion, are listed as 'A points'. These can cover a range of matters – from routine 'administrative' decisions to controversial new legislation that was agreed in principle at a previous ministerial meeting but upon which a formal decision was delayed pending final clarification or tidying up. 'A points' do not necessarily fall within the policy competence of the particular Council that is meeting, but may have been placed on the agenda because the appropriate formation of the Council is not due to meet for some time. Ministers retain the right to raise objections to 'A points', and if any do so the proposal may have to be withdrawn and referred back to COREPER. Normally, however, 'A points' are quickly approved without debate. Such is the thoroughness of the Council system that ministers can assume they have been thoroughly checked in both Brussels and national capitals to ensure they are politically acceptable, legally sound, and not subject to scrutiny reservations. Ministers then proceed to consider 'B points', which may include items left over from previous meetings, matters that have not been possible to resolve at COREPER or working group levels, or proposals that COREPER judges to be politically sensitive and hence requiring political decisions. All 'B points' will have been extensively discussed by national officials at lower Council levels, and on most of them a formula for an agreement will have been prepared for the ministers to consider. (There is a detailed analysis of the nature of 'A' and 'B' points and how they are managed by the Council in Van Schendelen, 1996.)

Ministerial meetings can have very wide and mixed agendas. Four observations are particularly worth making about the sorts of agenda items that arise.

- There are variations regarding what ministers are expected to do. The range of possibilities includes the taking of final decisions, the adoption of common positions, the approval of negotiating mandates for the Commission, the resolution of problems that have caused difficulties at lower levels of the Council hierarchy, and – simply – the noting of progress reports.
- Some items concern very general policy matters, whilst others are highly specialised and technical in nature.
- Most items fall within the sectoral competence of the ministers who have been convened, but a few do not. 'Extra sectoral' items are usually placed on agendas when everything has been agreed, a decision needs to be taken, and the relevant sectoral Council is not scheduled to meet in the immediate future.
- As well as policy issues, agenda items can also include administrative matters, such as appointments to advisory committees.

The position of the GAERC rather suggests that there would, in certain circumstances – such as when a policy matter cuts across sectoral divisions, or when sectoral Councils cannot resolve key issues – be a fourth decision-making stage in the Council involving the Foreign Ministers. In practice, recourse to such a stage is not common, although on very sensitive and important matters it can sometimes occur – as for example in 2005 when there were several rounds of negotiations on the 2007–13 financial perspective in the GAERC.

One problem for the GAERC is that, even post-Seville, it has no legal seniority over other Councils. Such seniority as it does have stems rather from a not altogether clear and informal understanding that the GAERC has a special responsibility for dealing with disputes that cannot be resolved by the sectoral Councils, for tackling politically sensitive matters, and for acting as a general coordinating body at ministerial level. A second problem for the GAERC is that it has a lot on its plate dealing with its own specific responsibilities and just cannot devote much time and attention to issues falling outside its spheres of competence and expertise. And a third problem is that Foreign Ministers are often not able, or willing, to act any more decisively in breaking a deadlock than is a divided sectoral Council. Members of the GAERC may, indeed, have no greater seniority in rank, and may even be junior, to their national colleagues in, say, the Ecofin or Agriculture Councils. Moreover, sectoral Councils are often not willing to refer their disputes 'upwards'. This is partly because Ministers of Environment, Employment, Finance and so on do, after all, have as much authority to make EU law as do Foreign Ministers. It is partly also because referring a dispute to the Foreign Ministers means the sectoral ministers lose control of the outcome. As Van Schendelen has noted with regard to the Agriculture Council, sectoral ministers want to find their own solutions rather than refer dossiers to the 'cross-sectoral' GAERC 'where agricultural interests might be traded off against quite different ones' (Van Schendelen, 1996: 54). All formations of the Council thus normally prefer, and are likely to continue to prefer, to take their own decisions – unless something that is likely to be very unpopular can be passed on elsewhere.

This absence of clear Council leadership and of an authoritative coordinating mechanism has played a part in encouraging the European Council to assume responsibilities in relation to the Council of Ministers, even though it is not formally part of the Council hierarchy. Increasingly the Heads of Government at their meetings have gone beyond issuing general guidelines to the Council of Ministers, which was intended to be the normal limit of European Council–Council of Ministers relationships when the former was established in 1974. Summits have sometimes been obliged to try to resolve thorny issues that have been referred to them by the Council of Ministers, and have also had to seek to ensure that there is some overall policy direction and coherence in the work of the Council of Ministers. The European Council can only go so far, however, in performing such problem-solving, leadership, and coordinating roles: partly because of the infrequency of its meetings; partly because some national leaders prefer to avoid getting too involved in detailed policy discussions; but, above all, because the Heads of Government are subject to the same national and political divisions as the ministers.

Decision-making procedures

Taking decisions

The treaties provide for three basic ways in which the Council can take decisions: by unanimity, by qualified majority vote, or by simple majority vote.

- *Unanimity* used to be the normal requirement when a new policy was being initiated or an existing policy framework was being modified or further developed. However, treaty reforms since the SEA have greatly reduced the circumstances in which a unanimity requirement applies and it is now largely confined to policy direction decisions under the CFSP and Police and Judicial Cooperation pillars of the EU and to such sensitive and particularly important matters under the EC pillar as 'constitutional' and financial issues. (See Part 2 and Chapter 16 for details.) Unanimity is also required when the Council wishes to amend a Commission proposal against the Commission's wishes.

  Abstentions do not constitute an impediment to the adoption of Council decisions that require unanimity. Furthermore, the Amsterdam Treaty provided for 'constructive abstentionism' under the CFSP pillar, whereby an abstaining state 'shall not be obliged to apply the decision, but shall accept that the decision commits the Union' (Article 23 TEU). If constructive abstentions represent more than one-third of the weighted votes, decisions cannot be adopted.

- *Qualified majority voting* now applies to most types of decision where legislation is being made under the EC pillar, to some types of decision under the CFSP pillar, and to a few types of decision under the Police and Judicial Cooperation pillar.

  Since 1 November 2004, the rules for QMV that were incorporated into the Treaty of Nice as part of the EU's preparations for enlargement have applied. These rules were described in Chapter 6 and the voting weights were set out in Table 6.1 (pp. 108–9). (For a detailed description and analysis of the implications of Nice for voting weights and QMV in the Council, see Galloway, 2001, Phinnemore, 2004.) Key features of the QMV arrangement post-Nice as compared with pre-Nice include:

  - An increase in the differentials of the voting weights of member states, with the position of larger states enhanced a little.
  - A small increase in the threshold for a qualified majority – from the pre-Nice 71.3 per cent to a possible (the precise figure depending on the course of the enlargement process) 73.4 per cent. In terms of numbers of votes, for a qualified majority to exist in the EU-25, 232 votes out of the total 321 votes must be cast in favour; the blocking

threshold is thus 90 votes. After Bulgaria and Romania become EU members, 255 votes will be necessary for a qualified majority, out of the total of 345 votes; 91 votes will constitute a blocking minority.
- The creation of two additional criteria when qualified majorities exist, which have the effect of creating the need for virtually a triple majority. The first of these additional criteria requires that QMV decisions on Commission proposals must be supported by at least a majority of states, and on Council proposals must be supported by at least two-thirds of states. This first stipulation is helpful to small member states. The second additional criterion requires that a qualified majority must comprise at least 62 per cent of the Union's total population when verification to this effect is requested by a member state. This second stipulation assists the position of large member states.

Under the Constitutional Treaty's provisions, the system of voting weights would have been abolished, leaving just the double majority system. The size of the majorities would rise, however, to 55 per cent of the member states (72 per cent where proposals did not come either from the Commission or the new Foreign Minister) and 65 per cent of the EU's population. A majority would have to include at least fifteen states whilst a blocking minority would have to include at least four.

- *Simple majority voting,* in which all states have one vote each, is used mainly for procedural purposes and, since February 1994, for anti-dumping and anti-subsidy tariffs within the context of the Common Commercial Policy (CCP).

Until the mid-1980s, proposals were not usually pushed to a vote in the Council when disagreements between the states existed, even when majority voting was permissible under the treaties. A major reason for this was the so-called Luxembourg Compromise of 1966, which was a political deal between the member states which was interpreted as meaning that, whatever the treaties might say about voting arrangements, any state had the right to exercise a veto on questions that affected its vital national interests – and states themselves determined when such interests were at stake. (For a fuller account of the Luxembourg Compromise and its consequences, see the fifth edition of this book, and Teasdale 1995). However, though majority voting has now come to be used and the Luxembourg Compromise is all but dead, the member states still prefer to take decisions by unanimity. They do so because there are strong positive reasons for acting on the basis of unanimity if at all possible, with the functioning and development of the EU likely to be enhanced if policy-making processes are consensual rather than conflictual. Thus, national authorities are unlikely to undertake the necessary task of transposing EU directives into national law with much enthusiasm if the directives are perceived as domestically damaging, or if they are imposed on a dissatisfied state following a majority vote in the Council. Nor is it likely that national bureaucracies will be helpful about implementing unwanted legislation. More generally, the over-use of majority voting on important and sensitive matters could well create grievances that could have disruptive implications right across the EU's policy spectrum.

For good reasons, as well as perhaps some bad, decision-making in the Council thus usually proceeds on the understanding that difficult and controversial decisions are not imposed on dissenting states without full consideration being given to the reasons for their opposition. When it is clear that a state or states have serious difficulties with a proposal, they are normally allowed time. They may well be put on the defensive, asked fully to explain their position, pressed to give way or at least to compromise, but the possibility of resolving an impasse by a vote is not the first port of call. Usually the item is held over for a further meeting, with the hope that in the meantime informal meetings or perhaps COREPER will find the basis for a solution. All states, and not just the foremost advocates of retention of the veto – initially France and since the early 1980s the UK – accept that this is the only way Council business can be done without risking major divisions.

But though there are good reasons for preferring consensus, it came to be accepted from the early 1980s that the unanimity principle could not be applied too universally or too rigidly. It was recognised that QMV would need to be increasingly used, and in practice it has been so. Several interrelated factors explain this increased use of majority voting.

- Attitudes have changed. There has been an increasing recognition, even amongst the most rigid defenders of national rights and interests, that decision-making by unanimity is a recipe not only for procrastination and delay, but often for unsatisfactory, or even no, decision-making. The situation whereby consensus remains the rule even on issues where countries would not object too strongly to being voted down, has come to be seen as unsustainable in the face of the manifest need for the EU to become efficient and dynamic in order, for example, to assist its industries to compete successfully on world markets.
- The 'legitimacy' and 'mystique' of the Luxembourg Compromise were dealt a severe blow in May 1982 when, for the first time, an attempt to invoke the Compromise was over-ridden. The occasion was an attempt by the British government to veto the annual agricultural prices settlement by proclaiming a vital national interest. The other states did not believe that such an interest was at stake and took the view that

Britain was attempting to use agricultural prices to force a more favourable outcome on concurrent negotiations over UK budgetary contributions.

- By increasing the number and variety of interests and views represented in the Council, EU enlargements have made unanimity all the more difficult to achieve and hence have increased the necessity for majority voting.
- All treaties since the SEA have extended the number of policy areas in which majority voting is constitutionally permissible (see Part 2 for details). Moreover, the discussions that have accompanied treaty reforms have been based on the assumption that the new voting provisions would be used.
- In July 1987, the General Affairs Council, in accordance with an agreement it had reached in December 1986, formally amended the Council's Rules of Procedure. Among the changes was a relaxation of the circumstances by which votes could be initiated: whereas previously only the President could call for a vote, since the amended Rules came into effect it has been the case that any national representative and the Commission also have the right, and a vote must be taken if a simple majority agrees.

Figures on the use of QMV are, in fact, lower than might be supposed, with analyses indicating that votes take place on only between 10 and 15 per cent of all Council decisions where QMV is possible. Wessels (2001: 206–9), for example, puts the figure at 10 per cent, whilst a director in the Council's Legal Service says that between 1999 and 2003 85 per cent of the decisions that could have been taken by QMV were taken by unanimity (Jaqué, 2004: 316). Most votes are on agriculture and fisheries and internal market issues.

Such low figures for the use of votes, which are confirmed by other observers – see, for example, Hayes-Renshaw and Wallace, 2006: Chapter 10; Mattila and Lane, 2001 – do not, however, provide a full picture of the impact of QMV on voting behaviour in the Council. This is because what really amounts to majority voting sometimes occurs without a formal vote being taken. This can take the form of a state that is opposed to a proposal that otherwise commands general support preferring to try to extract concessions through negotiation – perhaps at working group or COREPER stage – rather than run the risk of pressing for a vote and then finding itself outvoted. Or it can take the form of the Presidency announcing that 'we appear to have the necessary majority here', and this being left unchallenged by a dissenting state and therefore not formally voted on: unless an important point of principle or a damaging political consequence is at stake, a country in a minority may prefer not to create too much of a fuss.

But whatever the 'real' figures on the use of QMV may be, there can be no doubt that the impact of QMV has increased over the years and that its existence does very much affect the process of negotiations. When it is available it not only permits votes to be taken but it also forces states that are dissatisfied with a proposal to look for deals with other states. Where, by contrast, unanimity applies, states can be encouraged to grandstand and to look for 'compensations' in areas that have little to do with the proposal in hand.

That all said, the impact of QMV should not be overstated. Consensual decision-making remains and can be expected to remain a key feature of Council processes. Quite apart from the fact that unanimity is still required by the treaties in some important areas, there continues to be a strong preference for trying to reach general agreements where 'important', 'sensitive', and 'political' matters, as opposed to 'technical' matters, are being considered. This may involve delay, but the duty of the national representatives at all Council levels is not only to reach decisions but also to defend national interests.

The conduct of meetings

The formal processes by which Council meetings are conducted and business is transacted are broadly similar at ministerial, COREPER, and working group levels.

Meetings are held in large rooms, with national delegations sitting together. At one end or one side of the meeting table sits the Presidency – whose delegation is led by the most senior figure present from the country currently holding the Presidency; at the other end or side sit the Commission representatives; and ranged between the Presidency and the Commission are the representatives of the member states – with the delegation from the country holding the Presidency sitting to the right of, but separate from, the President.

As indicated earlier, the Presidency plays a key role in fixing the agenda of Council meetings, both in terms of content and the order in which items are considered. The room for manoeuvre available to the Presidency should not, however, be exaggerated, for quite apart from time constraints there are several other factors that serve to limit options and actions. For example, it is difficult to exclude from the agenda of Council meetings items that are clearly of central interest or need resolution; the development of rolling programmes means that much of the agenda of many meetings is largely fixed; and anyone in a COREPER or a ministerial meeting can insist that a matter is discussed provided the required notice is given. Therefore, a Presidency cannot afford to be too ambitious or the six-month tenureship will probably come to be seen as a failure. With this in mind, the normal pattern for an incoming President of a reasonably important sectoral Council is to take the view that of, say, eight proposed directives in his or her policy area, he or she will try to get four particular ones through. This is then reflected in the organisation of Council business, so that by the end of the Presidency two may have been adopted by the Council while another two may be at an advanced stage.

At ministerial level, Council meetings can often appear to be chaotic affairs: not counting interpreters there can be up to 150 people in the room – with each national delegation represented by a team of perhaps four or five at any one time, the Commission by a similar number, and the Presidency being made up of both General Secretariat and national officials; participants frequently change – with ministers often arriving late or leaving early, and officials coming and going in relation to items on the agenda; ministers are constantly being briefed by officials as new points are raised; there are huddles of delegations during breaks; requests for adjournments and postponements are made to enable further information to be sought and more consideration to be given; and communications may be made with national capitals for clarifications or even, occasionally, for authorisation to adopt revised negotiating positions. Not surprisingly, delegations which are headed by ministers with domestic political weight, which are well-versed in EU ways, which have mastered the intricacies of the issues under consideration, and which can think quickly on their feet, are particularly well-placed to exercise influence.

A device that used to be employed at Council meetings, especially when negotiations were making little progress, was the *tour de table* procedure, whereby the President invited each delegation to give a summary of its thinking on the matter under consideration. This ensured that the discussion was not totally dominated by a few, and more importantly it allowed the position of each member state to be established. It could thus help to reveal possible grounds for agreement and provide useful guidance to the President as to whether a compromise was possible or whether an attempt should be made to proceed to a decision. Enlargement has made the use of this procedure largely impractical because it is so time consuming. Presidencies now tend to be very cautious about using the procedure unless there seems to be no other way forward, and even then only representatives from states opposed to a proposal are encouraged to speak. It is usually better to use another approach, such as inviting the Commission to amend its proposal, or seeking to isolate the most 'hard-line' state in the hope that it will back down.

This last point highlights how important the Presidency can be, not only at the agenda-setting stage but also during meetings themselves. An astute and sensitive chairman is often able to judge when a delegation that is causing difficulties is not terribly serious: when, perhaps, it is being awkward for domestic political reasons and will not ultimately stand in the way of a decision being made. A poor chairman, on the other hand, may allow a proposal to drag on, or may rush it to such an extent that a state which, given time, would have agreed to a compromise may feel obliged to dig in its heels.

Informal processes and relationships

A final feature of Council decision-making procedures that must be noted is the extremely important role of informal processes and relationships. Three examples demonstrate this. First, many understandings and agreements are reached at the lunches that are very much a part of ministerial meetings. These lunches are attended only by ministers and a minimal number of translators (many ministers can converse directly with one another, usually in French or English).

Second, when difficulties arise in ministerial negotiations a good chairman will make advantageous use of scheduled or requested breaks in proceedings to explore possibilities for a settlement. This may involve holding off-the-record discussions with a delegation that is holding up an agreement, or it may take the form of a *tour* of key delegations – perhaps in the company of the relevant Commissioner and a couple of officials – to ascertain 'real' views and fall-back positions.

Third, many of the national officials based in Brussels come to know their counterparts in other Permanent Representations extremely well: better, sometimes, than their colleagues in their own national capitals or Permanent Representations. This enables them to judge when a country is posturing and when it is serious, and when and how a deal may be possible. A sort of code language may even be used between officials to signal their position on proposals. So if, for example, a national representative states that 'this is very important for my minister', or 'my minister is very strongly pressurised on this', the other participants recognise that a signal is being given that further deliberations are necessary at their level if more serious difficulties are to be avoided when the ministers gather.

Concluding Remarks

In recent years a number of important reforms have been made to the structure and functioning of the Council. These have sought to deal with the perceived problems of power being too dispersed, insufficient cohesion between and sometimes within sectoral Councils, and decision-making processes still often being rather cumbersome and slow. The most important of the changes have been the increased use of majority voting, the enhancement of the role of the Presidency, the increased cooperation that occurs between Presidencies, and the reduction in the number of Council formations.

Arguably the reforms have still not gone far enough. Many have argued that what is most needed to deal with at least some of the weaknesses is the creation of a 'super' Council of European Ministers, armed with the authority to impose an overall policy pattern on subsidiary sectoral Councils. However, though such a Council may indeed be useful for identifying priorities and knocking a few heads together, it would be unwise to hold out too many hopes for it, even if the practical obstacles to its establishment could be overcome. For, as the next chapter shows in respect of the operation of the European Council, the dream of authoritative national leaders rationally formulating policy frameworks in the 'EU interest' just does not accord with political realities.

Chapter 11

The European Council

Origins and Development

Although no provision was made in the Founding Treaties for summit meetings of Heads of Government, a few such gatherings did occur in the 1960s and early 1970s. At the Paris summit in 1974 it was decided to institutionalise these meetings with the establishment of what soon became known as the European Council.

The main reason for the creation of the European Council was a growing feeling that the Community was failing to respond adequately or quickly enough to new and increasingly difficult challenges. Neither the Commission, whose position had been weakened by the intergovernmental emphasis on decision-making that was signalled by the Luxembourg Compromise, nor the Council of Ministers, which was handicapped both by sectoralism and by its practice of proceeding only on the basis of unanimity, were providing the necessary leadership. A new focus of authority was seen as being necessary in order to make the Community more effective, both domestically and internationally. What was needed, argued France's President Giscard d'Estaing, who with West Germany's Chancellor Schmidt was instrumental in establishing the European Council, was a body that would bring the Heads of Government together on a relatively informal basis to exchange ideas, further mutual understanding at the highest political level, give direction to policy development, and perhaps sometimes break deadlocks and clear logjams. It was not anticipated that the leaders would concern themselves with the details of policy.

The formal creation of the European Council was very simple: a few paragraphs were issued as part of the Paris communiqué. The key paragraphs were as follows:

Recognising the need for an overall approach to the internal problems involved in achieving European unity and the external problems facing Europe, the Heads of Government consider it essential to ensure progress and overall consistency in the activities of the Communities and in the work on political cooperation.

The Heads of Government have therefore decided to meet, accompanied by the Ministers of Foreign Affairs, three times a year and, whenever necessary, in the Council of the Communities and in the context of political cooperation.

The administrative secretariat will be provided for in an appropriate manner with due regard for existing practices and procedures. (The full communiqué is reproduced in Harryvan and van der Harst, 1997: 181–3.)

Two points about this communiqué are particularly worth emphasising. First, it was vague and left important questions unanswered, especially regarding the precise role and functioning of the European Council. Second, it had no constitutional or legal standing. It announced a political agreement between the national leaders but it did not formally or legally integrate the European Council into the Community framework.

In a somewhat similar fashion to the Luxembourg Compromise and European Political Cooperation (EPC), the European Council was thus to be part of the 'unofficial' approach to integration rather than the 'official' treaty-based approach. Over the years, however, there has been something of a 'constitutionalisation' of the position and role of the European Council, albeit on a tentative and cautious basis. This has occurred in five steps. First, declarations by the European Council itself in the late 1970s and early 1980s – notably London (1977) and Stuttgart (1983) – did something, though not a great deal, to clarify its role. Second, in 1986 the European Council was given legal recognition for the first time via the SEA, though only in two short paragraphs that were confined to clarifying membership and reducing the minimum number of meetings per year from three to two. The paragraphs were not incorporated into the Community Treaties. Third, the Maastricht Treaty, expanding on the SEA, contained three 'sets of references' to the European Council: it was assigned responsibility for identifying the general direction of the EU's development; it was given certain duties and decision-making powers in respect of EMU; and it was provided with important powers in the CFSP pillar. Fourth, the Amsterdam Treaty confirmed the Maastricht provisions in respect of its general directional role and with regard to EMU, and greatly strengthened the European Council's position in respect of the CFSP. Fifth, the Nice Treaty gave *de jure* status to the *de facto* situation wherein the European Council nominates the person who is to be put forward for the position of President of the Commission.

This increasing legal recognition of the European Council has, however, stopped short of establishing it as a fully-fledged EU institution. It is omitted from the list of such institutions in Article 5 of the TEU, where only the EP, the Council of Ministers, the Commission, the ECJ, and the Court of Auditors appear. The Constitutional Treaty rectifies this situation, but the difficulties of ratifying the CT mean this legal consolidation of the European Council will, at best, be delayed for some time.

The European Council's treaty powers are thus presently as follows:

- The Common Provisions of the TEU specify the following under Article 4:

  The European Council shall provide the Union with the necessary impetus for its development and shall define the general political guidelines thereof.

  The European Council shall bring together the Heads of State or of Government of the Member States and the President of the Commission. They shall be assisted by the Ministers for Foreign Affairs of the Member States and by a Member of the Commission. The European Council shall meet at least twice a year, under the chairmanship of the Head of State or of Government of the Member State which holds the Presidency of the Council.

  The European Council shall submit to the European Parliament a report after each of its meetings and a yearly written report on the progress achieved by the Union.

The general role of the European Council in the EU is thus laid down in a legal document. It is so, however, in only vague terms and – because the Common Provisions are not incorporated into the Community Treaties – on such a legal basis that whatever interpretation the European Council gives to its role, or indeed to any of the other provisions of Article 4, it cannot be challenged in the Court of Justice.

- In Title VII of the TEC, which deals with Economic and Monetary Policy, there are two references to the European Council: under Article 99 it is given an important role in determining 'the broad guidelines of the economic policies of the Member States and of the Community'; and under Article 113 it is required to be presented with the annual report of the European Central Bank. Under Title VII the Heads of Government are also mentioned in a capacity separate from their membership of the European Council. In one formulation, under Article 112, members of the European Central Bank are to be appointed 'by common accord of the Governments of the Member States at the levels of Heads of State or of Government'. In the other formulation, which is used in Articles 121 and 122, certain key decisions in the transition to EMU – including the suitability of countries to join the third stage – are to be taken by qualified majority vote in the Council of Ministers 'meeting in the composition of Heads of State or of Government'.

- Article 13 of the TEU, as amended by the Amsterdam Treaty, places the European Council in a potentially very important position in respect of the CFSP:

  1. The European Council shall define the principles of and general guidelines for the common foreign and security policy, including the matters with defence implications.
  2. The European Council shall decide on common strategies to be implemented by the Union in areas where the Member States have important interests in common.
  Common strategies shall set out their objectives, duration and the means to be made available by the Union and the Member States.
  3. The Council shall take the decisions necessary for defining and implementing the common foreign and security policy on the basis of the general guidelines defined by the European Council.
  The Council shall recommend common strategies to the European Council and shall implement them, in particular by adopting joint actions and common positions.
  The Council shall ensure the unity, consistency and effectiveness of action by the Union.

- Under Article 214(2) of the TEC, as amended by the Nice Treaty, 'The Council, meeting in the composition of the Heads of State or Government and acting by a qualified majority, shall nominate the person it intends to appoint as President of the Commission; the nomination shall be approved by the European Parliament'.

It might have been thought that this limited treaty base of the European Council – not recognised until the SEA, largely outside the Founding Treaties, and a lack of legal clarity even today on its precise roles (especially in pillars one and three) – would have hindered the ability of the European Council to exercise influence and establish itself as an important decision-making institution. In practice it has not been a hindrance at all because the status of those who attend meetings – particularly the national leaders – is such that there is little to stop them from deciding amongst themselves what the European Council will and will not do. As a result, the evolution, operation and influence of the European Council have owed much more to the preferences of the participants and to political and practical necessities than they have to agreed rules and requirements. Indeed, in order to give itself maximum flexibility and manoeuvrability, the European Council has been careful to avoid being based on or subject to tight rules and requirements – especially those which might arise from ECJ jurisdiction if the European Council was to be placed firmly within the context of the Community Treaties.

The opportunity to decide for itself what it does has resulted in the European Council exercising a number of roles and performing a number of functions. The precise nature of these roles and functions are explained in some detail later in the chapter, so suffice it to note here that they add up to an extremely important and impressive portfolio. Indeed, they put the European Council at the very heart of EU decision-making – not on a day-to-day basis in the manner of the other four main EU institutions, but rather from a more distanced position where it is centrally involved in setting the overall parameters of the EU system. Final and legally binding EU decisions may be made by other EU institutions, but major political decisions concerning the institutional and policy development of the EU are now generally taken by, or at least are channelled through and given clearance by, the European Council.

Membership

As Article 4 of the Common Provisions of the TEU (see previous section) makes clear, there are two 'levels' of membership of the European Council: the Heads of State or Government of the member states and the President of the Commission; and the Foreign Ministers of the member states and one other member of the Commission, who attend to provide assistance. In practice the only Heads of State to take part in the European Council are those who are, in effect, also Head of Government, which means the French, Finnish and Cypriot Presidents.

In recent years, in response to the increasing importance of EMU, the practice has developed of Ecofin Council ministers also travelling to European summits, though not necessarily staying for the whole meeting. The Ecofin ministers usually hold at least a parallel meeting to discuss matters that fall within their sphere of competence, and at some point normally replace the Foreign Ministers in a plenary session to discuss and/or take decisions on economic and financial issues. If agenda items warrant it, other ministers also travel to summits, as at the June 2002 Seville summit when the prominence of immigration and asylum issues on the agenda resulted in Justice and Home Affairs Ministers attending. In response to this practice of 'sectoral' ministers attending summits and to make for greater flexibility in the operation of summits, the Seville meeting made provision for Foreign Ministers to be replaced in the meeting room by other ministers if agenda items so required it. It did so simply by specifying that 'Each delegation shall have two seats in the meeting room' (European Council, 2002a: Annex III – Rules for Organising the Proceedings of the European Council).

Apart from the 52 formal members of the European Council, only a very restricted number of other people are normally permitted to be present at formal sessions: the Council Secretary General (who is also the High Representative for the CFSP); the Council Deputy Secretary General; the Secretary General of the Commission; a very small number of Council Presidency, Council Secretariat, and Commission senior officials (all of whom sit back from the main table); national civil servants, but only on the basis of one adviser per country being allowed entrance at any one time; and interpreters.

Each member state has a suite in the vicinity of the summit meeting room, which is available to its official delegation and from which officials may be summoned as required. At Seville it was decided that official delegations would be restricted in size to twenty people. However, these are supplemented by numerous other officials who make up what are customarily described as the non-official or technical delegations.

The European Council membership is thus based on the Council of Ministers model in the sense that it is made up of national delegations, plus the Commission. Unlike in the Council of Ministers, however, the participants in formal European Council sessions are not accompanied by teams of national officials. The original thinking behind this restriction on access to the summit meeting room was that it would encourage relaxed informality, and in any event was not strictly necessary as the European Council was not a law-maker. However, in practice it has proved difficult to achieve the desired mood, not least because of the increased number of participants following EC/EU enlargements and the increased importance of decisions taken at European Council meetings.

Organisation

Number, location and length of summits

Number

Under Article 4 TEU (see p. 221) the European Council is required to meet at least twice a year. These two required meetings are held at the end of each six month Council Presidency, in June and December.

Since a special summit held in March 2000 in Lisbon to examine how the EU could best utilise new technologies to promote economic growth and employment, an annual Spring summit has also been held as part of what has become known as the Lisbon Strategy or Process. Other special summits have been held as and when they have been deemed to be necessary. Since member states holding the Council Presidency in the second half of the year have in recent years almost invariably decided that such a summit was indeed necessary (if only because they wished to maximise the publicity opportunities of their Presidency), this has meant that since the mid- to late 1990s there have almost always been at least four summits a year. The 2002 Seville summit decided to regularise this situation by specifying that the European Council would henceforth meet in principle four times a year: twice during each Council Presidency. The summit also decided that extraordinary meetings could be convened in extraordinary circumstances.

The only year in recent times when there has not been four European Council meetings was 2005. This was because the UK Presidency decided that an autumn summit was not strictly necessary, and indeed might be troublesome given ongoing differences between member states – especially France and the UK – over the content of the 2007–13 financial perspective. Tony Blair did however host, in October at Hampton Court Palace, what was officially labelled an 'Informal Meeting of Heads of State of Government'. In addition to the 25 member state Heads, the meeting was attended by the leaders of Bulgaria and Romania (because their countries were scheduled to join the EU in 2007), the Secretary General of the Council of Ministers, and the Presidents of the Commission and the EP. The meeting, which lasted for just five hours, including lunch, had as its main purpose a discussion on how the EU could best respond to the challenges of globalisation.

Location

Up to 2001 the twice-yearly end-of-Presidency summits were held in the country of the Presidency. However, the 2000 IGC annexed a declaration to the Nice Treaty stipulating that 'as from 2002, one European Council meeting per presidency will be held in Brussels. When the Union comprises 18 members [which, of course, it has since May 2004], all European Council meetings will be held in Brussels'. The declaration relates only to the end-of-Presidency summits, which are always held in June and December. Presidencies are, therefore, free to organise other summits wherever they like.

Length

The 'standard model' for end-of-Presidency summits is that they are held over a two-day period, beginning in the morning of day one and ending in the late afternoon of day two. From this model, there are various departures in practice, most of them arising from Presidency preferences and the politics of meetings. The longest summit to date was at Nice in December 2000, where disagreements over the contents over what became the Nice Treaty resulted in the meeting extending into a fifth day.

As part of a general attempt to streamline the operations of both the European Council and the Council of Ministers, the 2002 Seville summit changed the arrangements concerning the length of summits. Heads would still gather for two days, but on day one they would not be joined by ministers. The full European Council would normally last for just one full day, with the meeting closing at the end of the afternoon (European Council, 2002a: *Annex 1. Rules for the Organisation of the Proceedings of the European Council*). In practice, these revised arrangements have not been strictly applied and, as is shown below in the section on the conduct of business, most meetings proceed much as they did pre-Seville.

The timing and length of special summits depends largely on the reasons for which they had been called, but they usually last for just one day. The March 1999 Berlin summit, which was convened to take final decisions on the *Agenda 2000* proposals, was extremely unusual in that it was spread over three days,

Preparing summits

Prior to Seville, much of the responsibility for preparing European Council meetings rested with the Presidency – a post that is held concurrently with the Presidency of the Council of Ministers. How closely the Head of Government of the incumbent Presidency became involved in these preparations depended partly on circumstances, style and personal preference. However, as the profile of summits was raised, most national leaders came to play a very active and public preparatory role – including making a tour of some or all of the national capitals.

Whatever preparatory work national leaders themselves chose to do, national officials and Foreign Ministers were invariably extensively engaged in pre-European Council preparations. The 'standard' procedure for end-of-Presidency summits was for senior officials from the Presidency, working in liaison with the Secretariat of the Council of Ministers (the European Council does not have its own Secretariat), the Antici Group (see Chapter 10), and the Commission, to identify topics that could be, ought to be, or needed to be discussed. These were then channelled through COREPER and, in the case of CFSP matters, through the Political and Security Committee (see Chapters 10 and 19). About ten days before a summit meeting, Foreign Ministers, and often also Ecofin Ministers, met to finalise the general shape of the agenda and, usually, to engage in exploratory pre-summit negotiations. To this 'standard' procedure were often added – especially when it looked as though a European Council meeting would be difficult – numerous preparatory meetings of officials and the convening of extra ministerial meetings.

As part of the streamlining of the operation of the European Council that was agreed at Seville, the GAERC's role in preparing summits was elevated. The procedure would now be as follows:

> European Council meetings shall be prepared by the General Affairs and External Relations Council, which shall coordinate all the preparatory work and draw up the agenda. Contributions by other configurations of the Council to the proceedings of the European Council shall be forwarded to the General Affairs and External Relations Council not later than two weeks before the European Council meeting.

> At a meeting held at least four weeks before the European Council, the General Affairs and External Relations Council, acting on a Presidency proposal, shall draw up an annotated draft agenda distinguishing between:
> - items to be approved or endorsed without debate;
> - items for discussion with a view to defining general political guidelines;
> - items for discussions with a view to adopting a decision ... ;
> - items for discussion but not intended to be the subject of conclusions.

> For each of the items referred to in the second and third indents of [the previous] paragraph, the Presidency shall prepare a brief outline paper setting out the issues, the questions to be debated and the main options available.

> On the eve of the European Council meeting, the General Affairs and External Relations Council shall hold a final preparatory session and adopt the definitive agenda, to which no item may subsequently be added without the agreement of all delegations.

> Except for urgent and unforeseeable reasons linked, for example, to current international events, no Council or committee may meet between the final preparatory session of the General Affairs and External Relations Council and the European Council meeting (European Council, 2002a: Annex 1).

By and large these arrangements have been applied, albeit in a suitably fleshed-out manner based on the pre-Seville practices. So, it remains the case that the Council's various preparatory bodies – especially COREPER II, the Council Secretariat, and the Presidency – are centrally involved in preparations, via not only the formal channels but also a host of informal linkages and communications.

Setting the agenda

The agendas of end-of-Presidency summits are usually crowded. The sorts of matters that appear on their agendas are considered in a separate section later in the chapter, but the circumstances that can bring them onto agendas will be outlined here.

- Some issues are almost invariably on the agenda because of their intrinsic importance. So, time is usually allowed for a discussion of the general economic situation in the EU, and in recent years time has usually also been set aside for some consideration of developments relating to the SEM, to EMU, to the promotion of employment, and to enlargement.

- The Commission may be pressing a policy initiative towards which the Presidency and at least some of the states are sympathetic. This was, for example, an important part of the background to the June 2001 Göteborg summit agreeing on a strategy for sustainable development and adding an environmental dimension to the Lisbon Process (see below on the Lisbon Process).

- The Presidency, perhaps supported or even pressed by all or some of the other member states, may wish to use a European Council meeting to make or to formalise institutional change. Several summits, for example, have made decisions about the convening of IGCs, have reviewed the progress being made in IGCs, and of course have marked the culmination of IGCs.

- Decisions may be needed on matters that have come to be accepted as requiring European Council resolution, or at least approval. So, for example, the June and December 2005 summits were much taken up with the increasing need to reach an agreement on the 2007–13 financial perspective.

- Business may be left over from, or have been referred from, a previous summit. For example, the June 1998 Cardiff summit invited the Commission 'to report to future European Councils' on progress made in integrating environmental protection into EU policies so as to achieve sustainable development (European Council, 1998: 12). Another example concerns the Turkish membership application: at its December 2002 Copenhagen meeting the European Council promised Turkey that at its December 2004 meeting it would authorise the opening of accession negotiations if Turkey had made sufficient progress with its internal reform programme; the item thus duly appeared on the December 2004 meeting's agenda and the authorisation was given subject to certain conditions.

- Reports – usually from either the Council, the Commission, or the Presidency – may have to be considered, or at least noted. For instance, amongst reports submitted to the June 2002 Seville summit were: from the Council on illegal immigration and smuggling; from the Council on taxation; from the Commission on the management of the EU's external borders; from the Commission on using the internet to develop twinning between European secondary schools; from the Presidency on enlargement; and from the Presidency on the Lisbon Strategy.

- External relations usually require discussions, declarations and decisions. For example, amongst matters considered at the December 2004 summit were the situation in the Ukraine, the Middle East Peace Process, the European Security and Defence Policy, and the European Neighbourhood Policy.

Non end-of-Presidency summits have normally been convened around a specific theme or issue, so their agendas are narrower. The spring 'Lisbon Process' summits have as their general focus consideration of 'the economic, social and environmental situation in the Union'. More specifically, their remit is to follow up on the three key economic goals laid down at Lisbon for Europe by 2010: the creation of twenty million new jobs; the promotion of economic and social reform; and the creation of one of the world's leading knowledge-based economies. Usually, however, circumstances and events result in the spring summits also devoting at least some of their time to non-Lisbon Process matters. This happened, for example, with the March 2004 summit, which was held shortly after bombs in Madrid had killed over 200 people. Dealing with terrorism was added to the agenda and several measures were adopted, including a declaration on combating terrorism.

The autumn summits have taken a number of forms. Some, for example, have been convened to deal with a particular policy area, as with the October 1999 Tampere summit which considered measures that would need to be taken to create 'an area of freedom, security and justice in the European Union' (European Council, 1999c). Some have been convened to discuss potentially troublesome matters, such as the October 2000 Biarritz summit which had as its main purpose reviewing progress in the 2000 IGC. And some have been convened to consider particularly urgent matters, such as the September 2001 Brussels summit that was hurriedly called to consider the EU's response to the September 11 terrorist attacks in the USA. Post-Seville, it is possible that autumn summits will come to have more general agendas.

The conduct of business

As was noted above, the Seville summit sought to tighten the way in which summits are conducted by agreeing on 'Rules for the Organisation of the

Proceedings of the European Council (European Council, 2002a: Appendix 1). A component element of the rules is that 'in principle' there is a meeting on the first day that is restricted to the national leaders and the President of the Commission and only on the second day is there a meeting of the full European Council. Like, however, some other Seville provisions, this component of the rules has not been given full effect and most end-of-Presidency summits are being conducted in a not dissimilar manner to as in the past.

Summits naturally vary in terms of how precisely they are arranged and conducted. One variation arises from Presidential preferences with, for example, some Presidencies attaching more importance than others to the Seville spirit regarding the need to begin with a restricted session confined to Heads and the President of the Commission. Another variation arises from the contents of agendas. Depending on their length, these can result in some summits being assigned fewer working sessions than others. Depending on their controversiality, they can result in some summits either being cut short because the Presidency thinks no agreement can be reached on a key issue (as with the Italian Presidency and the Constitutional Treaty negotiations at the December 2003 summit) or being extended because the President is resolved to reach a settlement (as with the French Presidency and the Nice Treaty negotiations at the December 2000 summit).

Thus bearing in mind that variations do occur, the 'standard model' for the conduct of business at European Council meetings is as follows:

- Proceedings may begin with a restricted session attended only by Heads and the President of the Commission.
- On the basis of the agenda that has been agreed in advance, a full plenary session is held. From 1987 this session has included an address from the President of the European Parliament.
- Lunch is a drawn-out affair, which allows time for informal discussions and bilateral meetings. During lunch, and indeed during most breaks, there are meetings between the summit participants and their national delegations.
- Another full plenary is usually held in the afternoon, although sometimes the Heads of Government and the Foreign Ministers have separate meetings.
- In the evening, dinner provides another opportunity for further informal discussions. The Heads of Government and the President of the Commission on the one hand, and the Foreign Ministers and the other representative of the Commission on the other, usually dine separately, but sometimes a joint, grand, and largely ceremonial dinner is held, perhaps with the host Head of State presiding.

- What happens after dinner depends on what progress has been made during the day. In the early days of the European Council the Heads held informal 'fireside chats' while the Foreign Ministers discussed foreign policy issues. Over the years, however, such informal sessions have became less common. Occasionally there are reconvened plenaries in an attempt to make progress with uncompleted business, and often bilateral late-night meetings are held. During the night, Presidency and Council Secretariat officials work on a draft of conclusions on the first day's business ('pre-drafts' are written even before summits open) and/or on a form of words that can serve as a basis for further negotiations the next day.
- Another plenary session is held in the morning and sometimes the afternoon of day two. This usually picks up from the previous day's discussions, but with the draft that has been worked on during the night now tabled. With the participants trying to move towards conclusions, breaks in the proceedings are sometimes called, usually by the Presidency, so as to permit delegations to study the implications of proposals or to allow informal discussions to take place.
- The summit normally ends some time in the afternoon or early evening with the publication of a statement in the form of 'Presidency Conclusions'. Everything in the statement is customarily agreed to by all summit participants.
- Press conferences are held for up to 4000 journalists who attend European Councils and who do so much to turn the summits into major media events. The President of the European Council and the President of the Commission normally hold a joint press conference, and each delegation holds one of its own. Different versions of what has happened are often given on these occasions.

Roles and Activities

As was noted above, the European Council is relatively free to decide what it may and may not do. The few treaty and other legal provisions that relate to its responsibilities are, for the most part, vague, whilst the political status of its members is such as to put it generally beyond much challenge.

As a result, the activities undertaken by the European Council have tended to vary, according both to the preferences of the participants and changing circumstances and requirements. So, in the second half of the 1970s, when President Giscard d'Estaing and Chancellor Schmidt determined much of the direction and pace of European integration, considerable time was given over to general discussions of major economic and monetary problems. For much of the 1980s, by contrast, when some participants – notably Margaret Thatcher and the representatives of the Commission – began to press particular distributional questions, and when policy issues were increasingly referred 'upwards' from the Council of Ministers for resolution, the summits came to be much concerned with quite detailed decision-making. Towards the end of the 1980s another shift began to occur as summits devoted increasing time and attention to the general direction and development of the Community. This shift has continued and has resulted in the European Council increasingly assuming the role of a sort of board of directors: setting the overall framework and taking decisions about the major initiatives to be pursued, but tending to leave the operationalisation of its pronouncements and decisions to management (which in this case is essentially the Commission and the Council of Ministers).

The main topics and areas with which the European Council concerns itself can be grouped under five headings.

The evolution of the European Union

Although this item appears only occasionally on European Council agendas as a topic in its own right, reviewing and guiding the general evolution of the EU is what several specific items are, in effect, concerned with. The most important of these items – constitutional and institutional reform, EMU, and enlargement – are dealt with separately below, but others that are worth noting include: the monitoring of progress in the creation of the Single European Market; 'troubleshooting' when progress in building the European Union is threatened – as with measures agreed at the 1992 Edinburgh summit to deal with 'the Danish problem'; setting out framework principles when this is deemed necessary – as with periodic statements since the early 1990s emphasising the importance of subsidiarity; and framing the parameters of EU income and expenditure by determining the size and shape of the EU's multi-annual financial perspectives – as with the agreement at the special March 1999 Berlin summit on the 2000–6 financial perspective and the agreement at the December 2005 Brussels summit on the 2007–13 financial perspective (see Chapter 17 on financial perspectives and these two agreements).

Constitutional and institutional matters

These come up in the European Council in four main forms.

First, all key decisions relating to new accessions are taken at the summits. For example, amongst many key decisions taken in the process that led to the 2004 enlargement were: the agreement at the June 1993

Copenhagen summit that CEECs could become members of the EU; the setting out at the December 1994 Essen summit of a pre-accession strategy; the confirmation at the Luxembourg 1997 summit of the Commission's recommendation that negotiations should open with five CEECs and Cyprus in 1998; the similar confirmation at the Helsinki 1999 summit that negotiations should be extended in 2000 to the five remaining CEEC applicants and Malta; and the agreement at the December 2002 summit that ten states had completed the accession negotiations successfully and could join the EU on 1 May 2004.

Second, summits are also the venue to consider, and sometimes take action on, a range of specific institutional matters. For example, at the December 2003 summit a decision was taken on the location of several EU offices and agencies – including the European Food Safety Authority (which both Italy and Finland wanted), the European Chemicals Agency, and Eurojust.

Third, the European Council takes some important personnel decisions, notably on the nominee for Commission President, and on the appointment of the Council Secretary General and High Representative for the CFSP and the President of the European Central Bank (ECB). These decisions can become extremely politicised and very difficult. Taking the Commission President, the UK government vetoed the nomination of the Belgian Prime Minister, Jean-Luc Dehaene, as Commission President at the June 1994 Corfu summit, with the consequence that a special summit had to be held in Brussels a fortnight later when Jacques Santer was nominated. Similarly, in 2004, no agreement could be reached at the June summit on who should be nominated to succeed Romano Prodi, with the consequence that a special summit subsequently had to be convened after informal agreement had been reached that the nominee should be José Manuel Barroso. Taking the President of the ECB, France objected at the special Brussels summit in May 1998 to the appointment of Wim Duisenberg of the Netherlands Central Bank as the ECB's first President rather than Claude Trichet of the French Central Bank, and it was only after a deal was negotiated that involved Duisenberg agreeing to step down before his term of office had expired that the matter was resolved.

Fourth, the European Council takes important decisions in the context of the movement towards the 'constitutionalisation' of European integration. It has been a key player in all four major revisions of the Founding Treaties: (1) the June 1985 Milan summit established the IGC that paved the way for the SEA, which was agreed at the December 1985 Luxembourg summit; (2) the IGCs that worked on what became the Maastricht Treaty were established over a series of four summits in 1989 and 1990 (two regular and two special), and the final negotiations on the Treaty were conducted at the December 1991 Maastricht summit; (3) preparations and arrangements for the 1996–7 IGC were decided at summits between 1994 and 1996 – notably Corfu in June 1994, Cannes in June 1995, and Madrid in December 1995 – and the Amsterdam Treaty itself was finalised at the June 1997 Amsterdam summit; (4) the origins of the Nice Treaty lie in the protocol of the Amsterdam Treaty that made provision for the convening of another IGC to prepare for enlargement, but key decisions on the convening and agenda of the 2000 IGC were taken at the June 1999 Cologne summit, whilst the Treaty itself was finalised at the December 2000 Nice summit. And, as was shown in Chapter 7, the Nice summit provided for another IGC, which led to later summits determining the preparations for the Constitutional Treaty IGC – including creating the Constitutional Convention. The final contents of the CT were agreed at summits in December 2003 and June 2004 (the first of these summits reached agreement on virtually everything except national voting weights in the Council).

The economic and monetary policies of the European Union

Summits have long reviewed the overall economic and social situation within the EU and looked in a general way at questions relating to economic growth, trade patterns, inflation, exchange rates, and unemployment. Until the early 1990s, however, differences between the member states about what should be done, coupled with a widely shared determination to ensure that national hands remained firmly placed on key economic controls, meant that these discussions usually produced little beyond general exhortations on topics such as controlling inflation, tackling unemployment and encouraging investment. However, in recent years these economic deliberations have acquired more bite. One reason why they have done so is that the European Council is the place where the major features and timetable of the EMU programme are finalised. Another reason is that since EMU requires convergence between key national economic policies, proposals for concerted economic action are now considered in the European Council. And a third reason is that it has come to be accepted – not least in the framework of the 'Lisbon Process' – that the European Council should be providing broad guidance for EU economic programmes.

External relations

The European Council is involved in the EU's external relations in three principal ways.

First, many economic issues are not purely internal EU matters. They have vitally important global dimensions and summits often look at these either with a view to considering the EU's relations with other economic powers (especially the United States and Japan), or with a view to coordinating the EU's position in international negotiations (such as G8 summits or in the World Trade Organisation).

Second, the European Council has long issued declarations on important aspects of international political affairs. Sometimes the declarations have had policy instruments attached to them, but because these have been 'soft' instruments – usually in the form of mild economic sanctions or modest economic aid – there is little evidence of summits having had much effect on world political events. Nonetheless, a guidance role is specifically allocated to the European Council under Article 13 of the CFSP pillar (see p. 222) designed to ensure that all major EU policies, initiatives and actions are at its behest, or at least have its general approval.

Third, as was shown in Chapters 3 and 4, the European Council is directly involved with EU enlargement rounds, working closely with the Commission on the setting of guidelines and timetables.

Specific internal policy issues

Despite the original intention that the European Council should operate at a fairly general level, in practice it often concerns itself with quite specific internal policy issues. There are three main reasons for this: (1) some issues are so sensitive and/or so intractable that it requires the authority of national leaders to deal with them; (2) the European Council is, because of its non-sectoral nature, often the best-placed institution to put together broad-ranging policies or broker deals that cut across policy sectors; and (3) the status of the European Council in the EU system is now such that the general expectation and assumption is that most policy matters of significance ought at least to be given clearance, if not be determined, at European Council level.

These differing reasons have resulted in three broad types of policy involvement by the European Council. First, it sometimes plays a significant role in policy initiation. For example, since the late 1980s it has prompted initiatives in such areas as immigration, drugs and terrorism. Second, policy involvement can take the form of tackling issues that the Council of Ministers has been unable to resolve or which it is deemed necessary that the European Council should resolve. Such an instance occurred in connection with the institutional crisis that developed in the EU in 1996 following the export ban placed on British beef because of the high incidence of Bovine Spongiform Encephalopathy (BSE) in British cattle: the Commission drew up a plan for resolving the crisis, and it was referred to the June Florence summit for approval. Third, and this has been of increasing importance in recent years as the number of policy issues that are 'referred up' from the Council of Ministers for final resolution has declined (largely as a consequence of QMV resulting in fewer blockages at Council of Ministers level), the European Council has become less concerned with arbitrating and acting as a final court of appeal on internal policy issues and more concerned with encouraging and guiding. This is illustrated by the frequent messages it sends to other EU institutions via Presidency Conclusions: almost invariably these Conclusions are studded with phrases such as the European Council 'invites a report on', 'calls for action to be taken in regard to', 'confirms its full support for', 'welcomes the progress made by', 'endorses the steps taken in connection with' and so on.

*   *   *

The European Council thus concerns itself with various matters, the relative importance of which can vary from summit to summit. Six functions, which can be analytically separated but which in practice greatly overlap, are associated with these matters. First, the European Council is a forum, at the highest political level, for building mutual understanding and confidence between the governments of the EU member states. Second, it identifies medium- and long-term EU goals. Third, it is a policy initiator and dispenser of policy guidelines. Fourth, it makes an important contribution to the coordination of EU policy goals and activities. Fifth, it is a decision-maker – both on matters that have come to be accepted are its ultimate responsibility (most notably constitutional and major institutional issues), and on matters that, because of their importance or their political complexity and sensitivity, are not resolved by the Council of Ministers. Sixth, it exercises responsibilities in the sphere of external relations.

One function, it must be emphasised, that the European Council does not exercise is that of legislator. Its decisions are political decisions. When it is intended that its decisions should be given legal effect, the customary EU legislative procedures have to be applied. And in those procedures there is no guarantee that an agreement in the European Council will automatically produce ease of passage. One reason for this is that the guidelines laid down by the European Council are sometimes insufficiently precise to clear all political obstacles. Another reason is that governments occasionally decide after a summit that their delegations have given too much away and that ground must be recovered by taking a tough line in the Council of Ministers.

The European Council and the EU System

Institutionalised summitry in the form of the European Council has inevitably strengthened the position of national governments in the EU system. It has also added an extra intergovernmental element to the nature of the EU by virtue of the fact that the leaders virtually always act on the basis of unanimous agreement – either because they prefer to or, when subsequent legislation is required to give their decisions effect, because they may in practice be required to.

However, although the European Council has unquestionably become an important EU institution, its role, or more accurately roles, are still shifting. Certainly it has, since the mid- to late 1980s, come to approximate more to the original idea that it would provide overall strategic direction and not become too involved in policy detail, but this position is by no means fixed, or indeed applied with complete consistency. What happens at individual summits is not part of any regularised or consistent pattern. Thus some summits are relatively low-key affairs and do little more than pronounce on some aspects of current international developments, indicate one or two policy initiatives in fringe policy areas, and cobble together a concluding statement exuding general goodwill. Other summits, in contrast, are surrounded by an atmosphere of crisis and prophecies of catastrophe should they fail to produce firm decisions on key and pressing issues. Occasionally they do fail, but the catastrophes never quite happen, and the next summit, or next but one, is usually able to find an agreement via the customary EU method of compromise.

✻ ✻ ✻

The creation and development of the European Council has inevitably had implications for the role and functioning of the other principal EU institutions.

- The Commission has experienced some undermining of its special position regarding policy initiation. However, the Commission has to some extent been compensated for this by being permitted to enter into political discussions with national leaders at the summits, and also by being able – and sometimes required – to submit reports and documents to the summits.
- The Council of Ministers has lost power to the European Council by virtue of the increasing tendency of most major issues to go through summits in some form. As Hayes-Renshaw and Wallace (2006: 1) note, one role of the European Council is to act 'as a higher level of the Council of Ministers, by attempting to settle those issues on which the ministers have been unable to reach agreement'. However, the extent of the Council of Ministers loss of power should not be exaggerated. One reason why it should not be so is that there is no rigid hierarchical relationship between the two bodies in the sense that the Council of Ministers always feels obliged to refer all significant matters 'upwards'

for final decisions. It is true that most broad-based or very significant initiatives are referred to the European Council, but often that is for little more than political approval or for information. Certainly it would be quite erroneous to suppose that the European Council takes all 'first-order' decisions and the Council of Ministers is confined to 'second-order' decisions. A second reason why the extent of the loss should not be overstated is that there is no consistent line of division between the two regarding who does what, other than the Council of Ministers being responsible for making legislation. A third reason is that most issues considered by the European Council have already been prepared, channelled and filtered by the appropriate formation of the Council of Ministers. And a fourth reason is that since the European Council meets for only six to eight days a year, it cannot normally hope to do anything more than sketch outlines in a restricted number of areas.

- The EP has been largely by-passed by the European Council and so could be regarded as having experienced some net loss of power. It is true that the President of the European Council gives a verbal report on each summit meeting to the next EP plenary session, and it is also the case that the EP President addresses the opening sessions of summits in order to inform the national leaders of the EP's thinking on key issues. However, there is no evidence that either of these procedures produce much in the way of influence. Far more important is the almost complete lack of input by the EP into European Council agendas or deliberations, and the tendency of the Council of Ministers to take the view that proposals that stem from European Council decisions do not permit it much manoeuvrability when dealing with the EP.

- Since the European Council operates largely outside the framework of the TEC, and since its decisions are political rather than legal in character, its existence has had few implications for the Court of Justice. Or rather it has had few direct implications. It can, however, be argued that any increase in a non-treaty approach to integration necessarily constitutes a corresponding decrease in the influence of the Court, given its attachment to, indeed its restriction to, questions that have a legal base.

Concluding Remarks

The record of the European Council is mixed. On the one hand there have been failures, or at least the non-fulfilment of hopes. This was particularly so in the period from about 1980 to 1988: summits became rather routinised and immersed in specifics; too much time was devoted to policy detail rather than to mapping out the future; and disputes about distributional issues were seemingly always on the agenda. On the other hand there have been positive achievements: understandings between national leaders have been furthered; important goals have been identified/given an impetus/brought to a conclusion – such as on enlargements, the internal market, institutional reform, and EMU; and agreements have been worked out on matters that were either unsuitable for, or could not be resolved by, the Council of Ministers.

That there should be both pluses and minuses in the record is not altogether surprising. The summits are, after all, conducted on a relatively loosely structured basis and it is thus perhaps inevitable, given the participants, that they should be drawn into attempting to do a host of different things. It is also inevitable that summits should experience many of the problems of intergovernmental conflict that are so characteristic of the Council of Ministers.

Aware of the European Council's weaknesses, the government of the member states – led by the governments of the large member states – sought to use the Constitutional Treaty to strengthen the European Council's institutional capacity. They did so by replacing the six-month rotating Presidency of the European Council by a more permanent President. The office holder would be appointed by QMV for a tenure of two and a half years, which could be renewable once. The problems of ratifying the CT may have delayed the introduction of this measure, but such is its perceived importance amongst many key EU actors that it is likely to be resurrected in some form in the future.

The European Parliament

Powers and Influence

Since it was first constituted as the Assembly of the European Coal and Steel Community, the European Parliament – the title it adopted for itself in 1962 – has generally been regarded as a somewhat ineffectual institution. This reputation is no longer justified, for whilst it is true that the EP's formal powers are not as strong as those of national legislatures, developments over the years have come to give it a considerable influence in the EU system. As with national parliaments this influence is exercised in three main ways: through the legislative process, through the budgetary process, and through control and supervision of the executive.

Parliament and EU legislation

The EP has a number of opportunities to influence EU legislation.

First, it sometimes participates in policy discussions with the Commission at the pre-proposal legislative stage. The Commission may, for example, float a policy idea before an EP committee, or committee members themselves may suggest policy initiatives to the Commission.

Second, the EP can formally adopt its own ideas for suggested legislation. There are two main ways in which it can do this. One way is to adopt own initiative reports – that is, reports that the Parliament itself initiates. There is however a major weakness with these reports, which is that whilst the Commission may feel pressurised by them it is not obliged to act upon them. Partly because of this weakness, the number of such reports has declined over the years. As can be seen in Table 12.1 (p. 245), 82 own initiative reports, most of which were not calling for legislative proposals, were adopted in 2004. The other way of adopting ideas for legislation is under Article 192 TEC, which states that 'The European Parliament may, acting by a majority of its members, request the Commission to submit any

240

appropriate proposal on matters on which it considers that a Community act is required for the purpose of implementing this Treaty.' Political realities make it difficult for the Commission not to act on an Article 192 request, but, as Judge and Earnshaw (2003: 211–12) show, it has not always rushed to do so. Moreover, only a handful of Article 192 requests have been passed to date, largely because absolute majorities can be difficult to obtain. An example of a Commission legislative proposal stemming from this article is its 1998 proposal for a directive on settling the insurance claims of victims of traffic accidents occurring outside the victim's country of origin.

Third, the annual budgetary cycle provides opportunities to exercise legislative influence. In large measure this dates back to the *Joint Declaration of 30 June 1982 by the European Parliament, the Council and the Commission on various measures to improve the budgetary procedure*. Amongst the 'various measures', it was agreed that if the EP put appropriations into the budget for items for which there was no legal base – in other words if the EP opened new budget lines – the Commission and the Council would seek to provide the necessary base. It was further agreed that expenditure limits in respect of legislation should not be set in the legislative process, but in the budgetary process – where the EP has significant power. For the most part this understanding between the institutions has worked well and has enabled the EP to promote favoured policies: for example in 1998 it promoted a policy on employment generation in the area of small and medium-sized enterprises. It is an understanding, however, that requires the three institutions to work closely together, as was demonstrated in 1998 when the ECJ ruled in favour of four member states that claimed that a number of EU programmes approved under the budgetary procedure were illegal because they did not have an authorised legal base.

Fourth, the EP can influence, albeit perhaps rather indirectly, the Commission's annual legislative programme – which is essentially a planning tool of an indicative nature. The procedure is as follows. (1) The Commission adopts its annual work programme, which includes all proposals of a legislative nature, usually in November. Several factors determine the contents of the programme, most notably: commitments that are pending; initiatives that are deemed to be necessary to give effect to existing policy developments; preferences that have been indicated by the Council and the EP, perhaps in inter-institutional meetings; and priorities identified in Council planning programmes (see Chapter 10). (2) The programme is considered by appropriate EP committees, with a dialogue often taking place between MEPs and Commission representatives. (3) A resolution on the programme is voted on in plenary session, usually in December.

Fifth, and most importantly of all, the EP's views must be sought in connection with important/significant/sensitive legislation. Until July 1987 and the entry into force of the SEA all legislation referred to the EP was subject to what is known as the consultation procedure.

However, the SEA created two new procedures – the cooperation procedure and the assent procedure – and the Maastricht Treaty introduced a further one – the co-decision procedure. There are thus four possible procedures to which legislation may be subject (plus variations within these procedures). The nature of these procedures and the policy areas to which they apply are described in some detail in Chapter 16, so the discussion here will be restricted to how they affect the EP.

- *The consultation procedure.* Under this procedure the EP is asked for an opinion on Commission proposals for legislation. Once that opinion is given the Council may take whatever decision it wishes, even if the EP's opinion is negative.

  If the Council acts prematurely and does not wait for Parliament to make its views known, the 'law' will be ruled invalid by the ECJ. Any uncertainty on this point was removed by the isoglucose case ruling in 1980, when the Court annulled a Council regulation on the ground that it had been issued before Parliament's opinion was known. The isoglucose case ruling does not give the EP an indefinite veto over legislation under the consultation procedure, for it is obliged by treaty to issue opinions and in some of its judgements the Court has referred to the duty of loyal cooperation among EU institutions. However, the ruling does give the EP a very useful delaying power.

  What use the EP is able to make of the consultation procedure depends, in part at least, on its own subject competence and its tactical skills. The standard way of proceeding is to take advantage of Article 250 of the TEC, which states: 'As long as the Council has not acted, the Commission may alter its proposals during the procedures leading to the adoption of a Community act.' If the Commission can be persuaded to alter a proposal so as to incorporate the EP's views, the prospect of those views becoming part of the text that is finally approved by the Council is greatly enhanced. With this in mind, the EP attempts to convince or to pressurise the Commission. Normally, pressurising takes the form of voting on amendments to proposals but delaying voting on the resolution that formally constitutes the opinion until after the Commission has stated – as it is obliged to do – whether or not it accepts the amendments. If the Commission does accept the amendments the EP votes for the legislative resolution and the amendments are incorporated into the Commission's proposal. If the Commission does not accept the amendments, or at least not all of them, the EP may judge the Commission's position to be unsatisfactory and as a result may seek to delay the progress of the proposal by referring it back to the appropriate Parliamentary committee for further consideration.

- *The cooperation procedure.* Whereas under the consultation, or single reading, procedure the Council can take a final decision after the EP has issued its opinion, under the cooperation procedure there is a second reading process. On first reading the Council is confined to adopting a 'common position', which must then be referred back to the EP. When doing so, the Council is obliged to provide the EP with an explanation of its common position – including reasons for any EP amendments that have been rejected – and if the EP is dissatisfied it can exert further pressure at its second reading by amending or rejecting the common position by absolute majority vote. Such votes do not amount to vetoes, but because they carry considerable political weight, and because they can only be overcome in the Council by unanimous vote, they put considerable pressure on the Commission and the Council to take the EP's views seriously and to engage in inter-institutional bargaining.

- *The co-decision procedure.* This procedure is similar to the cooperation procedure up to the point when the EP issues its second reading, except that – under a change to the procedure made by the Amsterdam Treaty – if the Council and the EP reach agreement on the proposal at first reading, the proposal can be adopted at that stage. Assuming the Council and the EP are still at odds after the second reading, the proposal falls if the Parliament has rejected it by an absolute majority of its members and it is referred to a conciliation committee if the EP has amended it by an absolute majority. The conciliation committee is composed of an equal number of representatives from the Council and the Parliament. If agreement is reached in the conciliation committee, the text must be approved by the EP by a majority of the votes cast and by the Council acting by qualified majority. If no agreement is reached the proposal falls. (Under the Maastricht Treaty it was possible for the Council to attempt to press ahead with the proposal in the event of a conciliation committee failure, but the Amsterdam Treaty removed this possibility.) The key feature of the co-decision procedure is thus that it provides the EP with the potential to veto legislative proposals. The significance of the Parliament's powers under the procedure is symbolised by the fact that legislation that is subject to the procedure is made in the name of the EP and the Council, whereas legislation that is made under the consultation and cooperation procedures is made in the name of the Council only.

- *The assent procedure.* Under this procedure the EP must consider proposals at a single reading and with no provision for amendments. In some circumstances the assent requires an absolute majority of Parliament's members. Again, the EP thus has veto powers under this procedure.

Which procedure applies to a particular legislative proposal depends on which treaty article(s) the proposal is based. It is in the EP's interest that as much as possible is based on the co-decision procedure, where its powers are strongest, and as little as possible is based on the consultation procedure, where its powers are weakest. The Amsterdam Treaty benefited the EP in this regard, with some policy areas 'upgraded' from consultation to co-decision, and with the cooperation procedure virtually eliminated and the policy areas which had fallen within its remit moved to the co-decision procedure. The Nice Treaty further 'upgraded' some policy areas, but not on the scale of the Amsterdam Treaty.

Since the Amsterdam Treaty entered into force, most significant EU legislation has been subject to the co-decision procedure. The consultation procedure is largely confined to agriculture and to some justice and home affairs issues that are located in the TEC, the cooperation procedure is restricted to four areas of EMU, and the assent procedure is not – and never has been – used for 'normal' legislation but is reserved for special measures such as international agreements of certain kinds, EU enlargements, and the framework of the Structural Funds.

Table 12.1 shows the number of times the consultation, co-decision and assent procedures were used in 2004 for legislative proposals that were considered by the EP. The cooperation procedure was not used at all. Table 13.1 (p. 288) shows the total number of legislative acts that were adopted in the name of the EP – with, of course the Council, since the EP cannot adopt legislation by itself – in 2004: 40 regulations, 31 directives, and 4 decisions.

It is very difficult to estimate the precise effect of EP deliberations on the final form of legislative acts. One reason for this is that a great deal of EP persuading and lobbying is impossible to monitor because it is carried out via informal contacts with Commission and Council representatives. That is to say, EP influence is exercised not just by the formal acts of approving, rejecting, and amending legislative proposals. Second, statistical analyses of the extent to which EP amendments are incorporated into final legislation struggle with the following problems:

– Distinguishing between amendments that have a political edge and those that are essentially technical or procedural in nature.
– The fact that, as Corbett (2001: 363) has noted, the significance of EP amendments varies according to circumstances. For instance, some amendments under the co-decision procedure are adopted primarily for tactical reasons ahead of negotiations with the Council.

Table 12.1 *Parliamentary proceedings from January to December 2004 – resolutions and decisions adopted*

Part-session	Consultation[1]	Legislation — Co-decision: First reading[2]	Second reading[3]	Third reading	Assent	Budget and discharge	COS procedures[4]	Other: Own initiative procedures	Resolutions Art. 103, 108	Human rights Art. 115	Miscellaneous	Total
January I	13	3	1					15		1	3	36
January II	1	2		7		2		2	1	4		19
February I	16	9	1		2			11	1	4	3	47
February II	6	1			1	2		7		3		20
March I	17	15	8			2	1	13	3	4	3	66
March II	31	13	13	2	3	4	1	8	7	6		88
April	22	22	4	4	4	24		15	2	6	3	106
May	9						1					10
July											1	1
September	4					2		1	5	3	2	16
October I	2					1			3			7
October II	13	2				2		2	4	3		26
November	6	1						2	4	3	2	18
December I	3	1				1			3			8
December II	20		2		1	2		6	2	3	2	38
Total	163	69	29	13	11	42	3	82	35	40	19	506

1 Consultation: 66 cases in which Parliament proposed amendments to the Commission proposal.
2 Co-decision: 53 cases in which Parliament proposed amendments to the Commission proposal.
3 Co-decision: 17 cases in which Parliament amended the Council's common position.
4 COS procedure: opinions on Commission reports or communications.
Source: reproduced from European Commission (2005b).

- How to count when some, but not all, of an amendment is accepted by the Council. This is a particular problem under co-decision, with many amendments leading to compromises negotiated between the EP and Council in conciliation. As Judge and Earnshaw (2003) show, the EP and Council were initially wary of each other under co-decision, but they gradually came to recognise 'the advantages to be gained through negotiating strategies designed to secure compromise'. So, in 1994, 26 per cent of EP amendments were accepted as compromises, whereas in 1999 the figure was 59 per cent.

It is, therefore, extremely difficult – impossible many would say – to be precise about the extent of the EP's legislative influence. (For those who wish to consult attempts to be precise via statistical analyses see, for example, Kreppel and Tsebelis, 1999; Kreppel, 2000). Some indication of the influence being exercised by the EP can, however, be gauged from the fact that under co-decision only about 15 per cent of legislative proposals go to the final conciliation stage: about 40 per cent are agreed at first reading and about 45 per cent at second reading. In other words, 85 per cent of legislative proposals are in an acceptable form for the EP by the end of second reading. Of the 15 per cent that goes to conciliation, the EP claims that in the 1999–2004 Parliament, 27 per cent of its amendments were accepted as proposed, 51 per cent were accepted following a compromise with the Council, and 22 per cent were withdrawn (Hayes-Renshaw and Wallace, 2006).

But though the precision of statistical estimates of the EP's legislation can be questioned, two matters are incontrovertible. First, the EP is centrally involved with the Commission and the Council in the making of EU legislation. It is so both in formal settings – such as when it examines Commission proposals in committees and when it meets with the Council in conciliation committees – and through a variety of informal mechanisms – such as through trialogue meetings that bring together the key EP, Commission and Council actors on a proposal to explore the possibilities for a deal. Second, EP activity does have a significant impact on the outcome of legislative processes. Whilst only a handful of legislative proposals are actually blocked by the EP – under co-decision only nine had been blocked up to the end of 2005 – many proposals are significantly altered, including on matters of political substance.

* * *

Having established that the EP does have a genuine legislative influence – an influence that many national parliaments cannot match – the weaknesses to which it is subject will now be outlined.

The first and most obvious weakness is that the EP does not have full legislative powers. Unlike national parliaments, it does not have the final say over what is and what is not to become law. On the one hand it does not have the capacity to exercise a fully 'positive' legislative role by initiating, developing and passing into law its own proposals. On the other hand its 'negative' legislative role is also considerably circumscribed, for whilst the co-decision and assent procedures do give it a veto over many legislative proposals, under both the consultation and cooperation procedures the Council has the power to overturn EP amendments that have or have not been accepted by the Commission, and to ignore the EP's rejection of legislative proposals. The Council can also choose not to act at all on legislative proposals it does not like – and there are always many proposals upon which the Parliament has given an opinion that still await a Council decision. (Proposals subject to the cooperation and co-decision procedures are not exempt from such Council inaction, since the restricted timetable that is attached to the procedures only comes into play once the Council has adopted its common position.)

The second weakness is that although the EP usually attempts to deliver opinions as soon as possible to ensure they are available to the Council at an early stage of its deliberations, it is not unusual – although more so than it used to be – for the Council, before the opinion of the EP has been delivered, to take preliminary decisions or to adopt common positions 'in principle' or 'pending the opinion of the European Parliament'. This is especially common when the initial referral to the EP is delayed, when there is some urgency about the matter, or when a Council Presidency is anxious to push the proposal through. Whatever the reason, in such circumstances the EP's opinion, especially under the consultation procedure, is likely to have only a very limited effect.

The third weakness is that the EP is not consulted on all Council legislation. The greatest gaps in this regard are its lack of any right to be consulted on most of the external agreements the Council concludes with third countries on behalf of the EU. Most importantly, trade agreements concluded under Article 133 TEC do not require EP approval. In practice the Council, and more particularly the Commission (which conducts the actual trade negotiations), usually do discuss forthcoming and ongoing trade matters with the EP on an informal basis, but they are not obliged to do so and there is not much evidence of Parliament bringing influence to bear on the EU's negotiating stance. In only two sets of circumstances where EU law is being made with regard to external agreements is EP approval necessary, in both cases by the assent of an absolute majority of MEPs: under Article 49 TEU for new accessions to the EU, and under Article 300 TEC for specific types of agreement, including association agreements, some types of cooperation agreements, and agreements with important budgetary implications. The first of these circumstances is obviously only for very occasional use. The second, however, has a more recurring application and has been used to some effect, notably in putting pressure on countries to improve their human rights records if they wish to receive the financial assistance that is usually an important component of association and cooperation agreements. (It should perhaps be added here that the EP also has the right to be informed and consulted about various other forms of EU external relations – notably under the CFSP pillar of the EU – but these do not involve legislation, and the EP's powers are purely advisory.)

The fourth and final weakness is that the EP does not have to be consulted on – although in practice it is notified of – Commission legislation. This is despite the fact that, numerically, Commission legislation makes up most of EU legislation. There are different views on the significance of this. Pointing to the political and expenditure implications of some Commission legislation, MEPs have long argued that this is another example of executive power and legislative and democratic weakness. The Council and Commission, however, have emphasised that Commission legislation is usually highly technical and of a kind that needs quick decisions; as such, it is similar to the decrees, ordinances and other minor legislative acts that national administrations issue and which are commonly accepted as an inevitable aspect of decision-making in the modern world. (See the section on comitology in Chapter 9 for further discussion of this issue.)

Parliament and the EU budget

Thanks mainly to the 1970 *Treaty Amending Certain Budgetary Provisions of the Treaties* and the 1975 *Treaty Amending Certain Financial Provisions of the Treaties* the EP enjoys considerable treaty powers in relation to the EU budget. These powers include:

(1) The right to propose 'modifications' to compulsory expenditure (this principally means agriculture, which comprises over two-fifths of the total budget). Modifications that entail increases in total expenditure require qualified majority support in the Council to be accepted. Where increases are not involved, owing perhaps to a proposed increase being offset by a proposed decrease, a qualified majority vote is required for rejection – a negative majority as it is called.

(2) The right to propose 'amendments' to non-compulsory expenditure (which means most things apart from agriculture) subject to the ceilings set by the financial perspective (see below). Acting by a qualified majority the Council may modify these amendments, but

Parliament can reinsert and insist on them at its second reading of the budget.

(3) Under Article 272(8) TEC, Parliament, 'acting by a majority of its members and two-thirds of the votes cast, may, if there are important reasons, reject the draft budget and ask for a new draft to be submitted to it'. In other words the EP may reject the whole budget if it does not like the Council's final draft.

Following the introduction of direct elections for MEPs in 1979, in the 1980s extensive use was made of the powers just listed. Virtually all aspects of the rules, including the power of rejection, were tested to see how far they could be taken. Major confrontations with the Council, far from being avoided, seemed at times almost to be sought as the EP attempted to assert itself. For most of the 1980s, however, this assertion was limited in its effect, because although the EP formally enjoyed joint decision-making powers with the Council on the budget, the powers of the two bodies were not equally balanced. Parliament was still very much restricted in what it could do: restricted by the Treaty, which gave it very little room for manoeuvre in the major budgetary sector – compulsory expenditure; restricted by the Council's attitude, which tended to be one of wishing to limit Parliament's influence as much as possible; and restricted by its own inability – because of conflicting loyalties and pressures – to be wholly consistent and resolved in its approach.

For the most part these restrictions still apply. However, developments occurred in 1988 that increased the EP's influence. Following decisions taken by the European Council in February 1988 on budgetary matters, the EP, together with the Commission and the Council of Ministers, put its name, in June 1988, to *The Interinstitutional Agreement on Budgetary Discipline and Improvement of the Budgetary Procedure*. This committed all three institutions to a financial perspective for the years 1988 to 1992. Key features of the perspective were provisions for a significant increase in non-compulsory expenditure and a significant decrease in compulsory expenditure (thus realising aims the EP had been pressing for years), and the setting of clear ceilings for both types of expenditure. The main benefits of the Interinstitutional Agreement, in power terms, for the EP were twofold. First, its influence over compulsory expenditure, which in the past had been very limited, was potentially increased because Parliament's approval was now required for any upward movement of the ceiling. Second, the very act of the Council agreeing to sign a financial perspective with the EP gave to the latter an extra element of leverage in budgetary discussions.

When the 1988–92 financial perspective was revised in 1992–3 the EP's influence was not as great as MEPs had hoped or anticipated. Whilst it was accepted by the Commission and the Council that a precedent had been set in 1988 and that the next financial perspective would require the EP's endorsement, the key institutions in determining the size and shape of what became a seven-year financial perspective covering the years 1993–9 were the Commission, the Council of Ministers and the European Council. As it turned out there was much in the new financial perspective of which the EP approved – most notably further cuts in agricultural expenditure and further increases in non-agricultural expenditure – but this was more the outcome of battles fought in the Council of Ministers and at the December 1992 Edinburgh European Council meeting than EP influence. Dissatisfied with the negotiating role it had been allowed, the EP delayed ratifying the agreement until November 1993 – though this did enable it to wring concessions from the Council with regard to its future influence over compulsory expenditure.

As with the 1988–92 and 1993–9 financial perspectives, the key actors in shaping the 2000–6 perspective were the Commission – which set the contours of the debate and the negotiations in its *Agenda 2000* document (European Commission, 1997a) – and the member states. The EP exerted as much influence as it could – by producing reports and recommendations, questioning the Council and Commission, and holding debates and votes – but the main decisions were taken in the Council of Ministers and by the Heads of Government at the March 1999 Berlin summit. The EP subsequently managed to persuade the Council to make some modest adjustments to the perspective, but the endorsement that it gave to the perspective in May 1999 was essentially an endorsement of a Commission-sponsored and member state-negotiated deal.

The decision-making processes on the 2007–13 financial perspective operated very much on bases of those that produced the 1999–2006 perspective, with the Commission setting the broad agenda via initial and then revised proposals, with the governments in both the Council of Ministers and the European Council contesting key issues and acting virtually as if they were the sole decision-makers, and with the EP struggling to make its voice heard. An account of the making of the 2007–13 financial perspective is given in Chapter 17.

Control and supervision of the executive

Virtually all parliaments have difficulty exercising controlling and supervisory powers over executives. On the one hand, they are usually hampered by the executives themselves, which do not welcome the prospect of being investigated and therefore seek to protect themselves behind whatever constitutional, institutional or party political defences are available. On the other hand, parliamentarians themselves tend not to have the requisite information, the specialist knowledge, or the necessary resources that are required to monitor properly, and if necessary challenge, executive activity.

The EP shares these problems but also has two additional ones of its own. First, a key aspect of control and supervision of executives concerns policy implementation: is policy being implemented efficiently and for the purposes intended by the relevant law? The Commission is the most obvious body to be called to account on this question. But in many policy spheres the Commission's executive role is very limited and consists essentially of attempting to coordinate the work of outside agencies operating at different administrative levels. Such agencies, of which national governments are the most important, are often reluctant to open the books to or cooperate with EP investigators. Certainly there is little question of government ministers allowing themselves to be grilled by the EP on the competency and honesty of their national bureaucracies.

The second problem specific to the EP is that on broad controlling and supervisory issues – such as whether the EU executive is acting responsibly in the execution of its duties, and whether it is fulfilling its treaty obligations – problems arise from the blurring of roles between the Commission, the Council of Ministers and the European Council. Insofar as the Council of Ministers and the European Council undertake what are in effect executive powers, the EP's supervisory powers are weakened. This is because Parliament's treaty powers are not so strong in relation to the Council of Ministers as they are to the Commission, nor does it have the same access to the former as it does to the latter. As for the European Council, the EP has virtually no treaty powers in relation to it, and only very limited access.

The EP's ability to control and supervise the Commission, the Council of Ministers, the European Council, and other quasi-executive bodies, will now be considered separately.

The Commission

In relation to the Commission, the EP has eight main powers and channels at its disposal.

First, the nominee for Commission President must be approved by the EP. The narrow vote of approval given to Jacques Santer in 1994 showed that confirmation of the European Council's nominee cannot be assumed.

Second, the 'President and the other members of the Commission thus nominated shall be subject as a body to a vote of approval by the European Parliament' (Article 214 TEC). Since this power of approval was given to the EP by the Maastricht Treaty, each Commissioner-designate has been subject to a three hour or so grilling by the appropriate EP committee before the confirmation vote. The confirmation vote itself cannot be on individual Commissioners but must be on the College as a whole, but, as was shown in Chapter 9, the EP made it quite clear to President-designate Barroso in 2004 that if his College-designate continued to include individuals who were deemed to be totally unacceptable to the EP then approval would be withheld from the whole College.

Third, the EP can dismiss the College – but not individual Commissioners – by carrying a motion of censure by a two-thirds majority of the votes cast, including a majority of all MEPs. This power of dismissal is obviously too blunt a controlling instrument for most purposes and it has never been carried through. However, it came close to being so in January 1999 when a number of factors came together to produce a groundswell of dissatisfaction amongst MEPs with the Santer College. Amongst the factors were: a Court of Auditors report that revealed (yet again!) evidence of 'missing' EU funds and was strongly critical of aspects of Commission management practices; the suggestion that some Commissioners were favouring relatives and friends for appointments and the awarding of contracts; and a rather dismissive response by Jacques Santer to the criticisms that were being made about himself and some of his colleagues. It was only after Santer agreed to the creation of a special committee of independent experts to investigate the allegations of fraud, nepotism and mismanagement that the threat of dismissal receded, though even then the motion of censure was supported by 232 MEPs, with 293 voting against.

The special committee's report was issued two months later, in March, and was highly critical of aspects of the College's work and behaviour (Committee of Independent Experts, 1999a). Particular criticisms were made of: Santer in his capacity as the official responsible for the Commission's Security Office, for taking 'no meaningful interest in its functioning' and allowing it to develop as 'a state within a state' (point 6.5.7); Edith Cresson, the Commissioner responsible for Research, for showing favouritism to someone known to her when issuing contracts (points 8.1.1–8.1.38); and Commissioners as a whole for being reluctant to assume responsibility for their actions – 'The studies carried out by the Committee have too often revealed a growing reluctance among the members of the hierarchy to acknowledge their responsibility. It is becoming difficult to find anyone who has even the slightest sense of responsibility' (point 9.4.25). Meeting almost immediately after the report was published, faced with a refusal by Santer and Cresson to resign, and aware that MEPs were likely to carry a motion of censure on it by the necessary two-thirds majority, the Santer College collectively resigned. The resignation was widely interpreted as a triumph for the EP and as a highly significant step forward in its long campaign to exercise greater control over Commission activities.

A further step forward was taken in 2004 when the then Commission President-designate, José Manuel Barroso, gave way to pressures from MEPs that he should respond positively to any request from them to dismiss an individual member of his College. He promised that if what amounted to a motion of no confidence in a Commissioner was passed, he would require the individual to resign or at least would appear before Parliament to explain why he was not insisting on the Commissioner's resignation.

Fourth, under Article 200 TEC, the EP 'shall discuss in open session the annual general report submitted to it by the Commission'. This debate used to be one of the highlights of the Parliamentary year, but it has never produced significant results and is now of little consequence.

Fifth, under Article 275 TEC 'The Commission shall submit annually to the Council and to the European Parliament the accounts of the preceding financial year relating to the implementation of the budget. The Commission shall also forward to them a financial statement of the assets and liabilities of the Community.' On the basis of an examination of the accounts and the financial statement, and having examined also the annual report of the Court of Auditors, Parliament 'acting on a recommendation from the Council which shall act by a qualified majority, shall give a discharge to the Commission in respect of the implementation of the budget' (Article 276 TEC). Under its discharge powers the EP can require the Commission and other institutions to take appropriate steps to ensure action on the comments appearing in the decision on discharge. Sometimes the EP's discharge powers lead to confrontation with the Commission, as in 1998 when the Parliament initially postponed the discharge in order to give the Commission time to respond to charges of mismanagement and fraud in the running of some programmes, and then positively voted not to give discharge because of dissatisfaction with the way the Commission was dealing with these problems. This negative vote was an important factor in bringing about the January 1999 censure motion (see above). (The 1998 discharge dispute is considered further in the section on the Court of Auditors in Chapter 14.)

Sixth, the remits of EP standing committees are broad enough to allow them to attempt to exercise supervisory functions if they so choose. However, the Commission is not anxious to encourage investigations of itself, and the committees are not sufficiently well resourced to be able to probe very deeply. The Committee on Budgetary Control, which is specifically charged with monitoring policy implementation, is in a typically weak position: with only a handful of senior officers employed to assist it, it cannot hope to do anything other than cover a small fraction of the Commission's work.

Seventh, the Maastricht Treaty empowered the EP to establish temporary committees of inquiry 'to investigate ... alleged contraventions or maladministration in the implementation of Community law, except where the alleged facts are being examined before a court and while the case is still subject to legal proceedings' (Article 193 TEC). The rules governing the rights of EP committees of inquiry were subsequently set out in an EP–Council–Commission inter-institutional agreement signed in 1995. Clearly the work of committees of inquiry are not just concerned with Commission activities, but they certainly can focus on them, as demonstrated in 1996 when many of the recommendations that were made by the committee established to investigate the BSE crisis were directed at the Commission. According to one well-placed Commission insider, 'Parliament's debates with the Commission on 16 July 1996 and 18 February 1997 [on the BSE crisis, and framed by the work of the committee] can be seen as classic examples of a legislature holding the executive to account' (Westlake, 1997: 23). Following publication of the committee's report there was a move to censure the Commission, but – aware that blame for the crisis was widely shared – the EP opted to employ what it called a 'conditional censure', which involved imposing a deadline on the Commission to carry out the EP's recommendations. (The application of this concept of conditional censure – which has no legal base – is typical of the way the EP has long been extremely innovative in interpreting and using its formal powers to the full.)

Finally, questions can be asked of the Commission. These take different forms: written questions, oral questions in question time, and oral questions with debate (see Table 12.2).

Table 12.2   *Questions addressed by the European Parliament during 2004*

To the Commission	3676
of which:	
written	3254
oral with debate	53
during question time	369
To the Council	624
of which:	
written	379
oral with debate	37
during question time	208

Source: information from European Commission (2005b: point 796).

The Council

The EP is less able to control and supervise the Council of Ministers than it is the Commission. There are three main reasons for this.

The first reason arises from the role of the Council as the meeting place of the governments of the member states. To make it, or any of its members, directly responsible to the EP would be to introduce a measure of supranationalism into the EU that is unacceptable to most governments. The view has been taken that Council members should be principally responsible to their national parliaments. In other words, the Council as a collective body should not be responsible to anyone, whilst individual members should not be responsible to an EU institution. (It might be added that this does not always stop ministers, if they find themselves being pressed too hard in their national legislatures, from hiding behind Council meetings and 'immovable' EU partners.)

Second, in respect of certain key policy sectors – most notably the CFSP, Police and Judicial Cooperation, and aspects of EMU – the EP's powers are relatively weak. This is partly because decisions in these spheres sometimes need to be made quickly and in secret and partly because some member states favour intergovernmentalism as the prevailing decision-making mode in these sensitive areas. The EP is thus left to make the best it can of its powers to be consulted, to be kept informed, to ask questions, and to make recommendations.

Third, the very nature of the Council – with its ever-changing composition, its specialist Councils, and its rotating Presidency – means that continuity of relations between it and the EP is difficult to establish.

The amount of access the EP gets to the Council depends in large part on the attitude of the country holding the Presidency. There are, however, certain set points of contact which, if they do not enable the EP to exercise control over the Council, at least provide it with opportunities to challenge the Council on its general conduct of affairs. First, the Presidency of the Council – formerly usually represented by the Foreign Minister, but Heads of Government now normally do this – appears before EP plenaries at the beginning and end of each six-month term of office. On the first occasion the Presidency's priorities are explained and on the second an assessment of the Presidency is given. On both occasions MEPs are given the opportunity to ask questions. Second, ministers from the Presidency usually attend the EP committees that deal with their spheres of responsibility at least twice during their country's Presidency. MEPs can use these occasions for informal discussions with the Council, or to have wide-ranging question and answer sessions on the Council's priorities and performance. Third, ministers from the Presidency also regularly attend

EP plenary sessions and participate in important debates. Fourth, the EP can, through the Presidency, ask questions of the Council (see Table 12.2).

The European Council

If the EP is not able to call the Commission fully to account and is greatly restricted in its ability to exercise control over the Council of Ministers, it is almost wholly bereft of any supervisory power over the European Council. This is largely because of the nature of the European Council: it is an intergovernmental institution that is largely outside the framework of the TEC; it meets for only about six days a year; and most of its more important members, the Heads of Government, not only have no great wish to be accountable to MEPs but can also ensure that they do not become so since it is at European Council meetings that final decisions on the contents of the treaties – which set out the main operating principles of the EU – are taken.

The TEU and the TEC make provision in a few instances – such as in regard to EMU under the TEC – for the European Council, or the Heads of Government meeting in the composition of the Council of Ministers, to inform or consult the EP, but these are anticipated as being for only occasional use. In only two sets of circumstances does the European Council come into regular contact with the EP, and one of these is a consequence of political practice rather than legal requirement. The non-required contact is at the opening session of European Council meetings, when the EP President is permitted to address the summit to inform it of the views of MEPs on current issues. The second contact is as described above, when the President of the European Council delivers beginning and end of term reports and answers questions at EP plenary sessions.

What this all adds up to is that the EP can exert very little influence indeed on the European Council, let alone control over what it does. The fact is that there are very limited linkages between the two institutions, and there is no reason to suppose that the participants at summits make a habit of looking over their shoulders in anticipation of how the EP will view the outcome of their deliberations and negotiations.

Other bodies

The EP has a number of powers in relation to other EU bodies. Some of these bodies are of a quasi-executive nature.

The most prominent of the quasi-executive bodies is the European Central Bank where, under Article 114 TEC, the EP must be consulted on the nominees for the Bank's President, Vice-President and executive board members. As with the powers given to it on the appointment of the College of Commissioners, the Parliament has sought to use these treaty provisions to maximum advantage by use of confirmation hearings. Significantly, the first President-designate of the Bank, Wim Duisenberg, stated at the time of his confirmation hearing in 1998 that he would withdraw his candidature if the EP did not give him its approval. He also undertook to keep the EP fully informed about the work of the Bank and to appear personally before the EP's Economic Committee at least once a quarter.

Other quasi-executive bodies in which the EP has a role in the nomination process include the executive boards of some of the EU agencies which have been established in recent years. Amongst these agencies are the European Environment Agency and the European Medicines Agency.

Beyond quasi-executive bodies, the EP also has a role in the appointment and overseeing of certain other EU bodies. Two of these bodies are especially important. First, the EP is consulted on the appointment of members of the Court of Auditors. It is a consultation that, as with other appointment powers, has been examined via committee 'hearings' followed by a vote. However, on three occasions – once in 1989 and twice in 1993 – negative EP opinions have been ignored by the Council when making the formal appointments. Second, the European Ombudsman, who investigates cases of alleged maladministration, is appointed by the EP, with the Council having no input at all. Indeed, the Ombudsman is virtually a quasi-parliamentary post in that not only is the incumbent appointed by the EP but the duties of the post are regulated by Parliament and are annexed to the Parliament's Rules of Procedure.

Elections

Until 1979 MEPs were nominated by the national parliaments from amongst their members. Various consequences followed from this: parties not represented in their national legislature could not be represented in the EP; virtually all MEPs were pro-integrationist, since sceptics in national parliaments were generally unwilling to allow their names to be considered for nomination; and MEPs had limited time to devote to their European responsibilities.

However, Article 138 of the EEC Treaty included the following provision: 'The Assembly shall draw up proposals for elections by direct universal suffrage in accordance with a uniform procedure in all Member States.' The Assembly approved such proposals as early as 1960, but found itself frustrated by another Article 138 requirement which stated: 'The Council shall, acting unanimously, lay down the appropriate provisions, which it shall recommend to Member States for adoption in accordance with their respective constitutional requirements.' That the first set of direct elections were not held until 1979 is witness to the feeling of some member governments – initially mainly the French, later the Danes and the British – that direct elections were rather unwelcome, both because they had supranational overtones and because they might be followed by pressure for institutional reform in the EP's favour. Even after the principle of direct elections was eventually won and it was agreed they would be held on a fixed five-year basis, no uniform electoral system could be agreed, nor has been agreed since. Consequently, the six sets of direct elections held to date – in 1979, 1984, 1989, 1994, 1999 and 2004 – have all been contested on the basis of different national electoral arrangements (see Table 12.3). The 1999 elections, however, did bring a significant movement in the direction of standardisation in that the UK did not use its traditional single member constituency first past the post system but rather proportional representation on a regional basis, which meant that for the first time proportional representation – albeit in different forms – was used in all member states.

In addition to the differences arising from the usage of varying versions of proportional representation, two other differences between the states' EP electoral arrangements merit note. The first is that voting does not take place on the same day. In 2004, for example, voting was between 10 and 13 June, with the Netherlands and the UK voting on the 10th, the Czech Republic and Ireland on the 11th, Latvia, Malta, and Italy on the 12th (Italy voted on the 13th too), and all other states voting on the 13th. The second difference, and one that is important in terms of the democratic base of the EP, is that there is a considerable variation in the size of the electorate per MEP. The range is from one per 820 000 voters in Germany to one per 71 000 in Malta. The reason for this imbalance is that EP seats are distributed not just on grounds of national equitability but also with an eye to ensuring that the representations of small states are not totally swamped in EP decision-making processes. In most states the ratio is between one per 350 000 and one per 650 000.

* * *

A subject that has been much discussed in the context of EP elections is voter turnout. Many have argued that a high turnout would serve to enhance the EP's legitimacy and democratic base, and as a consequence would also place the EP in a strong position to press for increased powers.

In the event, turnout has been relatively low and has declined in every election since the first direct elections in 1979. In 1979 only 62 per cent of those eligible to vote did so, in 1984 the figure was 61 per cent, in 1989 it was 58 per cent, in 1994 it was 56.5 per cent, in 1999 it was 49.8 per cent,

Table 12.3 *Member states and the 2004 European Parliament elections*

	Number of MEPs	Electoral system	Number of constituencies	Electoral turnout 2004 (%)
Austria	18	PR with PV	1	42.3
Belgium	24	PR with PV	4	90.8
Cyprus	6	PR without PV	1	72.5
Czech Rep.	24	PR without PV	1	28.3
Denmark	14	PR with PV	1	47.9
Estonia	6	PR without PV	1	26.8
Finland	14	PR with PV	1	39.4
France	78	PR without PV	8	42.8
Germany	99	PR without PV	16	43.0
Greece	24	PR without PV	1	63.2
Hungary	24	PR without PV	1	38.5
Ireland	13	PR with STV	4	59.0
Italy	78	PR with PV	5	71.4
Latvia	9	PR without PV	1	41.3
Lithuania	13	PR with PV	1	48.4
Luxembourg	6	PR with vote splitting	1	91.2
Malta	5	PR with STV	1	82.4
Netherlands	27	PR with PV	1	39.3
Poland	54	PR without PV	1 (with partial use of 13 constituences)	20.9
Portugal	24	PR without PV	1	38.8
Slovakia	14	PR with PV	1	17.0
Slovenia	7	PR with PV	1	28.4
Spain	54	PR without PV	1	45.1
Sweden	19	PR with PV	1	37.9
United Kingdom	78	PR without PV (except Northern Ireland, which has 3 seats based on STV)	12	38.8
TOTAL	732			45.47
			EU-15	49.12
			EU-10	26.92

Notes:
PR with PV: proportional representation with preferential vote.
PR without PV: proportional representation without preferential vote
PR with STV: proportional representation with single transferable vote.
PR with vote splitting: proportional representation, with voters being able to choose candiates from different lists.

Sources: information from: for columns 1 and 4: European Parliament, *Session News*, 20–23 July 2004; for columns 2 and 3: European Parliament elections website at www.elections2004.eu.int/ep-election/sites/en/yourvoice/pl/law.html.

and in 2004 it was 45.5 per cent. As Table 12.3 shows, in 2004 turnout was highest in Belgium and Luxembourg – where voting is obligatory – and was lowest in Slovakia and Estonia. In some countries turnout was 'artificially boosted' by elections being held on the same day as national elections of some sort. Turnout in the new EU-10 states was, on average, significantly lower than in the EU-15 states: 26.9 per cent as compared with 49.1 per cent.

Three main factors combine to explain the low turnouts. First, because EP elections do not offer any prospect of a change of government, switches in policy, or the making or unmaking of political reputations, they stimulate little popular interest or political excitement. Second, the election campaigns have little overall coherence or coordination. They are essentially national contests, but of a secondary sort. 'European' issues have never made much of an impact. In 2004, for example, there was little sense of a majority defending its record, or of the Left or the Right seeking to gain control. Third, those actors who do much to focus attention on and generate interest in national electoral campaigns approach the EP elections in, at best, a half-hearted manner: few 'big names' have been candidates in recent elections; national political parties have been generally reluctant to commit resources to their Euro campaigns; party activists have tended to be uninterested; a conscious attempt has been made by some governments to play down the importance of the elections because they are frequently interpreted as being, in part at least, 'mid-term' national elections, or unofficial referendums on the government's performance in office; and media interest has been limited.

Political Parties and the European Parliament

Party political activity takes place at three main levels in relation to the EP: the transnational, the political groups in the EP, and the national.

The transnational federations

Very loosely organised transnational federations, grouped around general principles, exist for coordinating, propaganda, and electioneering purposes. They are based on affiliation by national parties, from both within and outside the EU.

The three main federations were created in similar circumstances in the mid-1970s out of existing, but extremely weakly-based, liaising and information-exchanging bodies, and as a specific response to the continuing development of the EC and the anticipated future use of direct elections to the EP. These three federations are: the European People's Party (EPP), which is composed of Centre-Right parties; the European Liberal, Democrat and Reform Party (ELDR); and the Party of European Socialists (PES).

Some supporters of European integration have hoped that the federations might develop into organisations providing leadership, vision and coordination at the European level, and perhaps might even serve as agents of unification to their heterogeneous memberships. They have failed to do so. Their principal weakness is that, unlike national parties or the EP political groups, they are not involved in day-to-day political activity in an institutional setting. Hence they have no clear focus and cannot develop attachments and loyalties. From this, other weaknesses flow: low status; limited resources – they are heavily dependent on the EP political groups for administrative and financial support; and loose organisational structures based on periodic congresses and bureaux meetings.

The federations, therefore, have not been able to do very much, even though there certainly are tasks that EU-wide transnational parties could usefully perform, such as long-term policy planning, the harmonisation of national party differences, and educating the electorate about Europe. Such influence as they have exercised has been largely confined to very loose policy coordination (effected partly through periodic meetings of national leaders, often before European Council meetings), and to EP elections when manifestos have been produced and a few joint activities have been arranged. Even the manifestos, however, have reinforced the general picture of weakness for they invariably have been somewhat vague in content (necessarily so given the need to reconcile differences), and have been utilised by only a few of the constituent member parties (because EP elections are contested, for the most part, along national lines).

Beyond the three main federations, other groupings of an even looser nature have surfaced from time to time, usually in order to coordinate election activities. They have included Green, Regional, Communist, and Extreme Right alliances. All have been internally divided and have been hard pressed to put together even minimal common statements. (For more detailed information on Europe's transnational party federations see Hix and Lord, 1997, especially Chapter 7.)

The political groups in the European Parliament

Partisan political activity in the EP is mainly channelled via political groups. The rules for the composition of political groups have changed over the years in response to the increasing size of the Parliament. Since the 2004 enlargement, nineteen MEPs drawn from at least five member states have been necessary to form a group.

Groups have been formed and developed for a number of reasons. The principal basis and unifying element of most of the groups is ideological identification. Despite the many differences that exist between them, MEPs from similar political backgrounds and traditions are naturally drawn to one another. All the more so when cooperation serves to maximise their influence, as it does in the EP in all sorts of ways – from electing the President to voting on amendments to Commission proposals.

Organisational benefits provide another inducement to political group formation. For example, funds for administrative and research purposes are distributed to groups on the basis of a fixed amount per group (the non-attached being regarded as a group for these purposes), plus an additional sum per member. No one, therefore, is unsupported, but clearly the larger the group the more easily it can afford good back-up services.

There are also advantages in the conduct of Parliamentary business that stem from group status, since the EP arranges much of what it does around the groups. Although non-attached members are not formally excluded from anything by this – indeed they are guaranteed many rights under the Rules of Procedure – in practice they can be disadvantaged: in the distribution of committee chairmanships for example, in the preparation of the agendas for plenary sessions, and in speaking time during debates.

In recent years there have usually been between seven and nine political groups in the EP. The main reason for there being so many is that, with proportional representation being used for EP elections, MEPs reflect the wide range of political opinion that exists across the EU with regard to ideological and national orientation. Since direct elections were introduced in 1979 there have never been fewer than sixty national political parties represented in the EP and since the 1994 EP elections there have never been less than one hundred.

The main characteristics of the political groups in the EP, as of early 2006, will now be outlined. The sizes of the groups are shown in Table 12.4. (Updated versions of this table and Table 12.3 will be posted when necessary at http://www.palgrave.com/politics/eu/.)

- *Group of the European People's Party and European Democrats (EPP-ED).* The EPP-ED used to be based on European Christian Democracy, and in particular the large Christian Democratic parties of Germany and Italy. Over the years, however, other Centre-Right parties, mostly from a conservative tradition, have been absorbed into the group. Indeed it was at the behest of these parties, especially UK Conservatives, that the group changed its name in 1999 from EPP to EPP-ED. The group, which contains at least one member from all member states, has had some difficulty maintaining internal ideological cohesion – not least on the nature of the integration process, with MEPs located in the Christian Democratic family tending to be stronger supporters of integration than other members of the group.

Table 12.4   *Political groups in the European Parliament*

	EPP-ED	PES	ALDE	Greens/ EFA	GUE/ NGL	IND/ DEM	UEN	NA	Total
Austria	6	7	1	2				2	18
Belgium	6	7	6	2				3	24
Cyprus	3		1		2				6
Czech Rep.	14	2			6	1		1	24
Denmark	1	5	4	1	1	1	1		14
Estonia	1	3	2						6
Finland	4	3	5	1	1				14
France	17	31	11	6	3	3		7	78
Germany	49	23	7	13	7				99
Greece	11	8			4	1			24
Hungary	13	9	2						24
Ireland	5	1	1		1	1	4		13
Italy	24	14	13	2	7	4	9	5	78
Latvia	3		1	1			4		9
Lithuania	2	2	7				2		13
Luxembourg	3	1	1	1					6
Malta	2	3							5
Netherlands	7	7	5	4	2	2			27
Poland	16	10	4			7	10	7	54
Portugal	9	12			3				24
Slovakia	8	3						3	14
Slovenia	4	1	2						7
Spain	24	24	2	3	1				54
Sweden	5	5	3	1	2	3			19
United Kingdom	27	18	12	5	1	10		4	78
TOTAL	**264**	**200**	**90**	**42**	**41**	**33**	**30**	**32**	**732**

Notes:
1. Situation in March 2006.
2. The full names of the political groups are given in the text.
3. Member states can have less than their full complement of MEPs for short periods if vacancies arise from resignations or deaths.

Source: information from European Parliament web pages on the Europa website.

- *Socialist Group in the European Parliament (PES).* The Socialist Group includes at least one MEP from 23 of the 25 member states. Reflecting the breadth of European Socialism and Social Democracy, the members of the group have sometimes found cooperation difficult. In part this has been because of ideological diversity within the group, with opinions ranging from 'traditional state interventionists' to 'moderate' and 'modernising' social democrats. In part it has been caused by national party groups being reluctant to concede national interests to wider European interests. And in part it has stemmed from differences within the group on the very bases and direction of European integration.

- *Group of the Alliance of Liberals and Democrats for Europe (ALDE).* Called before the 2004 elections the European Liberal, Democratic and Reform Party (ELDR), the ALDE is a strongly pro-European integrationist centrist group. It is comprised primarily of parties of the Centre and the Right, but there are also certain Leftist elements. In the 1999–2004 Parliament it worked with the EPP-ED on several matters, including contracting a deal under which the ELDR backed the EPP-ED's candidate for EP President for the first two and a half years of the Parliament (Nicole Fontaine was duly elected) whilst the EPP-ED would return the favour for the ELDR's candidate for the second two and a half years (Pat Cox was duly elected). After expanding its membership following the 2004 elections, the ALDE has members from twenty member states.

- *Group of the Greens/European Free Alliance (Greens/EFA).* This group was formed in 1999 largely as a marriage of convenience. Beyond a common concern with green issues, the Greens are not very homogeneous, with some of their MEPs coming from a clear Left background and others seeing themselves as neither Left nor Right. The parties in the group favour greater regional autonomy.

- *Confederal Group of the European Left/Nordic Green Left (GUE/ NGL).* This group is made up mainly of left Socialist and former Communist parties, plus a small number of Nordic Leftist Greens. It supports European integration, but wants a much greater emphasis to be given to social and environmental issues. Disparate views within the group coupled with a very loose group structure make for little internal group cohesion.

- *Independence and Democracy Group (Ind/Dem).* This group was created after the 2004 elections. Comprised of eurosceptics of various persuasions, including the UK Independence Party which campaigns for complete British withdrawal from the EU, its message is that there should be a 'Europe of Sovereign Nation States'.

- *Union for Europe of the Nations Group (UEN)*. This group has its origins in the Union for Europe (UFE) Group in the 1994–99 Parliament, which brought together French Gaullists and Irish Fianna Fail who were not numerous enough to constitute a group of their own but who, for different reasons, were reluctant to link up with one of the more established Centre-Right groups. The Gaullists subsequently joined the EPP-ED after the 1999 elections, but the group managed, and continues to manage, to continue, albeit with a very heterogeneous membership. Insofar as it has an identity it is one of conservatism and of opposition to the notion of a federal Europe.
- Non-attached MEPs are drawn from many different persuasions. After the 1999 elections many MEPs who did not wish to join one of the established political groups formed what they called *The Technical Group (TDI)* in a marriage of convenience aimed at enabling them to benefit from group privileges. The Group was initially refused recognition by the EP on the grounds that it breached the Parliament's Rules of Procedure that group members must show a political affiliation, but the EP then retreated when the Group appealed to the Court of First Instance against the decision. However, in October 2001 the Court ruled against the TDI (in joined cases T-222/99, T-327/99 and T-329/99), which resulted in the EP's President, Nicole Fontaine, announcing that the initial refusal of recognition was 'once again fully effective'.

As suggested in the above outlines, group formation and composition is highly fluid. The extent of this is demonstrated by the fact that although the number of groups has remained relatively stable over the years, since direct elections were first introduced only the two largest groups – the EPP-ED and the PES – have survived in recognisable form. Moreover, both of these have been subject to considerable changes in their memberships as a result of enlargements, election results, and – especially in the EPP-ED's case – defections from smaller groups.

As the above outlines also suggest, all the political groups have significant internal divisions, usually of both an ideological and a national character. This is especially so of the PES and the EPP-ED, which over the years have grown in size in relation to other groups as some smaller groups, recognising the advantages of large group membership, have joined them. Internal division within any group does, of course, undermine coherence, which has a weakening effect. So, for example, it is difficult, whatever their ideological principles might suggest to them, for French MEPs to vote for a cut in agricultural support measures or for Portuguese MEPs not to support increases in the Regional Fund.

Three other factors also make for looseness and a limited ability on the part of the groups to control and direct their members. The first of these factors arises from the political powers of the EP and the institutional setting in which it is placed. With no government to sustain or attack and no government-sponsored legislation to pass or reject, MEPs do not have the semi-automatic 'for' or 'against' reaction that is so typical of much national parliamentary behaviour. The second factor is structural. Unlike parties in national legislatures, the political groups are not part of a wider organisational framework from which emanate expectations of cooperative and united behaviour, and generally recognised notions of responsibility and accountability. Rather, most of them are weak, quasi-federal bodies functioning in a multicultural environment. This is evidenced in a number of ways: the constituent member parties of the larger groups hold their own separate meetings and have their own leaderships; in seeking to encourage group unity, group leaders can invoke no effective sanctions against, and can withhold few rewards from, MEPs who do not fall into line; and in looking to their political futures, it is not only their political group or its leadership that MEPs must cultivate but also their national parties at home. The third factor is that MEPs may have claims on their loyalties and votes that compete with the claims of the political groups. One source of such claims are the numerous interest groups with which many MEPs are closely associated. Other sources are the EP intergroups, which bring together, usually on a relatively informal basis, MEPs from different political groups who have similar views on particular issues. Over 100 intergroups exist, of which 25 or so meet on a regular basis. The intergroups come in many different forms and vary considerably in the nature and range of their policy focus. Amongst their number are the Federalist Intergroup for European Union, the Friends of Israel Intergroup, the Central American Intergroup, the Media Intergroup, the Rural Areas Intergroup, the Animal Welfare Intergroup, and the Elderly People Intergroup.

However, despite the many weaknesses of the groups, it is important to emphasise that they are of considerable importance in determining how the EP works.

Some of their functions and tasks and the privileges they enjoy are specifically allocated to them under the Rules of Procedure or by parliamentary decisions. These include guaranteed representation on key EP bodies and committees, and speaking rights in plenary sessions.

Other functions have not been formally laid down but have developed out of political necessity, advantage, or convenience. This is most obviously illustrated by the way the groups are the prime determiners of tactics and voting patterns in the EP, the decisions on which are normally taken in the week prior to plenary sessions, which is set aside for political group meetings. At these meetings efforts are made to agree a common group position on matters of current importance. For example: should a deal be attempted with another political group on the election of the President?, what is the group's attitude towards a Commission proposal for a directive?, what tactics can the group employ to prevent an unwelcome own initiative report being approved by a committee? In dealing with such questions internal group differences may have to be tackled, and sometimes they may not be resolved. But of the many influences bearing down on MEPs, political group membership is normally the single most important factor correlating with how they vote: in the three largest groups – the EPP-ED, the PES, and the ALDE (ELDR as was) – MEPs vote with their group over 80 per cent of the time, whilst for all groups the average is around 70 per cent (Judge and Earnshaw, 2003).

Regarding the implications of the political group composition of the EP for the overall balance of power in the Parliament, in very broad terms it can be said that from 1979–89 a nominal Centre-Right majority existed, from 1989–94 there was a nominal Left-Green majority, from 1994–99 there was no nominal majority either to the Right or to the Left, and since the 1999 elections there has been a Centre-Right majority. The nature of the political balance existing at any one time unquestionably affects the interests and priorities of the EP, with groups from the Left tending, for example, to be more sympathetic to social and environmental issues than groups from the Right. However, the significance of the nature of the overall balance is not as great as it normally is in national parliaments. There are four main reasons for this. First, important issues, sometimes of an organisational or domestic political nature rather than an ideological nature, can divide groups that otherwise appear to be obvious voting partners. The various liaising channels and mechanisms that exist in the EP via which groups attempt to reach agreements and strike deals cannot always bridge these divisions. On many issues it is by no means unusual for the views of political groups on the Centre-Left and Centre-Right, or at least of many MEPs within these groups, to be closer to each other than to the views of other Left and Right groups. The second reason is that many matters that come before the EP cut across traditional Left–Right divisions. Such is the case with much of the essentially technical legislation with which Parliament deals. Such too is the case with issues like action to combat racism in Europe, the provision of assistance to the countries of the developing world, and the further development of economic and political European integration. The third reason is that the EP frequently and consciously attempts to avoid being divided along Left–Right lines when it votes because it is in its institutional interests to do so. For example, under the co-decision procedure an absolute majority of MEPs must support EP amendments and rejections for votes to be effective. In consequence, it is necessary for groups from both Left and Right, and especially for the PES and the EPP-ED, to work together if the EP is to make full use of its powers. And the fourth reason is that most EU decision-making processes are characterised by bargaining and compromising. So, for example, the EP is almost constantly involved in inter-institutional dealings with the Commission and the Council. As a result, MEPs are accustomed to exchanging points and cutting deals in all sorts of ways: ways that often result in alliances being made that are not based on ideological identities (see Kreppel, 2000).

Given these circumstances it is not surprising that the most dominant voting pattern in the EP is not along 'hard' Left–Right lines but is grouped around an alliance of Centre-Left and Centre-Right. The PES, the EPP, and the ELDR used to vote together on average about 75–80 per cent of the time (Hix and Lord, 1997: 137). This figure has subsequently slipped, but the 'big three' groups still come together in a 'grand coalition' on about two-thirds of the votes (Judge and Earnshaw, 2003: Chapter 5). Left–Right divisions account only for about one-third of votes. The only modest Left–Right dimension of voting patterns in the EP is no more clearly seen than in figures provided by Hix (2002), which show that in the post-1999 EP the PES voted 65 per cent of the time with the furthest Left group, the European United Left, 74 per cent with the ELDR, 69 per cent with the EPP-ED, and 51 per cent with the furthest Right group, the UEN.

On a final point concerning the political groups, it is to be noted that the key position they occupy in organising and controlling much of the activity of the EP raises further questions – in addition to those arising from EP elections – concerning the relationship between the EP and EU democracy. For, as Judge and Earnshaw (2003) note, whilst voters in European elections are mobilised primarily around national party programmes and affiliations, the candidates who are elected by this process operate within the EP in transnational groups of which voters are almost completely unaware. Indeed, groups sometimes are not even in existence at the time of EP elections: as with, for example, the Ind/Dem group in the post-2004 Parliament.

National parties

National political parties are involved in EP-related activities in three main ways. First, most candidates in EP elections, and virtually all of those who are elected, are chosen by their national parties. This means that MEPs inevitably reflect national party concerns and are normally obliged, if they wish to be re-selected, to continue to display an awareness of these concerns.

Second, EP election campaigns are essentially national election campaigns conducted by national parties. Use may be made of transnational manifestos, but voters are directed by the parties primarily to national issues and the results are mainly assessed in terms of their domestic implications. That the European dimension is limited is no more evident than in the lack of any consistent Left–Right movement in voting patterns across the member states in European elections.

Finally, in the EP itself national party groups exist within the political groups. This is an obvious potential source of political group disharmony and sometimes creates strains. Problems do not arise so much from the national groups having to act on specific domestic instructions. This does sometimes occur, but in general the organisational links between the national groups and national party leaderships are weak and the former have a reasonably free hand within general party guidelines. The problem is simply that each national party group inevitably tends to have its own priorities and loyalties.

Composition

In addition to party political attachments, four other aspects of the composition of the EP are particularly worthy of comment.

The dual mandate

After the 1979 election some 30 per cent of MEPs were also members of their national legislature. This figure was inflated, however, because many MEPs had contested the election primarily for domestic political reasons and had no firm commitment to completing their terms of office. By the end of the Parliamentary term the number of dual mandates had been more than halved. What therefore seemed to be a big drop after the 1984 elections, to around 12 per cent of MEPs holding a dual mandate, in fact reflected a trend that was already well under way: a trend that was assisted from 1984 with the holding of a dual mandate being discouraged in most member states and being forbidden by national law in some. Only six per cent of MEPs who were elected in 1999 were simultaneously members of their national parliaments: 22 of these were from Italy and nine from the UK (with five of the latter being from the House of Lords).

Dual mandates have the advantage of strengthening links between the EP and national parliaments, but the disadvantage of reducing the amount of time and energy that is available for each post. Reacting to an increasingly accepted view that being an MEP should be a full-time job, a 2002 Council Decision abolished the dual mandate as from the 2004 EP elections, save for limited and temporary derogations given to Ireland and the UK. Accordingly, only eight people were elected to the EP in June 2004 who were also members of their national parliaments: six Irish and two British (with the latter both being members of the House of Lords) (Corbett *et al.*, 2005: 22).

Continuity

Change and turnover in personnel affects the way most organisations work. The EP is no exception to this: the more effective MEPs tend to be those who have developed policy interests and expertise in European affairs over time and have come to know their way around the EU system.

Lack of continuity in membership was a problem after the first EP elections in 1979, with nearly one-quarter of MEPs being replaced before the 1984 elections. However, as noted above, that was always likely as many of the prominent politicians who stood in 1979 had no intention of making a political career in the EP. Things have since settled down and now only a relatively small proportion of MEPs resign before the end of their term of office. However, the turnover of MEPs between parliaments is certainly higher than in most national parliaments: just over 50 per cent of those who were elected in 1989 were returnees, in 1994 the figure was just over 40 per cent, in 1999 it was 46 per cent, and in 2004 it was 54 per cent for MEPs from EU-15 states (Corbett *et al.*, 2005: 48).

Gender

As in national parliaments, women are proportionately under-represented in the EP. In the Parliaments elected in 1994, 1999 and 2004, the figure has hovered around 30 per cent.

The member states with the highest proportion of women MEPs in the 2004–09 Parliament are Sweden (58 per cent), France and the Netherlands (both 44 per cent), Slovenia (43 per cent) and Finland (44 per cent). The states with the lowest proportion are Cyprus and Malta (0 per cent – though they have only six and five seats respectively) and Poland (13 per cent). In most member states a higher proportion of women were returned as MEPs than had been returned to national parliaments in the previous national elections.

Competence and experience

It is sometimes suggested that MEPs are not of the same calibre and do not carry the same political weight as their counterparts in national legislatures. Because the EP is not high-profile, the argument runs, it mostly attracts second-rate parliamentarians, or those who regard it merely as a stepping stone to a national career or advancement.

There is some truth in this view. Major national figures have tended either not to contest EP elections or not to complete their terms of office. (The provision in the 1976 'Direct Elections Act' making national governmental office incompatible with EP membership has not helped in this regard.) Additionally, a few MEPs have transferred from the EP to national legislatures.

But the situation should not be exaggerated. The competition to become an MEP is normally fierce and requires all the customary political skills. Most MEPs have considerable public experience, either in national or regional politics, or in an executive capacity with a major sectional interest.

Perhaps the key point to be emphasised is that it should not be assumed that those who choose to stand for and work in the EP are necessarily settling for second best. Many are firmly committed to their responsibilities and have developed competences and experience that may be different from, but are not necessarily inferior to, those of national parliamentarians.

Organisation and Operation

The multi-site problem

The work of the EP is carried out on three sites in three different countries. Full plenary sessions are held in Strasbourg whilst mini-plenary sessions are held in Brussels. Committees usually meet in Brussels. Around half of the 4500 staff who work in the EP Secretariat (with another 120 in temporary posts) are based in Luxembourg, with the rest mainly in Brussels. (These figures do not include the 600 who work in the Secretariats of the political groups.)

This situation is clearly unsatisfactory and is a source of grievance and annoyance for most MEPs. Reasonably conscientious MEPs may well have to change their working location half a dozen times in an average month. An average work diary is likely to look something like this: four days attending the monthly plenary in Strasbourg; from two to five days in committee(s), probably in Brussels but sometimes elsewhere; two to four days in political group meetings and group working parties, probably in Brussels; whatever time remains is spent in the constituency (if the MEP has one), visiting somewhere as part of an EP delegation, in Brussels or Luxembourg consulting with officials on a report, or at home.

If the EP had just one base, and especially if that was Brussels, it is likely that the EP's efficiency, influence and visibility would all be increased. However, the Council has the power of decision on the matter, and hard lobbying from the Luxembourg and French governments has ensured that arguments for 'sense to prevail' and a single site to be agreed have not been acted upon.

Arranging parliamentary business

Compared with most national parliaments the EP enjoys considerable independence in the arrangement of its affairs. This is not to say it can do whatever it likes. The treaties oblige it to do some things – most notably deliver opinions on Commission proposals for Council and EP and Council legislation – and prevent it from doing others – such as censuring the Council. But on many agenda, timetable and other organisational matters the EP is, to a considerable degree, its own master.

A major reason for this independence is the special institutional setting in which the EP operates. The EU executive does not have to be as concerned to control what the EP does as do national governments with their legislatures. This is because although many EP pronouncements and activities can be unwelcome to the Council and the Commission, outside legislative procedures they do not normally have such politically damaging or unmanageable consequences as can be the case when national parliaments act in ways of which national governments disapprove.

A second, and closely related, reason is the lack of any clear and consistent identification, of either a positive or a negative kind, between the EP and the EU executive. In national parliaments business is shaped to a considerable degree by political attachments. But the Commission is made up of officials who are nominally non-partisan, whilst the Council is multi-party, multi-ideological, and multi-national in its membership. As for the 'persuasive devices' that national executives have at their disposal to encourage loyalty, neither the Commission nor the Council has patronage to dispense.

A third reason is that the EP is entitled to adopt its own Rules of Procedure. This it has done, amending and streamlining the Rules in order to make itself more efficient and more influential. Most decisions about the operation and functioning of the EP are not taken in plenary session but are delegated to the President, the Bureau, or the Conference of Presidents.

The President of the EP is elected to office for a two and a half year term. As was noted above, for the 1999–2004 Parliament, the EPP-ED and ELDR arranged a deal to enable each of them to assume the Presidency for a term. The EEP-ED and the PES made a similar deal at the beginning of the 2004–09 Parliament, which resulted in the Socialist Josep Borrell – a vastly experienced Spanish politician, but a newly elected MEP – being elected President for the first two and a half years of the Parliament.

According to Rule 19 of the Rules of Procedure, the President 'shall direct all the activities of Parliament and of its bodies under the conditions laid down in these Rules' (European Parliament, 2005). In practice this means that the President has many functions, such as presiding over debates in the chamber, referring matters to committees as appropriate, and representing the EP in dealings with other EU institutions and outside bodies. An effective President must be an administrator and a politician, skilled in organising and also in liaising and bargaining.

The Bureau consists of the President and the EP's fourteen Vice-Presidents. Like the President, the Vice-Presidents are elected for a two and a half year term of office, though by tradition the posts are distributed amongst the political groups and member states. Various financial and administrative organisational matters are dealt with by the Bureau, such as drawing up the EP's draft estimates and deciding on the composition and structure of the Secretariat. To assist it in the performance of its duties, and in particular to take responsibility for financial and administrative matters concerning members, five Quaestors, who are also elected, sit in the Bureau in an advisory capacity.

Organisational matters, other than matters of routine which are dealt with by the Bureau, are the responsibility of the Conference of Presidents. This is composed of the EP President and the chairs of the political groups. MEPs who are not attached to any political group can delegate two of their number to attend meetings. Matters that fall within the remit of the Conference of Presidents include the following: deciding on the seating arrangements in the Chamber – a potentially sensitive and highly symbolic issue when groups do not wish to be seated too far to the left or too far to the right of the hemicycle; arranging the EP's work programme, including assigning the drafting of reports to committees and drawing up the draft agendas for plenary sessions; and authorising the drawing up of own initiative reports. By and large the Conference responds to matters coming before it from EP committees and groups rather than imposing itself on Parliament. Decisions are made by consensus whenever possible, but if none exists matters are put to a vote, with group chairs (though not the non-attached delegates who do not have voting rights) having as many votes as there are members of the group.

Two other Conferences also have an organisational role: the Conference of Committee Chairs and the Conference of Delegation Chairs. The Conference of Committee Chairs brings together the chairs of EP committees on a monthly basis to undertake such tasks as arranging for necessary liaison between committees, settling inter-committee disputes, and generally monitoring the progress of business through the committee system. The Conference of Delegation Chairs brings together the chairs of the EP's 35 delegations. These delegations, each of which number about 15 MEPs, are of four types: interparliamentary delegations to maintain contacts with non EU countries that are not seeking EU membership; joint parliamentary committees to maintain contacts with the parliaments of countries that are seeking membership and/or have association agreements with the EU; the EP delegation to the ACP-EU Joint Parliamentary Assembly (see Chapter 19); and the EP delegation to the Euro-Mediterranean Parliamentary Assembly. The Conference of Delegation Chairs also meets monthly, in its case to discuss common organisational and planning matters.

The committees of the EP

Much of the EP's work is carried out by committees. These are of two main types. The first and by far the most important are standing or permanent committees, of which there are twenty in the 2004–09 Parliament (see Table 12.5). The second are *ad hoc* committees, which are established to investigate specific problems and topics.

MEPs are assigned to the standing committees at the beginning and half way through each five-year term. Assignment to the *ad hoc* committees is as required. According to the Rules of Procedure, all committee members are elected to their positions on the basis of proposals made by the Conference of Presidents to Parliament which are 'designed to ensure fair representation of Member States and of political views'. What this means in practice is that the political groups negotiate the share-out of committee memberships on a basis proportionate to their size. Most MEPs become a member of one standing committee – though a few are on as many as three – and a substitute member of another.

The standing committees, which in most cases have 40–60 members, perform various duties, such as exploring ideas with the Commission, fostering own initiative reports, and discussing developments with the President-in-Office of the Council. The most important task of most of them, however, is to examine Commission proposals for legislation. The customary way of proceeding (other than when a proposal is completely straightforward and uncontroversial, which may result in it being dealt with by special procedures allowing for rapid approval) is as follows:

(1) Each proposal is referred to an appropriate committee. Should a proposal overlap the competency and interest of several committees, up to three may be asked for their views, but one is named as the committee responsible and only it reports to the plenary session.

Table 12.5 *Standing committees of the European Parliament*

Foreign Affairs
 – Human Rights sub-committee
 – Security and Defence sub-committee
Development
International Trade
Budgets
Budgetary Control
Economic and Monetary Affairs
Employment and Social Affairs
Environment, Public Health and Food Safety
Industry, Research and Energy
Internal Market and Consumer Protection
Transport and Tourism
Regional Development
Agriculture and Rural Development
Fisheries
Culture and Education
Legal Affairs
Civil Liberties, Justice and Home Affairs
Constitutional Affairs
Women's Rights and Gender Equality
Petitions

(2) The responsibility for drawing up the committee's report is entrusted to *a rapporteur*. Though formally chosen by their fellow committee members, in practice *rapporteurs* are, as are committee chairs, appointed as a result of negotiations between the political groups: negotiations that in this case are carried out by group 'coordinators' from the different committees. When drawing up the report the *rapporteur* can call on various sources of assistance: from the EP Secretariat, from her or his own research services (the EP provides funds to enable each MEP to have at least one research assistant), from the Secretariat of his or her political group, from research institutes, and even from the Commission. Some *rapporteurs* hardly use these facilities and do most of the work themselves; others do little more than present what has been done on their behalf.

(3) A first draft is produced for consideration by the committee according to an agreed timetable. Drafts are normally presented in four main parts: Amendments to the Commission Proposal (if there are any); a Draft Legislative Resolution; an Explanatory Statement; and Annexes (if there are any), including the opinions of other committees. How much

discussion the draft provokes, and how many committee meetings are required before a text is adopted that can be recommended to the plenary, depends on the complexity and controversiality of the subject matter. Factors that are likely to shape the reactions of committee members include national and ideological perspectives, lobbying by outside interests, and views expressed by the Commission.

(4) The *rapporteur* acts as the committee's principal spokesman when the report is considered in the plenary. In this capacity he or she may have to explain the committee's view on amendments put forward by non-committee members, or be called upon to use his or her judgement in making recommendations to Parliament on what it should do when the Commission goes some, but not all, of the way towards accepting committee-approved amendments. Occasionally – as when, for example, the Commission offers a mixed package – committee meetings may be hurriedly convened during plenary sessions.

(5) Where the cooperation and co-decision procedures apply, the role and activity of committees at the second reading stage are similar to those at the first reading. That is, they examine the proposal (which is now in the form of the Council's common position) and make recommendations to the plenary. The responsibility for drawing up reports is conferred automatically on the committees involved in the first reading and the *rapporteur* remains the same. The reports normally have two main sections: Recommendations for the Second Reading (which may include approval of, rejection of, or amendments to, the common position – amendments are often aimed at re-establishing the EP's position as defined at the first reading, or producing a compromise with the Council); and Justifications or Explanatory Statements.

(6) The committee that has dealt with a proposal at the first and second readings is not directly concerned with the proceedings if a conciliation committee is convened under the co-decision procedure. However, the EP delegation to a conciliation committee always includes some members of the committee concerned, including the chairman and the *rapporteur*.

* * *

A number of factors help determine how the EP committees work and how much influence they exercise, the most important of which are as follows.

- *The significance of the policy area within the EU system.* The Committee on Agriculture and Rural Development, for example, deals with matters that loom larger in the EU scale of things than the Committee on Women's Rights and Gender Equality.

- *The extent of EU policy development.* There can be more opportunities to exercise influence when EU policy is in the process of formation than when it is well established. So, for example, the Committee on Environment, Public Health and Food Safety is advantaged in this regard, whereas the Committee on Agriculture is disadvantaged.
- *The power of the EP within the policy area.* The influence of the Committee on Budgets is enormously enhanced by the real budgetary decision-making powers that the treaties give to the EP. Similarly, the Committee on Budgetary Control would be much weaker if the EP did not have the statutory responsibility to grant, postpone, or refuse a discharge to the Commission in respect of the implementation of the EU budget. The Committee on Foreign Affairs, in contrast, though dealing with extremely important subject material, is greatly limited in what it can do because of the essentially intergovernmental and non-EC character of the policies with which it deals.
- *Committee expertise.* Many committee members just do not have the requisite specialised skills to be able to explore relevant issues in depth or to question the Commission on the basis of a fully informed understanding of policy. For example, few members of the Committee on Industry, Research and Energy have an appropriate technical background (though they may of course have, or may develop as a result of their committee membership, a great knowledge of relevant subject material). The Committee on Legal Affairs, on the other hand, is composed mainly of lawyers or legal experts.
- *Secretariat support.* In terms of numbers, all committees have restricted administrative back-up. On average, each has only about five or six policy officials and a similar number of support staff.
- *Committee chairmanship.* Committee chairs can be vital in guiding the work of committees. They can help to push business through; they can assist *rapporteurs* in rallying support for reports that are to be debated in plenaries; they can help to create committee harmony and a constructive working atmosphere; and they can do much to ensure that a committee broadens its horizons beyond simply reacting to initiatives presented to it by others.
- *Committee cohesiveness.* One of the reasons why, for example, the Committee on Development is rather more influential than a number of other committees is that it tends to display a high degree of cohesiveness. With members of the committee being united on the desirability of improving conditions in the developing countries, discussions tend to revolve around questions of feasibility rather than ideological desirability. The Agriculture Committee, on the other hand, attracts MEPs who are both supportive and critical of the CAP and hence it often tends to be sharply divided.

Plenary meetings

There are twelve full plenary meetings, or part-sessions as they are officially known, each year: one each month apart from August, plus an extra one in September/October when the EP holds its first reading of the budget. The sessions are held in Strasbourg and last from Monday to Thursday. The EP ceased holding Friday plenary meetings in 2001, largely because of poor attendance on that day.

Most MEPs do not believe the extra plenary in October is necessary, but they are obliged to convene it following a 1998 ruling by the Court of Justice that the EP is bound by a decision taken at the December 1992 Edinburgh summit that there should be twelve full plenaries, including the budget session, each year. The Edinburgh decision has subsequently been reinforced by a protocol to the same effect attached to the Amsterdam Treaty. The French government – concerned at the slow drift of many of the EP's activities to Brussels – was the main force behind both the Court case and the Amsterdam Treaty protocol.

In addition to full plenaries, four to six mini-plenaries are held each year. They normally take up two half-days (from lunchtime on day one to lunchtime on day two) and are held in Brussels.

The agenda for plenaries is drafted by the President and the Conference of Presidents in consultation with the Conference of Committee Chairs and the EP Secretariat. Their recommendations have to be approved by the plenary itself. With time so tight, items that many MEPs consider important inevitably do not get onto the agenda, and those that do make it normally have to be covered at pace. Strict rules govern who can speak, when, and for how long: the effect of the rules is often to restrict speakers to committee and political group spokesmen.

Full plenaries have three standard elements. First, the bread and butter business is the consideration of reports from committees. As indicated earlier, these reports usually lead either to resolutions embodying opinions or to resolutions embodying own initiatives. Second, time is set aside for debates on topical and urgent matters. As with the reports, these debates frequently result in the adoption of resolutions. Finally, there is a one and a half hour Commission Question Time and a one and a half hour Council Question Time. Who answers on behalf of the Commission and the Council depends on the policy content of the questions (which are known in advance), preferences expressed by the EP, and who is available. (Tables 12.1 and 12.2 provide a statistical breakdown of the 'outputs' of these three elements of EP activity.)

In addition to the three standard activities, there are a number of other possible agenda items. For example: statements by the Commission and the Council; addresses by distinguished foreign guests; and – at least twice a year – a report on European Council meetings by the Head of Government of the incumbent Presidency.

The EP in plenary does not, it should be said, give the impression of being the most dynamic of places. Attendance in the chamber is poor, the translation problem limits spontaneity, and much immediacy is lost by the practice of taking most votes in clusters at allocated voting times rather than at the end of debates. (These times are often not even on the same day as the debate.) Nonetheless, working procedures have been gradually improved over the years, most notably by the removal of much minor business from the floor of the chamber.

Concluding Remarks: Is the EP a 'Proper' Parliament?

The EP has clearly assumed an increased role in the EU over the years. Several factors account for this, not least the Parliament's own efforts to increase its powers.

In attempting to enhance its role and influence, the EP has pursued a dual strategy. On the one hand there has been *a maximalist* approach, which has been directed at achieving fundamental reform of inter-institutional relations, and especially increasing the powers of the Parliament *vis-à-vis* the Council of Ministers. In 1984 this approach led to the EP approving the *Draft Treaty Establishing the European Union,* which played a part – though perhaps not as important a part as its supporters have claimed – in helping to bring about the SEA. In the periods leading up to the treaty reforms agreed at Maastricht, Amsterdam and Nice the EP, taking advantage of the debate about the 'democratic defeat', approved reports calling for, amongst other things, co-decision-making legislative powers with the Council across the policy spectrum (significant progress was achieved at Maastricht and Amsterdam), the right to elect the President of the Commission on a proposal from the European Council (granted in the Amsterdam Treaty), and the co-decision-making procedure to apply whenever QMV applies in the Council (yet to be fully conceded by the governments of the member states). On the other hand there has been an *incrementalist* approach, in which the EP has used its existing powers to the full and done whatever it can to determine how far these powers can be pressed. As part of this approach the EP has, for example, interpreted its Maastricht-granted confirmation power on an incoming College of Commissioners as giving it the power to 'interview' Commissioners-designate, and it has contracted a number of inter-institutional agreements with the Commission and the Council (on such matters as the budgetary procedure and conciliation meetings) that have enhanced its institutional position.

But notwithstanding all its efforts and the increased influence it has secured for itself, the EP is still commonly regarded as not being quite a proper parliament. The main reason for this is that its formal powers remain weaker than those of national parliaments: in several important spheres of EU policy activity – including Economic and Monetary Union, the Common Foreign and Security Policy, external trade policy, and police and judicial cooperation – it is largely confined, at best, to information-receiving and consultative roles; it does not have full legislative powers; its budgetary powers are circumscribed; and it cannot overthrow a government.

However, when assessing the importance of the EP attention should not be restricted to its formal capabilities. For when the comparison with national parliaments is extended to encompass what actually happens in practice, the powers exercised by the EP are, in several key respects, comparable to the powers exercised by many national parliaments. Indeed, it is not difficult to make out a case that in exercising some of its functions – most particularly scrutinising legislative proposals and contributing to debates on future developments – the EP exerts a greater influence over affairs than do the more executive-dominated parliaments of many member states.

Chapter 13

European Union Law and the Courts

The Need for EU Law

An enforceable legal framework is the essential basis of decision-making and decision application in all democratic states. Although not itself a state, this also applies to the EU, because the EU is more than merely another international organisation in which countries cooperate with one another on a voluntary basis for reasons of mutual benefit. Rather it is an organisation in which states have voluntarily surrendered their right, across a broad range of important sectors, to be independent in the determination and application of public policy.

If there was no body of law setting out the powers and responsibilities of the institutions and the member states of the EU, and if there was no authority to give independent rulings on what that law is and how it should be interpreted, effective EU decision-making on policies would not be possible. Of course law is not the only factor shaping the EU's decision-making processes. As in any organisation, practice evolves in the light of experience of what is possible and what works best. The tendency not to press for a vote in the Council even when it is legally permissible is an obvious example of this. But the law does provide the basic setting in which decisions are made. It lays down that some things must be done, some cannot, and some may be. So, for example, it is by virtue of EU law that subsidies to farmers cannot be fixed in national capitals but must be agreed at EU level, that the Commission is entitled to take decisions on proposed company mergers, and that the EP is permitted to increase the annual budget within specified limits.

The existence of EU law is also crucial with regard to policy implementation. For if decisions only took the form of intergovernmental agreements, and if those agreements could be interpreted by member states in whatever way was most beneficial and convenient for them, common policies would not in practice exist and the whole rationale of the EU would be undermined. The likes of the EU's competition and fisheries policies, and the harmonisation of matters as diverse as maximum axle weights for lorries and minimum safety standards at work, can be fully effective only if they are based on *common laws* that are capable of *uniform* interpretation in *all* member states.

The Sources of EU Law

An EU legal order is thus an essential condition of the EU's existence. The sources of that order are to be found in a number of places: the treaties, EU legislation, judicial interpretation, international law, and the general principles of law.

The treaties

The legal standing of the treaties

The EU's treaty structure is, as was shown in Part 2 of this book, made up of several component parts. Some of these parts are subject to the jurisdiction of the European Court of Justice (ECJ) whilst others are not. Article 46 of the TEU makes it clear that the parts of the treaties that are subject to the jurisdiction of the Court are: the Founding Treaties, as amended over the years (since the ECSC Treaty expired in July 2002, this has meant the TEC and the Euratom Treaty only); certain aspects of the Police and Judicial Cooperation in Criminal Matters pillar, though quite explicitly not 'the exercise of the responsibilities incumbent upon Member States with regard to the maintenance of law and order and the safeguarding of internal security' (Article 35.5); the provisions for enhanced (closer) cooperation between a less than full complement of member states that are set out in both the TEU and the TEC; actions of the institutions in relation to respecting fundamental human rights; and the Final Provisions of the TEU, which include matters relating to treaty amendments and accession to the EU. The parts of the treaties that are not subject to the Court are: most of the Common Provisions of the TEU, which include the general objectives of the Union, the membership and role of the European Council, and the procedures to be used in the event of actions against a member state that is deemed to be at risk of breaching the fundamental principles of the Union; the Common Foreign and Security Policy (CFSP) pillar; and declarations attached to the treaties.

Clearly this all makes for a messy and untidy legal framework. It also makes for a rather confusing and potentially contentious one since in some circumstances there is considerable legal ambiguity and uncertainty. For example, the importance of subsidiarity is proclaimed in Article 2 of the TEU's Common Provisions, but the only definition of it is in Article 5 of the TEC – and that definition is so vague as to provide only limited guidance on how the principle should be applied in practice.

One of the consequences of the complicated legal nature of the treaties is that commentators on the EU have adopted different positions on whether to use the term 'EU law' or 'Community law'. Since there is not much that falls outside the Community Treaties that is subject to the jurisdiction of the Court, and since legislation can only be made in a Community context, many commentators – especially lawyers – prefer 'Community law'. Others, however, prefer 'EU law': partly because the Communities are within the EU; partly because some, albeit very limited, legal activity is not based on the Communities; and partly because to keep moving between 'EU' and 'Community' is a recipe for confusion. In this chapter, as elsewhere in the book, the term 'EU law' is used, except when this would be clearly inaccurate or potentially misleading.

Are the treaties the EU's constitution?

Amidst the political heat and debate surrounding the Constitutional Treaty (see Chapter 7), little has been made of the fact that in important respects the EU may be said to already have a constitution. Those parts of the treaties that are subject to the jurisdiction of the Court and which constitute the so-called primary law of the EU may be regarded as making up the EU's written and legal constitution. The treaties as a whole may be viewed as making up the EU's political constitution.

National constitutions in liberal democracies normally do two main things: they establish an institutional structure for decision-making, and they set out – often in a bill of rights or a declaration of liberties – the freedoms of the individual and restrictions on the power of decision-makers over the citizenry. The relevant component parts of the EU's treaties cover the first of these tasks, and up to a point the second too. The establishment of the institutional structure can be seen, most obviously, in the identification of the Commission, the European Council, the Council of Ministers, the Court of Justice, and the European Parliament as the key decision-making institutions, and by the laying down of rules governing relations between them and between them and the member states. As for the establishment of individual rights, the treaties (mainly through the TEC) are most specific about economic freedoms, but there is also the general provision of Article 6 of the TEU that 'The Union shall respect fundamental rights, as guaranteed by the [1950] European Convention for the Protection of Human Rights and Fundamental Freedoms … and as they result from the constitutional traditions common to the Member States, as general principles of Community Law.' Furthermore, political agreement on the EU Charter of Fundamental Rights was attached in a declaration to the Nice Treaty. Though the Charter was not incorporated into any of the EU's treaties and is legally non-binding, it has featured in some Court judgements. The Constitutional Treaty provides for the Charter to be given full treaty status, but that move is now on hold following the difficulties in ratifying the Treaty. (On the Charter, see Chapter 6.)

In addition to including not dissimilar content to national constitutions, the EU's treaties may also be said to be constitutional in nature in respect of the status of their contents and how they are determined. Treaty law is not 'ordinary' EU law that is made by 'ordinary' law-making procedures, but rather is a higher status law than is made by a special procedure. The special procedure takes the form of an Intergovernmental Conference (IGC), which is extensively pre-prepared, which usually is spread out over several months, which culminates at a European Council meeting, and whose outcome is subject to national ratification processes that in some member states can prove to be very high profile and difficult.

As well as covering 'traditional' constitutional matters, the treaties are also much concerned with something that is not normally considered to be appropriate subject matter for constitutions: policy. This takes the form of general principles on the one hand and the identification of policy sectors and activities that are to be developed on the other. The main general principles are those that are designed to promote competition and the free movement of goods, persons, services and capital, all behind a common external tariff (CET) and a common commercial policy (CCP). The policy sectors and activities that are identified, with varying degrees of precision on how they are to be developed, include: agriculture, social affairs, transport, regional affairs, the environment, and economic and monetary union (all in the TEC), foreign and security policy (pillar two of the TEU), and police and judicial cooperation in criminal matters (pillar three of the TEU).

The treaties may thus not formally be the EU's constitution, and they may contain much more and be much longer than most national constitutions, but they do have many constitutional features and in practical terms they do serve as the EU's constitution.

EU legislation

Laws adopted by the EU institutions under Article 249 TEC constitute secondary legislation. They are concerned with translating the general principles of the treaties into specific rules and are adopted by the European Parliament and the Council, by the Council, or by the Commission according to the procedures described in other chapters of this book. While there is no hard and fast distinction between EP and Council, Council, and Commission legislation, the first two tend to be broader in scope, to be concerned with more important matters, and to be aimed at laying down a legal framework in a policy sphere. Commission legislation – of which in terms of volume there is much more than EP and Council and Council-only legislation – is largely administrative/technical in nature and is usually subject to tight guidelines laid down in enabling EP and Council or Council legislation.

The treaties distinguish between different types of legislation: regulations, directives, decisions, and recommendations and opinions.

Regulations

A regulation is under Article 249 TEC:

(1) Of 'general application'; that is, it contains general and abstract provisions that may be applied to particular persons and circumstances.
(2) 'Binding in its entirety'; that is, it bestows rights and obligations upon those to whom it is addressed, and member states must observe it in full and as written.
(3) 'Directly applicable in all Member States'; that is, there is no need for national implementing measures to be taken in order for a regulation to have binding force within the member states. Regulations specify the date on which they are to take legal effect. Normally this is the same day as, or very shortly after, they are published in the *Official Journal of the European Union*. This in turn is usually only a day or two after they have been adopted.

Most regulations are adopted by the Commission and concern highly specific and technical adjustments to existing EU law. The majority relate to the CAP.

Directives

A directive 'shall be binding, as to the result to be achieved, upon each Member State to which it is addressed, but shall leave to the national authorities the choice of form and methods' (Article 249 TEC).

In theory, a directive is thus very different from a regulation: it is not binding in its entirety but only in 'the result to be achieved'; it is addressed to member states and does not claim general applicability; it is not necessarily addressed to all member states; and appropriate national measures need to be taken to give the directive legal effect. As a consequence directives tend to be rather more general in nature than regulations. They are less concerned with the detailed and uniform application of policy and more with the laying down of policy principles that member states must seek to achieve but can pursue by the appropriate means under their respective national constitutional and legal systems. (Such appropriate means can vary from administrative circulars to new laws approved by national legislatures.)

The distinction between regulations and directives should not, however, be exaggerated because in practice a number of factors often result in a blurring. First, directives are almost invariably addressed to all states. An important reason for this is that directives are frequently concerned with the harmonisation or approximation of laws and practices in fields of EU activity. Second, some directives are drafted so tightly that there is very little room for national authorities to incorporate adjustments when transposing directives into national law. Third, directives contain a date by which the national procedures to give the directive effect must have been completed. The Commission has to be notified of national implementing measures, and states that fail to comply by the due date are liable to have proceedings initiated against them, which can ultimately result in a case before the ECJ. Fourth, the Court has ruled that in some instances directives are directly applicable: for example, when national implementing legislation has been unduly delayed or when it has departed from the intent of the original directive.

Decisions

A decision 'shall be binding in its entirety upon those to whom it is addressed' (Article 249 TEC). It may be addressed to any or all member states, to undertakings, or to individuals. Many decisions are highly specific and, in effect, are administrative rather than legislative acts. Others are of a more general character and can be akin to regulations or even, occasionally, directives.

Decisions are adopted in a whole range of circumstances. For example: to enforce competition policy; to institute a pilot action programme; to authorise grants from one of the EU's funds; to allow an exemption from an existing measure; or to counter dumping from a third country.

Recommendations and opinions

Recommendations and opinions are explicitly stated by Article 249 as having no binding force and so, strictly speaking, do not formally constitute part of EU law. However, on occasions the Court has referred to them, so their legal status is not always completely clear. The same applies to some of the other non-binding devices used by the EU institutions for such purposes as floating ideas, starting a legislative process, promoting coordination, and encouraging harmonisation. These include memoranda, communications, conventions, programmes, guidelines, agreements, declarations, and resolutions.

✻ ✻ ✻

In order to accommodate the mosaic of different national circumstances and interests that exist on many policy issues the EU's legislative framework needs to be creative, flexible, and capable of permitting differentiation.

There are four main ways in which it is so:

- As has just been shown, the EU makes use of a variety of formal and quasi-formal legislative instruments.
- There are considerable variations between directives regarding the time periods permitted for incorporation into national law. For example, amending directives may have to be incorporated almost immediately, whereas innovative or controversial directives, or directives that require substantial capital expenditure in order to be properly applied – as is common with environmental directives – may not be required to be incorporated for some years.
- Devices that allow for adaptation to local conditions and needs are often either attached to legal texts or are authorised by the Commission after an act has come into force. Examples of such devices include exemptions, derogations, and safety clauses.
- Provided the Commission is satisfied that the relevant provisions 'are not a means of arbitrary discrimination or a disguised restriction on trade between Member States' (Article 95 TEC), member states are permitted to apply national legislation that is 'tougher' than EU legislation in respect of certain matters – notably protection of the environment and of the working environment.

There used to be several thousand legislative instruments issued each year, comprising around 4000 regulations, 2000 decisions, and 120 directives. However, the number has dropped considerably in recent years, partly because of the virtual completion of the Single European Market (SEM)

Table 13.1 Legislative acts adopted, repealed or expiring in 2004[1]

Enacting institution(s)	Number of acts	Regulations	Directives	Decisions	Recommendations
European Parliament and Council	Enacted in 2004	40	31	4	0
	Repealed or expiring in 2004	3	4	2	0
Council alone	Enacted in 2004	146	17	40	4
	Repealed or expiring in 2004	104	22	16	2
Commission	Enacted in 2004	672	59	468	45
	Repealed or expiring in 2004	391	18	190	1

[1] Data compiled on 19 January 2005 from CELEX, the inter-institutional computerised documentation system on Community law (→ point http://www.europa.eu.int/abc/doc/off/rg/en/2004/pt0782.htm 782), excluding acts not published in the *Official Journal* and acts published in light type (routine management acts valid for a limited period).

Source: reproduced from European Commission (2005b).

legislative programme, but mainly because of a drive by all decision-making institutions to simplify the EU legislative framework. Table 13.1 shows the number of legislative instruments enacted in 2004. The vast majority of these instruments consist of administrative measures of a routine, non-political, recurring kind. Many are replacements for instruments that have either been repealed (usually because, as with most CAP-related legislation, they have become outdated as a result of changing market conditions) or have expired.

Judicial interpretation

There are two EU courts: the European Court of Justice (ECJ) and the Court of First Instance (CFI). The former is the more senior of the two courts in that it deals with most cases raising major issues – including those of a 'constitutional' and/or 'political' nature – and in that also CFI judgements are, subject to specified conditions, subject to appeal to the ECJ. When, therefore, reference is made to EU law arising from judicial interpretation, the reference is normally to ECJ case law.

Although case law has not traditionally been a major source of law in most of the EU member states, the rulings of the EU's courts have played an important part in shaping and making EU law. This stems partly from the courts' duty to ensure that EU law is interpreted and applied correctly. It stems also from the fact that much of EU statute law is far from clear or complete.

The lack of precision in much of the EU's statute law is due to a number of factors: the relative newness of the EU and its constituent Communities; problems with the decision-making processes often lead to weak compromises and the avoidance of necessary secondary legislation; and the speed of change in some spheres of EU activity makes it very difficult for the written law to keep abreast of developments. In many fields of apparent EU competence the EU's courts thus have to issue judgements from a less than detailed statutory base. In the different types of case that come before them – cases of first and only instance, cases of appeal, and cases involving rulings on points of EU law that have been referred by national courts – the EU's courts therefore inevitably often go well beyond merely giving a technical and grammatical interpretation of the written rules. They fill in the gaps in the law and, in so doing, they not only clarify the law but also extend it.

International law

International law is notoriously vague and weak, but the ECJ has had occasional recourse to it when developing principles embodied in EU law.

Judgements have also established that insofar as the EU is increasingly developing an international personality of its own and taking over powers from the states, the same rules of international law apply to it as apply to them, for example with regard to treaty law and the privileges and immunities of international organisations.

The many international agreements to which the EU is a party – including association, cooperation and trade agreements – are sometimes viewed as another dimension of international law. However, since they are implemented by legislative acts they are better viewed as constituting part of EU legislation.

The general principles of law

The Community Treaties charge the ECJ and CFI with the task of ensuring 'that in the interpretation and application of this Treaty the law is observed' (Article 220 TEC, Article 136 Euratom). The implication of this and of certain other Treaty articles (notably 230 and 288 TEC), is that the courts need not regard written EU law as the only source of law to which they may refer.

In practice this has meant that the courts, when making their judgements, have had regard to general principles of law when these have been deemed relevant and applicable. Exactly what these general principles of law are, however, is a matter of controversy. Suffice to note here that the principles that have been cited by the courts include proportionality (the means used to achieve a given end should be no more than is appropriate and necessary to achieve that end), non-discrimination (whether between nations, product sectors, firms or individuals), adherence to legality, and respect for procedural rights.

The Content of EU Law

The content of EU law is described at some length in Chapter 15, in the context of the examination that is presented there of EU policies. Attention here will, therefore, be confined to three points of general significance.

The first point is that EU law is not as wide-ranging as national law. It is not, for instance, directly concerned with criminal law or family law. Nor does it have much to do with policy areas such as education or health. What EU law is primarily concerned with – and in this it reflects the aims and provisions of the treaties – is economic activity. More particularly, EU law is strongly focused in the direction of the activities of the EC which, as set out in Article 3 of the TEC, include a common commercial policy ... an internal market characterised by the abolition, as between Member States, of obstacles to the free movement of goods, persons, services and capital ... a common policy in the spheres of agriculture and fisheries ... a system ensuring that competition in the internal market is not distorted ... the approximation of the laws of Member States to the extent required for the functioning of the common market ... a policy in the sphere of the environment.

The second point is that no policy area, with the exception of the common commercial policy, contains a comprehensive code of EU law. Even in areas where there is a high degree of EU regulation, such as with the functioning of agricultural markets, national laws covering various matters still exist. As Tables 15.1 and 15.2 show (p. 388), EU law thus sits side by side with national law, constituting an important part of the overall legal framework of member states in some policy spheres, whilst being of only marginal significance in others.

The third point is that the range of EU law has broadened considerably over the years. As already noted, EU law is primarily economic in character, but less dominantly so than it was. A good illustration of this is seen in the considerable volume of EU environmental law that now exists: there are over 200 EU environmental laws in force, dealing with matters as diverse as air and water pollution, the disposal of toxic waste, and the protection of endangered bird species. This expansion of EU law into an increasing number of policy areas has occurred, and is still occurring, for several reasons, prominent among which are: recognition of the benefits that joint action can bring to many fields of activity; acceptance that the SEM can function smoothly, efficiently and equitably only if there are common rules not just on directly related market activities but also on matters such as health and safety at work, entitlement to social welfare benefits, and mutual recognition of educational and professional qualifications; and sectional interest pressures.

The Status of EU Law

In Case 6/64, *Costa v. ENEL*, the ECJ stated:

By creating a Community of unlimited duration, having its own institutions, its own personality, its own legal capacity of representation on the international plane and, more particularly, real powers stemming from limitation of sovereignty or a transfer of powers from the states to the Community, the Member States have limited their sovereign rights, albeit within limited fields, and have thus created a body of law which binds both their individuals and themselves.

EU law thus constitutes an autonomous legal system, imposing obligations and rights on both individuals and member states, and limiting the sovereignty of member states. There are two main pillars to this legal system: direct effect and primacy.

Direct effect

This term – which is sometimes also called direct applicability – refers to the principle whereby certain provisions of EU law may confer rights or impose obligations on individuals that national courts are bound to recognise and enforce. Having initially established the principle in 1963 in the case of *Van Gend en Loos* (Case 26/62), the Court, in a series of judgements, has gradually strengthened and extended the scope of direct effect so that it now applies to most secondary legislation except when discretion is explicitly granted to the addressee. Many of the provisions of the treaties have also been established as having direct effect, although the Court has ruled that it does not apply in some important spheres, such as the free movement of capital.

Primacy

Somewhat surprisingly, there is no explicit reference in the treaties to the primacy or supremacy of EU law over national law. Clearly the principle is vital if the EU is to function properly, since if member states had the power to annul EU law by adopting or giving precedence to national law, then there could be no uniform or consistent EU legal order: states could apply national law when EU law was distasteful or inconvenient to them. From an early stage, therefore, the Court took an active part in establishing the primacy of EU law. National courts, it has consistently asserted, must apply EU law in the event of any conflict, even if the domestic law is part of the national constitution. An example of Court statements on primacy may be taken from *Simmenthal v. Commission* (Case 92/78) where the Court concluded that:

> Every national court must, in a case within its jurisdiction, apply Community law in its entirety and protect rights which the latter confers on individuals and must accordingly set aside any provision of national law which may conflict with it, whether prior or subsequent to the Community rule.

In general, national courts have accepted this view and given precedence to EU law. A few problems remain – notably in relation to fundamental rights guaranteed by national constitutions – but for the most part the authority and binding nature of EU law is fully established.

The European Court of Justice

The European Court of Justice is based in Luxembourg and should not be, though it often is, confused with the Strasbourg-based European Court of Human Rights.

Membership and organisation

The ECJ consists of 25 judges – one from each member state. Each judge is appointed for a six-year term of office that may be, and frequently is, renewed. To ensure continuity, turnover is staggered in three-yearly cycles.

According to the Community Treaties, judges are to be appointed 'by common accord of the governments of the Member States' from amongst persons 'whose independence is beyond doubt and who possess the qualifications required for appointment to the highest judicial offices in their respective countries or who are juriconsults of recognised competence'. In practice there is something of a gap, in spirit at least, between these treaty provisions and reality. First, because each state is permitted one nomination and this is automatically accepted. Second, because when making their choices governments have tended not to be overly worried about the judicial qualifications or experience of their nominations and have instead looked for a good background in professional activities and public service. There is no evidence of 'political' appointments being made, in the way that they are to the United States Supreme Court, but the fact is that soundness and safeness seem to be as important as judicial ability. At the time of initial appointment the typical judge is a legally qualified 'man of affairs' (in early 2006 there were only two female judges!) who has been involved with government in his native country in some way, but who has served in a judicial capacity for, at best, only a limited period.

The judges elect one of their number to be President of the Court for a term of three years. The President's principal function is to see to the overall direction of the work of the Court by, for example, assigning cases to the Court's chambers, appointing *judge-rapporteurs* to cases, and setting schedules for cases. The President is also empowered, upon application from a party, to order the suspension of Community measures and to order such interim measures as he deems appropriate.

Assisting the judges in the exercise of their tasks are eight advocates-general. The duty of advocates-general is 'acting with complete impartiality and independence, to make, in open court, reasoned submissions on cases brought before the Court of Justice' (Article 222 TEC). This means that an advocate-general, on being assigned to a case, must make a thorough examination of all the issues involved in the case, take account of all relevant law, and then present his conclusions to the Court. The conclusions are likely to include observations on the key points in the case, an assessment of EU law touching on the case, and a proposed legal solution.

In principle, advocates-general are appointed on the same treaty terms and according to the same treaty criteria as the judges. In practice, since not all states can claim an advocate-general, appointments are more genuinely collective than is the case with judges – but only up to a point, since the larger states have usually been able to ensure that they have one post each. At the same time, the judicial experience of advocates-general tends to be even less than that of the judges; certainly few have ever served in a judicial capacity in their own states.

In addition to the judges and the advocates-general, each of whom is assisted by two legal secretaries, the Court, together with the CFI, employs a staff of around 1200 in permanent posts and 400 in temporary posts. Most of these are engaged either in administrative duties – such as registering and transmitting case documents – or in providing language services.

The increasing number of cases coming before the Court – in the 1960s there were around 50 in an average year, today there are over 500 (see Table 13.2) – has made it impossible for everything to be dealt with in full plenary session. There has therefore been an increasing tendency for cases to be assigned to one of the Court's six chambers. In general, a matter is referred to a chamber of three judges if it is based upon relatively straightforward facts, raises no substantial points of principle, or where the circumstances are covered by existing case law. Cases that involve more complex findings of fact, or novel or important points of law, and do not require to be heard by the full Court, are assigned to a chamber of five judges.

Table 13.2   *Cases before the European Court of Justice,*
2003–04: numbers and stage of proceedings[1]

	2003	2004
Cases completed	494	665
New cases	561	531
Cases pending	974	840

[1] The figures represent the total number of cases without account being taken of (the small number of) cases where cases are joined because of their similarity.

Source: reproduced from European Court of Justice (2005): 167–8.

Table 13.3   *Cases before the European Court of Justice, 2004:
bench hearing actions*

	Judgements/ Opinions	Orders[1]	Total
Full Court	21		21
Grand Chamber/Small Plenary	32	1	33
Chambers (5 judges)	257	18	275
Chambers (3 judges)	113	61	174
President		6	6
TOTAL	**423**	**86**	**509**

[1] Orders terminating proceedings by judicial determination (other than those removing a case from the register, declaring that there is no need to give a decision, or referring a case to the Court of First Instance).

Source: reproduced from European Court of Justice (2005): 170.

Following amendments made by the Maastricht Treaty, the only circumstance in which the Court was required to sit in full plenary session was 'when a Member State or a Community institution that is a party to the proceedings so requests' (Article 221 TEC). At Nice this was changed to enable such a request to be met by proceedings to be dealt with by a Grand Chamber, numbering thirteen judges since the 2004 EU enlargement. In practice the Court has sometimes continued to sit in full plenary session when cases have been deemed to be especially important.

Table 13.3 sets out the number of cases dealt with by the Court's different benches in 2004.

The procedure of the Court

The procedure of the ECJ involves both written and oral stages. The former are more important, with cases being conducted largely away from the public eye via the communication of documents between interested parties and Court officials. Not much happens in open court.

Without going into all the details and possible variations, direct action cases proceed broadly along the following lines.

● Relevant documentation and evidence is assembled. In complicated cases, involving for example the alleged existence of cartels, hundreds or even thousands of separate items of evidence may be collected. The

Court, under the direction of a duly appointed *judge-rapporteur,* may have to take a very proactive role in gathering the information that it needs and in soliciting the views of interested parties. This may involve holding a preparatory inquiry at which oral and documentary evidence is presented. (In preliminary ruling cases the procedure is very different: the national court making the reference should have provided with its submission a summary of the case and of all relevant facts, a statement of the legal problem, and the – abstract – question it wishes the Court to answer.)

- A public hearing is likely to be (but is not always) held at which the essentials of the case are outlined, the various parties are permitted to present their views orally, and the judges and advocates-general may question the parties' lawyers.
- Following the public hearing, the advocate-general appointed to the case examines it in detail. He and his staff look at all relevant EU law and then come to a decision that they consider to be correct in legal terms. A few weeks after the public hearing the advocate-general presents his submission to an open session of the Court.
- Acting on the advocate-general's submission, and on the basis of a draft drawn up by the *judge-rapporteur,* the Court prepares its decision. Deliberations are in secret and if there is disagreement the decision is made by majority vote. Judgements must be signed by all the judges who have taken part in the proceedings and no dissenting opinions may be published. (In their oath of office members swear to preserve the secrecy of the deliberation of the Court.)

Three problems associated with the Court's proceedings ought to be mentioned. First, there is a lengthy gap between cases being lodged at the Court and final decisions: on average, over 23 months for preliminary rulings and over 20 months for direct actions (European Court of Justice, 2005: 174). As of 31 December 2004, 840 cases were pending (see Table 13.2). In special cases, however, interim judgements are issued and accelerated procedures are used. Second, lawyers' fees usually mean that going before the Court can be an expensive business, even though there is no charge for the actual proceedings in the Court itself. This does not, of course, place much of a restriction on the ability of national governments or EU institutions to use the Court, but it can be a problem for individuals and small firms. There is a small legal aid fund, but it cannot remotely finance all potential applicants. Third, the use of majority voting, coupled with the lack of opportunity for dissenting opinions, has encouraged a tendency, which is perhaps inevitable given the different legal backgrounds of the judges, for judgements sometimes to be less than concise, and occasionally even to be fudged.

The Court of First Instance

Under the SEA, the ECJ was given a means of dealing more expeditiously and more effectively with its constantly expanding workload: the Council was empowered to establish, at the request of the ECJ, a Court of First Instance. Such a request was quickly made and in 1988 the CFI was established by Council Decision 88/591. The CFI began to function in November 1989.

The CFI is made up of one judge from each member state. The conditions of appointment and terms of office of the CFI judges are similar to those of the ECJ judges. Unlike, however, in the ECJ, no advocates-general are appointed to the CFI. When the exercise of the function of advocate-general is seen as being necessary – which it is not in all cases – the task is undertaken by one of the judges; the judge so designated cannot take part in the judgement of the case.

The jurisdiction of the CFI is covered along with that of the ECJ in the next section. It is appropriate, however, to point out here that the CFI's judicial role and importance has grown considerably over the years. Initially the CFI was limited to just three types of cases: disputes between the Community and its staff, actions brought against the Commission under the ECSC Treaty, and certain aspects of the competition rules. However, in 1993 the Council of Ministers agreed to give the CFI jurisdiction to hear and determine at first instance all actions brought by natural or legal persons other than anti-dumping cases, upon which a decision was deferred; jurisdiction in anti-dumping cases was eventually agreed in February 1994. The 1993 extension of the CFI's jurisdiction did not extend to preliminary rulings. New provisions agreed at the 2000 Nice summit subsequently further broadened the CFI's remit. Drawn up largely outside the 2000 IGC itself, by a group of legal experts known as 'Friends of the Presidency', some of the provisions agreed at Nice took the form of amendments to the TEC whilst others involved amendments to the Statute of the Court. Designed primarily to tackle the backlog of cases before the two courts and the long time periods before the issuing of judgements, two of the Nice reforms were especially important in respect of the CFI's work. First, so as to help lighten the ECJ's workload, the types of cases that the CFI would now be able to hear and determine were widened to include more direct action cases and certain types of preliminary rulings. Second, so as to lighten the CFI's own workload (see Table 13.4), authorisation was given for the establishment of specialised judicial panels which could hear and determine at first instance certain types of cases, including staff dispute cases.

As can be seen in Table 13.5, virtually all of the work of the CFI is undertaken in one of the Court's five chambers.

Table 13.4   *Cases before the Court of First Instance, 2003–04:*
numbers and stage of proceedings[1]

	2003	2004
Cases completed	339	361
New cases	466	536
Cases pending	999	1174

[1] The figures include certain groups of identical and related cases. If those sets of case are excluded, the numbers are reduced marginally.

Source: reproduced from European Court of Justice (2005): 191 and 193.

Table 13.5   *Cases before the Court of the First Instance, 2004:*
bench hearing actions

	Judgements and Orders
Chambers (3 judges)	276
Chambers (5 judges)	64
Single judge	14
President of the Court	7
TOTAL	**361**

Source: reproduced from European Court of Justice (2005): 197.

Types of Cases Before the Courts

The EU's courts cannot initiate actions. They must wait for cases to be referred to them. Cases coming before the courts take a number of forms, the most important of which are outlined below. They are outlined by taking the courts together rather than separately There are three reasons for this. First, the CFI's jurisdiction has now so grown that there are only a few types of cases with which it cannot deal. Second, in describing the responsibilities of the courts, the TEC mostly refers to 'the Court of Justice' when it is clearly describing both courts. Thirdly, most of the decisions of the CFI are subject to appeal to the ECJ on points of law.

As a preliminary, let it just be said that, in very broad terms, the ECJ's main – and unstated – role is to deal with matters that are of considerable importance to the EU's legal order, whilst the CFI is charged with dealing with matters that are generally more routine in nature. This division results in the ECJ being the competent court to deal with failures of member states to fulfil obligations, most preliminary references, and appeals against CFI decisions in direct actions. The CFI has responsibility for annulments, failures to act, disputes relating to compensation for non-contractual liability, and EU staffing disputes. Tables 13.6 and 13.7 indicate the numbers of the types of cases dealt with by the courts.

Table 13.6 *Cases before the European Court of Justice, 2003–04: nature of proceedings[1]*

	2003	2004
References for a preliminary ruling	233	262
Direct actions	193	299
Appeals	57	89
Appeals concerning interim measures and interventions	7	5
Opinions/rulings	0	1
Special forms of procedure	4	9
TOTAL	494	665

[1] The figures represent the total number of cases without account being taken of (the small number of) cases where cases are joined because of their similarity.

Source: reproduced from European Court of Justice (2005): 197.

Table 13.7 *Cases before the Court of First Instance, 2003–04: nature of proceedings[1]*

Nature of proceedings	2003	2004
Actions for annulment	174	199
Actions for failure to act	13	15
Actions for damages	24	19
Arbitration clauses	3	7
Intellectual property	100	110
Staff cases	124	146
Special forms of procedure	28	40
TOTAL	466	536

[1] The figures include certain groups of identical and related cases. If those sets of case are excluded, the numbers are reduced marginally

Source: reproduced from European Court of Justice (2005): 197.

Failure to fulfil an obligation

Under Articles 226 and 227 TEC, the ECJ rules on whether member states have failed to fulfil obligations under the Treaty. Actions may be brought either by the Commission or by other member states. In either eventuality, the Commission must first give the state(s) in question an opportunity to submit observations and then deliver a reasoned opinion. Only if this fails to produce proper compliance with EU law can the matter be referred to the Court.

In practice, failures to fulfil obligations are usually settled well before they are brought before the Court. When an action is brought the Commission is almost invariably the initiator. It is so partly because if a member state is behind the action it is obliged to refer the matter to the Commission in the first instance, and partly because member states are extremely reluctant to engage in direct public confrontation with one another (though they do sometimes try to encourage the Commission to, in effect, act on their behalf). Such cases have led to rulings against, for example, Italy (that its duties on imported gin and sparkling wine were discriminatory), against the UK (that it had introduced insufficient national measures to give full effect to the 1976 directive on sexual discrimination), and Belgium (for failing to implement directives to harmonise certain stock exchange rules).

The Maastricht Treaty gave to the Court, for the first time, the power to impose penalties on member states. As was explained in Chapter 9, under Article 228 TEC the Commission can initiate action against a state that it believes has not complied with a judgement of the Court in a case involving failure to fulfil an obligation under the Treaty. The first stages of the action involve giving the state in question the opportunity to submit its observations and issuing a reasoned opinion that specifies the points on which the state has not complied with the judgement of the Court and which also specifies a time limit for compliance. If the state does not comply with the reasoned opinion within a specified time limit, the Commission may bring it back before the Court. In so doing the Commission must specify the amount of the lump sum or penalty payment to be paid 'which it considers to be appropriate in the circumstances'. If the Court finds that the member state has not complied with its judgement, it may impose a lump sum or penalty payment. An example of such an imposition is that imposed on France in July 2005 for allowing fishermen to catch and sell fish that were smaller than permitted under EU legislation. The Court fined France €20 million and also required it to pay €57.8 million every six months until it complied with the rules.

Failure to fulfil an obligation cases constitute by far the largest number of direct action cases that come before the ECJ: of 219 new direct action cases before the Court in 2004, 193 were for failures to fulfil obligations. (European Court of Justice, 2005: 176).

Application for annulment

Under Article 230 TEC, the Court 'shall review the legality of acts adopted jointly by the European Parliament and the Council, of acts of the Council, of the Commission and of the ECB, other than recommendations and opinions, and of acts of the European Parliament intended to produce legal effects *vis-à-vis* third parties'. The Court cannot conduct reviews on its own initiative, but only in response to actions brought by a member state, the Council, the Commission, plus the EP under the Nice Treaty. Reviews may be based on the following grounds: 'lack of competence, infringement of an essential procedural requirement, infringement of this Treaty or of any rule relating to its application, or misuse of powers'. If an action is well founded, the Court is empowered under Article 231 TEC to declare the act concerned to be void.

The most high profile annulment case in recent years was in 2004, when the Commission brought an action against the Council in connection with EMU's Stability and Growth Pact (SGP). In the autumn of 2003 the Commission had recommended that the Council require France and Germany to take the necessary measures to reduce their budgetary deficits under Article 104(9) TEC. However, no majority existed for this in the Council, so as an alternative the Council decided, in effect, that the excessive deficit procedures should be suspended whilst France and Germany took other correcting action. Deciding that this Council decision undermined both its own authority and the credibility of EMU, the Commission brought an action for annulment against the Council. When it delivered its opinion, in July 2004 (in Case C – 17/04, *Commission v. Council*), the Court basically ruled in favour of the Commission, but refrained from insisting that the Council follow the Commission's recommendations. The judgement played an important part in the subsequent Council deliberations which led to the reform of the SGP in the spring of 2005.

An increasingly important aspect of Court activity in annulment cases arises in connection with the Treaty base(s) upon which EU legislation is proposed and adopted. There are several procedures by which EU law can be made (see Chapter 16 for details), each of which is different in terms of such key matters as whether qualified majority voting rules apply in the Council and what are the powers of the EP. Which procedure applies in a particular case depends on the article(s) of the Treaty upon which legislative proposals are based. So, for example, if a proposal concerned with the competitiveness of industry in the internal market is based on

Article 95 TEC (approximation of laws directly affecting the internal market), the co-decision procedure applies with QMV in the Council. This means that Council approval does not depend on all member states supporting the proposal, but the EP has a potential veto over the proposal. If, however, the proposal is brought forward on the basis of Article 157 TEC (industry), the consultation procedure applies, with unanimity in the Council. This means that a single member state can veto the proposal in the Council, whilst the EP's powers are weak. It thus naturally follows that if a legislative proposal is brought forward by the Commission on a legal base that a member state or the EP believe to be both damaging to their interests and legally questionable, and if political processes cannot bring about a satisfactory resolution to the matter, they may be tempted to appeal to the Court.

Similarly, institutions sometimes appeal to the Court when they believe their prerogatives have been infringed during a legislative procedure. The EP has been very active in this regard, taking a number of cases to the Court, usually on the grounds that either it should have been consulted but was not, or that the Council changed the content of legislation after it left the EP and the EP was not reconsulted. In general, the Court has supported the EP in such cases.

Article 230 also allows any 'natural or legal person' (that is private individuals or companies) to institute proceedings for annulment. Cases under Article 230 have included appeals by companies against Commission decisions to refuse to authorise subsidies and challenges to Commission decisions on abuse of dominant trading positions, restrictive practices, and company mergers. An instance of the CFI making an important decision in an application for annulment case occurred in June 2002 when the CFI overruled the Commission's 1999 veto of the merger between the UK holiday firms Airtours and First Choice on the grounds that the Commission had failed to provide enough evidence that the merger would harm competition. This was the first defeat for the Commission in one of the EU's courts in a merger case, but there have subsequently been others. Generally, however, rulings under Article 230 have tended to strengthen the hand of EU institutions and to serve as useful underpinnings to some EU policies, notably competition policy and commercial policy.

In certain policy spheres, notably competition, the Commission is empowered to impose financial penalties to ensure compliance with EU regulations. Under Article 229 TEC, the regulations governing such policy spheres may allow unlimited jurisdiction to the Court with regard to the penalties. This means that aggrieved parties may appeal to the Court against Commission decisions and the penalties it has imposed. As such, this is another form of action for annulment. The Court may annul or confirm the decision and increase or decrease the penalties. In the great majority of judgements the Commission's decisions are upheld. (See Chapter 9 for examples of fines imposed on firms for breaches of competition law.)

Failure to act

Under the Community treaties there are provisions for institutions to be taken to court for failure to act. These provisions vary in nature between the treaties. Under the TEC, should the EP, the Council or the Commission fail to act on a matter provided for by the Treaty, the member states, the institutions of the Community and, in restricted circumstances, 'natural or legal persons', may initiate an action under Article 232 to have the infringement established. Such actions are not common, but one that attracted much attention was initiated by the EP, with the support of the Commission, against the Council in 1983. The case concerned the alleged failure of the Council to take action to establish a Common Transport Policy, despite the provision for such a policy in the EEC Treaty. The judgement, which was delivered in May 1985, was not what the EP or the Commission had hoped for. The ECJ ruled that whilst there was a duty for legislation to be produced, it had no power of enforcement because the Treaty did not set out a detailed timetable or an inventory for completion; it was incumbent upon the national governments to decide how best to proceed.

Action to establish liability

'In the case of non-contractual liability, the Community shall, in accordance with the general principles common to the laws of the Member States, make good any damage caused by its institutions or by its servants in the performance of their duties' (Article 228 TEC). Under Article 235 the Court has exclusive jurisdiction to decide whether the Community is liable and, if so, whether it is bound to provide compensation.

This means that the Community may have actions brought against it on the ground of it having committed an illegal act. The complex mechanisms of the CAP have produced by far the greatest number of such cases, threatening indeed to overwhelm the ECJ in the early 1970s. As a consequence the Court became increasingly unwilling to accept non-contractual liability cases, at least on the basis of first instance, and made it clear that they should be brought before national courts.

In the 1970s the ECJ also ruled that the circumstances in which the Community could incur non-contractual liability and be liable for damages were strictly limited. Of particular importance in this context were judgements in 1978 on two joined cases concerning skimmed milk (Cases 83 and 94/76, and 4, 15 and 40/77). Community legislation obliged the food industry to add skimmed milk to animal feed as part of an effort to reduce the surplus of powdered milk. A number of users challenged the legality of this on the ground that the Community's solution to the problem was discriminatory. In its first judgement the Court ruled that the powdered milk regulations were, indeed, invalid because they did not spread the burden fairly across the agricultural sector. In its second judgement, however, it ruled that only in exceptional and special circumstances, notably when a relevant body had manifestly and seriously exceeded its powers, should the Community be liable to pay damages when a legislative measure of a political and economic character was found to be invalid.

Reference for a preliminary ruling

The types of case referred to in the sections above are known as direct actions. That is, the ECJ and CFI are called upon to give a judgement in a dispute between two or more parties who bring their case directly to court. References for preliminary rulings are quite different, in that they do not involve the courts (in practice the ECJ to date, although Nice did provide for the CFI to take some preliminary ruling cases) giving judgements in cases, but rather require them to give interpretations on points of EU law to enable national courts to make a ruling.

References are made under Article 234 TEC, which states that national courts may, and in some circumstances must, ask the Court to give a preliminary ruling where questions arise on the interpretation of the Treaty or the validity and interpretation of acts of the institutions of the Community. The Court cannot make a pronouncement on a case that happens to have come to its attention unless a reference has been made to it by the appropriate national court, and parties to a dispute have no power to insist on a reference or to object to one being made. It is the exclusive prerogative of the national court to apply for a preliminary ruling. Once a reference has been made, the Court is obliged to respond, but it can only do so on questions that have been put to it and it may not pronounce on, or even directly attempt to influence the outcome of, the principal action. Interpretations made by the Court during the course of preliminary rulings must be accepted and applied by the national court that has made the referral.

As can be seen in Table 13.6, preliminary rulings constitute a large part of the ECJ's work. With only occasional dips, references have progressively increased over the years: hence the Nice decision to enable the CFI to deal with some such cases. Preliminary rulings serve three principal functions, First, they help to ensure that national courts make legally 'correct' judgements. Second, because they are generally accepted by all national courts as setting a precedent, they promote the uniform interpretation and application of EU law in the member states. Third, they provide a valuable source of access to the Court for private individuals and undertakings who cannot directly appeal to it, either because there is no legal provision or because of insufficient funds.

Staff cases

In recent years over one-quarter of the cases coming before the CFI have involved disputes between the EU and its staff. This workload is somewhat 'low level' in nature and has long been seen as being not quite appropriate for the already over-loaded CFI. Accordingly, as was noted above, the Nice Treaty provided for the establishment of a special tribunal to deal with staff cases. On the basis of a Commission proposal of October 2003, a European Union Civil Service Tribunal was subsequently created by a Council decision of November 2004. The Tribunal is attached to the CFI and consists of seven judges who are appointed for six years by the Council. The first judges assumed office and began work on 1 October 2005.

Decisions of the Tribunal are subject to appeal to the CFI, within conditions.

Appeals

Under Article 225 TEC, certain decisions of the CFI are subject to appeal to the ECJ.

Appeals cannot be made on the substance of a case, but only on points of law. There are three broad grounds for appeal: the CFI lacked jurisdiction, it breached procedural rules, or it infringed Community law. There are usually over fifty appeals each year, most of which fail because the ECJ will only accept appeal on points of law, not points of substance, and also because the CFI follows previous case law of the ECJ.

The seeking of an opinion

Under Article 300 TEC, the Council, the Commission, or a member state plus the EP under the Nice Treaty, may obtain the opinion of the Court on whether a prospective international agreement is compatible with the provisions of the Treaty. Where the opinion of the Court is adverse, the agreement cannot enter into force without being suitably amended or without the Treaty being amended.

An example of an extremely important opinion is that issued in 1994 in respect of external powers. The Commission took the case before the Court, arguing that Article 113 (now 133), which gives the Commission sole negotiating powers in respect of certain international commercial agreements, should extend to trade in services and trade-related aspects of intellectual property rights. The Court ruled (Opinion 1/94) that the Community and the member states shared competence to conclude such agreements and therefore the Commission did not have sole negotiating powers.

The Impact and Influence of the Courts

The EU's courts have two main functions. First, they are responsible for directly applying the law in certain types of case. Second, they have a general responsibility for interpreting the provisions of EU law and ensuring that the application of the law, which on a day-to-day basis is primarily the responsibility of national courts and agencies, is consistent and uniform.

Inevitably, for the reasons explained earlier, these duties result in the courts – and especially the ECJ – making what, in effect, is judicial law. This is most clearly seen in four respects.

First, as noted above, the ECJ has clarified and strengthened the status of EU law. Landmark decisions of the 1960s and 1970s, such as *Van Gend en Loos,* were crucial in paving the way to the establishment of a strong legal system, but later decisions have also been important. For example, in its 1992 judgement in *Francovich and Bonifaci v. Italy* (Joined Cases 6/90 and 9/90) the Court ruled that individuals are entitled to financial compensation if they are adversely affected by the failure of a member state to transpose a directive within the prescribed period. And in its 2005 judgement in *Commission (supported by the European Parliament) v. Council (supported by eleven member states)* (Case C-176/03) the Court strengthened the EU's implementation capacity by ruling that in some circumstances criminal law sanctions could be used for offences against EU law.

Second, EU policy competence has been strengthened and extended by ECJ judgements. Social security entitlements illustrate this. Most governments have not wished to do much more about entitlements than coordinate certain aspects of their social security systems. The Court, however, through a number of judgements, often based on the TEC rather than on legislation, has played an important part in pushing the states towards the harmonisation of some of their practices, for example with regard to the rights of migrant workers. It has also extended the provisions of certain laws in ways the states did not envisage when they gave them their approval in the Council.

Another example of the ECJ strengthening and extending policy competence is a judgement it gave in May 1990 in a preliminary ruling case. The case – *Barber v. Guardian Royal Exchange Assurance Group* (Case 262/88) – had been referred by the UK Court of Appeal. The Court ruled that occupational pensions are part of an employee's pay and must therefore comply with (the then) Article 119 of the EEC Treaty dealing with equal pay for men and women. Regarding the particular issue that gave rise to the case, the Court stated that it was contrary to Article 119 to impose different age requirements for men and women as conditions for obtaining pensions on compulsory redundancy under a private pension scheme.

The area where the EU's courts have exercised the greatest influence in strengthening and extending EU policy competence is in regard to the SEM. In some instances this has been a result of practices being ruled illegal and in others it has been a consequence of judgements pressurising, enabling or forcing the Commission and the Council to act – as, for example, in de-regulating air transport following the 1986 *Nouvelles Frontières* case in which the ECJ held that the treaty rules governing competition applied to air transport.

Third, and of crucial importance in respect of the SEM, judgements have saved the EU the need to make law in existing areas of competence. A particularly influential judgement was issued in February 1979 in the *Cassis de Dijon* case (Case 120/78), which concerned the free circulation of the French blackcurrant liqueur of that name. The ECJ ruled that national food standards legislation cannot be invoked to prevent trade between member states unless it is related to 'public health, fiscal supervision and the defence of the consumer'. The principle of 'mutual recognition' – whereby a product lawfully produced and marketed in one member state must be accepted in another member state – was thus established, with the result that the need for legislation to harmonise standards in order to facilitate trade was much reduced. Of course the *Cassis de Dijon* judgement does not rule out challenges to the principle of 'mutual recognition', or to its application. For example, in the much publicised case *Commission v. Germany* (Case 178/84), the German government attempted to protect its brewers by arguing that whereas their product was pure, most so-called foreign beers contained additives and should be excluded from the German market on health grounds. In March 1987 the ECJ upheld the 'mutual recognition' principle and ruled that a blanket ban on additives to beer was quite disproportionate to the health risk involved; the German insistence on its own definition of beer amounted to a barrier to trade. In a similar ruling in July 1988 (Case

407/85) the Court ruled against an Italian prohibition on the sale in Italy of pasta products that are not made from durum (hard) wheat; the Court stated that German pasta – which is made from a mixture of hard and soft wheat – presented no threat to Italian consumers' health, nor did the product mislead consumers.

Fourth, the powers and functioning of the institutions have been clarified and in important respects significantly affected by the ECJ. Four important judgements will be cited to illustrate this. First, in 1980, in the isoglucose case (Case 138/79), the Court ruled that the Council could not adopt legislation until it had received the EP's opinion (see Chapter 12 for further consideration of this case). Second, in 1988, in the 'Wood Pulp' cases (Joined Cases 89, 104, 114–117, 125–129/85), the Court upheld and strengthened the power of Community institutions to take legal action against non-EC companies. (In this case the Commission had imposed fines on a number of American, Canadian and Finnish producers of wood pulp in respect of concerted practices that had affected selling prices in the Community. The Court ruled that the key factor in determining the Community's jurisdiction was not where companies were based, nor where any illegal agreements or practices were devised, but where illegalities were implemented.) Third, in 1992, in *Spain, Belgium and Italy v. Commission* (Joined Cases 271, 281 and 289/90) – which involved the liberalisation of the monopolistic telecommunications services market – the Court ruled that the Commission's powers in relation to competition policy were not limited to the surveillance of rules already in existence, but extended to taking a proactive role to break monopolies. The fact that the Council could have taken appropriate measures did not affect the Commission's competence to act. Fourth, in 2000, in *Germany v. European Parliament and Council* (Case 376/98) Germany successfully sought annulment of the Tobacco Advertising Ban Directive which would have gradually phased out virtually all tobacco publicity and sponsorship by 2006. The Court ruled that the Commission had been incorrect to use Article 100a (now 95) TEC – which provides for internal market harmonisation and elimination of competition measures – as the legal base of the Directive. This was because other treaty articles excluded harmonisation measures designed to protect and improve human health and Article 100a could not be a general power to regulate the internal market.

The EU's courts have thus had a very considerable impact on the content of EU law. They have done so for a number of reasons, not least because, as Alter (1996: 479) has pointed out, those EU politicians who have been dissatisfied with judicial activism (representing a minority on most issues) have found it difficult to constrain, let alone reduce, the powers of the courts.

The independent influence of the courts should not, however, be overstated. As Wincott (1999) has argued of the ECJ, it is not normally in a position to create a fully fledged policy by itself. There are two main reasons for this. First, the Court must usually have a treaty or legislative base upon which to act. This means that its judgements are normally constrained to at least some extent by an existing, albeit sometimes very sketchy, policy framework. Second, judgements can only be issued on cases that are referred to the Court. It cannot initiate cases itself. Consequently, as Wincott says, 'where the Court has made a striking contribution to the character of a particular policy, usually its contribution has been to unsettle an established policy regime or to break up a gridlock ... rather than to create a policy itself'. Court judgements have certainly impacted on EU policy, but the most important impact has often been not so much direct as rather 'the provocation of further legislation' (Wincott, 1999: 94–5).

Concluding Remarks

The legal framework described in the previous pages constitutes the single most important feature distinguishing the EU from other international organisations. The member states do not just cooperate with one another on an intergovernmental basis but have developed common laws designed to promote uniformity. The claim to legal supremacy in the interpretation, application and adjudication of these laws constitutes a central element of the supranational character of the EU.

This has necessarily involved the member states in surrendering some of their sovereignty, since they are obliged to submit to a legal system over which they have only partial control. In consequence of this, the governments of member states are sometimes obliged to apply laws they do not want and are occasionally prevented from introducing laws they desire.

The EU's courts have played an extremely important part in establishing the EU's legal order. This is because between them they exercise three key legal roles (Lenaerts, 1991). First, there is the role of constitutional court – adjudicating, for example, inter-institutional disputes and disputes about the division of powers between EU institutions and member states. Second, there is the role of supreme court, as most obviously with preliminary rulings that have as their purpose the uniform interpretation and application of EU law. And third, there is the role of administrative court, as when the ECJ and the CFI are called upon by private parties to offer protection against illegal executive acts by EU institutions.

In exercising their responsibilities, the courts, and particularly the ECJ, sometimes not only interpret law but also make it. Of course judges everywhere help to shape the law, but this is especially so in the EU where the courts have much more manoeuvrability available to them than is customary within states. They have used this to considerable effect: to help clarify relations between the institutions and between the institutions and the member states; to help clarify and extend policy content in many different spheres; and to help develop and foster the *esprit communautaire*.

Chapter 14

Other Institutions and Actors

The European Economic and Social Committee
The Committee of the Regions
The European Investment Bank
The European System of Central Banks
The Court of Auditors
Interests

The European Economic and Social Committee

Origins

In the negotiations that led to the Rome Treaties it was decided to establish a consultative body composed of representatives of socio-economic interests.

There were four principal reasons for this decision. First, five of the six founding states – West Germany was the exception – had such bodies in their own national systems. The main role of these bodies was to provide a forum in which sectional interests could express their views, and in so doing could supplement the popular will as expressed via parliaments. Second, the essentially economic nature of the Community meant that sectional interests would be directly affected by policy developments and would be key participants in, and determiners of, the development of integration. Third, it was not thought that the Assembly (as the EP was then called) would be an effective forum for the expression of sectional views. Fourth, the institutional framework of the Rome Treaties was based on the Treaty of Paris model, and that had provided for a socio-economic advisory body in the ECSC Consultative Committee.

Accordingly, the EEC and Euratom Treaties provided for a common Economic and Social Committee (ESC). It was to have an advisory role and it was to be made up of representatives of various types of economic and social activity.

Since 2003, the ESC has called itself the European Economic and Social Committee (EESC).

Membership

The EESC has 317 members. France, Italy, Germany and the UK have the largest national representations, with 24 members each, whilst Malta has the smallest representation, with five members (see Table 6.1, pp. 108–9).

The members of the EESC are proposed by national governments and are formally appointed by the Council of Ministers, by QMV since the ratification of the Nice Treaty. The term of office is four years, which may be renewed.

To ensure that a broad spectrum of interests and views is represented, the membership is divided into three groups that are just about equal in size. Each national complement of members is supposed to reflect this tripartite division. The three groups are as follows:

- *Group I: Employers.* Just less than half of this group are drawn from industry. The rest are mostly from public enterprises, commercial organisations, banks, insurance companies etc.
- *Group II: Employees.* The great majority in this group are members of national trade unions.
- *Group III: Various interests.* About half of this group are associated with either agriculture, small and medium-sized businesses, or the professions. The rest are mostly involved with public agencies and local authorities, consumer groups, environmental protection organisations and so on.

All members are appointed in a personal capacity and not as delegates of organisations. However, since most members are closely associated with or are employees of national interest organisations (organisations that in many cases are affiliated to Euro-organisations) it is inevitable that they do tend to act as representatives of, and be spokesmen for, a cause.

*   *   *

The administrative support for the EESC is organised by its Secretariat General. In 2004 the institution had an authorised staffing of 594 permanent posts and 24 temporary posts, including some posts in joint services with the Committee of the Regions (European Commission, 2005b: point 830).

Organisation

Every two years the EESC elects a President, two Vice Presidents, and a Bureau from amongst its members. The Presidency rotates amongst the three groups, with the two groups that do not occupy the Presidency each assuming a Vice Presidency. There are 37 members of the Bureau: the President, the two Vice Presidents, and 34 members drawn from the three groups in equal proportion.

The main role of the President is to see to the orderly conduct of the EESC's business and to represent the EESC in its relations with other EU institutions, member states, and outside bodies. The Vice Presidents assist the President in these tasks. The main tasks of the Bureau are to provide guidelines for the EESC's work, to coordinate that work, and to assist with external representation.

The groups operate in a somewhat similar fashion to the political groups in the EP. That is to say, they meet on a regular basis – there are about 90 group meetings per year – to review matters of common concern, to discuss ongoing EESC work, and (particularly in the more cohesive groups I and II) to attempt to agree voting positions on proposals and issues that are due to be considered in plenary sessions. Group representatives in sections and study groups (see below) also sometimes meet together to coordinate their activities.

Most of the work of the EESC consists of giving opinions on EU-related matters. In a manner similar to the way in which the detailed work on opinions in the EP is undertaken by committees, so in the EESC it is undertaken by sections, each of which draws its membership from the groups. There are six sections: Agriculture, Rural Development and the Environment; Economic and Monetary Union and Economic and Social Cohesion; Employment, Social Affairs and Citizenship; External Relations; The Single Market, Production and Consumption; and Transport, Energy, Infrastructure and the Information Society. The sections appoint *rapporteurs* to prepare draft opinions on their behalf. How *rapporteurs* go about this depends on circumstances and preferences. Usually use is made of a sub-committee or study group; assistance may be called for from the EESC Secretariat; and – a common occurrence – help may be sought from, or be offered by outside interests. In the sections attempts are usually made to develop common positions on opinions, though on controversial issues this is not always possible to achieve. In an average year there are usually around 70–80 section meetings and some 300 meetings of subcommittees and study groups. (In addition, there are 300–400 miscellaneous meetings and meetings sponsored by the three groups. Many of these are concerned in some way with the preparation of opinions.)

Plenary meetings are held in Brussels, over a two-day period, usually nine or ten times a year. Agendas are dominated by consideration of reports from the sections. The standard procedure for dealing with reports is for each to be introduced by its *rapporteur,* for a debate to be held, and for a vote to be taken. On uncontroversial items the vote may be taken without discussion or debate.

Functions

The EESC engages in a number of activities:

(1) It issues information reports on matters of contemporary interest and concern.
(2) It liaises, via delegations, with a host of other international bodies and groupings.
(3) It seeks to promote understanding between sectional interests by, for example, organising conferences, convening meetings, and being represented at congresses and symposia.
(4) It seeks to take advantage of various contacts it has with other EU institutions to press its views. The most regularised of these contacts is with the Commission: Commission officials, and sometimes Commissioners themselves, attend plenaries and meetings of sections. Occasionally ministers address plenaries.
(5) Above all, as noted above, it issues opinions on a range of EU matters. Opinions are issued in one of three sets of circumstances:

- *Mandatory referral*. Under Article 262 TEC and Article 170 of the Euratom Treaty 'The Committee must be consulted by the Council or by the Commission where this Treaty so provides.' Compared with the EP there are fewer policy areas where the Treaties do so provide, but extensions made by the SEA, the Maastricht Treaty and the Amsterdam Treaty have resulted in most important policy areas now being subject to EESC mandatory referral. So, under the TEC, amongst the policy spheres on which the EESC must be consulted are agriculture, freedom of movement of workers, internal market issues, economic and social cohesion, social policy and the European Social Fund (ESF), regional policy and the European Regional Development Fund (ERDF), the environment, and research and technological development. Under the Euratom Treaty the EESC has to be consulted on such matters as research and training programmes, health and safety, and investment.
- *Optional consultation*. The EESC may be consulted by the Council or the Commission 'in all cases in which they consider it appropriate' (Article 262, TEC; Article 170, Euratom Treaty). Until the entry into force of the SEA some 80 per cent of EESC opinions were based on optional consultation. With the widening of the scope of mandatory referral this figure has fallen to around 50 per cent.

- *Own initiatives*. The ESC has the right to issue opinions on its own initiative. Thus, in theory it can pronounce on almost any matter it wishes.

The EESC normally issues around 200 consultative documents per year, of which the vast majority are opinions on Commission proposals and communications, 30–40 are own initiative opinions, and 3–4 are information reports. Amongst the policy matters covered in Commission proposals and communications on which it issued opinions in 2004 were the organisation of working time, the integration of people with disabilities into the workforce, and the legal prerequisites for the creation of a single retail payments area in the EU. Amongst the policy matters covered by EESC own opinions in 2004 were the employment situation in agriculture, the issues involved in using nuclear power in electricity generation, and the transatlantic dialogue.

The EESC tends to operate in a reasonably consensual manner, with most of its opinions issued unanimously or with a very large majority. A point of contrast, however, worth noting between EESC and EP opinions is that the EESC is not as concerned as the EP to reach a single position that excludes all minority views. It is quite possible for minority positions to be attached as annexes to EESC opinions that have received majority support in the plenary.

Influence

The influence exercised by the EESC on EU policy and decision-making is limited. Evidence of this is provided, for example, by the Commission's follow-up reports to EESC opinions: these rarely constitute unambiguous acceptance of EESC recommendations and include many evasive comments along the lines of 'The Commission has taken note of the EESC opinion' or 'The opinion will be useful to the Commission staff in their exchanges of views with the Council'. Such EESC recommendations as are taken up usually cover relatively minor points, and are often as much a consequence of pressure exerted by other institutions and interests as by EESC pronouncements (this point is discussed further in Chapter 16).

There are a number of reasons why the EESC has only limited power. First, there has always been, as Jeffery (2002) has observed, a lack of clarity as to its role in the EU system: is it mainly a body to represent interests that otherwise would be neglected or is it a sort of panel of experts charged with improving the quality of decision-making? Added to this lack of clarity is the fact that both of these roles have become increasingly difficult for the EESC to use with effect: the first because the nature of its membership has increasingly come to have a rather old-fashioned look and also because corporatist structures themselves are now not so in vogue as they were; the second because the EESC is but one of many sources of specialised advice available to the EU's decision-making institutions.

Second, the Council and the Commission are not obliged to act upon its views. Of course, this also applies to the EP outside the co-decision procedure, but in its case even when co-decision does not apply it has to be consulted on most important proposals, its opinion must be delivered before proposals can be given legislative effect, and delaying powers are available to strengthen its bargaining position. The EESC is not so well placed: the range of issues upon which consultation is mandatory is more restricted; the deliverance of its opinion is often therefore not necessary for further progress; and even when its opinion is required it can be made subject to a timetable that is so tight as not to allow sufficient time for a considered response – the Council and the Commission can, if they consider it necessary, set a time limit as short as one month for the submission of an EESC opinion.

The third weakness follows on from this last point: it is by no means uncommon for proposals to be referred to the EESC at a stage of policy advancement when agreements between the key decision-makers have already been made in principle and are difficult to unscramble.

Fourth, the EESC is not the only, and in many circumstances is not even the most important, channel available to sectional interests wishing to exert pressure on EU decision-makers. EU policy processes are highly sectorised and multi-levelled and offer numerous contact points for interests. Direct access to Council representatives and Commission officials, and representation in advisory committees, are seen by many as being more useful than activity in the EESC – not least because these other channels often offer greater opportunities than does the EESC for influencing policy at the pre-proposal stage.

Finally, the members of the EESC serve only on a part-time basis and are therefore very limited in what they can do. In addition, the fact that they serve – in theory at least – in a personal rather than a representational capacity means that there are rarely strong reasons for the Commission or the Council to listen to them if they do not wish to do so.

The EESC is perhaps best thought of as a functional complement to the EP. It should not, however, be thought of as in any way comparable to the EP, for it simply does not have anything like the same capacity, status, influence or power.

The EESC basically does two things. First, it provides a forum in which representatives of sectional interests can come together on a largely cooperative basis to exchange views and ideas. Second, it is a consultative organ that provides some limited – though in most cases only very limited – opportunities for interests to influence EU policy and decision-making.

The Committee of the Regions

Origins

Regionalism, regional issues and regional politics have come to assume a significant role and importance in the EU. The main factors accounting for this are as follows:

- There are considerable variations in wealth and income between member states and between regions in the member states. In the early 2000s the ten most prosperous regions, headed by Groningen in the Netherlands and Hamburg in Germany, were three times richer and invested three times more in their basic economic fabric than the then ten poorest regions in Greece and Portugal. Such disparities have long produced calls for compensatory and rectifying measures to be taken at EU level, and these calls have increased since the SEM programme was launched in the mid-1980s.
- Since the ERDF was established in 1975, regional and local groupings have had a clear focus for their attention at EU level: the attraction of funds. The Commission has encouraged subnational levels of government to play a full part in ERDF management, especially since the launching of its partnership programme under the 1988 reform of the Structural Funds.
- Partly as a consequence of the financial opportunities offered by the ERDF and other funds, but partly too because they do not wish to be wholly controlled by their national governments, many subnational levels of government have established direct lines of communication with decision-makers in Brussels. In those states where subnational governments have strong constitutional positions – such as Germany and Belgium because of their quasi-federal systems – it is customary for the regional governments to have their own offices in Brussels.
- Over the years several transnational organisations that bring together the subnational governments of different member states have been established to promote common interests and, where appropriate, to make representations and exert pressure at the EU level. These organisations include the Association of European Border Regions, the Assembly of European Regions, the Association of Regions of Traditional Industry and the Association of Frontier Regions.

In response to this developing regional dimension of Community affairs, in 1988 the Commission established the Consultative Council of Regional and Local Authorities. For some governments, notably the German and Belgian, the Consultative Council did not go far enough and they took advantage of the 1990–1 IGC on Political Union to press the case for a stronger body to be established. Differing views were expressed in the IGC – with France, Spain and the UK putting up some resistance to the creation of a new body – but it was eventually agreed to establish, as part of the EU, a Committee of the Regions (CoR).

Membership, organisation, functions and powers

The size and national composition of the *membership* of the CoR is the same as that of the EESC (see Table 6.1, pp. 108–9). The members are appointed for a renewable four-year term of office by the Council of Ministers – by QMV post-Nice – on the basis of proposals from the member states.

As to the qualities and characteristics of the CoR's members, at the time of the creation of the institution the TEC simply stated the Committee should consist of 'representatives of regional and local bodies' (Article 263). The lack of insistence in the Treaty that members should be elected representatives of regional and local bodies led to considerable debate in some member states as to who should be proposed for membership, but in the event virtually all of those nominated to the CoR were and have continued to be elected representatives of subnational levels of government of some kind. Those countries with clear regional structures – including Belgium, France, Germany, Italy, the Netherlands and Spain – have allocated at least half of their places to regional representatives. The more centralised countries have mostly sent representatives from local councils and authorities. The ambiguity about whether or not members should hold elected office was removed by the Nice Treaty which requires them to be elected members of regional or local authorities, or to be politically answerable to an elected assembly.

* * *

The *organisational structure* of the CoR is similar to that of the EESC. The planning and overseeing of the work of the Committee is undertaken by its 56-member Bureau, which is made up of the CoR's President, first Vice President, 25 other Vice Presidents (one for each member state), 25 other members, and the chairs of the four political groups (see below). The members of the Bureau are elected for a two-year term.

Most of the work of the CoR is channelled through six specialised committees, called commissions. These are the commissions for: Territorial Cohesion Policy; Economic and Social Policy; Sustainable Development; Culture and Education; Constitutional Affairs and European Governance; and External Relations. The commissions report to CoR plenary sessions, of which there are normally five each year.

Unlike in the EESC, political groups paralleling the main groups in the EP exist in the CoR. There are four such groups: the European People's Party (EPP), the Party of European Socialists (PES), the Group of the Alliance of Liberals and Democrats for Europe (ALDE), and – not quite the same as in the EP – the Union for Europe of the Nations-European Alliance Group (UEN-EA). The groups, which have official status in the CoR, meet before plenaries to discuss and try to agree positions on tactics on upcoming business.

In 2004 the CoR had an authorised staffing of 382 permanent posts and 25 temporary posts. Some routine work is undertaken by services shared with the EESC.

*   *   *

The *functions and powers* of the CoR are, like those of the EESC, of an advisory nature. The key Treaty references to what the CoR can do are set out in Article 265 TEC:

> The Committee of the Regions shall be consulted by the Council or by the Commission where this Treaty so provides and in all other cases, in particular those which concern cross-border cooperation, in which one of these two institutions considers it appropriate ...
>
> Where the Economic and Social Committee is consulted ... the Committee of the Regions shall be informed by the Council or the Commission of the request for an opinion. Where it considers that specific regional interests are involved, the Committee of the Regions may issue an opinion on the matter.
>
> The Committee of the Regions may be consulted by the European Parliament.
>
> It may issue an opinion on its own initiative in cases in which it considers such action appropriate.

The Maastricht Treaty provided for the CoR to be consulted about: education, training and youth; economic and social cohesion, including the Structural Funds; trans-European transport networks and energy infrastructure networks; public health; and culture. The Amsterdam Treaty provided for some extensions to this list, most notably to transport policy, EU enlargement, combating social exclusion, the environment, and cross-border cooperation.

As they can with the EESC, the Council or the Commission can set a time limit on the CoR for the delivery of its opinion, which can be as little as one month. Upon expiry of the time limit, the absence of an opinion cannot prevent the Council or the Commission from proceeding.

An indication of the volume of work undertaken by the CoR is seen in its adoption in 2004 of 55 opinions and three resolutions. Of the opinions, 13 were on matters where it must be consulted, 39 on matters where consultation is optional, and three were own initiatives. Not surprisingly, a theme running through many of the positions it adopts is that subnational levels of government should play an important role in the identification, management, and evaluation of EU policies that affect them.

Within the spheres of its competence, and especially where mandatory consultation applies, the influence of the CoR appears to be at least comparable to that of the EESC. Like the EESC it is weakened by the fact that those it is charged to represent – primarily subnational authorities in its case – also have other policy process options to utilise, including the Council of Ministers itself in those cases where the national governments of countries with strong regional governmental structures allow regional representatives to participate in their 'delegations' on some issues. As Jeffery (2002: 345) states, the CoR is only one of a number of channels available for regional interests to make a mark on Europe.

The European Investment Bank

The European Investment Bank (EIB) was created in 1958 under the EEC Treaty. Its members are the member states of the EU. The Bank is located in Luxembourg.

Responsibilities and functions

The responsibilities and functions of the EIB are referred to in several articles of the TEC. Article 267 is especially important: it sets out the task of the EIB as being to contribute, on a non-profit-making basis, via the granting of loans and the giving of guarantees, to the 'balanced and steady development of the common market in the interests of the Community'. What this means in practice is that the Bank's main job is to act as a source of investment finance for projects that further certain EU goals. In so doing, it is by far the largest provider of EU loan finance. In 2004 the EIB granted loans totalling €43.2 billion, of which €39.7 billion was in the EU-25 member states and €3.5 billion was in what the EIB calls 'partner countries' – mainly underdeveloped countries, with the funds being used for development aid and cooperation (European Investment Bank, 2005).

With regard to the loans made within the EU, two main conditions have to be satisfied for the EIB to consider providing finance.

First, projects must comply with the policy objectives laid down in Article 267 and with credit directives from the Bank's Board of Governors.

These objectives are interpreted fairly broadly but at least one of the following criteria normally has to be met:

(1) Projects must further economic and social cohesion by contributing to the economic development of the EU's less prosperous regions. Almost two-thirds of EIB loans within the EU are assigned for regional development purposes and for helping the poorest areas. This finance is used primarily to assist with communications and other infrastructure, the productive sector, and capital spending on energy installations.

(2) Projects must support innovation, contribute to the competitiveness of EU industry, and help implement the 'Lisbon Strategy'. Under this heading, particular support is given to the introduction and development of advanced technology and to the integration of industry at the European level.

(3) Projects must be of common interest to several member states or to the EU as a whole. In this connection, major transport and telecommunications developments and the EU's energy objectives are given a high priority. The EU's environmental policies also receive considerable support, with around half of the 'environmental loans' being made to the water sector (catchment, treatment and supply) and the rest going to projects dealing with such problems as atmospheric pollution, waste management, land conservation, and urban improvement.

Second, projects must be financially and technically viable, and loans must be guaranteed by adequate security. This is because although the EIB is not a profit-making body it is not a loss-making one either: apart from certain specified and strictly limited circumstances, the Bank's loans are not subsidised from the EU budget but must be financed from its own capital. This capital comes from two sources: paid-in or due-to-be-paid-in capital by the member states, and borrowing – in the EIB's own name and on its own credit – on capital markets inside and outside the EU. Of these two sources, borrowing is by far the largest element, and since the sums raised must be repaid from the Bank's own financial operations it must take appropriate steps to protect itself.

A major attraction for potential EIB borrowers is that loans are offered at very competitive rates. They are so partly because the Bank enjoys a first class international credit rating and is thus itself able to borrow at favourable rates and partly also because the Bank is not profit-making and is thus able to pass on its favourable rates. Other advantages of EIB loans are that they are generally made available at fixed interest rates, repayments can often be deferred for the first two or three years, and the repayment periods are usually medium to long term (between five and twelve years for industrial projects and up to twenty years or more for infrastructure projects).

Two other features of EIB loans are also worth noting. First, the Bank does not usually lend more than 50 per cent – the average is about 30 per cent – of the investment cost of a project unless it is part of a special programme. Borrowers need to find additional sources of loan finance, with the consequence that the Bank very frequently operates on a co-financing basis with other banks. Second, the Bank generally only deals directly with large loans – of more than about €25 million. This does not however mean that only large-scale investment is supported because, mainly via its global loan facility, the Bank opens lines of credit to intermediary institutions – such as regional development agencies and, more commonly, national financial institutions – which lend on the money in smaller amounts. Global loans account for around 30 per cent of total EIB lending and are directed principally towards small and medium-sized enterprises (SMEs). An administrative problem with global loans is that the intermediary agencies that act on the EIB's behalf and are delegated responsibility for appraising applications and negotiating with potential borrowers on the basis of the EIB's lending criteria tend sometimes to make their decisions according to traditional banking criteria and with little eye to EU objectives.

✻ ✻ ✻

In addition to the activities just described – which may be thought of as the Bank's 'standard' activities – certain other activities are undertaken, including the following:

- Some projects are eligible for both EIB loan finance and EU grant aid. When this is the case – and it applies mainly in connection with the ERDF and the Cohesion Fund – the Bank works closely with other interested parties, especially the Commission, to work out appropriate financial arrangements.
- The December 1992 Edinburgh European Council laid the foundations for a European Investment Fund (EIF), which was established in 1994 and which is designed primarily to assist high technology SMEs and those with a high growth potential. This is done via a venture capital facility, loan guarantees, and direct investment operations. Guarantees are particularly important, with the volume of outstanding guarantees standing at €7.73 billion at the end of 2004. The Fund's subscribed capital is drawn from three sources: 40 per cent is provided by the EIB, 30 per cent by other EU sources (channelled through the Commission), and 30 per cent by public and private banks. The EIF has its own administrative and decision-making structure within the EIB.

Organisation

The EIB's main decision-making bodies are as follows:

The *Board of Governors* decides on the Bank's subscribed capital and lays down general directives on the Bank's activities. It is also responsible for formally appointing the members of the Board of Directors and the Management Committee. The Board of Governors is composed of one minister per member state – usually the Minister of Finance – and normally meets once a year. Certain major Board decisions have to be made unanimously, whilst others can be made by a majority of members representing at least 45 per cent of subscribed capital.

The *Board of Directors* has general responsibility for ensuring that the Bank is managed according to the provisions of the TEC, the Bank's Statute, and directives issued by the Governors. More specifically, the Board has sole responsibility for deciding on loans and guarantees, raising funds, and fixing interest rates. There are 26 Directors: one Director is nominated by each member state and is invariably a senior figure in a national financial institutions or national Ministries of Finance/ Economics/Industry, and one Director is nominated by the Commission. The Board of Directors normally meets every four to six weeks.

The *Management Committee* controls current operations, makes recommendations to the Board of Directors and is responsible for implementing decisions made by the Directors. The Committee consists of the Bank's President and eight Vice-Presidents. It meets at least weekly.

* * *

Supporting, and operating under, these decision-making bodies is the EIB's administration. This is divided into thirteen departments, included amongst which are: the General Secretariat and Legal Affairs; the Directorate for Lending Operations in Europe; the Directorate for Lending Operations Outside Europe; the Finance Directorate; and the Projects Directorate. In all, the EIB employs around 900 staff.

The importance of the EIB

The EIB is a bank, not a grant-dispensing body. This means that it must observe certain basic banking principles. At the same time, however, it is an EU institution charged with furthering a number of policy objectives. These two roles – banker and EU institution – do not always sit easily together.

The scale of EIB borrowing and lending is small when compared with the total operations of commercial banks across the member states. The importance of the Bank should not, however, be underestimated. Indeed, it is the largest international financial institution on capital markets, and within the EU it is an important source of finance for capital investment.

The EIB acts as a useful source of medium- and long-term finance for EU-oriented projects. It complements other public and private funding resources for the promotion of capital investment projects that, in general terms, promote economic development and further integration within the EU.

The European System of Central Banks

The operating context

As the EU moved forward during the 1990s with the construction of Economic and Monetary Union (EMU), an institutional structure was created to manage it. The nature of what the structure should be was extensively debated, with two issues particularly strongly contested. First, given that the single currency – which the December 1995 Madrid European Council meeting decided would be called the euro – would require common monetary policies, what should the balance be between politicians and bankers in the determination of those policies? Second, given that the single currency would require some harmonisation of macroeconomic policies – though the extent of this was disputed – should harmonisation and other EMU-related policy issues be considered and determined by the representatives of all EU governments or only by the representatives of single currency members?

The first of these questions was agreed by all national governments from an early stage: it was specified in the Maastricht Treaty that bankers should be responsible for the day-to-day management of common monetary policies. However, it was also agreed – more enthusiastically by some than by others – that in exercising their management role the bankers should not have a completely free hand: they should be subject, albeit at a general level, to some political direction and accountability.

On the second question, agreement was difficult to reach. Those countries that were not to be part of the first wave of the single currency – Denmark, Greece, Sweden, and the UK – were concerned that they might be excluded from important decision-making forums. The UK in particular pressed the view that single currency members should not create forums from which non-members were excluded. The impasse was only resolved by a fudged deal in which it was agreed that the single currency ministers would sometimes meet as a group, but their gatherings would be for the purpose of consultation and cooperation rather than decision-making.

As a result of these debates and agreements, the principal components of the EMU institutional structure are as follows.

- *The Ecofin Council of Ministers.* Composed of national Ministers of Finance from all EU member states, the Ecofin Council (whose position in the Council structure was explained in Chapter 10) is responsible for the broad outlines of EU macroeconomic policy. The Ecofin Council also has a number of specific EMU-related responsibilities, including deciding upon whether to take action against euro zone states with excessive government deficits and deciding on a range of issues in connection with external monetary and foreign exchange matters.
- *The Eurogroup.* Composed of Ministers of Finance from single currency member states, the Eurogroup has no legal status, although it is given one by the Constitutional Treaty. The Eurogroup ministers normally convene before Ecofin meetings to discuss matters of shared interest concerning the eurozone. Non-eurozone states, especially the UK, have been concerned that the Eurogroup might develop into a sort of pre-Ecofin Council, whilst the French government has sometimes indicated that it would like the Eurogroup to be a political counterweight to the European Central Bank. In practice it is becoming both of these. The most striking demonstration to date of its decision-making capacity occurred in the spring of 2005 when it agreed to loosen the terms of the Stability and Growth Pact and then presented its agreement to Ecofin – formally the decision-making body – virtually for ratification.
- *The European Central Bank* (ECB). The ECB, whose tasks and structure are examined in detail below, operates within the framework of the *European System of Central Banks* (ESCB). The ESCB is composed of the ECB and the EU national central banks (NCBs). NCBs of the member states that are not part of the euro area have a separate status within the ESCB: because they continue to have their own national monetary policies, they do not take part in decision-making on the single monetary policy of the euro area.
- Other EU institutions and actors with significant EMU-related responsibilities are:

  - The *European Council,* which is obliged to discuss, under Article 99 TEC, 'a conclusion of the broad guidelines of the economic policies of the Member States and of the Community', and in practice can consider anything else that it wishes.
  - The *Commission,* which is responsible for monitoring and producing reports on national economic, and especially budgetary, performances, and for making recommendations to the Council when states are deemed to be in breach of their Treaty and Stability and Growth Pact requirements. As was shown in Chapter 13, in the autumn of

2004 the Council did not accept the Commission's recommendations on action to be taken against France and Germany for breaching the requirements, which led to the Commission taking the Council to the ECJ.
- The *Economic and Financial Committee,* whose remit includes financial policy, capital movements, and international monetary relations (see Chapter 10 for the membership of the Committee).
- The *European Parliament,* which has few powers in relation to EMU, but does have a range of consultation and information-receiving rights.

Objectives and tasks

Article 105 TEC states that

> The primary objective of the ESCB shall be to maintain price stability. Without prejudice to the objective of price stability, the ESCB shall support the general economic policies in the Community with a view to contributing to the achievement of the objectives of the Community as laid down in Article 2 [of the TEC].

These two sentences of Article 105 contain the seeds of possible disputes over ESCB policies, since Article 2 identifies Community tasks as including 'a high level of employment and of social protection' and 'economic and social cohesion and solidarity among Member States'. These are tasks that in some circumstances might be seen as not sitting easily alongside policies aimed at ensuring low inflation. In public statements, several EU politicians have already sought to exert pressure on ESCB decision-makers for not paying enough attention to policies beyond the control of inflation. For example, in June 2004 the French Finance Minister, Nicolas Sarkozy, accused the Bank of concentrating too much on keeping inflation below its target of two per cent and not enough on promoting economic growth and employment. Later in 2004 the Italian Prime Minister, Silvio Berlusconi, plus several leading German politicians, called on the Bank to sell euros and buy dollars so as to stop the rise in value of the euro which was damaging export potential. However, ESCB decision-makers are given a certain amount of protection from such political pressures in that the Treaty emphasises that the ESCB must be independent. When performing ESCB-related tasks 'neither the ECB, nor a central bank, nor any member of their decision-making bodies shall seek or take instructions from Community institutions or bankers, from any government of a Member State or from any other body' (Article 108 TEC).

Article 105 also states that the basic tasks to be carried out through the ESCB are 'to define and implement the monetary policy of the

Community', 'to conduct foreign exchange operations', 'to hold and manage the official foreign reserves of the member states' and 'to promote the smooth operation of payment systems'. In addition, the ESCB is charged with providing advice to the Community and national authorities on matters that fall within its competence, especially where legislation is envisaged, and contributing to the smooth conduct of policies pursued by the competent authorities relating to the prudent supervision of financial institutions.

The ECB's capital of €5 billion and foreign reserve assets of €40 billion are drawn from the NCBs of eurozone states, according to criteria based on the size of GDP and population.

Organisational structure

'The ESCB shall be governed by the decision-making bodies of the ECB which shall be the Governing Council and the Executive Board' (Article 107 TEC).

The Governing Council

The main responsibilities of the ECB Governing Council are:

- To adopt guidelines and make the necessary decisions to ensure the performance of the tasks entrusted to the ESCB.
- To formulate the Community's monetary policy, including, as appropriate, decisions relating to intermediate monetary objectives, key interest rates and the supply of ESCB reserves, and to establish the necessary guidelines for their implementation (European Central Bank, 1999).

The Governing Council, which meets twice a month, is made up of the members of the Executive Board and the governors of euro member NCBs. The President of the Ecofin Council and a member of the Commission may attend Governing Council meetings, but do not have the right to vote.

The Executive Board

The main responsibilities of the ECB Executive Board are:

- To implement monetary policy in accordance with the guidelines and decisions laid down by the Governing Council, and in so doing to give the necessary instructions to the national central banks.
- To execute such policies as have been delegated to it by the Governing Council (European Central Bank, 1999).

Though these responsibilities suggest that the Executive Board is the servant of the Governing Council, in practice it is very much involved in the formulation of policy, not least in helping to set the agenda and shape the decisions of the Council (McNamara, 2002: 171–3).

The Executive Board consists of the ECB President, Vice-President, and four other members. They are appointed 'from among persons of recognised standing and professional experience in monetary or banking matters by common accord of the governments of the Member States at the level of Heads of State or Government, on a recommendation from the Council, after it has consulted the European Parliament and the Governing Council of the ECB' (Article 112 TEC, ex 109a). The term of office is a non-renewable eight years.

As was shown in Chapter 11, in 1998 the appointment of the first Executive Board, and more especially of the first President, became highly politicised when France pressed for the appointment of its candidate, Jean-Claude Trichet, as President, rather than the Dutchman, Wim Duisenberg, who was favoured by other states. The impasse was only resolved by what most participants regarded as an unsatisfactory informal understanding – the terms of which later came to be disputed – in which Duisenberg agreed to step down well before his eight-year term expired, at which point he would be replaced by Trichet. In the event, Trichet replaced Duisenberg in 2003.

* * *

In addition to its Governing Council and Executive Board, the ECB also has a General Council. Its membership comprises the ECB President and Vice-President and the governors of all the NCBs (that is, from both euro and non-euro zone states). The four other members of the ECB Executive Board may participate in General Council meetings, but do not have the right to vote.

The General Council has a number of tasks to perform, including supervision of the functioning of the post-single currency Exchange Rate Mechanism, considering the monetary and exchange rate policies of the member states that are not in the euro zone, and undertaking various advisory, administrative, and technical duties.

The governing bodies of the ECB are supported by an ECB staff complement of around 600 employees.

Functioning

The early experiences of the ESCB, and more especially of its core institution the ECB, have highlighted a number of difficulties that may be expected to continue, perhaps even increase in intensity, in the foreseeable future.

One of these difficulties is tensions arising from the fact that whilst the ECB is broadly responsible for the monetary policies of 'euroland' the member states retain responsibility for economic policies. When the Bank's policies have been thought not to chime wholly with the economic goals of national governments it has found itself the object of public criticism from the state(s) concerned.

A related difficulty has been some uncertainty and also disagreement as to whether the ECB should pursue exchange rate objectives. Should, as Duisenberg argued in 1998, the external value of the euro be mainly a consequence of the ECB's monetary policy, or should there be 'general orientations' and, if so, should these be set by the bankers or the politicians? A sharp decline in the value of the euro against the dollar in its initial period of operation stoked disagreements amongst practitioners and commentators on these questions: disagreements that remain unresolved.

A third area of difficulty has concerned, as McNamara (2002: 180) puts it, 'how the ECB can maintain independence and profit from the benefits of political autonomy and at the same time be viewed as legitimate and accountable to the European public'. Some important EU actors are not happy about aspects of the powers and structures of the ECB. Matters about which there is unease include: should bankers have so much power?; and, given that the bankers have been given considerable power, should they not be made to be more accountable?

And a fourth difficulty has been that the ECB has become the main focus for complaints about the economic performance of the eurozone. That the performance has been disappointing is undeniable, with growth consistently below two per cent since the single currency was launched and with unemployment around ten per cent in several eurozone states – including the key states of France and Germany. Whether, however, the ECB should be held partly to account for this is highly questionable. Most economists point to underlying economic structural problems as the main 'culprit'. But the fact is that, as the main physical embodiment of the eurozone, the Bank has been a useful and much-used scapegoat.

The Court of Auditors

The 1975 *Treaty Amending Certain Financial Provisions of the Treaties . . .,* which entered into force in 1977, replaced the two existing Community audit bodies – the Audit Board of the EEC and Euratom and the ECSC Auditor – with a single Court of Auditors. The Maastricht Treaty enhanced the Court of Auditors' standing by raising it to the rank of a fully fledged Community institution. The Court is based in Luxembourg.

Membership and organisation

There are as many members of the Court of Auditors as there are EU states. Each member is appointed by the Council of Ministers, by QMV post-Nice, on the basis of one nomination per member state and after consultations with the EP. As with Commissioners-designate, the EP uses its right of consultation to hold hearings with nominees: before the Budgetary Control Committee.

At its November 1989 part-session, the EP voted, for the first time, to reject nominations – one made by France and one by Greece. The EP vote was not binding on the Council, but France nonetheless submitted a new name. Greece claimed difficulty in finding a suitable alternative candidate, so at the following December part-session the EP decided to accept both appointments so that the two posts could be filled by the new year. The EP hoped that this episode established its right to veto any nominee whom it considered to be unsuitable, but this proved not to be the case for in 1993 the Council confirmed the appointment of two candidates about whom the EP had expressed reservations. In 2004 the Council again overrode the EP's views when in appointing members from the new member states it confirmed the Slovak nominee even though he had been rejected by the EP. (The EP did, however, have a partial 'success' in 2004 when the Cypriot nominee withdrew his name following a negative vote by the Budgetary Control Committee.)

At the time of their appointment, members of the Court of Auditors must belong to, or have belonged to, an external audit body in their own country, or be appropriately qualified in some other capacity. The appointment is for a renewable six-year period. As with other 'non-political' EU bodies, a condition of appointment is that the members will act in the general interest and will be completely independent in the performance of their duties.

The members elect one of their number to be the President of the Court. The term of office is three years and is renewable. The President sees to the efficient running of the Court and also represents it in its external relations.

The members are assigned a specific sector of activity for which they hold a particular responsibility regarding the preparation and implementation of the decisions of the Court. Each sector falls under one of four audit groups which act primarily as coordinating agencies and filters for plenary sessions of the whole Court. All important decisions are taken in plenaries, by majority vote if need be.

* * *

As with several other EU institutions, the administration supporting the Court of Auditors is rather small in size given the potential importance of the work to be done. In 2004 just over 600 people were employed by the Court, of whom almost 100 were in temporary posts. Of the 600, around 350 were directly engaged in audit duties, 100 were in the language service, and 100 were in administrative departments. Inevitably such modest staffing resources greatly restricts the number of things the Court can attempt to do.

Activities of the Court

The main tasks of the Court of Auditors are to examine all EU revenue and expenditure accounts, the same for bodies set up by the EU unless the relevant legal instruments preclude such examination, and to provide the Council and the EP with a Statement of Assurance on the reliability of the accounts and the legality and regularity of the associated transactions. In exercising its responsibilities the Court engages in two main types of activity.

The first is to carry out audits to see whether revenue has been received and expenditure has been incurred in a lawful and regular manner, and also to examine whether the financial management of EU authorities has been sound. The auditing powers of the Court cover the general budget of the EU, plus certain financial operations that are not included in the budget such as aid to developing countries that is financed by national contributions.

The auditing of the general budget and the related process of granting a discharge to the Commission on its implementation of the budget, proceed as follows:

- The Commission is required to draw up, for each financial year, accounts relating to the implementation of the budget, a financial statement of the assets and liabilities of the EU, and an analysis of the financial year. The main responsibility for collecting and presenting this information (the internal audit) lies with financial controllers in the Commission. The documentation must be forwarded to the Council, the EP, and the Court of Auditors by no later than 1 June of the following financial year.
- The Court undertakes its audit (the external audit) partly on the basis of an examination of Commission documentation and partly on the basis of its own independent investigations. The latter is an ongoing process and involves the examination of records supplied by and requested from EU institutions and member states (which in the case of member states means liaising closely with national audit bodies and appropriate

national agencies), and when necessary carrying out on-the-spot investigations. The purpose of this Court audit is not to replicate what has already been covered by the internal audit, but rather to add an extra dimension to the EU's overall auditory control by examining the adequacy of internal procedures – particularly with regard to their ability to identify significant irregular and unlawful transactions – and to evaluate the extent to which correct financial management (in terms of economy, efficiency and effectiveness) is being practised. The Court transmits to all relevant institutions any comments that it proposes to include in its annual report to which it believes there should be a reply, or to which an institution may wish to reply. After receipt of the replies, the Court completes the final version of its annual report. This has to be communicated to the other EU institutions by 30 November.

The format of the annual report changed with the report on the 1997 financial year so as to allow the Court's work to be more manageable and measured. Whereas the report used to contain the detailed results of enquiries, it now consists largely of general observations grouped into chapters – on, for example, the CAP, structural measures, and external aid – and a summary of the audit conclusions of special reports, of which about ten are produced each year, and special annual reports on particular activities and EU agencies. Whilst the annual reports have increasingly testified in recent years to improvements in the EU's, and more especially the Commission's, financial control and operating systems, they have also emphasised that the Court is able only to examine a small proportion of EU expenditure and is just not in a position to give a statement of assurance on the reliability and regularity of all financial transactions.

- The EP, acting on a recommendation of the Council, is supposed to give discharge to the Commission in respect of the implementation of the budget by 30 April of the following year. To this end, the EP's Budgetary Control Committee examines all relevant documentation, particularly that produced by the Court of Auditors, and makes a recommendation to the EP. Normally discharge is given by the due date, but not always and there have been occasions when discharge has been deferred until after the Commission has taken remedying measures to deal with the problem. Most dramatically in this context, in March 1998 the EP deferred discharge on the 1996 budget after a series of cases involving alleged Commission mismanagement and fraud came to light, particularly in respect of the PHARE and TACIS programmes, aid for Eastern Europe, and the Mediterranean aid programme. When the discharge vote was eventually held, in December 1998, the EP – angered by what it saw as an insufficiently robust Commission response to its concerns and aware that in November the Court had again strongly criticised the Commission in its report on the 1997 financial year – voted against giving discharge, even though the Budgetary Control Committee had voted narrowly (by 14 votes to 13) to recommend that discharge be given. The President of the Commission, Jacques Santer, responded by calling on the EP either to back or to sack the College of Commissioners. As was shown in Chapters 9 and 12, the sacking option came close to being taken when other causes of dissatisfaction with the Commission became caught up in a vote of censure on the College in January 1999. Though the vote was not passed, the circumstances that led to it being held paved the way for the events that resulted in the resignation of the College two months later.

The second main activity of the Court of Auditors is to submit observations and deliver opinions on a range of subjects. This it does in two main sets of circumstances. First, an EU institution may ask the Court to submit an opinion on a matter, usually concerning financial aspects of draft legislation. Second, when the Council enacts a financial regulation it is obliged to seek an opinion from the Court on the draft text.

Under the Nice Treaty the Court is permitted to set up chambers for certain categories of opinion or report.

The effectiveness of financial controls

As the Court invariably reports each year, controls over EU revenue and expenditure could be improved. For example, procedures could be tightened so as to prevent member states from imposing the limitations they occasionally apply to the audit enquiries considered necessary by the Court. The Court's own attempts to extend its influence beyond questions of financial rectitude into considerations of policy efficiency could be encouraged, and even formalised. And the particular problem of fraud – which is generally thought to account for at least 10 per cent of the EU budget, most of it in connection with agriculture payments and foreign aid contracts – could be tackled more effectively if resources at both EU and member state levels were increased and if more of the proposals that have long been advocated by the Court for streamlining administrative practices were adopted.

However, considerable progress has been made in recent years in improving financial control and overseeing, especially since the College of Commissioners was forced to resign in 1999 because – in large part – it was seen to have been lax in respect of financial management. Much of the credit for this progress, which is seen throughout the EU both in tighter financial control mechanisms and in the development/strengthening of a culture of financial responsibility, can be claimed by the Court of Auditors.

Its reports have been sharp, critical, and increasingly difficult for those who are responsible for managing EU expenditure to ignore. One reason for this is, as Laffan (2002: 251) has observed, that its reports have provided the raw material for the EP to exercise its discharge procedure in a manner that has strengthened its control over the Commission.

One final point about EU expenditure that should be recognised amidst the hype that sometimes greets allegations of financial mismanagement: the total sums involved are relatively modest (see Chapter 17 for details). EU decision-makers, far from being able to be financially profligate with surplus funds are, for the most part, obliged to work to tight budgets and within limited resources.

Interests

Different types

Brussels has come to compete with Washington as the world's 'most lobbied city'. The exact number of lobbyists in Brussels is impossible to gauge with precision, partly because many who lobby do not do so on a full-time basis but also act as lawyers, accountants, businessmen, and so on, and partly also because many of those who are really full-time lobbyists prefer to call themselves 'consultants', 'advisers', 'policy specialists', and the like. Nonetheless, the normal estimates of between 15 000 and 20 000 people making a living from 'lobbying Brussels' give an indication of the scale of lobbying activity.

Lobbyists represent and seek to act on behalf of a range of non-governmental interests. These interests are of four main types.

Subnational levels of government

As noted above in the discussion on the Committee of the Regions, many subnational governmental bodies from the member states seek to influence, or even play a direct role in, EU decision-making processes. The degree of their involvement and activity depends largely on the degree of autonomy and manoeuvrability they enjoy at the national level. Where regional and local governments with real powers exist, then direct lines of communication have usually been opened up with EU institutions, notably the Commission, and offices have been established in Brussels. In total, over 100 subnational authorities maintain representative offices in Brussels (Jeffery, 2002: 344). More commonly, however, regional and local authorities work with the EU mainly through their national governments and, where appropriate, through liaison organisations and the locally based 'European office' that many have created.

Private and public companies

Many large business firms, especially multinational corporations, are very active in lobbying EU institutions. Around 250 firms have established offices in Brussels. Adopting, usually, multiple strategies, business lobbying is channelled through both national and Euro interest groups (see below), and is also conducted on a direct basis. Direct lobbying has the advantage of not requiring a collective view to be sought with other firms, and also enables sensitive issues to be pursued when there is no desire to 'go public', for example when competition and trading matters are involved. The car industry is an example of a sector where direct lobbying by firms, and not just European firms, is common – as is indicated by the fact that most large car firms in Europe have lobbying/information offices in Brussels.

National interest groups

Many circumstances result in national interest groups attempting to involve themselves in EU processes. For example, several national environmental interest groups have pressed for more effective implementation of existing EU legislation on the disposal of sewage into the sea. In some policy areas, especially those concerned with business and trade matters, many national interest groups are from non-EU countries: one of the most influential of all is the EU Committee of the American Chamber of Commerce (AMCHAM-EU). In seeking to play a part in EU processes, most national interest groups are confined to working from their national offices or via a European interest group, but a few of the larger industrial and agricultural groups have, in addition to a domestic and a European group base, their own representatives and agents permanently based in Brussels.

Eurogroups

Eurogroups are groups that draw their membership from several countries and operate at – and in so doing seek to represent the interests of their sector or cause at – the EU level. As with lobbyists, the number of Eurogroups is difficult to estimate, with there being no central register of such groups and with the differences between groups that might be considered to be Eurogroups being so great that considerable difficulties arise in deciding which ones should be counted. As an indication, however, of the scale of activity, Greenwood (2003: pp. 8–13) estimates there are 1450 formally constituted EU level groups that exist to address EU activities.

Given their particular EU orientation it is worth looking at Eurogroups in detail.

Their *policy interests* naturally reflect the policy priorities and concerns of the EU. According to Greenwood (2003: 19) 66 per cent represent business, 20 per cent represent public interests (the environment, consumers, youth, etc.), 11 per cent represent the professions, and 3 per cent represent trade unions. Within these broad categories a multiplicity of specific interests and groups are to be found. For example, within the business category, agricultural interests are a major and diverse component, ranging in nature from the broadly based Committee of Agricultural Organisations in the European Union (COPA) and the General Confederation of Agricultural Co-operatives in the European Union (COGECA), which work very closely with one another, which share a secretariat, and which seek to represent most types of farmer on most issues, to highly specialised groups representing the likes of yeast producers and pasta manufacturers.

The reason why such an array of Eurogroups has been constituted and is active at the EU level is quite simple: pressure groups go where power goes. As policy responsibilities – in agriculture, in the regulation of the market, in the protection of the environment and so on – have been transferred from national capitals to the EU, so has a Euro-lobby developed to supplement – not to replace – the domestic lobbies.

The *membership* of Eurogroups also varies considerably. It does so in four main respects. First, there are variations in the breadth of the membership base. Some groups – the so-called umbrella groups – have a broad membership base and are usually trans-sector or sectoral-wide in character. Examples of umbrella groups are the Union of Industrial and Employers Confederation of Europe (UNICE), the European Trade Union Confederation (ETUC), the European Environmental Bureau (EEB), the European Bureau of Consumers' Associations (BEUC), and COPA/COGECA. Because of the breadth of their membership some of these umbrella groups have considerable difficulty in maintaining internal cohesion and presenting a common front: ETUC, for example, has traditionally had to try to reconcile differences between socialist, communist, and Christian trade unions, whilst COPA/COGECA has had problems with managing the varying agricultural sectoral implications of reforms to the CAP. Most groups, however, are more narrowly focused than the umbrella groups and seek to speak on behalf of a specific industry, process, service, or product. Examples of such groups are the Construction Industry Federation (FIEC), the Savings Banks Group (ESBG), and the European Cocoa Association (ECA).

Second, there are variations in terms of whether membership is direct or via affiliation. In most cases membership is based on affiliation by national sectoral or, in the case of a few of the larger Eurogroups, national peak (cross-sectoral) organisations. Since the mid-1980s, however, there has been a growth in direct membership groupings and organisations. The most important development in this regard has been the coming together of major industrial, often multinational, companies, frequently as a supplement to their involvement in affiliation-based sectoral groups. Examples of Eurogroups that are dominated by large companies are the Association of European Automobile Constructors (ACEA), which represents most of the EU's major non-Japanese car manufacturers, and the Association of Petrochemical Producers and Exporters (APPE). A few lobbying-related linkages between major companies are relatively informally based and in some respects are perhaps more like think tanks and forums for the generation of ideas than Eurogroups. The best known example of such a 'think tank' is the European Round Table of Industrialists which brings together, on an invitation-only basis, fifty or so heads of major European industries. The Round Table produces reports that are intended to identify how the right conditions can be created for business to flourish.

Third, there are variations in the representativeness of groups. Since most Eurogroups are based on national affiliates, the number of people they can claim to represent naturally reflects the factors determining group membership at the national level. Hence, sectional interests are usually better placed than promotional interests. Similarly, amongst sectional interests, Eurogroups representing interests that are well mobilised at the national level, such as dairy farmers and textile manufacturers, naturally tend to be much more genuinely representative than groups acting on behalf of poorly mobilised sections of the population such as consumers or agricultural labourers.

Fourth, there are variations in the width of the EU base of groups. At one end of the spectrum, a few groups draw members from virtually all EU states and often also several European states beyond. ETUC, for example, comprises 77 member organisations from 34 countries and 12 European industry federations, whilst UNICE comprises 36 national member federations from 30 countries. Membership of this latter sort, stretching into non-EU states, has advantages and disadvantages: on the one hand it can help to promote international cooperation and increase group resources; on the other hand, and this is a charge that has frequently been laid against ETUC, it can serve to dilute group concentration on, and therefore influence within, the EU. More typical, however, of Eurogroups than ETUC or UNICE is the European Passengers' Federation (EPF), which seeks to promote rail use and to look after the interests of rail passengers by promoting rail infrastructure and rail facilities. The EPF has18 member organisations drawn from eleven EU member states plus Switzerland.

Clearly this narrower membership weakens the representational claims that the EPF can make.

In terms of *resources*, the best resourced groups are mostly either large business groups – such as the European Chemical Industry Council (CEFIC), COPA/COGECA, UNICE, the European Insurance Committee (CEA), and the European Federation of Pharmaceutical Industry Associations (EFPIA) – or global public interest groups such as Friends of the Earth and the World Wide Fund for Nature. The most poorly resourced groups, which are not of a particular type but exist amongst business, public interest, and other groups, usually do not have strong corporate backing and/or have a narrow membership base.

There are thus wide variations in group resources. On the one hand there are very well resourced groups with twenty or more staff (CEFIC is the largest with over 100 and COPA/COGECA the second largest with around 50) and ample and well-appointed accommodation. On the other hand some groups, such as the EPF, do not even stretch to one employee and work through affiliates, consultants, and part-time and temporary representatives whose services are called upon as and when they are needed. (It is not difficult to find people prepared to act as contract agents: there are around 140 professional public consultancies and 160 law firms based in Brussels that are willing to take on 'EU business'.)

The *organisational structure* of most Eurogroups is extremely loose. The central group organs usually enjoy only a very limited independence from the national affiliates, whilst the affiliates themselves are autonomous in most respects and are not subject to central discipline. In addition, key decisions made at the centre are frequently taken only on the basis of unanimous votes, though some groups do have provisions for weighted majorities on some issues. These loose structures can weaken the effectiveness of Eurogroups by making them slow to react and making it difficult for them to put forward collective views that are anything more than rather vague lowest common denominators. At the same time, however, moves to create stronger structures risk groups not affiliating, or national affiliates concentrating almost exclusively on their national activities.

The extent and complexity of groups' organisational structures varies. The more specialised and poorly resourced groups usually operate on a fairly rudimentary basis, often merely via an annual meeting and an executive committee that meets as required. The large umbrella groups, in contrast, usually have an extensive structure that typically includes a general meeting at least once a year, an executive committee that meets once every four to six weeks, specialist policy committees whose frequency of meeting depends on the business in hand, a President, and a full-time Secretariat headed by a Secretary General. COPA is an example of a group with a highly developed structure (see Figure 14.1).

Figure 14.1 *Organisational structure of COPA*

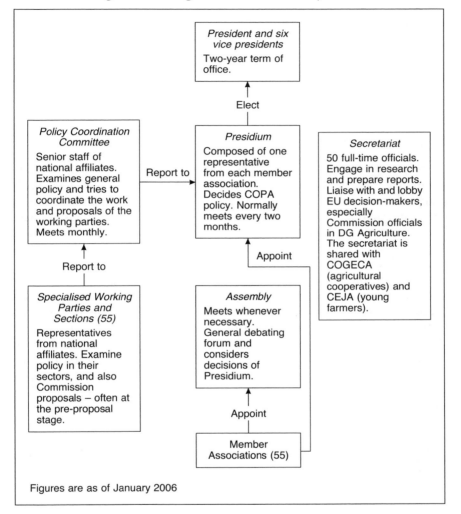

Figures are as of January 2006

Finally, with regard to their *functions,* Eurogroups normally attempt to do two main things. First, they seek to gather and exchange information, both in a two-way process with EU organs and with and between national affiliates. Second, they seek to have their interests and views incorporated into EU policy, by persuading and pressurising those who make and implement policy. Not all Eurogroups, of course, attempt or are able to exercise these functions in equal measure: for example, in those sectors where EU policy is little developed, Eurogroups often choose to give a higher priority to the first function than they do to the second.

Access to decision-makers

The long, complex and multi-layered nature of EU processes provides many points of access for interests, and hence many opportunities for them to keep themselves informed about developments and press their cases with those who influence, make, and implement decisions. The main points of access are national governments, the Commission, and the European Parliament.

National governments

A major problem for interests is that they cannot normally directly approach either the European Council or the Council of Ministers. This is partly because there are practical problems with lobbying what are in effect international negotiations, it is partly because the meetings are held behind closed doors, but it is mainly because neither body wishes to make itself available, as a collective entity, for regularised or intensive interest targeting. Only a few direct linkages therefore exist, and these are largely restricted to the most powerful interests. So, the President-in-Office of a sectoral Council may occasionally meet the president of a powerful Eurogroup, or a written submission from an influential interest may be officially received and circulated prior to a European Council or Council of Ministers meeting. More usually, however, the only way an interest can hope to establish contact with, and perhaps exert pressure on, the European Council or the Council of Ministers is indirectly: through a government or governments looking favourably on its cause or feeling obliged to act on its behalf.

Much time and effort is therefore spent by interests, especially national interests, in attempting to influence the positions adopted by governments in EU negotiations. In the case of the European Council, this task usually has to be undertaken at least at one stage removed because national leaders do not normally allow themselves to be lobbied directly. With the Council of Ministers, however, one of a number of factors may result in doors being opened. Amongst such factors are: some interests, such as most of the major national agricultural groups, enjoy – for a mixture of political, economic, technical and other reasons – insider status with the relevant government departments, which means they are consulted as a matter of course on proposals and developments within their sphere of interest; when a technically complicated matter is under consideration, governments usually seek the advice of relevant interests at an early stage of the Council process – with perhaps Council working group members communicating directly with interest representatives; and when the cooperation of an interest is important for the effective implementation of an EU proposal, its views may well be actively sought, or received and listened to if an approach is made.

This last point touches on another reason (in addition to trying to influence Council decision-making), why interests may approach national governments: they may wish to influence the way EU decisions are implemented. One way in which they can attempt to do this is by making their views known to governments when measures are being devised to incorporate EU directives into national law. And if relevant ministries can be persuaded to delay, or not to monitor too closely, the implementation of directives on, say, the disposal of pollutants or safety standards in the workplace, some interests may well have much to gain financially.

The Commission

The Commission is the main target for most interests. It is so, primarily, because of its central importance in so many respects: in policy initiation and formulation; in taking many final decisions; in following proposals through their legislative cycle; in managing the EU's spending programmes; and in policy implementation. An important contributory reason why the Commission attracts so much attention is simply that it is known to be approachable.

The Commission makes itself available to interests because several advantages can accrue to it from so doing. First, interests often have access to specialised information and to knowledge of how things are 'at the front' which the Commission needs if it is to be able to exercise its own responsibilities efficiently. Second, the Commission's negotiating hand with the Council of Ministers is strengthened if it can demonstrate that its proposals are supported by influential interests – as, for example, many of its attempts to approximate European standards are supported by multinational corporations, and indeed in some cases may have originated from them. Third, and this is in some ways the other side of the coin of the previous point, if the Commission does not consult with and try to satisfy interests, and comes forward with proposals to which influential interests are strongly opposed, the proposals are likely to meet with strong resistance in the Council. Fourth, with specific regard to Eurogroups, when groups come forward with broadly united and coherent positions they can greatly assist the Commission by allowing it to deal with already aggregated views and enabling it to avoid entanglement in national and ideological differences between sectional interests. For this reason, DGs generally keep 'recognised' Eurogroups informed about matters that are of interest to them and are usually prepared to consult them too. (There are, however, no explicit Commission rules on recognition, in the sense that there is no proper system of accreditation or registration, but informal consultation lists do exist. The main reasons for non-recognition are either that the Commission does not regard the group as a proper Eurogroup – perhaps because it consists of just two or three large companies – or that it is not seen as being very effective in 'delivering' aggregated and coordinated views.)

Until about the mid-1970s the Commission displayed a strong preference for talking to Eurogroups rather than national groups, and to national governments rather than subnational levels of government. This attitude, however, has since been relaxed and most interests of significance, and most interests which can provide useful information that is presented in a clear manner, are able to have their views at least considered by the Commission. The procedures by which the contacts and communications occur are many and are of both a formal and an informal nature. They include the following:

- The extensive advisory committee system that is clustered around the Commission primarily exists for the precise purpose of allowing interests to make their views known to EU authorities, and in particular to the Commission (see Chapter 9).
- The Social Dialogue provides for an exchange of views between the Commission and the two sides of industry. Since 1985 it has regularly brought together, at the most senior and at working group levels, representatives from the Commission, trade union representatives from ETUC and representatives from the two main employers' and industrial organisations – UNICE and the European Centre of Enterprises with Public Participation (CEEP). The Maastricht Treaty's Social Charter greatly extended the scope of the Commission's consultations with management and labour and it is even possible for legislative proposals to be developed within its framework.
- Commissioners and DG officials receive numerous delegations from interests of all sorts.
- Representatives of the Commission travel to member states to meet interests and to attend conferences and seminars where interests are represented.
- A few of the larger Eurogroups invite Commission representatives to attend some of their working parties and committee meetings.
- Informal meetings and telephone conversations between Commission and interest representatives occur constantly.
- Interests present the Commission with a mass of written communications in the form of information, briefing, and policy documents.

Naturally, the extent and nature of the communications between interests and the Commission vary considerably according to a number of factors. A small national interest in a specialised area may only require occasional contact at middle-ranking official level with one particular DG. In contrast, an active umbrella group may wish to be permanently plugged into the Commission at many different points. As an indication of how extensive the links can be, some of the access channels available to COPA are worth noting: about every three months the Presidium of COPA meets the Commissioner for Agriculture; the Secretary General of COPA and the Director General of DG Agriculture meet regularly and often speak to each other on the telephone; at all levels the staff of COPA are in almost constant touch with staff in DG Agriculture and, less frequently, are also in close contact with staff in other DGs – notably DG Budget and DG Environment; and COPA is strongly represented, both in its own right and via affiliates, on all the agricultural advisory committees and also on certain other leading advisory committees such as the Standing Committee on Employment and the Harmonisation of Legislation Committee.

The European Parliament

It has been very noticeable, not least in the swelling ranks of lobbyists who attend the Strasbourg plenaries, that as the role and influence of the EP in the EU system has grown it has increasingly attracted the attention of interests. Among the lobbying possibilities available to interests in respect of the EP are the following:

- The EP considers most important legislative proposals and is in a position, especially when the co-decision procedure applies, to exercise considerable influence over the content of legislation (see Chapters 12 and 16). It can thus be very fruitful for interests to lobby MEPs, especially *rapporteurs* and members of committees dealing with relevant legislation. The relative lack of political group discipline in the EP (relative, that is, to the party discipline that applies in the legislatures of most member states) enhances the possibility of individual MEPs being 'persuadable'.
- The power conferred on the EP by the Maastricht Treaty to request the Commission to submit legislative acts created the possibility of interests using MEPs to get legislative initiatives off the ground. This is, however, very difficult to achieve with only a small number of such requests having been made by the EP since the power was granted.
- MEPs and officials engaged in preparing reports for EP committees often approach appropriate interests for their views, or allow themselves to be approached. This can be for a number of reasons but is usually because they wish to make use of the knowledge and expertise of interests and/or because the future progress of reports is likely to be eased if they do not come up against stiff oppositional lobbying from interests.

- Interests have some opportunities for direct contact with EP committees and political groups. Committees, for example, sometimes hold 'hearings' and occasionally travel to member states for the precise purpose of meeting interest representatives, whilst political groups sometimes allow themselves to be addressed when they judge it to be appropriate.
- Attempts can be made to encourage MEPs to draw up own initiative reports. If progress is made the Commission and/or the Council might conceivably be prompted into action of a desired sort.
- Intergroups, which (as was explained in Chapter 12) are loosely organised and voluntary groupings of MEPs with shared concerns about particular issues or areas of activity, are natural targets for interests. For example, interests acting on behalf of disabled people will clearly wish to be in contact with the Handicapped Intergroup, while those acting on behalf of citrus fruit producers will wish to be in touch with, amongst others, the Israel and the Mediterranean Intergroups.
- A general circulation of literature amongst MEPs may have the effect of improving the image of an interest or changing the climate of opinion in the interest's area of concern.
- Attempts can be made to persuade individual MEPs to take matters up with governments and the Commission.

All of these avenues are used by interests, with the bigger and better researched ones – which, for the most part, are business interests – making use of most of them to at least some extent.

* * *

Many possible avenues are thus available to interests to enable them to promote their causes. Which are the most suitable, the most available, and the most effective, naturally varies according to circumstances. For example, a local authority that wishes to attract ERDF funds would be well-advised to establish contact with DG Regional Policy, but it should also court good relations with regional and national civil servants since the ERDF functions on an EU–national–regional partnership basis. In contrast, an environmental group in a country where the government is not noted for its sympathy to green issues might be most effective working as part of a Eurogroup in order to: launch public information and relations campaigns that help persuade the EP to pass a resolution; pressurise the Commission to produce legislative proposals and increase its efforts to ensure that existing legislation is properly implemented; find a route to the Council of Ministers via some of the national affiliates that are leaning on their governments.

Influence

The factors that determine the influence exercised by interests in the EU are similar to those which apply at the national level. The more powerful and more effective interests tend to have at least some of the following characteristics:

Control of key information and expertise

Effective policy-making and implementation requires a knowledge and understanding that often can only be provided to EU authorities by interests. This obviously puts some interests in a potentially advantageous position – as evidenced by the fact that the influence that interests exercise via official forums is often much greater in specialised advisory committees than it is in more general settings such as the EESC or the CoR.

Adequate resources

The better resourced an interest is, the more likely it is to be able to make use of a variety of tactics and devices at a number of different access points. So, with regard to proposed legislation, a well-resourced interest is likely to be in a position to feed its views through to the Commission, the EP, and perhaps the Council from the initiating stage to the taking of the final decision. Similarly, a regional or local authority hoping for EU funds is more likely to be successful if it employs people who know what is available, how to apply, and with whom it is worth having an informal word.

Economic weight

Important economic interests – be they major companies or cross-sectoral representational organisations – usually have to be listened to by EU decision-makers, not least because their cooperation is often necessary in connection with policies designed, for instance, to encourage EU-wide investment, expand employment in less prosperous regions, stimulate cross-border rationalisations, or improve industrial efficiency. Examples of economic weight being an important factor in political influence include: the way in which the chemical industry – via its Eurogroup CEFIC – has managed to persuade the Commission to investigate numerous cases of alleged dumping; the way in which EUROFER (the steel manufacturers' association) has worked closely with the Commission and governments to limit the damage caused to its members by steel rationalisation programmes; and the way in which the pharmaceutical industry – acting through EFPIA – has persuaded the Commission to allow it to regulate itself rather than be regulated.

Political weight

Many interests have political assets that can be used to advantage, usually via governments. For example, a national pressure group that is closely linked to a party in government may be able to get that government to act virtually on its behalf in the Council of Ministers. At a broader level, electoral factors can be important, with ministers in the Council not usually anxious to support anything that might upset key voters, especially if an important national or local election is looming. Farmers' organisations in France, Italy, Germany and elsewhere are the best examples of interests that have benefited from the possession of electoral significance.

Genuine representational claims

National pressure groups and Eurogroups that genuinely represent a sizeable proportion of the interests in a given sector are naturally in a stronger position than those which do not. The representativeness of CEFIC, for example, is one important reason why the chemical industry has been permitted to exercise a certain degree of self-regulation.

Cohesion

Some interests find it difficult to put forward clear and consistent views and are thereby weakened. As was noted earlier, this often applies to Eurogroups, especially umbrella Eurogroups, because of their varied membership and loose confederal structures. Increasing difficulty in maintaining internal coherence and consensus has contributed to a decline in COPA's lobbying influence over the years.

Access to decision-makers

Most of the characteristics just described play some part in determining which interests enjoy good access to decision-makers and which do not. Clearly, those which do have good access – especially if it is at both national and EU levels – are more likely than those which do not to be fully aware of thinking and developments in decision-making circles, and to be able to present their case to those who matter. At the EU level, COPA is, notwithstanding its declining influence, an obvious example of such an 'insider' interest, whilst at the national level COPA affiliates usually also enjoy an advantageous position.

Interests and EU policy processes

There are both positive and negative aspects to the involvement of interests in EU processes. Of the positive aspects, two are especially worth emphasising. First, interest activity broadens the participatory base of the EU and ensures that policy- and decision-making are not completely controlled by politicians and officials. Second, interests can provide EU authorities with information and viewpoints that improve the quality and effectiveness of their policies and decisions. Of the negative aspects, the most important is that some interests are much more powerful and influential than others. This lack of balance raises questions about whether interests unduly, perhaps even undemocratically, tilt EU policy- and decision-making in certain directions – towards, for example, a legislative framework that tends to favour producers more than such 'natural' opponents as consumers and environmentalists.

But irrespective of whether interest activity is judged to be, on the whole, beneficial or not, its importance is clear. Interests are central to many key information flows to and from EU authorities, and they bring considerable influence to bear on policy- and decision-making processes from initiation through to implementation. There are no EU policy sectors where interests of at least some significance are not to be found.

Policies and Policy Processes of the European Union

Part 4 examines what the EU does and how it does it.

Chapter 15 looks at EU policies. The origins, the range, and the context of the policies are all considered. Particular themes of Chapter 15 are the breadth and diversity of EU policy interests, and the less than complete nature of many of the policies.

Chapter 16 focuses on patterns, practices and features of the EU policy-making and decision-making machinery. Having examined the EU institutions and political actors in Part 3, Chapter 16 considers how the various pieces fit together. What sort of policy-making and decision-making system are they part of and have they helped to create? A central concern of Chapter 16 is to emphasise that even the most general statements about how the EU operates normally have to be qualified. For one of the few things that can be said with certainty about EU processes is that they are many, complex and varied. A comprehensive and complete account of how the EU functions therefore requires something that just cannot be attempted here: an analysis of the procedures and practices that apply in every policy area with which the EU is involved.

In Chapter 17 the EU budget is examined. From where does the EU get its money and on what does it spend it? The budgetary decision-making processes, which in important respects are distinctly different from the processes that apply in policy areas, are also examined.

Chapter 18 considers one particular policy area in depth. As such, the chapter offers something of a contrast to the necessarily rather general approach taken in Chapters 15 and 16. Agriculture has been selected for this special examination, not because of any suggestion that it is typical – the variability of EU policy processes precludes any policy area being described as such – but simply because of its significance in the EU context.

The external relations of the EU are increasingly important and these constitute the subject matter of Chapter 19. The examination is undertaken on the basis of the four main component parts of the EU's external policies: trade policy, foreign, security and defence policies, development policy, and the external dimension of internal policies.

Finally, Chapter 20 focuses on one of the most important and certainly one of the most distinctive features of EU processes: the mechanisms and arrangements used by the member states to control their relations with the EU and, insofar as it is possible, to control the EU itself.

Chapter 15

Policies

The Origins of EU Policies

The origins of EU policies lie in a number of places. At a general level, the changed mood in Western Europe played a part in the early post-war years, just as more recently has the spread of the integration process to Central and Eastern Europe. The increasingly interdependent nature of the international system has also been important, resulting in national borders becoming ever more ill-matched with political and economic forces and realities. This interdependence has helped to persuade European states to transfer policy responsibilities to a 'higher' level in an attempt to shape, manage, control, take advantage of, and keep pace with the modern world.

At a more specific level, the treaties are generally seen as key determinants of EU policy. However, their influence is not as great as is commonly supposed. Certainly they are important stimuli to policy development and they also provide the legal base upon which much policy activity occurs. For example, such 'core' EU policies as the Common Commercial Policy (CCP), the Common Agricultural Policy (CAP), and the Competition Policy have their roots – though by no means all their principles – in the EEC (now EC) Treaty. Similarly, EU involvement with coal and steel cannot possibly be fully understood without reference to the Treaty of Paris. But treaty provision for policy development does not guarantee that it will occur. The limited progress made towards the establishment of a Common Transport Policy, despite it being provided for in the EEC/EC Treaty, illustrates this. So too does the non-fulfilment of most of the hopes that were held for Euratom. Another, and crucially important in its implications for the nature of the EU, example of limited development of treaty provisions is the only very partial implementation, until the late 1980s, of Part 3 Title 2 of the EEC Treaty, under which member states were supposed to treat their macroeconomic policies 'as a matter of common concern' and were to coordinate, cooperate and consult with one another on key economic and financial questions. In practice, although there was cooperation and consultation in these areas – carried out mainly under the Ecofin Council of Ministers by committees of very senior national officials – the states did not work or act as closely together as the Treaty envisaged. Furthermore, one of the key steps towards cooperation – the creation in 1979 of the European Monetary System (EMS) which, amongst other things, was designed to fix maximum and minimum rates of exchange for currencies in the system – was created outside the treaty system because of concern in some quarters about the rigidities that a treaty-based approach might entail, and also because not all member states (notably the UK) wished to be full participants. It was only in 1987–8, thirty years after the EEC Treaty was signed, that clear, significant, formal, and Community-based moves towards economic and monetary integration between the member states began to be initiated and implemented.

If treaty provision is no guarantee of policy development, lack of provision is no guarantee of lack of development. Environmental policy illustrates this. Until it was given constitutional status by the Single European Act (SEA), environment was given no specific mention in the treaties. Yet from the early 1970s Community environmental policy programmes were formulated and legislation was approved. Legal authority for this was held to lie in the (almost) catch-all Articles 100 and 235 of the EEC/EC Treaty (Articles 94 and 308 post-Amsterdam). The former allowed the Community to issue directives for the approximation of laws 'as directly affect the establishment or functioning of the common market' and the latter enabled it to take 'appropriate measures' to 'attain, in the course of the operation of the common market, one of the objectives of the Community'. Environmental policy was therefore able to find a treaty base, but only a weak one.

However, even the most liberal readings of Articles 100/94 and 235/308 could not/cannot stretch to some policy areas, but this has not prevented policy development from occurring. Foreign policy cooperation prior to the SEA illustrates this. Aware that there were no treaty provisions for such cooperation, and unenthusiastic about subjecting such a sensitive area to the formalities and restrictions of treaty processes, the EC member states in the early 1970s simply created a new machinery – which they entitled European Political Cooperation (EPC) – alongside, rather than inside, the formal framework of the treaties. EPC was first given legal (but not EEC Treaty) status by the SEA, and this subsequently provided much of the basis for the Common Foreign and Security Policy (CFSP) pillar of the Maastricht Treaty. This 'constitutional evolution' of foreign policy highlights a key feature of the nature of EU policy development: the treaties are facilitators and enablers of policy development, but they are not always the main causes. Indeed, many of the amendments made over the years to the Founding Treaties have taken the form of acknowledging and giving recognition to changes that have been occurring outside their frameworks.

If the treaties thus provide only a partial explanation for policy development, what other factors have been influential? There has been, and still is, an extensive academic debate on this question. Since much of this debate is examined at length in Chapter 21, suffice it here to focus on three factors that have been especially important: the leadership offered by the Commission; the perceptions of the member states of what is desirable; and the individual and collective capacities of the member states to translate their perceptions into practice.

To begin with Commission leadership, it is generally recognised that the Commissions led by Walter Hallstein (1958–66), Roy Jenkins (1977–81), and Jacques Delors (1985–95) were more dynamic and forceful than other Commissions. This is not to suggest that all their ideas and proposals were translated into practice, but it is to say that they were particularly innovative in helping to bring issues onto the policy agenda and in pointing to what could, and perhaps should, be done. The ability of the Commission, in favourable circumstances, to have a real effect on policy development is no more clearly illustrated than in the way the Delors-led Commissions helped to force the pace on such key issues as the Single European Market (SEM) programme, Economic and Monetary Union (EMU), and the social dimension.

Regarding the perceptions of the states – or, to be more precise, of national governments – a fundamental precondition of successful policy development is that the advantages of acting together are judged to outweigh the disadvantages. The advantages are mainly, though not entirely, economic in kind: those that stem from having, in an increasingly interdependent and competitive world, a single and protected market, a common external trading position, and some collective action and some pooling of resources in particular functional and sectoral areas. The principal disadvantage is the loss of national decision-making powers and sovereignty that transfers of power and responsibilities to the EU inevitably entails. Some states are more concerned about this than others, but even the strongest supporters of integration are hesitant about ceding powers that may, at a later stage, result in their national room for manoeuvre being limited in areas that are important to them.

As for the capacity of the states to operationalise their perceptions of what is desirable, there are many problems. At the individual state level, a government may be favourably disposed towards an EU initiative but be inhibited from supporting it in the Council of Ministers because of opposition from a powerful domestic interest or because it could be electorally damaging. Following this through to the EU level, opposition from just one state, whether it is principled or pragmatic, can make policy development difficult to achieve given the practice of the European Council to take its decisions only by unanimity, the continuing treaty requirement of unanimity in the Council of Ministers on several issues, and the preference in the Council for progress through consensus – especially on major issues – even when majority decisions are legally permissible.

The EU's Policy Interests and Responsibilities

The EU's main policy interests and responsibilities can be grouped under five broad headings: establishing the Single European Market, macroeconomic and financial policies, functional policies, sectoral policies, and external policies.

Establishing the Single European Market

The single most important reason why the dynamism and profile of the EC was raised so high in the 1980s was that the Community embarked on a programme to complete the internal market by 1992.

This programme was really a development of the Community's long-established goal of creating a common market. After years in which only modest progress had been made in this direction, a number of factors combined in the 1980s to convince the governments of the member states that a greater thrust was needed: the sluggish economic growth of the second half of the 1970s was continuing; the Community was clearly falling behind its competitors (notably Japan and the United States) in the new technologies; there was an increasing appreciation that the continuation of still essentially fragmented national markets was having a damaging effect on the economic performance of the member states; and the accession of three new countries (Greece in 1981 and Spain and Portugal in 1986) made it clear to all that to continue on the same path and in the same way would mean that the common market would never be properly established.

Against this background, in April 1985 the Commission produced the White Paper *Completing the Internal Market* (European Commission, 1985). The White Paper identified some 300 measures that would have to be taken to enable the internal market to be completed, and suggested that 31 December 1992 should be set as the deadline for the adoption of the measures. The European Council, at its June 1985 Milan meeting, accepted the White Paper, and at its December 1985 Luxembourg meeting agreed that both the internal market objective and the 1992 deadline be included in the Single European Act. Crucially, their inclusion in the SEA

involved additions and amendments to the EEC Treaty. Article 13 of the
SEA, incorporating a new Article 8A of the EEC Treaty, was especially
important:

> The Community shall adopt measures with the aim of progressively
> establishing the internal market over a period expiring on 31 December
> 1992 ... The internal market shall comprise an area without internal
> frontiers in which the free movement of goods, persons, services and
> capital is ensured in accordance with the provisions of this [the EEC]
> Treaty.

The White Paper sought, in essence, to establish the conditions in which
market activities – buying and selling, lending and borrowing, producing
and consuming – could be done as easily on a Community basis as they
could on a national basis. The hope was that by removing the obstacles
and barriers that sectionalised and fragmented the Community market,
efficiency, growth, trade, employment, and prosperity could all be
promoted. In the context of a general deregulatory approach, three sorts
of obstacle and barrier were identified as needing to be removed: physical,
technical, and fiscal.

The Commission was not of course starting from scratch with its
internal market programme. A free and open market had been provided
for in the EEC Treaty and much progress had been made. What the White
Paper was intended to do was to inject a new focus, impetus and
dynamism into a fundamental treaty objective that was proceeding far
too slowly, and in some respects had gone rather off the rails. Much of
what was proposed in the White Paper, therefore, was not new, but had
been around for some time – awaiting decisions by the Council of
Ministers.

The White Paper thus needs to be placed in the context of the
Community's long-standing aim to create a common market – or, as it
has come to be known in recent years, an internal market or a Single
European Market (SEM). That aim was being pursued, but with only
limited success, before the White Paper appeared, and it has been
vigorously pursued since, not only via the implementation of the White
Paper but also via new measures that did not appear in the White Paper.

These new measures have largely been a response to, on the one hand,
an increasing recognition by EU elites and decision-makers of the importance of the SEM project and, on the other hand, an increasingly
expansive view of what the SEM should encompass – either to make the
market function as effectively as possible or to cushion some of the
market's costs.

The SEM rests on four main pillars.

The free movement of goods, persons, services and capital between the member states

Of these four freedoms, the *free movement of goods* was the first to be tackled. It is a freedom that, it might be thought, would be fairly easy to realise: all barriers to trade must be dismantled according to the guiding principles of the TEC, which states that customs duties, quantitative restrictions, and measures having equivalent effect are not permitted. Great steps were quickly made in the 1960s with the first two of these and by 1968 customs duties and quantitative restrictions had been removed. Measures having equivalent effect, however, have been more difficult to deal with and have frequently acted, and been used, as obstacles to trade. Attempts to eliminate such measures have generated a considerable amount of secondary legislation, much activity in the Union's Courts, and constituted a central part of the White Paper programme.

In seeking to establish the conditions for the *free movement of persons*, the Treaty provides for both the employed and the self-employed. The free movement of the former is to be attained by 'the abolition of any discrimination based on nationality between workers of the Member States as regards employment, remuneration and other conditions of work and employment' (Article 39 TEC). The free movement of the latter is concerned principally with rights of establishment, that is with the right of individuals and undertakings to establish businesses in the territory of other member states. As with the free movement of goods, secondary legislation and Court rulings have done much to clarify and extend the free movement of persons. They have done so in two main ways. First, by providing for mutual recognition of many educational, professional, and trade qualifications. Second, by providing key facilitators, notably in the form of the establishment of various legal entitlements, irrespective of nationality and place of domicile, to education and job training, health care, and social welfare payments.

Some of the legislation and Court judgements that have promoted the free movement of persons, and more particularly rights of establishment, have also helped to give some effect to the Treaty declaration that *there should be free movement of services*. Services, which account for approaching 70 per cent of EU GDP are, however, far from having been wholly liberalised, with many barriers preventing firms from providing services in, or establishing themselves in, other member states. As a central plank in its attempt to tackle this problem, in January 2004 the Commission issued a draft services directive aimed at opening up most of the non-financial services market: in total, around 50 per cent of economic activity in the EU would be covered. Up to the time of writing (January 2006 – two years after the draft was issued), however, the directive has not been enacted, is steeped in political controversy, and is gradually being diluted.

Differences between and within EU institutions have turned on two points in particular. First, the Commission's proposal that the directive be based on the country of origin principle, which means that the provider is subject only to the law of the country in which the business is established. For many, this is too liberal and risks standards and levels of social and consumer protection being 'driven to the bottom'. Second, which sectors and industries, if any, should be excluded from the directive, and on what grounds? Are, for example, health, educational and cultural criteria grounds for exclusion, and in what circumstances? Running through both of these areas of disagreement are a mosaic of factors influencing political actors, not least calculations about how national providers are likely to fare in a more open market and ideological preferences concerning regulatory levels in the market.

As for financial services (banking, insurance, securities, asset management), considerable progress in opening up and strengthening markets was made under the 1999–2005 Financial Services Action Plan (FSAP). In December 2005 the Commission issued a White Paper, *Financial Services Policy 2005–2010* (European Commission, 2005f) identifying objectives and proposed actions over the next five years. The focus is mainly on consolidation between service providers, and improving supervisory cooperation and convergence.

Until the late 1980s only limited progress was made in establishing *the free movement of capital*. Treaty provisions partly explain this, since the elimination of restrictions on the movement of capital under Article 67 EEC Treaty (now abolished) was required only 'to the extent necessary to ensure the proper functioning of the common market'. More importantly, however, and notwithstanding the creation of the EMS in the late 1970s, the necessary political will did not exist in the first three decades of the Community's life. For many states, control of capital movements was an important economic and monetary instrument and they preferred it to remain largely in their own hands. However, as part of the SEM programme, much of this former resistance was withdrawn or overcome, and all the major capital markets have – subject to a few derogations and some national protective measures – been more or less open since 1990. (This does not, however, mean that in practice there is complete free movement of capital, since taxation rates have not been made common and banking rules have not yet all been standardised.)

The approximation of such laws, regulations or administrative provisions of the Member States as directly affect the establishment or functioning of the common market

This pillar of the SEM rests on Article 94 TEC, which used to be Article 100. Prior to the Maastricht Treaty, Article 100 referred to 'the approximation, *or harmonisation* of such legal provisions in the Member States' (emphasis added), but the word harmonisation was dropped from the amended EC Treaty to reflect the more flexible and less rigid approach that had developed towards differences in national standards and requirements. This development followed upon the 'breakthrough' *Cassis de Dijon* case in 1979, when the ECJ ruled that products that conform with the standards of one member state cannot be excluded from the markets of other member states unless they can be shown to be damaging to health, safety, the environment, or other aspects of the public interest. The ruling allowed the Community to be less concerned with the harmonisation of technical details and to adopt a 'new approach' under which a simpler and speedier process would apply. There are three main aspects to this process: (1) whenever possible, legislation does not seek to harmonise but rather to approximate in that it is restricted to laying down the essential requirements that national standards and specifications must meet – on health and safety requirements for example; (2) as long as the essential conditions are met, member states must mutually recognise each other's specifications and standards; and (3) national specifications and standards are gradually being replaced by European specifications and standards drawn up by European standards organisations.

The need for approximation arises because, as noted above, the dismantling of barriers is not in itself sufficient to guarantee free movement. This is most clearly seen with regard to the movement of goods, where prior to the 1992 programme many non-tariff and non-quantitative barriers existed that inhibited, even prevented, free movement across the Community's internal borders. These barriers had, in the words of the Treaty, the 'equivalent effect' of tariffs and quantitative restrictions, and as such were obstacles to the creation of a market based on free and open competition. Moreover, they tended to be barriers of a kind that could not be removed simply by issuing general prohibitions. Many took the form of different national standards, national requirements, and national provisions and practices that had been adopted over the years. Sometimes they had been adopted for perfectly good reasons, but sometimes they had been adopted as a deliberate attempt to protect a domestic market from unwanted competition without actually infringing Community law. Whatever the intent, the effect was often the same: because of the need to adapt products to meet the different national standards of different states, and because of the need for products to be subject to re-testing and re-certification procedures, efficiency was not maximised and producers in one member state often could not compete on an equal basis with producers in another. Examples of non-tariff barriers (NTBs) included different national technical specifications for products, different health and safety standards, charges for the inspection of certain categories of imported goods, and taxes that, though nominally general in their scope, were discriminatory against imported goods in their effect.

Approximation, and before it harmonisation, is thus concerned with the removal of NTBs and is vital if free movement across national boundaries is to be achieved. EU directives are the main instruments for achieving approximation, although many Court rulings have also been supportive and helpful. Most approximation law is to be found in relation to the free movement of goods, and consists largely of matters such as the setting of common standards on technical requirements, design specifications, product content, and necessary documentation. Critics of the EU often present such measures as seeking unwanted and unnecessary conformity, and sometimes proposals do indeed appear to smack of insensitivity to national customs and preferences. Sight should not be lost, however, of what approximation is all about: creating conditions that allow, encourage and increase the uniform treatment of persons, goods, services and capital throughout the EU.

Competition policy

The basic rules on competition are outlined in Articles 81–9 TEC. They have three principal aspects to them. First, under Article 81 there is a prohibition on 'all agreements between undertakings, decisions by associations of undertakings and concerted practices which may affect trade between Member States and which have as their object or effect the prevention, restriction or distortion of competition within the common market'. Second, under Article 82, 'Any abuse by one or more undertakings of a dominant position within the common market or in a substantial part of it shall be prohibited or incompatible with the common market insofar as it may affect trade between Member States'. Third, under Article 87, state aid 'which distorts or threatens to distort competition by favouring certain undertakings or the production of certain goods shall, insofar as it affects trade between Member States, be incompatible with the common market'.

All of these Treaty prohibitions – on restrictive practices, dominant trading positions, and state aid – have been clarified by subsequent EC/EU law, both in the form of legislation and Court judgements. It has been established, for example, that a 'dominant position' cannot be held to apply on the basis of an overall percentage market share, but only in relation to factors such as the particular product, the structure of its market, and substitutability. Similarly, exemptions to state aid prohibitions, which are only generally referred to in the Treaty, have been confirmed as being legally permissible if they are for purposes such as regional development, retraining, and job creation in potential growth industries.

Much of the work and time of the Commission's Competition DG is taken up examining allegations of breaches in competition law and considering applications for exemptions (see Chapter 9). Under the SEM momentum it has been much more vigorous than it used to be and has, for example, as Peterson and Bomberg (1999) note, boldly wielded competition powers in relation to 'revenue-producing monopolies' to open up hitherto protected telecommunications markets. Political resistance has, however, resulted in less success in liberalising certain other markets with, for example, France being prominent in resisting liberalisation of energy markets.

An effective competition policy is of course necessary for an open and integrated market. To try to improve the policy and ensure that it is sufficiently effective the EU has adopted a twin-track approach in recent years. First, the Commission has become much more active in examining cases of apparent malpractice. For example, using its powers as investigator, prosecutor, judge and jury (though with its decisions subject to appeal to the ECJ) it has been more willing to take action against member states in connection with state aid. Second, legislation designed to broaden the competition policy base has been approved. An important instance of such legislation is the 1989 Company Merger Regulation, which gives considerable powers to the Commission to disallow or set conditions on mergers that it judges will have an adverse effect on competition. Other examples of legislation, in a very different area of competition policy, are the directives that are designed to open up public procurement – an area of activity that accounts for around 15 per cent of EU GDP.

The Common External Tariff

The purpose of the Common External Tariff (CET) or Common Customs Tariff (CCT) as it is also known, is to further the course of fair and equal trading by surrounding all the member states with common trade barriers so that goods entering the EU via, say, the ports of Liverpool or Rotterdam do so on exactly the same terms as they do via airports at Athens or Prague. No member state can therefore gain a competitive advantage by having access to cheaper raw materials and none can make a profit from exporting imported goods to an EU partner. The CET takes the EU beyond being just a free trade area – where, at best, external tariffs are only approximated – and makes it a customs union.

The external tariffs were in place by 1968, to coincide with the removal of the internal tariffs, and since then governments have had no independent legal authority over the tariff rate on goods entering their country. The terms of trade of the member states are established and negotiated on a EU-wide basis via the Common Commercial Policy (CCP) (see Chapter 19). If a member state wishes to seek exemptions from, or changes to, these terms of trade it must go through the appropriate EU decision-making processes. Naturally there have been frequent disagreements between the states over different aspects of external trade and the CCP – with tariff rates, trade protection measures, and alleged dumping amongst the issues that have created difficulties – but the existence of a clear and binding legal framework has ensured that, for the most part, the common external front – protection system it might be called – has worked.

✵ ✵ ✵

Clearly much has been and still is being achieved in the move towards a single market. Some of the most intractable problems – such as the removal of internal border controls and setting limitations on the rates of indirect taxation – have witnessed progress. However, there is no foreseeable prospect of the SEM being as open or as integrated as national markets. This is because not all of the barriers to free movement will be removed, and not all of the national policies that serve to fragment the market will be made common. The obstacles to a completely open and integrated market are of three main types.

First, there are the somewhat intangible, but nonetheless very important, obstacles arising from different historical experiences, cultures, traditions and languages. These obstacles are unquestionably being broken down, but only slowly. EU laws may, for example, oblige public authorities to receive tenders for contracts from throughout the EU, but laws cannot control the many informal processes that often incline decision-makers to award contracts whenever possible to fellow national, or even locally-based, companies.

Second, there is still some member state resistance – almost invariably based on reasons of national interest – to fully developing and applying specific aspects of the SEM project. Whilst virtually all of the original legislative programme has now been processed, some of the legislation is rather loose (because this was seen as necessary to overcome opposition in the Council) whilst some of it is only being weakly applied. Spheres of market activity so affected include aspects of financial services, veterinary and phytosanitary controls, and the recognition of some diplomas and professional qualifications.

Third, there are economic factors that were not included in the 1985 White Paper and which have never formally become part of the SEM project that act as obstacles to complete market integration. Economists and politicians dispute exactly what economic factors do constitute such obstacles, and what their relative importance is, but prominent amongst the factors that are generally recognised are the following: the non-participation of some member states in the single currency system and hence also their non-involvement in the single monetary and exchange rate policies of 'Euroland'; the only partial development of common regional, social, environmental, transport, and consumer protection policies; and the diversity of corporate direct taxation systems.

Macroeconomic policies

The background to and creation of Economic and Monetary Union

Notwithstanding certain EEC Treaty provisions, and despite declarations by the Heads of Government in 1969 and 1972 that their intention was to establish an economic and monetary union by 1980, only limited practical progress was made until the late 1980s in moving towards Economic and Monetary Union (EMU).

Ministers and senior national officials did regularly convene to consult and to exchange ideas on macroeconomic policy, and at their meetings they periodically considered Commission submissions for the adoption of common guidelines and for short-term and medium-term strategies. But ultimately it was up to the states themselves as to what they did. For example, when the Commission in its quarterly economic report published in February 1987 stated that Germany had the greatest margin for manoeuvre to stimulate domestic demand, and France and the UK could do more to boost their productive capacity, there was no guarantee that national policies would thereby be adjusted. A state may have been unwise to fall too much out of step with its partners – as the French government was in 1981–2 when it attempted to stimulate its economy against the general trend – but it was perfectly entitled and able to embark on such a course of action.

Monetary policy was the subject of particularly frequent contacts between the states – at ministerial, official and central bank levels – but, as with other branches of macroeconomic policy, most of what came out of such exchanges was of an exhortive rather than a directionist nature. That said, however, the creation in 1979 of the European Monetary System (EMS) did provide Community monetary policy with some central structure and some powers, since amongst its features were: a common reserve fund to provide for market intervention; the European Currency Unit (ecu) to act as a reserve asset and a means of settlement; and, in the Exchange Rate Mechanism (ERM) of the EMS, fixed – though adjustable when necessary – bands of exchange for participating currencies.

Until the late 1980s the Community's macroeconomic policies thus had only relatively weak policy instruments attached to them. Attempts to strengthen these instruments, in order to build up a more effective policy framework, traditionally met with at least four obstacles. First, there were differences over which – the economic or the monetary – naturally came first and should be accorded priority. Second, the Community's rather sectionalised policy-making mechanisms inhibited an overall and coordinated approach. Third, different aspects of economic and monetary integration had different implications for the states, which resulted in them being viewed with different degrees of enthusiasm. Fourth, for some states the possibility of ceding key macroeconomic powers to the Community raised fundamental sovereignty questions.

But notwithstanding the many obstacles in the way of policy development, real progress towards EMU began to be made in the late 1980s. It was, and still is, driven by two rationales:

- *A political rationale.* For those who wish to see a more integrated Europe, perhaps a fully federal Europe, EMU is an important building block. As with the coal and steel community, the customs union, and the SEM, EMU helps to create political integration by economic means.
- *An economic rationale.* There are several economic advantages of EMU, including greater price transparency and elimination of currency exchange costs, but the main economic benefit has been seen by most practitioners and observers to be the removal of exchange rate volatility between member states. This makes for much greater market stability and in so doing is believed to promote investment and growth.

With the potential advantages of EMU increasingly being appreciated by national leaders and with the EEC Treaty having been amended by the SEA to include a new chapter on 'Co-operation in Economic and Monetary Policy', the Community formally embarked on the road to EMU at much the same time as the SEM programme was beginning to be applied. Differences remained between the states over what precisely EMU should consist of and what should be the timetable for its full implementation, but all (apart from the UK) subscribed to the broad outlines of the scheme that was put forward in April 1989 by the Delors Committee in its *Report on Economic and Monetary Union* which laid foundations for EMU. The Committee proved to be the forerunner of the 1990–1 IGC on EMU, in that not only did it clear much of the ground for the establishment of the IGC, but many of its proposals – including the principle of a three-stage transition to EMU – were accepted by the IGC and incorporated in the Maastricht Treaty.

The Maastricht provisions on EMU and their subsequent application were described in Chapters 3 and 5, so will not be repeated here. Suffice it to say that the Treaty established a scheme and a timetable for progression to EMU. The main feature of the scheme was increasing coordination and convergence of the economic and monetary policies of all member states, leading to a single currency in which monetary policy would be made within the framework of a European System of Central Banks (ESCB). The main feature of the timetable was a three-stage transitional process leading to the adoption of a single currency by January 1999 at the latest.

The single currency duly came into operation in January 1999, with eleven of the EU's fifteen member states as members – Denmark, Sweden and the UK chose not to participate, and Greece did not meet the qualifying convergence criteria. The eleven became twelve in January 2001 when Greece, having then been deemed to meet the criteria, joined the single currency system.

Under the terms of their accession treaties, the states that joined the EU in 2004 would not be eligible for eurozone membership until they had completed at least two full years of EU membership. During this period they would be required to pursue macroeconomic policies that would enable them to meet the terms of the Maastricht convergence criteria. Since they became EU members, all of the new states have signalled their continued desire and willingness to join the eurozone, though variable economic performances mean that it is extremely likely they will become euro members on a staggered basis rather than in one 'big bang'.

The nature of Economic and Monetary Union

There are three principal features of EMU.

First, eurozone members no longer have national currencies. (From January 1999 the exchange rates between single currency members were irrevocably fixed. In January and February 2002 the national banknotes and coinage of members were replaced by euro banknotes and coins.)

Second, eurozone countries can no longer take individual decisions on what monetary policies – including interest rate policies – they should pursue. The eurozone has common monetary policies, which are determined through the zone's own institutional structures. At the heart of these monetary policies is a strong anti-inflationary ethos. (See the section on the ESCB in Chapter 14 for an account of the nature of the eurozone's institutional structure and the policy remit within which it must act.) The macroeconomic policies of eurozone countries must be closely aligned, though they are not common as are monetary policies. The framework for this alignment is known as the Stability and Growth Pact (SGP), which is based on the budget and public debt elements of the Maastricht convergence criteria and which obliges members to practise prudent fiscal policies and, more particularly, to maintain broadly balanced national budgets over the economic cycle. The key SGP rule is that the annual budgetary deficits of eurozone states may not exceed 3 per cent of national GDP. Non-compliance with the terms of the SGP can lead to financial sanctions being imposed on offenders: initially in the form of the lodging of a non-interest bearing deposit, and if excessive deficits continue in the form of a fine.

No financial penalties have been applied up to the time of writing, even though several of the eurozone states have breached SGP rules. These breaches have resulted in sharp differences between the Commission and the ECB on the one hand and some eurozone member states on the other. So, in February 2002 the Commission wanted to issue an early warning to Germany that its budgetary deficit was becoming unsustainable – though there was no breach of the Pact's ceiling of 3 per cent of GDP, the budget was forecast to rise during the year to 2.7 per cent. However, the German Finance Minister succeeded in persuading his British, French, Italian and Portuguese colleagues in the Ecofin Council that the Commission was being too rigid and was not allowing sufficiently for fluctuations in the economic cycle. In a compromise under which Germany undertook to eliminate its budget deficit by 2004, no rebuke was issued and no formal vote was taken by the ministers. Clearly politics had prevailed over tight management of the Pact, with the original main proponent of the Pact able to use its size and power to avoid a political embarrassment.

In 2003, tensions became even sharper, when the Commission proposed taking formal action against both France and Germany for repeatedly breaching the 3 per cent ceiling. At an acrimonious Ecofin meeting in November, France and Germany managed to persuade Finance Ministers to lift the threat of disciplinary action being taken against them, which resulted in the Commission initiating a case against the Council in the ECJ. In July 2004 the Court ruled largely in favour of the Commission (Case C-27/04). However, political realities then led not to the disciplinary action being imposed but to the terms of the Pact being changed by Ecofin in March 2005. The key change was a recognition that there were exceptional and temporary circumstances in which the 3 per cent limit could be breached without risk of financial penalty. The circumstances were not listed, as some member states wanted, but rather were left to the discretion of the Commission to judge. The most likely circumstance was generally recognised as being when a national economy is experiencing temporary difficulties, with low growth and high unemployment, but the underlying structure is sound.

Third, whilst non-euro member countries are not tied to the terms of eurozone monetary and fiscal policy, they are expected to coordinate their economic policies with the others. They cannot be subject to financial penalties for breaching SGP rules, but they are obliged to comply with the 'multilateral surveillance' system of national economies that was established as part of the preparation for the single currency and are obliged to endeavour to avoid excessive budgetary deficits. For EU-10 states this obligation is, of course, part of the preparations they are expected to make for eventual eurozone membership. For the three states that have chosen not to be eurozone members – Denmark, Sweden and the UK – it is an obligation of EU membership: they are subject to the EU's excessive deficit procedure, which means that if they exceed, or seem likely to exceed, the 3 per cent budgetary deficit limit, the Commission can recommend to the Eurofin Council that the state in question be required to adopt appropriate rectifying measures (though neither the Commission nor Ecofin can state what these measures should be). Such a reprimand – for that is essentially what it is – was given to the UK in January 2006.

The significance of Economic and Monetary Union

Clearly the establishment of the single currency marks a major step forward in the European integration process. On the one hand, it has considerable symbolic significance, with the replacement of the French franc, the German deutschemark, the Italian lira, the Spanish peseta and so on with the euro. It may well be that this will provide much impetus to the development of a common European identity. On the other hand, single currency states have transferred to Euro-level bodies responsibility for two key policy instruments – exchange rate and interest rate levels – and have accepted stiff limitations on what they can do in respect of budgetary and fiscal policy.

But though the single currency system advances European integration, it remains to be seen whether it will be judged a success. The rationale is that by creating a more stable European economic and monetary environment and thus providing greater predictability for investments and markets, the single currency will promote growth and prosperity. But to date growth rates have been disappointing, unemployment rates in several eurozone countries have been high, and pre-existing and significant variations in measures of competitiveness between member states have persisted. In consequence, problems have already arisen from the 'one size for all' nature of EMU, and that is before the system has had to cope with a major economic downturn and/or with asymmetric shocks. The fact is that the eurozone system does not contain the two main instruments that single currency systems arguably need to deal with problems of internal variations in economic performance, namely mobility of labour and the ability of the centre to effect significant fiscal transfers. As has been shown, both here and in Chapter 14, there have already been open differences over the contents of policies between 'expansionist' politicians on the one hand and 'cautious' bankers and Commission SGP 'guardians' on the other. There have been differences too between national governments over policies, with the governments of countries with high levels of unemployment showing some reluctance to accept – given that they no longer have interest rate or exchange rate adjustments available to them – tight fiscal policies that are judged to be in the general interest of euroland. There have also been differences arising from the desire of some governments to promise tax cuts during election campaigns. Such differences, and the tensions associated with them, show no sign of settling down and could become even sharper if any member states are seen to be seriously endangering the euro system.

As to whether the euro can match the dollar as an international currency, there is a long way to go. There is certainly considerable potential with, for example, a GDP that is comparable in size, a population that is much larger, and an economy that is more reliant on international trade. In important respects, however, the foundations of the euro are not so solid and its future is less certain than that of the dollar. For example, the US has a much more developed financial system than the eurozone. The eurozone is sometimes seen to be divided – with differences, for instance, between the Commission, the ECB, the Ecofin Council, and the member states. And in the coming years the eurozone is likely to be enlarged to include many new member states, most of which are small and have faster growing economies than existing member states.

Functional policies

The EU has interests and responsibilities in many functional policies: that is, policies with a clear functional purpose and a more specific nature than the policies considered under the previous heading.

Probably the best known of the EU functional policies are the justice and home affairs, cohesion, and research and technological development policies. Less prominent functional policies include education policy, cultural policy, and consumer protection policy. Since it is not possible to examine all of the EU's functional policies here, attention will be directed to six of the more important ones. The examinations that follow will, in addition to explaining the features of the six policy spheres in question, also illustrate the range and varying depth of EU involvement in different functional areas.

Justice and home affairs policies

In the mid-1970s the EC member states began to exchange information and cooperate with one another on matters relating to the monitoring and control of terrorism, drugs, and organised crime. A series of mechanisms, which were quite outside the framework of the Community Treaties and which came to be known as the Trevi process, were developed and brought together, often on a semi-secret basis, officials from Interior and Justice ministries, senior police and intelligence officers, and ministers. Over the years the issues covered by Trevi developed – due in no small part to the need to dismantle internal border controls as part of the SEM programme – and by the late 1980s the original 'threats' of terrorism, drugs and organised crime had been joined by a variety of matters relating to immigration, visas, public order, and customs controls.

This array of policy interests, and the plethora of *ad hoc* arrangements developed to deal with them, were brought together and strengthened by the Maastricht Treaty. They were so mainly under the third pillar of the Treaty – dealing with Provisions on Cooperation in the Fields of Justice and Home Affairs (JHA). The contents of the Maastricht third pillar were set out in Chapter 5, so they will be only summarised here. First, the member states were to regard nine policy areas – including asylum policy, immigration policy, and the combating of drug addiction – as 'matters of common interest'. Visa policy was incorporated into the TEC, with the requirement that a common visa policy should be adopted, by qualified majority voting rules in the Council, by 1 January 1996. Second, the Council was empowered to adopt joint positions and joint actions (through, for example, the issuing of resolutions and recommendations), and to draw up conventions. Third, new institutional arrangements to promote cooperation and coordination, and to enable the EU to fulfil its obligations under the Treaty, were to be established.

The Maastricht-created third pillar led to much activity in the JHA field with, for example, the adoption of numerous declarations and conventions and the establishment of a European Police Office: Europol. But progress was only modest in respect of governments becoming committed to adopting tough collective responses to the JHA problems facing them. A major reason for this was that many JHA policies are of a highly sensitive kind, raising deep cultural issues – on, for example, the exchange of sensitive information and individual rights – and touching directly on national sovereignty concerns. Because of this sensitivity, the third pillar was established on an intergovernmental basis, making Council decision-making very difficult. Another problem with JHA is that much of it is intrinsically complex in nature with, for example, numerous – often non-congruent – national agencies involved and very different national civil laws applying.

Dissatisfaction with the operation of the third pillar resulted in it being much discussed in the 1996–7 IGC and in it being the policy area most strengthened by the Amsterdam Treaty. The ways in which this strengthening was undertaken were set out in some detail in Chapter 5 so, as with the contents of the JHA elements of the Maastricht Treaty, only the major points of the Amsterdam Treaty will be summarised here. First, several JHA policy areas – including immigration, asylum, and refugees and displaced persons – were 'communitarised' by being transferred from the intergovernmental pillar three to the much more supranational pillar one. Within the EC pillar, most decisions were to be taken by unanimous vote in the Council (apart from visa policy), but provision was made for the possible introduction of QMV after five years. Second, policy objectives were clarified. Third, the Schengen Agreement – of which most member states were signatories and which had been used, on an extra-treaty basis, to remove most internal border controls – was incorporated into the EU framework, though with Ireland and the UK not participating. Fourth, pillar three, which was to continue to be intergovernmental in character, was refocused and retitled 'Provisions on Police and Judicial Cooperation in Criminal Matters'.

As part of the Amsterdam changes, explicit provision was made for the aim of JHA and JHA-related policies to be the creation of 'an area of freedom, security and justice' in which there is free movement of persons behind common external borders. To help give effect to this aim, Amsterdam was followed up by a special European Council meeting on JHA matters at Tampere in 1999. At Tampere the national leaders gave further impetus to the policy area by establishing goals for the 1999–2004 period. Amongst the goals were: reaching agreement on the introduction of a common asylum system; the adoption of measures to improve progress in access to justice and in the mutual recognition of judicial decisions; and the creation of two new agencies – a prosecution agency, Eurojust, and a European Police College (European Council, 1999c).

After Maastricht, and more especially after Amsterdam, the JHA policy area advanced rapidly. The pace has been quickened even further in the 2000s, largely in response to two developments. The first development has been growing concerns about the porousness of the EU's borders. Common, and tighter, policies on immigration, asylum, and visa controls have increasingly been seen as being necessary – all the more so with the already vulnerable southern borders being joined by vulnerable eastern borders with the 2004 EU enlargement. Particular attention was given to these matters at the June 2002 Seville summit when political agreement was reached on a package of measures including: closer cooperation between the member states on border controls, including the creation of a network of immigration control officers; closer cooperation with third countries on illegal immigration, with the EU prepared to offer financial and technical assistance where appropriate and prepared also to make it clear that inadequate cooperation could hamper the forging of closer ties;

and, so as to make 'asylum shopping' more difficult, the issuing of an instruction to JHA ministers to adopt proposals to make the Dublin Convention – which states that the EU country where asylum seekers first enter the EU is responsible for processing any asylum application – legally binding (European Council, 2002a). The second development has been the revealing, initially through the September 11 2001 terrorist attacks in the USA and subsequently through attacks in Europe – of the extent of the threat posed to the West by international terrorism. The terrorist threat has resulted in the adoption of a number of anti-terrorist measures, including an EU-wide arrest warrant to replace former lengthy extradition procedures.

In November 2004 the European Council approved what is known as the Hague programme to succeed the Tampere programme. Covering the years 2005–09, the Hague programme is inevitably less innovatory than its predecessor. Most of it is concerned with either completing or extending existing policy developments. Amongst specified policy aims of the programme are: the creation of a comprehensive European asylum policy by 2010; the provision by 2006 of crime 'threat assessments' by Europol; and the strengthening of the Schengen information system by 2007.

On the institutional front, the Hague programme reiterated earlier commitments that in practice had not been acted upon to change communautarised JHA law-making from the consultation procedure with unanimity in the Council to the co-decision procedure with QMV in the Council. In December 2004 the member states eventually made these changes. In consequence, since January 2005, decisions on asylum, illegal immigration, external border controls, and certain civil law cooperation issues are all subject to co-decision and Council qualified majority voting (Monar, 2005: 145). Intergovernmentalism does, of course, continue to be the decision-making method in JHA policy areas that are still located in pillar three, but the December 2004 decision does unquestionably constitute a very significant extension of the 'Community method' in the JHA policy sphere.

*   *   *

In response, therefore, to a number of factors, numerous policies and legislative acts in the JHA policy area have been put in place in recent years and new institutions and agencies have been established. As Jörg Monar, a long-time JHA expert has observed, 'There is no other example ... of an area of loose intergovernmental cooperation having made its way so quickly to the top of the Union's political and legislative agenda' (Monar, 2002: 189).

Cohesion policy

There are a number of policies, grouped under the general name of cohesion policy, that are designed to provide a partial counterbalance to the 'natural' effects of the internal market by promoting a more balanced distribution of resources and economic development across the EU.

Increased importance has been attached to cohesion policy since the mid-1980s. This partly reflects feelings that a vigorous cohesion policy is necessary for reasons of social justice; it partly reflects beliefs that weaker parts of the EU economy can become stronger if they are given focused and directed assistance; and it partly reflects hard political bargaining by the governments of those member states that are the main beneficiaries of cohesion policy – Spain, in particular, has threatened on more than one occasion to cause problems in other policy areas if cohesion policy is not prioritised/protected/structured in a manner that is to Spain's advantage.

The main policy instruments of cohesion policy are the supporting financial instruments. These are second only to the CAP in the allocation of EU budgetary resources, accounting for over 35 per cent of total budgetary expenditure for the 2000–06 financial period and assigned over 40 per cent for the 2007–13 period (see Chapter 17 for details). Key principles on which the financial instruments are based include additionality, which means EU resources should add to rather than replace national resources, and co-financing, by which programmes and projects are co-financed by the EU and member states.

Under the 2000–06 financial perspective there were two main financial instruments, or funds, concerned with cohesion policy: the European Regional Development Fund (ERDF), which accounted for 49 per cent of funding and the European Social Fund (ESF) which accounted for 30 per cent. Additional funding was available from four other sources: the European Agricultural Guidance and Guarantee Fund (EAGGF) (mainly from the Guidance Section), the Financial Instrument for Fisheries Guidance (FIFG), the Cohesion Fund, and a number of Community Initiatives managed directly by the Commission. Under the 2007–13 financial perspective, support for agriculture and fisheries is transferred to separate financial instruments and the number of cohesion financial instruments is reduced to three: the ERDF, the ESF, and the Cohesion Fund.

The reduction in the number of financial instruments is part of an attempt to make cohesion policy simpler, more transparent and, above all, more focused. The re-focusing involves the orientation of cohesion policy around three priority themes: innovation and the knowledge economy; accessibility and services of general economic interest; and environment and risk prevention. These priority themes, which are designed to complement major EU policy initiatives such as the European Employment

Strategy and the Lisbon Process, are given practical effect under three operational headings:

- *Convergence*: supporting growth and job creation in the least developed member states and regions. This is the main priority of the cohesion policy, accounting for nearly 82 per cent of total cohesion funding. It is directed at regions whose per capita GDP is less than 75 per cent of the EU average.
- *Regional competitiveness and employment*: anticipating and promoting change. Designed to fund activities outside the least developed member states and regions, this objective aims, through regional and national programmes, to promote competitiveness, full employment, and social inclusion. It accounts for nearly 16 per cent of cohesion funding.
- *European territorial cooperation*: promoting the harmonious and balanced development of the Union territory. Accounting for around 2.5 per cent of cohesion funding, this objective involves supporting joint and integrated approaches to problems being tackled by member states at cross-border, transnational and inter-regional levels. Examples of activities that qualify for funding include joint urban, rural and coastal development schemes, networked and partnership research and development, and integrated water development.

Social, employment, and economic growth policies

The EEC Treaty provided for the development of a Community social policy. It did so in two ways: Articles 117–22 stated that there should be closer cooperation between the member states in the social field, and particularly specified (in Article 119) that member states should apply the principle that men and women should receive equal pay for equal work; Articles 123–8 laid the foundation for the ESF.

Although the ESF was quickly established, little was done for many years to give effect to Articles 117–22, apart from some developments – via legislation and ECJ judgements – in areas linked to employment matters such as working conditions, entitlement to benefits, and equal opportunities. However, in 1989 a major boost was given to Community social policy when the Commission – believing that the SEM programme should have a 'social dimension' – produced *The Community Charter of Fundamental Social Rights for Workers*. The Charter was inevitably somewhat general in character and terminology, but it contained the fundamental principles that should apply to twelve main themes. Amongst these themes were: free movement of workers on the basis of equal treatment in access to employment and social protection; employment on the basis of fair remuneration; improvement of living and working conditions; freedom of association and collective bargaining; and protection of children and adolescents. The Charter was adopted by all the member states except the UK at the 1989 Strasbourg summit and formed the basis for the subsequent Social Chapter that the same eleven states had attached to the Maastricht Treaty in the form of a Protocol and Agreement on Social Policy (see Chapter 5).

The Amsterdam Treaty strengthened the treaty base of social policy in two significant ways. First, the UK, now with a Labour government, removed its objections to the Maastricht Agreement on Social Policy, with the consequence that the Agreement was incorporated into the TEC. Second, a new Employment Title was created in the TEC, with a focus on encouraging and exhorting member states to regard the promotion of employment as a matter of high priority and common concern.

To determine how to give effect to the new TEC Employment Title, a special 'jobs summit' was held in Luxembourg in November 1997. At the summit, a procedure for giving employment promotion a higher priority and more focused approach was agreed. The main stages of the procedure are: employment guidelines, which are subject to annual review, are adopted by the Council on the basis of a proposal from the Commission; the guidelines are incorporated into national employment action plans, which are analysed by the Commission; and the Commission draws up an annual employment report for Council approval which, amongst other things, reviews progress, makes suggestions for modifications of the guidelines, and issues country-specific recommendations to the member states. A central theme of the guidelines and of the Commission's reports has been the need to reform labour markets by, for example, the need for active policies to combat youth and long-term unemployment, to increase labour supply and participation, and to have in place a comprehensive lifelong learning strategy.

Employment was also at the heart of a special European Council meeting held in Lisbon in March 2000. At this summit a ten-year strategic goal was set for the Union 'to become the most competitive and dynamic knowledge-based economy in the world, capable of sustaining economic growth with more and better jobs and greater social cohesion' (European Council, 2000a: 2). Amongst specific goals set at Lisbon were raising the employment rate from an average of 61 per cent in 2000 to as close as possible to 70 per cent by 2010 and increasing the number of women in employment from an average of 51 per cent to 60 per cent by the same year. Various mechanisms were identified to enable the summit's goals to be achieved, many of which focused around 'innovation', 'entrepreneurship' and 'the information society'. Progress in achieving the Lisbon strategic goal is reviewed and, where appropriate, updated and extended each spring at 'Lisbon Process'/'Lisbon Strategy' summits.

As the scheduled mid-term review of the Lisbon Strategy approached, it was becoming clear that progress towards achieving the Strategy's aims was disappointing and that the core goals would not be met. Responding to this, the March 2004 European Council meeting established a high-level group of experts under the chairmanship of the former Dutch Minister, Wim Kok, to investigate ways in which the Strategy could be re-vamped. The group presented its report – *Facing the Challenge: The Lisbon Strategy for Growth and Employment* (Kok, 2004) – in November 2004. The central message of the report was that member governments lacked 'the engagement and political determination' to adopt and implement the structural measures that were necessary to enable the Lisbon goals to be met. They further needed to narrow the number of goals and make them more specific and achievable. Difficult matters that needed to be grasped including cutting taxes, liberalising services, and re-structuring social protection schemes, pensions, and labour markets.

Although not all of its recommendations were accepted, the Kok report subsequently provided much of the basis of a Commission communication to the spring 2005 European Council. In its communication, which was entitled *Working Together For Growth and Jobs – A New Start for the Lisbon Strategy* (European Commission, 2005e), the Commission agreed with Kok that the Strategy needed to be given a sharper focus and be made more deliverable. A range of specific measures and actions were identified including further reforms to complete the SEM, more public and private sector spending on research and development, competition rules to be applied more proactively, and more active employment policies to help people into work and to provide incentives for them to stay there.

The March 2005 European Council meeting welcomed the Commission's communication and agreed to a re-launching of the Lisbon Strategy. As part of the re-launching, the headline goal of making the EU 'the most competitive and dynamic knowledge-based economy in the world' was dropped. Reflecting criticisms from leftist and trade union quarters, the European Council in its Conclusions gave a higher priority to social market aspects of the Strategy than the Commission had done in its communication (European Council, 2005a).

Three aspects of these recent developments in the EU's social, employment, and economic growth policies are particularly significant and merit highlighting. First, although the policies are in important respects separate, they have in practice increasingly become inter-linked and inter-twined. This has been most obviously so in the context of Lisbon Strategy discussions and actions. Second, although many different preferences and points of view have been articulated during policy processes, an especially notable division has been between those who take a broadly liberal approach to how the European economy should be framed and those who take a social market approach. The depth of division should not be over-stated for, with all EU governments much concerned about market competitiveness, none has been over-willing to adopt new and strong employee protection measures that might threaten labour market flexibility. The main thrust of all governments has been in the direction of greater liberalisation of markets. But clear differences of emphases have, nonetheless, been present and this has led to some policy frictions. Third, policy approaches, especially in the employment and economic growth domains, have displayed significant differences in character from the SEM and EMU building programmes. Whereas they were constructed on legal foundations and on the basis of tight plans and timetables, employment and economic growth objectives are partly being pursued via more voluntaristic and loose routes in which the submission of annual national reports, peer pressure, bench marking, and the adoption of best practices are amongst the preferred methods of achieving aims and targets. This looser approach, which is coming to be used in a limited way in other policy areas too, is generally referred to as the open method of coordination (OMC). (For an analysis of OMC, with particular reference in this case to its application to the operation of EMU, see Hodson and Maher, 2001.) The main disadvantage of the OMC approach is that governments are not legally bound by agreements and so may not feel so committed to implementing them. Advantages are that policy remains primarily a national responsibility, national diversities are respected, and governments may agree to orientations and actions they otherwise would not accept.

Having emphasised that much of social policy is about employment promotion policy, the extent of EU involvement in protective social policy measures should not be underestimated. By way of illustration of this, just a few of the policy areas covered by directives may be cited: health and safety of temporary workers; safety signs at work; protection of pregnant women at work and women who have recently given birth; organisation of working time; protection of young people at work; and parental leave from work. In addition, the EU runs social policy programmes of various kinds, including public health programmes and programmes to assist the elderly and the disabled.

Energy policy

Given the existence of the ECSC and Euratom Treaties, the centrality of energy to any modern economy, the disruption and damage that was caused by oil price increases in the 1970s, and the immense savings that the Commission has for years identified as accruing from an integrated energy market, it is perhaps surprising that until the late 1980s very little progress was made towards a common energy policy (as opposed to having some policies for particular energy sectors). The main obstacle to progress was that the member states – with their differing domestic energy resources, differing energy requirements, and large, state-owned, monopolistic energy industries – preferred essentially national solutions.

Since the late 1980s, however, there has been greater receptivity to the idea of a common energy policy. This has been stimulated in no small part by the realisation that energy cannot be isolated from the increasingly integrated SEM, and also by increased appreciation of the over-reliance of the EU on external suppliers – the EU depends on non-member countries for almost half of its energy requirements, with this dependence being as high as 70 per cent in the case of oil. Attitudes have thus been changing, and this is bringing about a rapid evolution in energy policy. The policy is based on a number of pillars:

- *Developing an internal market in energy.* Progress has been made in a number of areas, including opening up public procurement in the energy equipment sector, standardisation of energy equipment and products, and some liberalisation of the electricity and gas markets.
- *Developing external energy relations and ensuring security of supply.* Initiatives in this sphere have largely focused on: establishing binding rules at the international level for the sale and transportation of energy; engaging in an ongoing dialogue and establishing partnerships with major suppliers, most notably Russia and Middle East states.
- *Managing demand.* Various schemes and programmes exist to reduce energy consumption.
- *Diversifying sources.* The EU does not exclude any options, including the nuclear energy option, and funds research programmes in renewable sources.
- *Minimising the negative impact on the environment of energy use and production.* Measures here include a variety of programmes with such purposes as developing alternative sources of non-polluting energy and reinforcing domestic and industrial efficiency. However, several proposals to give the environmental dimension of energy policy real teeth by establishing fiscal incentives (for energy saving and the reduction of environmental pollution) and disincentives (for polluting) have met with resistance in the Council of Ministers.

Clearly there has been significant progress in the energy policy field, though much still remains to be done. Amongst priorities are further liberalisation of energy generation and distribution and the establishment of networks to allow more open access to grids. The UK and the

Scandinavian countries, for example, have almost wholly liberalised their markets for electricity and gas, but most EU countries retain significant market protection.

Research and technological development policy

There was no mention of research and technological development (R&TD) policy in the original EEC Treaty, but it nonetheless began to be developed from the late 1970s in response to a growing concern that the EC's member states were not sufficiently promoting innovation or adapting to innovation, especially in high-tech and other advanced sectors. Recognising, and wishing to promote further, the importance of this policy area, the member states added a new title on 'Research and Technological Development' to the EEC Treaty via the SEA. The title was then developed a little by the Maastricht Treaty, whilst preserving the same broad objective of 'strengthening the scientific and technological bases of Community industry and encouraging it to become more competitive at international level, while promoting all the research activities deemed necessary' (Article 163 TEC).

The EU's R&TD policy is pursued, on the one hand, by directly managing and financing research activities and, on the other hand, by attempting to create a framework and environment in which research that falls within the EU's priorities is encouraged and facilitated. More specifically, research activity takes four main forms:

(1) Research is undertaken directly by the EU itself at its Joint Research Centre (JRC). The JRC consists of seven establishments and employs over 2000 people. Most of the work of the JRC is concerned with nuclear energy (especially safety issues), materials, remote sensing and, increasingly, industrial research related to the SEM.

(2) The largest part of EU R&TD consists of shared-cost or contract research. This research is not undertaken by Commission employees but by tens of thousands of researchers in universities, research institutes, and public and private companies. The EU's role is to develop and agree the principles, aims, and conditions of the programmes under which the research is conducted, to coordinate activities, and to provide some of the finance (usually around 50 per cent of the total cost of the research). The better known programmes in this approach to research activity include ESPRIT (information technology), BRITE (industrial technology) and RACE (advanced telecommunications).

(3) There are concerted action-research projects where the EU does not finance the actual research, but facilitates and finances the coordination of

work being done at the national level. The EU's medical research programme takes this form.

(4) Some of the research activity takes none of the above three 'conventional' forms, but consists of arrangements in which, for example, only some member states participate, or in which the EU cooperates with non-member states and international organisations. Work undertaken within the framework of the European Research Coordinating Agency (EUREKA) is of this type, with EUREKA's membership being extended to several non-EU European states, including Russia.

The EU uses multi-annual framework programmes to coordinate and give strategic direction to its R&TD policies and activities. The First Framework Programme covered 1984–7, the Second 1987–91, the Third (which overlapped with the Second) 1990–4, the Fourth 1994–8, the Fifth 1999–2002, the Sixth 2000–6, and the Seventh 2007–13. The Seventh Programme builds on the Sixth Programme, which was framed within the context of the Lisbon Process aim of creating a dynamic and knowledge-based EU economy. As part of this aim, the Sixth Programme sought to create a European Research Area (ERA). The ERA seeks: to concentrate research support on priority research areas and to strengthen the coordination and coherence of research at European and national levels; to strengthen bridges between research and innovation and promote the human potential for research and the mobility of researchers; and to promote the particular scientific and technological research needs arising from EU policies.

The Seventh Programme (FP7) almost doubles the size of EU research funding, from around €5 billion per year to almost €10 billion. This represents an increase from about 5 per cent of total public spending in the EU on research to approaching 10 per cent. FP7 has four objectives, each supported by its own programme: the Co-operation programme promotes collaboration between universities, industry, research centres and public authorities across the EU and assists them to 'gain leadership' in science and technology; the Ideas programme supports 'frontier research'; the People programme reinforces the existing Marie Curie support for researchers, helping with skills, mobility, and career development; and the Capacities programme supports research infrastructures, regional research clusters, small and medium-sized enterprises, and science and technology cooperation policy. As with the Sixth Programme, FP7 emphasises research themes. Existing themes such as biotechnology, information technology, nanotechnology, energy, and transport are retained, whilst a new theme of security and space is added.

Environmental policy

As with R&TD policy, there was no mention of environmental policy in the original EEC Treaty, but it was incorporated by the SEA through a new title – 'Environment'. The Maastricht Treaty and (to a lesser extent) the Amsterdam Treaty built on the SEA provisions, though less in terms of objectives – which remain so vague as to be virtually meaningless – than in terms of operating principles. There are two key TEC articles in this respect:

> Environmental protection requirements must be integrated into the definition and implementation of the Community policies and activities referred to in Article 3 [which lists the other main areas of EC policy activity], in particular with a view to promoting sustainable development. (Article 6)

> Community policy on the environment shall aim at a high level of protection taking into account the diversity of situations in the various regions of the Community. It shall be based on the precautionary principle and on the principles that preventive action should be taken, that environmental damage should as a priority be rectified at source and that the polluter should pay. (Article 174(2))

Since Community environmental legislation began to appear in the early 1970s, a number of operating principles have been developed, amongst which are sustainability, preventative action, the polluter pays, shared responsibilities (of different levels of government), and integration of environmental concerns into other policy areas. As they have been developed, these principles have been incorporated into EU legislation where possible and as appropriate. There are over 200 such legal instruments, most of them in the form of directives, covering matters as diverse as water and air pollution, disposal of chemicals, waste treatment, and protection of species and natural resources. Alongside, and supporting, this legislation are several other policy instruments, ranging from information campaigns to arrangements for the collection of environmental data – the latter being the particular responsibility of the European Environment Agency, which after long delays caused by disagreements in the Council over its siting, was eventually established in Copenhagen in 1994.

Many of the environmental policy instruments, both legislative and non-legislative, have been designed to give effect to the series of Environmental Action Programmes that have been adopted since 1973. The Sixth Programme, entitled *Environment 2010: Our Future, Our Choice*, covers the 2001–10 period. Building on, but also extending, existing practices, the Programme sets out five approaches to be applied across environmental policy:

- Implementation of existing environmental legislation to be improved.
- Integration of environmental concerns into other policy areas to be deepened.
- Working with the market to be intensified, by encouraging business and consumer interests to contribute to more sustainable production and consumption patterns.
- Individual citizens to be given better quality and more easily accessible information on environmental issues, with a view to making them more environmentally sensitive.
- Development of a more environmentally conscious attitude towards land use.

Alongside these approaches, particular attention is being paid to four priority areas:

- *Tackling climate change.* The Programme declares that if air pollution and climate change are to be tackled effectively, the EU will have to exceed its Kyoto Protocol commitment to reduce greenhouse gases by 8 per cent of 1990 levels by 2012. There is an aim of a 20–40 per cent reduction by 2020, but this appears to be over-ambititous.
- *Nature and bio-diversity.* Amongst priorities here are completion of the Natura habitat network (which promotes conservation measures to protect endangered species and natural habitats in decline), increased sectoral bio-diversity, and plans for the protection of landscapes, the marine environment and soils.
- *Environment and health.* The Programme seeks to promote a more holistic approach to environmental improvement with a particular focus on problems concerning chemicals, water and air quality, and noise.
- *Sustainable use of natural resources and wastes.* In this area a strategy, including such measures as taxes and incentives, is being sought that ensures the consumption of renewable and non-renewable resources does not exceed the delivery capacity of the environment. In addition, there is an intensification of measures to encourage the recycling and recovery of wastes.

A major problem in the environmental policy sphere is implementation of EU laws. Because of the way in which the EU is structured, and because of the Commission's limited resources, implementation of laws is also a problem in other EU policy spheres and sectors. It is so, however, particularly in respect of the environment. There are a number of reasons for this, of which expense is frequently the most crucial. It is, for example, very costly to implement the measures required to meet the standards set out in the 1975 bathing water directive – a directive that is notorious for poor implementation.

Beyond its 'internal' environmental policy activities, the EU promotes international cooperation on environmental issues and actively participates in international environmental forums.

Sectoral policies

Some EU policies are directed towards specific economic sectors. A few such policies – covering coal and steel, atomic energy, agriculture and transport – were explicitly provided for in the Founding Treaties. Others have their origins in a combination of factors: difficulties in adjusting to changed market conditions; rapid sectoral decline; and effective political lobbying by interested parties.

The most obvious example of a sectoral policy is the Common Agricultural Policy (CAP), which consumes by far the largest proportion of EU expenditure and where most policy-making responsibilities have been transferred from the member states to the EU (the CAP is examined in some detail in Chapter 18). Another, though more modest and less comprehensive example of a sectoral policy is atomic energy where, for example, important research work is undertaken on the more economical use of atomic energy and on safety standards.

Two of the EU's most important sectoral policies cover fishing and shipbuilding.

Fishing

After years of discussion and the periodic issuing of laws regulating aspects of the industry, a legally enforceable Common Fisheries Policy (CFP) was agreed in 1983. The essential rationale of the CFP, based on reforms that were adopted at the end of 2002, is to ensure that, with resources diminishing, existing fish stocks are exploited responsibly, with due care for the marine ecosystem and with the interests of fishermen and consumers protected as far as possible. The main pillars of the CFP are as follows:

- *Access*. All waters within the EU's exclusive fishing zone, which extends to 200 nautical miles from its coastlines, are open to all EU fishermen. However, within a 12-mile limit of their own shores member states may reserve fishing for their own fishermen and those with traditional rights.

- *Conservation*. Fish stocks are controlled by the annual setting of total allowance catches (TACs), which are set within multi-annual management framework plans that are designed to protect, and in appropriate cases to enable the recovery of, stocks. TACs are divided into national quotas. The size of TACs and quotas are set in December each year by the Council, on the basis of proposals from the Commission which acts on scientific advice. Political pressures invariably result in the Council setting higher limits for at least some species than are proposed by the Commission.

  TACs and quotas are notoriously difficult to enforce and there is known to be widespread abuse, with the landing of fish that are over quota or undersized. The EU has tried to tackle the problem by strengthening policy implementation mechanisms. Amongst the mechanisms in place are the following: all EU fishing vessels are required to have a fishing licence on board; Commission inspectors (of which there are only a few) have the right of unannounced arrival in ports and on vessels; and use is made of satellite technology to monitor fishing activities. In March 2005 the Council approved the establishment of a Fisheries Control Agency to strengthen enforcement coordination and efficiency. Amongst the responsibilities of the Agency are the development of EU-wide standards for training inspectors and organising the deployment of surveillance resources.
- *Structural measures*. Funding is made available from the EU budget for matters such as processing and market development projects, conversion and safety schemes, and redeployment.
- *External negotiations*. Negotiations with non-EU countries on fishing – which mostly concern access to waters and the conservation of fish stocks – are conducted by EU representatives on behalf of all member states.

Shipbuilding

Rather like fisheries, shipbuilding's central problem has been over-capacity. But whereas with fisheries the over-capacity has been created by insufficient fish stocks, with shipbuilding it has been caused by insufficient competitiveness on world markets. This lack of competitiveness has arisen essentially from two factors: on the one hand, years of state aid by European governments to national shipbuilders so as to keep them in business; on the other hand, very low prices being charged by competitors, especially in Japan and Korea. By the mid-2000s the EU accounted for only around 11 per cent of world production, as compared with Japan's 32 per cent and Korea's 29 per cent.

To deal with shipbuilding's over-capacity and lack of competitiveness, EU shipbuilding policy has been focused around three broad and inter-related objectives:

- rationalisation by means of a controlled cut-back in capacity;
- enhancing productivity and competitiveness of the industry, especially in those segments of shipbuilding where the EU maintains a world position – which essentially is in the highest technological area of production, such as advanced container vessels, tankers, chemical and gas carriers, and small specialised ships;
- providing re-structuring opportunities for areas affected by rationalisation and re-training opportunities for individuals who are made redundant.

A key policy instrument in respect of the first and second of these objectives has been increasingly tight rules on state aid. The rules are now comparable to those for other industries, with aid being permissible for some modernisation and restructuring activities but largely prohibited for contract-related operating aid. Another policy instrument, of vital importance in respect of the second objective, has been liaising and negotiating with competitors on ending aid to the shipbuilding industry. In 1994, the EU, Japan, South Korea, Norway and the USA reached an agreement under OECD auspices aimed at eliminating all existing measures or practices constituting obstacles to normal competitive conditions. There have, however, been problems with the full application of this agreement, as there have been with WTO rules on state subsidisation of support. A third policy instrument, used for the third objective, has been ERDF and ESF assistance for regional development and for the re-training of workers.

External policies

The nature of the EU's external policies are examined at length in Chapter 19, so just two key points will be made here. First, there are many aspects to the external policies but they can be grouped broadly under four headings: external trade policies, foreign, security and defence policies, development policy, and the external dimension of internal policies. Second, external policies constitute an extremely important part of the overall EU policy agenda, and they are likely to loom even larger in the future as foreign and security policies are more fully developed.

Characteristics of EU Policies

Four features of EU policies are particularly striking.

The range and diversity of EU policies

Many of the EU's policies and laws centre on the promotion and defence of an internally free and externally protected market. Hence, there are policies that are designed to encourage the free movement of goods, persons, services, and capital; there is the competition policy, which seeks to facilitate fair and open competition within and across the borders of the member states; and there is the common external tariff and the common commercial policy. In practice, however, not all of these policies are complete or wholly successful. There are still, for example, barriers related to company law and company taxation that can make it difficult for firms in different member states to engage in joint commercial activities, and despite strenuous activity on harmonisation and approximation non-tariff barriers to internal trade still exist. In consequence, the EU is, in some respects, less than the integrated internal market it is commonly supposed to be.

But in other respects it is more than an internal market, in that many of its policy concerns range far beyond matters that are part and parcel of an internal market's requirements. The policy concerns of the EU are not, in other words, just concerned with dismantling internal barriers and providing conditions for fair trade on the one hand, and presenting a common external front on the other. There are two main aspects to this.

First, with regard to the EU's economic policies, many of these are not based solely on the non-interventionist/*laissez faire* principles that are often thought of as providing the ethos, or even the ideology, of the EU. In some spheres the EU tends very much towards interventionism/managerialism/regulation, and in so doing it does not always restrict itself to 'market efficiency' policies. This is most obviously seen in the way in which the regional, social, and consumer protection policies, plus much of the CAP, have as their precise purpose the counteracting and softening of nationally unacceptable or socially inequitable market consequences. On a broader front, there are the euro-related policies which clearly take the EU – and especially euroland – far beyond being 'just' an internal market and give it many of the characteristics of an economic and monetary union.

Second, the EU has developed policies that are not only non-market focused but also non-economic focused. Of these the most obvious are those where the member states consult and attempt to coordinate their positions on key foreign policy and some defence policy questions. In addition to foreign policy and defence policy there are many other policy areas – such as public health, broadcasting, and combating crime – which were long thought of as not being the EU's concern, but where important developments have occurred.

The regulatory emphasis

A classic way of distinguishing between policy types is in terms of regulatory, redistributive and distributive policies (Lowi, 1964). Regulatory policies lay down rules governing behaviour. Redistributive policies transfer financial resources from groups of individuals (most commonly social classes), regions or countries to others. And distributive policies also generally involve allocations of financial resources, but not from one 'side' to another (as from the better off to the worse off) but rather between alternative users and usually on the basis of *juste retour* (which in the EU context means member states draw from the resources available for distributive policies in appropriate proportion to what they contribute).

This scheme of policy types is by no means exhaustive or mutually exclusive. Nonetheless, it is a much-used schema and one that is helpful in throwing light on the nature of the EU's policy portfolio.

EU policies have a strong *regulatory* emphasis. Such indeed is the emphasis that Giandomenico Majone has suggested that the EU can be thought of as being a regulatory state (Majone, 1992, 1994, 1996; see also Chapter 21). The regulatory emphasis of EU policies is most obviously seen in respect of the SEM, where an extensive legislative framework is laid down to govern actors' behaviour in the market. This framework covers not just 'pure' market activities, such as the rules governing product specifications and market movements, but also many policies that are partly regulated for their own sake but mainly because they have market implications. Examples of policy areas that are so subject to heavy EU regulation are working conditions, consumer protection, and the environment.

The reason that EU regulatory policy is so wide-ranging and, as Pollack (2000) has shown, has displayed little sign of slowing down in its advance, is that there is both a demand and a supply for it. The demand comes from various quarters, but most especially from large business which wants as integrated a market as possible – which means common rules in all member states – so as to be able to pursue business activities with maximum ease. The supply comes mainly from the Commission, which through its policy and legislative proposals plays a crucial role in setting the regulatory framework. The Commission produces this supply for a number of reasons. One reason is simply that it is much more able to do so than it is with redistributive or distributive policies. This is partly because the technical nature of much regulatory policy tends to make it less contentious than the other two policy types, and it is partly too because most of the costs of implementing regulatory policies fall not on the EU budget but on the budgets of private firms and public authorities in the member states. Another reason why the Commission produces the supply is, in the view of public choice theorists, that expanding EU regulatory powers also expands the Commission's own powers (see, for example, Hix, 2005).

The EU has *redistributive* policies – most notably in the form of the cohesion funds and the CAP – but nothing like to the same extent as member states have such policies in the form of social welfare, health and educational policies There are two main reasons why EU redistributive policies are not well developed. First, no pressing reasons have presented themselves for redistributive policies to be transferred to the EU level, so transfers of sovereignty have been seen as being unnecessary. Second, most national governments have wished to keep a tight rein on EU budgetary expenditure, which means the EU has only modest funds to redistribute. As is shown in Chapter 17, expenditure on the Regional and Social Funds was doubled in 1988 and then again in 1992, but even with the 1992 increase the overall size of the EU budget was capped at 1.27 per cent of total EU GDP. Since the 1992 increase, cohesion spending has been kept more or less level, and overall spending has been marginally cut as an increasing number of member states have adopted tighter attitudes towards EU spending. Key factors accounting for these attitudes are: they conform with ideological shifts in favour of a more restrictive stance towards all forms of public expenditure; the emphasis given in the EU since the early 1990s to the doctrine of subsidiarity weighs against EU budgetary expansion; the EMU convergence and Stability and Growth Pact criteria place a strong emphasis on budgetary discipline; the prospect and then the reality of many relatively poor countries joining the EU has not encouraged EU-15 states to expand redistributive policies – from which most of them have little to gain but for which they must pay; and Germany, long the major net contributor to the EU budget, has come to suffer from 'donor fatigue' – largely because of the costs incurred by German unification.

Distributive policies are not much developed in the EU. Examples of EU distributive policies include research and technological development, education (where there are some training and exchange programmes), and – if it can be called a policy – the siting of EU agencies. On this last 'policy', many specialised agencies – ranging from the European Agency for the Evaluation of Medicinal Products to Europol – have been created in recent years and their location has almost invariably been the occasion for wrangling and for dispersal amongst the member states. Much of the explanation for why distributive policies are not well developed at EU level is similar to the explanation for the under-development of redistributive policies: they are seen as being primarily national responsibilities, so only limited budgetary resources are made available for them. In Pollack's view (1994) another key reason is that distributive policies are not so tied in with the operation of the market as regulatory or redistributive policies. Whereas regulatory policies are very much a consequence of economic spillover and redistributive policies are at least in part a consequence of countries with specific market difficulties being given compensation or 'side-payments', distributive policies are not so 'advantaged' and are highly dependent on Commission entrepreneurship for advancement.

The differing degrees of EU policy involvement

The EU's responsibility for policy-making and policy management varies enormously across its range of policy interests. In those spheres where significant responsibilities are exercised, arrangements are usually well established, and effective policy instruments – legal and financial – are usually available. Where, however, EU involvement is marginal, policy processes may be confined to little more than occasional exchanges of ideas and information between interested parties, whilst policy instruments may merely be of the exhortive and persuasive kind such as are common in many international organisations. Table 15.1 provides an indication of the varying extent of EU involvement in different policy areas, and Table 15.2 gives an indication of the varying nature of EU policy involvement.

Examples of extensive EU involvement are the CCP, the CAP, and the CFP. Here, most major policy decisions, such as those on external tariffs, agricultural support mechanisms and payments, and fishing quotas are taken at the EU level, whilst their detailed and supposedly uniform implementation is left to the states, acting as agents of the EU. In areas where these so-called common policies are not in reality totally common – and both the CAP and the CFP allow room for governments to provide national aids and assistance – decisions of any significance normally require at least clearance from Brussels.

Moving along the spectrum of EU policy involvement, there are many spheres in which the EU's interests and competence, though less comprehensive than in the examples just given, are still very significant, and complement and supplement the activities of the states in important ways. Competition policy is one example. This seeks to encourage free and open competition throughout the EU by, for instance, setting out rules under which firms can make and sell their products, laying down conditions under which national authorities may assist firms, and imposing restrictions on certain types of company merger. Social policy is another example, with much of the focus in this sphere being on job training and re-training, labour mobility, working conditions, and the general promotion of employment.

Table 15.1   *The extent of EU policy involvement*

Extensive EU policy involvement	*Considerable EU policy involvement*	*Policy responsibility shared between the EU and the member states*	*Limited EU policy involvement*	*Virtually no EU policy involvement*
Trade Agriculture Fishing	Market regulation Monetary (for euro members)	Regional Competition Industrial Foreign Environmental Equal opportunities Working conditions Consumer protection Movement across external borders Macroeconomic (especially for euro members) Energy Transport Cross-border crime	Health Education Defence Social welfare	Housing Civil liberties Domestic crime

Table 15.2   *The nature of EU policy involvement*

Heavy reliance on legal regulation	*Very considerable reliance on legal regulation*	*A mixture of legal regulation and inter-state cooperation*	*Some legal regulation but a considerable reliance on inter-state cooperation*	*Largely based on inter-state cooperation*
Trade Agriculture Fishing	Regional Competition Consumer protection Working conditions Equal opportunities Market regulation	Industrial Evironmental Transport Movement across external borders Macroeconomic Energy	Social welfare Energy Defence Law and order	Health Education Foreign

Turning finally to policy spheres where the EU's involvement is at best limited, examples include education, health, housing, pensions, and social welfare payments. As these examples make clear, many of the policies that fall into this category of low EU involvement are public welfare policies and policies that have major budgetary implications.

This complex mosaic of policy involvement has over the years moved almost unceasingly in an incrementally integrationist direction. The pace of the movement has varied, both over time periods and within policy areas, but it has been constant. So, if one looks back to, say, the mid-1970s, many issues that would have been listed then as being in the category of very limited policy involvement – such as environment and foreign policy – are now by no means marginal. Environment has spawned policy pro-grammes and legislation, foreign policy has evolved its own machinery and has seen increasingly coordinated policy development, and both have been awarded treaty recognition. At the same time, some policy spheres which in the mid-1970s the Community would not have been thought of as having any competence in at all have assumed significant places on the EU's policy agenda. Examples include defence policy and the various JHA policies.

The patchy and somewhat uncoordinated nature of EU policies

The overall EU policy framework can hardly be said to display a clear pattern or coherence. Some effort is now being made to pull it together and give it a rationale, notably via the so-called subsidiarity principle which implies that only those policies which it is agreed are best dealt with at EU level rather than national level do become the EU's concern. The problem with this principle, however, both as a description of the present reality and as a prescription for future action, is that it is vague and question-begging. Descriptions of the present and evolving policy framework as being centred on 'managed and tempered capitalism' or 'a controlled open market' are perhaps of more use in capturing the essence of the EU's policy interests, but they too are still far from wholly satisfactory in that they do not embrace the full flavour of the array and varying depths of EU policy interests, nor do they draw attention to the conflicting principles that underlie different parts of the policy network.

The fact is that the considerable national and political differences that exist in the EU make it difficult to develop coordinated and coherent policies based on shared principles and agreed objectives. This is so because any policy development at EU level is usually only possible if searching questions are answered to the satisfaction of a large number of actors. From the viewpoint of the member states these questions include: is the national (or at least government) interest being served?; is the cooperation and integration that the policy development involves politically acceptable?; and, if the policy sphere does require closer relations with other states, is the EU the most desirable arena in which it should occur? As the EU's extensive range of policies demonstrates, these questions have often been answered in the affirmative, though normally only after being subject to caveats and reservations which sit uneasily beside, and sometimes clash with, one another. But often, too, the responses have been in the negative, or at least have been so on the part of a sufficient number to prevent progress.

Policy development has consequently been as much about what is possible as what is desirable. In the absence of a centre of power with the authority and internal coherence to take an overall view of EU requirements and impose an ordered pattern, policies have tended to be the outcome of complex and laboured interactions where different, and often contrasting, requirements, preferences, reservations and fears have all played a part. As a result, the EU's overall policy picture is inevitably patchy and rather ragged. A few spheres – such as the CAP and the operation of the SEM – are well developed. Other spheres, however, which it might have been expected would be developed, are either developed only in uncoordinated and partial ways or are barely developed at all.

Concluding Remarks

A central theme of this chapter has been the range and diversity of the EU's policy responsibilities and interests. There are now few policy areas with which the EU does not have at least some sort of involvement.

But another theme has been that there are many deficiencies in EU policies. Industrial policy, energy policy, and regional policy are but three examples of key policy areas where there are not, if EU effectiveness is to be maximised, sufficiently strong or integrated policy frameworks with clear and consistent goals. They are too partial and too fragmented. They are also, in general, under-funded.

Of course, similar critical comments about under-development and lack of cohesion can also be levelled against most national policy frameworks. But not to the same extent. For, at the individual state level, there is, even when the political system is weak and decentralised, usually more opportunity than there is in the EU for direction from the centre. This is partly because national decision-makers have access to more policy instruments than do EU decision-makers. It is mainly, however, because at state level there is normally some focus of political authority capable of offering leadership and imposing a degree of order: a Head of Government perhaps, a Cabinet or Council of Ministers, a Ministry of Economics or

Finance, or a dominant party group. In the EU, the Commission, the Council of Ministers and the European Council are the main foci of political authority and leadership, but none is constituted or organised in such a way as to enable it to establish an overall policy coherence or to enforce a clear and consistent policy direction.

However, as Chapter 16 will show, the situation has greatly improved from what it used to be.

Chapter 16

Policy Processes

Variations in EU Processes
Factors Determining EU Policy Processes
The Making of EU Legislation
EU Legislation after Adoption
Characteristic Features of EU Policy Processes
The Efficiency of EU Policy Processes

Variations in EU Processes

There cannot be said to be a 'standard' or 'typical' EU policy-making or decision-making process. A multiplicity of actors interact with one another via a myriad of channels.

The actors

There are three main sets of actors: those associated with the EU institutions, with the governments of the member states, and with Euro and national interests. As has been shown in previous chapters, each of these has responsibilities to fulfil and roles to perform. But so variable and fluid are EU policy processes that the nature of the responsibilities and roles may differ considerably according to circumstances. For instance, in one set of circumstances an actor may be anxious to play an active role and may have the power – legal and/or political – to do so. In a second set of circumstances it may not wish to be actively involved, perhaps because it has no particular interests at stake or because prominence may be politically damaging. And in a third set of circumstances it may wish for a leading part but not be able to attain it because of a lack of appropriate power resources.

The channels

The channels vary in four principal respects:

(1) *In their complexity and exhaustiveness.* Some types of decision are made fairly quickly by a relatively small number of people using procedures that are easy to operate. In contrast, others are subject to complex

and exhaustive processes in which many different sorts of actor attempt to determine and shape outcomes.

(2) *In the relative importance of EU, member state, and subnational processes and in the links between the three levels.* One of the EU's major structural difficulties is that it is multi-layered, with differing degrees and sorts of power and influence being exercised in different ways at different levels. Moreover, there are often no clear lines of authority or hierarchy between the different levels.

(3) *In their levels of seniority.* EU policy processes are conducted at many different levels of seniority, as illustrated by the numerous forums in which representatives of the governments of the member states meet: Heads of Government in the European Council; Ministers in the Council of Ministers; Permanent Representatives and their deputies in COREPER; and officials and experts in committees and working groups.

(4) *In their degree of formality and structure.* By their very nature, the fixed and set-piece occasions of EU policy processes – such as meetings of the Council of Ministers, plenary sessions of the EP, and Council of Ministers/EP delegation meetings called to resolve legislative and budgetary differences – tend to be formal and structured. Partly because of this, they are often not very well equipped to produce the horse trading, concessions, and compromises that are so necessary to build majorities, create agreements and further progress. As a result, they have come to be supported by a vast network of informal and unstructured channels between EU actors, ranging from the after-dinner discussions that are sometimes held at European Council gatherings to the continuous rounds of soundings, telephone calls, e-mails, lunches, and meetings and pre-meetings that are such a part of EU life in Brussels, Strasbourg, Luxembourg and national capitals.

Factors Determining EU Policy Processes

The central point made in the previous section – that EU policy-making and decision-making processes are multi-faceted in nature – is illustrated in some detail in Chapters 17, 18 and 19 on the budget, agricultural policy, and external relations. Taken together, these chapters demonstrate how difficult it is to generalise about how the EU functions.

It would of course be expected that, as in individual states, there would be some differences between EU processes in different policy arenas. What is distinctive about the EU, however, is the sheer range and complexity of its processes: a host of actors, operating within the context of numerous EU and national institutions, interact with one another on the basis of an array of different decision-making rules and procedures.

In trying to bring an overall perspective to the complexity of EU processes a number of factors can be identified as being especially important in determining the particular mix of actors and channels that are to be found in any particular context.

The treaty base

As was explained in Part 1, the EU is based on treaties. One of the most important things the treaties do is to lay down many different decision-making procedures and to specify the circumstances in which they are to be used. As a result the treaties – and especially the TEU and the TEC – are of fundamental importance in shaping the nature of the EU's policy processes and determining the powers exercised by institutions and actors within these processes. This may be illustrated by giving just a few examples of the variety of policy-making and decision-making procedures provided for in the TEU and the TEC (these procedures are all explained at length elsewhere in the book, either later in this chapter or in following chapters).

- There are four 'standard' procedures for 'non-administrative' legislation: the consultation, cooperation, co-decision and assent procedures. Key points of difference between these procedures include: (1) the EP can exercise veto powers under the co-decision and assent procedures but cannot do so under the consultation and cooperation procedures; and (2) there are single readings in the Council and the EP under the consultation and assent procedures, two readings under the cooperation procedure, and potentially three readings – or, perhaps more accurately, two readings and a third stage – under the co-decision procedure.
- External trade agreements negotiated under Article 133 of the TEC have their own special procedure, under which the Commission and the Council decide and the EP, at best, is only able to offer advice.
- The annual budget also has its own arrangements, under which the Council and the EP are joint budgetary authorities.
- Under the 'flexibility' provisions added to the TEU and the TEC by the Amsterdam Treaty and made easier to apply by the Nice Treaty, it is possible for a group of EU member states – constituting less than the full membership – to establish 'closer cooperation' between themselves and to make use of EU institutions, procedures and mechanisms. A decision to so act can be taken by qualified majority, though with safeguards built in for member states which object to such a decision being taken (see Chapters 5 and 6 for details).
- Pillars two and three of the EU (dealing respectively with foreign and security policy and police and judicial cooperation in criminal matters) set out largely, though not wholly, intergovernmental decision-making frameworks that enable non-legislative decisions of various sorts to be

taken. In broad terms, most major policy decisions under both pillars require unanimity in the Council and consultation with the EP, whilst operational and procedural decisions can usually be taken by QMV if the Council so decides and without consulting with the EP. Whether or not the EP is consulted, the Council must keep it regularly informed of developments under the two pillars.

The proposed status of the matter under consideration

As a general rule, procedures tend to be more fixed when EU law is envisaged than when it is not. They are fixed most obviously by the treaties, but also by Court of Justice interpretations (for example, the obligation that the Council must wait upon EP opinions before giving Commission proposals legislative status) and by conventions (for example, the understanding in the Council that when a member state has genuine difficulties the matter will not normally be rushed and an effort will be made to reach a compromise even when QMV is permissible).

When law is being made, Commission legislation is usually subject to less review and discussion than EP and Council or Council legislation. The reason for this is that Commission legislation is normally of an administrative kind – more technical than political. Indeed, much of it consists of updates, applications or amendments to already existing legislation, usually in the sphere of external trade or the CAP. As a result, Commission legislation, prior to being introduced, is often only fully discussed by appropriate officials in the Commission, and perhaps by national officials in a comitology committee. Some Council legislation, on the other hand, and all EP and Council legislation, is broader in scope and is subject to a full legislative procedure. As such it becomes the subject of representations and pressures from many interests, is assessed by the EP and often also by the EESC and the CoR, and is scrutinised in detail in national capitals and in Council forums in Brussels.

Where policy activity does not involve law making, considerable discretion is available to decision-makers, especially governments, as to which policy processes will be used and who will be permitted to participate. A common procedure when states wish the EU to do something, but do not necessarily wish a new law to be made (which may be because there is no agreement on what the law should be or because, as with foreign policy pronouncements, law is inappropriate), is to issue Council resolutions, declarations, or agreements. These can be as vague or as precise as the Council wishes them to be. Often, resolutions and the like can have a very useful policy impact, even if it is just to keep dialogue going, but because they are not legal instruments they are not normally as subject as EP and Council or Council legislation to examination and challenge by other EU institutions and actors.

The degree of generality or specificity of the policy issue

At the generality end of the scale, EU policy-making may consist of little more than exchanges of ideas between interested parties to see whether there is common ground for policy coordination, the setting of priorities, or possible legislation. Such exchanges and discussions take place at many different levels on an almost continuous basis, but the most important, in the sense that their initiatives are the ones most likely to be followed up, are those which involve *les grands messieurs* of the Commission and the member states – especially if the outcome of deliberations find their way into European Council Conclusions.

Far removed from *grands tours d'horizon* by *les grands messieurs* is the daily grind of preparing and drafting the mass of highly detailed and technical regulations that make up the great bulk of the EU's legislative output. Senior EU figures, especially ministers, are not normally directly involved in the processes that lead to such legislation. There may be a requirement that they give the legislation their formal approval, but it is Commission officials, aided in appropriate cases by national officials, who do the basic work.

The newness, importance, controversiality, or political sensitivity of the issue in question

The more these characteristics apply, and the perception of the extent to which they do may vary – what may be a technical question for one may be politically charged for another – the more complex policy processes are likely to be. If, for example, it seems likely that a proposal for an EP and Council directive on some aspect of animal welfare will cause significant difficulties for farmers, it is probable that the accompanying decision-making process will display all or most of the following features: particularly intensive pre-proposal consultations by the Commission; vigorous attempts by many sectional and promotional interest groups to make an input; very careful examination of the proposal by the EP and the EESC; long and exhaustive negotiations in the Council; considerable activity and manoeuvring on the fringes of formal meetings, and in between the meetings; and, overall, much delay and many alterations *en route* to the (possible) eventual adoption of the proposal.

The balance of policy responsibilities between EU and national levels

Where there has been a significant transfer of responsibilities to the EU – as, for example, with agricultural, commercial, and competition policies –

EU-level processes are naturally very important. In such policy spheres, EU institutions, particularly the Commission, have many tasks to perform: monitoring developments, making adjustments, ensuring existing policies and programmes are replaced when necessary, and so on. On the other hand, where the EU's policy role is at best supplementary to that of the member states – education policy and health policy are examples – most significant policy and decision-making activity continues to be channelled through the customary national procedures, and policy activity at EU level is limited in scope.

Circumstances and the perceptions of circumstances

This is seemingly rather vague, but it refers to the crucially important fact that policy development and decision-making processes in the EU are closely related to prevailing political and economic circumstances, to the perceptions by key actors – especially national governments – of their needs in the circumstances, and to perceptions of the potential of the EU to act as a problem-solving organisation in regard to the circumstances. Do the advantages of acting at EU level, as opposed to national level, and of acting in the EU in a particular way as opposed to another way, outweigh the disadvantages?

The Justice and Home Affairs (JHA) policy area provides an example of how changing circumstances can bring about related changes in policy processes. The policy area began to be initially developed at EU level from the mid-1980s, largely as a result of spillover from the SEM project and the opening-up of borders. However, the development was very tentative and was conducted on a strictly intergovernmental basis. Two sets of changing circumstances have, however, resulted in national governments giving JHA issues a much greater priority in recent years and being willing to see intergovernmental policies at EU level giving way in many JHA areas to supranational processes. One of these changing circumstances has been EU enlargement to CEECs, which has intensified already existing concerns in many EU-15 states about border controls and such related issues as illegal inward movements of people (from non-EU states to the EU), cross-border crime, and drug trafficking. The other changing circumstance has been the increased threat to 'the West' from international terrorism, which was first dramatically demonstrated by the September 11 2001 events in the US and has since been brought closer to home by bombings in Europe – notably in Madrid in 2004 and in London in 2005. Both of these changing circumstances have been instrumental in promoting the more 'communitaurised' approach to much of JHA that has been evident since the late 1990s.

The Making of EU Legislation

Having established that there are considerable variations in EU policy-making and decision-making processes, it is necessary to emphasise that there are some common, shared, and recurring features. This is no more clearly seen than in relation to EU legislation, most of which is made via one of three 'set routes'. The general framework of two of these routes – those dealing with 'domestic legislation' – is modelled in Figure 16.1.

(1) Administrative/management/regulatory/implementing legislation is issued mainly in the form of Commission regulations and decisions. The basic work on this type of legislation is undertaken by officials in the relevant DG. Commissioners themselves are only involved in the making of such legislation when it is not straightforward or someone asks them to take a look.

National officials usually have the opportunity to voice their comments in a comitology committee, but whether or not they have the power to stop legislation to which they object depends on which procedure applies. As was explained in Chapter 9, the Commission is in a much stronger position when it works through advisory committees than it is when it works through management and, in particular, regulatory, committees.

When this type of legislation is issued as Council legislation it naturally results in national officials playing a more active role, and formal ministerial approval is required.

(2) Much of the legislation that is enacted in connection with EU external trade policies is based on agreements with third countries, and is therefore subject to special decision-making procedures. These procedures are described in Chapter 19. Amongst their distinctive features are the following: the Commission usually acts as the EU's main negotiator in economic negotiations with third countries; the Council seeks to control and monitor what the Commission does during negotiations; the EP does not normally exercise much influence – except when cooperation and association agreements are proposed; and most legislation produced as a result of negotiations, including virtually all legislation that is intended to establish the principles of a legal framework, is enacted in the form of Council regulations and decisions and therefore requires formal ministerial approval.

(3) Most of what remains consists of legislation that is deemed to require examination via one of the EU's full legislative procedures. There are no hard and fast rules for deciding which Commission proposals do require such an examination, but in general they are those that are thought to be significant or concerned with establishing principles. The broader in scope they are, the more likely they are to be in the form of directives.

Figure 16.1 *Principal features of the EU's legislative procedures*

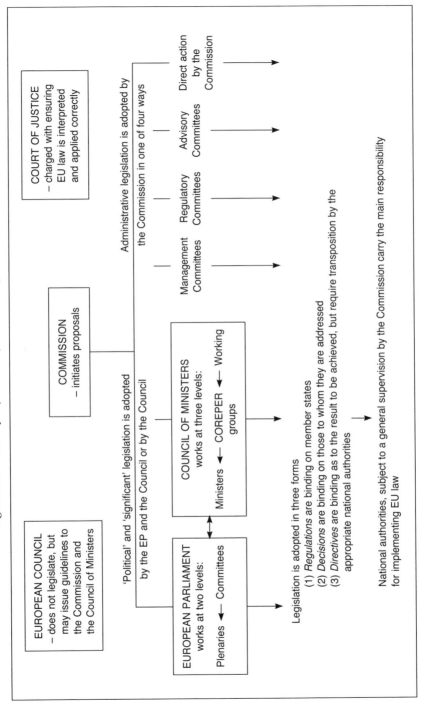

Because of their obvious importance, the EU's full legislative procedures need to be examined here. However, since much of the detail of how the EU institutions exercise their particular legislative responsibilities has already been set out in Part 3 of this book, a comprehensive account is not attempted in what follows. Attention is restricted to highlighting the principal features of the legislative procedures.

Since the Maastricht Treaty entered into force there have been four different legislative procedures: the consultation, cooperation, co-decision, and assent procedures. There are also internal variations within these procedures, the most important of which is that under the consultation, co-decision, and assent procedures, QMV is possible in the Council when legislation is being made under certain Treaty articles whereas unanimity is required under other articles. Descriptions of the consultation, co-decision, and assent procedures now follow. The cooperation procedure is not described since, although it used to be very important, it was virtually abolished by the Amsterdam Treaty. Indeed, it would have been completely abolished had the member states not been reluctant to tamper with its application to four aspects of EMU for fear of opening up the whole EMU issue in the Amsterdam IGC. Should any reader wish to know about the nature of the cooperation procedure, it is outlined on pp. 243 of this book and described fully in the third edition (1994).

The consultation procedure

Prior to the SEA, the consultation procedure was the only procedure for non-administrative legislation. However, the creation of the cooperation procedure by the SEA and of the co-decision procedure by the Maastricht Treaty, coupled with the 'elevation' of policy areas from the consultation procedure to these other procedures by the SEA and the Maastricht, Amsterdam and Nice Treaties (the last made only marginal changes), has meant that the number of policy areas to which the consultation procedure applies has been reduced over the years. The main policy area still covered by it is agriculture.

The consultation procedure is a single reading procedure in which the Council is the sole final decision-maker. However, it cannot take a final decision until it has received the opinion of the EP. On some proposals it must also await the opinions of the European Economic and Social Committee (EESC) and the Committee of the Regions (CoR).

Initiation

The starting point of any legislative proposal is when somebody suggests that the EU should act on a matter. Most likely this will be the

Commission, the Council, or the EP: the Commission because it is the only body with the authority formally to table a legislative proposal, and because of its special expertise in, and responsibility for, EU affairs; the Council because of its political weight, its position as the natural conduit for national claims and interests, and its power under Article 208 TEC to request the Commission 'to undertake any studies the Council considers desirable for the attainment of the common objectives, and to submit to it any appropriate proposals'; and the EP because of the desire of MEPs to be active and because under Article 192 TEC 'The European Parliament may, acting by a majority of its members, request the Commission to submit any appropriate proposals on matters on which it considers that a Community act is required for the purpose of implementing this Treaty'. (In practice only a handful of such EP requests have been made since the EP was given this power under the Maastricht Treaty.)

Beyond the Commission, the Council, and the EP there are many other possible sources of EU legislation, but little progress can be made unless the Commission decides to take up an issue and draft a proposal. Many factors may result in it deciding to do so, the most frequent being that such legislation is required as part of an ongoing policy commitment or programme. Sometimes, however, it is very difficult, when looking at specific proposals, to determine why the Commission decided to act and to identify precisely who originated the initiative. For example, a Commission proposal that seems to have been a response to a Council request may, on inspection, be traced beyond the Council to a national pressure group influencing a minister, who then gradually and informally introduced the issue into the Council as an option to be considered. Similarly, a Commission proposal may seem to have been a response to points raised in an EP committee or to representations from Europe-wide interests, but in fact the Commission may itself have dropped hints to MEPs or to interests that they should look at the matter (thus reinforcing the Commission's own position *vis-à-vis* the Council).

Preparation of a text

In preparing a text, a number of matters must be carefully considered by the Commission in addition to the direct policy considerations at issue.

- The proposal must have the correct legal base – that is, it must be based on the correct treaty article(s). Normally this is a straightforward matter and there is no room for argument, but sometimes disputes arise when a proposal cuts across policy areas and the Commission chooses a legal base that is deemed by a policy actor to be unsatisfactory. For example, a member state that is concerned about the possible implications of a policy proposal is likely to prefer a procedure where unanimity rather than QMV applies in the Council, whilst the EP always prefers the co-decision procedure to be used rather than the consultation procedure because this gives it a potential veto. The question of legal base can therefore be controversial, and has resulted in references to the ECJ.

- Justification of the proposal must be given in terms of the application of the subsidiarity principle. This takes the form of answers to a series of questions on subsidiarity in the explanatory memorandum that is attached to each proposal.
- Where appropriate, justification must be given in terms of the environmental impact of the proposal. This usually applies, for example, to transport and agriculture proposals.
- The probable financial implications for the EU budget of the proposal must be assessed.

The standard way in which proposals are prepared is as follows. The process begins with a middle-ranking official in the 'lead' DG assuming the main responsibility for the dossier: that is for preparing and looking after the Commission's draft. This way of working emphasises individual responsibility, means that officials are or become highly expert in particular policy areas, and results in the distribution of information about policy proposals being very dependent, in the early stages at least, on the preferred approach of officials responsible for dossiers.

Formal communications within the Commission about a proposal tend initially to be of a vertical rather than of a horizontal kind. That is to say, they tend primarily to be up and down the lead DG – known as the *chef de file* – rather than across and between DGs. This rather hierarchical and compartmentalised approach can make for difficulties, though creative and imaginative officials make appropriate, and if necessary extensive, use of informal communications – through telephone calls, e-mails and meetings – with potentially interested officials elsewhere in the services so as to ensure that there are not too many inter-service problems at a later stage of proceedings.

Whether or not they are kept fully informed of developments from an early drafting stage, other DGs with a possible interest in a proposal must be given the opportunity at some point to make their views known. This may involve the convening of one or more inter-service meetings. Other Commission services with which there must be exchanges and agreements include the Secretariat General (which has amongst its responsibilities the overall coordination of the Commission's work schedule) and the Legal Service (which amongst other things checks the legal base of proposals).

When all directly involved Commission interests have given their approval, the draft is sent to the *cabinet* of the Commissioner responsible for the subject. The *cabinet*, which may or may not have been involved in informal discussions with Commission officials as the proposal was being drafted, may or may not attempt to persuade Commission officials to re-work the draft before submitting it to the Commissioner for approval.

When the Commissioner is satisfied, she or he asks the Secretariat General to submit the draft to the College of Commissioners. The draft is then scrutinised, and possibly amended, by the *chefs de cabinet* at their weekly meeting. If the draft is judged to be uncontroversial the Commissioners may adopt it by written procedure; if it is controversial the Commissioners may, after debate, accept it, reject it, amend it, or refer it back to the relevant DG for further consideration.

In preparing a text officials usually find themselves the focus of attention from many directions. Knowing that the Commission's thinking is normally at its most flexible at this preliminary stage, and knowing too that once a proposal is formalised it is more difficult for it to be changed, interested parties use whatever means they can to press their views. Four factors most affect the extent to which the Commission is prepared to listen to outside interests at this pre-proposal stage. First, what contacts and channels have already been regularised in the sector and which ways of proceeding have proved to be effective in the past? Second, what political considerations arise and how important is it to incorporate different sectional and national views from the outset? Third, what degree of technical knowledge and outside expertise is called for? Fourth, how do the relevant Commission officials prefer to work?

Assuming, as it is normally reasonable to do, Commission receptivity, there are several ways in which external views may be brought to the attention of those drafting a proposal. The Commission itself may request a report, perhaps from a university or a research institute. Interest groups may submit briefing documents. Professional lobbyists, politicians, and officials from the Permanent Representations may press preferences in informal meetings. EP committees and EESC sections may be sounded out. And use may be made of the extensive advisory committee system that is clustered around the Commission (see Chapter 9).

There is thus no standard consultative pattern or procedure. An important consequence of this is that governmental involvement in the preparation of Commission texts varies considerably. Indeed, not only is there variation in involvement, there is also variation in knowledge of the Commission's intentions. Sometimes governments are fully aware of Commission thinking, because national officials have been formally consulted in committees of experts. Sometimes sectional interests represented on consultative committees will let their governments know what is going on. Sometimes governments will be abreast of developments as a result of having tapped sources within the Commission, most probably through officials in their Permanent Representations. But occasionally governments are not much aware of proposals until they are published.

The time that elapses between the decision to initiate a proposal and the publication by the Commission of its text naturally depends on a number of factors. Is there any urgency? How keen is the Commission to press ahead? How widespread are the consultations? Is there consensus amongst key external actors and does the Commission want their prior support? Is there consensus within the Commission itself? Not surprisingly, elapses of well over a year are common.

The opinions of the European Parliament, the European Economic and Social Committee, and the Committee of the Regions

On publication, the Commission's text is submitted to the Council of Ministers for a decision and to the EP and, if appropriate, the EESC and the CoR, for their opinions.

The EP is by far the most influential of the consultative bodies. Though it does not have full legislative powers under the consultation procedure, it has enough weapons in its arsenal to ensure that its views are at least taken into consideration, particularly by the Commission. Its representational claims are one source of its influence. The quality of its arguments and its suggestions are another. And it has the power of delay, by virtue of the requirement that the EP's opinion must be known before the proposal can be formally adopted by the Council.

As was shown in Chapter 12, most of the detailed work undertaken by the EP on proposed legislation is handled by its standing committees and, to a lesser extent, its political groups. Both the committees and the groups advise MEPs on how to vote in plenary.

The usual way in which plenaries act to bring influence to bear is to vote on amendments to the Commission's proposal, but not to vote on the draft legislative resolution – which constitutes the EP's opinion – until the Commission states, as it is obliged to do, whether or not it will change its text to incorporate the amendments that have been approved by the EP. (Under the consultation, cooperation and co-decision procedures, the Commission can amend, or even withdraw, its text at any time, apart from at the third stage of the co-decision procedure.) If the amendments are accepted by the Commission a favourable opinion is issued, and the amended text becomes the text that the Council considers. If all or some of the amendments are not accepted by the Commission, the EP can exert pressure by not issuing an opinion and referring the proposal back to the committee responsible. A reference back can also be made if the whole proposal is judged to be unacceptable. Withholding an opinion does not, it should be emphasised, mean that the EP has power of veto, because it is legally obliged to issue opinions and the ECJ has referred to the duty of loyal cooperation between EU institutions. What the withholding of opinions does do, however, is to give the EP the often useful bargaining and pressurising tool of the power of delay.

For the reasons outlined in Chapter 12 and which are considered further below, it is difficult to estimate the precise impact the EP has on EU legislation. In general terms, however, it can be said that the record in the context of the consultation procedure is mixed.

On the positive side, the Commission is normally sympathetic to the EP's views and accepts about three-quarters of its amendments. The Council is less sympathetic and accepts well under half of the amendments, but that still means that many EP amendments, on many different policy matters, find their way into the final legislative texts.

On the negative side, there are three main points to be made. First, there is not much the EP can do if the Council rejects its opinion. The best it can normally hope for is a conciliation meeting with the Council (not to be confused with a conciliation committee meeting under the co-decision procedure), but such meetings usually achieve little – mainly because the Council has no wish to re-open questions that may put at risk its own, often exhaustively negotiated, agreements. Second, the Council occasionally – though much less than it used to – takes a decision 'in principle' or 'subject to Parliament's opinion', before the opinion has even been delivered. In such circumstances the EP's views, once known, are unlikely to result in the Council having second thoughts. Third, it is possible for the text of proposals to be changed after the EP has issued its opinion. There is some safeguard against the potential implications of this insofar as the ECJ has indicated that the Council should refer a legislative proposal back to the EP if the Council substantially amends the proposal after the EP has issued its opinion. Moreover, there is a Council–EP understanding that the former will not make substantial changes without referring back to the EP. In practice, however, the question of what constitutes a substantial amendment is open to interpretation and references back do not always occur.

* * *

The EESC and the CoR are not so well placed as the EP to influence the control of legislative proposals. As was explained in Chapter 14, a major reason for this is that their formal powers are not as great: while they must be consulted on draft legislation in many policy spheres, consultation is only optional in some. Furthermore, when they are consulted the Council or the Commission may lay down a very tight timetable, can go ahead if no opinion is issued by a specified date, and cannot be frustrated by delays if either the EESC or the CoR wants changes to a text. Other sources of weakness include the part-time capacity of their members, the personal rather than representational nature of much of their memberships, and the perception by many interests and regional bodies that advisory committees and direct forms of lobbying are more effective channels of influence.

Decision-making in the Council

The Council does not wait for the views of the EP, the EESC and the CoR before it begins to examine a proposal. Indeed, governments may begin preparing their positions for the Council, and informal discussions and deliberations may even take place within the Council itself, before the formal referral from the Commission.

The standard procedure in the Council is for the proposal to be referred initially to a working group of national representatives for detailed examination. The representatives have two principal tasks: to ensure that the interests of their country are safeguarded, and to try to reach an agreement on a text. Inevitably these two responsibilities do not always coincide, with the consequence that working group deliberations can be protracted. Progress depends on many factors: the controversiality of the proposal; the extent to which it benefits or damages states differentially; the number of countries, especially large countries, pressing for progress; the enthusiasm and competence of the Presidency; the tactical skills of the national representatives and their capacity to trade disputed points (both of which are dependent on personal ability and the sort of briefs laid down for representatives by their governments); and the flexibility of the Commission in agreeing to change its text.

Once a working group has gone as far as it can with a proposal – which can mean reaching a general agreement, agreeing on most points but with reservations entered by some countries on particular points, or very little agreement at all on the main issues – reference is made upwards to COREPER or, in a few cases a specialised committee – most notably the Special Committee on Agriculture (SCA). At this level, the Permanent Representatives (in COREPER II), their deputies (in COREPER I), or senior officials (as in the SCA) concern themselves not so much with the technical details of a proposal as with its policy and, to some extent, its political, implications. So far as is possible differences left over from the working group are sorted out. When this cannot be done, bases for possible agreement may be identified, and the proposal is then either referred back to the working group for further detailed consideration or forwarded to the ministers for political resolution.

All proposals must be formally approved by the ministers. Those that have been agreed at a lower level of the Council machinery are placed on the ministers' agenda as 'A' points and are normally quickly ratified. Where, however, outstanding problems and differences have to be considered a number of things can happen. One is that the political authority that ministers carry, and the preparatory work undertaken by officials prior to ministerial meetings, may clear the way for an agreed settlement: perhaps reached quickly over lunch, perhaps hammered out in long and frequently adjourned Council sessions. A second and increasingly utilised possibility is that a vote is taken when the treaty article(s) upon which the proposal is based so allows. This does not mean that the traditional preference for proceeding by consensus no longer applies, but it does mean that it is not quite the obstacle it formerly was. A third possibility is that no agreement is reached and a vote is either not possible under the treaties or is not judged to be appropriate.

If no agreement can be reached in the Council – either by consensus or by the use of QMV – the legislative process does not necessarily end in failure. On the contrary, the proposal may well be referred back down the Council machinery for further deliberations, referred back to the Commission with a request for changes to the existing text, or referred to a future meeting in the hope that shifts in position will take place in the meantime and the basis of a solution will be found. If agreement is reached, the decision-making process at EU level ends with the Council's adoption of a text.

The co-decision procedure

The co-decision procedure was created by the Maastricht Treaty. However, it was not named as such in the Treaty, but rather was referred to by reference to the article that set out its provisions – Article 189b. The Amsterdam Treaty similarly did not provide for a formal naming of the procedure, so under the re-numbered TEC it is the Article 251 procedure.

The procedure grew out of and extended the cooperation procedure, which was created by the SEA. The cooperation procedure was established for two main reasons. First, it was seen as being necessary, especially with the SEM programme in mind, to increase the efficiency, and more especially the speed, of decision-making processes. This was achieved by enabling QMV to be used in the Council when decisions were made under the procedure and by laying down time limitations for the institutions to act during the later stages of the procedure. Second, it was a response to concerns about 'the democratic deficit', and more particularly pressures for more powers to be given to the EP. This was achieved by introducing a two-reading stage for legislation, and increasing the EP's leverage – though not to the point of giving it a veto – over the Council at second reading.

Democratic deficit concerns and pressures from the EP were also very much behind the creation of the co-decision procedure in the Maastricht Treaty. While the cooperation procedure had certainly increased the EP's influence, it still did not have the power of veto under the procedure if the Council was resolved to press ahead with a legislative proposal. The co-decision procedure gave the EP this power of veto.

The power was restricted to 15 treaty articles under the Maastricht Treaty, but was extended to 37 by the Amsterdam Treaty. Eleven of the new 22 articles made subject to the procedure by the Amsterdam Treaty were previously subject to cooperation, two to consultation, one to assent and eight were additional articles. As a result of the extensions to the remit of the procedure under the Amsterdam Treaty, most EU legislation apart from agriculture, justice and home affairs, trade, fiscal harmonisation, and EMU issues now became subject to co-decision. As was explained in Chapter 15, the Treaty also made provision for much of the JHA policy area to be later changed from consultation to co-decision. In the case of visa policy this was to be done automatically after five years. In the case of other JHA policies that the Treaty had transferred from pillar three to the EC pillar, the Council, acting by unanimity, could decide to make the change after five years – which it eventually did in 2004 to enable the co-decision procedure to be used from January 2005. The Nice Treaty further extended the reach of the procedure, but only marginally: seven additional treaty articles were embraced, but none of these covered a core policy area (see Chapter 6).

The nature of the co-decision procedure will now be described. It will be seen that it is a one, two, or three stage procedure. Proposals only advance to the third stage if the EP and the Council cannot reach agreement at the first or second stage. It will also be seen that it is a procedure that strongly encourages the EP, the Council, and the Commission to engage in intensive and extensive inter-institutional bargaining. Such bargaining was already developing before the co-decision procedure was established as a result of the creation of the cooperation procedure, and under co-decision it has become an absolutely central part of the legislative process. The nature of the procedure is such that if the three institutions do not liaise and work closely with one another, protracted delays may occur in the early legislative stages and impasses may occur in the later stages. Since, though they may disagree on points of detail, each of the institutions normally wants legislative proposals to become legislative texts, the inevitable requirement is that they spend a lot of time communicating with one another – in forums ranging from a mushrooming number of formal inter-institutional meetings to casual off-the-record conversations between key institutional policy actors. Figure 16.2 provides a diagrammatic representation of the procedure.

First stage

The pre-proposal processes are much as they are under the consultation procedure, though with the Commission taking rather more care as to the EP's likely reactions given its greater powers under co-decision.

After the Commission has published its proposal, of which there are around 70–80 in an average year, it is examined by the EP and the Council through their normal mechanisms: that is, with most of the detailed work being undertaken by the relevant committee in the EP and by working groups and COREPER in the Council.

Prior to the Amsterdam Treaty it was not possible for a text to be adopted at this first legislative stage under co-decision. However, as part of a general attempt to streamline what was widely agreed to be a somewhat cumbersome procedure, the Treaty made provision for a text to be adopted at first reading providing the Council and the EP agree on its contents and that other 'standard' legislative requirements are met – notably the EESC and the CoR are consulted as appropriate, and amendments with which the Commission does not agree receive unanimous support in the Council. (This latter requirement applies to all stages of all legislative procedures, apart from the final – conciliation – stage of the co-decision procedure.)

Since the Amsterdam Treaty change, around 30 per cent of legislative proposals are agreed at first reading stage. Most of these cover technical matters, consolidated texts, or relations with third countries, though a few are also in 'mainstream' policy areas.

If the Council and the EP do not reach agreement at the first reading, the Council, on receipt of the EP's opinion, adopts a common position – with QMV usually, but not quite always, being available for this purpose.

Second stage

At its second reading, the EP can approve, amend, reject, or take no action on a common position. To assist it in its deliberations, the Council must provide the EP with an explanation of the common position and the Commission must also explain its position, including in respect of whether or not it will accept EP amendments.

If the EP approves or takes no action on a common position the Council can, within three months, adopt it as a legislative act (using the same voting rules as applied at the first reading). If the EP rejects the common position by an absolute majority of its members the proposal falls. (Up to the end of 2005 there had been only one instance of this happening: in July 2005 when MEPs, dissatisfied with the responses of the Commission and Council to the EP's first reading amendments, voted overwhelmingly to

Figure 16.2 *The co-decision (Article 251) procedure*

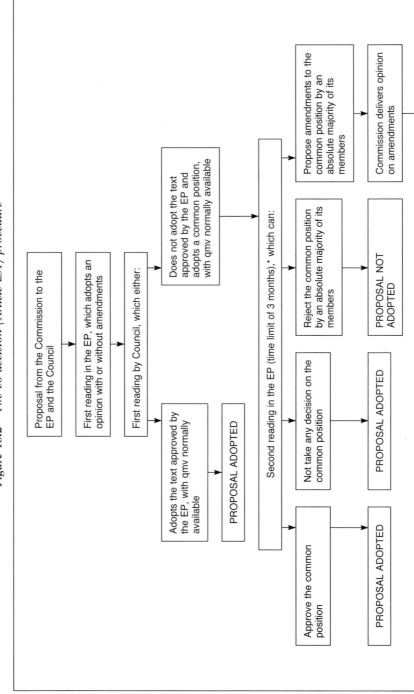

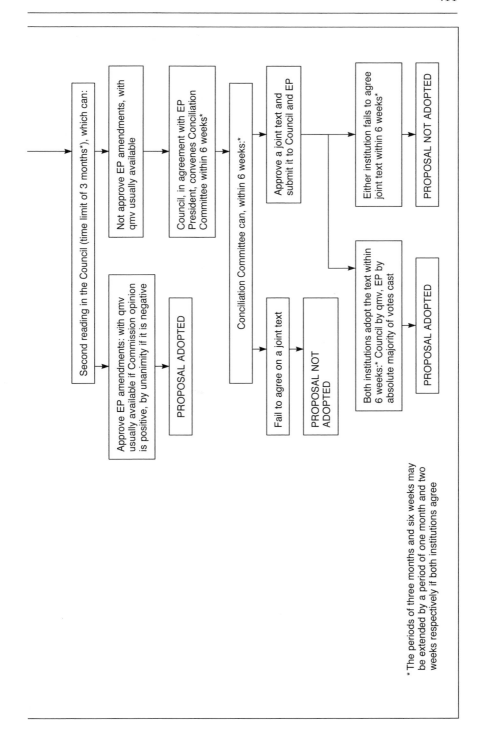

Second reading in the Council (time limit of 3 months*), which can:

Approve EP amendments: with qmv usually available if Commission opinion is positive, by unanimity if it is negative

PROPOSAL ADOPTED

Not approve EP amendments, with qmv usually available

Council, in agreement with EP President, convenes Conciliation Committee within 6 weeks*

Conciliation Committee can, within 6 weeks:*

Fail to agree on a joint text

PROPOSAL NOT ADOPTED

Approve a joint text and submit it to Council and EP

Both institutions adopt the text within 6 weeks:* Council by qmv, EP by absolute majority of votes cast

PROPOSAL ADOPTED

Either institution fails to agree joint text within 6 weeks*

PROPOSAL NOT ADOPTED

*The periods of three months and six weeks may be extended by a period of one month and two weeks respectively if both institutions agree

reject the Council's common position on a software patent law.) And if the EP amends the common position by an absolute majority of its members and the Council at its second reading is unable to accept the text approved by the EP, a third legislative stage occurs.

Prior to the entry into force of the Amsterdam Treaty changes, about 60 per cent of legislative procedures were completed by the end of stage 2. This figure has subsequently risen to about 80 per cent – with, as noted above, around 30 per cent of the completions at first reading and about 50 per cent at second reading (Hayes-Renshaw and Wallace, 2006: 216).

Third stage

This stage opens, within six weeks of the Council failing to approve the text supported by the EP, with the contested proposal being referred to a conciliation committee composed of an equal number of representatives of the Council and the EP. As can be deduced from the figures given above, about 20 per cent of legislative proposals require the convening of a conciliation committee.

In conciliation committees, the Council is normally represented by senior officials from the national Permanent Representations to the EU and the EP is represented by a mixture of semi-permanent conciliation committee members and members of relevant Parliamentary committees. Up to 100 people can be in the room during conciliation meetings, which makes them rather unwieldy and unsuitable for real negotiations.

Accordingly, they are almost invariably preceded by smaller tripartite meetings, known as trialogues, which bring together on a more informal basis key Commission, Council and EP representatives. Normally about 25 people attend trialogues. In around half of the cases that are referred to a conciliation committee a joint text is agreed in a trialogue meeting, leaving the full conciliation committee to approve the text without discussion.

It might be added here that the perceived success of trialogues at conciliation stage has resulted in them also coming to be increasingly used 'upstream' at first and second reading stages since a 1999 EP/Council/Commission Joint Declaration on practical arrangements for co-decision (*Official Journal*, C148/1, 28 May 1999). There now are many more trialogue meetings – about twenty per year – than there are conciliation committee meetings – about ten per year.

If the conciliation committee agrees on a joint text – and it normally has six weeks to do so – the proposal is referred back to the Council and the EP for final adoption within a period of six weeks. In this final vote the Council acts by QMV and the EP by a majority of the votes cast. (When the co-decision procedure was created in the Maastricht Treaty, the Council could attempt to impose the common position in the event of non-agreement in the conciliation committee, but this possibility was removed by the Amsterdam Treaty, with the consequence that failure by the Council and the EP to agree on a text means the proposal cannot be adopted.)

It is unusual for legislative proposals to fail at this third legislative stage: only three did so before the Amsterdam changes were introduced and only two did so from their introduction until the end of the 1999–2004 Parliament (Hayes-Renshaw and Wallace, 2006). The first failure under the post-Amsterdam co-decision procedure occurred in July 2001, when a proposed directive on corporate takeover bids that had been agreed in conciliation committee failed by just one vote to be given Parliament's approval (the vote was tied at 273 in favour, 273 against, and 22 abstentions). A number of factors contributed to the EP vote, one of them being that the German government, after heavy lobbying from German companies, withdrew its support from the Council's common position and encouraged German MEPs to vote against the agreed text – which virtually all of them did.

When a legislative proposal does fail at the conciliation stage, it is common for the Commission to subsequently re-present it in a form that enables it to be approved by the Council and the EP.

The assent procedure

The assent procedure, which was established by the SEA, appears at first sight to be simple in form, being a single stage procedure in which proposed measures that are subject to it have to be approved by both the Council and the EP. The procedure does not allow the EP to make amendments.

However, close inspection reveals the procedure to be rather more complex than initially it appears. This is primarily because although unanimity is normally required in the Council it is not always so, whilst in the EP a majority of those voting suffices for some measures but an absolute majority is required for others. The complexity is extreme in respect of breaches and potential breaches by member states of the fundamental principles on which the EU is founded, as the extracts from Article 7 TEU post-Nice on p. 142 show.

The assent procedure is not used for 'normal' legislation but is reserved for special types of decision. These include international agreements of certain kinds, EU enlargements, the framework of the cohesion funds, and – since the Amsterdam Treaty – serious breaches, or – post-Nice – risks of serious breaches, of the principles on which the EU is based.

The precise rules and powers exercised by the EU institutions under the procedure vary according to the type of decision for which assent is being sought. For example, if the decision involves a matter that has involved the preparation of detailed proposals, as in relation to the cohesion funds, or complex negotiations with third countries, as with association and cooperation agreements, then the Commission is in a very strong position to influence and shape the outcomes, especially if, as is sometimes the case, unanimity is not required in the Council. If, however, unanimity is required and matters of political principle are of crucial importance, for example with regard to citizenship issues and with the devising of a uniform electoral procedure for EP elections, then the Commission is much less favourably placed and the views of the national governments, and of the Council collectively, are crucial.

As for the EP, it might be thought that because under the rules of the procedure it can only pronounce on final proposals and cannot table amendments, it would be confined to a rather limited confirmatory/withholding role. To some extent it indeed is, but not completely, because by having the power to say 'no' to proposals the EP also has the power to indicate to what it would say 'yes'. It has used this power most notably to take action on the human rights records of third countries that have signed association and cooperation agreements with the EU, and to put pressure on the Commission and the Council to amend and change the terms of some of these agreements.

EU Legislation After Adoption

There are considerable variations in what happens to proposals after they are adopted as EU legislation, what use is made of them, and how they are applied. Many of these variations are considered at some length in other chapters – notably in Chapters 9, 13 and 20 – but it will be useful to pull together the more important variations here in order to give an indication of the overall picture.

The need for additional legislation

Much legislation requires the adoption of additional legislative/regulatory measures:

- Much European Parliament and Council and Council legislation needs to be supplemented by implementing legislation so as to fit it to particular circumstances, to adapt it to changing conditions, and to keep it up to date. Indeed, on a quantitative basis the vast bulk of EU legislation is implementing legislation, usually issued in the form of Commission regulations. The ways in which this legislation is issued are examined in Chapter 9, in the section on comitology.

- Some European Parliament and Council and Council legislation needs to be followed up not just with implementing legislation but with further 'policy' legislation. This is most obviously the case in respect of 'framework' legislation, which is legislation that lays down general principles and basic rules that states have to follow in a policy area, but which needs usually to be complemented by more narrowly focused legislation that covers in a reasonably detailed manner issues/initiatives/ actions that fall within the remit of the framework. An example of framework legislation is the Council *Directive of 12 June 1989 on the introduction of measures to encourage improvements in the safety and health of workers at work* (89/391/EEC). That this legislation was intended to be a base and a focus for further legislation is seen in Article 16 of the Directive, which states: 'The Council acting on a proposal from the Commission, based on 118a of the Treaty, shall adopt individual Directives, inter alia, in the areas listed in the Annex.'
- Legislation that also requires further measures, but measures that are very different in character from those just outlined, is the 'new approach' legislation that constitutes an important part of the internal market legal framework. Under the approach, the EU does not try to harmonise all the specifications and technical standards of marketed goods, but confines itself to producing relatively short texts that lay down 'essential requirements', in particular requirements relating to health and safety and to consumer and environmental protection. As long as member states abide by the 'essential requirements' they can have their own national standards which are subject to mutual recognition by other states. However, national standards are generally supposed to be replaced by European standards which are agreed by European standards bodies. The main such bodies are the European Committee for Standardisation (CEN) and the European Committee for Electrotechnical Standardisation (CENELEC). Both CEN and CEN-ELEC include non-EU countries amongst their membership, and both use weighted voting procedures for the taking of final decisions on standards. Once European standards are agreed, EU states must adopt them within a fixed time limit, and within the same time limit must remove all conflicting national standards.

The need to transpose legislation

Regulations and most decisions do not require any measures to be taken at national level before they apply, but directives do not assume legislative force until they have been transposed into national law by the appropriate national authorities. The member states themselves determine which are the appropriate national authorities in their case and by what process the transposition is to be made. As a result, the mechanisms by which directives are transposed at the national level varies between member states according to differing national legislative procedures and differing perceptions of the importance of particular directives. The general pattern, however, is for transposition to be achieved by attaching appropriate administrative measures to existing primary or secondary legislation, introducing new secondary legislation, or adding new clauses to already planned primary legislation. States are given anything from a few weeks to a few years to effect the transposition – the final date being specified in the directive – and are obliged to notify the Commission of the national legislation, regulations, or administrative provisions that have been adopted to give formal effect to each directive.

Some states – including Denmark, Germany, and the UK – have a considerably better record of transposing directives than others. In consequence, there are variations between the states in terms of the speed at which, and extent to which, directives are applied, and variations too in terms of the frequency with which states are subject to Commission and Court action for non/incomplete/incorrect transposition of EU law.

The need to apply legislation

Responsibilities for applying EU legislation are shared between EU authorities and external agencies. The main EU authorities are the various DGs that are responsible for particular policies: Agriculture, Fisheries, Regional Policy, Research and so on. The external agencies include public, private, and semi-private bodies of various sorts, but are mainly the numerous national and subnational authorities whose responsibility it is to collect excise duties, read tachographs, monitor fishing catches, check that agriculture produce for which payments are made is of the quality that is claimed, and so on.

In very broad terms the division of responsibilities between the two levels in terms of day-to-day policy implementation is that the Commission oversees and the national and subnational authorities do most of the 'front line' work. Only in a few policy areas, of which competition is the most important, does the Commission directly implement itself. This means that the Commission needs to move carefully and, because it does not wish to stoke up national resentments, must negotiate and discuss implementing problems with authorities in member states rather than rush to initiate legal proceedings against them.

However, despite – or in some respects because of – the range of agencies that have some responsibility for policy implementation and implementation control, it is evident that all is not well with the application of some EU policies. This is seen most obviously in respect of those policies involving budgetary expenditure, where the Anti-Fraud Office and the Court of Auditors have identified serious implementation failings. The problem is partly one of fraud, which according to some estimates might account for 5–10 per cent of the EU budget. The main problem, however, is administrative irregularities: that is, not deliberate deception but incorrect understanding and application of EU law. The control mechanisms and administrative procedures have been strengthened in recent years, not least in respect of flows of information between the Commission and the national agencies. But the fact is that with the Commission being unable to conduct very much direct surveillance of its own because of limited powers and resources, and with much EU legislation being so complicated that it is barely comprehensible even to the expert, it probably will never be possible to ensure that all laws are fully, properly and uniformly implemented.

Some sense of the difficulties the EU has in attempting to apply its policies in a uniform and efficient manner can be gauged by reference to the sheer volume of overlapping laws that exist in some areas of EU activity and the large number of contracts the EU has to deal with in some funded areas. Regarding the former, towards the end of 2005 there were, for example, approximately 56 directives in force on labelling, 38 on professional qualifications, 22 on approval of types of vehicles, 15 on packaging, and 12 on consumer contracts (*EUobserver*, 26 October 2005). Regarding the latter, development policy makes the point, with over 40 000 development aid projects running at one time.

Characteristic Features of EU Policy Processes

A number of general features are characteristic of EU policy processes. They include variable institutional roles and powers, compromises and linkages, inter-institutional cooperation, difficulties in effecting radical change, tactical manoeuvring, and different speeds.

Variable institutional roles and powers

As was stressed at the beginning of this chapter, there are many EU policy processes. Indeed, the Constitutional Convention identified no less than 28 distinct procedures on the basis of the decision-making rules in the Council, the nature of the EP's involvement, and the consultative status of the EESC and the CoR.

Unsurprisingly in light of this, the roles and powers of the EU's institutions and of the political actors associated with them, vary considerably between policy areas. This point may almost be regarded as a theme of this book, so often is it made – either implicitly or explicitly – in other chapters. Attention here will, therefore, be confined to the making of a few core observations.

Where the Community method applies, which essentially means when legislation is being made under the EC pillar, decision-making processes are based on an institutional triangle of the Commission, the Council, and the EP. The precise powers and influence of each of the institutions under the method can, however, vary considerably according to just what is being proposed and what procedure applies. The Commission, for example, has very considerable control over administrative legislation, but is likely to have to make extensive changes to draft directives that provoke controversy and/or opposition in the other institutions.

But not all policy processes within the EC pillar are based on the Community method and a triangular relationship within which the Commission, the Council and the EP all exercise considerable power and influence and are constantly interacting. Where, for example, a non-legislative and 'softer' policy approach is taken, the EP is normally disadvantaged and policy processes resemble more a Commission–Council tandem. This is the case in respect of those parts of the Lisbon Process that are based on the open method of coordination. And in respect of EMU, processes are different yet again with, most notably, the EP once more on the margins, much of the Council's role undertaken in practice by the Eurogroup of ministers, and key monetary decisions being taken by the European Central Bank (the Eurogroup and the ECB are examined in Chapters 14 and 15).

Beyond the EC pillar, the Council is the main institutional actor. This is because of the intergovernmental nature of pillars two and three, which means not only that the unanimity principle prevails in the Council but also that the Commission does not have exclusive proposing rights and the EP is largely restricted to being consulted and being able to tender advice. In addition to the Council, the European Council sometimes also exercises a significant role in respect of CFSP and non-EC pillar JHA issues (as indeed it does from time to time on some EC policy issues). Another important CFSP institutional actor is the High Representative for the CFSP, who too is part of the Council system and who has become crucial in driving the policy area forward (see Chapter 19).

Compromises and linkages

The diversity of competing interests across the member states, coupled with the nature of the EU's decision-making systems, means that successful policy development is frequently heavily dependent on key actors, especially governments, being prepared to compromise. If they are not so prepared, effective decision-making can be very difficult.

As part of the process wherein compromises provide the basis for agreements, deals are frequently formulated in which different and sometimes seemingly unrelated policy issues are linked. Linking issues together in 'package deals' can open the door to agreements by ensuring that there are prizes for everybody and not, as might be the case when only a specific issue is taken, for just a few.

The European Council has been instrumental in formulating some of the EU's grander compromises and linked deals. For example, the December 2005 summit, which was focused on the 2007–13 financial perspective, pulled together an agreement on a range of matters that had been causing considerable difficulties. They included the overall size of the perspective, a proposed review of CAP expenditure, and national net contributions to and receipts from the EU's budget (see Chapter 17).

One of the reasons the European Council has become involved in the construction of overarching deals of the kind just described is that other EU institutions and actors, and EU processes as a whole, are ill-adapted to the linking of different policy areas and the construction of complex package deals. The GAERC and Ecofin Councils have some potential in this regard, especially the former since its coordinating potential was enhanced by the 2002 Seville summit. However, in practice, these Councils are only occasionally able to 'impose' comprehensive solutions on sectoral Councils. As for the sectoral Councils, they do not normally become involved in discussions beyond their immediate policy concern, and they certainly do not have the means of linking difficulties in their own areas with difficulties being experienced by ministers elsewhere.

Much EU policy-making and decision-making thus tends to be rather compartmentalised, and it is within rather than across policy compartments that the trading, bargaining, linkaging and compromising that are so characteristic of EU processes are mainly to be found. At Council working group level, trading may consist of little more than an official conceding a point on line eight of a proposed legal instrument in exchange for support received on line three. At ministerial level, it may result in what amounts to an exchange of resources as, for example, can happen in the Agriculture Council in respect of decisions on product and income support systems.

A useful case study by Langenberg (2004) of decision-making on the Sixth Framework Programme for Research and Technological Development (covering the years 2000–06) may be cited to illustrate the sort of compromises that frequently have to be made to enable agreements to be reached within policy sectors. Langenberg shows that as decision-making processes have become more complex, not least because of the increasing number of member states and the enhanced part played by the EP in deliberations, then so has it become ever more necessary for political actors, especially the member states, to work collaboratively and flexibly with one another. 'Stubbornly defending an isolated position ... is often costly and ineffective in the end' (p. 67). The Sixth Framework Programme decision-making process, which formally lasted from the Commission's issuing of its proposal in early 2001 to EP and Council agreement in June 2002, was therefore necessarily studded with give-and-take from the outset. Without such an approach by the member states no agreement could have been reached, although of course with it no state was one hundred per cent happy with the outcome. Amongst changes that were made to the draft proposal as it proceeded were the removal of some of the Commission's most controversial proposals (including on a number of ethical matters) and the referral of some disputed points to later decision-making when specific programmes could be considered.

Inter-institutional cooperation

As this and other chapters show, policy processes are frequently marked by disagreements and disputes between the EU institutions. These disagreements and disputes mostly concern policy matters, but they can also concern institutional matters – especially if an institution is seen to abuse its powers in some way.

But the extent of inter-institutional disagreements and disputes should not be exaggerated, for EU policy processes are also characterised by close, even intense, inter-institutional cooperation of many different kinds. Indeed, not only are the processes characterised by such cooperation but they are highly dependent on it. If cooperation was not to be generally forthcoming, policy processes would be much more difficult, protracted and halting than they are. For example, processes would always be highly conflictual if the Commission and Council were seen by MEPs to be over-dismissive of EP amendments to legislative proposals, whilst they would be extremely inefficient if the Commission, the Council, and the EP did not cooperate with each other on legislative planning and timetabling.

Inter-institutional cooperation has grown over the years as the range of policy activities in which the EU is involved has spread, and more especially as policy processes have become more numerous and more complex. The growth has taken many different forms. So, for example, there has been a mushrooming of informal contacts between officials of the Commission, the Council, and the EP, and it is now commonplace for these officials to liaise closely with their counterparts on policy dossiers. At a rather more formal level, there are tripartite meetings – that is, meetings between representatives of the three institutions – of various kinds. For instance, there is a monthly meeting to monitor the progress of proposals identified in the Commission's annual work programme. There is also a monthly meeting of the Presidents of the three institutions during the EP

Strasbourg plenary week to consider relevant issues. At an even more formal level, several inter-institutional agreements have been signed to regularise, clarify and generally facilitate inter-institutional relations. An example of such an inter-institutional agreement is the 2003 European Parliament, Council and Commission *Interinstitutional Agreement on Better Law-Making* which sets out a series of initiatives and procedures to improve the coordination of their legislative activity and thereby improve the quality of EU law making. (*Official Journal*, C321/1, 31 December 2003).

The co-decision procedure illustrates in a specific way the growth in inter-institutional cooperation. Amongst its consequences it has: (1) encouraged the institutions to devise/accept a compromise text at an early legislative stage (an encouragement that is even stronger since the Amsterdam Treaty, which allows a text to be agreed at first reading); (2) increased the need for the Council to be sensitive to the EP's views; (3) made trialogue meetings between representatives of the Commission, the Council and the EP a vital feature of much EU law-making; and (4) promoted (the already extensive) informal exchanges between representatives of institutions to sound out positions, discover what may be possible, and identify areas where progress may be made. In short, the co-decision procedure has given a powerful stimulus to a 'cultural' change in the relations between the Commission, the Council and the EP that has been under way since the creation of the cooperation procedure by the SEA. At the heart of this cultural change is the notion that the three institutions must work closely with one another, and when legislation is being made they must operate on the basis of a genuinely triangular relationship.

Figures on the proportions of final legislation that are 'attributable' to the Commission, Council and EP must always be treated with care. They cannot fully measure the dynamics of inter-institutional dynamics and bargaining and the relative 'success' of institutions in championing their policy preferences. There are problems, for example, in evaluating the relative importance of Council and EP amendments, as there are also in assessing precisely what has happened when drafts are re-worked to accommodate some, but not all, of Council and EP amendments. Given, however, that all three institutions must judge a draft to be at least acceptable for it to be approved by the end of second reading, the fact that 80 per cent of legislation is so approved is testimony to the 'give-and-take' that is characteristic of legislative processes. As for the conciliation stage, the EP estimates that in the 1995–2004 period, 23 per cent of its amendments were accepted as proposed by the Council (they do not have to be accepted by the Commission in conciliation), 60 per cent were accepted following compromise, and 17 per cent were withdrawn (Hayes-Renshaw and Wallace, 2006: 227).

Difficulties in effecting radical change

Partly as a consequence of the prevalence of compromise, much EU policy-making and decision-making displays a deep gradualism and increment-alism. It is just not possible for the Commission, the Council Presidency, a national government, or anyone else, to initiate a clear and comprehensive policy proposal, incorporating bold new plans and significant departures from the *status quo,* and expect it to be accepted without being modified significantly – which usually means being watered down. Ambitious proposals customarily find themselves being smothered with modifications, escape clauses, and long transitional periods before full implementation.

The obstacles to innovation and radical change are powerful, and stem from a range of different national, institutional and ideological positions and perspectives. Moreover, some of the obstacles have increased in force over the years. One reason for this is that the way forward is not as clear as it was in the 1960s, when specific treaty obligations were being honoured and 'negative integration' (that is, the dismantling of barriers and the encouragement of trade liberalisation) was generally accepted as the main policy priority. Another reason is that the EU has become more politically and ideologically heterogeneous. This is partly because of enlargement and partly because the broad Keynesian consensus on social and economic policy that existed in most Western European countries until the mid-1970s no longer exists. Although there has been a measure of consensus on the benefits of moving towards a more liberal model of integration, there have been significant differences between the governments of the member states on the extent to which and the ways in which economic life should be directed and managed. A third reason why some obstacles to change have increased in force is that policy development has inevitably created and attracted interests that have a stake in the *status quo.* This is most obviously the case in agriculture, where Commission proposals for reform invariably produce protests from powerful sectional groups and electorally sensitive governments.

All this is not, however, to suggest that change and reform are not possible. On the contrary, since the mid-1980s there clearly have been major changes and reforms of both an institutional and a policy kind. Additions and amendments to the treaties, the SEM programme, the creation of EMU, the enlargement process, the Lisbon Strategy, and the movement of the CAP away from price support towards income support are but amongst the most obvious examples of ongoing changes and reforms. These changes and reforms have been driven by a range of external and internal factors, and have been guided and shaped by complex interactions between EU and national political forces. The existence of obstacles to change does not, therefore, preclude it occurring, but what it does do is to ensure that since just about any policy innovation is likely to meet with at least some resistance from some quarter(s), bold initiatives are always likely to be weakened/checked/delayed.

Tactical manoeuvring

Tactical manoeuvring and jockeying for position are universal characteristics of policy processes. However they are especially apparent in the EU as a result of its multiplicity of actors and channels and the diversity of its interests.

It is not possible to present a comprehensive catalogue of tactical options here, but a sample of the questions that often have to be considered by just one category of key EU actors – national representatives in the Council – will give a flavour of the intricacies and potential importance of tactical considerations:

- Can a coalition be built to create a positive majority or a negative minority? If so, should it be done via bilateral meetings or in an EU forum?
- Is it necessary to make an intervention for domestic political purposes? (Although most Council business is conducted behind closed doors, much of what goes on, especially in ministerial meetings, is reported back, either through unofficial channels or through formally minuted national objections to Council decisions.)
- Is it possible to disguise opposition to a proposal by 'hiding' behind another state?
- Should concessions be made in a working group or in COREPER to ensure progress, or should they be held back until the ministers meet in the hope that this will be seen as conciliatory and helpful, with the consequence that it might reap dividends on another occasion?
- Where is the balance to be struck between being seen to be tough in defence of the national interest and being seen to be European-minded and ready to compromise? (Often, on a particular issue, some states have a vested interest in an agreement being reached, whilst the interests of others are best served by the absence of any agreement and, as a result, the absence of EU obligations.)

Different speeds

EU processes are often criticised for being cumbersome and slow. Unquestionably they can be, but it should be recognised that they are not always so. Procedures exist that allow certain types of decision to be made as and when necessary. So, for example, annual budgetary decisions are made according to a pre-determined timetable, Commission legislation can be issued almost immediately, and Council regulations and decisions can be pushed through via urgent procedures if the circumstances require it.

As for 'standard' EU legislation, decision-making processes have speeded up over the years, despite the movement from the one reading consultation procedure to the potentially three reading co-decision procedure. Whereas the average time between the transmission and adoption of a directive was around 36 months in the mid-1980s, it is now just less than 18 months where conciliation is not necessary (about 80 per cent of co-decisions), just over 29 per cent where conciliations are necessary (about 20 per cent of co-decisions), and just over 20 months as an overall average (Hayes-Renshaw and Wallace, 2006: 67). There are three main factors determining the speed at which particular proposals are adopted. First, whether or not they command initial general support in the Council and the EP. Second, the legislative procedures that apply and the use that is made of them. Third, whether QMV rules apply in the Council. If QMV is available, ministers are not normally prepared to wait – as they must if unanimity is required – for everyone to agree to all aspects of a proposal. Rather it is customary to give a government that objects strongly to a proposal time to adjust to the majority view – perhaps with encouragement via compromises and derogations – and then proceed, either on the basis of an implicit vote by officials or an explicit vote by ministers.

Voting is used most frequently in established policy areas such as trade, agriculture and the internal market. As Hayes-Renshaw and Wallace (2006: 298) put it, 'it seems to be the case that routinized explicit voting at ministerial level or implicit voting at official level occurs more readily in those policy fields where there is a settled rhythm to EU decision-making; where the default position is that an existing agreement continues rather than that there is no agreement; where national positions are quite clear; and where habits of doing business together are fairly well established'.

Decision-making is thus likely to be at its slowest when a proposal is in a policy area still under construction, when it is highly contested, when it creates difficulties of principle for the Council and/or EP, when it is not subject to the dictates of a timetable, and when QMV cannot be used. In such circumstances the EU's decision-making capacity can be relatively weak and it can be very difficult for progress to be made. There may not even be much of a concerted effort to force progress if it is felt in the Council that one or more minority states genuinely have considerable difficulties with the proposal, for governments tend to be very sensitive to the needs of one another – not least because they are aware that they themselves may be in a minority on a future occasion.

An example of a legislative proposal moving only slowly through the EU's legislative processes is the Commission's proposal of October 2003 for an EP and Council regulation concerning the registration, evaluation, authorisation and restriction of chemicals (REACH), together with the creation of a European Chemicals Agency. Designed to commit firms that manufacture and import chemicals to identify and manage risks, the effect of the directive would be to replace more than 40 existing EU laws and to shift the burden of proof that chemicals on the market are safe from the public to the private sector. At the time of writing the regulation is still far from being adopted – over two years after the proposal was issued! The reason for the delay is the existence of sharply differing views within all three institutions: differences that have been buttressed by intense lobbying from the chemical industry on the one side and environmental and consumer interests on the other. Very broadly speaking, the Council has taken a more 'business-friendly' approach, the Parliament has pressed (not least through the tabling of hundreds of amendments) for a tighter regulatory framework, and the Commission has sought, whilst being closer to the Council's position, to find a consensual way forward.

The Efficiency of EU Policy Processes

The EU lacks a fixed, central, authoritative point where general priorities can be set out and choices between competing options can be made. In other words, there is no single framework or mechanism for determining and implementing an overall policy view in which the requirements of agriculture, industry, the environment and so on are weighed and evaluated in relation to one another and in relation to resources. As is shown below, new policy planning instruments have been adopted in recent years, but no EU institution has the power or resources to set a comprehensive EU policy programme and then ensure it is carried through.

Within individual policy sectors there are, as has been shown, many obstacles to coherent and properly-ordered policy development. For example, resistance by states to what they regard as an excessive transfer of powers to the EU has undoubtedly resulted in many policy spheres being less integrated and comprehensive in their approach than is, from a policy efficiency perspective, ideally desirable. Regional policy, industrial policy, and environmental policy are examples of policy areas where policy responsibilities are shared between the EU and the states, where frequently the activities of the two levels (three if subnational authorities are added) are not always properly coordinated, and sometimes where they are not even mutually complementary.

EU policy thus tends not to be the outcome of a rational model of decision-making. That is to say, policy is not normally made via a procedure in which problems are identified, objectives are set, all possible alternatives for achieving the objectives are carefully evaluated, and the best alternatives are then adopted and proceeded with. Rather, policy tends to evolve in a somewhat messy way, which means that models of decision-making other than the rational model are often more useful for highlighting key features of EU processes. For example:

- *Political interest* models of decision-making draw attention to the interaction of competing interests in the EU, to the variable power exercised by these interests in different decision-making situations, and to the ways in which decisional outcomes are frequently a consequence of bargaining and compromise between interests.
- *Policy network* are useful in focusing on the ways in which EU decision-makers and outside interests come together on an at least semi-regular basis for such purposes as information sharing, reconciling differences, and making decisions. As is shown in Chapter 21, policy networks can vary considerably in character, with some, for example, being tight in structure and making provision for frequent intra-network communications, whilst others are loose in structure and provide for only occasional communications.
- *Political elite* models highlight the considerable concentrations of power, at official and political levels, that exist across the EU's decision-making processes. Concentration is especially marked in areas such as monetary policy and foreign policy, where processes are more secret and closed than they are in regional or agriculture policy for example. Political elite models also draw attention to the paucity of mechanisms available to EU citizens to ensure direct accountability on the part of EU decision-makers. The fact is that decision-making in the EU is not so tied to or restricted by elections and electoral outcomes as is decision-making at the national level.
- *Institutional* models of decision-making emphasise how the rules and understandings via which EU decisions are made do much to shape the nature of the decisions themselves. That is, the institutional structures and processes are not neutral. So, for example, when a wide range of national, regional and sectional interests are entitled to be consulted before policy can be developed and decisions can only be made by unanimity in the Council, progress is frequently slow and the outcome is often little more than the lowest common denominator. When, on the other hand, the process is more streamlined – and permits, for example, QMV in the Council of Ministers or the Commission to disburse funds directly – then decision-making is likely to be more decisive and

decisions themselves perhaps more adventurous and coherent. (On models and conceptualisations of EU policy processes, see also Chapter 21.)

Having identified weaknesses in the quality of EU policy processes, some re-balancing is now in order lest the impression be given of a system that is wholly and uniquely disordered and undemocratic. There are three main points to be made.

The first point is that, in many respects, EU policy processes are not so different from national processes. This is not, of course, to say that important differences do not exist. The international nature of the EU, for example, makes for more diverse and more powerful opposition to its policy initiatives than customarily exists within states. It is also the case that EU decision-makers are less directly accountable than national decision-makers to those who are subject to their decisions. Another difference is that the EU's policy structures are more complex, and in some respects collectively weaker, than their national counterparts.

But recognition of these and other differences should not obscure similarities of type – if not perhaps intensity – between EU and national processes: political interest, policy networks, political elite, institutional and other models of decision-making can, after all, throw light on features of the latter as well as the former. For example, in all member states, especially those with coalition governments (which is the norm in most EU states), political accommodation is an everyday occurrence and policy trimming is common. Furthermore, in countries like Germany and Belgium where there is a considerable geographical decentralisation of power, tensions between levels of government over who does what and who pays for what are by no means unusual. In short, many of the EU's policy-making 'problems' – such as the prevalence of incrementalism and of policy slippages – are by no means absent in national political systems.

The second point is that not all EU policy processes consist of cobbling together deals that can satisfy the current complexion of political forces. This certainly is a crucially important feature, but it does not amount to the complete picture. In recent years greater efforts have been made to initiate rather than just react, to look to the medium term rather than just the short term, and to pull at least some of the pieces together into coordinated programmes.

At the level of overarching policy coordination, progress towards more forward-looking and coordinated policy planning has, it must be said, been only modest, but it is developing. For example, as is shown in Chapter 17, the financial perspectives that have framed budgetary policy since 1988 have been based on Commission documents that have sought to deal with at least some central priorities on a multi-annual basis.

The Prodi and Barroso Commissions have further sought to strengthen medium-term planning by issuing at the beginning of their terms of office documents setting out policy priorities. Designed to provide guidelines for their five-year terms, the documents have been followed up by the issuing of annual policy strategies setting out political priorities for the following year. These in turn have fed into the annual legislative work programmes, which are now presented in November rather than, as before, at the beginning of the year in which they are to apply.

Of course, effective EU planning requires that Commission plans and priorities be tied in with those of the other main institutions. This has been something of a problem, with both the Council and the EP being protective of their right to determine their own priorities – as witnessed, for example, by Council Presidencies setting out the goals for their six months tenure, and by both the Council and the EP specifying their political objectives at the beginning of the annual budgetary process (see Chapter 17). Nonetheless, collaboration on planning between the institutions is improving, with a variety of consultative and information-exchange mechanisms now in place designed to try and ensure that the three institutions work in the same policy direction.

New medium-term planning mechanisms agreed at the June 2002 Seville European Council meeting are also improving the EU's ability to look beyond the immediate and the pressing. The European Council now adopts three-year multi-annual strategic programmes that are drafted by the six member states that occupy the Presidency over the period. These programmes inform annual operational programmes of Council activities that are proposed to the GAERC Council by the two Presidencies for each year working in collaboration with the Commission. Each Presidency then draws on these operational programmes when planning its work programme.

Coordinated forward thinking and planning has also improved over the years in particular policy sectors, with the existence of medium- to long-term policy objectives and multi-annual programmes. These are drawn up by the Commission, usually in consultation with appropriate consultative committees and committees of experts, and have to be approved by the Council to be given effect. They appear in various forms. For example: Green Papers, such as the 2005 Green Paper *Doing More With Less: Green Paper on Energy Efficiency* (European Commission, 2005d); communications, such as the 2005 communication *i2010–A European Information Society for Growth and Employment,* which set out a strategy for modernising and deploying policy instruments to stimulate the development of the digital economy (European Commission, 2005c); framework and legislation programmes, such as the multi-annual programmes for the environment and for research and technological development (see Chapter 15) ; and action programmes.

It is worth saying a little about action programmes to illustrate how, within specified fields of activity, a measure of coordinated development over a planned medium-term period is possible. Action programmes vary in nature, from the broad and general to the highly specific. Broad and general programmes typically include measures to improve the monitoring and supervision of existing legislation, ideas for new legislation, running a pilot scheme, and spending programmes. Amongst the fields of activity where such action programmes exist are equal opportunities, public health, and access to educational training programmes. In contrast, specific action programmes are more specialised in their areas of concern and tighter in their provisions. Examples are the social research programmes on such matters as safety in coalmines and industrial hygiene, which are given appropriations for a given period and provide up to about 60 per cent of the cost of approved research projects.

The third and final 're-balancing' point to be made about EU policy processes is that critical judgements of them ought to be placed in the context of the very considerable degree of policy cooperation and integration that has been achieved at the EU level. There is no comparable international development where states have voluntarily transferred so many policy responsibilities to a collective organisation of states, and in so doing have surrendered so much of their national sovereignty. It is hardly surprising, given the enormity of the exercise, that pressures and desires for cooperation and integration should so often be challenged, and held in check, by caution, uncertainty, conflict and competition.

Chapter 17

The Budget

The Budget in Context

Despite the considerable attention it has received over the years, and despite the political tensions it has sometimes generated, the size of the EU's budget is relatively small. In 2006 it totalled €111.97 billion in payment appropriations, which represented only 1.01 per cent of the total Gross National Income (GNI) of the member states and about 2.5 per cent of their total public expenditure.

The reason why the budget is so small is that most of the policy sectors that make up the bulk of public expenditure – defence, education, health, social welfare and so on – remain primarily the responsibility of the member states. Many of the EU's policy activities, such as those concerned with the regulation of the market, involve little in the way of operational costs. When EU policies do involve significant operational costs, for example where they impose an obligation to introduce measures to conform with EU environmental legislation, the financial impact usually falls not on the EU budget but on private firms and public authorities in the member states.

The modesty of the size of EU budget should therefore be borne in mind when assessing the budget's financial and policy impact. The budget does from time to time, especially when financial perspectives are being considered and negotiated, become the subject of very great political controversy and media focus. But the fact is that in overall economic terms the impact of the budget is slight. It cannot and does not, serve to effect a major transfer of financial resources from national exchequers to the EU level or *vice versa*. It does not move great amounts of money around and across the EU on distributive and redistributive bases. And, as Begg (2005: 10) observes, 'compared with established federations in which the federal level has substantial resources and plays an important part in macroeconomic policy, the *economic* significance of the EU budget is minor' (italics in original).

That all said, however, the budget certainly merits examination. One reason why it does so is that it generates very considerable political heat and attention. A second reason is that whilst the size and economic impact of the budget are small, they are far from being wholly negligible. A third reason is that an understanding of the nature of the debates and discussions surrounding the EU's budget is important to an understanding of the nature of the EU's policy portfolio. And a fourth reason is that a theme of this book, and especially of Part 3, is the highly variegated nature of EU policy and decision-making processes. Budgetary processes illustrate this variegation, with the existence both of special processes and special allocations of powers between process actors.

The Financial Perspectives

In the early 1980s the EC was plagued by budgetary crises. There were three main reasons for this. First, there were increasing financial obligations, particularly in respect of the Common Agricultural Policy (CAP) which at that time accounted for around 70 per cent of total budgetary expenditure. Second, budgetary resources – which consisted of customs duties, agricultural levies, and a proportion of Value Added Tax (VAT) up to a one per cent ceiling – could not generate enough income to meet the financial obligations. The member states could have resolved this problem by altering the resources base, but some states – the UK in particular – were reluctant to do this. Third, the UK government under Mrs Thatcher was campaigning vigorously to reduce what it saw to be excessive UK net budgetary contributions.

The crises of the early 1980s eventually led to the conclusion of a complicated deal at the 1984 Fontainebleau European Council. Key elements of the deal included new rules on budgetary discipline, a formula for reducing UK budgetary contributions, and an expansion of resources through the setting of a new 1.4 per cent ceiling for VAT from 1986. The Fontainebleau agreement was, however, too little too late, in that no sooner had the 1.4 per cent ceiling been introduced in 1986 than it was exhausted and the Commission was forced to open a new campaign for a further expansion of the revenue base.

That campaign culminated in the 1988 Brussels summit which brought a further, and compared with Fontainebleau much more radical, reform designed to deal with the EC's recurring budgetary difficulties. The Brussels reform was operationalised in an *Interinstitutional Agreement on Budgetary Discipline and Improvement of the Budgetary Procedure,* which was signed by the Presidents of the Council of Ministers, the Commission, and the European Parliament (European Communities, 1987). The importance of the Interinstitutional Agreement was that it contained a formal commitment by all three institutions to the framework of a financial perspective for the years 1988–92. Included in the perspective were: a phased reduction in CAP expenditure, a continuation of special abatement arrangements for the UK, a much tighter framework for ensuring budgetary discipline, and a significant expansion of resources through the creation of a new budgetary resource based on the Gross National Product (GNP) of each state. An increase in resources was thus linked to an expanding spending programme, subject to the limitation that the total amount of resources for any one year could not exceed specified percentages of the total GNP of the Community for the year in question: the perspective started with 1.15 per cent for 1988 and rose to 1.20 per cent for 1992.

In 1992 the Commission put forward proposals for a new financial perspective under the title *From the Single Act to Maastricht and Beyond: the Means to Match Our Ambitions* (European Commission, 1992). After negotiations between the member states in the Council of Ministers and the European Council, which took up much of 1992, a financial perspective for the years 1993–9 was agreed at the December 1992 Edinburgh summit. The core elements of this new financial perspective, which were incorporated in 1993 into another inter-institutional agreement, were based on the principles of the 1988 financial perspective: further stabilisation of agricultural expenditure and a further increase in funding for structural operations; a specified annual ceiling for categories of expenditure; an increase in resources, up to a ceiling of 1.27 per cent of GNP in 1999; continuation of the existing four revenue resources, though with some modifications to make them weigh less heavily on the poorer states; continuing tight budgetary discipline; and no changes in the abatement arrangements for the UK.

In 1997–8, as part of its *Agenda 2000* package of reforms, the Commission put forward proposals for a third financial perspective covering the period 2000–6 (European Commission, 1997a). As with the Commission's proposals for the 1988–92 and 1993–9 financial perspectives, the *Agenda 2000* proposals were scrutinised thoroughly by the member states and prompted extensive political debate and controversy. That there should be controversy in such circumstances is almost inevitable since not only is the EU budget – like all budgets – an expression of political priorities, but it also has significant implications for national exchequers. Amongst the concerns of national governments were the following: the governments of net contributor states, especially Germany, wanted the size of their contributions reduced; the UK government wanted to retain the

UK abatement; and the governments of states benefiting from spending programmes – such as France from the CAP and Spain from the structural funds – were resistant to these programmes being reduced, even if the released funds were to be directed to the 'good cause' of assisting Central and Eastern European countries (CEECs) to prepare for EU membership. (The structural funds are now normally called the cohesion funds.)

After numerous rounds of negotiations between the member states – channelled through many formations of the Council, but primarily Foreign, Ecofin, and Agriculture Ministers – the Heads of Government agreed on a seven-year financial perspective for the years 2000–6 at the special Berlin summit in March 1999. The EP endorsed the perspective in May following Council agreement to make modest increases to internal policy expenditure. A new inter-institutional agreement was then concluded between the Council, Commission and EP (see Table 16.1 on p. 369 of the fifth edition of this book). The main features of this third financial perspective were as follows: overall expenditure was stabilised, with an anticipation that over the period of the financial perspective total expenditure would increase approximately in proportion to economic growth; the 1.27 per cent ceiling on own resources was maintained, even though it was assumed enlargement would occur during the lifetime of the financial perspective; the revenue base was modified, with the VAT element being reduced and the GNP element being increased – the main aim of this modification being to make national funding of the budget less regressive; CAP expenditure was increased marginally; Structural Fund expenditure was decreased marginally, but there was to be a greater concentration of structural spending on the areas of greatest need; over €3 billion was made available annually for pre-accession aid to CEECs, with more being available when CEECs became EU members; and the UK abatement was virtually unchanged.

The processes leading to the adoption of the EU's fourth financial perspective, covering the years 2007–13, were always likely to be even more heated than those which led to the Berlin agreement on the 1999–2006 perspective. One reason for this was that many national positions would inevitably be re-activated, most particularly with net contributors to the budget wanting their contributions cut and net beneficiaries wanting their benefits protected. A second reason was that the states that joined the EU in May 2004 would be party to the negotiations, and since most of these believed they had been treated ungenerously under the terms of the 1999–2006 financial perspective they would be looking for a considerable improvement in their positions. A third reason was that some states, most notably the UK, believed that the 2007–13 financial perspective should tackle a major problem that previous financial perspectives had left largely unresolved – the budgetary imbalance caused by the fact that the CAP accounted for around 45 per cent of budgetary expenditure. And a fourth reason was that 24 of the 25 member states wanted to remove, or at least greatly reduce the size of, the UK abatement, which was seen as being no longer justified given the accession in 2004 of so many poorer states and given too the increased prosperity of the UK since the principle of the abatement had been established in 1984.

The deliberation and negotiation process 'should' have started with the publication of proposals from the Commission. However, before the proposals were issued there were two 'pre-emptive strikes'. The first of these occurred in October 2002, when France and Germany were success-ful in engineering an agreement in the European Council to the effect that the amount of money spent on the CAP (which is not the same as the proportion of the budget assigned to the CAP) would be virtually frozen during the period of the new financial perspective. This agreement subsequently greatly limited the Commission's room for manoeuvre when devising its proposals for the financial perspective. (See Chapter 18 for further information on the CAP element of the October 2002 agreement.) The second pre-emptive strike occurred in December 2003 when the leaders of the six net contributor states to the budget – Austria, France, Germany, the Netherlands, Sweden, and the UK – sent a joint letter to the President of the Commission, Romano Prodi. In their letter, the leaders urged that a ceiling of one per cent of EU GNI should be set on EU commitments' expenditure in the financial perspective. This one per cent figure was lower than the expenditure ceiling of the 1999–2006 financial perspective, but was close to current 'real' expenditure which, because of under-spending, was just under one per cent.

The Commission's proposals were issued in February 2004 in the form of a communication to the Council and the EP under the title *Building Our Common Future: Policy Challenges and Budgetary Measures of the Enlarged Union 2007–2013* (European Commission, 2004). The main features of the proposals were:

- The total size of the budget to increase by around 35 per cent, with most of this being attributable to the incorporation of new member states.
- The ceiling on total expenditure to be 1.14 per cent for payments and 1.24 per cent for commitments.
- The titles of expenditure headings to be changed to reflect policy developments and priorities. In the 1999–2006 perspective there were seven headings: agriculture, structural operations, internal policies, external action, administration, reserves, and pre-accession aid. In the new perspective six headings were proposed: sustainable growth (mainly cohesion and Lisbon-related policies); preservation and management of natural resources (essentially the CAP); citizenship, freedom, security and

justice; the EU as a global partner; administration, and – for three years only – compensations.

- Spending on market-related CAP measures to stay fairly flat in money terms in line with the decision taken at the October 2002 summit, but to gradually decrease as a proportion of the budget – to an average of 29 per cent over the period of the financial perspective and to 26 per cent in 2013.
- Increased spending under the other headings apart from administration to be priorities for the financial perspective. Spending on sustainable growth to increase by 28 per cent over the period, on European citizenship by 122 per cent, and on the EU as a global partner by 38 per cent.
- The UK abatement problem (which was referred to only indirectly) to be tackled within the framework of the creation of a generalised corrective mechanism. The mechanism would be designed to ensure that no state made excessive net contributions to the budget.

Over the following months the Commission's proposals were considered by policy actors in the member states and at EU level. Numerous suggestions/demands for changes were put forward, mostly along predictable lines. The general intention was to try and reach an overall settlement at the June 2005 European Council meeting and to this end the Luxembourg Presidency liaised closely with the member states to try to find a compromise that would be acceptable. In the event, however, this proved not to be possible, with five member states – Denmark, Germany, the Netherlands, Sweden, and (most strongly) the UK – rejecting the Presidency's final draft. The key features of the draft were: the spending ceiling on commitments to be capped at 1.06 per cent of EU GNI; there to be deliberations in 2010 on ways to cut CAP expenditure, but any agreed reforms not to come into effect during the lifetime of the financial perspective; and the UK rebate to be frozen in 2007 and to be set on a downward path.

The failure to reach an agreement in June 2005 was not a disaster. After all, the financial perspective was not scheduled to come into force for another eighteen months. But the failure did greatly increase the pressures on the succeeding UK Presidency to find an acceptable compromise, not least since a political deal on the perspective would need to be followed by implementing legislation and because also CEECs in particular were pressing for an agreement so they could plan spending programmes. But the UK government was in a difficult position because, rather like the German government under the German Presidency in the first half of 1999, whilst it was anxious to be seen to have run a successful Presidency and a deal on the financial perspective would be very helpful in that regard, its own national position was the one that was most detached from the positions of other states: it wanted the overall size of the budget to be as near as possible to one per cent of EU GNI, it wanted to retain the UK abatement, and it wanted a review of CAP spending to be both conducted and implemented during the course of the perspective.

As part of its strategy to try and find an agreement, the UK Presidency decided not to issue revised proposals until a matter of days before the end-of-Presidency summit in December 2005. This approach, it reasoned, would reduce oppositional grandstanding and the premature adopting of hard-line oppositional stances. In that an agreement was indeed duly reached at the December 2005 summit it is a strategy that may be said to have worked, assisted by other facilitating factors – most notably the willingness of the leaders to compromise.

Table 17.1 sets out an overview of the ceilings on expenditure contained in the agreed 2007–13 financial perspective, using the official expenditure headings. Under what are perhaps more recognisable headings, the percentages assigned to the appropriations for commitments are as follows:

– Farm and rural support	42.8
– Cohesion aid	35.4
– Competitiveness	8.3
– Foreign policy	5.8
– Administration	5.8
– Justice and security	1.2
– Other	0.7

These percentages are not much different from those applying in recent EU annual budgets.

As can be seen in Table 17.1, the figure for commitment appropriations is 1.045 per cent of EU GNI, which is much closer to the 1.0 per cent urged by 'the contributor six' in December 2003 than it is to the 1.24 per cent originally proposed by the Commission and supported by many beneficiary states. But it is a compromise figure nonetheless. All other aspects of the agreement also involved compromise. One compromise included new arrangements to calculate net contributions, which will have the effect of making for greater parity between the richer states. As part of this, the UK rebate is to be reduced (by about one-fifth), but not eliminated – as the French government in particular wanted. Another compromise involved an agreement to launch in 2008 a review by the Commission into budgetary expenditure, including on the CAP. The proposal for a review had been resisted by the French, but they gave way when the British agreed not to include a firm commitment that the outcome of the review would necessarily begin to be implemented during the lifetime of the financial perspective.

✳   ✳   ✳

Table 17.1   *Financial perspective 2007–13**

Commitments and Appropriations	2007	2008	2009	2010	2011	2012	2013	Total 2007–2013
1. Sustainable growth	51 090	52 148	53 330	54 001	54 945	56 384	57 841	379 739
1a Competitiveness for growth and employment	8 250	8 860	9 510	10 200	10 950	11 750	12 600	72 120
1b Cohesion for growth and employment	42 840	43 288	43 820	43 801	43 995	44 634	45 241	307 619
2. Preservation and management of natural resources	54 972	54 308	53 652	53 021	52 386	51 761	51 145	371 244
of which: market related expenditure and direct payments	43 120	42 697	42 279	41 864	41 453	41 047	40 645	293 105
3. Citizenship, freedom, security and justice	1 120	1 210	1 310	1 430	1 570	1 720	1 910	10 270
3a Freedom, security and justice	600	690	790	910	1 050	1 200	1 390	6 630
3b Citizenship	520	520	520	520	520	520	520	3 640
4. EU as a global player	6 280	6 550	6 830	7 120	7 420	7 740	8 070	50 010
5. Administration	6 720	6 900	7 050	7 180	7 320	7 450	7 680	50 300
6. Compensations	419	191	190					800
Total appropriations for commitments	120 601	121 307	122 362	122 752	123 641	125 055	126 646	862 363
as a percentage of GNI	1.10%	1.08%	1.06%	1.04%	1.03%	1.02%	1.00%	1.045%
Total appropriations for payments	116 650	119 535	111 830	118 080	115 595	119 070	118 620	819 380
as a percentage of GNI	1.06%	1.06%	0.97%	1.00%	0.96%	0.97%	0.94%	0.99%
Margin available	0.18%	0.18%	0.27%	0.24%	0.28%	0.27%	0.30%	0.25%
Own resources ceiling as a percentage of GNI	1.24%	1.24%	1.24%	1.24%	1.24%	1.24%	1.24%	1.24%

* 2004 prices, EUR billion.
Source: reproduced from Council of the European Union (2005).

As has just been shown, financial perspectives generate much political heat and controversy. In 2005 the two end-of-Presidency European Council meetings, and much of the EU-related political debate before and after them, were dominated by attempts to find an agreement between the member states on the 2006–13 financial perspective. But if the attention given to financial perspectives is perhaps excessive, it should be recognised that they do serve at least three useful purposes. First, by acting as medium-term budgetary planning instruments they allow the EU and the member states to use EU funds in more measured and ordered ways than otherwise would be possible. Second, by specifying ceilings on all categories of EU expenditure they impose budgetary discipline. Third, by greatly restricting what can be done within the annual budgetary process, they help to ensure that although there may be disagreement between the participants in that process there are not full scale political fall-outs every year.

The Composition of the Budget

Revenue

Following a decision by the member states in 1970, the funding of the budget was changed between 1970 and 1975 from a system based on national contributions to one based on 'own resources'. A major reason for introducing this change was that it would provide the Community with greater financial independence. The member states would determine the upper limit of the own resources, but the resources themselves would belong to the Community and not the states.

Since the creation of the GNP-based resource in 1988, the own resources have consisted of the following.

- *Common Customs Tariff duties and other duties,* which are collected in respect of trade with non-member countries.
- *Agricultural levies, premiums and other duties,* which are collected in respect of trade with non-member countries within the framework of the CAP. These differ from customs duties in that they are not fixed import taxes, but are fluctuating charges designed to have the effect of raising import prices to EU levels. There are also certain internal agricultural levies and duties, notably connected with the framework of the common organisation of the market in sugar.
- *The application of a uniform percentage rate to the VAT assessment base,* which is determined in a standardised manner for member states. In order to protect countries whose VAT base was high, under the 1988–92 financial perspective the assessment base for VAT could not exceed 55 per cent of GNP at market prices. To reduce further the

regressive aspect of this element of budgetary resources, it was decided at the 1992 Edinburgh summit to lower the uniform rate of VAT from 1.4 per cent to 1 per cent between 1995 and 1999, and to cut the assessment base for the VAT resource from 55 per cent to 50 per cent of GNP. At the 1999 Berlin summit it was decided to cut the 1 per cent rate to 0.75 per cent from 2002 and to 0.5 per cent from 2004. (It should be emphasised that these VAT rules still allow countries some variation in their national VAT rates.)

- *The application of a rate to a base representing the sum of member states' GNI at market prices.* The rate is determined under the budgetary procedure in the light of the total of all other revenue and the total expenditure agreed. Since this resource is very much like a national contribution, it has been suggested by some observers that it does not have quite the own resource character of the other resources. Key features of this resource are that it introduces into the EU's revenue system a link with ability to pay, and it can be easily adjusted to bring budgetary revenue into balance with budgetary expenditure. The agreements at the Edinburgh and Berlin summits to reduce the VAT component of budgetary resources have meant this GNI component has become the EU's most important income resource.

Precisely what proportion of total budgetary revenue comes from each resource is naturally determined primarily by the rules governing the resources. As has just been shown, these rules change periodically. However, the proportions also vary a little from year to year according to such factors as trade flows, world agricultural prices and output, and national growth rates. At the time of writing, the projected proportions from the four resources for 2006 are as follows: customs duties – 11.5 per cent; agricultural and sugar levies – 1.2 per cent; VAT – 14.2 per cent; GNI resource – 72.0 per cent; plus miscellaneous – 1.2 per cent (European Commission, 2006: 24).

As regards the member states and budgetary resources, the larger states – Germany, France, Italy, and the UK – are naturally the largest gross contributors to the revenue pool. However, France, Italy and the UK are not so large net contributors: France because it is a major beneficiary of the CAP; Italy because it benefits significantly from the CAP and the Structural Funds; and the UK because of the abatement on its contributions. Germany is by far the largest net contributor, followed by, in relative terms (as a percentage of GNP), the Netherlands, the UK, Sweden, and Austria.

Expenditure

The EU makes a distinction between expenditure that is a direct result of treaty application or acts adopted on the basis of the treaties – called compulsory (or obligatory) expenditure – and that which is not – called non-compulsory (or non-obligatory) expenditure. In recent years compulsory expenditure has accounted for around 45 per cent of the total budget and non-compulsory expenditure for around 55 per cent.

The most striking feature of EU expenditure is that virtually all compulsory expenditure is used for the CAP. Two main factors account for the very strong position of agriculture in the budget. First, agriculture has seen a greater transfer of financial responsibility from national budgets to the EU budget than any other major policy area. Second, as will be explained in Chapter 18, agriculture is heavily subsidised – formerly through price support, now more through direct income support.

On a rational and commonsense basis this can hardly be justified. Agriculture appears to be proportionately overfunded, whilst policy areas drawing on non-compulsory expenditure – such as regional policy, research policy and energy policy – appear to be underfunded. Certainly the relatively modest sums available in all categories other than the CAP means that the EU's financial ability to tackle such pressing problems as under-investment, technological change, unemployment, and resource imbalances is limited. However, budgetary expenditure, like budgetary income, is not determined by 'objective' criteria but by political interplay. And in that interplay there are many powerful forces that wish to maintain high levels of spending on agriculture: governments anxious to receive farmers' votes do not normally wish to upset this often volatile section of the electorate; net beneficiaries of the CAP (both states and sectional interests) are not inclined voluntarily to surrender their gains; and, as will be shown in Chapter 18, agriculture is regarded by many decision-makers as 'special'.

However, notwithstanding these obstacles to reform, pressures to 're-balance' budgetary expenditure have been considerable since the mid- to late 1980s. Attention has focused primarily on the imbalance between CAP and non-CAP spending, on the levels and types of assistance that should be assigned to assisting less prosperous states and regions, and on the financial support to be given to new policy needs and initiatives. Reflecting the outcomes of deliberations and negotiations on these questions, measures designed to bring about a partial shift in the EU's pattern of expenditure have been important features of financial perspectives. The most important outcome of the measures has been a reduction in expenditure on the CAP from around 70 per cent in the late 1980s, to around 45 per cent since the mid-1990s, to a projected 33 per cent by the end of the 2007–13 financial perspective.

As for current levels of expenditure, the 2006 budget of €111.97 billion (payment appropriations) is grouped by the Commission under the following headings:

● *Natural resources*, of which CAP support measures account for 36 per cent of the total budget and rural development and environment account for 11 per cent. Most CAP funding was formerly used for price guarantee purposes but following reforms to the CAP since the early 1990s it is now used mainly for direct income support to farmers (see Chapter 18).

● *Competitiveness and cohesion* accounts for 39 per cent of the budget. Most of this is directed to cohesion, especially the two main component part of the EU's cohesion operations in the form of the European Regional Development Fund (ERDF) and the European Social Fund (ESF) (see Chapter 15). The less prosperous member states are the main beneficiaries of the EU's cohesion policies.

● *The EU as a global partner.* Accounting for 7 per cent of the EU's budget, this funding allocation is used to support a wide range of external activities, from peacekeeping operations to humanitarian aid. Geographically, it is particularly concentrated on the Balkans, the Mediterranean area, and former Soviet states.

● *Citizenship, freedom, security and justice.* Making up just one per cent of the budget, funding under this heading mainly covers matters relating to the protection of external borders and the upholding of law within the borders.

● *Other expenditure.* This accounts for 6 per cent of the budget and is made up primarily of expenditure on administration.

Budgetary Decision-Making

As has been shown, financial perspectives lay down ceilings on EU financial resources and expenditure over a number of years. As such, they provide the financial frameworks in which the EU's annual budgets are made. Decisions about the size and nature of the EU's budget are thus made via two different processes: those that lead to the financial perspectives and those that produce the EU's annual budgets.

Financial perspectives

An account of the main stages and issues involved in the making of the 2007–13 financial perspectives was given above. Attention here, therefore, will be confined to the identification of four general points about financial perspective decision-making processes.

The first point to be made is that the processes are protracted. If they are measured just from the Commission's issuing of its proposals to adoption by the European Council, each of the last two financial perspectives – those of 1999–2006 and 2007–13 – have taken almost two years to resolve.

If, however, preparation by the Commission is added on to the beginning of the process and approval by the EP and the adoption of necessary implementing legislation is added on to the end, then the time period is at least doubled.

The second point is that the processes are highly politicised and contentious – a key reason, of course, why they are protracted. Differences between the states take different forms, reflecting the nature of national economic needs and political preferences, but most boil down to each state wanting to contribute as little as possible to, and extract as much as possible from, the budget. The differences that exist are sharpened by the fact that because decisional outcomes are expressed in numerical figures, it is quite clear who 'the winners' and 'the losers' are when decisions are made – which is not generally so much the case when, for example, internal market or environmental decisions are being made.

The third point is that all final decisions are taken at the highest political level on an intergovernmental basis. That is to say, they are taken by the European Council acting by unanimity. Two factors combine to explain this. One is the importance of the decisions being made: as was shown in Chapter 11, there are now few major EU decisions that are not either made by or at least approved by the national leaders. The other factor is that financial perspectives have no treaty base, so there are no financial perspective decision-making processes specifying who should be taking final decisions.

The overarching nature of matters covered by financial perspective decisions coupled with the fact that final decisions are taken by the European Council, also means that at Council level most of the work is channelled through the General Affairs Council rather than the Ecofin Council.

The fourth point is that, unlike in the annual budgetary procedure where it is the co-decision-maker with the Council, the EP has no formal powers and in practice has exercised little influence over financial perspectives. This is because, as noted above, financial perspectives have no treaty base and are, essentially, political agreements between the governments of the member states. The EP is not a direct participant in the main decision-making processes.

This notwithstanding, the EP does what it can to influence the content of financial perspectives. It does so primarily by attempting to engage in meaningful discussions with the Commission and the Council and indicating its preferences in formal plenary votes, both before and after the European Council takes a decision. So, in respect of the 2007–13 financial perspective, as the decision-making process got under way the EP established a special temporary committee to help establish its position. On the basis of the committee's report the EP voted in June 2004 for a financial perspective of €975 billion in commitments and €883 billion in payments – 1.18 per cent and 1.07 per cent respectively of EU GNI. When certain funds that the EP opted not to include in the financial perspective are factored in, the EP's position was very close to the Commission's original position. That, however, did not help it much, with its proposals for payments being a full €64 billion more than the sum eventually agreed upon by the Heads of Government and the proposals for commitments being €113 billion more. As for the EP's efforts to exercise influence after the national leaders have taken their decision, there is some leverage available by virtue of the fact that an inter-institutional agreement between the Commission, Council and EP on the financial perspective is deemed to be politically necessary before the perspective can be regarded as having been adopted. So, in January 2006 the EP rejected the December 2005 budget deal and called for a number of reforms. The reforms requested were, however, somewhat modest in nature, and many of them – such as stronger auditing rules, simpler spending procedures, and a greater role for MEPs in controlling foreign policy expenditure – focused on matters that would not directly affect financial perspective figures. The reason for the EP's seeming 'defeatism' (given its original financial perspective position) was that it recognised that it would not be realistic to expect the national governments to re-open financial 'basics' that had been resolved only with great difficulty.

The annual budget

A timetable and set of procedures for drawing up and approving the annual budget is laid down in Article 272 TEC. However, in practice, Article 272 gives only an approximate and rather formal guide to what actually happens. It provides a framework that has been fleshed out and adapted over time in response to pressures, necessities, and convenience.

In broad terms, and assuming no major problems exist or arise to disrupt the process severely, the pattern of budgetary decision-making is as follows.

Preparation of the Preliminary Draft Budget

The budgetary process is constantly ongoing. The preparation of each annual budget may, however, be said to begin during the winter of the year before it is due to come into effect, for it is then that the Commission prepares spending plans. In attempting to look this far ahead – over twelve months to the beginning of the financial year (in January) and twenty four months to its close – the Commission is necessarily faced with many uncertainties on both the revenue and expenditure sides. Agriculture used to be especially problematical when the CAP was based primarily on open-ended price support, for then the amount of expenditure on agriculture was highly dependent on unpredictable crop yields and world agriculture prices and currency movements. As, however, production outputs have been capped and price support has mainly given way to direct income support (see Chapter 18) then so has CAP expenditure become more manageable.

But even though agricultural spending is not so problematical as it was, the Commission still has to make many assumptions when preparing the draft budget, some of which may not be realised. If changed situations become apparent during the course of the budgetary cycle corrections can be made fairly easily by sending rectifying or amending letters to the Council and the EP. If, however, the situation changes during the budgetary year the position is more awkward. It used to be the case that 'temporary' solutions, such as the postponement of payments, delays in the introduction of new programmes, and supplementary budgets were used. Since the 1988 Brussels agreement, however, the Commission has had available, and has used, a range of stronger management powers to enable it to take appropriate action at an early stage if unforeseen circumstances and/or problems arise. It can, for example, directly intervene to alter certain types of payments in agriculture product markets.

The prime responsibility within the Commission for drawing up what is known as the Preliminary Draft Budget (PDB) falls to the Budget Commissioner and the Budget DG. Inevitably they are subject to pressures from many sides: from other parts of the Commission, which forward their own estimates and bids; from national representatives, both through the Council and on a direct lobbying basis; from the EP, especially leading figures on its Committee on Budgets; and from sectional interests. The Budget Commissioner and officials from the Budget DG hold many meetings, both formal and informal, to enable many of these interested parties to have their say. Naturally, those with the best chance of achieving some satisfaction are those that carry political weight and/or are already in tune with the Commission's thinking.

In preparing the PDB the Budget Commissioner and Budget DG have had to make significant adjustments to traditional ways of working as a result of developments in recent years aimed at improving strategic planning and programming and matching budgetary expenditure more closely with political priorities. The first development involves the College of Commissioners, the Ecofin Council, and the EP each setting out their political priorities for the budget before the PDB is finalised. This they do between January and early April. Those responsible in the Commission for preparing the PDB are expected to take note of the priorities of the three institutions. The second development, which was first used in 2001 for the

2002 budget and which is framed within the broader development of the use by the Commission of activity-based management for planning, budgeting, managing, and reporting on results, involves the use of activity-based budgeting (ABB). In essence this involves structuring costs and expenditure around policy areas and activities so that a clear comparison can be made between the results achieved for a policy with the resources used for that policy.

Under the terms of a 1993 Interinstitutional Agreement between the Commission, Council and EP that was designed to improve relations and understandings between the three institutions during the budgetary procedure, at some point before the Commission takes a final decision on the PDB there is a trialogue meeting (delegations from the three institutions). The purpose of the meeting is 'to discuss the possible priorities for the budget of that year, with due account being taken of the institutions' powers'.

Once the Budget DG has its proposals ready, they are presented by the Commissioner to the other Commissioners and all must agree on the package. When they do, the proposals officially become the Preliminary Draft Budget. This is normally done by late April or early May.

Prior to the 1988 reform, the PDB usually disappointed those who wanted to see the budget used as the motor for change in EC priorities. The Commission did make several attempts to use the PDB to effect at least modest shifts in policy emphasis – notably by proposing the containment of agricultural expenditure and expansion of the structural funds – but its manoeuvrability was always severely restricted by existing expenditure commitments, and also by the knowledge that any significant proposed change from the *status quo* would be fiercely resisted in the Council. The existence since 1988 of financial perspectives has changed this situation since the PDB must be set within the framework of the financial perspective applying.

The financial perspective does not, it should be emphasised, totally constrain the Commission when it draws up the PDB. It does have some manoeuvrability below expenditure ceilings and it does have options within expenditure headings. Indeed, in recent years the Commission theoretically has had considerable potential manoeuvrability, for budgets have been well below the ceilings of the financial perspectives. In practice, however, this potential has not been utilised, and it certainly would have been opposed by the Council had it been so.

The Commission presents the PDB in two forms: payment appropriations, which cover actual expenditure during the financial year; and commitment or engagement appropriations, which cover expenditure during the financial year plus liabilities extending beyond the year. Commitment appropriations are naturally higher than payment appropriations. The spending plans of the PDB are grouped under broad headings. Until the 2005 budget these headings were agriculture, structural operations, internal policies, external policies, administration, reserves, and pre-accession aid. As, however, was explained earlier in the chapter, these headings have now been changed and for the 2006 budget the following headings were used: natural resources (sub-divided into CAP support measures and rural development and environment); competitiveness and cohesion (mainly cohesion funds' operations); the EU as a global partner; citizenship, freedom, security and justice; other expenditure (mainly administration). Within each heading, hundreds of budget lines identify the funding proposed for specific policies, programmes and projects.

Council first reading

Assuming there are no major or special problems, the PDB is usually referred to the Council in May or June. Prior to the June 2002 Seville European Council meeting there was a separate Budget Council, but as part of the streamlining of Council formations that was agreed at Seville responsibility for the budget was assumed by the Ecofin Council.

Most of the Council's detailed examination of the budget is undertaken by the Budget Committee, a working group of national officials who, in what can be long and exhaustive sessions, examine the PDB chapter by chapter, line by line. As the date of the Ministers' meeting in the Council approaches, the Committee is likely to meet with increasing frequency in order to resolve as many issues as possible. The negotiators are in frequent contact with their national capitals about what transpires in the meetings, and hence they mostly have a prepared view when items come up for discussion. When this produces a rigidity in negotiating positions, much of the responsibility for finding a solution falls to the Council Presidency. The Commission provides assistance with this task.

From the Budget Committee the draft proceeds to COREPER. The number of unresolved items put before the Permanent Representatives naturally depends on what has happened in the Committee. Normally, much remains to be done, and COREPER attempts, like the Committee, to clear as many items as possible before the Ministers meet. It is usually most successful with those issues that do not have a potentially conflictual political aspect.

The Ecofin Ministers customarily hold a two-day meeting in mid-July, with the second day being reserved for the budget. Their examination of the PDB is preceded by a meeting with a delegation from the EP, made up mainly of members of the Budget Committee.

Prior to the establishment of financial perspectives, the July Budget Council normally lasted for a couple days and involved 15 to 20 hours of negotiations in formal sessions, plus extensive informal discussions and manoeuvrings in the wings. Qualified majority voting usually allowed a draft to be eventually agreed, but on controversial proposals a blocking minority sometimes existed. On two occasions the divisions between the member states were such that the July meeting was unable to approve a draft, which meant there had to be a reference back to officials. The officials then produced a new package for the Ministers to consider when they returned in September, by which time the timetable was pressing and an agreement had to be reached.

The reason why the July meeting was often so difficult was that the states differed both in their views about the balance to be struck between restraint and expansion and in their perceptions of problems and priorities. What emerged, therefore, was a draft reflecting accommodations and compromises. Almost invariably, however, the general thrust of the draft was, on the one hand, to propose a tighter overall budget than that envisaged in the PDB and, on the other hand, to propose some shift from non-compulsory expenditure to compulsory expenditure – that is, from items such as regional, social and research expenditure (which were relatively 'soft' because of their non-compulsory character) to agriculture (which was difficult to touch given the existing commitments).

Financial perspectives plus a now considerable use of multi-annual programming within policy areas have constrained the Council, as they have the Commission, in what it can do. This has had two effects on the Council's first reading stage. First, the decision-making process is now less divisive and troublesome than it was in the past. Second, though the Council still customarily cuts the PDB, its hands are largely tied and it is obliged to produce a draft that is very similar to the PDB: normally the cuts amount to no more than between €1–2 billion.

Parliament first reading

On being approved, the Council's first draft is referred to the EP. However, as noted above, this is not the first point at which the EP becomes involved in the budgetary process. It will have been attempting to exert its influence for some time: through its resolution on budget guidelines; through at least one trialogue meeting with the Commission and the Council to discuss budgetary plans; and through its Committee on Budgets which begins its considerations even before the PDB is issued.

Now, with the Council's draft available, the pace is stepped up. There is a brief debate in plenary session, but the detailed work is given over to committees. The Committee on Budgets naturally has most responsibility. It examines the budget in detail and also acts as a coordinating agency for reports submitted to it by other EP committees that look at the budget to see how their sectors will be affected. The Committee on Budgets does not, however, have the power completely to control what goes forward to the plenary: it cannot, for example, stop an amendment that has support elsewhere, especially if it is backed by any of the larger political groups. Partly in consequence of this, hundreds of proposed changes are usually put forward, many of which conflict with one another or are even mutually exclusive. Much, therefore, rests on the liaising, organising, and leadership skills of the chair of the Committee on Budgets and the appointed *rapporteur*.

The intention is normally to hold the plenary session dealing with the budget in mid- to late October, although on occasion it has been delayed until November. At the plenary, MEPs can do three things with the contents of the Council's draft: accept them; propose amendments to non-compulsory expenditure (which requires the majority support of MEPs); or propose modifications to compulsory expenditure (which requires a majority of the votes cast).

As with both the drafting of the PDB and the Council's first reading, the EP's first reading has been affected by the establishment of financial perspectives and multi-annual programming. There is not now much potential for using the annual budget for new policy advancement purposes, with the consequence that there is not now such a gap as there used to be between the positions of the Council and the EP: typically, whereas the Council proposes a budget that in total is about €1–2 billion smaller than the PDP, the EP proposes a budget that is about €1–2 billion larger.

Since 1988 disagreements between the Council and the EP in the budgetary process have focused primarily on two sorts of issues. First, the EP has customarily pressed for higher levels of non-compulsory expenditure than the Council. Second, the EP has urged that expenditure be classified in ways that increase its institutional powers, and to this end it has long campaigned for the abolition of the distinction between compulsory and non-compulsory expenditure.

In October, after the EP has debated the draft budget in plenary session and after all amendments and modifications have been voted upon, a resolution on the budget is adopted.

Council second reading

From the EP the draft goes back to the Council, where officials prepare it for the ministerial second reading, which is usually held in mid- to late

November. If important issues between the institutions remain unresolved, activity can be feverish, with all sorts of communications taking place between officials and representatives of the Commission, Council and EP. Trialogue meetings may be held.

Before the November Ecofin meeting formally gives a second reading to the draft budget, ministers normally meet again with an EP delegation, which invariably has much the same composition as the delegation that met with the Council at the first reading. The purpose of the meeting is to try to iron out remaining differences and identify grounds for compromise.

On matters where there is still disagreement with the EP, the options available to the Council depend on the type of expenditure concerned and whether the EP has proposed expenditure increases. In broad terms, the situation is that the Council has the last word on compulsory expenditure so can reject EP amendments if it wishes, whilst the EP has the last word on non-compulsory expenditure so the Council can only modify EP amendments.

The usual approach of the Council at the second reading is to strike a balance between accommodating the EP on the one hand whilst reaffirming its first reading position on the other.

Parliament second reading

The EP holds its second reading on the budget in mid-December. What happens before, at, and after the plenary depends very much on the extent to which contentious issues remain unresolved.

If the situation is relatively straightforward and most problems have been sorted out, then the normal procedure is for the Committee on Budgets to meet, to re-insert such non-compulsory expenditure as it legally can and, on this basis, to recommend adoption. The plenary then votes, and if the budget is approved the President formally signs it and declares it to be adopted.

But when, as was frequently the case prior to the creation of financial perspectives, major differences between the Council and the EP remain, the two sides are obliged to get down to negotiations. Various procedures can come into play: the President of the Council, accompanied by the Budget Commissioner, may meet with the Committee on Budgets; the President of the Council may make an appeal to the plenary; a trialogue meeting may be held; or a special Council may be hurriedly called – perhaps to meet again with an EP delegation, perhaps to give the budget what is, in effect, a third reading. If all efforts to reach a Council–EP agreement fail, the Parliament can reject the budget by a majority of its members, including two-thirds of the votes cast.

Non-approval of the budget

In five of the first nine years after the introduction of direct elections in 1979, budgets were not approved in time to be implemented at the beginning of the financial year on 1 January. These were the budgets of 1980 and 1984–8.

If a legal budget is not approved by the EP before 1 January a fall back position applies. This allows for funding to continue, but only on the basis of what are known as 'provisional twelfths', which means that spending is limited to the monthly average expenditure of the previous year. Therefore policies do not collapse, but some payments may have to be suspended, and programmes, especially new ones, may have to be delayed. A speedy agreement on the budget of what by this stage is the current financial year is thus desirable.

There is no formal procedure or set pattern of action in the event of non-adoption. The expectation and assumption is that the process will be resumed at the point at which it broke down, but practice has shown that matters are not so simple. Developments following non-adoption have varied considerably, depending principally on the reasons for the non-adoption. For example, the 1986 budget was, like those for 1985 and 1988, not approved until halfway through the financial year. The problem with the 1986 budget was not that a budget was not approved by the EP in December 1985, but rather that the Council judged that the budget adopted by the EP was illegal on the ground that it included more non-compulsory expenditure than was legally permissible. The Council therefore asked the Court of Justice for a ruling. On 3 July 1986 the Court eventually delivered its judgement, and in essence upheld the Council's claim that the budget was illegal. The next week saw hectic activity, a truncated budgetary procedure and, on 10 July, the adoption of a budget in which creative accountancy and financial ingenuity played prominent parts.

The adoption of financial perspectives and inter-institutional agreements has removed, or at least blunted the sharpness of, many of the problems that occasioned the non-adoption of budgets in the 1980s. In particular, agricultural expenditure has been made subject to stronger budgetary discipline, the Structural Funds have been increased, mechanisms have been established to improve the match between income and expenditure, there has been clarification on what falls under the compulsory and non-compulsory headings, and decision-making procedures have been made less confrontational. Of course, not all differences or potential problems have been totally erased. But the prospect of budgets being adopted at December plenaries has been considerably enhanced, and all budgets since 1988 have indeed been so adopted.

The budgetary procedure has thus become much less dramatic than it used to be. As Shackleton (2002: 108) puts it, the procedure is now 'more an exercise in joint management than in providing direction for the Union'.

Implementation of the budget

The implementation of, and the monitoring of the implementation of, the budget may also be considered as part of the budgetary process. Only a couple of general points will be made here about these activities, however, since both receive attention elsewhere in the book, notably in Chapters 9, 14 (in the section on the Court of Auditors), and 16.

The first point is that, as with other aspects of EU policy implementation, much of the 'front-line' budgetary implementation is undertaken by national agencies in the member states. The Commission makes transfer payments to the agencies – which are mainly, although by no means exclusively, national and regional governmental bodies – and they manage them on the Commission's behalf. This delegation to agencies does not, however, absolve the Commission from overall responsibility for the execution of the budget, and for this purpose it has a battery of administrative structures and arrangements to deal with such matters as the drawing up of tenders, the issuing of contracts, and the handling – either directly or indirectly – of payments.

An indication of the scale of the activities involved is provided by the fact that the Commission is responsible for some 400 000 financial transactions a year, including approaching 300 000 payment orders. These range from large CAP and Structural Fund transfer payments to employees' travel expenses.

The second point is that the implementation of the budget has attracted considerable attention in recent years, not least from the media and the EP. This is partly, perhaps, because attention has been less focused on budgetary decision-making as that process has become much less fraught. It is mainly, however, because the Court of Auditors in a series of reports has exposed mismanagement and fraud in the implementation of EU policies. The Commission is not slow to point out that many of the problems identified by the Court must be laid at the doors of the national agencies that are responsible for around 80 per cent of direct payments, but the fact is that the Court has also exposed inadequacies in the Commission's financial control systems. As was shown in Chapters 12 and 14, it was the exposure of such inadequacies that initiated the events that led to the resignation of the College of Commissioners in March 1999. As was shown in Chapter 9, this resignation and the events leading up to it have resulted in major changes in EU financial management and implementation practices.

Key Features of Budgetary Processes

Some features of the budgetary processes merit particular comment.

First the most fundamental budgetary decisions are taken quite outside the framework of the EU's treaties. Whereas there are clear treaty provisions covering the making of the EU's annual budgets, financial perspectives have no treaty base and the decision-making processes that are used to determine them are a consequence of political necessities and understandings.

Second, financial frameworks are essentially the outcome of exhaustive intergovernmental negotiations that culminate in European Council decisions. The Commission does, of course, structure these negotiations with its initial proposals and then helps to facilitate them in association with Council Presidencies. The EP has a role to play too, not least since financial perspectives require its approval. But the national governments are the key decision-makers.

Third, the power balance between the institutions is different in respect of the annual budgetary process than it is in respect of financial perspectives. In respect of the making of the annual budget the Council of Ministers and the EP jointly constitute the budgetary authority. The Commission is important, but after the presentation of the PDB it is cast in an essentially servicing capacity: responding to what happens in the Council and the EP and doing what it can to bring the two sides together. As for the particular nature of the balance between the Council and the EP, the former is the stronger, but changes since 1988 have improved the position of the EP. They have done so in three ways: by binding the institutions into a financial framework that can only be revised by common agreement; by significantly increasing the proportion of the budget over which the EP has most control – non-compulsory expenditure; and by giving the EP some control over compulsory expenditure – a condition of the EP's agreement to the 1993–9 financial perspective was that it would have the right to scrutinise the compulsory expenditure part of the budget, with a view to forcing the Commission to justify the legal base of compulsory budget lines.

Fourth, the annual budgetary procedure is unusual in the EU decision-making context in that it operates according to a stipulated timetable. Legislative proposals can be pushed along if they are strongly supported, and the greater use of QMV in the Council has greatly quickened the pace of much legislative decision-making, but it is only in the later stages of the cooperation and co-decision procedures that a timetable applies. It is still the case that legislative proposals can drag on in the Council until some sort of agreement is reached, and if this proves not to be possible they may be indefinitely postponed or even dropped altogether. With the budget such a relaxed and open-ended approach is not possible, since expenditure and resource decisions have to be made each year. The existence and exigencies of the timetable thus introduce an urgency into budgetary decision-making that is not always found in other spheres of EU decision-making.

Fifth, many of the arguments and confrontations that have occurred during the annual budgetary process have been occasioned not so much by the financial sums involved – which have been relatively small – but more by a broader institutional struggle, especially between the Council and the EP. With the EP dissatisfied with its overall position in the EU system, it is only natural that it should have sought to use the budget to maximum advantage. There are a number of ways in which it has gone about this. One was a willingness in the 1980s to reject the budget. Another has been interpreting the treaties, along with inter-institutional agreements and understandings about budgetary decision-making, in ways that are advantageous to itself – as on matters such as the bases for budgetary calculations and the classification of expenditure in terms of compulsory and non-compulsory. And yet another way has been by attempting to exploit differences within the Council, for example by seeking to exert pressure in a particular direction through the indication of preferences in plenary votes or, less formally, in inter-institutional exchanges such as conciliation meetings.

Sixth, and finally, because of the desire of member states, especially net contributor states, to ensure that EU income and expenditure are relatively small, budgetary processes have provided only limited opportunities to forge and drive policy change. Financial perspectives have allowed for some use of the budget to guide incremental policy development and have enabled the budget to become the instrument for modest policy reform. But they can hardly be said to have been mechanisms for effecting radical policy shifts.

Concluding Remarks

The EU budget is necessary for the financing of many EU activities and operations. But it is relatively small in size, and therefore its policy impact is limited. This is no more clearly demonstrated than in the fact that whereas public expenditure by the member states accounts for about 45 per cent of EU GNI, EU expenditure accounts for less than three per cent.

But notwithstanding its relatively smallness, the EU's budget has been the focus of very considerable political attention and controversy. Since the late 1980s, the multi-annual financial perspectives within which the annual budgets are framed have been the main subject of such a focus. They have been so because of a mixture of a number of factors, not least the very high political profile that has been given to them. The annual budgets, by contrast, have been negotiated in atmospheres of relative peace. They used to be to be strongly contested, but financial perspectives and multi-annual programming have imposed tight constraints and an ordered framework on what now can and cannot be done within the annual budgetary cycle.

Chapter 18

Agricultural Policy and Policy Processes

The Common Agricultural Policy in Context
What is Special about Agriculture?
How the Common Agricultural Policy Works
The Impact and Effects of the Common Agricultural Policy
Policy Processes
Concluding Remarks

The Common Agricultural Policy in Context

Despite the fact that, even after the 2004 enlargement, it accounts for only 2.7 per cent of EU GDP and 5.2 per cent of EU employment, agriculture looms large in the life of the EU. It does so for five main reasons. First, the economic impact of agriculture is greater than indicated by the figures just given, for in addition to farming itself there are many industries that are closely linked to agriculture and are dependent on its success. These industries include agro-chemicals and fertilisers, agricultural equipment, food processing, veterinary medicines, and financial services. Second, the EU has, via the Common Agricultural Policy (CAP), major policy-making and decision-making responsibilities for agriculture. Indeed, agriculture is the most integrated of the EU's sectoral policies. Third, as the major recipient of EU funds – costing currently over €50 billion, which accounts for almost half of total annual expenditure – agriculture is central to EU budgetary deliberations. Fourth, there is a greater institutional presence and activity in the agricultural field than in any other: the Agriculture Ministers normally meet more frequently than the ministers of all other Councils except for the Foreign and Ecofin Ministers; Agriculture Council meetings are prepared not by COREPER but by a special body, the Special Committee on Agriculture (SCA); the Agriculture Directorate General is the second largest of the Commission's DGs (only Personnel and Administration is larger and that does not deal with a policy sector); and there are far more Council working groups and Commission management and advisory committees in the sphere of agriculture than in any other single policy area. Fifth, agriculture is the most controversial of the EU's policies, with the member states disagreeing on many issues, most notably the extent to which and the ways in which the sector should be protected.

For its supporters, the most important benefits accruing from the CAP are a plentiful and stable food supply and the maintenance of productive activity in the countryside. The CAP is seen also as an important symbol and indicator that real policy integration is possible at EU level. Those who criticise the CAP are thus liable to be attacked both on technical and efficiency grounds – with the claim that national solutions would be much less satisfactory – and more broadly for being *non communautaire* – with the assertion that this most integrated of EU policies should not be undermined. For opponents of the CAP, economic efficiency is the key issue, with criticisms focusing especially on the subsidisation of wealthy farmers and agri-companies, high prices for consumers, the production of farm surpluses, the cost of disposing of the surpluses, and the damage caused to agriculture in the underdeveloped world when the surpluses are disposed of via export subsidy 'dumping' on the world market.

Yet even amongst those who are most critical of the CAP, few seriously challenge the view that there should be an EU agriculture policy of some kind. Certainly no member state believes that the agricultural edifice should be wholly uprooted and policy returned completely to national capitals. The view that there is something special about agriculture, something that distinguishes it from other sectoral activities and merits it receiving advantageous treatment, whilst not commanding such strong support as in the early days of the EC, still strikes a chord with EU decision-makers.

What is Special about Agriculture?

The attention given to agriculture in the EEC Treaty, and the subsequent creation of the CAP after long and often tortuous negotiations, is often seen as being part of a trade-off between France and Germany. There is some truth to this view. In exchange for the creation of a common market in industrial goods, which the French feared would be greatly to Germany's advantage, France – with its large but uneconomic agricultural sector – would benefit from an agricultural system that, though also in the form of a common market, would be based not on free and open market principles but on foundations that would protect farmers from too much competition.

Important though it was, however, the Franco–German 'deal' is only part of the explanation of why agriculture, from the earliest days of the Community, was given an elevated policy status. For the fact is that when the CAP was being created in the late 1950s and early 1960s, none of the then six member states seriously objected to it in principle – the Netherlands, for example, was a strong supporter – though there were differences between the states on the pace of the CAP's construction and the precise nature of its policy instruments. This consensus on the existence of the CAP was a result of a shared recognition that agriculture required special treatment.

Today, despite the original EC having greatly increased in size, despite the circumstances and conditions of agriculture having dramatically changed, and despite the CAP having caused major difficulties and disruptions to the whole EU system, agriculture is still generally regarded by the national governments as requiring special treatment. Many of the reasons for this are much the same as they were in the EC's early days. Others are more recent. The reasons can be grouped under two general headings: the distinctive nature of agriculture, and political factors.

The distinctive nature of agriculture

Most governments of the industrialised world take the view that agriculture is not like other areas of economic activity. It is special and as such merits special treatment to encourage, assist and protect it. In the EU five main arguments have been advanced in support of this view, the relative importance of which have varied over time.

The first argument stems from the fact that agricultural prices are subject to considerable fluctuation if they are not subject to public intervention and regulation. This is largely because, even with modern farming techniques, agricultural supply is heavily dependent on the weather. Agricultural price instability is seen as being undesirable for two reasons. First, if prices suddenly go up, inflation is immediately fuelled (given that food constitutes around 20 per cent of the budget of the average EU citizen). Second, if prices fall too low, farmers may not be able to make an adequate living and may be forced off the land; even those who are able to stay in farming may experience severe difficulties as a result of high debt loads on land and capital purchases.

The second argument is that reliance on imports for vital foodstuffs creates a potential vulnerability to outside pressures. In the early years of the EC, when memories were still fresh of wartime shortages and the international trading climate was strained, this argument played an important part in encouraging a drive for greater self-sufficiency. However, in the relatively calm international trading conditions that now exist, and with many of the foodstuffs produced in the EU being in surplus – including cereals, dairy produce and beef – it is an argument that, though still heard, is less weighty than it used to be.

The third argument asserts that because people must have food, insufficient domestic production means the gap between output and demand has to be met by imports, with potentially damaging consequences for the balance of payments. Moreover, since the demand for food is fairly inelastic up to necessity levels (as long as income allows it, food will still be bought even if prices go up) the economic vulnerability of an importing state is high. This balance of payments argument used to be important in helping to underpin the CAP, but it has not been so forceful since the early to mid-1970s when Community prices became significantly higher than world prices and Community production began to move significantly into surplus. High domestic prices mean that EU processors cannot maximise their value added exports by buying at the cheapest possible prices, and surpluses mean that national treasuries have to pay – via the EU budget – for their disposal.

The fourth argument suggests that farmers should be encouraged to stay on the land for social and environmental reasons. Sometimes such calls, which have been voiced increasingly in recent years, have an idealistic tone to them, with pleas that a populated countryside is part of the natural fabric, or the suggestion that management of the land is a desirable end in itself. Rather more hard-headed perhaps are the arguments that land that is not managed often reverts to scrub which is inimical to bio-diversity, and that it is both undesirable and potentially dangerous to allow farm incomes to deteriorate to the point that poor farmers and agricultural workers are forced to move to the towns in search of employment that often does not exist.

The fifth argument is that agriculture must be treated with particular care because it is intrinsically linked with food health and safety. A series of food scares in Europe since the mid-1990s has brought this consideration firmly onto the political agenda. The BSE/CJD crisis in particular – which first erupted in 1996 and focused on the extent to which BSE in (primarily British) beef was being passed on to humans in the form of CJD – has obliged decision-makers to take a broader view of what should be the content and priorities of agricultural policy.

Political factors

The agriculture sector enjoys political assets that have been translated into influence on EU policy. Four of these assets are especially important.

(1) Since the CAP was established, the governments of those states which benefit most from CAP financial transfers have been strong defenders of the system. The line-up of these states has not been wholly consistent over time as circumstances have changed, but in recent years the most

prominent opponents of radical CAP reform have included France (which accounts for 22.5 per cent of total EU agricultural production and which is the most notable permanent member of the 'anti-reform' club), Ireland, Belgium and Spain.

(2) At the national decision-making level, Ministries of Agriculture have traditionally tended to be slightly apart from mainstream policy processes, and since 1958 this has been reproduced at the EU level with the position of the Agriculture DG in the Commission. All policy-makers in all areas of policy do, of course, attempt to use their own expertise, knowledge and information to provide themselves with some insulation from the rest of the decision-making system, but agriculture is particularly well placed to do this. Its supposedly distinctive nature, the complexity of much of its subject matter, and the customary close relations between agricultural decision-makers and producers, all combine to make it difficult for 'outside' decision-makers to offer an effective challenge or alternative to what is presented to them. That all said, in a few member states this 'separateness' of Agriculture Ministries is now becoming not quite what it was, with – as in the UK, for example – agriculture becoming part of more broadly based environment/rural affairs departments.

(3) Farmers enjoy considerable electoral weight. Even though their relative numerical importance has declined sharply over the years – in 1958 around 25 per cent of total EC employment was in agriculture, by 2002 it was less than 5 per cent, and in the post-2004 enlarged EU it is just over 5 per cent – the agricultural vote is still significant. The significance varies from state to state. The size of the domestic population engaged in agriculture is one important factor in determining this significance: proportions vary considerably, with around 19 per cent of the working population in Poland, 14 per cent in Greece, 11 per cent in Portugal, 2 per cent in Belgium, and 1.5 per cent in the UK. Another consideration is the direction of the agricultural vote. In some member states the agricultural vote is disproportionately directed towards small parties which, benefiting from proportional representation, can be key players in national politics and government. On the whole, farmers, especially richer farmers, incline towards Centre-Right and Right parties, with the consequence that it is they, rather than parties of the Left, that are usually the strongest defenders of agricultural interests in EU forums. But this inclination to the Right does not, in most countries, amount to an exclusive loyalty, so few parties can afford to ignore the farmers: at a minimum, all parties must give the impression of being concerned and solicitous.

(4) In most EU countries farmers have long had very strong domestic organisations to represent and articulate their interests. When it became clear in the late 1950s and early 1960s that much agricultural policy and

decision-making was to be transferred to Brussels, similar organisations were quickly established at Community level. As early as 1963 approaching 100 Community-wide agriculture groups had been formed. Today the number is around 130. The most important of these groups is the Committee of Agricultural Organisations in the European Union/General Confederation of Agricultural Co-operatives in the EU (COPA/COGECA), which is an alliance of umbrella or peak organisations attempting to represent all types of farmers on the basis of affiliation through national farming groups. Beyond COPA/COGECA and a few other overarching organisations, specialist bodies exist to represent virtually every product that is produced and consumed in the EU and also all participants in the agricultural process – farmers most obviously, but also processors, traders, retailers and so on.

The influence of this agricultural lobby has declined over the years, but it is still a significant force in the EU. It is worth setting out the reasons why this is so.

The sheer size of the lobby is formidable. It operates at two levels, the national and the EU.

At the national level there are considerable variations in the pattern and strength of agricultural representation. But in all member states there are groups of some kind that have as part of their purpose the utilisation of whatever devices and channels are available to them to influence both national agricultural policy (within the general principles of the CAP, states enjoy a considerable policy discretion) and EU agricultural policy. Thus, the National Farmers' Union for England and Wales employs a full-time professional staff of 160 at its London headquarters plus around 1000 staff in 310 local offices. In addition, it funds – in conjunction with the NFU of Scotland and the Ulster Farmers' Union – a Brussels office, known as the British Office of Agriculture, which has a regular staff of between five and ten who are topped up as and when required.

At the EU level the large number of Euro-agric groups means that lobbying activities across the agricultural sector are almost continuous. COPA/COGECA moves on the broadest front, and with over 50 full-time officials is by far the best resourced and staffed organisation (for further information on COPA/COGECA see Chapter 14; Grant, 1997; COPA/COGECA's website at www.copa-cogeca.be). The more specialised groups – such as the mustard makers (CIMCEE) and the butchers (COBCCEE) – are much more modestly provided for and at best may have just one full-time member of staff working in an office made available by a national affiliate. But since the interests of these small groups are usually narrowly drawn this is just about enough to allow basic lobbying requirements to be fulfilled – holding meetings and consultations with decision-makers, feeding information through to the EU institutions, preparing policy and briefing documents. If necessary, reinforcements are usually available from national and Euro-umbrella associations.

Agricultural interests generally enjoy good contact with, and access to, decision-makers. Again, this factor operates at both national and EU levels. At the national level, influence with governments is vital, not only because of their control over nationally determined policies but also because they are the route to the Council of Ministers. Most governments are at least prepared to listen to representations from national agricultural interests, and some engage in a virtually automatic consultation on important issues. There are a number of reasons why governments are generally approachable in this way: there may be a pre-existing sympathy for the interests' views; a fuller picture of what is going on in the agricultural world is made possible; policy implementation may be made easier; and political support may be generated by being supportive, or at least by giving the impression that the government and the interest are as one. If, despite being sympathetically listened to by its government, a national agricultural interest is dissatisfied with what is agreed in the Council of Ministers, the government can always try to blame 'the awkward Italians', 'the impossible Greeks' or 'the immovable Poles'.

At the EU level, the Commission is the prime target for agricultural interests. For the most part it is very willing to listen. Indeed, it has encouraged the establishment of Euro-agric groups and readily makes itself available to them. Close Commission–group relations are viewed by the Commission as being extremely useful: the groups can contribute their knowledge and experience, which may improve policy; the Commission can explain to the groups why it is engaging in certain actions and thus try to sensitise them to Commission concerns and aims; face-to-face meetings can help break down barriers and resistance arising from suspicions that 'the Eurocrats' do not really understand farming practicalities; and if Eurogroups can do something to aggregate the conflicting national interests and demands that arise in relation to most proposals they can considerably simplify the Commission's task of developing policies that are acceptable and can help to legitimise the Commission as a decision-maker in the eyes of the Council and the EP. All that said, however, it is the case that since the mid-1980s the Commission, though maintaining close links with the agricultural lobby, has been less influenced by it. A major reason for this is that the Commission has been obliged to try to reform the agricultural sector, whilst organisations such as COPA/COGECA have been, in Grant's words, 'seeking to defend the ancient regime' (Grant, 1997: 170; on the declining influence of COPA/COGECA, see also Clark and Jones, 1999).

The agricultural organisations are not counterbalanced by strong and vigorous groups advancing contrary attitudes and claims. 'Natural opponents' do exist – consumers and environmentalists most notably – but they are relatively weak in comparison. A major reason for their weakness is that whereas farmers constitute a clear section of the population with a readily identifiable common sectoral interest, consumers and environmentalists do not have such a group consciousness, are more widely dispersed and, in consequence, are just not so easy to mobilise or organise. So although there are many more consumers than there are farmers in the EU, the largest of the Euro-consumer groups – the European Bureau of Consumers' Associations (BEUC) – has a staff of only fifteen or so. This is sizeable enough when compared with most Eurogroups, but it pales in comparison with the massed ranks of the agricultural associations. Moreover, the BEUC has to cover the whole spectrum of relevant EU policies; agriculture takes up only part of its time.

In terms of access to decision-makers, the farmers' 'rivals' do not as a rule enjoy the 'insider status' granted to much of the agriculture lobby. They rarely have a 'sponsoring' ministry in the way that agricultural interests do. Nor are they necessarily consulted by the Commission on agricultural matters as a matter of routine, nor automatically called in for discussions when something of importance or potential interest arises. The fact is they do not have the political and economic power of farmers, they cannot offer trade-offs in the way of cooperation on policy implementation, they are – in some instances – relative latecomers, and a few – notably the more radical greens – are seen as not conforming to established values and the rules of the game. Some of the more respectable of these 'oppositional' agriculture groups have their foot in the EU door – BEUC, for instance, is a recognised 'social partner' – but none has quite entered the room in the manner of the agricultural lobby.

Agriculture has powerful friends. While farmers and those directly engaged in the agricultural industries have been the most obvious beneficiaries of the CAP, others have gained too, notably the owners of land. Huge profits have been made by investment institutions, financiers, banks, industrial corporations and private landlords from the rising value of land that has been associated with the CAP. Many of these interests have direct access to decision-makers, indeed are themselves amongst the decision-makers in some governments, and have sought to use their influence accordingly.

Unity has been a source of strength. Despite the great range of interests represented, the agriculture lobby was, until the early 1980s, more or less united in its aims: it pressed for comprehensive market regimes for as much produce as possible, and it sought the largest price increases it could get.

Since that time, however, as significant steps to bring spending on agriculture under control have been taken and as EC/EU enlargements have made the interests of the agricultural sector more divergent, the unity of the lobby has been subject to increasing strains and its effectiveness has accordingly been weakened. Sectors have vied with one another as increasing attention has had to be paid not only to the size of the cake but also to the way in which it is cut. Increasing competition *within* the agricultural sector has been no more clearly demonstrated than by the division in recent years between COPA/COGECA and the European Farmers Coordination (CPE) which represents small farmers. In the context of agricultural reform discussions and negotiations, CPE has been much more in favour than COPA/COGECA of the redistribution of support to small farmers and of broadly-based rural development activities.

Farmers sometimes resort to direct action. In some EU countries, most notably France, farmers sometimes take matters into their own hands if they are dissatisfied with policies and decisions affecting their sector. Whilst decision-makers never care to admit that they have been swayed by direct action, there is no doubt that farmers' militancy has affected at least some of those who are responsible for running EU agriculture. Certainly, for example, the tough stance adopted by the French government in the Council of Ministers in respect of the reform of the CAP in 1991–2 and in respect of the agricultural aspects of the GATT Uruguay Round in 1992–3, was at least partially influenced by the knowledge that angry farmers had already demonstrated their fear of a possible 'sell-out' by holding large demonstrations and causing widespread disruption of the French transport network.

How the Common Agricultural Policy Works

Title II of the TEC (Articles 32–8) – which is still as written in 1957 in the EEC Treaty, save for the removal of redundant transition measures – sets out the general rationale and framework of the CAP. The objectives are laid down in Article 33:

(a) to increase agricultural productivity by promoting technical progress and by ensuring the rational development of agricultural production and the optimum utilisation of the factors of production, in particular labour;

(b) thus to ensure a fair standard of living for the agricultural community, in particular by increasing the individual earnings of persons engaged in agriculture;

(c)   to stabilise markets;

(d)   to assure the availability of supplies;

(e)   to ensure that supplies reach consumers at reasonable prices.

Many matters concerning the nature of the CAP are barely touched on in Title II because, in 1957, they were deliberately left aside for later consideration by representatives of the states. Amongst the first fruits of these deliberations was the adoption by the Council of Ministers in December 1960 of the three major operating principles of the CAP. These still apply today.

A single internal market

Agricultural goods are supposed to be able to flow freely across internal EU borders, unhindered by barriers to trade and unhampered by devices such as subsidies or administrative regulations that might distort or limit competition. However, it is not a free trade system based on pure market principles because price and/or income support mechanisms exist for most agricultural products.

The CAP used to be based almost exclusively on a price support system. It was a system that was extremely expensive to finance. This was for three main reasons. First, many products were produced in amounts that were surplus to EU requirements. High guaranteed prices were the main reason for these surpluses, but improved farming techniques and the concentrated use of agri-chemicals also played a part. Second, most products were protected and supported by a market regime, known as a common organisation of the market (COM). Different regimes provided different forms of protection and support – so that in practice there were many agricultural policies rather than just one – but about 70 per cent of products were beneficiaries of support prices of some kind. For some products the support prices were available on an unconditional and open-ended basis, but more commonly, following reforms in the 1980s designed to tackle the problem of surpluses and reduce CAP expenditure, they were subject to restrictions. The nature of the restrictions varied from product to product, but they usually took one, or some combination, of four main forms: quotas, co-responsibility levies, quality controls, and stabilisers – the latter consisting of a mechanism in which production thresholds (maximum guaranteed quantities) were set and if these were exceeded the guaranteed payments were automatically reduced. (For a description of the different forms of COMs, see pp. 393–4 of the fifth edition of this book.) Third, apart from a brief interlude in 1974–5, EU agricultural prices were consistently above world prices, which meant that it was not possible to export surpluses without suffering a financial loss. Several devices were used to deal with the surpluses: exporting them and providing an export refund to exporters to ensure that no loss was incurred on transactions; storing them until EU prices rose; donating them as food aid; or converting them to animal foodstuffs. All these devices had to be financed from the EU budget.

The reforms of the 1980s designed to curb agricultural output had some effect, but not enough. Accordingly, internal demands for further reform soon arose, with pressures focused especially on the large proportion of the EU budget – over 60 per cent in the late 1980s – that was allocated to the CAP and the waste of agricultural over-production. At much the same time – the late 1980s and early 1990s – the EC came under increasing pressure from outside – most particularly from the USA – to reform fundamentally the CAP so that both the EC market would be made more open and subsidised EC produce would not be 'dumped' on world markets. These twin pressures, internal and external, led, after extensive internal deliberations and external negotiations – the latter in the context of the General Agreement on Tariffs and Trade (GATT) Uruguay Round – to agreement in 1992 on major reforms of the CAP. At the heart of these reforms was a bearing down on prices on the one hand and a shift from price support to income support on the other. Included amongst the income support measures were various compensation schemes designed to enable farmers to take agricultural land out of production, to diversify land use, and to take early retirement.

But just as the reforms of the 1980s alleviated rather than solved the CAP problem, so similarly did the more radical reforms of 1992. By the mid- to late 1990s pressures for further fundamental reform were again building. The pressures came from three directions. First, with the CAP still accounting for around half of the EU budget, several of the net contributor member states started pressing for another attempt to reduce the size of the CAP budget. Second, as enlargement to Central and Eastern European countries (CEECs) loomed, it became clear that the CAP just could not continue in its existing form, or at least not without a very large increase in the EU budget – which would not be politically possible. The large increase would be necessary because most of the CEECs, especially Poland, have large and relatively inefficient agricultural sectors and so would be major beneficiaries of an unreformed CAP Third, international pressures, again led by the USA, to open up the EU agricultural market were continuing. The EU was already required, as a result of the Uruguay Round, to partially dismantle its protectionist system, and a further liberalising round was scheduled under the World Trade Organisation (WTO – which replaced GATT in 1995).

Proposals for responding to these pressures and for further reforming the CAP were set out by the Commission in its July 1997 *Agenda 2000* document (European Commission, 1997a), which was followed up in

March 1998 with more detailed proposals. The main features of the proposals followed upon the principles of the 1992 reforms with, on the one hand, further significant cuts in support prices – especially for beef, milk, and cereals – and on the other hand a strengthening of direct compensatory aid to farmers and of incentives for diversification. The Commission also proposed extending rural development policy, by allocating to it around ten per cent of the total CAP budget, by strengthening existing rural development programmes such as those designed to improve the competitiveness of rural areas and to preserve the environment and rural heritage, and by making rural development the 'second pillar' of the CAP (the first pillar being market support measures and direct payments to producers). Following extensive negotiations between the member states, in which there was some dilution of the Commission's proposals, the Agriculture Ministers agreed in March 1999 on a package of reforms based on *Agenda 2000*. A fortnight later, however, some of the key components of the package were further diluted when the Heads of Government met in Berlin to decide upon the whole *Agenda 2000* reform programme. The softening was mainly at the insistence of President Chirac, who – looking to the interests of French farmers and the French exchequer – was not prepared to accept the Agriculture Ministers' agreement as it stood.

As with the 1992 reforms, the 1999 reforms were quickly seen as not having been sufficiently radical. One reason for this was that they did not make provision for any significant overall decrease in CAP expenditure; indeed over the period of the 1999–2006 financial perspective there was to be a slight increase. Another reason was that they did not go far enough to meet WTO demands for the reduction of agricultural trade distorting support mechanisms – demands that included the abandonment of export refunds. It was made clear to the EU, by both developed and developing countries, that the issue would have to be addressed during the new round of WTO trade negotiations that was launched at Doha in November 2001. And a third reason was that they did not address how to deal with the increased demands that would be placed on the EU budget by the impending EU membership of CEECs.

This last problem was dealt with in October 2002 by the European Council, on the basis of proposals submitted to it by the Commission (see p. 476 below). The key element in the resolution of the problem was that the states that would soon join the EU would not receive full CAP support until 2013: that is, until the end of the financial perspective that would cover the years 2007–13. Their 'entitlements' would be only gradually phased in. This clearly was a major blow for the new member states but then, as was explained in Chapter 4, EU accession negotiations are largely about applicants meeting the EU's terms of admission rather than negotiating what those terms actually are. For the most part applicants have to 'take it or leave it', and since they are anxious to become EU members they have little choice but to take it.

Ways of dealing with the other post-1999 problems were put forward by the Commission in July 2002 as part of a mid-term review of the 1999 settlement (see p. 476 below). After some modifications to satisfy national interests and preferences, the proposals were accepted by the Council of Ministers in June 2003. The principal measures contained in the agreed reform package continued in the tradition of the 1992 and 1999 reform rounds, with a further bearing down on support prices where they continued to exist, with an intensification of support measures for environmental protection and rural development, and with a further major movement in the direction of separating – or 'de-coupling' to use the technical term – the provision of financial support for agriculture from production levels. As part of the de-coupling, most financial payments to farmers are to be made in a single payment based on past payments, acreage, and land use. In a system known as 'cross-compliance', payments are conditional on farmers meeting specified standards on a range of farming practice matters, including food safety and animal welfare requirements. To ensure that the much-criticised practice of most of CAP funding being given to large farmers and agri-companies is curtailed, limits are placed on the maximum size of individual payments and ensuing savings are directed to rural development – in a system called 'modulation'.

Since the June 2003 settlement, the process of attempting to improve the management of the CAP has continued. As part of this, in October 2005 the Council accepted a suggestion from the Commission that it draft before the end of 2006 a proposal to replace the existing CMOs with a single CMO in which there is a single and much simpler set of rules on such matters as market intervention and refunds. The Commission's suggestion reflected the fact that as the CAP system has moved away from price to income support, so have CMOs become less critical policy instruments.

✻   ✻   ✻

A number of factors have thus combined since the late 1980s to produce very strong pressures for fundamental reform of the CAP. The most important of these factors have been: market imbalances arising from the CAP's structure – especially high prices and over-production; the dominating position of the CAP in the EU's budget; rising international dissatisfaction with the distorting effects of the CAP on world agricultural trade; and the increasing importance on policy agendas of newer issues that are of concern to society, notably food safety and environmental protection.

The pressures to which these factors have given rise have been such as to produce major rounds of CAP reform in 1992, 1999, and 2003. The reforms have been so extensive as bring about, albeit in an incremental manner, a fundamental change in the nature of the CAP's internal market. The three main dimensions of the changes have been:

- A movement away from the former policy of high guaranteed price levels. Intervention prices have either been removed or reduced to much lower levels – levels that for most products are, in effect, safety net levels.
- Price level support for farmers has been largely replaced by income support payments. Most, though by no means all, payments have been de-coupled from payments for production outputs. The extent of the de-coupling varies by commodity, and to some extent also by member state – the latter of which is evidence of a measure of re-nationalisation of agricultural policy.
- A much higher priority is being given to 'newer' policy concerns, including rural development, environmental protection, and food safety. There is less emphasis on highly intensive and productive farming and more on resource protective farming.

The CAP market system may thus be said to have been transformed, with income support generally having replaced price support, with EU prices now much closer to world prices, and with farmers being seen not just as agricultural producers but also as custodians of the land.

However, sight should not be lost of the fact that not all has changed. As Garzon (2006) has observed 'Europe has not fully embraced the new paradigm of market liberalism. Public intervention remains high, in particular in supporting farmer income. The logic of alleviating market instability in the name of the social objective of providing farmers with a fair standard of living is still present.' This public intervention, even though it is of a very different kind to formerly, ensures that the CAP will continue to dominate the EU's budget and ensures too that the EU will continue to be pressed by trading partners to move further in the direction of market liberalisation.

Community preference

The EU market is protected from the international market. Since world prices are normally lower than EU prices, free access onto the EU market would clearly undermine the CAP system. Community preference (the term 'EU preference' is not used) is, therefore, required. The mechanics of the preference system and of the tariffs imposed vary according to the market regime for the product concerned.

Protectionist measures do not apply to all agricultural imports into the EU from all states. As is explained in Chapter 19, the EU has negotiated arrangements whereby a large number of countries are given special access to EU markets for at least some of their products, including agricultural products. So, the EU grants 'generalised preferences' to more than 120 developing countries and one effect of this has been the abolition or reduction of tariffs on over 300 agricultural products intended for processing. Under the Cotonou Agreement virtually all of the agricultural exports of the African, Pacific and Caribbean (ACP) countries are allowed free access to the EU market. (It should perhaps be pointed out that these 'concessions' do not stem simply from generosity and goodwill. Much of the produce falling under generalised preferences and the Cotonou Agreement is tropical in nature and not in competition with EU produce.)

Over and above the various special forms of access to the EU market given to developing countries, it should be noted that the general impact and extent of the Community preference system has been greatly reduced since the early 1990s. This has occurred as tariffs have been generally reduced in response to GATT/WTO pressures and as the CAP has moved away from price guarantee to income support.

Joint financing

The CAP is financed jointly by the member states out of the EU budget. Hitherto the channel for agricultural expenditure has been the European Agricultural Guidance and Guarantee Fund (EAGGF) of the budget. This has been divided into two sections. The Guarantee section has financed expenditure on direct payments and agricultural market organisations, on certain rural development measures that accompany market support, and on veterinary expenditure and information measures. The Guidance section has financed other rural development expenditure. When the CAP was established, the intention was for the Guarantee section to be larger than the Guidance section by a ratio of two or three to one, but in practice this was never even remotely approached and the Guidance section constantly hovered at just under 10 per cent of total EAGGF expenditure. The demands on the Guarantee section, occasioned initially by high EU prices and in later years more by direct payments, explain this imbalance.

In June 2005 the Agriculture Ministers reached political agreement on changes to the CAP funding arrangements from 2007. Their decision was taken partly to modernise financial control and management practices and partly to reflect the changing nature of the CAP – in particular the fact that under the reform programme agricultural policy has come to be based on two pillars, with pillar one focusing on direct financial support measures and pillar two on rural development. Under the June 2005 agreement, agricultural expenditure will in the future be made from two new funds: the European Agricultural Guarantee Fund (EAGF) and the European Agricultural Fund for Rural Development (EAFRD).

Financial support available for agriculture in the EU is not, it should be stressed, confined to the direct funding provided for agriculture in the EU budget. Some funds are available from other EU sources, including the European Investment Bank (EIB). By far the greatest additional funding source, however, is national exchequers: member states are allowed to assist their farmers in many ways provided they do not – in the judgement of the Commission – distort competition or infringe the principles of the market. In some states national subsidies to agriculture far outstrip those provided by the EU.

A fourth, 'unofficial', operating principle: allowance for national variations

As the previous paragraph implies, in addition to the three treaty-prescribed CAP operating principles, a fourth, unofficial, principle may also be said to exist: allowance for national variations.

The CAP is not as common or as integrated as it usually is portrayed as being. To be sure, the CAP lays down a policy framework within which member states must operate. But that framework has never been a complete straitjacket.

One reason for national variations is the differing nature of agricultural economies and structures across the EU: a phenomenon that has increased in scope and intensity as the EU has enlarged. Such are the differences – arising from such factors as topography, weather conditions, and the average size of land holdings – that it has always been necessary to have a policy framework that allows for variations that meets specific needs and circumstances. A second reason for national variations is differing policy choices of governments. Some governments, for example, have been much more inclined than others to make available to their farmers – after receiving Commission approval that CAP rules are not being breached – national financial and other forms of assistance. And a third reason is that, as Greer (2005: 3) puts it, 'There are still important areas that are not covered by EU-level policy-making or where the reach of the CAP is weak. These include important supply side matters such as research, education and advice, and some sectors are not subject to common market organisation (potatoes for human consumption, for example)'.

Significantly, the reform rounds since 1992 are resulting in the CAP become ever more diversified and less common. One reason for this is the increased emphasis on 'non agricultural' aspects of land use. Another reason is that the reforms have a considerable measure of national discretion and allowance built in. The 2003 reforms go particularly far in allowing for national flexibility and discretion with, for example, states that fear the possibility of a rush from the land – such as France, Spain and Ireland – being able to introduce special national measures if necessary, and states that think the reform do not go far enough – including the Netherlands, Sweden and the UK – being permitted to introduce certain more radical reforms.

The calls that are sometimes made for a 're-nationalisation' of agriculture have made little headway, and are unlikely to do so in the foreseeable future. However, it is undeniable that the *Common* Agricultural Policy displays a considerable measure of nationality.

The Impact and Effects of the Common Agricultural Policy

Whether the CAP is to be regarded as a success or not naturally depends on the priorities and interests of those making the judgement. Since, however, the issue has caused so much controversy it is a question that merits some attention here. This will be done initially via the five aims set out in Article 33 TEC, which were listed above.

- Agricultural efficiency has increased enormously as a result of modernisation and rationalisation. Because of the large number of variables involved, it is notoriously difficult to be precise about agricultural efficiency, but one indication of the advances made under the CAP is seen in the fact that at a time when the number of people engaged in agriculture has dropped by over 60 per cent on average in the EU-12 states (the pre-1995 EU members) since the CAP was created, volume outputs have steadily increased – at an average of 1.3 per cent since the early 1970s (Ackrill, 2000: 195–6). That said, it might be asked whether the overproduction of certain products at great cost, and the encouragement that high levels of support have given to many who would otherwise have left the land to stay on their farms, is wholly consistent with 'ensuring the rational development of agricultural production'.
- Agricultural incomes have grown roughly in parallel with incomes in other sectors. However, this overall average masks enormous variations, both between large farmers (who have done very well for the most part) and small farmers, and between producers of northern temperate products (notably dairy produce, cereals, and beef, which have been the main product beneficiaries of the CAP) and producers of other (mainly Mediterranean) products. The post-1992 direct payment

systems are partly designed to offset these distortions, with support targeted more towards small farmers.

- Markets have been stabilised, in the sense that there have been no major food shortages and EU prices have escaped the price fluctuations that have occurred in the world market on some products.
- The EU is now self-sufficient in virtually all of those foodstuffs its climate allows it to raise and grow. In 1958 the then six member states produced about 85 per cent of their food requirements; by the early 1990s the then twelve member states were producing around 120 per cent. This latter figure has now dropped in the wake of the CAP reforms, but surpluses still exist in most product sectors. The movement beyond self-sufficiency to the production of surpluses has been expensive in that it has only been possible to dispose of the surpluses at considerable cost.
- The exclusion of cheaper (often much cheaper) produce from outside the EU means that the aim of 'reasonable prices' to the consumer has had a low priority. The undeniable fact is that within the EU the principal beneficiaries of the CAP have been large agri-companies and farmers, whilst the main losers have been poor consumers.

Beyond an assessment of the CAP through its five Treaty aims, five other significant consequences of the policy are also worth noting.

First, the CAP's dominance of the budget has unquestionably made it more difficult for other policies to be developed. The financial perspectives that have been in operation since 1988, coupled with the series of reforms to the CAP, have brought agriculture under greater financial control, but it still accounts for almost half of the total budget.

Second, the CAP has been the source of many disagreements and tensions both within the EU and between the EU and non-EU states. For example, within the EU, France's generally protectionist attitude towards the CAP – which is explained by France accounting for almost a quarter of the EU's food production – has frequently caused it to be at loggerheads with other member states, especially the UK, over aspects of agricultural policy. As for its effect on relations between the EU and non-EU states, the CAP has fuelled many trading disputes between the EU and other agricultural exporters, both within the WTO framework and bilaterally.

Third, the intense farming practices that the CAP has encouraged have had damaging implications for the environment, and arguably also for food safety. It is only in recent years that these damaging implications have begun to be properly addressed. In the case of the environment, this has been achieved by making protection of the countryside a theme of the reform rounds since 1992 – for example, by making some direct aid conditional on farmers adopting production methods that respect the environment and bio-diversity. Food safety issues have been addressed in a number of ways, including by detaching most of the responsibility for it from DG Agriculture and attaching it to DG Health and Consumer Protection and by the creation of the European Food Safety Authority which was established in 2002.

Fourth, protecting the EU market from cheaper world produce, and the release onto the world market of heavily subsidised EU produce, has distorted the international division of labour and the rational utilisation of resources.

Fifth, in international debates and negotiations concerning development policies and the problems of 'the Global South', there has been an increasing emphasis in recent years on the perceived damaging effects of the CAP. This has been partly because NGOs such as Oxfam have given more attention to anti-CAP campaigning.

Policy Processes

Prior to the reform process that began with the 1992 reforms, agriculture was a highly distinctive policy-making sphere. This was mainly because many key decisions were made as part of a regular, and usually highly complicated, process: the annual price review. Many non-price elements were swept up in reviews and became components of what customarily were highly complex and interconnected packages by the time final agreements were made. The core of the packages usually consisted of a range of price increases, adjustments to produce regimes, and statements of intent about future action.

The phased reductions in prices since 1992 coupled with the associated switch from price support to income support have resulted in the annual price review disappearing. As this has happened, policy-making and decision-making processes for agriculture have become more like the processes that exist in other policy sectors. However, the importance, range, and complexity of the CAP, plus the ever-changing nature of the world's agricultural markets, means that there are still significant variations from the 'standard' EU model. The principal variations are as follows.

Commission initiation and formulation: driving for reform

Whereas the policy initiation and formulation responsibilities of the Commission in many sectors are mainly concerned with creating a policy framework, in agriculture they are inevitably directed more towards improving the efficiency of one that already exists.

As part of this drive for greater efficiency, since the late 1960s the Commission has been proactively in the forefront of attempts to bring about fundamental reform of the CAP. However, as has been shown above, there are formidable obstacles in the way of the Commission forwarding proposals that both go to the heart of the agricultural problem and are acceptable to the Council. As long ago as 1968, the then Commissioner for Agriculture, Sicco Mansholt, launched a major plan to reduce the size of the agricultural sector and improve the efficiency of what remained, but his proposals had little effect and were not followed up with sufficient Council legislation. As a result, in the 1970s the Commission approached its policy initiation and formulation responsibilities in a very cautious way. It became reluctant to advance wide-ranging schemes aimed at fundamental reform and concentrated more on short-term measures of an essentially reactive nature: reacting, that is, to specific problems in particular market sectors.

In the 1980s and 1990s circumstances changed in such a way as to enable, even oblige, the Commission to bring a longer-term view back onto the agenda and force real and properly integrated reform to be seriously discussed. The most important of these circumstances were deteriorating market conditions and increasing surpluses, recurring budgetary problems, international pressures against the EC's high levels of protectionism and subsidisation, and the enlargement of the Community to states that would not do especially well out of the CAP as constituted. It was against this background that in 1985 the Commission launched a consultative Green Paper – *Perspectives for the Common Agricultural Policy* – which outlined policy options for the future of agriculture until the end of the century. After wide-ranging discussions with interested parties the Green Paper was followed up with more detailed guidelines in the form of a communication to the Council and the EP entitled *A Future for European Agriculture*. At the heart of the Commission's proposals lay an ambitious long-term strategy for a move towards a more market-based and restrictive pricing policy, greater flexibility in guarantees and intervention mechanisms, and a much greater degree of producer co-responsibility for surpluses. These objectives were re-stated in the Commission's influential 1987 document *The Single Act: A New Frontier for Europe,* and constituted the basis for important agricultural reforms that the Agriculture Ministers agreed to in December 1986 and the Heads of Government agreed to at their special summit at Brussels in February 1988.

In 1991 the Commission proposed even more fundamental reforms. The views of trading partners were, however, much more important on this occasion than they had been previously, for agriculture featured prominently in the GATT Uruguay Round of international trade negotiations conducted in the late 1980s/early 1990s. As in 1985 the reforms were launched in two stages, starting with a consultation document – entitled *Communication ... The Development and Future of the CAP. Reflections Paper of the Commission* – followed six months later by specific proposals under the title *Communication ... The Development and Future of the Common Agricultural Policy. Follow-up to the Reflections Paper. Proposals of the Commission*. Although subsequently watered down, these proposals provided the general framework for the radical reforms of the CAP to which Agriculture Ministers agreed in May 1992.

As was explained above, further agricultural reforms were agreed at the 1999 Berlin summit. As with the previous reform rounds, the 1999 reforms were again based on Commission proposals, with the key document this time being *Agenda 2000*. Two of the main considerations guiding the Commission's thinking in preparing *Agenda 2000* were similar to the considerations that had guided it when making its earlier reform proposals: the continuing high proportion of the EU budget consumed by agriculture and international pressures on the EU to reduce subsidised exports and open up its market. A new consideration, however, was the looming prospect of EU enlargement and the accession of Central and Eastern European countries (CEECs) with large, and for the most part relatively inefficient, agricultural sectors. The main thrust of the Commission's *Agenda 2000* proposals involved an intensification of the 1992 reforms – that is, further movement towards a more market-based system in which farmers would be protected by an elaborate system of direct payments.

The *Agenda 2000* proposals were, as was noted above, watered down by the national governments. This was partly because some governments pressed for a stronger defence of particular national interests and partly too because the *Agenda 2000* negotiations were not conducted in an atmosphere of imminent crisis and so the pressures for radical reform were not so intense as they had been in the 1980s and early 1990s (Ackrill, 2000). The dilution of the Commission's proposals resulted in the planned mid-term review of the 2000–6 arrangements assuming rather more importance than had originally been foreseen. One reason for this was that the 1999 agreement quickly came to be viewed as not having responded sufficiently to international pressures for reductions in agricultural financial support, especially in the form of export refunds. Another reason was that the 1999 reforms had not been sufficiently radical in preparing the EU for enlargement: CAP expenditure in the EU-15 was not planned to fall – because direct payments come mainly from the EU budget – whilst applying existing policies to accession states would greatly increase CAP expenditure. Accordingly, in the first half of 2002 the Commission issued two major documents:

- In January, in a paper entitled *Enlargement and Agriculture: Successfully Integrating the New Member States into the CAP* (European Commission, 2002a), proposals were made for incorporating acceding countries into the CAP. The key elements of the proposals were: long transitional periods – of up to ten years – before new member states would benefit fully from support measures, with direct aids beginning at just one-quarter of the full level in the year after accession (this being justified with the argument that the immediate introduction of 100 per cent direct payments would freeze existing structures and hamper modernisation in the CEECs); production quotas set at low levels; and confirmation that the costs of accession could be met within the 2000–6 financial framework agreed at the 1999 Berlin summit.
- In July, a communication to the Council and the EP – *Mid-Term Review of the Common Agricultural Policy* (European Commission, 2002e) – was issued. The Review proposed a range of radical reforms, the most prominent of which were: an end to the array of payments based on levels of output and production; support for farmers to be based on a single direct payment linked to past income, with the maximum amount to be paid to any one farm to be capped at €300 000 and with payments to be reduced over time for larger farmers; payments to farmers to be dependent on them observing environmental, food safety, and animal welfare standards; savings in direct payments to be re-directed towards rural development and environmental protection schemes; and the introduction of a new farm audit scheme.

Justifying the proposals, Agriculture Commissioner Franz Fischler said: 'In future, farmers will not be paid for overproduction, but for responding to what people want: safe food, quality production, animal welfare and a healthy environment. While guaranteeing farmers a stable income, the new system will free them from the straitjacket of having to gear their production towards subsidies. They will be able to produce the crop or the type of meat where they see the best market opportunities and not the highest subsidies' (*Europa* website).

As was widely anticipated, the proposals met with a mixed and predictable reaction. The traditional supporters of CAP reform – most notably Germany, Sweden and the UK – broadly welcomed the thrust of the proposals, though regretted they did not go far enough in that they would have little effect on the overall size of the CAP budget. The traditional opponents, by contrast – with France, Ireland and Spain in the lead – expressed concerns bordering on outright opposition, and accused Fischler of having exceeded his mandate of being restricted to conducting just a mid-term review – which they understood to mean a technical rather than a policy review. Overall, however, the differences between the member states were less than they had been in respect of the 1992 and 1999 reform rounds. Key factors for this were that some shifts of policy principle had already been accepted in the earlier rounds and the force of international pressures for further reform was quickly recognised. Accordingly, negotiations on the Commission's proposals lasted just one year – much shorter than with the previous rounds – and the broad thrust of the Commission's proposals were incorporated into the compromise package that was agreed by the Council in June 2003. (For a much fuller account of the Commission's thinking and behaviour, and of the negotiations between the member states on the Commission's proposals, in all three reform rounds, see Garzon, 2006.)

✳ ✳ ✳

The Commission thus has been and is a crucial agenda-setter in the long drawn-out and ongoing process of CAP reform. In this process the lead within the Commission has inevitably been taken by the Agriculture Commissioner and DG Agriculture. However, they no longer have the near-monopoly control over agriculture policy they used to enjoy. As pressures for reform of the CAP have increased and as perceptions of the nature and the implications of agricultural policy have been broadened, so have other parts of the Commission come to have a say and to exercise an influence. Amongst the other parts of the Commission to have inserted themselves/to become drawn into agricultural policy are health and consumer protection, environment, and trade. Taking trade, the Trade Commissioner and DG Trade have become key players as international trade pressures have played an increasing role in driving the agricultural reform process. So, although the Agriculture Commissioner, Marian Fischer Boel, was present at the December 2005 Doha Round negotiations in Hong Kong where agreement was reached, amongst other things, on the phasing-out by 2013 of all first world agricultural export refunds, the EU's 'main player' was the Trade Commissioner, Peter Mandelson.

Council decision-making, and control problems for the Agriculture Council

An important feature of Council decision-making in the agriculture sphere is that formal processes are relatively straightforward, with legislation mostly being made on the basis of the consultation procedure and with QMV applying in the Council. Use of the consultation procedure means that the EP's ability to press its preferences on the Council is limited, and certainly much weaker than under the other legislative procedures. Use of

QMV means that governments wishing to dissent from majority Council opinion – and such dissents are common in respect of CAP matters – can be, and frequently are, outvoted.

But though formal processes are relatively straightforward, in practice the reality can be somewhat complex. Of all the formations in which the Council of Ministers meets, the Agriculture Council has traditionally been the most reliant on issue linkages and package deals for the conduct of its business. However, in recent years this use of linkages and packages to increase negotiating flexibility and create room for agreements has not been so prevalent, except in major reform rounds. This is because the margins for manoeuvre available to the Council have been reduced by the use of multi-annual planning within financial perspectives, by the disappearance of the price review, and by the gradual phasing-out of separate product market organisations. But though wide-ranging wheeling and dealing is not now so characteristic of the Council as it used to be, it certainly still exists – most especially when important decisions have to be taken on, for example, Commission reform proposals or positions to be adopted in external agricultural trade negotiations. In such situations, agreements are usually only possible if they are based on a recognition of the different interests and priorities of the member states: some states, for example, are net exporters of agricultural produce whilst others are net importers; some have temperate climates whilst others have Mediterranean; some have mainly large and efficient farms whilst others have many small and inefficient family-based units; and some have vast tracts of 'less favoured' land whilst others have very little.

Another feature of Council agriculture policy processes is that they are less insulated from other policy areas than they used to be. In this, they mirror the processes within the Commission that were noted above that have arisen from agriculture becoming increasingly enmeshed with other policy areas. As Grant (1997: 148) has noted, the circle of actors involved in agricultural policy formation in the EU has widened considerably in recent years. The most obvious impact of this widening at Council level is that non-Agriculture Councils – especially the GAERC (which is responsible for external trade), Ecofin, and Environment – sometimes express views and make decisions that have direct implications for agriculture. Given the segmented nature of Council structures, this can create problems in terms of developing rounded and properly integrated policy.

Retaining complete control over policy can also be difficult for the Agriculture Council when policy issues assume a high political profile, as they are more prone to do than is generally the case with most other formations of the Council apart from the GAERC and Ecofin. Three examples may be taken to illustrate this. The first is the crisis that arose in the beef industry in 1996 as a result of BSE in British cattle (on the crisis, see Westlake, 1997). Foreign Ministers in the General Affairs Council and Heads of Government in the European Council quickly became directly involved in the policy process when there was perceived to be an urgent need for action and a requirement that agricultural policy should be linked more closely to consumer protection policy. The second example is the agricultural reforms that were part of the Commission's *Agenda 2000* proposals. With the reforms being vital to agreement on the overall *Agenda 2000* package, Agriculture Ministers were left in no doubt by the General Affairs and Ecofin Councils (both of which discussed the agricultural component of *Agenda 2000* on several occasions) that their room for manoeuvre was limited. As the scheduled date for final agreement on *Agenda 2000* drew close in the first half of 1999, the German Presidency made it clear to the Agriculture Ministers – not least in statements by Chancellor Schröder himself – that they must recognise the need to be flexible and make concessions so as to open the way for a deal on the package as a whole (*European Voice*, 14–20 January 1999). As was noted above, the Agriculture Ministers eventually reached agreement on a range of reforms in March 1999, but parts of their agreement were changed later that month by Heads of Government at the Berlin summit. The third example is discussions concerning agriculture in the context of the 2007–13 financial perspective. Aware that when negotiations on the contents of the perspective got under way in 2003–04 there would be intense pressures to cut agricultural spending, President Chirac allied with Chancellor Schröder in the autumn of 2002 to pre-empt such pressures. This was done by them jointly putting to, and virtually steamrolling through, the October 2002 European Council meeting the proposition that the proportion of the EU budget assigned to agriculture should be only marginally reduced over the period of the perspective. This October 2002 decision did, as anticipated, effectively preclude the possibility of significant cuts in CAP spending during the lifetime of the financial perspective and resulted in the ensuing discussions and negotiations on the expenditure side of the perspective having to focus primarily on the 55 per cent of the budget accounted for by non-agricultural spending. However, in the later part of the negotiations, when much attention came to focus on the UK abatement (rebate), Prime Minister Blair sought to link a reduction in the abatement to a fundamental review of agricultural spending to be conducted by the Commission. Though initially resisted by President Chirac, this linkage was eventually agreed at the December 2005 summit, with the start of the review scheduled for 2008 – though with no firm commitment as to when the implementation of recommendations emanating from the review would begin.

The role of the European Parliament

As was noted in Chapter 12, the powers of the EP have increased greatly over the years. Apart from the special cases of the policy areas covered by pillars two and three of the TEU (CFSP and Police and Judicial Cooperation) of the TEU, the EP now commands very considerable powers – notably via the co-decision procedure – in virtually all policy areas.

The most notable policy area where the EP does not command such powers is agriculture. There are two principal aspects to its weakness. First, although the EP is a co-decision-maker with the Council on the EU's annual budget and although agriculture accounts for approaching fifty per cent of that budget, the EP can do little about agricultural expenditure. The reason for this was explained in Chapter 17, but in essence it is because whereas the EP has powers to amend what is known as non-compulsory expenditure it can only make recommendations to amend what is known as compulsory expenditure: and compulsory expenditure consists almost entirely of agriculture. Second, agriculture is one of the very few remaining policy areas where the co-decision legislation procedure does not apply. The consultation procedure which, as was shown in Chapter 17, allows the EP to make recommendations to and exert pressure on the Commission and the Council in respect of legislative proposals, but does not permit it to insist that its views be accepted, remains the decision-making process. The Constitutional Treaty makes provision for agricultural policy to be 'upgraded' to the co-decision procedure, but the future of the Treaty is now uncertain.

This is not to suggest that the EP does not exert some influence on agricultural policy. It scrutinises both policy and legislative proposals and does have some successes in helping to shape outcomes. Garzon (2006), for example, suggests that the Agriculture Committee played a crucial role in helping to devise an acceptable formula on de-coupling in the 2003 reform round. It is also the case that the Parliament's influence over agriculture has increased as agriculture policy has been broadened out to include aspects of related policy areas such as environment and food safety. Overall, however, agriculture remains an area of comparative EP institutional weakness.

Management and implementation of the Common Agricultural Policy

Because of the nature of the CAP, the EU is much more involved in the management and implementation of agricultural policy than it is in most other policy spheres. The Commission, and particularly DG Agriculture, are central in this regard. They oversee the general operation of the whole system, adjust it as necessary and, as far as possible, try to ensure that the national agencies that undertake the front-line implementation of policy – national Ministries of Agriculture, intervention agencies, customs and excise authorities and so on - fulfil their obligations in a proper manner.

Much of what the Commission does in managing the CAP is of an essentially technical nature. This is, for example, the case in respect of the almost continuous adjustments it has to make to CAP prices to match ever-changing market conditions. To cite just three Commission regulations that were issued on a typical day in January 2002, there was nothing especially 'political' about the regulations 'establishing the standard import values for determining the entry price of certain fruit and vegetables', 'fixing the import duties in the rice sector', and 'on the registration of establishments keeping laying hens' (*Official Journal*, Vol. 45: L30, 31 January 2002).

But some management work does involve the Commission doing things that amount to rather more than the simple application of tightly drawn rules. Many decisions on, for instance, intervention and support systems are taken within margins of manoeuvre that give the Commission at least some flexibility. This flexibility can result in the Commission's choices having important financial implications for producers, traders, processors, and the EU budget.

The Commission also has some room for manoeuvre in how it deals with the national agencies which undertake most of the direct policy implementation. Moreover, this room for manoeuvre has broadened as the CAP has been reformed, because a significant degree of decentralisation is built into the reform programme. Key features of this decentralisation are: some direct payments are allocated to member states in the form of 'national envelopes' which national authorities manage according to their own criteria and requirements; rural development measures are co-financed with member states; and member states must have in place rural development programmes which require Commission approval before EU funds can be released. Such decentralisation requires the Commission to frame its relations with national agencies more in terms of being a partner than an overseer.

When quick management decisions have to be taken, the Commission is authorised to act. However, as was explained in Chapter 9, the Commission's agricultural management responsibilities are not undertaken by Commission officials alone but via management committees made up of civil servants from the member states. There are around twenty such CAP committees, including one for each category of products, and implementing measures that the Commission intends to enact are submitted to the appropriate committees for their opinion. There are usually between 300 and 400 meetings of CAP management committees each year. The

Commission determines the direction and sets the pace in the committees, but the existence of the committees does mean that the member states have a direct input into, and ultimately a degree of control over, all but the fine details of agricultural policy and the management of that policy.

Concluding Remarks

Despite all the obstacles and hurdles that litter its decision-making processes, the CAP has been the subject of considerable reform in recent years. One aspect of the reform has resulted in a system that used to be based primarily on support prices being replaced by one that now is based primarily on direct payments. Some price supports do remain, though at much lower levels, but direct payments now account for over three quarters of CAP expenditure. The other main aspect of the reform has resulted in the CAP becoming less focused on matters related to food production and more concerned with wider environmental, rural development, and consumer protection issues.

However, the reforms that have been and are being made have not solved all of the CAP's problems. *Outside the EU*, many countries, not least the USA, continue to be dissatisfied with what they regard as a still over-protected EU market and still over-subsidised EU produce on world markets. *Inside the EU*, sharp differences still exist over many aspects of agricultural policy: where should the balance be struck between market efficiency on the one hand and the granting of support to the agriculture sector on the other, and insofar as support is to be given to agriculture, how ought it to be distributed, and in what form?

Agricultural policy will thus continue to loom large on the EU agenda.

Chapter 19

External Relations

External Trade
Foreign, Security and Defence Policies
Development Policy
The External Dimension of Internal Policies
The Consistency and Representational Problems
Concluding Remarks

The EU is an important actor on the world stage. It is so partly because of its size and resources and partly because of its ability to act in a united, or at least coordinated, manner in a range of external policy contexts and settings.

There are four main aspects to the EU's external relations: trade; foreign, security and defence; development; and the external dimension of internal policies. Each of these will be examined in this chapter.

External Trade

The EU in the world trading system

The member states of the EU present a united front to the world in respect of international trade and they act as one in contracting the terms of trade agreements. If they did not do so the unified internal market would not be possible.

The main foundations of the united front are the Common External Tariff (CET) – or Common Customs Tariff (CCT) as it is also known – and the Common Commercial Policy (CCP). Together, the CET and the CCP enable, indeed oblige, the member states to act in common on matters such as the fixing and adjusting of external customs tariffs, the negotiation of customs and trade agreements with non-member countries, and the taking of action to impede imports – this being most likely when unfair trading practices, such as dumping and subsidies, are suspected.

The EU conducts trade negotiations in many forums: with single states; with other regional groupings, such as the European Free Trade Association (EFTA) and the Association of South-East Asian Nations (ASEAN); and in international frameworks, of which the most important is the

World Trade Organisation (WTO) – which at the end of 2005 had 149 members, who collectively accounted for 90 per cent of world trade. In these forums the EU is able to bring very considerable economic and trading strengths to bear:

- The combined Gross Domestic Product (GDP) of the EU-25 in 2005 was around €10,000 billion, as compared with around €9,850 billion for the USA. In percentage terms this results in the EU accounting for around 25 per cent of world GDP, as compared with around 23 per cent for the USA and 12 per cent for Japan.
- The EU accounts for around one-fifth of world exports and imports (excluding internal EU trade), which is comparable to the USA but much larger than Japan which accounts for around 7 per cent. (The main sources used for the figures given in these first two bullet points are Eurostat and the WTO, as reproduced at < www.eurunion.org/ profile/facts.htm > .)
- In terms of population, the EU market, with almost 460 million people (about one-seventh of the world's population), is much larger than both the US market, which numbers just over 290 million people, and the Japanese market, which numbers around 127 million.
- Many of the countries and groupings with which the EU negotiates on trade matters are heavily reliant on the EU market for their exports – either for reasons of geography (as most obviously with non-EU European countries) or for reasons of historical linkage (as with former French and UK colonies).

The combination of these economic and trading strengths, and the fact that in trading forums it acts as a single bloc, means that the EU is an extremely powerful world trading force.

Trade policies

The EU presents itself as being committed to a liberal trade policy and as having as its main priority in external trade negotiations the opening up of markets. The most important international trade negotiations of recent years – the 1986–93 General Agreement on Tariffs and Trade (GATT) Uruguay Round and the WTO Doha Development Round which was launched in 2001 – are seen as providing evidence in support of this view of the nature of the EU's trading stance. Priorities for the EU during the negotiations have included: the lowering of international customs duties; the removal of non-tariff barriers to trade; and the opening up of hitherto restricted spheres of trading activity, especially those, such as financial services, in which the EU, or at least some of its member states, are strong.

It is a liberal trading policy, however, which is not always pursued with complete consistency or uniformity. The governments of the member states frequently seek to cope with 'special' national economic circumstances and accompanying political pressures by pressing for protectionist measures. EU trade policy is thus concerned not only with promoting the general liberalisation of trade, but also with ensuring that the consequences of this are not damaging for its member states. This results in trade policy also being much taken up with matters such as the seeking of special exemptions from general trade agreements, the negotiation of 'orderly marketing' agreements with more competitive countries, and the imposition of anti-dumping duties (the latter being taken mainly against Asian countries).

The most obvious sectoral sphere of EU protectionism is agriculture, which has long been sheltered from the full rigours of external competition by domestic support to agricultural producers and traders on the one hand and high tariffs on imports on the other. Under WTO pressures, however, the EU has been changing these policies and since the mid-1990s has been moving away from price support to income support, has been reducing export refunds (which have been a particular target for other agricultural exporting countries because of their distortion of world agricultural markets), and has been lowering agricultural tariffs (see Chapter 18 for details). Other sectors that have attracted EU special protection include the motor vehicle industry, which has been assisted by export restraint agreements with Japan, and textiles, where there have long been restrictions of various sorts on imports from the Far East.

Beyond 'strict' trade issues, the EU often has to deal with, and indeed brings, other issues into trade negotiations. This is part of a general process whereby the international trade agenda has been expanded and politicised over the years. So, politically sensitive trade-related matters such as labour standards and environmental protection increasingly feature in trade talks, as do issues concerning human rights. The EU takes, in relative terms, an 'advanced' position on such matters.

Trade and trade-dominated agreements

The EU – or strictly speaking the EC in the context of external trade – has trade agreements, or agreements in which a substantial part of the content is concerned with trade, with just about every country in the world. These agreements take a number of different forms, both in terms of the extent to which they remove barriers to market access and the number and range of non-trade matters that are covered. Some of the agreements are best viewed as being part of the EU's development cooperation policies and, as such, are considered in the section on development cooperation later in the chapter. Trade agreements that are not part of development cooperation policy are of three main types. In 'ascending' order – from minimalist to maximalist – they are:

Trade agreements

These are based on Article 133 (ex 113) of the TEC, which obliges the EU to operate a common commercial policy: 'The common commercial policy shall be based on uniform principles, particularly in regard to changes in tariff rates, the conclusion of tariff and trade agreements, the achievement of uniformity in measures of liberalisation, export policy and measures to protect trade such as those to be taken in the event of dumping or subsidies.' Article 133 agreements may be preferential or non-preferential in kind, but they are all subject to the general framework of international trading rules established within the framework of the WTO and these rules prohibit preferential agreements unless waivers are negotiated.

The Commission has long sought to persuade the member states to adopt an expansive approach towards what may be included in Article 133 agreements, arguing this is necessary to reflect the fact that EU and global economic activity and trade have changed considerably in nature since the EEC Treaty was negotiated in the 1950s. In particular, from the early 1990s the Commission came to campaign vigorously for the rapidly expanding trade areas of services and intellectual property to be located within the framework of Article 133. The campaign received setbacks when the ECJ ruled in 1994 (in Opinion 1/94) that the responsibility for negotiating services and intellectual property was shared between the EU and its member states and in the 1996–97 IGC when the member states decided not to amend the TEC so as to include services and intellectual property in Article 133. (Though provision was made in the Amsterdam Treaty for Article 133 to be extended to services and intellectual property if in the future the Council, acting unanimously, decided to do so.) However, some movement towards the Commission's position was incorporated into the Nice Treaty, which included a compromise between the 'maximalist' option – where all responsibilities for trade in services and intellectual property would be communautarised – and the 'minimalist' position – which would retain the existing mixed competence status of these issues. Regarding trade in services, this now became – under Article 133.5 TEC – an exclusive competence, though with: (1) unanimity required for certain types of decisions; (2) a list of policy areas which are excepted – including cultural and audiovisual services (at French insistence), education, and social and human health services. Regarding trade in intellectual property, this is divided into 'commercial aspects of intellectual property', which are assigned to exclusive competence, and all other aspects of intellectual property, which are to remain a shared competence but with the Council being able to decide by unanimity that they should be an exclusive competence. (On the trade provisions of the Nice Treaty, see Meunier and Nicolaidis, 2001.)

Trade and economic cooperation agreements

The Treaty base of these agreements depends on their precise nature, but there is usually some combination of Article 133 and at least one other article. So, Article 300 of the TEC which sets out procedures for the contracting of external agreements, is almost invariably used, whilst Article 181 applies when there is a development cooperation dimension to agreements. The number of trade and cooperation agreements has increased enormously over the years and their scope has steadily expanded. At their core are trade preferences of various kinds and usually also assistance of some sort from the EU to the other signatory(ies). In some cases, as with partnership agreements with states that were part of the former Soviet Union such as Georgia, Moldova and the Ukraine, free trade is an eventual objective. Since the late 1980s, political conditions – usually concerning human rights and democratic processes – have routinely been part of cooperation agreements.

Association agreements

These are based on Article 310 of the TEC, which states that 'The Community may conclude with one or more states or international organisations agreements establishing an association involving reciprocal rights and obligations, common action and reciprocal procedure'. Typically, association agreements include highly preferential access to EU markets, the prospect of a free trade area eventually being formed between the signatories, economic and technical cooperation of various sorts, financial aid from the EU, political dialogue, and – in some cases – the prospect of the associated countries eventually becoming members of the EU. There are currently three broad categories of countries that either have, or are in the process of negotiating, association agreements with the EU. First, there are countries that are seeking and have realistic prospects of EU membership. Turkey is in this category. Prior to their accession, all CEECs had association agreements with the EU. Developed out of earlier cooperation agreements, these were very much part of the CEECs' pre-accession strategy and were seen by both the EU and CEEC sides as a means of assisting economic liberalisation, market adjustment, and political democratisation in the CEECs. A similar process is now ongoing with most of the states of the Western Balkans – Albania, Bosnia-

Herzegovina, Croatia, Macedonia, and Serbia-Montenegro. All of these states are part of the EU's Stability Programme for South East Europe which includes the negotiation of association agreements that contain trade, cultural and political cooperation aspects that have as their main purpose the promotion of, and assistance with, internal reforms and development. The agreements explicitly hold out the prospect of future EU membership. Second, there are several Mediterranean states – including the Mashreq and Maghreb countries – that constitute part of the EU's Mediterranean policy. The prospect of EU membership is not part of these association agreements. Third, there are the non-EU members of the European Economic Area (EEA) – Iceland, Norway and Liechtenstein. The EEA is the deepest of the EU's trading agreements in that it involves not only free trade in goods but also extends the EU's other so-called freedoms (of services, capital, and people) to the three EEA states.

With each of these three types of agreement – trade, cooperation, and association – containing variations in both scope and depth, the EU is thus involved in a wide and complicated range of agreements with trading partners. The agreements can be thought of as constituting a hierarchy of preferences in which the EU and the other signatory(ies) of agreements are, moving from the bottom to the top of the hierarchy, bound together in complex and, for the most part, open, market access and other arrangements.

Policy processes

Trade agreements made on the basis of Article 133 and in the context of the CCP are essentially the responsibility of the Commission and the Council. The normal procedure for contracting agreements is as follows:

- The Commission makes a recommendation to the General Affairs and External Relations Council (GAERC) that the EU should seek to conclude a trade agreement with a third country or organisation. (There is no separate Trade Council, but at the GAERC trade matters are usually handled by Trade Ministers rather than Foreign Ministers.)
- The Committee of Permanent Representatives (COREPER) discusses the recommendation and places it on the agenda of the Council. The Council takes a decision as to whether negotiations should proceed. In making its decision the Council may, on the basis of proposals drawn up by the Commission and subsequently discussed, and perhaps modified, by COREPER, give to the Commission negotiating directives, guidelines or – to use the most commonly used, but not most accurate term – mandates. The Council may act, as it may act on any decisions

taken in connection with Article 133 agreements, by qualified majority vote, but in practice it usually proceeds by consensus.

- Working within the framework of mandates it has been given by the Council, the Commission negotiates on behalf of all twenty five EU states. The Trade DG normally takes the lead role on behalf of the Commission but other DGs – including Development, Competition, and Agriculture – are also involved if they have a direct interest. How much room for manoeuvre the Commission has when conducting negotiations varies according to the circumstances. Usually, differences of both principle and special interest between the member states result in negotiating mandates being fairly tightly drawn, often reflecting a compromise between those countries which tend towards protectionism and those which favour free trade. While Commission officials acknowledge privately that Council mandates are usually less of a dead weight than is often supposed, there is no doubt that the Commission's flexibility in negotiations can be constrained by the necessity of not disturbing compromises that have been agreed only with difficulty in the Council. (Although it should also be said that it is not unknown for the Commission to use Council reins to the EU's advantage: during negotiations it can be helpful to say in response to an unwanted proposal, 'the Council would never agree to that'.)

- Throughout the period of the negotiations, the Commission is in touch with the Article 133 Committee. This is a Council committee that normally meets weekly to review, discuss, and make decisions on trade agreements that come within the scope of Article 133. The Committee meets at two levels: full members and deputies. At full members' meetings, which are held at least once each month, national 'teams' are headed by senior officials from the national ministries responsible for trade. The Commission 'team' is headed by the Director General of DG Trade. Full members' meetings focus on general and particularly problematical policy issues. At deputy members' meetings, which are held three times a month, national 'teams' are composed of officials from either relevant national ministries or the permanent representations in Brussels and the Commission is represented by officials from DG Trade. Deputies' meetings deal with detailed policy matters. The 133 Committee is supported by specialised sub-committees that deal with particular trade matters, including services, textiles, and motor vehicles.

- During particularly difficult or important negotiations the Commission may return to the Council for clarification of the negotiating mandate, or for an amended mandate that might break a deadlock. The Article 133 Committee can adjust negotiating mandates, but anything that is especially sensitive or political is normally referred to COREPER and, if necessary, the GAERC. (In the closing stages of the Uruguay Round negotiations in November and December 1993, the chief Commission negotiator, Sir Leon Brittan, presented written and verbal reports and made requests to several Council meetings.)

• At the (apparent) conclusion of negotiations the Commission may initial negotiated settlements, but Council approval is necessary for agreements to be formally authorised and signed.

The powers of and relations between and within the EU institutions in connection with the CCP are such that tensions of various sorts are by no means uncommon. Four areas cause particular difficulties.

First, the power balance between the Council and the Commission can be very delicate, with the Council trying to ensure that the Commission remains under its control and the Commission wanting and needing enough manoeuvrability to enable it to be an effective negotiator.

Second, the different national interests and preferences of the member states can create difficulties in the Council. Apart from differences that arise on specific issues, there is a broad underlying difference, with some countries – including France, Italy, Spain and Greece – tending to favour a measure of protectionism and other countries – led by Germany and the UK – tending more towards trade liberalisation.

Third, problems can arise within the Commission with disputes between Commissioners and between DGs about where policy responsibilities lie and who has a legitimate interest in particular external trade policies and agreements. Thus in June 1990 the Farm Commissioner – Raymond MacSharry – stressing that he was determined to defend the Community's position on farm reform in the GATT Uruguay Round talks, felt obliged to state publicly that he, not the Trade Commissioner – Frans Andriessen – was 'in charge of agricultural negotiations'. In November 1992, when the much troubled bilateral negotiations with the USA on the agricultural aspects of the Uruguay Round were at their most difficult, MacSharry temporarily resigned from his position in the Commission negotiating team because of alleged excessive interference by the Commission President, Jacques Delors.

Fourth, MEPs are dissatisfied that the EP has no automatic right to be consulted, let alone to insist that its views be considered, in connection with Article 133 agreements. In practice, the EP is notified about agreements, and the Commission and to a lesser extent the Council do discuss external trade matters with the EP – primarily in the forum of Parliament's International Trade Committee – but it is clear that Parliament's influence is usually limited. However, there are signs that it is increasing. One reason for this is that the EP has constantly voiced its dissatisfaction and has done what it can to maximise its influence, not least by incorporating into its Rules of Procedure a range of measures aimed at persuading the Council to take note of the EP as regards the opening, negotiating, and concluding of trade agreements.

✻ ✻ ✻

Turning to procedures in respect of cooperation and association agreements, the rules are set out in Article 300. These result in similar decision-making procedures to those which apply in respect of Article 133 agreements, but with two important exceptions. First, unanimity rather than a qualified majority is required for Council decisions when the agreement covers a field for which unanimity is required for the adoption of internal rules and when association agreements are being contracted. (Unanimity tends to weaken the negotiating position of the Commission, since it cannot afford to sideline the wishes of any member state.) Second, the powers of the EP are much greater, for it must at least be consulted on cooperation agreements and its assent is required for some types of cooperation agreement and for all association agreements. The power of assent gives the EP a useful lever to try to influence the course of negotiations, for it can block the outcome of negotiations if it finds them to be unsatisfactory. Such a block has sometimes been threatened, and occasionally imposed, usually as a protest against lack of democracy or abuse of human rights in the state with which the agreement is being contracted. In the mid-1990s the EP withheld its assent from the EU–Turkey customs union agreement because of concerns about the human rights situation in Turkey and only 'relented' after Turkey agreed to amend its constitution.

Foreign, Security and Defence Policies

Resources and problems with their usage

The EU is often described as being a 'civilian' or 'soft' international power. This means that whilst it does exercise influence on matters related to economics, trade, the environment and so on, it contributes little in 'traditional' and 'hard' areas of foreign and defence policy.

There unquestionably is much in this portrayal of the EU, although as will be shown below it is a portrayal that is becoming increasingly less accurate. The key reason it is becoming less accurate is that the EU is slowly making better use of the resources it has at its disposal in the foreign and defence policy areas. And resources that give it the potential to be a major international foreign and defence policy actor it most certainly does have. Unlike, however, with trade policies, the resources are accompanied by many obstacles which have made the effective marshalling of the resources difficult and have left much of the potential unrealised.

What then are the resources and the accompanying obstacles? The principal resources are:

- The EU's membership of 25 member states. Some of these states – notably Germany, France, Italy, Poland, Spain and the UK – are, in global terms, of at least middle-ranking size and status.
- Many EU member states, and increasingly the EU itself, have extensive diplomatic experience and skills, and also special links with many parts of the world.
- Two EU states – France and the UK – are nuclear powers.
- Two EU states – again France and the UK – occupy two of the five permanent seats on the United Nations Security Council.
- The collective spending of the member states on defence is second only to that of the US amongst the world's powers. In 2005 the US spent around €400 billion, the EU spent around €160 billion, whilst the third largest spender, China, spent an unofficial estimate of around €70 billion (Beatty, 2005: 18). One result of EU defence expenditure is that there are more full-time European troops than there are American.
- The EU's powerful economic and trading positions (see above) are becoming all the more important as much of international relations become less focused on 'traditional' political and military issues and more focused on economic issues and economic-related issues such as environmental protection and energy supplies.

What then are the problems in the way of being able to fully use these resources and opening the way to the development of genuinely common EU foreign, security and defence policies? The main obstacles are the following:

- The EU is not a state and therefore does not have the (usually) long-established 'givens' that help to focus national foreign policy. Most notably, there is no national territory to protect and no national political, economic, social and cultural interests to promote. The EU's territory does not 'belong' to it in the way national territory 'belongs' to member states, and the EU's political, economic, social and cultural interests are by no means clearly defined.
- Many member states, especially the larger ones with long histories of being influential on the world stage in their own right, are reluctant to lose control of a policy area that is so associated with national influence, sovereignty, and identity.
- Some member states traditionally have had special relationships with particular parts of the world that they are anxious to maintain.

- There are sometimes differences between EU states on foreign policy questions arising from conflicting ideological orientations.
- In the especially sensitive area of defence policy, there are differing national perspectives on whether a distinctive, let alone a comprehensive, European defence orientation and capacity is desirable. This feeds into many specific policy questions, including whether and to what extent the defence resources of individual states should be matched and made mutually compatible. (As long as defence expenditure decisions are taken solely within a national framework, there are naturally major problems at European level of duplications, of the non inter-operability of equipment, and of shortfalls in expensive and sophisticated high-tech hardware.)

Notwithstanding these many difficulties and obstacles, important and significant developments have however occurred in the foreign security and defence policy areas since foreign policy acceptance was first launched under the name European Political Cooperation (EPC) in 1970. Although the policy areas are, of course, closely entwined, they have tended, until very recently at least, to be developed in somewhat separate ways, so the story of their evolution will be taken separately here too.

Evolution of foreign policy

Initially on a tentative basis, and quite outside the framework of the Community Treaties, in the 1970s and 1980s the member states increasingly cooperated with one another on foreign policy matters – to such an extent that by the mid-1980s there were few major international issues upon which the EC did not pronounce. The developing importance of foreign policy cooperation was recognised when EPC was accorded its own section – Title III – in the SEA. Amongst other things, Title III stated that 'The High Contracting Parties [the member states], being members of the European Communities, shall endeavour jointly to formulate and implement a European foreign policy'. However, unlike certain other policy areas that were also recognised in the SEA, Title III was not incorporated into the treaties. This was mainly because the member states were unwilling to allow the normal Community decision-making processes to apply to foreign policy. As a result, EPC continued to be much looser and more voluntaristic in nature than most other policy areas with which the Community concerned itself. No laws were made within EPC, most decisions were arrived at by consensus, and no state could be prevented from engaging in independent action if it so chose.

But although the SEA signalled the increasing importance of EU foreign policy and facilitated its further development, until the early 1990s the

EU's international standing continued to be very much that of an economic giant on the one hand and of a political pygmy on the other. That is to say, it exercised considerable international influence in respect of economic, and especially trade, matters, but its voice did not count for a great deal in respect of political and, more particularly, security and defence matters. Since the early 1990s, however, this situation has been changing as it has come to be increasingly accepted by the member states that the EU ought to be doing rather more than issuing general, and often anodyne, declarations, or, very occasionally, imposing mild economic sanctions against a state to indicate the EU's disapproval of a policy or action. Five factors have been especially important in stimulating this change.

First, the ending of the Cold War and the collapse of communism in the Soviet bloc and the Soviet Union have transformed the nature of international power relationships. In particular: the international political context in which Europe finds itself has changed dramatically, with a shift of focus from the global East–West dimension to regional issues and conflicts; strategically, Europe is no longer squeezed between two superpowers, with little choice but to ally itself to one – the United States – in a more-or-less subservient manner; and the bases of power relationships have altered, with nuclear and military capacity becoming less important and economic strength and geographical position – especially in relation to the troubled Middle East – becoming more important. In this 'new' world, in which international relations are much more fluid and the nature and future development of the European continent is far from clear, the EU countries naturally wish to play a leading part in guiding and managing events. In so doing they are being given encouragement by the USA which, though sometimes troubled when the EU is seen to be acting *too* independently, is anxious to lighten some of its international and, more especially some of its European, commitments.

Second, German reunification has increased the pressure on the foreign and security policy front, as it has too on the economic and monetary union front, to create an EU framework within which Germany is clearly located and to which it is firmly attached. The much-quoted determination of EU leaders, not least German leaders themselves, to ensure there is a European Germany rather than a German Europe, has been seen by many as needing to apply particularly to foreign and security policy given the sensitivities associated with Germany's past and the actual and potential political turbulence to Germany's east and south. That Germany must be 'tied in' more tightly was confirmed for many by the way in which, in late 1991, Germany successfully pressed other EU states to grant diplomatic recognition to Croatia and Slovenia much earlier than most would have preferred, thus obliging the EU states to accept the disintegration of the Former Republic of Yugoslavia (FRY).

Third, the 1990–1 Gulf War and the events leading up to it demonstrated that EPC would always be restricted in its effectiveness if security and defence policy continued to be kept apart from foreign policy. The Community's response to Iraq's invasion of Kuwait was to coordinate diplomatic action and jointly impose economic sanctions, but on the key issues of the appropriate military response and national contributions to that response, the member states reacted in a piecemeal and uncoordinated fashion.

Fourth, the EU's response to the post-1991 break-up of FRY and the subsequent hostilities in the Balkans was widely recognised as being inadequately prepared, developed and mobilised. EU states contributed in various ways and through various forums to policy formulation and the setting up of peacekeeping and humanitarian operations, but there was no clear, consistent or coordinated EU response to the situation. What leadership was provided to deal with the turbulence in the Balkans came mainly from the USA.

Fifth, and in response to the factors just identified, treaties, especially the Maastricht and Amsterdam Treaties, have provided for significant advances in foreign and security policy cooperation, albeit on a basis that has maintained their essentially intergovernmental nature and non-EC status. The relevant contents of these treaties were set out in Chapter 5, so only a brief reminder of the most salient points will be given here. The Maastricht Treaty provided for a Common Foreign and Security Policy (CFSP) to constitute the EU's second pillar. The key elements of the pillar were: (1) the general objectives of the CFSP were identified; (2) systematic cooperation was to be established between the EU states on any matter of foreign and security policy that was of general interest; (3) where it was deemed to be necessary the Council of Ministers would, on the basis of unanimity, define common positions to which the member states should conform; (4) on the basis of general guidelines from the European Council, the Council of Ministers could decide that a matter should be the subject of a joint action; (5) the CFSP was to include security issues, 'including the eventual framing of a common defence policy, which might in time lead to a common defence'; and (6) the Western European Union (WEU) was to be 'an integral part of the development of the Union'. The Amsterdam Treaty strengthened the Maastricht provisions in a number of ways: policy instruments were streamlined and extended; there was an extension of QMV provisions on implementation decisions; a 'constructive abstention' device was introduced, allowing a state not to apply a decision that otherwise bound the EU; security policy was advanced a little, with the Petersberg tasks – which were first identified at a 1992 WEU conference and which are focused on crisis management, peace-keeping and humanitarian tasks – incorporated in the TEU and with the reference to 'the eventual framing of a common defence policy' being replaced by 'the progressive framing of a common defence policy'; and support mechanisms were strengthened with the creation within the Council of a CFSP High Representative and a Policy Planning and Early Warning Unit.

As was explained in Chapter 6, the Nice Treaty further strengthened the potential of CFSP, principally by enabling enhanced cooperation – which had been provided for under the Amsterdam Treaty to enable some member states to go forward with an initiative – to be used for the implementation for joint actions and common positions that do not have military or defence implications.

This exclusion of actions and positions with military or defence implications highlights what has been a major weakness in the development of the CFSP: the exclusion of security and defence policies. However, in recent years this weakness has begun to be tackled. It has been so under the CFSP umbrella, but since many of the issues and processes are highly distinctive they are best considered separately.

Evolution of security and defence policies

Security and defence policies have been a particularly difficult area in which to develop EU inter-state cooperation, let alone integration. One reason why they have been so is that security and defence are closely associated with the very essence of national sovereignty. Another reason is the different security and defence capabilities of the member states. A third reason is the varying degrees of willingness by the member states to use armed force when pressed. And a fourth reason is differences between member states regarding their attitudes and degrees of commitment to the various security/defence organisations that exist in the modern world. On this last point, NATO and the transatlantic relationship have been especially problematical, with four EU states not being NATO members (Austria, Finland, Ireland and Sweden) and with a range of opinion existing amongst the EU states as to how tightly Europe should be tied in with the USA. Of the large member states, the UK has taken the most pro-US position – as witnessed, for example, in its strong and active support for the military campaign in Afghanistan following the 2001 September 11 terrorist attacks and the spring 2003 invasion of Iraq – whilst France has been the most reticent and the most forceful champion of European independence.

However, notwithstanding these difficulties, the EU did, as was shown above, begin to engage with security and defence policies from the early 1990s, albeit initially somewhat tentatively. The engagement was occasioned largely by Europe's fragmented and hesitant responses to the conflicts in the Gulf and then in FRY, where it showed itself to be capable of contributing to post-war stabilisation and reconstruction but only marginally to military intervention during hostilities. Towards the end of the 1990s the crisis in Kosovo displayed Europe's weaknesses and reliance on the political will and military assets of the USA in a particularly stark manner: notwithstanding the fact that the EU could hardly claim to have been taken by surprise by the crisis, the military situation was such that the USA launched 80 per cent of the precision-guided munitions and 95 per cent of the cruise missiles, and flew most of the air sorties. Kosovo thus demonstrated the need for a greater European independent capability in relation to security operations.

The conflicts in the Balkans were instrumental in producing pressures from the USA for more burden-sharing by Europeans. They also resulted in the Europeans being obliged to recognise and act upon the unsatisfactory features of their military position: as long as the EU lacked an effective military operational capability, the USA would take the policy lead in dealing with conflicts on the continent of Europe; there might be circumstances in which the EU would wish to adopt a different stance towards conflicts than the USA; and the management of conflicts requires rapid and efficient decision-making processes – and the EU did not have these in the security and defence domains.

These considerations led from 1994 to steps being taken to develop a European Security and Defence Identity (ESDI). Based firmly within the NATO framework, the ESDI was concerned essentially with military re-structuring so as to enable the Europeans to exercise a greater, and where necessary more independent, influence within NATO.

The big defence policy 'breakthrough' within the EU framework came, however, in December 1998 when, at a Franco–British summit in St Malo, the two countries that had been almost at opposite ends of the debate about European and American orientations in foreign and defence policy, signalled a convergence in their positions by calling for the creation of a clearer and stronger EU security capability within the NATO framework. The convergence was occasioned by a number of factors, including successful military cooperation on the ground in Bosnia, irritation with American leadership in the Balkans, and frustration – especially on the part of Tony Blair, who in May 1997 became the most pro-European British Prime Minister for over twenty years – that whilst European governments spent two-thirds as much as the USA on defence they could deploy only 10 per cent as many troops (Forster and Wallace, 2000: 481–5). The principal significance of St Malo was that not only did the UK end its opposition to defence policy being considered in the EU context, but it was made clear that the UK wished to encourage such discussion and play a leading role in developing the policy sphere. The references to security and defence in the TEU, which had been incorporated by the Maastricht and

Amsterdam treaties (see pp. 72 and 77), could thus start to be given some real effect.

Since St Malo events have unfolded rapidly. Four European Council meetings have been especially important:

- At the June 1999 Cologne summit a declaration was issued 'On Strengthening the Common European Policy on Security and Defence'. Included in the declaration was the following:

    In pursuit of our Common Foreign and Security Policy objectives and the progressive framing of a common defence policy, we are convinced that the Council should have the ability to take decisions on the full range of conflict prevention and crisis management tasks defined in the Treaty on European Union, the 'Petersberg tasks'. To this end, the Union must have the capacity for autonomous action, backed up by credible military forces, the means to decide to use them, and a readiness to do so, in order to respond to international crises without prejudice to actions by NATO (European Council, 1999b: Appendix III).

- At the December 1999 Helsinki summit the contents of the Cologne declaration were confirmed and clarified. There was also agreement on a 'Headline Goal' under which, by 2003, a European Rapid Reaction Force (ERRF) of up to 50 000–60 000 persons would be created, capable of being deployed within 60 days, of being sustained for at least a year, and focused on the full range of Petersberg tasks (European Council, 1999d).

    Subsequent to Helsinki, deliberations and negotiations between the governments of the member states led to the 1999 Headline Goal being virtually replaced in May 2004 by a new *Headline Goal 2010*. This resulted in the ERRF concept being enhanced by what were seen to be more flexible policy instruments in the form of rapid reaction 'battle groups'. These will normally be made up of around 1500 personnel from three or four states. Each battle group will have specified responsibilities, will normally go into action as part of a UN approved operation, and will be capable of being deployed anywhere in the world within two weeks and for a period of at least thirty days. At the time of writing (early 2006), a total of around twenty battle groups are envisaged, with most becoming operational in 2007–08.

- At the June 2000 Feira summit a non-military 'headline goal' was added, with member states committing themselves to providing up to 5000 civilian police officers within 30 days for crisis situations. There was also agreement on the creation of a Rapid Reaction Mechanism (RRM) to enable emergency civilian aid to be available quickly to help stabilise crises (European Council, 2000b).

- At the December 2003 Brussels summit, the national leaders adopted the proposal for a European security strategy – entitled *A Secure Europe in a Better World* – that had been drawn up under the direction of the High Representative for the CFSP (European Council, 2003). At the heart of the strategy was an emphasis on 'effective multilateralism' through the UN and regional organisations, a focus on conflict prevention and crisis management, maintenance of close relations with NATO, and provision for autonomous EU operations in some circumstances.

Since the St Malo breakthrough, security and defence policies have thus advanced rapidly. As part of this advance, an increasingly broad view has been taken of what is necessary if the EU is to have effective security and defence policies – or, as they have been collectively known since the Helsinki summit – a European Security and Defence Policy (ESDP). (The Helsinki summit actually used the name *Common* European Security and Defence Policy, but the 'Common' is not now used, even in official documents.) The broadening has, however, not strayed from several core positions:

- The focus of the ESDP is limited in its security ambitions (the Petersberg tasks). 'Traditional' defence is being left to NATO or national efforts.
- The ESDP is firmly located within NATO and the transatlantic alliance. The EU will act 'autonomously' only when NATO chooses not to act.
- The main decision-making processes of ESDP are intergovernmental. (A position that is no more clearly demonstrated than by it being left entirely to national governments to decide which, if any, battle groups they wish to contribute to, and in what ways and by how much.)
- There is not to be a European army. Certainly the battle groups are capable of being mobilised by autonomous European action, they do have a European command chain, and they do draw on European military resources. However, they are not to be a standing force, each country retains control over the number and deployment of its troops, and there is no common uniform. Battle groups are best thought of as a mechanism for allowing troops to be called up to undertake military-based fire-fighting operations.
- The ESDP project is open in that the EU wishes to receive contributions from non-EU NATO members and from EU applicant states.

A useful way of thinking of just how far EU security and defence policies have developed is to distinguish between three types or levels of policy.

Soft security policy focuses on the promotion of peace and security and uses non-military tools for this purpose. Examples of EU soft security devices include, at a general level, the EU enlargement process, and at a more specific level the Stability Pact for South Eastern Europe in which a range of trade, aid, and political cooperation instruments feature. The appointment of EU 'special representatives' to address problems in trouble-spots may also be regarded as essentially soft policy instruments. At the time of writing (early 2006) there are seven such representatives in place – in the former Yugoslavia, Afghanistan, the Middle East, and Africa. *Hard security policy* involves being prepared to use a military capability for such purposes as conflict resolution, peace-keeping and peace monitoring. These are precisely the sort of tasks that make up the Petersberg Tasks that were incorporated into the TEU at Amsterdam. Some of the softer of such tasks, including the monitoring of political and security developments and contributing to early warning and confidence building measures, have already been undertaken by EU police and military missions, including in Bosnia and Herzegovina, Macedonia, and the Congo. To date, the European Force (Eurofor) in Bosnia and Herzegovina, which took over from a NATO-led force in late 2004, has been, with 7000 personnel, the largest operation to be mounted by the EU. *Defence policy,* as traditionally understood, has at its core using military force, if necessary offensively, for the defence of territory and for 'high security' reasons. The EU is not seeking such a capability. It sees its main security contribution as being to contribute to conflict prevention, to peace missions, and to post-conflict reconstruction – by both civilian and military means.

Policy content and policy action

Two main criticisms were traditionally made of EPC. First, that it was essentially reactive. Apart from a very small number of initiatives – such as pressing, from 1980, for the Palestine Liberation Organisation (PLO) to be included in Middle East peace talks – the EC was seen as following events rather than making and shaping them. Second, that it was too declaratory: policy positions were not followed up with the use of effective policy instruments; at best, as in its opposition to the former apartheid regime in South Africa, weak and essentially symbolic economic sanctions were employed against states engaging in activities of which the EC disapproved.

The CFSP pillar of the EU is designed, in large part, to enable the EU to tackle these weaknesses. The principal means being used to do this are the more conscious pursuit of common policies and the development of properly coordinated policy actions and policy instruments.

Regarding common policies, Article 11 of the TEU states the following:

The Union and its Member States shall define and implement a common foreign and security policy covering all areas of foreign and security policy, the objectives of which shall be:

- to safeguard the common values, fundamental interests, independence and integrity of the Union in conformity with the principles of the United Nations Charter;
- to strengthen the security of the Union in all ways;
- to preserve peace and strengthen international security, in accordance with the principles of the United Nations Charter, as well as the principles of the Helsinki Final Act and the objectives of the Paris Charter, including those on external borders;
- to promote international cooperation;
- to develop and consolidate democracy and the rule of law, and respect for human rights and fundamental freedoms.

Article 12 of the TEU states that the CFSP's objectives are to be achieved by:

- defining the principles of and general guidelines for the common foreign and security policy;
- deciding on common strategies;
- adopting joint actions;
- adopting common positions;
- strengthening systematic cooperation between Member States in the conduct of policy.

(Joint actions and common positions were created by the Maastricht Treaty and common strategies were created by the Amsterdam Treaty.)

The TEU does, of course, identify policy objectives and instruments only in general terms and it is left to policy actors – notably the European Council, the GAERC Council, and the Council Presidency – to develop more specific objectives and to specify the precise nature of policy instruments and the circumstances in which they should be used. Regarding policy objectives, insofar as the EU can be said to have developed core foreign policy goals they are the promotion of peace, democracy, liberty, and human rights, especially in the wider Europe and the 'near abroad'. As such, enlargement policy, with all of the conditionalities that are associated with it, is a key part of EU foreign policy. So too is the European Neighbourhood Policy (ENP) which was launched in March 2003 with the aim of developing 'a zone of prosperity and a friendly neighbourhood – a 'ring of friends' – with whom the EU enjoys, close, peaceful and co-operative relations' (European Commission,

2003). The ENP is based on existing bilateral relations between the EU and the ENP states. As such, ENP action plans (covering mainly trade, aid and political and cultural cooperation) are negotiated with each state rather than there being an overall ENP action programme. The aim of the ENP is to place the bi-lateral relations with neighbours within a more coherent and ordered framework. The Western Balkan countries are not part of the ENP because they have their own 'special arrangement' with the EU in the form of the Stability Pact for South East Europe. Fifteen countries – all either former Soviet states or north African states – are, however, covered by the ENP policy, as is the Palestinian Authority.

Regarding policy instruments, the two policy instruments created by the Maastricht Treaty – joint actions and common positions – have been used quite extensively, but both have tended to be rather innocuous in content. In 2004 twenty new common positions and seven new joint actions were adopted. As for the common strategies created by the Amsterdam Treaty (which must be decided unanimously by the European Council on a proposal from the Council of Ministers) they have been sparingly used with only three concluded by the end of 2005: on Russia, the Ukraine, and the Mediterranean region. None of the three added much to existing policy aims and commitments.

Beyond the policy instruments set out in Article 12, the EU also has available, and makes use of, other instruments. These include diplomacy, political pressure – there are few significant foreign policy issues upon which an EU statement or declaration is not issued, often in harness with associated states – trade sanctions, economic and financial assistance, and technical, scientific, cultural and other forms of cooperation. The last three types of instrument involve the CFSP pillar 'using' the economic strength of the EU via its EC pillar. They have been applied in a number of contexts, including to put pressure on states to improve their human rights records.

As for that most sensitive of foreign policy instruments, military force, it was shown above that a capability is being developed and has begun to be used, even though its use is only for restricted purposes. A consequence of this development is that the WEU has withered. The Maastricht and Amsterdam treaties prepared its demise by providing for it to undertake at least some of its work within the EU framework, and the Nice Treaty incorporated the WEU into the EU, with the exception of its collective defence commitment.

The incorporation of the WEU symbolises how far the EU has gone in just a few years in developing a military dimension. But it is to be emphasised that it is a dimension that is limited in scope, both as regards military capacity and potential use. There is little prospect in the foreseeable future of a significant breaking beyond the limitations that have been (self) imposed. This is because at least five obstacles stand in the way of the

EU developing fully fledged security and defence policies and capabilities for at least some time to come. First, a number of member states, especially those with a tradition of neutrality, are reluctant to over-develop security and defence policies for ideological/historical reasons. Second, security and defence policies raises sovereignty concerns for virtually all member states. Third, security and defence issues still sometimes divide member states in terms of both ends and means. This was demonstrated, for example, in 1995 when France conducted nuclear tests in the South Pacific despite the disapproval of most EU governments, in 1999 when the UK joined the US to bomb Iraq despite clear disquiet in most EU capitals, and most dramatically of all in 2003 when the EU split over the US-led invasion of Iraq – with the UK leading supporting and more pro-'Atlanticist' states (which included Denmark, Italy, Spain and most of the soon to become EU members CEECs), and with France, Germany, Belgium and Finland being amongst the oppositionist states. Fourth, many member states see no need to take EU security and defence policies too far given the other defence options that are available to them. The most obvious of these options is NATO, to which, as was noted above, most EU states belong. There is no desire by these states to downgrade NATO's role or to loosen the EU's bonds with the US. Additional security and defence options include the Organisation for Security and Cooperation in Europe (OSCE), which has been active in the Balkans, and the *ad hoc* coalitions of 'the able and the willing' that are constituted from time to time. An example of such a coalition is the military intervention force that was put together by Italy in 1997 in response to a major outbreak of violence in Albania. Numbering 6000 personnel, the force involved Italian, French, Spanish, Greek, Austrian and Danish participation from inside the EU, and Turkish and Romanian participation from outside (Allen and Smith, 1998: 71). Fifth and finally, without significantly higher levels of expenditure on security and defence the EU will continue to be heavily reliant on NATO/the US for such key military resources as satellite technology, heavy airlift, logistical support, and some armaments. Within the ESDP framework a variety of means are being used to enhance the capacity of European security and defence – including much closer cooperation to improve the availability, mobility and deployability of forces, the interoperability of equipment, and the procurement of munitions – but the reality is that there is no immediate prospect of the EU being able, let along willing, to embark on a major military campaign without US assistance.

Policy processes: foreign policy

The functioning of the CFSP is centred on a network of cooperative and consultative activities between representatives of the member states, with regular rounds of meetings at political and official level at their heart. The aim of all this activity is to try to ensure a maximum information flow and cooperative effort between the member states, to enable the EU to issue joint statements on important foreign policy issues wherever possible, and to enable the EU to develop and use its post-Maastricht policy instruments when it is deemed necessary and appropriate.

The CFSP is based primarily on intergovernmental – predominantly inter-Foreign Ministry – arrangements. There are a number of interlinkng and overlapping reasons for this, but they basically boil down to the fact that because of the politically sensitive nature of much of the content of foreign and security policy, the CFSP has been kept outside the framework of the TEC and the Community system.

Notwithstanding, however, this exclusion from the 'mainstream' EC system, over the years foreign policy has come to assume at least some of the characteristics of 'normal' Community policy-making, with all of the main EU institutions having at least some policy role to play. The policy-making processes of the CFSP, and the powers of the EU institutions within these processes, will now be described. Figure 19.1 outlines the processes in diagrammatic form.

The European Council

Article 13 of the TEU – which is set out on p. 222 – assigns to the European Council responsibility for defining the principles and general guidelines of the CFSP and deciding on common strategies. Working through and with the GAERC, the European Council is thus responsible for the overall direction of the CFSP.

The 1992 Lisbon summit provided an early example of the European Council giving such direction when it set out CFSP ground rules. It was agreed, for example, that when assessing whether important common interests are at stake and defining the issues and areas for joint action, account should be taken of the following factors: the geographical proximity of a given region or country to the EU; the existence of an important EU interest in the political and economic stability of a region or country; and the existence of threats to the security interests of the EU (European Council, 1992: 32). Since Lisbon, numerous policy directional decisions have been channelled through the European Council, on matters such as the former Yugoslavia, the Middle East Peace Process, and the European Neighbourhood Policy.

In addition to laying down guiding principles, the European Council also commonly pronounces on foreign policy issues of current concern. To cite, by way of example, just one European Council meeting, the June 1998 Cardiff summit included statements on South Africa, Russia, India/

Figure 19.1 *CFSP and ESDP decision-making structures*

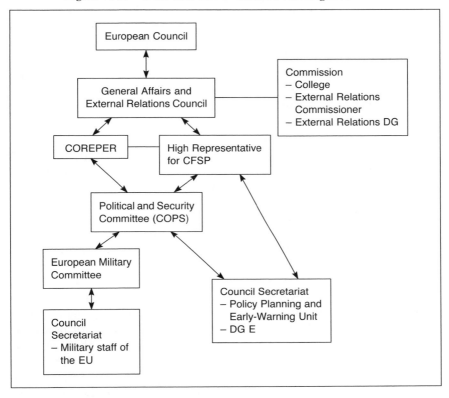

Pakistan nuclear tests, Indonesia's activities in East Timor, the Ethiopia-Eritrea dispute, and the establishment of an International Criminal Court (European Council, 1998: 26–33).

The Council of Ministers

The Council is at the very heart of the CFSP processes. Most of the work is channelled via a tiered structure of meetings which bring together representatives of the member states. In 'descending' hierarchical order, the nature of the tiered structure is as follows:

- *The General Affairs and External Relations Council.* The Foreign Ministers of the member states, with the Commission in attendance, normally meet about once a month, but additional meetings are convened when necessary. In addition to formal GAERC meetings, Foreign Ministers also meet in other forums, notably at European Councils and at twice-yearly informal weekend gatherings.

The GAERC is the main decision-making body of the CFSP. Operating within the context of such general policy guidelines as have been issued by the European Council, it makes, or for routine matters formalises, most CFSP decisions – including those on defining common positions and adopting joint actions. As was explained in Chapter 5, the Amsterdam Treaty established QMV as the norm for adopting and implementing common positions and joint actions, though with the proviso that no vote can be taken if a member state 'for important and stated reasons of national policy' declares its opposition to the adoption of a decision by qualified majority.

Within the Council, the Presidency has a particular responsibility to 'represent the Union in matters coming within the common foreign and security policy' and to be 'responsible for the implementation of decisions taken under [the CFSP]' (Article 18 TEU). This responsibility results in the Presidency being much to the fore when the EU takes foreign policy initiatives, be they peace brokering efforts in international crisis situations or attempts to upgrade the EU's political relations with third countries.

The Presidency used to work closely with the previous and succeeding Presidencies in the so-called 'troika'. The purpose of the troika was to ensure a smooth transition between Presidencies, to help promote policy consistency and stability, and to facilitate work sharing (of particular value to small countries). Since the late 1990s, however, the troika has virtually disappeared as the Presidency has come to work closely with the occupants of two new positions – the High Representative for the CFSP and the Commissioner for External Relations (see below) – plus, when appropriate, the succeeding Presidency.

- *The Committee of Permanent Representatives* (COREPER). As was explained in Chapter 10, COREPER is composed of the Permanent Representatives of the member states to the EU. The Commission is always present and is usually represented by its Deputy Secretary General.

  Meeting weekly, COREPER acts on CFSP matters primarily as a transit and filtering agency between the Political and Security Committee on the one hand (whose decisions it can discuss, but not change) and the GAERC on the other.

- *The Political and Security Committee* (COPS) was created in 2000/01 as part of new structural arrangements to handle the ESDP. It replaced the former Political Committee (PoCo) whose membership was headed by the Political Directors of the member states (who are very senior officials based in national Foreign Ministries) and the Political Director of the Commission (who is the Director General for External Relations). COPS' membership is headed by officials at 'senior/ambassadorial level'

(European Council, 1999b) from the member states' Permanent Representations to the EU in Brussels, plus a senior official from the External Relations DG. The CFSP High Representative, though not a member, often also attends COPS meetings. From time to time COPS meets at the level of Political Directors – though the Directors gather periodically on an informal basis in any event. Following its creation, COPS was soon being identified by the European Council as the 'lynchpin' of both the CFSP and ESDP (European Council, 2000b, Annex III to Annex VI). As the lynchpin, it meets normally twice a week to exercise a number of key responsibilities including keeping track of the international situation as it concerns the CFSP, assisting with the definition of CFSP/ESDP policies, providing political direction on the development of military capabilities and on dealing with crisis situations, and monitoring the implementation of agreed policies.

COPS has been involved in some mild institutional rivalry with COREPER, with both bodies displaying a willingness to assert themselves. Turf battles have, however, always been contained, on the basis of COPS recognising that its communications with the ministers must be channelled via COREPER and COREPER accepting that it does not interfere too much with COPS' decisions.

COPS is supported by a number of specialised groups and committees including the European Union Military Committee (see below) a Committee for Civilian Aspects of Crisis Management.

- *The Correspondents' Group.* Composed of those officials who are responsible for the coordination of CFSP inside Foreign Ministries, and with the Commission in attendance, the Correspondents' Group meets at least once a month. As well as acting as a key liaising mechanism between Foreign Ministries, it regularly deals with business coming up from the working groups with which COPS does not have the time or the inclination to deal. Correspondents are responsible for most of the day-to-day liaison between the Foreign Ministers of the member state.

- *Working groups.* There are usually around thirty or so working groups in existence, most of which are permanent but a few of which are *ad hoc*. A total of between 250 and 300 working group meetings are held each year, with permanent working groups meeting at least once during each Presidency. The groups are composed of senior diplomats – often departmental heads – from the member states, plus a Commission representative. Some working groups deal with regions, for example the Middle East, Central and South America, and Africa; some deal with themes, for example the OSCE, disarmament, and human rights; and some deal with operational matters, for example EU representation in third countries, and joint actions.

✳ ✳ ✳

Council CFSP meetings are prepared and serviced by the Council's Secretariat, which has three principal CFSP components. The first is the *High Representative for the* CFSP. This position was created by the Amsterdam Treaty, partly for the purpose of raising the profile of EU foreign policy by giving it a human face and partly in an attempt to improve cooperation between the member states on foreign policy matters. The remit of the High Representative is to 'assist the Council in matters coming within the scope of the common foreign and security policy in particular through contributing to the formulation, preparation and implementation of policy decisions, and, when appropriate and acting on behalf of the Council at the request of the Presidency, through conducting political dialogue with third countries' (Article 26 TEU). So as to emphasise the importance attached by the member states to the position of High Representative it was decided that it would be held co-terminously with that of Secretary General of the Council. A new post of Deputy Secretary General was created to manage the day-to-day running of the General Secretariat. So as to ensure that the occupant of the position would command respect and be high profile, Javier Solana, the Secretary General of NATO, was appointed to be the first High Representative. In practice, Solana has met most of the expectations of the member states, which is to say that he has used his position to project the EU's stance on foreign policy issues, to offer EU mediation and assistance in such troubled areas as the Balkans and the Middle East, and to coax the member states into adopting a unified policy wherever possible.

The Amsterdam Treaty also created a new *Policy Planning and Early-Warning Unit,* more commonly known simply as the Policy Unit, which is the second principal CFSP component in the Council Secretariat. Operating under the responsibility of the High Representative, the tasks of the unit include: monitoring and analysing developments in areas relevant to the CFSP; providing assessments of the EU foreign and security policy interests and identifying areas for CFSP focus; providing assessments and early warnings of events or situations that may have significant repercussions for EU foreign and security policy; and producing policy option papers (Declaration 6 of the Amsterdam Treaty). In practice, the Unit has tended to be used as an extension of the High Representative's private office, with much of its work focused on day-to-day matters rather than on strategic planning.

The third principal CFSP Council Secretariat component is the DG that deals with foreign policy – Directorate General E. Charged with providing administrative and advisory support, about half of the 70 or so officials who work in the DG are permanent Council employees and about half are on secondment from member states.

The Commission

Since the 1981 London Report the Commission has been 'fully associated' with the work carried out in the foreign policy field. However, the intergovernmental and extra-Community nature of foreign and security policy has meant that the Commission's position has always been much weaker in the foreign policy context than it has in the EC context. This is no more clearly illustrated than by the fact that it was not until the Maastricht Treaty that the Commission gained the right, and then it was a non-exclusive right, to refer foreign policy matters and proposals to the Council.

Concerns within the Commission that the institution should take full advantage of the policy openings provided by the creation of the CFSP pillar have played an important part in stimulating a number of internal structural changes – at both College and DG levels – since 1993 in the external relations area (for details, see Nugent and Saurugger, 2002). In the Prodi and Barroso Colleges the approach to the structural question has been to divide the external relations portfolios and Directorates General along functional lines and include in the arrangements a Commissioner and a Directorate General with explicit responsibility for foreign policy – though political sensitivities have resulted in them being named as being responsible for External Relations rather than Foreign Policy.

The functional arrangements do appear to have enhanced the Commission's CFSP role, assisted in considerable degree by the fact that the External Relations Commissioners in the Prodi and Barroso Colleges – Chris Patten and Benita Ferrero-Walmer respectively – have proved to be accomplished performers. They have not, however, been able to match the profile or status of the Council's High Representative. How much influence the Commission actually exercises over particular policy matters always depends very much on individual circumstances. It is, for example, in a strong position when CFSP actions involve the use of EC policy instruments, such as the use of economic sanctions, for then the Council can only act on the basis of Commission proposals. Similarly, its position can be strong when the Council is reliant on it for specialised information and advice. In this context, one of the ways in which the Commission has sought to enhance its position is by developing policies and policy instruments in the field of conflict prevention and in civilian aspects of conflict management and post-conflict reconstruction.

The Commission's position is usually at its weakest when matters in hand are 'purely political' and when the incumbent Presidency is a large member state with a big and effective Foreign Ministry and/or is a member state which prefers foreign policy matters to be conducted mainly on an intergovernmental basis.

The European Parliament

Under Article 21 TEU:

> The Presidency shall consult the European Parliament on the main aspects and the basic choices of the common foreign and security policy and shall ensure that the views of the European Parliament are duly taken into consideration. The European Parliament shall be kept regularly informed by the Presidency and the Commission of the development of the Union's foreign and security policy.
>
> The European Parliament may ask questions of the Council or make recommendations to it. It shall hold an annual debate on progress in implementing the common foreign and security policy.

What these provisions tend to mean in practice is that unless special circumstances apply – as, for example, when a foreign policy issue is linked to an association agreement and the assent procedure thus needs to be used – the EP is largely confined to an advisory role on foreign policy under the TEU.

All the EP can thus do is make maximum use of such mechanisms as it has at its disposal to try to ensure that the Commission and, more importantly, the Council really do consult and really do listen. Prior to the Amsterdam Treaty the main mechanisms were: exchanging views with the Council Presidency in the Committee on Foreign Affairs and Security; asking questions – written and oral – of the Council; holding debates in plenary sessions; and making recommendations, passing resolutions and tendering opinions. The Amsterdam Treaty created another mechanism by formalising the already common practice of charging most administrative and operational CFSP expenditure to the EU budget. This gives the EP the opportunity to raise foreign policy issues during the budgetary procedure.

Embassies, delegations and missions

The development since the Second World War of rapid international travel and instantaneous electronic communications has undermined much of the role and value of diplomatic representations as a means for countries to communicate with one another. Nonetheless, embassies, delegations and missions are still used to promote and defend interests abroad.

Because it is not a state the EU is not able to maintain overseas embassies, but it does have an extensive network of external delegations – technically, delegations of the Commission. There are over 130 such delegations in third countries, and five delegations to international organisations. (It might also be added – and this exemplifies the importance of the EU to the outside world – that over 170 countries have diplomatic missions officially accredited to the EU.)

Overseas representations are, of course, concerned with many issues other than foreign policy – most notably, the promotion of trade and, in the case of national representations, the safeguarding of citizens' interests. The CFSP is, however, a matter that embassies of the member states and Commission delegations seek to promote. In this context Article 20 TEU states that 'The diplomatic and consular missions of the Member States and the Commission Delegations in third countries and international conferences, and their representations to international organisations, shall cooperate in ensuring that the common positions and joint actions adopted by the Council are complied with and implemented'.

Article 20 is assisting the continued development of processes that have been under way for some time, whereby embassies of EU member states in third countries and delegations attached to international organisations exchange information and coordinate activities. For example member state ambassadors to the UN meet weekly to coordinate policy, and vote together on over 90 per cent of Security Council votes.

Policy processes: defence policy

The ESDP institutional structure was sketched out at the June 1999 Cologne summit, developed and confirmed at the December 1999 Helsinki summit, launched on a transitory footing in March 2000, and established on a permanent basis in the first half of 2001.

The structure is much the same as that of the CFSP in respect of the positions of the European Council, the Council of Ministers (with the exception that Defence Ministers join Foreign Ministers in the GAERC when appropriate, and occasionally meet by themselves), the High Representative, the Commission and the EP. The principal difference, as can be seen from Figure 19.1, is that two bodies are exclusively concerned with the ESDP. These bodies – which along with COPS were each created by a Council decision in January 2001 (see *Official Journal*, 44: L27, 30 January 2001) – are:

- *The European Union Military Committee* (EUMC) is composed of the Chiefs of Defence, represented by their military delegates except in circumstances which require the Chiefs themselves to meet. The functions of EUMC include providing military advice and making recommendations to COPS, acting as the forum for military consultation and cooperation between the member states in the field of conflict prevention and crisis management, and undertaking various evaluative and advisory tasks in crisis management situations. The Committee normally meets weekly.

- *The Military Staff of the European Union* (EUMS) consists of military personnel seconded from the member states. The staff are part of the General Secretariat of the Council, but because of concerns about security they are not based in the same building as the rest of the Secretariat. Working under the direction of the EUMC, the military staff provide military expertise and support for the ESDP, including on early warning, situation assessment and strategic planning.

Development Policy

The EU and its member states are major actors in international development policy. This is no more clearly demonstrated than in the fact that the EU's member states provide around 45 per cent of all international development aid whilst the EU itself provides another 10 per cent. In the related area of international humanitarian aid, the EU's member states provide around 25 per cent of the total and the EU provides around 30 per cent (Holland, 2002: 109).

Policy content

The general principles of EU development policy are laid down in Title XX – Development Cooperation – of the TEC. Article 177 of Title XX states:

1. Community policy in the sphere of development cooperation, which shall be complementary to the policies pursued by the Member States, shall foster:
   - the sustainable economic and social development of the developing countries, and more particularly the most disadvantaged among them;
   - the smooth and gradual integration of the developing countries into the world economy;
   - the campaign against poverty in the developing countries.
2. Community policy in this area shall contribute to the general objective of developing and consolidating democracy and the rule of law, and to that of respecting human rights and fundamental freedoms.
3. The Community and the Member States shall comply with the commitments and take account of the objectives they have approved in the context of the United Nations and other competent international organizations.

These principles are periodically given a sharper focus in multi-annual strategy papers. In 2005 a new strategy paper – *The European Consensus on Development* – was adopted in the form of a joint statement by the Council and the representatives of the governments of the member states meeting within the Council, the European Parliament and the Commission (Joint Statement, 2005). The key objectives identified in the joint statement are:

> The primary and overarching objective of EU development cooperation is the eradication of poverty in the context of sustainable development, including pursuit of the Millennium Development Goals (MDGs).
>
> The eight MDGs are to: eradicate extreme poverty and hunger; achieve universal primary education; promote gender equality and empower women; reduce the mortality rate of children; improve maternal health; combat HIV/AIDS, malaria and other diseases; ensure environmental sustainability and develop a global partnership for development (Joint Statement, 2005: 4 and 5).

The reasons for the EU's active engagement in development policy are a mixture of the historical, the moral, and the economic: historical in that some EU countries, notably France and the UK, have long-established ties with parts of the developing world as a result of their colonial past; moral in that EU governments believe, although with different degrees of enthusiasm, that something should be done about world poverty and hunger; and economic in that developing countries account for around 30 per cent of EU exports, and the EU is highly dependent on the developing world for products such as rubber, copper and uranium.

Some of the forms of assistance made available by the EU apply to the whole of the developing world. Amongst these are:

(1) *Generalised preferences.* All developing countries can export their industrial products to the EU without paying tariffs (subject to strict rules of origin requirements and subject also to volume limits for some products). Many agricultural products can also be exported free of duty. As an addition to the Generalised System of Preferences scheme, under a Council regulation of February 2001 all goods apart from arms and ammunition from the world's 50 Least Developed Countries (LDCs) are given duty free access to the EU market (for analysis of this 'Everything but Arms' arrangement, see Holland, 2002: Chapter 8). (It might be noted here that generalised preferences are much less significant than they used to be as a result of GATT/WTO policies and actions to lower trade tariffs and to equalise trade treatment.)

(2) *Food aid.* Foodstuffs are sent to countries with serious food shortages.

(3) *Emergency aid*. Aid of an appropriate sort is made available to countries stricken by natural disasters and other crises.

(4) *Aid to non-governmental organisations*. The EU makes available aid to projects sponsored by non-governmental organisations in a number of developing world countries.

In addition to these general forms of assistance, the EU provides additional assistance and aid to countries with which it has special relationships. Most of these special relationships take the form of economic, trade, industrial, technical and financial cooperation agreements. The most important and most wide-ranging agreement is the Cotonou Partnership Agreement, which was signed in the capital of Benin in June 2000 and was updated by a revised agreement signed in Luxembourg in June 2005. The Agreement links the EU with 78 African, Caribbean and Pacific (ACP) countries, most of which are countries with which at least one member state has historical links, most commonly as a colonial power. The Cotonou Agreement, which is to last for twenty years but with five-year reviews built in, replaces the Lomé Conventions which framed EU–ACP relations from 1975. The Cotonou Agreement continues with many of Lomé's core features, including: duty-free access to the EU market for virtually all ACP exports (of declining importance given world trade liberalisation); schemes to stabilise export earnings; and the European Development Fund (EDF), which provides financial assistance for development projects in ACP countries.

But Cotonou also involves very significant changes to the Lomé system. These changes were driven primarily by: a recognition that many ACP states had not improved their economic independence under Lomé and were not becoming properly integrated into the world economy; an acknowledgement of the increasing diversity of ACP states; and WTO pressures in the direction of global liberalisation. The main changes introduced by Cotonou are:

– The Lomé system of uniform preferential trade access is being replaced by a phased move towards the creation of reciprocal and regionally-based Economic Partnership Agreements (EPAs) involving groups of ACP countries. Cotonou thus allows for more differentiation between ACPs than did Lomé. In particular, the more advanced ACPs are moving more quickly with trade liberalisation than are the less developed ACPs, which is seen as being crucial in creating trade development and investment opportunities that match local conditions.
– Increased emphasis is being attached to the role of the private sector in stimulating enterprise in the ACP states.

– Political cooperation and conditionality is being stepped up, with greater emphasis being given to strengthening democratic processes, good governance, respect for human rights, and civil society in the ACP states.

Development aid is financed in two ways. First, non-EDF aid is funded by the EU budget. Accounting for around four per cent of the budget, about half of this aid is used to provide financial assistance to non-ACP countries and about half is used for food aid purposes. Second, EDF aid is funded by special contributions from the member states. Taking EDF and non-EDF aid together, the principal beneficiaries are sub-Saharan Africa (which receives almost 60 per cent), southern Asia (about 10 per cent), and Latin America and the Caribbean (also about 10 per cent).

It should be stressed that EU development policy is conducted alongside national policies. Unlike with trade policy, the EU does not have exclusive competence in the area of development policy. In some aspects of development policy the EU takes the leading role whilst in others the member states are the main players and the EU is confined to, at most, supplementing, complementing and coordinating national development policies. So, the trade aspects of development policy are necessarily the EU's responsibility, but the states are much more prominent in respect of financial assistance.

Strains have sometimes arisen between member states and between member states and EU institutions (especially the Commission) regarding development policies. This has been largely because there are differences between the member states regarding their aims, priorities and interests on development policy issues. As Holland (2002: 171) puts it, 'For example, French development policy remains largely neo-colonial, Italy follows a more commercial approach, the UK stresses good governance whereas the Nordic states focus principally on the alleviation of poverty'. Particular problems have arisen when states have used aid for the purpose of promoting national political and economic interests. In an attempt to ensure the policies and activities of the EU and its member states match, much of the focus of development policy in recent years has been on advancing cooperation, consistency, coherence and complementarity between the EU and member state levels (see Holland, 2002).

Policy processes

The EU makes all sorts of decisions in connection with its development policy. Just as in other policy areas, the actors involved and the procedures that apply vary enormously.

With regard to the actors, the most important players are: the GAERC Council (the separate Development Council was disbanded as part of the Seville reforms of the Council, so Development Ministers now attend the GAERC when agenda items concern them); the Commissioner for Development and Humanitarian Aid; the Development DG; the EP Committee on Development; the diplomatic missions of developing countries in Brussels that are accredited to the EU (which undertake a variety of liaising and information-providing functions); and the Commission delegations in developing countries (which, amongst a wide range of functions, have management responsibilities for development aid projects).

With regard to decision-making procedures, these are dependent on the type of decision envisaged. For example, if the Council is simply intending to issue a declaration or a resolution on a matter, it is not obliged to consult the EP and can move at its own pace – which may mean proceeding very cautiously and only after the receipt of proposals from the Commission and/or from a specially convened Council *ad hoc* working party. If a trade-only agreement is envisaged, Article 133 applies – which, as noted above, means that the Commission and the Council are the key actors, QMV can be used in the Council, and the EP has no formal role. If cooperation or association agreements are proposed, Article 300 applies – which means QMV for cooperation agreements and unanimity for association agreements, and the power of assent for the EP on all association agreements and some cooperation agreements.

As was shown above, the Cotonou Agreement is the most important of the numerous agreements to which the EU is party in connection with its policy on development cooperation. It is therefore worth saying a little about how it functions, for the Agreement has its own institutional structure, which is largely the structure passed down from the Lomé Convention. There are three principal bodies in the structure. The first is the Council of Ministers, which is composed of the members of the EU Council of Ministers, a member of the Commission, and a member of the government of each ACP country. The Council meets at least once a year to take whatever major political and policy decisions are necessary under the Agreement. Decisions are taken by 'common agreement'. If there is a dispute between the 'two sides' binding arbitration applies, with the procedures of the Permanent Court of Arbitration for International Organisations normally being used. The second body is the Committee of Ambassadors, which is composed of a representative of each EU state, a representative of the Commission, and a representative of each ACP state. The Committee meets at least twice a year and is charged with assisting and advising the Council of Ministers, monitoring the implementation of the Agreement and the progress towards its objectives, and generally supervising and coordinating the work of the many committees and subsidiary bodies that exist under the general umbrella of the Agreement. Finally, there is the joint Assembly, which is made up of equal numbers of MEPs and ACP members of parliament or national representatives. It meets twice a year and acts as a general advisory and deliberating body.

The External Dimension of Internal Policies

Many of the EU's internal policies have significant external dimensions. For example, transport policy involves dealing with neighbouring countries on road transit arrangements and with countries throughout the world on numerous air and maritime transport issues. Energy policy includes dealing with countries that are energy suppliers about rights, guarantees, and terms of access. And environmental policy includes dealing with countries near and far on such issues as climate change and many aspects of air, land, and water damage and pollution.

The EU does not have explicit treaty powers to act as the external representative of the member states in such policy areas. However, the Court of Justice has established that the EU (more precisely the Community) does have implied external powers in respect of policy areas that fall within its internal jurisdiction. Just how extensive these implied powers are, and in what circumstances they apply, has been frequently contested over the years, but the key principle of 'parallelism' has been firmly established, by which the exercise of internal law-making powers by the EU in a particular policy area is taken to imply that it also has the power to negotiate and conclude international agreements in that area.

The procedural arrangements by which the EU contracts external agreements on internal policy issues are set out in Article 300 of the TEC. Different procedures apply depending on the nature of the agreement concerned. A relatively straightforward agreement with no major institutional or budgetary implications is subject to much the same procedure as applies under Article 133, though with the difference that the EP must be consulted. In contrast, agreements that are constituent elements of more wide-ranging cooperation or association agreements are subject to the 'more difficult' procedures that apply to these latter agreements – that is, unanimity in the Council for association agreements and EP assent for some cooperation agreements and all association agreements.

To these already rather complicated arrangements, another complication is added by the fact that the EU does not necessarily have the exclusive right to negotiate external agreements on internal policies. Rather, there are many mixed competences where policy responsibilities are shared between the EU and the member states. This results in there being two main ways, with variations within each, as to how the EU is represented and conducts itself in international negotiations in such policy areas. On the one hand, where there is exclusive EU competence, as with fisheries, the Commission is the sole EU representative and negotiator. On the other hand, where there is a mixed competence, as with transport policy, the Commission acts on behalf of the EU and national representatives act on behalf of the member states.

The distribution of competences is highly complex in some policy areas. Bretherton and Vogler (1999: 89) provide a good example of such complexity, with the Basel Convention on hazardous waste: 'It has trade aspects where there is full Community competence, science and development assistance aspects (where there is Member State competence), and environmental aspects – where mixed competence prevails'. Such complexity and overlapping competences can naturally make it difficult for the EU fully to coordinate its inputs in international forums and negotiations. In turn, this can weaken its influence, but the extent of the weakening should not be overstated. In the environmental policy sphere, for example, the EU is a major global player, as Bretherton and Vogler show. It is, for instance, party to, and an influential voice within, more than 30 different multilateral environmental agreements – including agreements on the protection of the ozone layer, the transboundary movement of hazardous wastes and their disposal, desertification, and the protection of the marine environment (there are several marine environment agreements covering different sea areas). Moreover in a few environmental policy areas – including climate change and biological diversity – it is not going too far to describe the EU as virtually a policy leader. On climate change, for example, it was instrumental in helping to bring about the 1997 Kyoto Protocol aimed at reducing the emission of gases into the atmosphere and has not been diverted from meeting its target cuts by the withdrawal of the USA from the Protocol in 2001.

A key reason why the EU is often able to exert a significant policy influence, even when there are problems with its 'actorness', is that it is usually well prepared for negotiations with third parties. Even when there have been internal disputes, accommodations – on competences, policy goals, and who is to take the negotiating 'lead' – are usually agreed before external negotiations begin. Furthermore, during the course of external negotiations EU 'coordination' meetings are normally held as and when they are deemed necessary.

An example of an accommodation being worked out occurred in the months preceding the first WTO Ministerial Conference, which was held in Singapore in December 1996. Since some of the subject matter at the Conference was of a mixed character – including services and intellectual property rights – both the Commission and the Council spent much time and effort examining and establishing 'the overall aims to be pursued by the Community and its Member States' (Council Press Release 8913/96, 15–16 July 1996). As part of these preparations, there were several meetings of Foreign Ministers and one informal meeting of Trade Ministers, at which much of the work focused on reports, communications, and proposals produced by the Commission on topics such as trade and the environment, the negotiation of an information technology agreement, and negotiations on basic telecommunications.

Such preparations do not always succeed in establishing agreed EU positions and a shared discipline, but for the most part they do.

The Consistency and Representational Problems

Article 3 of the Common Provisions of the TEU states that 'The Union shall in particular ensure the consistency of its external activities as a whole in the context of its external relations, security, economic and development policies. The Council and the Commission shall be responsible for ensuring such consistency and shall cooperate to this end.'

Consistency is a key factor in determining the extent to which would-be global actors can establish themselves on the world stage and be effective. Yet ensuring policy consistency is a major problem for the EU in the conduct of its external relations. There are many examples – including policies towards the European Neighbours, the Middle East Peace Process, Somalia, and Rwanda – of either the EU itself not being consistent over time or of member states clearly not being in line with one another (see Regelsberger *et al., 1997* for case studies of policy inconsistencies). There are several overlapping and interrelating reasons why EU policy consistency is often difficult to achieve:

- The great spread of EU external relations' interests and activities.
- The diversity of actors and processes that are involved in EU external relations policy processes.
- The differing powers of the EU in different policy contexts, with particular problems arising when competence is shared between the EU and the member states – as it is for most of the internal policies that have an external dimension.
- The differing powers of EU actors in differing spheres of external relations.
- The conflicting orientations and preferences of the member states on many policy issues.
- The varying levels of EU policy development – from the common commercial policy to the emerging military security policy.

Procedures, mechanisms and arrangements do, of course, exist to try and minimise consistency problems. Crucial in this respect is the convening, at different levels of seniority, of numerous intra- and inter-institutional meetings that have as their purpose the coordination of external policies and activities. Within the Commission, for example, the coordinating structure is broadly as follows:

- The Commissioners' Relex Group, which brings together the External Relations, Trade, Development, Enlargement, and Economic and Monetary Affairs Commissioners, plus other Commissioners when agenda items require their presence. This group is chaired by the President of the Commission.
- The Directors General Relex Group, which is attended not only by the Directors General of the five DGs covered by the Commissioner's Group but also by the Secretary General, the Head of the Legal Service, and also Directors General from such DGs as Agriculture and Competition when necessary.
- Inter-service groups. These bring together officials from all DGs with an interest in a particular issue. There are a few standing inter-service groups, such as that on the WTO, but most are convened as and when they are deemed to be necessary. So, there are no standing inter-service groups on particular countries, but if a cross-cutting issue concerning a country arises, a paper – probably drafted from the country desk in the External Relations DG – may be circulated, which may then well be followed up by a one-off inter-service meeting in which all interested parties are brought together.

That such coordinating arrangements do have at least some success is witnessed by the increasing multi-dimensionality of external programmes. For instance, the numerous cooperation and association agreements that the EU has concluded with third countries typically include a battery of, as appropriate, trade, development, and democracy-building/human rights measures, plus provisions for a political dialogue between the partners.

The consistency problem is closely related to the representational problem that is encaptured in the question first allegedly posed by the US Secretary of State, Henry Kissinger, in the early 1970s – who speaks for Europe? When the EU acts in international forums and situations the nature of its representation can vary considerably according to circumstances. So, for example, in charged political situations the representation is likely to involve some combination of the Foreign Minister from the Presidency-in-Office, the High Representative for CFSP, and the External Relations Commissioner. In addition, some member states may also seek to act in an individual capacity. Where, by contrast, international monetary matters are under consideration, the representation is likely to involve some combination of the Finance Minister from the Presidency-in-Office, the Economic and Monetary Affairs Commissioner (both of these seeking to represent the EU 25), the President of the European Central Bank (representing the 'euroland' 12), and national Finance Ministers and national Central Bank Governors (especially from the three member states outside the euro area).

The nature of the representational problem is perhaps best exemplified in the positions of the High Representative for the CFSP and the External Relations Commissioner. Whilst the individuals occupying these positions have been able to establish a reasonable working relationship – with the High Representative being responsible for putting together the views of the member states on CFSP matters and making them into a coherent and effective policy, and the Commissioner focusing more on the implementation aspects of policy – the fact is that it clearly would be simpler and more efficient if the two posts were combined. As was shown in Chapter 7, this is something the Constitutional Treaty provided for, but the ratification difficulties have made the prospects for the merger of the posts uncertain.

Concluding Remarks

This chapter has demonstrated that the EU can be thought of as being a partially constructed international actor which exercises a major influence on the world stage in respect of trade policy, a significant influence in respect of development, environment and certain other policies, and a modest but growing influence in respect of foreign and security policies. As Ginsberg (1999 and 2001) has argued and demonstrated, the EU not only has external policy outputs but also an external policy impact on non-member state international actors and international issue areas.

A central question that is likely to loom large in the foreseeable future is whether the EU will advance from being a modest player to becoming a major player in the foreign and security policy fields. Mechanisms to enable it to do so have been strengthened over the years, but they are still essentially intergovernmental in character. As several observers have noted, the CFSP has been 'Brusselised' – with, for example, the creation of the High Representative, COPS, and the External Relations Commissioner – but it has barely been 'communautarised' in the sense of becoming subject to supranational drive, decision-making, supervision and enforcement.

But the development of a greater institutional capacity will not in itself be enough to enable the CFSP and the related ESDP to deepen. The political will to use and take advantage of the capacity is also required. For reasons that have been outlined in this chapter, such political will is not always forthcoming. To cite just one example of an area where a stronger collective political will is required, it is accepted by virtually all informed observers that defence expenditure in the EU is not used to maximum effect. For example, too many operating systems and forms of hardware are not inter-operable, there are duplications, and in a world where the nature of security threats has changed dramatically in recent years too many states are spending too much on personnel and not enough on research and sophisticated weaponry. An attempt is being made to improve the situation, via an EU created and funded European Defence Agency (EDA) which began operations in 2005. Included in the EDA's remit is the promotion of European armaments cooperation within a framework of a more competitive European defence equipment market. Whether the EDA will have much success in persuading EU governments to work more closely together in this highly sensitive policy area remains to be seen.

But however the prospects of the EDA may be judged, it should not be assumed that all political will is lacking and that further integrationist advances cannot be made in the CFSP and ESDP spheres. There may be major obstacles in the way, but many of what used to be seen as almost insurmountable barriers have been removed in recent years. For example: the special relationships that some EU countries have with particular parts of the world have become less problematical as historical ties have been loosened; the difficulties created by the quasi-neutrality of some member states have largely been overcome since the end of the Cold War; and, for a host of reasons, EU member states – including those which are most concerned with the preservation of national sovereignty – have increasingly come to regard both foreign and security issues as proper and legitimate matters for the EU agenda.

Chapter 20

National Influences and Controls on European Union Processes

Governments
Parliaments
Courts
Subnational Levels of Government
Citizens' Views
Political Parties
Interests
Concluding Remarks

The most obvious price states pay for membership of the EU is a substantial loss of national decision-making powers. In a few policy spheres – such as fishing and external trade – most key decisions are now taken at the EU level, whilst in many other spheres – such as environmental policy and competition policy – decision-making responsibilities are shared between the EU and the member states.

The reason why member states have been prepared to countenance this loss – or pooling – of sovereignty and have been willing to participate in collective decision-making in important policy areas is that their national decision-makers, supported by, or at least with the acquiescence of, large sections of their populations have believed it to be in their national interests to do so. The particular balance of perceived advantages and disadvantages arising from EU membership has varied from state to state, but each has judged that there is more to be gained from being inside the EU than from being outside.

A consequence of being on the inside is that the political systems of the member states are increasingly being 'Europeanised'. That is to say, national political structures, political actors, policy processes, and policies are increasingly orienting, or are being oriented, in a European direction. The extent of the orienting, and of the associated national adaptations, varies between states and within states varies between policy sectors. However, no states and no sectors are exempt from the need to accommodate themselves within EU requirements and rules, be they large member states or policy sectors that are only slightly touched by the EU's presence.

Because it is mainly concerned with the impact of the EU on the member states, Europeanisation – or 'EU-ization' as Bulmer and Lequesne (2005:11) suggest it may be better termed – is normally thought of as being a top-down process. (There is now an extensive academic literature on Europeanisation. See, for example: Featherstone and Radaelli, 2003; Goetz and Hix, 2001; Green Cowles *et al*, 2001; Olsen, 2002.) However, it has an important bottom-up element too in that a key reason national agencies and forces have adjusted to the EU is so as to enhance their ability to communicate with and influence decision-making at the centre. It is with this latter aspect of Europeanisation that this chapter is mostly concerned. That is to say, whilst top-down Europeanisation is not ignored, the main focus is on national inputs into EU policy and decision-making processes and how they have been designed and adjusted in attempts to enable them to feed into the processes in an effective manner.

The precise nature of these inputs varies between states, reflecting such factors as different national political systems, traditions, and cultures. In broad terms, however, they can be seen as being directed through seven principal channels: governments, parliaments, courts, subnational levels of government, citizens' views, political parties, and interests.

Governments

Governments are naturally in the strongest position to control or influence EU processes. This is most obviously seen in their relationships with the Commission and the Council of Ministers.

Influencing the Commission

As was shown in Chapter 9, the system of appointment to the Commission ensures that all member states are represented within it. This, however, does not mean that Commissioners or Commission officials act as governmental representatives. Rather, for the most part they look to the EU-wide interest and are not open to instructions from national capitals. But they may, quite naturally, be inclined to take a particular interest in the impact of proposals on their own country. And governments looking for sympathetic ears in the Commission may well make fellow nationals their first port of call (though not necessarily: competent government officials, especially from the Permanent Representations, cultivate a broad range of contacts in the Commission).

As well as the use of national contacts, there are many other ways in which governments try to persuade, influence or bring pressure to bear on the Commission. Use is made of formal channels, such as the groups of experts who advise the Commission on all sorts of matters, the comitology committees through which the Commission exercises many of its executive functions, and the numerous decision-making meetings that take place within the Council system from working group level upwards – meetings which the Commission virtually always attends. Informal methods range from a minister ringing up a Commissioner, to a working group representative meeting a Commission official for lunch.

It should be emphasised that government influence on Commission thinking is not necessarily a bad thing. On the contrary, it can be positively helpful by, for example, improving the prospect of legislative proposals being adopted. However, it can become unhealthy if governments try to lean too heavily on their fellow nationals in the Commission, or if clusters of nationals have a disproportionate influence on policy development in a key sector (as, for example, has frequently been alleged of the French in respect of agriculture).

Influencing the Council

The potential for any government to influence what happens in the Council depends on a number of factors.

The size of the state it represents

On most policy issues the EU's larger member states carry more weight than its smaller member states. This is not just because the larger states have greater voting weight in the Council but also because the smaller states tend to defer to the size and resources of the larger states. The case should not, however, be overstated for, as Thorhallsen (2000) and Archer and Nugent (2002) have shown, the smaller states do – ironically because of their more limited administrative capacities – often display characteristics that make it possible for them to participate successfully in EU decision-making processes. Amongst these characteristics are: more informal domestic lines of policy communication; more flexible internal decision-making; the issuing of guidelines rather than instructions to Council negotiators; and a focus on a narrower range of policy issues.

The importance of the state to particular negotiations

When an issue is important to a state, its government will be actively involved in Council processes and is likely to ensure that it is represented by senior figures in Council meetings. When, however, a state is not much affected by an issue its representatives may not engage actively in Council deliberations and may send junior people to represent it. For example, in Common Fisheries Policy (CFP) deliberations the Spanish government is likely to be a much more central actor than the Austrian government.

The desire of the government to play an active role

Where governments have strong policy preferences they are likely to be to the fore in the preparation of position papers and to be highly active in relevant policy debates and deliberations. This may result in them playing a crucial role in helping to set policy agendas and establish 'framework ideas'. Examples of governments exercising such a role include Germany in respect of the 'sound money' principles of EMU and the UK in respect of the liberal principles of the SEM.

The capacity of the government to play an active role

A government may have clear 'views on an EU initiative and may wish to play an active role in supporting or opposing it, but be restrained by domestic political considerations such as a finely balanced coalition government, opposition from key interest groups, or possible electoral damage.

Relations with other governments

Cohesive and fixed alliances within the EU between particular govern-ments do not exist. The governments of small states, for example, do not come together as a group, except on some treaty reform issues. Rather, governments come together in different combinations on different issues. However, some governments do make more of a conscious effort than others to seek general understandings and cooperation with one or more of their EU partners. So, for example, in 2001 the prime ministers of the three Nordic member states – Denmark, Sweden and Finland – decided they would meet before each European Council meeting to discuss issues of common concern. The best example of countries establishing a close relationship is that between France and Germany, which has been consciously fostered and maintained by most French and German governments since the early 1960s. The so-called Franco–German axis is no longer as commanding as it was when there were only six member states, or when Chancellor Schmidt and President Giscard d'Estaing and later Chancellor Kohl and President Mitterrand worked closely together, but it still plays an important part in helping to shape and set the pace of EU developments.

An increasingly important aspect of governmental strategies in the EU is multilateral bilateralism, which sees governments linking up with just one or two other governments on specific issues, often for the purpose of launching initiatives.

The procedures applying

Of particular importance is whether qualified majority voting is permissible under the relevant treaty article(s) and is politically acceptable in the circumstances applying. If it is, concessions and compromises might be preferable to being outvoted. If it is not, any government can cause indefinite delay, though by so doing it may weaken goodwill towards it and thus damage its long-term interests. An example of governments forgoing the use of a veto they would have liked to have exercised is Austria and Cyprus, which in 2004 and 2005 resisted vetoing the opening of accession negotiations with Turkey.

The competence of governmental negotiators

Given the extensive tactical manoeuvrings involved in EU processes, and given that many negotiations are not about the broad sweep of policy but are about highly technical matters, the competence of individual negotiators can be crucial. Are they well-briefed and able to master details? Can they judge how far their negotiating partners can be pushed? Can they avoid being isolated? Can they build coalitions? Can they time their interventions so as to clinch points? The evidence suggests that variations in such competencies are not so much between states as between individual negotiators.

The arrangements for linking representatives in the Council with national capitals

This point is worth developing in a little detail because there are significant variations in the ways in which governments attempt to manage and control their input into the Council via their representatives. Two aspects of this are particularly worth mentioning.

First, some countries – including Belgium, Italy, and the Netherlands – generally allow their representatives to work within a relatively flexible framework. This is demonstrated by the way in which representatives are often able to negotiate on important policy matters not just at the ministerial level but also at lower levels. As well as assisting the functioning of the Council as a whole – by reducing the need for awkward issues to be referred upwards – manoeuvrability of this kind can be used to the national advantage by competent negotiators. At the same time, however, too much independence on the part of representatives can lead to the need for awkward backtracking at a later negotiating stage if a misjudgement is made. In contrast, the representatives of some other states – including France and the UK – are generally reluctant and/or are not able to negotiate on policy issues below ministerial level. Whether, as is sometimes claimed, this greater rigidity improves the consistency and effectiveness of a country's negotiating position is doubtful. Undoubtedly, the more that countries lean in this direction, and all do at times, the more that negotiations at the lower Council levels are limited to technical matters and the more the overall Council process is protracted.

At the most senior Council level – ministerial meetings – there is, of course, not such a problem of control from national capitals. It is important to ensure that the minister is fully briefed on the national implications of proposals and is accompanied by national officials who fully understand all aspects of agenda items, but the political weight of the participants usually means that, if the will is there, commitments can be entered into without having to refer back for clearance. This is not to say that those in attendance at ministerial meetings can do as they like. At a minimum they are obliged to operate within the general guidelines of their government's policies. They may also be subject to special national constraints: perhaps occasioned by an inability of the minister to attend personally; perhaps linked to domestic political difficulties caused by the existence of a coalition government; perhaps caused by a national parliamentary committee having indicated concerns; or perhaps a consequence of a particular national interest having resulted in the establishment of a rigid governmental position in advance.

Second, in all member states arrangements have been established to enable governments to coordinate their policy towards and their participation in the EU. According to Peters and Wright (2001: 162) four general observations can be made about these arrangements: major political and constitutional EU issues are handled by the Heads of Government, assisted by their Foreign and Finance Ministers; the formal link between the domestic capital and Brussels is generally coordinated through the Foreign Ministry, the Finance/Economics Ministry, or both; most ministries in all member states have adjusted their internal structures to meet EU requirements; and despite some convergence, the nature of the coordination arrangements varies considerably between the member states.

Some flesh can be put on these general observations by comparing the arrangements made by two member states: the UK, which has a centralised coordinating system, and Germany, which has a more fragmented system.

In the UK, the centralised governmental system and the majority party political system provide a favourable base for effective coordinating mechanisms. The mechanisms themselves are formalised, structured, and seemingly well integrated. At the general policy level, the Foreign and Commonwealth Office (FCO), the Cabinet Office, and the UK Permanent Representation to the European Union (UKREP) are the key bodies: the FCO has two European Union Departments – Internal and External; the

Cabinet Office contains a European Secretariat which, amongst other things, convenes each year around 200 interdepartmental meetings of civil servants attended by representatives from appropriate ministries, including one regular weekly meeting which is attended by the Permanent Representative; and UKREP – which is formally an FCO overseas post – acts as the eyes and ears of the UK in Brussels. Working together, these three bodies attempt to monitor, coordinate and control overall EU developments: by giving general consideration to important matters due to come up at forthcoming meetings; by looking at whether a broadly consistent line is being pursued across different policy areas; by trying to ensure that ministries have issued sufficiently clear guidelines for representatives in Council meetings; and, in the cases of the FCO and UKREP, giving briefings to representatives when appropriate. 'Above' these three bodies, but not involved in such a continual manner, there is a Cabinet Committee on European Issues chaired by the Foreign Secretary, the Cabinet itself, and the Prime Minister. 'Below' them, each ministry has its own arrangements for examining proposals that fall within its competence and for ensuring that specialist negotiators are well briefed and fully aware of departmental thinking. When EU matters loom large in a ministry's work, special divisions or units exist for coordination purposes. (For a more detailed account of the UK government's coordinating arrangements see Bulmer and Burch, 1998; Forster and Blair, 2002.)

Some of Germany's coordinating arrangements are not dissimilar from those of the UK. There is, for example, a European Division in the Foreign Office and regular meetings are held of representatives from relevant ministries at (normally junior) ministerial and senior official levels. However, in Germany a number of factors combine to make coordination more difficult than it is in the UK: the existence of a coalition government and the need to satisfy (though not on a consistent basis across policy areas) the different elements of the coalition; the relative autonomy of ministers and ministries within the federal government (seen, most notably, in the long-running disagreement between the Finance Ministry and the Agriculture Ministry over the cost of the CAP); the lack of an authoritative coordinating centre – the Chancellor's Office and the Foreign Ministry both have a responsibility for major EU issues, whilst the Finance Ministry has a responsibility for many coordination matters; the relative independence from government of the Bundesbank (not so important since the establishment of the euro); the considerable powers of the federal states (the Länder) in certain policy areas; and strong sectoral specialisation, allied with loyalties to different federal ministries, amongst the staff of the German Permanent Representation in Brussels. As a result, Germany's European policies are sometimes less than consistent. Fortunately for Germany, having effective domestic arrangements for coordinating inputs into EU processes is not the only factor in determining policy influence in the EU and its position as the strongest single EU state seemingly enables it to avoid being too seriously damaged by this internal weakness. (For more information on Germany and the EU, see Anderson, 2005.)

But whatever the particulars of their arrangements for controlling and influencing their EU policy activities, all governments have found the task increasingly difficult in recent years. Three factors are especially important in accounting for this:

- Many more decisions are now being taken by the EU. This applies both to major and long-term decisions – on EMU, institutional reform, enlargement and so on – and to more specific and technical decisions, such as much of the SEM-related legislation.
- Not only are more decisions being made, but many are being made much more quickly. The greater use of QMV means that governments can no longer always delay progress on a proposal until they are ready and satisfied.
- The increased scope of EU policy interests means that there are no longer just a few domestic ministries – Agriculture, Trade, Finance and so forth – which are directly involved with the EU. The 'Europeanisation' of domestic politics and administration has resulted in most ministries in most states being affected by, and becoming actively involved in, EU affairs. So, for example, Wessels (2001) has estimated that approximately one-third of all senior (A-level) German Federal Ministry officials are involved directly in different phases of the Brussels policy cycle, whilst nearly two-thirds are in contact with the EU system in some way as part of their normal administrative work.

Parliaments

Parliaments have much less influence than governments over EU developments. Of course, governments normally reflect the political composition of their national legislatures and must retain their confidence, so – in an indirect sense – government activity in relation to the EU could be said to reflect the parliamentary will. But that is a quite different matter from direct parliamentary control.

One of the main reasons for the comparative lack of direct parliamentary control is that national parliaments have no formal EU treaty powers, so governments can choose what to consult their parliaments about. All governments consult their parliaments on fundamental matters when the treaties refer to ratification in accordance with 'respective constitutional requirements' (enlargements, treaty amendments, and the EU's budgetary base carry this provision), but otherwise there are variations between the states. Another reason for the weakness is the particular difficulties that arise in relation to what might be expected to be the major sphere of influence of national parliaments: advising on EU legislation. The difficulties here are legion: a high proportion of EU legislation is, or is regarded by governments as being, 'administrative' legislation and is therefore not within parliamentary competences; much EU legislation is so technical that it is almost incomprehensible to the average legislator; there is little opportunity to consider even the most important legislation at the formative and crucial pre-proposal stage; proposed legislation that is considered is often well advanced in, and may even be through, the Council system before it is examined by parliaments; and QMV in the Council means that a parliament whose government has been outvoted has no way at all of calling the real decision-makers to account.

But notwithstanding these problems and difficulties, all national parliaments have established some sort of specialised arrangements for attempting to deal with EU affairs. In different ways and with different degrees of effectiveness, these arrangements focus on examining proposed EU legislation, scrutinising ministerial positions and performances, producing reports on EU-related matters, and generally monitoring EU developments. Amongst the many differences that exist between the national arrangements three are particularly worth noting:

- All parliaments have established an EU committee of some sort. However, whereas in some cases these serve as the main forum for dealing with EU matters, in others they serve more as coordinating committees with the detailed work being undertaken by appropriate 'domestic' committees.
- The regularity and circumstances in which ministers with EU policy responsibilities appear before appropriate parliamentary bodies to explain and be questioned about these policies varies considerably.
- Some parliaments have established close working relationships with their national MEPs, whilst others have not. In a few parliaments – including the Belgian, German, and Greek – the specialised EU committees include MEPs, whilst in a growing number of parliaments MEPs are used as experts when appropriate.

Despite the changes and adjustments made by parliaments in recognition of the importance of the EU, it is still the case, however, that parliaments are mostly confined to a relatively minor role.

The position of the Irish Parliament is fairly typical. Following Irish accession to the Community in 1973 arrangements were made that were supposed to give Parliament monitoring, advisory, and deliberating responsibilities in respect of Irish participation in the Community. In particular, these arrangements consisted of an obligation on the part of the government to present a six-monthly report to Parliament on developments in the Community, and the creation of a new committee – the Joint Committee on Secondary Legislation, comprising 25 Dail Deputies and Senators – to examine Community proposals and advise the government on their implications and suitability for Ireland. The arrangements had but a marginal effect on Irish policy in Europe and in 1993 the Committee was subsumed within a new Joint Committee on Foreign Affairs, which has since been followed by the establishment of a Joint Committee on European Affairs. The changed arrangements have certainly strengthened the Dail's ability to scrutinise and debate EU affairs, though for the most part EU policy still is largely in the hands of a small, government-dominated, network of politicians and officials who listen to Parliament only when they deem it appropriate. In the case of agriculture, for example, the Minister of Agriculture, senior officials in the Department of Agriculture, and leaders of relevant organisations – particularly the Irish Farmers' Association – hold the key to decision-making and decision implementation, and they are not unduly inconvenienced by parliamentary probing.

The three Scandinavian EU member states – Denmark, Finland, and Sweden – have similar arrangements to each other and are the major exceptions to the general pattern of legislative weakness. Of the three, the Danish parliament – the Folketing – is probably the strongest. There are two main sources of its strength. First, there has been a powerful anti-integration sentiment among the people of Denmark since accession in 1973. No Danish government has been able to ignore the articulation of this in the Folketing, especially since Danish governments are invariably coalitions or minorities. Second, the Folketing has a committee system – formerly based on a very influential European Committee, since 2004 broadened out to include 'mainstream' policy committees – that includes amongst its activities close working relationships between Danish parliamentarians and ministers in advance of the latter attending Council meetings. The principal advantage of the system is that it helps to ensure that agreements reached by Danish ministers in the Council are not subsequently queried or endangered at home. The principal disadvantage is that it can make it difficult for Danish representatives to be flexible in the Council and can result in them being isolated if new solutions to problems are advanced during the course of negotiations.

Courts

National courts might be thought to have a significant role to play as the guarantors and defenders of national rights against EU encroachment, but in practice they do not.

The reason for this, as was explained in Chapter 13, is that the principle of primacy of EU law is accepted by national courts. There were some initial teething problems in this regard, but it is now extremely rare for national courts to question the legality of EU proceedings and decisions. The treaties, EU legislation and the case law of the ECJ are seen as taking precedence when they clash with national law. The frequent practice of national courts to seek preliminary rulings from the ECJ in cases where there is uncertainty over an aspect of EU law is testimony to the general desire of national courts not to be out of step with EU law.

That said, national courts have occasionally sought to assert national rights and interests against the EU. For example, in a few instances national courts have refused to acknowledge the legality of directives that have not been incorporated into national law by the due date, even though the ECJ has ruled that in such circumstances they may be deemed as having direct effect. Constitutional law, especially as applied to individual rights, has been another area where some assertion of national independence has been attempted by national courts, though less often since the principle of EU law having precedence over national constitutional law was confirmed by ECJ rulings in the early 1970s.

In recent years the most important instances of national court intervention have been in connection with Irish ratification of the SEA and German ratification of the Maastricht Treaty. The Irish intervention occurred in December 1986 when the Irish Supreme Court, by a margin of three to two, found in favour of a Raymond Crotty, who had challenged the constitutional validity of the SEA. The judges ruled that Title III of the Act, which put foreign policy cooperation on a legal basis, could restrict Ireland's sovereignty and might inhibit it from pursuing its traditionally neutral foreign policy. The SEA must therefore, they indicated, be endorsed by a referendum. As a result, the SEA was unable to come into effect in any of the twelve Community states on 1 January 1987, as had been intended, and was delayed until the Irish gave their approval in the duly held referendum. The SEA eventually entered into force on 1 July 1987. The German intervention occurred when several people – including four Green Party MEPs – appealed to the country's Constitutional Court to declare that the Maastricht Treaty was in breach of the German constitution, the Basic Law. The appeal was made shortly after the Bundestag and the Bundesrat had ratified the Treaty by huge majorities in December 1992, with the consequence that, instead of being one of the first countries to ratify the Treaty, Germany became the very last as the Constitutional Court did not issue its judgement until October 1993. In its judgement the Court declared that the TEU did not infringe Germany's constitution, but made it clear that certain conditions would have to be satisfied in respect of further integration.

Subnational Levels of Government

The parts played and the influence exercised by subnational levels of government in the EU were considered in Chapter 13 in the sections on the Committee of the Regions and on interests. Here, therefore, only a few observations will be made on key points.

Subnational levels of government have grown in importance within the EU system in recent years, not least as a result of decentralisation and regionalisation in several member states. A consequence of this has been that national authorities, especially governments, have lost some of their power to articulate and advance 'the national position' in EU decision-making forums. The extent to which national authorities' gatekeeping roles have been undermined naturally varies according to a number of factors, most particularly the national constitutional status of subnational levels of government, but even in countries where central powers remain strong – for example Ireland and Denmark – by no means all EU-national official communications are channelled through the central authorities.

Channels of communication between the EU and subnational levels of government include the following:

- Most EU states have subnational levels of government of some kind that have offices or representations in Brussels. For example, all of Germany's Länder and Spain's autonomia have offices, as do most of France's regions. The tasks of these offices include lobbying, information gathering, generally establishing contacts and 'keeping in touch' with appropriate officials and decision-makers, and acting as intermediaries between the EU and the regions/localities.
- Many of the subnational levels of government that do not have their own offices in Brussels make use of Brussels-based consultancies and/or have domestically-based EU offices and officers.
- The Committee of the Regions exists for the precise purpose of enabling EU decision-makers to seek the views of regional representatives on regional issues.
- A few governments – including the Belgian, the German and the British – are sometimes represented in the Council of Ministers by regional ministers when agenda items are the responsibility of regional governments.

The EU may be a long way from the Europe of the Regions that some advocate and others claim to detect, but clearly the national dimension of EU affairs has an increasingly powerful subnational element attached to it.

Citizens' Views

Referendums

One way in which citizens can have their say on issues is in referendums. Leaving aside the special case of accession referendums, which most, though not all, post-foundation states have held prior to their EC/EU accessions, up to early 2006 there had been nineteen referendums in member states on EC/EU related matters. As can be seen from Table 20.1, most of these referendums have been concerned with the ratification of EC/EU treaties.

Whilst referendums do inject an element of direct democracy into public decision-making, it must be doubted whether the referendums listed in Table 20.1 have really done much to deal with the much-publicised and debated problem of the EU's so-called 'democratic deficit'. For a number of reasons:

- There have not been many of them.
- Most have been, or have become, tangled up with national politics and have not been primarily about, or focused on, the EU. For example, the 1972 French referendum was really designed to boost the legitimacy and status of President Pompidou, whilst the 2001 Irish referendum focused largely around 'non-EU' issues – including dissatisfaction with the government and the protection of 'family values'.
- Few have been on issues that citizens really understand in terms of how the referendum outcome will impact on them. For example, surveys in the 2005 French and Dutch referendums showed that citizens had little knowledge of the contents of the treaties on which they have voted.
- Most referendums have not been on issues that engage citizens – with the two referendums on euro membership being the clearest exceptions.

The fact is that on major EU issues to which citizens can relate and have an opinion (albeit, arguably, an ill-informed opinion), few referendums have been held. This is, of course, primarily because the political systems of the member states are based on representative rather than on direct democracy. But, it is also partly because when there have been pressures on member state governments to hold referendums on EU-related issues they have usually not taken the 'risk' for fear of citizens giving the 'wrong' answer. It is significant, for example, that not one referendum on euro membership has been held in the member states that have become euro

Table 20.1   *Referendums in member states on EC/EU issues**

Date	Country	Subject of referendum	Referendum decision
1972	France	Ratification of EU enlargement	Yes
1975	UK	Continued EC membership	Yes
1986	Denmark	Ratification of SEA	Yes
1987	Ireland	Ratification of SEA	Yes
1989	Italy	Transformation of the EC into an 'effective union'	Yes
1992	Denmark	Ratification of Maastricht Treaty	No
1992	Ireland	Ratification of Maastricht Treaty	Yes
1992	France	Ratification of Maastricht Treaty	Yes
1993	Denmark	Ratification of Maastricht Treaty	Yes
1998	Ireland	Ratification of Amsterdam Treaty	Yes
1998	Denmark	Ratification of Amsterdam Treaty	Yes
2000	Denmark	Whether to join the euro	No
2001	Ireland	Ratification of Nice Treaty	No
2002	Ireland	Ratification of Nice Treaty	Yes
2003	Sweden	Whether to join the euro	No
2005	Spain	Ratification of the Constitutional Treaty	Yes
2005	France	Ratification of the Constitutional Treaty	No
2005	Netherlands	Ratification of the Constitutional Treaty	No
2005	Luxembourg	Ratification of the Constitutional Treaty	Yes

* Up to February 2006. Voting figures in the referendums are given in the Chronology.

members, even though – or more precisely because – there was evidence of substantial opposition in several of the states, including Germany. In the two states where euro membership referendums have been held – Denmark and Sweden – the people voted 'no'.

This is not, however, to say that there have not been referendums that have not had a significant impact on the integration process. Four 'sets' of referendums have been especially important.

First, there have been the referendums that have delayed treaty ratifications: the 1992 Danish referendum on the Maastricht Treaty and the 2001 Irish referendum on the Nice Treaty (see Chapters 5 and 6 for the extent of the delays).

Second, there have been the referendums that have affected public, and especially elite, thinking about the integration process. The 1992 Danish and French referendums drew attention to how European integration is essentially an elite-driven process and emphasised that it is important for decision-makers not to get too out of step with public opinion. In recognition of this, the rhetoric of supporters of European integration tended to be more tempered from mid-1992, decision-makers moved more cautiously for a while, and much came to be made by all concerned of the merits of subsidiarity, transparency, and decentralisation. The 2001 Irish referendum might also be placed in this 'set' in that it drew attention to the 'dangers' in an ever-larger EU of permitting national electorates a decisive influence on EU-wide issues. For, as Rees and Holmes (2002: 49) have observed of the referendum: 'A country of less than four million people, an electorate of less than three million, a turnout of less than a million and a No vote of slightly over half a million derailed a process designed to allow the EU to enlarge to almost 500 million'.

Third, there have been the referendums that have had a very direct and specific policy consequence. Amongst the fall-out of the 1992 Danish referendum was that Denmark was given, as an inducement to approve the Maastricht Treaty, 'opt-outs' from EMU and from the projected common defence policy. The 2000 Danish and 2003 Swedish referendums resulted in those countries not joining the single currency system.

Fourth, there have been the two 2005 referendums – in France and the Netherlands – where negative majorities were cast against the ratification of the Constitutional Treaty. Whilst the consequences of these referendums is not altogether clear at the time of writing, it is most likely that they have done much more than merely delayed the Treaty's ratification.

Of course, there is one way in which referendums could potentially act as a direct and effective channel for citizen's views on EU issues and that is to hold EU-wide referendums on matters of major importance. Such has been suggested by many 'pro-integrationists' in the context of the ratification of the Constitutional Treaty. The prospect of referendums of this sort being held in the foreseeable future is, however, very remote. One reason for this is that it would likely involve highly contentious treaty changes – especially if it was envisaged that the outcomes of such referendums would be binding. And another, related, reason, is that some states would fiercely resist such an open 'transfer' of sovereignty from 'national voters' to 'European voters'.

European Parliament elections

In contrast with the only occasional and localised opportunities for participation offered by referendums, elections to the EP provide citizens with regular and direct opportunities to participate in the political process on an EU-wide basis. (See Chapter 12 for details of EP elections.) As such, the elections are seen by some observers as providing the EU with a democratic base. This view, however, must be counterbalanced by recognition of the fact that since the elections are not in practice contested by European parties standing on European issues, but are more like second-order national elections, they can hardly be regarded as occasions when the populace indicate their European policy preferences. The fact that voter turnout is, in most cases, low by national standards, and furthermore has declined across the EU in every set of EP elections since they were first held in 1979 – to such an extent that the overall level in 1999 and 2004 was below 50 per cent – raises further questions about the democratic legitimacy given to the EU by the elections.

National elections

Another way in which citizens can exert an influence on EU affairs via the ballot box is through national elections, since most important EU decisions are taken by the elected national representatives in the European Council and the Council of Ministers. This influence, however, is indirect in the sense that national elections are two or three stages removed from the EU: voters elect legislatures, from which governments are formed, which send representatives to EU summits and Council meetings. The influence is also somewhat tangential in that in national elections voters are not much concerned with 'European issues' or with the competence of candidates to deal with European matters: beyond some limited attention by far-right and nationalist parties – occasioned by their generally 'anti-Europe' stance – there is not much evidence of 'Europe' as such being an issue or of it swaying many votes.

Public opinion

Public opinion towards the EU and its policies is closely and extensively monitored, both at the EU level through regular Commission-sponsored Eurobarometer polls and at national levels through countless polls conducted on behalf of governments, research agencies, and the media. In broad terms it can be said that this ongoing trawling of public opinion reveals three main sets of findings. First, across the EU as a whole around one-third of citizens strongly support European integration, just over one-half are ranged between ambivalence and cautious support, and just over one-tenth are strongly opposed. Second, there are variations between countries, with, in 2005, Austria, the UK and Latvia displaying the lowest levels of support on most indicators, and Ireland, Luxembourg and Spain being amongst the highest. Third, support usually dips when citizens are asked whether they would like further integration in particular issue areas, such as taxation or social welfare. There are probably a number of reasons why there is limited enthusiasm for the EU becoming more involved in such policies: the implications can seem to be threatening, parts of the media are frequently hostile, and it can look like (and indeed can be) another example of political elites trying to force unwanted integration.

The extent to which governments respond to public opinion depends very much on their own ideological and policy preferences, their perception of the importance and durability of issues, and the time remaining until the next election. The existence of, for example, less than enthusiastic support for European integration amongst a sizeable proportion of national electorates may both restrain and encourage politicians depending on their viewpoint, but there certainly is no automatic relationship between what the people think about EU matters and what governments do. The UK Conservative government, for example, made no move to withdraw from the Community in the early 1980s even though a majority of the British population thought it should, and it did not weaken its opposition in the 1990s to the Social Charter even though polls suggested that the Charter was supported by about two-thirds of the British people. Similarly, in the late 1990s the German government did not weaken in its resolve to take Germany into the single currency even though polls showed that a majority of Germans were opposed to the deutschemark being subsumed within the euro.

That said, public opinion does exercise an influence in at least setting the boundaries in which national leaders must operate. For example, domestic scepticism about the euro means that Tony Blair has had to be very careful in advocating the case for UK adoption of the currency, whilst anti-Turkish sentiments in France and Germany and very low levels of support for EU enlargement to include Turkey have led French and German leaders to display a wariness about the prospect of Turkey eventually acceding to the EU.

Public opinion can also be important in that if an issue is generally accepted as constituting a national interest, or at least commands strong domestic support, then governments of whatever political persuasion are likely to pursue it in the Council. Even if they themselves do not wish to be too rigid, they may well be forced, by electoral considerations and domestic pressures, to strike postures and make a public display of not being pushed around. For example, Irish and French governments invari-

ably favour generous settlements for farmers, Danish and German governments press for strict environmental controls, and CEEC governments
argue for increased cohesion operations to enable them to modernise their
economies.

Political Parties

Political parties normally wish to exercise power, which in liberal
democratic states means they must be able to command popular support.
This in turn means they must be able to articulate and aggregate national
opinions and interests. At the same time, parties are not normally content
simply to act as mirror images of the popular will. Drawing on their
traditions, and guided by leaders and activists, they also seek to direct
society by mobilising support behind preferred ideological/policy positions. Judgements thus have to be made about the balance to be struck
between 'reflecting' society and 'leading' it. Those parties which lean too
much towards the latter have little chance of winning elections, although
in multi-party systems they may well still find themselves with strong
negotiating hands.

Of course, the precise extent to which parties are, on the one hand,
reflecting and channelling opinions on particular issues and, on the other,
are shaping and determining them is very difficult to judge since, in most
instances, the processes are two-way and interrelated. But whatever the
exact balance may be between the processes, both are very much in
operation in relation to the EU. The experiences of Denmark, Greece
and the UK in the 1980s and early 1990s illustrate this. In each of these
countries there was widespread popular scepticism in the early to mid-
1980s about Community membership and this found both expression and
encouragement at the party political level, with some parties advocating a
complete withdrawal from Community membership and others expressing
considerable concern about aspects of the implications of membership –
especially in relation to sovereignty. As the 'realities' of membership began
to seep through, however, both public opinion and party attitudes began to
change. So much so that by the early 1990s Greece had become one of the
more enthusiastic Community states in terms of public opinion and a
'typical' one in terms of the attitudes of its political parties, whilst
Denmark and the UK, though still in the slow stream, were not lagging
as far behind as formerly they had been.

Apart from their interactive relationship with the attitudinal climate in
which EU processes work, political parties also feed directly into EU
decision-making. First, by providing much of the ideological base of the
policies of governments and most, if not all, of the leading personnel of

governments, they do much to determine and shape the attitudes, priorities and stances of the member states in the Council. While it is true that many policy positions are barely altered by changes of government, shifts of emphasis do occur and these can be significant, as was clearly demonstrated in 1997 when the replacement of the Conservatives by Labour in Britain resulted in very important changes in governmental policy towards the EU. Second, even when in domestic opposition political parties can influence government behaviour in the Council because governments do not wish to be accused of being weak or not strongly defending national interests. Third, national political parties are the main contestants in the European elections and their successful candidates become the national representatives in the EP.

Interests

Acting either by themselves or through an appropriate Eurogroup, national sectional and promotional interests have a number of possible avenues available to them to try to influence EU policies and decisions. Some avenues are at the domestic level, such as approaches through fellow national MEPs, government officials, and ministers. Others are at the EU level, such as using contacts in the Commission and the EP. These avenues were discussed in some detail in Chapter 14, so will not be repeated here.

In very general terms, the most successful national interests tend to fulfil at least one of two conditions. Either they are able to persuade their government that there is little distinction between the interests' aims and national aims. Or they have sufficient power and information resources to persuade at least some EU decision-makers that they ought to be listened to. A major reason why farmers have been so influential is that both of these conditions have applied to them in some countries. In France, Portugal, Ireland, and elsewhere this has resulted in Ministries of Agriculture perceiving that a major part of their responsibility in the Council is to act virtually as a spokesman for the farmers.

Concluding Remarks

The existence of different and frequently conflicting inputs from member states is the major obstacle in the way of the realisation of a smooth, efficient and decisive EU policy and decision-making machinery. But it is vital that national views and requirements should be able to be articulated and incorporated into decisions if the EU is to work at all, for ultimately the EU exists to further the interests of those who live in the member states. If the citizens of the states and, more particularly, the political elites in governments and parliaments were to feel that the EU was no longer serving that purpose, then there would be no reason for continued membership. The member states, in short, need to have confidence in the EU. The EU must therefore be responsive to its constituent parts.

There is an emerging body of evidence to indicate that these constituent parts are becoming increasingly similar in the nature of their inputs into the EU and the way they handle EU business. Though, as has been shown in this and earlier chapters, at present there are still significant differences between the member states on both these counts, convergences are none-theless apparent. This is particularly the case in respect of policy inputs, but there are also signs of 'institutional fusion' (Rometsch and Wessels, 1996). Such convergences can be expected to increase as the EU and national levels become ever more enmeshed.

Stepping Back and Looking Forward

Part 5 steps back from the detailed study of European integration and the European Union to consider a number of general issues and matters. It also looks forward to how the integration process and the EU might develop.

Chapter 21 is quite different in character from the previous chapters of the book. It examines conceptual and theoretical tools that have been used to capture and analyse the key features of the integration process, the main organisational characteristics of the EU, and particular aspects of the functioning of the EU.

Chapter 22 provides a conclusion for the book. It does so by placing the EU in its global context, by looking at factors that are likely to affect the EU's future development and by examining the main challenges facing the EU.

Chapter 21

Conceptualising and Theorising

Conceptualising the European Union
Three Key Concepts: Sovereignty, Intergovernmentalism and
  Supranationalism
Theorising European Integration: Grand Theory
Theorising the Functioning of the EU: Middle-Range Theory
Concluding Remarks

The previous chapters of this book have been concerned with identifying and analysing the principal features of the evolution and nature of European integration and the European Union. This chapter has much the same focus, but takes a different approach. It does so by moving away from logging and analysing 'the facts' to examining the insights that are provided by conceptual and theoretical perspectives.

Conceptualising, which essentially means thinking about phenomena in abstract terms, and theorising, which means positing general explanations of phenomena, have constituted the base of much academic writing on European integration. There are, it should be said, some who question the value of much of this conceptualising and theorising, with doubts and reservations usually focusing on what are seen to be poor, and potentially misleading, 'matches' between over-simplistic models on the one hand and complex realities on the other. This is, however, a minority view and most EU academic commentators take the general social science position that the development and use of concepts and theories enhances the understanding of political, economic, and social phenomena by structuring and directing observation and interpretation. (Fuller arguments for the usefulness – indeed indispensability – of theory in European integration studies can be found in Chryssochoou, 2001: Chapter 1; Rosamond, 2000: Chapter 1; Wiener and Diez, 2004: Chapter 1).

There are three broad types of conceptual and theoretical work on European integration and the EU.

- There are attempts to conceptualise the organisational nature of the EU. Such conceptualisations, which can be thought of as attempts to determine 'the nature of the beast', are explored in the first two sections of this chapter. The first of these sections examines conceptualisations of the EU as a political system and the second examines three key concepts that are habitually employed when assessing the political character of the EU.

- There are attempts to theorise the general nature of the integration process. Such theorising is not as fashionable today as it once was, but it is still seen by many scholars as worthwhile, and it certainly marks the point of departure for a great deal of other conceptual and theoretical work. Grand theory, as general integration theory is commonly known, is studied in the third section of the chapter.

- There are attempts to develop conceptual and theoretical approaches to particular aspects of the functioning of the EU, especially policy and decision-making. Operating at the middle range, or as it is sometimes called the meso, level rather than at the general level, this has been a major growth area in scholarly work on the EU in recent years. It is the subject of the fourth section of the chapter.

As will be shown, within each of these three broad types of conceptual and theoretical work there is a wide range of different approaches. An underlying theme of the chapter is that the existence of many approaches is inevitable given the multi-dimensional nature of European integration as a process and the EU as an organisation. No single theory is capable of explaining everything. The complexities of the process and the organisation are such that different sets of conceptual and theoretical tools are necessary to examine and interpret them.

Before proceeding, three cautionary notes must be issued. First, there is considerable overlap and intertwining between the many different dimensions of the conceptual and theoretical ideas that are described and analysed below. Although, for ease of presentation, the dimensions are sectionalised in the account that follows, it should be recognised that in practice there is considerable overlap between the sections. So, for example, most broad theoretical work draws heavily on a wide range of more narrowly focused conceptual work. Second, the range of conceptual and theoretical approaches to the study of European integration and the EU is so great that only some of them can be considered here. Attention is necessarily restricted to examining some of the more important approaches and giving a flavour of their varying characters. Third, the focus here is largely restricted to political science approaches to theorising and conceptualising. Other disciplines do, of course, have their own approaches.

Conceptualising the European Union

What type of political organisation/system is the EU? This is a difficult question to answer. It is so for at least four reasons.

First, the EU itself has never sought to describe or define its political character in any clear manner. The closest it has come is in the Common Provisions of the TEU, especially as revised by the Amsterdam Treaty. Article 1 TEU states that 'This Treaty marks a new stage in the process of creating an ever closer union among the peoples of Europe, in which decisions are taken as openly as possible and as closely as possible to the citizen'. According to Article 6 'The Union is founded on the principles of liberty, democracy, respect for human rights and fundamental freedoms, and the rule of law, principles which are common to the Member States'. The TEU thus tells us something about the political character of the EU, but not much.

Second, as the above quotation from Article 1 TEU suggests, the EU is, and always has been, in constant transition. Its character has changed considerably over the years as the integration process has deepened and widened. Its nature has never been settled. For example, its decision-making processes have become progressively more supranational since the mid- 1980s, as evidenced by the much greater use of QMV in the Council of Ministers and the growing power of the EP.

Third, the EU is a highly complex and multi-faceted system. This means that there are abundant opportunities for different characteristics of the system to be generated by different focuses of analysis. Is, for example, the focus to be on the EU as an actor or as an arena? If the latter, is the focus to be on its territorial or its sectoral character?

Fourth, in important respects the EU is unique. It is so, for example, in the way it embodies both supranational and intergovernmental features in its system of governance, and in the extent to which it embodies shared policy responsibilities between different levels of government and different nation states. A perfectly reasonable answer to the question 'What type of political organisation/system is the EU?' is thus that it is not of any type – or, at least, not of any established type – at all. Rather it is *sui generis* – the only one of its kind.

But recognition of the fact that the EU is in important respects unique, does not mean that attempts should not be made to conceptualise it. The reason for this is that conceptualisation can help to highlight the EU's essential features, and in so doing can draw attention to those features that are distinctive and those that are found elsewhere.

States and intergovernmental organisations

A useful starting point in attempting to conceptualise the EU is to compare it with the most important political unit of the international system, the state, and with the customary way in which states interrelate with one another on a structured basis, the intergovernmental organisation (IGO).

Definitions of the state are many and various. Generally speaking, however, the key characteristics of the state are: *territoriality* – the state is geographically based and bound; *sovereignty* – the state stands above all other associations and groups within its geographical area and its jurisdiction extends to the whole population of the area; *legitimacy* – the authority of the state is widely recognised, both internally and externally; *monopoly of governance* – the institutions of the state monopolise public decision-making and enforcement.

These four features do not all need to be present in a pure, undiluted and uncontested form for a state to exist. They do, however, need to feature prominently and to constitute the essential bedrock of the system. With the EU there is no doubt that all four features are present, but they are so only in partial ways. So, *territoriality* is present in the sense that the EU's territory is the sum total of the member states' territory. However, the EU can hardly be said to 'own' that territory in the sense that member states can be said to own their territory. In part to add credence to this territorial dimension of its existence, the EU has created some of the symbols of statehood with a flag, an anthem, and (almost) a common passport. The EU enjoys some *sovereignty* – as witnessed by the primacy of EU law and the fact that EU jurisdiction applies to the whole EU population – but the reach of that sovereignty is confined to the policy areas where the EU's remit is established. Likewise the EU does command *legitimacy*, but opinion surveys show that its internal authority is somewhat thinly based, whilst its external authority is generally weak beyond the Common Commercial Policy. And as for *monopoly of governance,* far from being in a position of dominance the EU monopolises governance in only a very few policy areas, and even then it is highly dependent on the member states for policy enforcement. To these 'weaknesses' might be added the very limited development of EU citizenship and the EU's comparatively limited financial resources.

The EU thus falls a long way short of being a state, as statehood is traditionally understood. However, the concept of the state is still of some use in helping to promote an understanding of the nature of the EU. It is so for two reasons. First, as has just been shown, the EU does display some of the traditional characteristics of a state, and the continuing development of the integration process inevitably means that these characteristics will strengthen. It is, for example, the case that Jacques Delors was largely correct when he predicted in 1988 – to the accompaniment of much scoffing – that by the end of the 1990s 80 per cent of socio-economic legislation applying in the member states would be made at EU level. Second, the realities of traditional statehood are breaking down in the modern world, most particularly under the pressures of international interdependence. So, for example, no modern state can now be regarded as being fully sovereign in a *de facto* sense, and the EU member states cannot even claim that they are fully sovereign in a *de jure* sense. These changes in the realities of statehood mean there must also be changes in how the state is conceptualised. And in such new conceptualisations – involving, for instance, notions of the regulatory state and the postmodern state – the EU displays, as James Caporaso (1996) has argued, many state-like features.

The notion of the EU as a regulatory state is a conceptualisation that has attracted much attention, due in large part to the extensive work of Giandomenico Majone (1992, 1994, 1996) on the subject. The regulatory state model conceptualises the EU in terms both of its functions and its institutional structure. Regarding its functions, the EU is seen as not being greatly involved in distributive or redistributive policies but as being extensively involved in regulating such policy areas as competition, environment, product quality, and health and safety at work. A number of factors are identified by Majone as explaining this regulatory focus, including pressure from business firms for there to be a fully integrated internal market and a reluctance on the part of member state governments to permit the large budget that redistributive policies require. Regarding the EU's institutional structure, Majone argues that a range of regulatory and non-majoritarian institutions exist – most notably in the form of the Commission, the Court of Justice, and regulatory agencies – that collectively constitute virtually an independent fourth branch of government.

Turning to IGOs, these are organisations in which representatives of national governments come together to cooperate on a voluntary basis for reasons of mutual benefit. IGOs have very little if any decision-making autonomy and cannot enforce their will on reluctant member states. Amongst the best known examples of IGOs are the UN, the OECD, NATO, and the Council of Europe.

Paul Magnette (2005) argues for the usefulness of the IGO conceptualisation when trying to understand the nature of the EU. The EU is, he acknowledges, more sophisticated and developed than the likes of NATO and the Council of Europe but nonetheless 'the best way to understand the EU's structure and functioning is to see it primarily as an intergovernmental organization' (ibid.: 3). Central to Magnette's position is that EU institutions are best viewed not as external agencies imposing their views on unwilling national authorities but rather as frameworks or networks in which national actors attempt to coordinate their interests and policy preferences. The EU 'is a set of institutions and rules designed to strengthen the European states by encouraging them to cooperate ... The EU is not about depriving the states of their sovereignty. Rather it is about encouraging them to exercise their prerogatives in new and more cooperative ways' (ibid.: 3).

Magnette's view, whilst thought-provoking and interesting, is not, it has to be said, widely shared. Most observers see striking differences between the EU and IGOs:

- The EU has a much more developed and complex institutional structure than is found in IGOs. The standard pattern of advanced IGOs – permanent secretariats and attached delegations – is perhaps, in a much grander and more elaborated form, replicated in the EU with the Commission and the Permanent Representations, but to these are added many other features. Among the more obvious of such features are the regular and frequent meetings at the very highest political levels between representatives of the governments of the member states; the constant and many varied forms of contact between national officials; the Court of Justice; and the EP – the only directly elected multi-state assembly in the world.
- No IGO has anything like the policy responsibilities of the EU. In terms of breadth, few significant policy areas have completely escaped the EU's attention. In terms of depth, the pattern varies, but in many important areas, including external trade, agriculture, and competition policy, key initiating and decision-making powers have been transferred from the member states to the EU authorities.
- The EU has progressed far beyond the intergovernmental nature of IGOs to incorporate many supranational characteristics into its structure and operation. The nature of the balance within the EU between intergovernmentalism and supranationalism will be examined later in the chapter.

In terms of state and IGO conceptualisation, the EU is thus perhaps best thought of as being less than the former but more than the latter. Are there, therefore, other conceptualisations that come closer to capturing the essence of the EU?

Three of the more commonly used conceptualisations of the EU are now explored.

Federalism

Interpretations of the nature of federalism vary. This is not surprising, perhaps, when systems as diverse as Germany, India, Switzerland and the United States all describe themselves as federal.

Different interpretations within the EU of the nature of federalism were no more clearly demonstrated than in the run-up to the 1991 Maastricht summit, when the UK government became embroiled in a sharp clash with the governments of the other member states over whether there should be a reference in the TEU to the EU 'evolving in a federal direction'. The clash centred in large part on different understandings of what 'federal' entails and implies, with the UK government giving the word a much more centralist spin than other governments. Indeed, the solution that was eventually agreed upon – to remove the offending phrase and replace it with a statement that the Treaty 'marks a new stage in the process of creating an ever closer union among the peoples of Europe' – seemed to many EU governments far more centralist in tone than did the original formulation.

Academic commentators too have not been in complete accord on the precise nature of federal systems. In broad terms, however, most would regard the key characteristics of such systems as being as follows:

- Power is divided between central decision-making institutions on the one hand and regional decision-making institutions on the other.
- The nature of this division of power is specified in and is protected by constitutional documents. Disputes over the division are settled by a supreme judicial authority.
- The division of power between the central and regional levels is balanced in the sense that both have responsibilities – although not necessarily wholly exclusive responsibilities – for important spheres of public policy.
- Modern realities dictate that in practice the division of power cannot be over-rigid. Rather, some policy responsibilities inevitably overlap and intertwine. In short, the only viable form of federalism in the modern world is cooperative federalism.
- Whilst the policy content of the division of power can vary, some policy areas are primarily the responsibility of the central level because they are concerned with the identity, coherence, and protection of the system as a whole. Such policy areas normally include foreign affairs, security and defence, management of the (single) currency, and specification and protection of citizens' rights – or at least the more important of these rights.

In applying the federal model to the EU it is readily apparent that the EU does display some federal traits:

- Power *is* divided between central decision-making institutions (the Commission, the Council, the EP and so on), and regional decision-making institutions (the governing authorities in the member states).
- The nature of the division *is* specified in constitutional documents (the treaties) and there *is* a supreme judicial authority (the ECJ) with the authority to adjudicate in the event of disputes over the division.

- Both levels *do* have important powers and responsibilities for public policy – with those of the central level appertaining particularly, but by no means exclusively, to the economic sphere.

At the same time, however, it is also clear that in some respects the EU falls short of the federal model:

- Although power is divided between the central and regional levels, some of the responsibilities that lie at the centre are heavily dependent on regional acquiescence if they are to be exercised. This is most obviously the case where the unanimity rule applies in the Council, as for example, in respect of decisions on treaty reform, enlargement, and fiscal measures.
- The policy balance is still tilted towards the member states. The degree of tilt is much less than it was before the 're-launch' of the Community in the mid-1980s, but for all but economic policies the member states are still mostly in control of public decision-making. This is reflected in the fact that policy areas that involve heavy public expenditure – such as education, health, social welfare, and defence – are still essentially national policies, with the control of taxation and financial resources still lying overwhelmingly with the member states.
- Those policy spheres which in 'conventional' federal systems are normally thought of as being the responsibility of the central authorities, in the EU are primarily national responsibilities. Foreign affairs, security and defence, and citizenship rights are being developed at the EU level, but so far only to a limited degree and on a largely intergovernmental basis. Currency control is the most obvious exception to this, but not all member states are members of the single currency system.
- The central authorities are not able to use 'legitimate violence' in 'EU territory'.

This balance of characteristics combines to suggest a system that does not fully embrace all the traits of the classical federal system, but is not as far removed from the federal model as is usually supposed (see Sbragia, 1992, for a supporting argument along these lines). At a minimum, the EU may be said to embody the federal principle of combining in a territorial and contractual sharing of power a degree of unity on the one hand with a respect for the interests and partial autonomy of regional units on the other. Moreover, it is clear that over the years the movement of the EU progressively has been in a federal direction. The Maastricht Treaty was, as Koslowski (1999) has observed, especially significant in this respect. It was so most obviously with its provisions for institutional deepening. But it was so also with its establishment of Union citizenship, albeit in a weak form, and its 'codification' of the principle of subsidiarity which may be seen as an embryo federal principle 'governing the scope of EU policy-making and thereby fram[ing] the political relationship between the EU and its member states in federal terms' (ibid.: 574).

So the EU may certainly be thought of as at least perhaps being a federal system in the making. This might lead one to agree with Warleigh (1998, 2000), who suggests that the most appropriate way of labelling the EU at present is as a confederation. The distinction between federation and confederation is fuzzy, but in essence it rests on the amount of power exercised at the central and regional levels, with confederations being systems in which the balance is very much tilted to the regional level. Insofar as the EU is a union of previously sovereign states created by treaty in which supranational institutions exist but whose range of powers fall short of the powers exercised by their counterparts in federal systems, it may be thought of as a confederation.

State-centrism and consociationalism

State-centric models of the EU are advanced by those who take an intergovernmental view of the integration process. As such, they portray the EU as having the following features at its core:

- The system rests primarily on nation states that have come together to cooperate for certain specified purposes.
- The main channels of communication between EU member states are the national governments.
- The national governments control the overall direction and pace of EU decision-making.
- No governments, and therefore no states, are obliged to accept decisions on major issues to which they are opposed.
- Supranational actors such as the Commission and the ECJ do not have significant independent powers in their own right, but function essentially as agents and facilitators of the collective will of the national governments.

From this shared core, state-centric models branch out into a number of different forms, most of which involve some 'softening' of the core's hard edges. Variations occur in respect of such matters as the dynamics of inter-state relations, the nature of the policy role and impact of non-state actors, and the importance that is accorded to national domestic politics.

The last of these variations has produced a conceptualisation of EU policy dynamics as conducted on the basis of a two-level game, in which state-centrism is combined with a domestic politics approach (see Bulmer, 1983, on this latter approach). In the two-level game conceptualisation, most famously advanced by Putnam (1988), the governments of member states are involved in EU policy-making at two levels: at the domestic level, where political actors seek to influence the positions adopted by governments, and at the intergovernmental level, where governments negotiate with one another in EU forums.

A much employed variation of the core state-centric model is consociationalism. Originally developed – notably by Arend Lijphart (1969) – to throw light on how some democratic states which are sharply divided internally are able to function in a relatively smooth and stable manner, consociationalism has been championed as a model that can provide valuable insights into central features of the functioning of the EU.

Consociational states are normally portrayed as displaying the following main features:

- There is societal segmentation (which may or may not be geographically demarcated) and there are several politically significant lines of division.
- The various segments are represented in decision-making forums on a proportional basis, though with the possibility of minorities sometimes being over-represented.
- Political elites of the segments dominate decision-making processes. Interactions between these elites are intense and almost constant.
- Decisions are taken on the basis of compromise and consensus. The majoritarian principle, whereby a majority can proceed even if it is opposed by a minority, is not normally employed, especially when major or sensitive issues are involved. Decisional processes are characterised by bargaining and exchanges, whilst decisional outcomes are marked by compromise and are frequently little more than the lowest common denominator.
- The interactions between the segments, and particularly between the elites of the segments, can be both positive and negative with regards to promoting solidarity: positive in that links are established and community-wide attitudes can be fostered between the segments; negative in that since the very rationale of consociationalism is the preservation of segmented autonomy within a cooperative system, segments may be tempted to over-emphasise their distinctiveness and moves towards over-centralisation may become occasions for resentment and unease within the segments.

Just as there are variations of the core state-centric model, so have the main features of the consociational model been developed and directed by analysts in various ways. In the EU context, a leading such analyst is Paul Taylor (1991, 1996), who sees the model as extremely valuable in helping to explain the nature of the balance between fragmentation and cooperation/integration in the EU, the mutual dependence between the member states and the collectivity, and the ability – which does not imply inevitability – of the system as a whole both to advance and maintain stability.

At the heart of Taylor's analysis of the EU is the notion of there being a symbiosis – a mutual dependence – between the participating segments of the consociation (the member states) and the collectivity of the consociation (EU structures and frameworks). This symbiosis is seen as enabling many of the costs of fragmentation to be overcome, whilst at the same time preserving, and in some ways even strengthening, the power and authority of *both* the segments and the collectivity.

A particularly important aspect of this last point is the assertion that EU member states do not lose significant power or authority by virtue of their EU membership. Taylor is quite explicit about this:

> the system works not on the basis of what functionalists, or federalists, would call the Community interest, but much more on the basis of the low level consensus among segmented elites identified within con-sociationalism. There is a strong sense that the Community exists to serve the member states ... there is no evidence to suggest that common arrangements could not be extended a very long way without necessarily posing any direct challenge to the sovereignty of states (Taylor, 1991: 24–5).

Dimitris Chryssochoou (1994, 1995, 1998, 2001) and Costa and Magnette (2003), who too are exponents of the consociational model, also emphasise this point about the resilience of states within the EU and their retention of fundamental sovereignty. For Chryssochoou (1994: 48), the EU is a confederal consociation in that it is a system in which there is 'the merging of distinct politically organised states in some form of union to further common ends without losing either national identity or resigning individual sovereignty'. The internal mechanisms of the EU – which are seen as being largely under the control of state executive elites – are constituted, Chryssochoou suggests, so as to ensure that vital national interests are not 'mystically subsumed by the force of common interests in a neofunctionalist fashion' (ibid.: 55).

The view that EU membership does not of itself fundamentally undermine the sovereignty of member states is of course widely contested. Some of the contestants suggest that multi-level governance provides a more useful way of conceptualising and modelling the EU.

Multi-level governance

The conceptualisations considered so far are, broadly speaking, located within a comparative perspective. Their concern is whether and to what extent the EU 'matches' established models of governance. However, those who are firmly of the view that the EU is very much *sui generis* – or, as it is sometimes put, $n = 1$ – naturally wish to develop new conceptual ideas and models.

In this context, some EU scholars have drawn on the developing political science interest in what is commonly referred to as 'the new governance' and given it a particular emphasis and spin. At the general political science level, viewpoints included in the new governance approach are that government now involves a wide variety of actors and processes beyond the state, the relationships between state and non-state actors have become less hierarchical and more interactive, and the essential 'business' of government has become the regulation of public activities rather than the redistribution of resources. As applied to the EU, the new governance perspective 'is that the EU is transforming politics and government at the European and national levels into a system of multi-level, non-hierarchical, deliberative and apolitical governance, via a complex web of public/private networks and quasi-autonomous executive agencies, which is primarily concerned with the deregulation and reregulation of the market' (Hix, 1998: 54).

Taking just one of these strands of the new governance, much has been heard since the early 1990s of the merits of conceptualising the EU as a system of multi-level governance. Advocates of this conceptualisation usually specifically set themselves against the state-centric model, suggesting that the latter is too simple in its emphasis on the pre-eminence of state executives as actors and decision-makers. The great importance of national governments is not denied, but the claim that they dominate and control decision-making processes most certainly is.

Following the scheme advanced by Marks, Hooghe and Black (1996), three main characteristics can be seen as lying at the heart of the multi-level governance model of the EU:

- Decision-making competences are deemed to lie with, and to be exercised by, not only national governments but also institutions and actors at other levels. The most important of these levels is the EU level, where supranational actors – of which the most important are the Commission, the EP, and the ECJ – are identified as exercising an *independent* influence on policy processes and policy outcomes. In many member states subnational levels are also seen as important, with regional and local authorities able to engage in policy activities that are not (wholly) controllable by national governments.
- Collective decision-making by states at the EU level is regarded as involving a significant loss of national sovereignty, and therefore a significant loss of control by national governments. The intergovernmental view that states retain the ultimate decision-making power is rejected, largely on the grounds that '(l)owest common denominator

outcomes are available only on a subset of EU decisions, mainly those concerning the scope of integration' (Marks *et al.*, 1996: 346).

- Political arenas are viewed as interconnected rather than nested. So, rather than national political activity being confined to the national arena and national inputs into EU decision-making being channelled via state-level actors, a variety of channels and interconnections between different levels of government – supranational, national, and sub-national – are seen as both existing and being important. 'The separation between domestic and international politics, which lies at the heart of the state-centric model, is rejected by the multi-level governance model. States are an integral and powerful part of the EU, but they no longer provide the sole interface between supranational and subnational arenas, and they share, rather than monopolize, control over many activities that take place in their respective territories' (ibid.: 347).

Multi-level governance thus conceives of the EU as a polity, or at least as a polity in the making, in which power and influence are exercised at multiple levels of government. National state executives are seen as extremely important actors in the EU arena, but the almost semi-monopolistic position that is ascribed to them by many state-centrists is firmly rejected.

Critics of the multi-level governance conceptualisation naturally focus particularly on whether the supranational and subnational levels really do have the power and influence they are claimed to have. Supranational levels are seen by state-centric observers as being largely subject to state-level controls (mainly through the various organs of the Council), while subnational levels are considered to have little room or potential to make a significant impact on policy outcomes. Is it not the case, multi-level governance critics argue, that in some member states there is no robust subnational level of government, and is it not also the case that there is little evidence of subnational actors exercising much of a policy role beyond the sphere of cohesion policy from which the advocates of multi-level governance draw most of their empirical evidence?

Three Key Concepts: Sovereignty, Intergovernmentalism and Supranationalism

As indicated in earlier parts of this book and throughout this chapter, much of the debate amongst practitioners and observers about the nature of the EU has centred on the related concepts of sovereignty, intergovernmentalism and supranationalism. These concepts therefore merit special attention.

Defining the terms

Sovereignty is an emotive word, associated as it is with notions of power, authority, independence, and the exercise of will. Because of its emotiveness and its associations, it is a word to which several meanings are attached. The most common meaning, and the one which will be employed here, refers to the legal capacity of national decision-makers to take decisions without being subject to external restraints. This is usually called national, or sometimes state, sovereignty.

Intergovernmentalism refers to arrangements whereby nation states, in situations and conditions they can control, cooperate with one another on matters of common interest. The existence of control, which allows all participating states to decide the extent and nature of this cooperation, means that national sovereignty is not directly undermined.

Supranationalism involves states working with one another in a manner that does not allow them to retain complete control over developments. That is, states may be obliged to do things against their preferences and their will because they do not have the power to stop decisions. Supranationalism thus takes inter-state relations beyond cooperation into integration, and involves some loss of national sovereignty.

The intergovernmental/supranational balance in the EU

In the 1960s the governments of five of the Community's then six member states were willing to permit, even to encourage, some movement towards supranationalism. President de Gaulle, however, who wished to preserve 'the indivisible sovereignty of the nation state', was not. In order to emphasise this point, and more particularly to prevent certain supranational developments that were due to be introduced, he withdrew France in 1965 from most of the Community's key decision-making forums. The outcome of the crisis that this occasioned was the 1966 Luxembourg Compromise (see Chapter 10) which, though it had no legal force, had as its effect the general imposition of intergovernmentalism on Community decision-making processes: the powers of the Commission and the EP were contained, and decisions in the Council came customarily to be made – even where the treaties allowed for majority voting – by unanimous agreement.

The first enlargement of the Community in 1973 reinforced intergovernmentalism, bringing in as it did two countries – Denmark and the UK – where there was strong domestic opposition to membership and where supranationalism was viewed with suspicion. International economic uncertainties and recession also encouraged intergovernmentalism, since they forced states to look rather more critically at the distributive consequences of Community policies, produced a temptation to look for national solutions to pressing problems, and resulted in greater caution about the transfer of powers to Community institutions.

However, intergovernmental attachments and pressures were never able, and never have been able, completely to stop the development of supranationalism. The treaties, increasing interdependence, and the logic of the EU itself, have all ensured that national sovereignties have been progressively undermined. Indeed, not only has supranationalism become more embedded, but since the mid-1980s it has been given a considerable boost as the states have adopted a much more positive attitude towards its development. They have done so partly because the effects of the delays and the inaction that intergovernmentalism spawns have become more obvious and more damaging, and partly because it has been recognised that as the number of EU member states has grown, over-rigid inter-governmentalism is a greater recipe than ever for stagnation and sclerosis.

The EU thus displays both intergovernmental and supranational characteristics. The principal intergovernmental characteristics are as follows.

- In most of the major areas of public policy – including foreign affairs, defence, fiscal policy, social welfare, education, health, and justice and home affairs – decisions are still mainly taken at the national level. Each state consults and coordinates with its EU partners on aspects of these policies, and is increasingly subject to constraints as a result of EU membership, but ultimately a state can usually decide for itself what is to be done.
- Virtually all major decisions on the general direction and policy priorities of the EU are taken in the European Council: that is, in the forum containing the most senior national representatives. Only rarely does the European Council take decisions by majority vote. As for EU legislation, all important decisions need the approval of ministers in the Council of Ministers, with some key Council decisions, including those of a constitutional or fiscal nature, requiring unanimous approval. Where qualified majority voting is permissible, attempts are always made to reach a consensus if a state declares it has important national interests at stake.
- The Commission and the EP, the two most obvious 'supranational political rivals' to the European Council and the Council of Ministers in that their responsibility is to look to the EU as a whole rather than to specific national interests, are restricted in their decision-making powers and cannot impose policies that the representatives of the member states do not want.

Of the supranational characteristics of the EU, the following are particularly important.

- The Commission does much to frame the EU policy agenda. Moreover, though it may have to defer to the European Council and the Council of Ministers where major decisions are involved, it is an extremely important decision-maker in its own right when it comes to secondary and regulatory decision-making. Indeed, in quantitative terms most EU legislation is issued in the name of the Commission.
- In the Council of Ministers, qualified majority voting is now common. This is partly a result of changing norms and expectations, and partly a result of the treaty reforms that have brought about extensions of the policy spheres in which QMV is permissible.
- The influence of the EP on EU decision-making is considerable. This influence has been greatly enhanced over the years by treaty reforms, especially by the creation of the co-decision procedure by the Maastricht Treaty and its extension by the Amsterdam and Nice Treaties.
- The force and status of decision-making outcomes is crucial to EU supranationalism, for clearly the EU could hardly be described as supranational if its decisions had no binding force. Indeed, some do not and are merely advisory and exhortive. But many do, and these constitute EU law. It is a law that constitutes an increasingly prominent part of the legal systems of all member states, that takes precedence over national law should the two conflict, and that, in the event of a dispute, finds its final authority not in national courts but in the interpretations of the EU's own courts.

Both intergovernmentalism and supranationalism are thus important features of the functioning and nature of the EU. This is no more clearly demonstrated than in the influence exercised by the Commission: on the one hand it is an important motor in the European integration process, but on the other it is constrained by the preferences of the governments of the member states. As Mark Pollack has put it in analysing the role of the Commission in terms of principal–agent relationships, 'Supranational autonomy and influence ... is not a simple binary matter of obedient servants or runaway Eurocracies, but rather varies along a continuum between the two points' (Pollack, 1998: 218).

A pooling and sharing of sovereignty?

The EU is quite unique in the extent to which it involves states engaging in *joint* action to formulate *common* policies and make *binding* decisions. As the words 'joint', 'common' and 'binding' imply, the process of working together is resulting in the EU states becoming ever more intermeshed and interdependent. This is no more clearly seen than in the 'tying' effect of many aspects of their relationships and shared activities: tying in the sense that it would not be possible for them to be reversed without creating major constitutional, legal, political and economic difficulties at both the EU and the national level.

Clearly a central aspect of the intermeshing and the interdependence, and one of the principal distinguishing characteristics of the EU, is the way in which the member states have voluntarily surrendered some of their national sovereignty and independence to collective institutions. However, viewed from a broader perspective, the EU is not only the cause of a decline in national powers but is also a response to decline. This is because much of the rationale of the EU lies in the attempt – an attempt for which there is no international parallel – on the part of the member states to increase their control of, and their strength and influence in, a rapidly changing world. Although all of the states have reservations about, and some have fundamental criticisms of, certain aspects of the EU, each has judged that membership enhances its ability to achieve certain objectives. The precise nature of these objectives varies from state to state, but in virtually all cases the main priorities are the promotion of economic growth and prosperity, the control of economic and financial forces that are not confined to national boundaries, and the strengthening of political influence. Insofar as these objectives are being attained, it can be argued that the diminution in the role of the state and the loss of sovereignty that arises from supranationalism is counterbalanced by the collective strength of the EU as a whole.

Indeed, since international change and developing interdependence have resulted in all of the member states experiencing a considerable *de facto,* if not *de jure,* loss of national sovereignty quite irrespective of the loss that is attributable to EU membership, it can be argued that the discussion about national sovereignty, in the classical sense of the term at least, is no longer very meaningful. Rather it should be recognised that the only way in which EU states can retain control of their operating environments is by pooling and sharing their power and their sovereignty.

Theorising European Integration: Grand Theory

Many scholars of European integration have explored ways in which the overall nature of the integration process might be theorised. The purpose of such exploration has been to develop a broad understanding of the factors underlying European integration and in so doing to facilitate predictions of how integration is likely to proceed.

This search for what is commonly referred to as 'grand' theory – that is, theory which explains the main features of the integration process as a whole – began soon after the European Community was established in the

1950s, with US scholars leading the way. However, after about fifteen years of considerable activity and published output, interest in grand integration theory declined from the mid-1970s as disillusionment set in with what had been and could be achieved by such theory. Furthermore, the EC itself became less interesting, with its seeming retreat into retrenchment and even sclerosis. There followed a lull of ten years or so in which little was published in the sphere of grand integration theory. This lull ended in the mid- to late 1980s, when interest was re-stimulated by the 're-launch' of the integration process through the SEM and SEA in 1985–6, and with the appearance on the academic scene of new scholars who believed that, though early grand theory may have had its limitations, the *raison d'être* of grand theory – to further understanding of the general character of European integration – was as valid as ever.

A notable feature of the re-awakened interest in grand theory in recent years has been that much of it has centred on debating the respective merits of, and developing more sophisticated versions of, the two theories – the foundational theories one may call them – that dominated the early years of European integration theory: neofunctionalism and intergovernmental-ism. Another prominent feature has been the extensive use that has been made of interdependency theory, which is not especially focused on European integration but is widely seen as being of much use in helping to explain the reasons for, and the course of, the European integration process.

This section of the chapter is thus primarily concerned with neofunc-tionalism, intergovernmentalism, and interdependency.

Neofunctionalism

The foundations of neofunctionalism were laid in the late 1950s and during the 1960s by a number of US academics, of whom the most prominent were Ernst Haas (1958) and Leon Lindberg (1963).

In its classic formulation, neofunctionalism revolves largely around the concept of spillover, which takes two main forms. The first form – functional spillover – arises from the interconnected nature of modern economies, which makes it difficult to confine integration to particular economic sectors. Rather, integration in one sector produces pressures for integration in adjoining and related sectors. The second form – political spillover – largely follows on from economic integration and has a number of dimensions: national elites increasingly turn their attention to suprana-tional levels of activity and decision-making; these elites become favour-ably disposed towards the integration process and the upgrading of common interests; supranational institutions and non-governmental actors become more influential in the integration process, while nation states and governmental actors become less influential; and the increasing importance of integration generates pressures and demands for political control and accountability at the supranational level.

Early neofunctionalism thus suggested, though it certainly did not regard as inevitable, the progressive development of European integration. Drawing heavily on the experience of the ECSC, which had played such an important part in paving the way for the EEC, integration was seen as promoting further integration. The slowing down of the integration process following the 1965–6 crisis in the EC and the world economic recession of the early 1970s was thus something of a jolt for advocates of neofunctionalism. For far from policy integration proceeding apace and political behaviour and decision-making becoming increasingly supranational in character, policy integration did not develop in the manner that had been anticipated whilst political behaviour and decision-making remained essentially nationally-based and conditioned. As a result, neofunctionalism lost much of its gloss and appeal, not least when its foremost figures – Haas and Lindberg – retreated from it and suggested that future integration theory would need to give greater recognition to, among other things, nationalism and the role of political leadership.

Since the late 1980s, however, as the pace of integration has again picked up, there has been a re-assessment and a partial comeback of neofunctionalism, albeit often in a 'disguised' form. As Phillippe Schmitter (2004: 45) has observed 'Real live neofunctionists may be an endangered species, but neofunctionist thinking [is] very much alive, even if it [is] usually ... re-branded as a different animal'.

Jeppe Tranholm-Mikkelsen (1991) has argued that much of the 'new dynamism' in Western Europe from the mid-1980s can be explained in neofunctionalist terms, though he also emphasises the importance of factors that were not part of the original neofunctionalist position – such as forceful political actors and changes in the external security environment. His main conclusion is that although neofunctionalism may be dealing only with 'some parts of the elephant ... it appears that those parts are amongst the ones that make the animal move' (ibid.: 319). Tranholm-Mikkelsen exemplifies those who argue that although original neofunctionalism may have had its limitations and faults – most notably by being overdeterministic and not giving due allowance to the continuing importance in the European integration process of the (often distinctive) interests of member states and their representatives – it still has, especially when updated and modified, considerable theoretical value. Evidence cited to support neofunctionalism's case relates both to functional and to political spillover. In respect of functional spillover, reference is most commonly made to the SEM, where the original 'requirements' for the completion of the internal market have steadily been expanded to include, amongst other things, the social dimension, the single currency, and a measure of fiscal harmonisation. In respect of political spillover, the great advances in supranational decision-making since the mid-1980s are commonly cited, with 'the motor role' of the Commission, the common use of QMV in the Council, and the Court's support for much integrationist activity all seen as falling within the neofunctionalist framework. Indeed, with regard to the role of the Court, Burley and Mattli (1993: 43) have explicitly argued that 'the legal integration of the Community corresponds remarkably closely to the original neofunctionalist model', and that the ECJ has not only had considerable scope to pursue its own agenda but has frequently done so in a manner that favours integration.

Much of the work of Wayne Sandholtz and Alec Stone Sweet (Sandholtz and Stone Sweet, 1998; Stone Sweet and Sandholtz, 1997) is informed by neofunctionalism, though like Tranholm-Mikkelsen and others they too look on original neofunctionalism as wanting – not least, in their view, in an inability to explain why integration should advance via spillover in some policy sectors and not in others. Building from a broadly neofunctionalist base, Sandholtz and Stone Sweet draw on other approaches and perspectives – notably globalisation and transactionalism – to advance a theory to explain the development of supranational governance in the EU and why the extent of the development varies so much between policy sectors that, they suggest, the EU is best regarded not as a single regime but as a series of different regimes. The starting point of their explanation is that globalisation has led to a growth in cross-border economic transactions (trade, investment, production, distribution) and communications which have produced pressures both for the removal of cross-border barriers and for the creation of EU-wide rules and regulations. These pressures lead to EU policies and policy arenas in which supranational institutions have key policy management and policy promotion roles. Integration is then sustained in a number of ways, including by a continued expansion of transnational exchanges and by the supranational institutions seeking to widen and strengthen the frameworks with a view to further controlling the transnational exchanges. As they make clear, the key constituent elements of their theory are thus 'prefigured in neofunctionalism: the development of transnational society, the role of supranational organizations with meaningful autonomous capacity to pursue integrative agendas, and the focus on European rule-making to resolve international policy externalities' (Sandholtz and Stone Sweet, 1998: 6). They build on these elements to develop a theory in which '[t]ransnational exchange provokes supranational organizations to make rules designed to facilitate and to regulate the development of transnational society' (ibid.: 25). In seeking to answer the question why integration proceeds faster and further in some policy areas than in others they 'look to variation in the levels of cross-border interactions and in the consequent need for supranational coordination and rules' (ibid.: 14).

Intergovernmentalism

Intergovernmentalism has its origins in international relations theory, and more particularly the realist tradition within that theory. Put simply, realism is centred on the view that nation states are the key actors in international affairs and the key political relations between states are channelled primarily via national governments. Unlike neofunctionalism, realism does not accord much importance to the influence of supranational or transnational actors and only limited importance to non-governmental actors within states.

As applied to European integration, intergovernmentalism thus explains the direction and pace of the integration process mainly by reference to decisions and actions taken by the governments of European states. There is a recognition that other actors, both within and beyond states, can exercise some influence on developments, but not a crucial, and certainly not a controlling, influence. This focus on states – and the associated perception of states having their own distinctive national interests which they vigorously defend, especially in the spheres of high politics (foreign policy, security and defence) – has resulted in intergovernmentalists tending to emphasise, as Stanley Hoffmann (1966) put it, 'the logic of diversity' rather than 'the logic of integration'.

For many years Hoffmann was the foremost proponent of this interpretation of European integration, but in recent years Andrew Moravcsik (1991, 1993, 1995, 1998) has established himself as its leading exponent. (Other exponents of forms of intergovernmentalism include Garrett, 1992, 1993, and Grieco, 1995.) Just as Tranholm-Mikkelsen and others have built on early neofunctionalism to develop a more sophisticated theoretical framework, so has Moravcsik performed a similar service for intergovernmentalism. He calls his framework liberal intergovernmentalism.

There are three main components of liberal intergovernmentalism. First, there is an assumption of rational state behaviour, which means that the actions of states are assumed to be based on utilising what are judged to be the most appropriate means of achieving their goals. Second, there is a liberal theory of national preference formation. This draws on a domestic politics approach to explain how state goals can be shaped by domestic pressures and interactions, which in turn are often conditioned by the constraints and opportunities that derive from economic interdependence. Third, there is an intergovernmentalist interpretation of inter-state relations, which emphasises the key role of governments in determining the relations between states and sees the outcome of negotiations between governments as essentially being determined by their relative bargaining powers and the advantages that accrue to them by striking agreements.

Because liberal intergovernmentalism advances such a clear and, in important respects, almost uncompromising framework, and because it is seen by many as just not fitting the facts in an era of multiple international actors and complex interdependence between states, it has inevitably attracted criticism. Four criticisms are particularly worth noting.

First, it is suggested that Moravcsik is too selective with his empirical references when seeking to demonstrate the validity of his framework in the EU context. More particularly, he is considered to focus too much on 'historic' decisions and not enough on more commonplace and routine decisions. To over-focus on historic decisions is seen as distortional, since not only are such decisions untypical by their very nature, they also necessarily emphasise the role of national governments since they are channelled via the European Council.

Second, it is argued that liberal intergovernmentalism concentrates too much on the formal and final stages of decision-making and pays too little attention to informal integration and the constraints that such integration imposes on the formal decision-makers. For example, Wincott (1995) argues that the SEM programme and the SEA, which Moravcsik suggests were the outcome of negotiations between national actors, are in important respects better viewed as the formalisation by national governments of what had been happening in practice for some time.

Third, critics argue that insufficient attention is paid to the 'black box' of the state, and more especially to disaggregating the different parts of government. According to Forster (1998: 364), this means that liberal intergovernmentalism provides an inadequate account of how governments choose their policy options. 'The formation of objectives, the pursuit of strategies and the final positions adopted are every bit as disorderly and unpredictable as domestic policy-making. Politics is not always a rational process: ideology, belief and symbolism can play as important a role as substance' (ibid.: 364).

Fourth – and this is probably the most commonly voiced criticism of liberal intergovernmentalism, and indeed of any form of intergovernmenalism – it is said that it grossly understates the influence exercised in the European integration process by supranational actors such as the Commission and the ECJ, and transnational actors such as European firms and interest groups. For example, in a collection of essays edited by Sandholtz and Stone Sweet (1998), several academic commentators provide evidence of EU supranational bodies seeking to enhance their autonomy and influence and having considerable success in so doing. Moravcsik's portrayal of the Commission as exercising the role of little more than a facilitator in respect of significant decision-making has attracted particular criticism, with numerous empirically-based studies claiming to show that the Commission does exercise an independent and influential decision-making role, be it as – the metaphors abound – an *animateur,* a policy entrepreneur, or a motor force. Such studies do not, it has to be said, convince Moravcsik that the Commission and other supranational actors are doing much more than responding to an agenda set by the governments of the member states. As he puts it '*intergovernmental demand* for policy ideas, not the *supranational supply* of these ideas, is the fundamental exogenous factor driving integration. To a very large extent, the demand for co-operative policies creates its own supply' (Moravcsik, 1995: 618, emphasis in original).

Forster (1998: 365) has suggested that liberal intergovernmentalism's weaknesses mean that it is 'perhaps best regarded less as a theory of intergovernmental bargaining, than as a pre-theory or analytical framework'. This may be so, but it should not be forgotten that although weaknesses in liberal intergovernmentalism can readily be identified, the approach has considerable strengths. In particular, it provides a reminder of the role of states and governments in the EU and it does so in a much more nuanced and sophisticated manner than did early intergovernmentalism.

Interdependency

Whilst both neofunctionalism and intergovernmentalism recognise that external factors have at times triggered the pace and nature of European integration, both theories are concerned primarily with the internal dynamics of integration. Interdependency, in contrast, has been used by scholars of European integration to place integration in the wider context of growing international interdependence.

Interdependency theory was initially developed in the 1970s, most famously by Robert Keohane and Joseph Nye (1977). Its central thrust when applied to European integration is that the integration process should not be viewed in too narrow a context. Many of the factors that have influenced its development have applied to it alone, but many have not. This is seen most obviously in the ways in which post-Second World War international modernisation in its various forms – including increased levels of wealth, vast increases in world trade, the technological revolution, and the transformation of communications – has promoted many different forms of political and economic interdependency. These in turn have produced a transformation in the ways in which different parts of the world relate to and come into contact with one another. For example, there has been a steady increase in the number and variety of international actors – both above and below the level of the nation state – and a corresponding weakening of the dominance of states. An increasing range of methods and channels are used by international actors to pursue their goals, with relationships between governments, for instance, no longer being so controlled by Foreign Offices and Ministries of External Affairs. The range of issues on international agendas has grown with, in particular, traditional 'high' policy issues (those concerned with security and the defence of the state) being joined by an array of 'low' policy issues (those concerned with the wealth and welfare of citizens). And paralleling the change in the policy content of international agendas there has been a decline, in the Western industrialised world at least, in the use of physical force as a policy instrument, with conflicts over the likes of trade imbalances and currency exchange rates not resolved by armed conflict but by bargaining, adjusting and compromising.

Interdependence theory is thus useful in helping to set European integration within the context of the rapid changes that are occurring throughout the international system. This system is becoming, like the EU system itself, increasingly multi-layered and interconnected. Whether the purpose is to regulate international trade, promote the efficient functioning of the international monetary system, set international standards on packaging for the transportation of hazardous material, or control the hunting and killing of whales, states now come together in many different ways, in many different combinations and for many different purposes.

Interdependency theory is distinctive from neofunctionalism and inter-governmentalism in that it emphasises that much of the European integration process is explained by factors that are global in nature, and it emphasises too that many of the systemic features of the EU are found elsewhere in the international system, albeit less intensively. Interdependency is also different from neofunctionalism and intergovernmentalism in that it has been less intensively applied to European integration and partly in consequence is less rigorous and systematic in the explanation it offers. Whilst most of those who have engaged in the theoretical debate on the nature of the integration process have recognised the importance of interdependency, they have tended to do so as part of the framing background rather than as central causation. It is not possible to point to any major scholar who has advanced interdependency as *the sole cause* of the European integration process. As Carole Webb wrote in the early 1980s, 'For most students the concept of interdependence has been used to explain the conditions under which governments and other economic actors have to contemplate some form of collaboration; but unlike the approach of integration theory, it does not necessarily help to define the outcome very precisely' (Webb, 1983: 33). This lack of precision in interdependency theory is most obviously seen in the fact that, as O'Neill

(2000: 131) puts it, its 'narrative apparently confirms neither an inter-governmental, confederal nor a supra-national prognosis ... Governance per se is not the central issue.' Rather, the central issue for interdependency theory is the role of inexorable transnational forces buffeting nation states. As such, interdependency in the European integration context is perhaps best thought of as an approach and/or a perspective rather than as a theory.

The future of grand theory

Social science theories rarely satisfy everyone. Whatever phenomena they are seeking to explain and whatever forms they take, they almost invariably attract criticism for being deficient in important respects. Commonly identified deficiencies include focusing on only part of the phenomena under examination, being too general in scope and/or formulation, being excessively time-bound, and being insufficiently empirically grounded.

European integration grand theory has not been exempt from such criticisms. Indeed, it has been especially prone to them given that the European integration process is so complex, so constantly changing, and so capable of being viewed from different angles. But, as with other social science theories, European integration theories do not lose all value because critics can show them to be less than complete and final in the explanations they offer. Rather, grand theories can be of considerable value in furthering understanding of the integration process by offering particular insights into it, by providing partial explanations of it, and by promoting further work and thought on it.

Of course, as long as existing theory is seen to be deficient in certain respects there will be attempts to improve upon it. In this context an increasingly important feature of the theoretical debate on European integration is the attempt by many theorists to move beyond what is now widely viewed as the over-narrow and restrictive nature of the jousting between classical intergovernmentalism and classical neofunction-alism.

One aspect of this new theorising is the development of theoretical explanations that, although emerging from one or other of these two schools of thought, are much more complex, sophisticated and nuanced than the theories in their original formulations. Moravcsik and Sandholtz and Stone Sweet are the best known of those who are theorising in this way, but there are many others. Another aspect of the new theorising is the attempt to bring together key features of the traditional theories and link them, as appropriate, to relevant parts of other theories. Robert Keohane and Stanley Hoffmann (1991) adopt such an eclectic and synthesising approach in their analysis of the quickened pace of integration, particularly institutional integration, in the mid-1980s. Essentially they argue that neofunctionalism, interdependency, and intergovernmentalism all have something to contribute to the explanation of why the Community was 'relaunched'. Regarding neofunctionalism, '[s]pillover took place not as a functional expansion of tasks but rather in the form of the creation, as a result of enlargement, of incentives for institutional change' (ibid.: 22). Regarding interdependence, '[t]he 1992 program was ... strongly affected by events in the world economy outside of Europe – especially by concern about international competitiveness' (ibid.: 19). Regarding intergovernmentalism, they consider that the precise timing of the burst of integration was due 'not only to incentives for the world political economy and spillover but also to intergovernmental bargains made possible by convergence of preferences of major European states' (ibid.: 25).

Janne Matlary (1993) is another who argues that the limitations of traditional models – especially, in her view, the limitations of intergovernmentalism, which she regards as failing to recognise the crucial interaction between EU institutions and member states and also between formal and informal integration processes – make a synthesising approach essential. There seems, she says, to be 'an emerging view that a comprehensive theory of integration must include not only realist assumptions of state behaviour, but also analysis of domestic politics and the role of the different EC institutions' (ibid.: 376). Stephen George (1994) is less optimistic than Matlary that a comprehensive theory of integration can be developed, but he too is convinced of the need for a model that 'combines the insights' of the intergovernmentalist and neofunctionalist schools.

Searching for points of contact and overlap, perhaps even for a synthesis, between ever more sophisticated intergovernmentalist and neofunctionalist-inspired models is thus likely to be a feature of future integration theory. Whether, however, synthetic theory will ever be able to escape its basic problem, namely that attempts to develop it are almost inevitably drawn back into one of the dominant perspectives, must be doubted. For as Alexander Warleigh (1998: 9) has observed, 'rapprochement of neo-functionalism and neo-realism would effectively deprive both theories of their respective *raison d'être* and guiding principles, a step which neither set of scholars [advocating the theories] can take without emasculating their theory'.

Another likely feature of the future course of integration theory is its placement within the context of wider globalisation theory. As Ben Rosamond (1995) has pointed out, globalisation theory should help to establish how integration is occurring in so many different ways in so many parts of the world: at the 'official' level between international, supranational, national, regional and even local institutions of government, but at the 'unofficial' level too as a result of changes in technology, communications, travel patterns and culture.

Michael O'Neill (1996: 81) has observed that European integration theory 'has been a constantly shifting dialectic between events as they have unfolded on the ground, and the efforts of scholars to track and accurately explain them ... the paradigms and the intellectual tension generated by [the theoretical discourse on integration] have helped to map more accurately the actual developments in European integration, and to clarify our understanding of what the process means'. These observations will doubtless also apply to future theory. Theorising will become more sophisticated and nuanced as new theory builds on previous theory and as the integration process itself continues to unfold. But the essential purpose of grand theory will remain unchanged: to assist understanding and explanation of the integration process.

Theorising the Functioning of the EU: Middle-Range Theory

Whereas grand theory looks at the nature of the integration process as a whole, middle-range theory looks at particular aspects of the process. More especially, it normally focuses on aspects of how the EU functions.

In recent years, much scholarly attention has shifted in the direction of this less embracing theoretical endeavour. There are two main reasons for this. First, there has been an increasing feeling that grand theory is inherently limited in what it can achieve. It is prone, critics argue, to falling between two stools. On the one hand, if it restricts itself to identifying only major causational factors it inevitably misses, or at least does not adequately recognise, the many different dimensions of the integration process. On the other hand, if it attempts to encompass all the dimensions of integration it becomes too complicated and difficult to operationalise. Better, the argument runs, to be less ambitious and to focus only on parts of the integration process and the EU, especially the more important parts. Second, as the European integration process has intensified, so has the EU attracted the attention of an increasing number and range of scholars. It used to be the case that most of the European integration scholars who were interested in theorising and conceptualising were steeped in and made extensive use of international relations theory. This has become much less so in recent years with many scholars today taking the view that European integration should be studied not just through a traditional international relations approach but also, and arguably more so, through other subdisciplines of political science. If it is the case, as many of these scholars suggest, that the EU is a polity, albeit one without the usual lines of authority and control, then does it not follow that approaches that are deemed to be suitable for the study of conventional polities – most notably states – might also be suitable for the study of the EU? Those who answer this question in the affirmative have particularly advocated the merits of using comparative politics and public policy studies approaches. As Hix (1994) states, they have used these approaches not to follow the international relations route and examine European integration, but rather to examine EU *politics*.

Of course, EU politics are complex, so unsurprisingly a large number and variety of middle-range theoretical approaches have been used to assist explanation of them. This is intellectually healthy for furthering understanding of the nature of the EU since no one approach is likely to be capable of capturing the essential nature of the many different facets of EU politics. To take, for example, the area of activity that has been the main focus for middle-range theorising, policy processes, there is no reason to expect any one theoretical approach to be wholly satisfactory. After all, there are many different types of EU policy process with some, for instance, being essentially intergovernmental in character and others being more supranational. Within each policy process there are several stages – from the initial stages of problem identification and then policy initiation through to the final stage of policy evaluation. And each policy area has its own troupe of policy actors.

To illustrate middle-range theoretical approaches to the study of EU politics, and more especially EU policy processes, two of the more important will now be considered: new institutionalism and policy networks. They are both best thought of as being *theoretical approaches* rather than full-blown theories because they are still very much in development, arguably have greater descriptive than explanatory uses and powers, and have only a very limited predictive capability.

New institutionalism

Much has been heard since the late 1980s about the merits of new institutionalism. In essence, new institutionalism has at its core the assertion that institutions matter in determining decisional outcomes. As such, new institutionalism is partly a reaction against behaviouralism, which was so influential in social and political science circles in the 1970s and 1980s, especially in the United States.

In what ways is 'new' institutionalism different from 'old' institutionalism? In general terms the main difference is that whereas old or traditional institutionalism did not go much beyond analysing the formal powers and structures of decision-making institutions, new institutionalism defines institutions in a very broad sense to incorporate a wide range of formal and informal procedures, practices, relationships, customs, and norms. As such, new institutionalism is much more all-embracing and expansive in its concerns and interests.

Beyond a core shared interest in institutions broadly defined, new institutionalism spreads out in different directions. As Hall and Taylor (1996) have noted, there are at least three analytical approaches within new institutionalism: historical institutionalism, rational choice institutionalism, and sociological institutionalism. Among the main concerns of historical institutionalism are the distributions of power that are produced by institutional arrangements, the ways in which these arrangements result in path dependence and unintended consequences, and the relationships between institutions and other factors that shape political activities and outcomes such as economic developments and ideological beliefs. Rational choice institutionalism is especially interested in the extent to which and the ways in which institutions shape, channel, and constrain the rational actions of political actors. And sociological institutionalism focuses particularly on how institutional forms and practices can often be culturally explained.

All three variants of new institutionalism have been employed in respect of European integration and the functioning of the EU. Brief summaries of these employments now follow (for fuller overviews see Dowding, 2000; Pollack, 2003 and 2004; and Schneider and Aspinwall, 2001).

Historical institutionalism has been used most particularly to show how decisions of member state governments have constrained their future behaviour and have increased the independence and positions of supranational institutions. Prominent users and developers of historical institutionalism have included Simon Bulmer (1994, 1998) and Paul Pierson (1996) who have both advanced the merits of the approach for analysing and, as Bulmer puts it, 'capturing', political and policy activity in the increasingly multi-layered system. More specifically, Bulmer has advocated and employed the framework of a 'governance regime' for analysing the EU at the policy-specific or sub-system level.

Rational choice institutionalism has been employed primarily to throw light on the motivations of member state governments in the integration process and to demonstrate the consequences of different EU decisional rules for actors' behaviour and influence. In respect of governmental behaviour, a common theme of rational choice analysis is that governments actively participate in the EU and cede powers to it because they derive a variety of benefits from so doing, prominent amongst which are reducing transaction costs through enhanced policy development, policy effectiveness, and policy compliance. In respect of the consequences of decisional rules, amongst the things rational choice analysts have shown are the different restrictions placed on policy actors under different decision-making procedures and the varying inter-actor relations and policy impacts that are thereby created (the work of Garrett and Tsebilis is especially notable in this context – see, for example, Garrett and Tsebilis, 1996 and Tsebilis and Garrett, 1997 and 2001). For instance, QMV in the Council has been shown not only to produce the expected increased efficiency in Council decision-making but also to have beneficial effects for the Commission and EP, with policy outcomes being closer to their preferences as a result of dissenting national government positions being more easily by-passed.

As applied to the EU, sociological institutionalism is the most under-used of the three branches of new institutionalism. Insofar as it has been used, much of it has been for the purpose of examining the attitudes, motivations and behaviour of people working for and in the EU institutions. There is, for example, now a body of literature on Commission officials, showing amongst other things how they identify much more than do ordinary citizens with Europe and with a supranational perspective of how the EU should function (see especially Hooghe, 2001). Staying with the Commission, authors such as Bellier (1997) and Cini (2000) have highlighted clashes in the administrative culture of the Commission with, for example, officials in DG Competition displaying a stronger attachment to liberal market principles than officials in DG Regional Policy and DG Environment who display more sympathy for selected public intervention in the pursuit of non-market goals. More broadly, sociological institutionalism has blended with constructivist approaches to the study of European integration and the EU, where attention is directed to examining and establishing how the likes of political space and institutional and individual identities, roles and values are socially constructed. (On social constructivism and European integration, see the special edition of *Journal of European Public Policy*: 6(4), 1999. Schimmelfennig 2001 and 2002 provides interesting applications of social constructivism to EU enlargement policy.)

Policy networks

The policy networks approach can be thought of as an application of new institutionalism in its broadest sense. The approach is used to describe and analyse policy processes and policy outcomes.

Simply put, policy networks are arenas in which decision-makers and interests come together to mediate differences and search for solutions. Policy networks vary in character according to three key variables: the relative stability (or instability) of network memberships; the relative insularity (or permeability) of networks; and the relative strength (or weakness) of resource dependencies (Peterson, 1995: 77). From these variables a continuum emerges, 'At one end are tightly integrated policy *communities* in which membership is constant and often hierarchical, external pressures have minimal impact, and actors are highly dependent on each other for resources. At the other are loosely integrated issue *networks,* in which membership is fluid and non hierarchical, the network is easily permeated by external influences, and actors are highly self-reliant' (ibid.: 77).

The EU is seen by those who champion the policy network approach as particularly lending itself to the emergence of such networks (see, for example, the volume by Kohler-Koch and Eising (1999) which views EU policy processes as being essentially based on a system of network governance). Amongst factors identified as being conducive to policy networks are: the informal nature of much EU policy-making; the multiplicity of interests at EU level that are anxious to have access to policy makers; the highly technical – almost non-political – nature of much EU policy content; the powerful policy positions held by senior officials, especially in the Commission and especially in the early stages of policy-making; and the heavy reliance of officials on outside interests for information and advice about policy content and policy implementation. As Schneider *et al.* (1994: 480) state on this last point, 'The highly pluralist pattern exhibited by the EC policy networks is a consequence not only of numerous actors' efforts to influence the European policy process in an early stage of formulation, but also of a deliberate networking strategy employed by the European institutions, especially the Commission'.

The existence, the types, and the influence of networks vary considerably across the policy spectrum. Networks of a policy community type are often found in areas where EU policy is well-established, where an organised 'clientele' exists, and where decision-makers benefit from the cooperation of interests. Examples of such policy areas include agriculture and research and development. In contrast, issue networks are more common where EU policy is not well-developed, where the policy debate is fluid and shifting, and where such organised interests as do exist have few resources to 'exchange' with decision-makers. Consumer protection policy and much of environmental and social policy are examples of policy areas where issue networks are commonly found.

The usefulness of the policy networks approach is not, it should be said, accepted by all EU analysts. Amongst the reservations that have been expressed are that it cannot deal with the making of major directional decisions and it cannot capture the extreme fluidity and fragmented nature of EU policy processes (see Kassim, 1994, for a critique of the usefulness of policy networks in analysing EU policy processes). There is doubtless something in such criticisms, but they are arguably partly based on misplaced understandings of what advocates of the model claim on its behalf. As Rhodes *et al.* (1996: 381) suggest, when arguing that the-approach is helpful in the EU context, ' Policy networks is a useful tool for analysing the links between types of governmental units, between levels of government, and between governments and interest groups. It aids understanding of the policy process but it is only one variable in that process'.

Concluding Remarks

A wide variety of conceptually and theoretically informed approaches to the understanding and study of European integration and the EU have been explored in this chapter. All have been shown to be subject to criticism and to expressions of reservation about their usefulness. For example, of the three grand theories that were considered, amongst the central 'charges' laid against neofunctionalism and intergovernmentalism are that both press their side of the case too hard and both disappoint when applied empirically over time, whilst the central weakness of interdependence is seen to be its lack of a regional focus.

But concepts and theories, and the methodological approaches based on them, should be judged not only on their deficiencies but also on what they can contribute to knowledge. In this regard there is, as has been shown, extensive merit in much of the conceptual and theoretical work that has been undertaken on European integration and the EU. There may be no one body of work that has been able to capture and explain all aspects of European integration and the EU reality, but that is only to be expected. After all, as Hix (1998: 46) has observed, there is no general theory of American or German government, so why should there be one of the EU? Rather, we should recognise, as Sandholtz (1996: 426) puts it, 'that different kinds of theories are appropriate for different pieces of the EU puzzle'.

This notion that different kinds of theories should be used for different purposes – that different approaches should be seen as potentially complementary rather than competing tools of analysis – is now a working assumption of most EU analysts. It is seen indeed as being essential to ensure that no one type of theory is the victim of over-stretch and that no aspect of integration is analysed via inappropriate conceptual and theoretical tools. To guide thinking on what types of theories might be most useful in what circumstances, a few commentators have suggested frameworks for 'fitting' theories with circumstances. For example, Peterson (1995) and Peterson and Bomberg (1999) suggest a framework based on the level and type of EU decisions being made, with macro theories being most appropriate to analyse super-systemic, or history-making, decisions, new institutional approaches being best for systemic decisions (that is, decisions about policy content), and policy network approaches being best for sub-systemic decisions (that is, decisions about policy details). Alex Warleigh (2000) also provides a three-level framework, but in his case the focus is not just EU decisions but, more broadly, categories of EU activity: confederal theory is advocated to explain the creation and nature of the EU, multi-level governance theory to explain the functioning of the EU, and policy network and new institutional theory to explain EU policy-making and output.

A mixture of conceptual and theoretical tools must thus be utilised when analysing European integration and the EU. This chapter has examined the most frequently used of these tools. They have been shown to further understanding by drawing attention to, and highlighting, key features of processes, structures, contexts, and outcomes.

Chapter 22

Present Realities and Future Prospects

The European Union and the Changing Nature
of the International System
The Uniqueness of the European Union
The Future of the European Union

The European Union and the Changing Nature of the International System

The European Union should not be viewed in too narrow a context. Whilst many of the factors that have influenced its development apply to it alone, many do not. This is most clearly seen in the ways in which modernisation and interdependence, which have been crucial to the creation of many of the central features of the EU, have produced similar effects elsewhere in the international system – albeit usually to a more modest degree.

Of the many ways in which modernisation and interdependence have transformed the international system, one of the most important has been in the challenges it has posed to politicians to control events and forces. Of course, states have never been completely islands in the sense of being able wholly independent to take whatever decisions they liked concerning their political and economic preferences. In Europe this has been so especially for small states such as the Benelux states, but it has applied also to large states such as France and Germany in as much as many of their policies – most obviously their trade policies – have necessitated establishing relations and concluding agreements with other countries.

Since the Second World War, and more especially since the 1970s, international considerations have borne down more strongly than ever before on domestic decision-making in the developed world. This is seen most strikingly in respect of economic and monetary policies, where the increasing importance of non-state actors and of international financial mobility have resulted in the representatives of states having to be extremely watchful when taking what may appear to be purely domestic decisions. So, for example, a government wishing to increase corporate tax rates to help finance social welfare policies has the legal authority to act, but in practice it may well be prevented from doing so for fear that such a decision will result in nationally-based multinational corporations transferring investment to other countries that provide more favourable fiscal locations.

The international system has thus become more complex and interconnected. As it has done so, states have come to work much more closely with one another, both in terms of the issues they discuss and negotiate, the mechanisms through which they do business with one another, and the instruments they use to pursue policy goals. Regarding the issues, traditional foreign policy and security issues remain important, but so now are issue areas that used to barely feature on the international agenda, such as the environment and justice and home affairs. Regarding the mechanisms, whereas relations between governments used to be dominated and controlled by national leaders and diplomatic corps, now many branches and layers of government are involved in 'external relations' of some sort. And regarding the policy instruments, policy matters such as trade disputes, sluggish global economic growth, and protection of species cannot be tackled by that most traditional policy instrument of larger states, armed force, but rather must rely on international bargaining and compromising.

Another and very important way in which states have reacted to modernisation and interdependence has been via the creation of international organisations. Countless such organisations – each with different memberships, functions, powers, and structures – have been constituted since the Second World War. By way of illustration, the following are just a few of the more important international organisations that have been, and still are, used by European states: global organisations include the United Nations (UN), the International Monetary Fund (IMF), and the World Trade Organisation (WTO); Western-dominated organisations include the Organisation for Economic Cooperation and Development (OECD), the North Atlantic Treaty Organisation (NATO), and the Group of Eight (G8) (the last of these is not perhaps quite officially an organisation, but it is increasingly structured and increasingly meets not just at summit level but also at sub-summit levels); and European organisations include the Council of Europe and the Organisation for Security and Cooperation in Europe (OSCE).

Amongst this array of organisations with which European states have been and continue to be associated, the EU stands out as by far the most important. Within its framework, the transformations in the international system noted above – in issues, mechanisms and policy instruments – have all been developed to an intense degree. This development has made the EU unique amongst international organisations.

The Uniqueness of the European Union

The nature of the EU's uniqueness was explored at length in Chapter 21, but a few key points regarding its uniqueness as compared with other international organisations bear further emphasis and development here.

First, the EU is structurally highly complex, with many more institutions, decision-making arrangements and processes, and policy actors than are found in other international organisations. *Regarding the institutions*, there are five 'core' institutions – the Commission, the Council of Ministers, the European Council, the European Parliament, and the Court of Justice – and a battery of subsidiary institutions, including the European Economic and Social Committee, the Committee of the Regions, and the European Central Bank. The responsibilities and powers of these institutions varies considerably between policy areas, with there being few policy areas in which there is not a considerable interdependency between at least three of the core institutions. *Regarding the decision-making arrangements and processes*, there are nearly 30 distinctive procedures laid down in the treaties, many with their own internal variations. *Regarding the policy actors*, in addition to those associated with the EU's own institutions there are international actors of various sorts plus a host of actors associated with the member states, non-member states, and sectional and promotional interests.

Second, other international organisations do not have so broad a range of policy responsibilities as the EU. Whereas the EU is involved, to at least some degree, in just about every sphere of public policy, other international organisations tend either to have a very broad focus but with decision-making mechanisms that make it extremely difficult for the potential to be realised – such as the UN or the Council of Europe – or to have a restricted focus – such as the WTO, NATO, or the International Maritime Organisation.

Third, whereas other international organisations are essentially intergovernmental in character, the EU is in many important respects supranational. This supranationalism is seen most particularly in the frequent usage of QMV in the Council of Ministers, in the Commission's wide-ranging executive powers, in the EP's considerable legislative powers, and in the primacy of EU law.

These characteristics do not make the EU a state, but they do make it a highly developed political system.

The Future of the European Union

Factors affecting prospects

Integration in Europe has not evolved in quite the way, or as quickly, as was envisaged by many of the EC's founders. The expectation that policy interests and responsibilities would grow, with achievements in initially selected sectors leading to developments in other sectors, has been partly borne out, but only up to a point, and certainly not consistently – in the 1970s and early 1980s policy development was extremely sluggish. Similarly, the anticipation that national institutions and political and economic actors would become progressively entwined with one another has been partially realised, but it has also been partially frustrated – not least because of the continuing reluctance of governments to transfer particular responsibilities and powers to the EU institutions. The assumption that the focus of political activities and attentions would switch from national capitals to Europe has happened to an extent, but in many policy areas – particularly those involving heavy government expenditure such as education, health, and social welfare – the national level is still more important than the EU level. And the belief that a European spirit would emerge, based on shared perceptions of a common interest, has proved to be over-optimistic.

There has, in short, been no semi-automatic movement in an integrationist direction. But if integration has not inevitably and of itself led to greater integration, it has certainly stimulated pressure for greater integration. It has done so, for example, by creating 'client groups' – of which, in the EU context, Eurocrats are not the least prominent – that have vested interests in sustaining and extending integration. Integration has also provided an institutional framework into which integrationist pressures, of both an exogenous and an endogenous kind, have been channelled. Among such pressures on the EU today are: the international trade challenge presented by the United States, Japan, and the newly-industrialising countries; the transnational character of problem areas such as the environment and terrorism; and the need to respond to the integration that is occurring outside formal EU processes through developments as diverse as industrial mergers, closer cross-border banking and other financial arrangements, and population movements.

How the EU will respond to these and other pressures will depend on a number of factors, the most important of which are perceptions, support and opposition, and leadership.

The importance of *perceptions* is evidenced by the way in which the prospect of progress is considerably enhanced when all of the member states perceive an initiative to be broadly desirable, or at least regard the costs of not proceeding as being too high. Very frequently, of course, there is no such common perception, especially when new types of development are envisaged and/or initiatives have sovereignty or clear distributional implications.

The extent to which key actors are motivated to *support or oppose* an initiative depends on many things. Perception of merit is obviously central, but this can be offset by other considerations. For example, a government may fiercely resist a proposal in the Council of Ministers not because it regards it as innately unsound but because acceptance could be electorally damaging or could lead to problems with an important domestic pressure group.

Leadership has long been a weakness of the EU in that there is no strong and central focus of decision-making authority. The Commission, the European Council, and the Council of Ministers are in many ways the key decision-making bodies, but their ability to get things done is subject to limitations. When attempts are made to provide forceful leadership – by, perhaps, an informal coalition of states, by an ambitious Council Presidency, or by a forceful Commission President – there is usually resistance from some quarter.

Perceptions, support, and leadership are of course not static, but are in constant transition. Since the early to mid-1980s they have undergone significant changes, in ways that have facilitated integrationist developments. The factors accounting for the changes are many and varied, and range from the specific, such as the appointment of the highly dynamic Jacques Delors to the Commission Presidency in 1985, to the general, such as the opening up of the internal market and the related increasing interdependence of international economic and political life. These changes have helped to produce a climate wherein, for example, the European Council and the Commission have both offered bold leadership in such important areas as EMU and EU enlargement.

But although the integration process continues to move forward, there are still formidable obstacles to further integration. This is no more clearly seen than in the different public positions taken by the governments of the member states on the future shape of the EU. On the one hand, there are those who tend towards a 'maximalist' position – such as the Italians and the Belgians – who are generally enthusiastic about economic, monetary and political union and who do not automatically recoil at the prospect of a federal Europe. On the other hand, there are those who are more cautious – most notably the Danes, the Swedes and the British – who tend to prefer cooperation rather than integration and still make much of the importance of preserving national independence and sovereignty.

Challenges

Of critical importance in determining the future evolution of the EU will be how it handles the many challenges that are facing it. Five challenges feature particularly prominently on the agenda.

Consolidating the euro

The launch of the euro clearly marked a major advance in the integration process. Not only do the participating states now share a single currency, but they have ceded independent control of basic levers of macroeconomic policy to central institutions.

However, the euro cannot as yet be judged to have been a success. Growth rates within the eurozone have generally been low, unemployment rates have been high, and the anchor of the euro system – the Stability and Growth Pact – had to be considerably loosened in 2004–05 to accommodate the needs of some states, especially France and Germany, which found it too restrictive. In addition to these 'policy delivery' problems, there have also been institutional difficulties, with the Commission and the Ecofin Council clashing over the SGP and with the ECB clearly disapproving of what it has seen to be the over lax spending policies of some eurozone states.

The capacity of the euro system to meet the needs of the member states is thus not yet proven. But even before it is proven it is likely that states which joined the EU in May 2004 will be seeking to join the euro – thus ensuring further possible problems given that most of the potential newcomers have significantly higher economic growth rates than existing euro members and given too that they mostly have only partially developed financial systems.

Policy development and reform

As was shown in Chapter 15, EU policies are in constant evolution. In recent years this has been demonstrated with, for example, the development of an embryonic external security policy capability, the movement of the CAP from being a price support system to an income support system, and the 'communitaurisation' of many JHA policies.

Many factors fuel debate on, and force the pace of, policy development and policy reform. A number of such factors can be identified as being of current, and likely future, importance. For example, the legacy of the tensions and upheavals in the Balkans, the security uncertainties on Europe's fringes, and pressures from the USA for Europe to make a greater military contribution to international, and especially European, security, are all pressing in the direction of the EU's foreign and defence policies being further strengthened. The continuing terrorist threat is obliging the EU to give internal security policies a high priority. The commitment to a review of EU spending policies in 2008 (see Chapter 17) ensures that CAP reform will continue to feature prominently in budget-related deliberations. And with the EU becoming increasingly dependent on the Middle East and Russia for energy supplies, energy policy in the broadest sense is likely to be given greater attention.

But, of course, differences between the EU's policy actors will ensure that deliberations on many of the policy challenges facing the EU will be difficult. EU political dynamics are favoured by the fact that many of the policy differences between the member states are cross-cutting rather than cumulative – thus ensuring that the large states do not consistently dominate and also that no state or states are continually in a minority and thus permanently aggrieved. But that does not mean that some of the differences are not significant and capable of threatening policy development. For example, differences between those who take a 'liberal' and a 'social market' view of economic policy may be exaggerated, but they certainly exist and make coordinated and coherent EU-wide macroeconomic and social policy development difficult.

Managing flexibility

In response to the different requirements and propensities of the member states, the EC/EU has long provided for a limited flexibility and diversity in its structures and policies. When 'standard' methods have been judged as inappropriate or over-rigid, inter-state relations have taken other forms. For example, European Political Cooperation was developed from the early 1970s alongside but outside the formal Community structures. This was taken a stage further in the Maastricht Treaty when the three pillar structure was established.

Since the mid- to late 1990s the increasing use of new modes of governance have further increased flexibility within the EU. The 'new governance', which has impacted widely on Western public policy and administration, has a number of dimensions. One is the 'outsourcing' of public policy functions to agencies that are not fully part of the central administrative system. European agencies such as the European Medicines Agency, European Environmental Agency, and European Food Safety Authority are of this sort. The powers and roles of the EU's agencies – of which there were eighteen in early 2006 – vary, but most are focused primarily on information gathering and making policy recommendations.

Another dimension of the new governance involves public policy and administration placing less emphasis on traditional, 'top-down', legislation-based forms of operation and more emphasis on flexible, often network-based, and frequently semi-voluntary forms of policy development and practice. In the EU context, use of this approach is seen in the open method of coordination (OMC), which has been used particularly in social policy-related areas. OMC involves a relatively loose form of policy activity, based essentially on the identification of policy targets that member states are pressurised – but are not compelled – to meet by benchmarking and peer review.

A particularly important form of flexibility in the EU is differentiation: that is, policy development and activity in which not all member states are involved. The European Monetary System which was developed from the late 1970s on a partial membership basis, was the first instance of differentiation. It was followed from the mid-1980s by the Schengen System. Differentiation was then given treaty authorisation by the Maastricht Treaty, which identified EMU and the social dimension as policy areas that could be developed without the participation of the full complement of EU states. The Amsterdam Treaty generalised the Maastricht 'dispensation' by providing for 'Provisions on Closer Cooperation' which authorised a majority of member states to develop a policy within the Community framework, subject to conditions. The Nice Treaty then made closer cooperation easier to operationalise by replacing the stipulation that a majority of member states must be involved in a closer cooperation initiative by a stipulation that only eight must be so. With enlargement in May 2004, the proportion of participating member states was thus reduced from over one-half to less than one-third.

Flexibility in various forms has thus become an accepted part of the EU system. It is likely that it will become even more so in the future as enlargement continues to bring in not only more member states but also member states that are increasingly varied in terms of their political and economic requirements and capacities. Such flexibility raises questions about the possible future fragmentation of the EU. If the EU is to continue to be obliged to narrow the base of the required *acquis* – that is, the common core that all member states must accept – how far can it go without undermining the Union's very essence?

Treaty reform

The Constitutional Treaty was a disappointment to many. It did not provide a simple and clear document which citizens could understand or to which they could readily relate. It did not advance the integration process to any great degree. And it did not address the EU's so-called leadership deficit. Indeed, if anything, it made the leadership issue even more complex, with the present institutional leadership – which is based primarily on the College of Commissioners and the Council Presidency – joined, not replaced, by a semi-permanent head of the European Council and a Union Minister for Foreign Affairs.

But although the Constitutional Treaty is not the document pro-integrationists in particular had hoped to see, it does contain, as was shown in Chapter 7, many important changes and provisions. These include the abolition of the pillar structure, arrangements for a reduction in the future size of the College of Commissioners, extensions to QMV availability in the Council, a strengthening of the legal base of the Charter of Fundamental Rights, and the above mentioned creation of the new posts of European Council President and Union Minister for Foreign Affairs.

The French and Dutch referendums of 2005 mean that, for the present, the EU continues to operate on the basis of the Nice Treaty. But it cannot do so forever. The debates on the Constitutional Treaty may have highlighted differences between the member states on aspects of the future nature of the EU, but the fact is that the Treaty was planned and negotiated because of a general recognition that some changes to the EU's existing treaty structure were necessary.

Enlargement

EU enlargement is an ongoing process rather than a series of discrete steps or stages. Since the early 1970s there has never been a time when the EU has not been engaged in some combination of considering membership applications, conducting accession negotiations, and fitting in new member states to EU processes and policies.

There is every reason to assume that this challenge of enlargement will continue into the foreseeable future: the full assimilation of Central and Eastern European countries will not be completed for some considerable time; in October 2005 the EU opened accession negotiations with Croatia and Turkey; Macedonia applied for membership in 2005, and applicants from other Western Balkan states can be anticipated; and some former Soviet states, including the Ukraine and Moldova, harbour hopes of eventual membership.

A central problem for the EU in permitting the enlargement process to continue is that it is adding to the EU's diversity. Apart from the special cases of Iceland, Norway and Switzerland, all of the states that could be 'easily' fitted into the EU are now in. As the EU extends further to the east and south east it is inevitably increasingly dealing with countries whose political traditions, economic circumstances, and cultural inheritance are significantly 'different'. Fundamental questions are thus raised about the EU's absorption capacity. They are questions which in large part can only be answered in terms of what sort of EU is envisaged ... and desired.

Chronology of Main Events in the European Integration Process

1947	March	Belgium, Luxembourg and the Netherlands agree to establish a customs union. Subsequently an economic union is established in October 1947 and a common customs tariff is introduced in January 1948.
	March	France and the United Kingdom sign a military alliance, the Treaty of Dunkirk.
	June	General George Marshall, United States Secretary of State, offers US aid for the economic recovery of Europe.
	September	Sixteen nations join the European Recovery Programme.
1948	March	Brussels Treaty concluded between France, the UK and the Benelux states. The aim is to promote collective defence and improve cooperation in the economic, social and cultural fields.
	April	Founding of the Organisation for European Economic Cooperation (OEEC) by sixteen states.
	May	A Congress is held in The Hague, attended by many leading supporters of European cooperation and integration. It issues a resolution asserting 'that it is the urgent duty of the nations of Europe to create an economic and political union in order to assure security and social progress'.
1949	April	Treaty establishing North Atlantic Treaty Organisation (NATO) signed in Washington by twelve states.
	May	Statute of Council of Europe signed in Strasbourg by ten states.
1950	May	Robert Schuman, the French Foreign Minister, puts forward his proposals to place French and German coal and steel under a common authority. He declares 'it is no longer the moment for vain words, but for a bold act – a constructive act'.
	October	René Pleven, the French Prime Minister, proposes a European Defence Community (EDC).

1951	April	European Coal and Steel Community (ECSC) Treaty signed in Paris by six states: Belgium, France, West Germany, Italy, Luxembourg and the Netherlands.
1952	May	EDC Treaty signed in Paris by the six ECSC states.
	July	ECSC comes into operation.
1954	August	French National Assembly rejects EDC Treaty.
	October	WEU Treaty signed by the six ECSC states plus the UK.
1955	June	Messina Conference of the Foreign Ministers of the six ECSC states to discuss further European integration. Spaak Committee established to study ways in which a fresh advance towards the building of Europe could be achieved.
1956	June	Negotiations formally open between the six with a view to creating an Economic Community and an Atomic Energy Community.
1957	March	The Treaties of Rome signed, establishing the European Economic Community (EEC) and the European Atomic Energy Community (Euratom).
1958	January	EEC and Euratom come into operation.
1959	January	First EEC tariff cuts and increases in quotas.
1960	January	European Free Trade Association (EFTA) Convention signed in Stockholm by Austria, Denmark, Norway, Portugal, Sweden, Switzerland and the UK. EFTA comes into force in May 1960.
	December	Organisation for Economic Cooperation and Development (OECD) Treaty signed in Paris. OECD replaces OEEC and includes Canada and the United States.
1961	July	Signing of Association Agreement between Greece and the EEC. Comes into effect November 1962.
	July–August	Ireland, Denmark and UK request membership negotiations with the Community.
1962	January	Basic features of Common Agricultural Policy (CAP) agreed.
	July	Norway requests negotiations on Community membership.
1963	January	General de Gaulle announces his veto on UK membership.
	January	Signing of Franco–German Treaty of Friendship and Cooperation.

July	A wide-ranging association agreement is signed between the Community and 18 underdeveloped countries in Africa – the Yaoundé Convention, which enters into force in June 1964.
1964 May	The GATT Kennedy Round of international tariff negotiations opens in Geneva. The Community states participate as a single delegation.
1965 April	Signing of Treaty Establishing a Single Council and a Single Commission of the European Communities (The Merger Treaty).
July	France begins a boycott of Community institutions to register its opposition to various proposed supranational developments.
1966 January	Foreign Ministers agree to the Luxembourg Compromise. Normal Community processes are resumed.
1967 May	Denmark, Ireland and the UK re-apply for Community membership.
July	1965 Merger Treaty takes effect.
July	Norway re-applies for Community membership.
December	The Council of Ministers fails to reach agreement on the re-opening of membership negotiations with the applicant states because of continued French opposition to UK membership.
1968 July	The Customs Union is completed. All internal customs duties and quotas are removed and the common external tariff is established.
1969 July	President Pompidou (who succeeded de Gaulle after his resignation in April) announces he does not oppose UK membership in principle.
July	Signing of the second Yaoundé Convention. Enters into force in January 1971.
December	Hague summit agrees on a number of important matters: strengthening the Community institutions, enlargement, establishing an economic and monetary union by 1980, and developing political cooperation (i.e. foreign policy).
1970 April	The financial base of the Community is changed by the Decision of 21 April 1970 on the Replacement of Financial Contributions From Member States by the Communities' Own Resources. The Community's budgetary procedures are regularised and the European Parliament's budgetary powers are increased by the Treaty Amending Certain Budgetary Provisions of the Treaties.

1970 June   Preferential trade agreement signed between the Community
                 and Spain. Comes into effect in October 1970.
     June   Community opens membership negotiations with Denmark,
                 Ireland, Norway and the UK.
     October   The six accept the Davignon report on political cooperation.
                 This provides the basis for cooperation on foreign policy
                 matters.

1972 January   Negotiations between the Community and the four applicant
                 countries concluded. Signing of treaties of accession.
     May   Irish approve Community accession in a referendum.
     July   Conclusion of Special Relations Agreement between Com-
                 munity and EFTA countries.
     September   Majority vote against Community accession in a referendum
                 in Norway.
     October   Danes approve Community accession in a referendum.
     October   Paris summit. Heads of Government set guidelines for the
                 future, including reaffirmation of the goal of achieving
                 economic and monetary union by 1980.

1973 January   Accession of Denmark, Ireland and the UK to the
                 Community.
     January   Preferential trade agreement between the Community and
                 most EFTA countries comes into effect. Agreements with
                 other EFTA countries come into force later.

1974 December   Paris summit agrees to the principle of direct elections to the
                 EP and to the details of a European Regional Development
                 Fund (ERDF) (the establishment of which had been agreed at
                 the 1972 Paris and 1973 Copenhagen summits). It is also
                 agreed to institutionalise summit meetings by establishing the
                 European Council.

1975 February   Signing of the first Lomé Convention between the Commu-
                 nity and 46 underdeveloped countries in Africa, the
                 Caribbean and the Pacific (the ACP states). The Convention
                 replaces and extends the Yaoundé Convention.
     March   First meeting of the European Council in Dublin.
     June   A majority vote in favour of continued Community member-
                 ship in UK referendum.
     June   Greece applies for Community membership.
     July   Signing of the Treaty Amending Certain Financial Provisions
                 of the Treaties. This strengthens the European Parliament's
                 budgetary powers and also establishes the Court of Auditors.

1976 July   Opening of negotiations on Greek accession to the
                 Community.

| 1977 | March | Portugal applies for Community membership. |
| | July | Spain applies for Community membership. |

| 1978 | October | Community opens accession negotiations with Portugal. |

1979	February	Community opens accession negotiations with Spain.
	March	European Monetary System (EMS) (which had been the subject of high-level negotiations for over a year) comes into operation.
	May	Signing of Accession Treaty between Community and Greece.
	June	First direct elections to the EP.
	October	Signing of the second Lomé Convention between the Community and 58 ACP states.
	December	For the first time the EP does not approve the Community budget. As a result the Community has to operate on the basis of 'one-twelfths' from 1 January 1980.

| 1981 | January | Accession of Greece to Community. |
| | October | Community Foreign Ministers reach agreement on the London Report, which strengthens and extends European Political Cooperation (EPC). |

| 1983 | January | Common Fisheries Policy (CFP) agreed. |
| | June | At the Stuttgart European Council meeting approval is given to a 'Solemn Declaration on European Union'. |

1984	January	Free trade area between Community and EFTA established.
	February	The EP approves The Draft Treaty Establishing the European Union.
	June	Second set of direct elections to the EP.
	June	Fontainebleau European Council meeting. Agreement to reduce UK budgetary contributions (which Margaret Thatcher had been demanding since 1979) and agreement to increase Community resources by raising the VAT ceiling from 1 per cent to 1.4 per cent.
	December	Signing of the third Lomé Convention between the Community and 66 ACP countries.
	December	Dublin European Council meeting agrees budgetary discipline measures.

1985	June	Signing of accession treaties between the Community and Spain and Portugal.
	June	The Commission publishes its White Paper Completing the Internal Market.
	June	Milan European Council meeting approves the Commission's White Paper. It also establishes an Intergovernmental

1985 June *cont.*   Conference to examine various matters, including treaty reform. The decision to establish the Conference is the first time at a summit meeting that a decision is taken by a majority vote.

December   Luxembourg European Council meeting agrees to the principles of the Single European Act (SEA). Amongst other things the Act incorporates various treaty revisions and confirms the objective of completing the internal market by 1992.

1986 January   Accession of Spain and Portugal to Community.

1987 June   Turkey applies for Community membership.
July   After several months delay caused by ratification problems in Ireland, the SEA comes into force.

1988 February   A special European Council meeting in Brussels agrees to increase and widen the Community's budgetary base. Measures are also agreed to significantly reduce expenditure on the CAP and to double expenditure on the regional and social funds.

June   The Community and Comecon (the East European trading bloc) sign an agreement enabling the two organisations to recognise each other. As part of the agreement the Comecon states officially recognise, for the first time, the authority of the Community to negotiate on behalf of its member states.

June   Hanover European Council meeting entrusts to a committee chaired by Jacques Delors the task of studying how the Community might progress to Economic and Monetary Union (EMU).

1989 April   The 'Delors Committee' presents its report (the Delors Report). It outlines a scheme for a three-stage progression to EMU.

June   Third set of direct elections to the EP.

June   Madrid European Council meeting agrees that Stage 1 of the programme to bring about EMU will begin on 1 July 1990.

July   Austria applies for Community membership.

September–   The collapse of communist governments in Eastern Europe.
December   The process 'begins' with the appointment of a non-communist Prime Minister in Poland in September and 'ends' with the overthrow of the Ceausescu regime in Romania in December.

December   Signing of the fourth Lomé Convention between the Community and 68 ACP countries.

December   Community and USSR sign a ten-year trade and economic cooperation agreement.

	December	Commission advises Council of Ministers to reject Turkey's application for Community membership.
	December	Strasbourg European Council meeting accepts Social Charter and agrees to establish an Intergovernmental Conference (IGC) on EMU at the end of 1990. Both decisions taken by eleven votes to one, with the UK dissenting in each case.
1990	April	Special Dublin European Council meeting confirms the Community's commitment to political union.
	June	Dublin European Council meeting formally agrees that an IGC on Political Union will be convened.
	July	Cyprus and Malta apply for Community membership.
	October	Unification of Germany. Territory of former East Germany becomes part of the Community.
	October	Special Rome European Council meeting agrees that Stage 2 of EMU will begin on 1 January 1994.
	December	The two IGCs on EMU and on Political Union are opened at the Rome summit.
1991	July	Sweden applies for Community membership.
	August–December	Break-up of the USSR.
	December	Maastricht European Council meeting agrees to The Treaty on European Union. The Treaty is based on three pillars: the European Communities, a Common Foreign and Security Policy (CFSP), and Cooperation in the Fields of Justice and Home Affairs (JHA). The European Communities pillar includes the strengthening of Community institutions, the extension of the Community's legal policy competence, and a timetable for the establishment of EMU and a single currency.
	December	Association ('Europe') Agreements signed with Czechoslovakia, Hungary, and Poland.
1992	February	Treaty on European Union formally signed at Maastricht by Foreign and Finance Ministers.
	March	Finland applies to join the EU.
	May	After several months' delay caused by a Court of Justice ruling, the EEA agreement between the EC and EFTA is signed.
	May	Switzerland applies to join the EC.
	June	In a referendum the Danish people reject the TEU by 50.7 per cent to 49.3 per cent.
	September	Crisis in the ERM. Sterling and the lira suspend their membership.
	September	In a referendum the French people endorse the TEU by 51 per cent to 49 per cent.

1992	November	Norway applies to join the EU.
	December	In a referendum the Swiss people vote not to ratify the EEA by 50.3 per cent to 49.7 per cent. Amongst other implications this means that Switzerland's application to join the EU is suspended.
	December	Edinburgh European Council meeting agrees on several key issues, notably: (1) Danish opt-outs from the TEU and any future common defence policy; (2) a financial perspective for 1993–9; and (3) the opening of accession negotiations in early 1993 with Austria, Finland, Sweden and Norway.
1993	February	Accession negotiations open with Austria, Finland, and Sweden.
	April	Accession negotiations open with Norway.
	May	In a second referendum the Danish people vote by 56.8 per cent to 43.2 per cent to ratify the TEU.
	June	Copenhagen European Council. It is agreed that CEECs wishing to become members of the EU shall do so once they meet specified economic and political conditions (the Copenhagen criteria).
	August	Following great turbulence in the currency markets, the bands for all currencies in the ERM, apart from the deutschemark and the guilder, are increased to 15 per cent.
	October	German Constitutional Court ruling enables Germany to become the last member state to ratify the TEU.
	November	TEU enters into force.
	December	Settlement of the GATT Uruguay Round.
1994	January	Second stage of EMU comes into effect.
	January	EEA enters into force.
	March	Committee of the Regions meets for the first time.
	March	Austria, Finland, Sweden, and Norway agree accession terms with the EU.
	April	Hungary and Poland apply for membership of the EU.
	June	Fourth set of direct elections to the EP.
	June	In a referendum on accession to the EU, the Austrian people vote in favour by 66.4 per cent to 33.6 per cent.
	June	Corfu European Council. The UK vetoes Belgian Prime Minister, Jean-Luc Dehaene, as the new Commission President.
	July	Jacques Santer, the Luxembourg Prime Minister, nominated as the new Commission President at a special half-day European Council meeting in Brussels.
	October	Referendum in Finland on EU membership. The people vote in favour by 57 per cent to 43 per cent.
	November	Referendum in Sweden on EU membership. The people vote in favour by 52.2 per cent to 46.9 per cent.

November	Referendum in Norway on EU membership. The people reject accession by 52.2 per cent to 47.8 per cent.
1995 January	Austria, Finland and Sweden become EU members.
January	EP votes to confirm the Santer Commission: 418 votes in favour, 103 against, and 59 abstentions. The Commission is subsequently formally appointed by the representatives of the member states.
March	Schengen Accord implemented by seven EU member states: Germany, France, Belgium, Luxembourg, the Netherlands, Spain, and Portugal.
June	Romania and Slovakia apply to join the EU.
October	Latvia applies to join the EU.
November	Estonia applies to join the EU.
December	Lithuania and Bulgaria apply to join the EU.
1996 January	The Czech Republic and Slovenia apply to join the EU.
March	The IGC provided for in the Maastricht Treaty is formally opened at a special Heads of Government summit in Turin.
May	The UK government announces a policy of non-cooperation with EU decision-making following a Council of Ministers decision not to agree to a timetable for the lifting of the export ban on UK beef products.
June	A formula for ending the UK's non-cooperation policy agreed at the Florence European Council.
1997 June	Amsterdam European Council agrees to the Treaty of Amsterdam. The Treaty fails to provide for the institutional change that enlargement will require, but does contain some strengthening of EU institutions and policies.
July	Commission issues its *Agenda 2000* programme, which contains recommendations on how enlargement to the CEECs should be handled and how EU policies – especially the CAP and the Structural Funds – should be reformed.
October	Amsterdam Treaty formally signed by EU Foreign Ministers.
1998 March	Accession negotiations formally opened with Hungary, Poland, the Czech Republic, Slovenia, Estonia and Cyprus.
May	At a special European Council meeting in Brussels it is agreed that eleven states will participate when the euro is launched in 1999: France, Germany, Italy, Belgium, Luxembourg, the Netherlands, Ireland, Spain, Portugal, Finland and Austria.
May	Denmark and Ireland hold referenda in which the Treaty of Amsterdam is approved.
1999 January	Stage 3 of EMU and the euro come into operation, with eleven of the EU's fifteen states participating. The non-participants are Denmark, Greece, Sweden and the UK.

1999	March	The College of Commissioners resigns following the publication of a highly critical report by the Committee of Independent Experts.
	March	At a special European Council meeting in Berlin, the Heads of Government reach agreement on Agenda 2000 measures. The measures include a financial perspective for 2000–6, and CAP and Structural Fund reforms. It is also agreed to nominate Romano Prodi, the former Italian Prime Minister, to succeed Jacques Santer as Commission President.
	May	Treaty of Amsterdam enters into force.
	May	EP endorses Romano Prodi as Commission President-designate by 392 votes to 72, with 41 abstentions.
	June	Fifth set of direct elections to the EP.
	September	Prodi Commission assumes office after the EP endorses it by 414 votes to 142, with 35 abstentions.
	December	Helsinki European Council meeting takes key decisions on EU enlargement. These include that negotiations will be opened in early 2000 with six more applicant states and that Turkey will be viewed as having candidate status. The summit also decides that the EU will establish a Rapid Reaction Force, 50 000–60 000 strong, by 2003.
2000	February	The IGC provided for in a protocol attached to the Amsterdam Treaty is opened.
	February	Accession negotiations are opened with Latvia, Lithuania, Bulgaria, Slovakia, Romania, and Malta.
	June	The Cotonou Agreement, a twenty-year Partnership Agreement replacing the Lomé Convention, is signed by the EU and 77 ACP countries.
	September	In a referendum the Danish people reject membership of the euro by 53.1 per cent to 46.9 per cent.
	December	Nice European Council agrees to the Treaty of Nice. The Treaty consists mainly of a range of institutional reforms designed to prepare the EU for enlargement.
2001	January	Greece becomes a member of the euro zone.
	February	Treaty of Nice is formally signed by EU Foreign Ministers.
	June	In a referendum, the Irish people reject the Treaty of Nice by 54 per cent to 46 per cent on a low 35 per cent turnout.
2002	January	Euro coins and notes come into circulation and the national currencies of the twelve euroland countries are phased out.
	March	The Convention on the Future of Europe opens under the chairmanship of Valery Giscard d'Estaing.
	October	In a referendum the Irish people approve the Treaty of Nice by 63 per cent to 37 per cent on a 48 per cent turnout.

December	Copenhagen European Council meeting takes key decisions on enlargement. These include: ten states (Cyprus, the Czech Republic, Estonia, Hungary, Latvia, Lithuania, Malta, Poland, Slovakia, and Slovenia) are deemed to have completed accession negotiations and will join the EU on 1 May 2004 subject to ratification procedures having been completed; Bulgaria and Romania will be able to join the EU in 2007 if they make satisfactory progress in complying with the membership criteria; the December 2004 summit will authorise the immediate opening of accession negotiations with Turkey if the Commission makes a recommendation to this effect based on Turkey having continued with its reform process.
2003 February	The Treaty of Nice enters into force. Croatia applies to join the EU.
March	In the first referendum to be held in the '2004 enlargement' round, the Maltese people vote to join the EU by 53.6 per cent to 46.4 per cent on a 91 per cent turnout.
April	In a referendum, the Slovenian people vote to join the EU by 89.6 per cent to 10.4 per cent on a 60.3 per cent turnout. The Treaty of Accession is signed in Athens by representatives of the EU-15 and the 10 applicant states with which negotiations have been completed. In a referendum, the Hungarian people vote to join the EU by 84.0 per cent to 16.0 per cent on a 45.6 per cent turnout.
May	In a referendum, the Lithuanian people vote to join the EU by 91.0 per cent to 9.0 per cent on a 63.4 per cent turnout. In a referendum, the Slovak people vote to join the EU by 92.5 per cent to 6.2 per cent on a 52.1 per cent turnout.
June	The European Convention on the Future of Europe agrees on the contents of the Draft Treaty Establishing a Constitution for Europe. In a referendum, the Polish people vote to join the EU by 77.5 per cent to 22.5 per cent on a 58.8 per cent turnout. In a referendum, the Czech people vote to join the EU by 77.3 per cent to 23.7 per cent on a 55.2 per cent turnout.
July	The Cypriot House of Representatives votes unanimously to approve Cyprus's Treaty of Accession to the EU. (Of the ten states to sign the April 2003 Accession Treaty, Cyprus is the only one not to hold a referendum.)
September	In a referendum, the Estonian people vote to join the EU by 66.8 per cent to 32.2 per cent on a 64.0 per cent turnout. In a referendum, the Latvian people vote to join the EU by 67.0 per cent to 32.3 per cent on a 72.5 per cent turnout. In a referendum, the Swedish people vote against membership of the euro by 56.1 per cent to 41.8 per cent on an 81.2 per cent turnout.

2003 October   The IGC charged with negotiating a Constitutional Treaty is opened.

December   The Brussels European Council meeting fails to agree on the contents of the Constitutional Treaty and the IGC is suspended.

2004 March   Macedonia applies to join the EU.
The Brussels European Council meeting decides to re-start the IGC, with a view to the Constitutional Treaty being agreed at the June European Council.

May   Ten countries become members of the EU: Cyprus, the Czech Republic, Estonia, Hungary, Latvia, Lithuania, Malta, Poland, Slovakia and Slovenia.

June   Sixth set of direct elections to the EP.
The European Council agrees on the contents of the Constitutional Treaty.
At a special meeting of the European Council it is agreed that Portuguese Prime Minister, José Manuel Barroso, will be nominated to be President of the European Commission.

July   José Manuel Barroso is approved by the EP by 413 votes to 251.

October   Barroso withdraws his College-designate from the process of EP approval so as to avoid the possibility of rejection.
Following two personnel changes and other portfolio changes the EP gives its approval to the Barroso College by 449 votes to 149, with 82 abstentions.
The leaders of the EU's member states sign the Constitutional Treaty in Rome.

December   The European Council agrees that accession negotiations should be opened with Croatia in March 2005 and with Turkey in October 2005, provided certain conditions are met.

2005 March   The Spanish people vote in a referendum to ratify the Constitutional Treaty by 76.7 per cent to 23.3 per cent on a 42.3 per cent turnout.

May   The French people vote in a referendum not to ratify the Constitutional Treaty by 54.9 per cent to 45.1 per cent on a 69.7 per cent turnout.

June   The Dutch people vote in a referendum not to ratify the Constitutional Treaty by 61.7 per cent to 38.3 per cent on a 63 per cent turnout.

July   The Luxembourg people vote in a referendum to ratify the Constitutional Treaty by 56.5 per cent to 43.5 per cent on a 90.5 per cent turnout.

October   The EU opens accession negotiations with Turkey and Croatia.

December   The European Council agrees on the contents of the 2007–13 financial perspective.

Guide to Further Reading

Official European Union Sources
National Government Sources
Periodicals, Newspapers and Journals
Web Sources
Books

Official European Union Sources

The EU issues a vast amount of material, most of which is available in paper and electronic forms. Paper copies are usually published by the Office for Official Publications of the European Communities (EUR-OP). Electronic copies are usually accessible via the EU's website, Europa, the URL of which is < www.europa.eu.int >

The treaties should naturally be consulted by all those who wish to understand the nature and functioning of the EU. They have been published in several editions by, amongst others, EUR-OP and Sweet & Maxwell. The editions of the *Official Journal* in which the Maastricht, Amsterdam and Nice treaties are published are listed in the Bibliography. The treaties are also directly available on the Europa website.

The *Official Journal of the European Union (OJ)* is issued on most weekdays and provides an authoritative record of decisions and activities of various kinds. It consists of two series. The 'L' (Legislation) series is the vehicle for the publication of EU legislation. The 'C' (Information and Notices) series contains a range of information, including appointments to advisory committees, minutes of EP plenary proceedings and resolutions adopted by plenaries, EESC opinions, Court of Auditors reports, cases referred to the Court of Justice and Court judgements, Commission communications and notices, and Commission proposals for Council legislation. There is also an 'S' series which supplements the *OJ* which is mainly concerned with public contract and tendering announcements. An index to the 'L' and 'C' series of the *OJ* is available in monthly and annual editions.

The monthly *Bulletin of the European Union* provides a general account of most significant developments. Some of the information contained amounts to a summary of material included in the *OJ* (with appropriate references). Much else is additional: there are, for example, reports – albeit rather brief ones – of Council of Ministers meetings, updates on policy developments, a monitoring of progress in the annual budgetary cycle, and information on initiatives, meetings and agreements in the sphere of external relations.

The *General Report on the Activities of the European Union* is published annually and provides an excellent summary of both institutional and policy developments. Where necessary it can be supplemented by the annual reports published by most of the institutions.

Information about the annual budget is available in the *Bulletin* and in the *General Report*. The full budget, which runs to about 1800 pages of text, is published in the *OJ* (L series) about one month after it has been approved by the EP. A useful publication is *The Community Budget: the Facts in Figures*, which usually appears on an annual basis.

The most detailed analysis of and information on EU policies is usually to be found in documents produced by the Commission. Leaving aside one-off publications, these appear in three main forms. First, serialised reports are issued on a regular basis and cover just about every aspect of EU affairs. As an indication of the sort of reports that are produced, four might be mentioned: *European Economy* covers economic trends and proposals and is issued quarterly, with monthly supplements; *Social Europe* provides information on the many facets of social and employment policy and is issued three times a year; *Eurobarometer* reports on public opinion in the EU and appears twice a year; and the *Agricultural Situation in the Community* is an annual report. Second, an enormous volume of information is issued by the Statistical Office – known as *Eurostat* – on matters ranging from energy consumption patterns to agricultural prices. Useful general publications are *Europe in Figures* and *Eurostat Yearbook*. Third, there are Commission documents (COMDOCS), which cover many matters including programme reports, policy reviews and, most importantly, proposals for legislation.

Useful material stemming from other EU institutions on a regular basis includes: *Reports, Dossiers,* and *Research Documents* of the EP; the monthly *Bulletin of the EESC*; and *Reports of Cases Before the Court.*

National Government Sources

The governments of the member states produce a considerable volume of documentation on the EU. The precise nature of this material varies, but it mostly consists of a mixture of 'state of play' reports, reports from relevant parliamentary committees, and information pamphlets/booklets/packs. Because many of the latter are intended to stimulate a greater public awareness of the EU, or are designed to encourage business to take advantage of EU policies, hard copies are often available free of charge.

The Foreign Offices of all member states have websites with useful information on the EU.

Periodicals, Newspapers and Journals

A daily bulletin of events is provided in *Europe* – commonly known as *Agence Europe* – which is published by Agence Internationale D'Information Pour La

Presse. *European Report*, published by Europe Information Service, also provides a detailed monitoring of events, in its case on a twice-weekly basis.

European Voice, published by the Economist Group, is an excellent weekly newspaper on the EU.

EUobserver provides an extremely useful daily report on issues currently concerning the EU. It is available online at < www.EUobserver.com >

In most member states the 'quality' press provides a reasonable review of EU affairs. In the United Kingdom the most comprehensive coverage is provided by the *Financial Times*.

Academic articles on the EU are to be found in a number of places. Particularly useful academic journals include *Journal of Common Market Studies*, *Journal of European Public Policy*, *Journal of European Integration*, *European Union Politics*, *Current Politics and Economics of Europe*, *Common Market Law Review*, and *European Law Review*.

The European Union: Annual Review of the EU is very useful for monitoring each year's developments. It is published by Blackwell and also appears as the fifth issue of the *Journal of Common Market Studies*.

Web Sources

An enormous amount of information about European integration and the EU is available on the web. Attention here is directed to a few of the most useful websites, most of which are gateway sites in that they provide links to more specialised sites. All the sites listed have free access.

As was noted above, the Europa website is immensely valuable for accessing official EU information. It provides links to an enormous number of webpages covering EU institutions, policies, documentation and developments. The many different webpages on Europa can be accessed either by logging on to the Europa site and then following links or by accessing webpages directly. So, for example, the URL of EUR-Lex, which gives access to the full text of EU law and to the latest editions of the *Official Journal*, is < www.europa.eu.int/eur-lex/ > .

Other EU sites well worth visiting include those of the European Commission offices around the world. The site of the Commission's Delegation to the USA, for example, is quite excellent. It is at < www.eurunion.org > .

Non-EU websites that cover all aspects of the EU and provide numerous links to other sites include:

- *Europe Sources Online* provides a wide variety of information on the EU and Europe at < www.europeansources.info > .
- *The Archive of European Integration*, is a repository of research materials and articles on European integration at < http://aei.pitt.edu >

Online academic papers on European integration, based on several series of research papers, can be accessed at < eiop.or.at/erpa/ > .

Tables of the contents of journals relevant to European integration can be accessed at < www.jeanmonnetprogram.org/TOC/index.html > .

Two prominent academic associations with helpful websites are:

- The European Union Studies Association at < www.eustudies.org > .
- The University Association for Contemporary European Studies at < www. uaces.org > .

Finally, Palgrave Macmillan has its own EU web page for this book and other books in the European Union Series. The page provides updating information on important developments and also links to other internet sites on the EU. The URL is < www.palgrave.com/politics/eu/ > .

Books

The number of books published on the EU is now voluminous. Only a brief indication of what is available is attempted here, with references being confined to books in English and with preference being given to recent publications.

The titles listed are grouped into very broad sections. The boundaries between the sections are far from watertight.

General books on the government and politics of the EU

Cini (2003), Dinan (2005), McCormick (2005), George and Bache (2001), Nicoll and Salmon (2001), and Wood and Yesilada (2002) are all good introductory texts.

Green Cowles and Dinan (2004) and Richardson (2006) are valuable for those who are already familiar with 'the basics'.

The historical evolution

Dinan (2004) provides a highly informed and readable account of the integration process since the Second World War. Stirk (1996) examines the integration process since 1914 and Urwin (1995) does so from 1945.

It is always helpful to consult primary sources and an easy way of doing this is through readers. The following are all useful: Giustino (1996), Harryvan and van der Harst (1997), Salmon and Nicoll (1997), and Stirk and Weigall (1999).

Memoirs of the Founding Fathers merit attention. See especially Monnet (1978) and Marjolin (1989).

Milward (1984, 2000) has written detailed and challenging analyses of the early years of European integration.

On the EU's treaties see Church and Phinnemore (2002). On the Maastricht Treaty see Church and Phinnemore (1994), Corbett (1993), and Duff *et al.* (1994). On the Amsterdam Treaty see Dehousse (1999), Duff (1997), and Monar and Wessels (2001). On the Nice Treaty see Bond and Feus (2001), Galloway (2001), and Laursen (2006). On the Constitutional Treaty see Church and Phinnemore (2005).

The institutions and political actors

Peterson and Shackleton (2006) and Warleigh (2002) are the most comprehensive books focused solely on the EU's institutions.

On the Commission see Dimitrakopoulos (2004), Hooghe (2001), Nugent (2000 and 2001). On the Council see Hayes-Renshaw and Wallace (2006), Westlake (1999), and Sherrington (2000). The most comprehensive books on the European Parliament are Corbett, Jacobs and Shackleton (2005), Corbett (1998), and Judge and Earnshaw (2003). Hix and Lord (1997) examine political parties in the EU. Stevens and Stevens (2001) analyse the administrative apparatus and personnel of the EU institutions. For non-lawyers, amongst the best books on the EU's courts and EU law are Dehousse (1998), Hartley (2003), Mathijsen (2004), and Steiner *et al.* (2003). Greenwood (2003) provides a comprehensive review and analysis of interests in the EU.

Policies and policy processes

Peterson and Bomberg (1999) and Wallace and Wallace (2005) both provide excellent overviews of EU policies and policy processes.

On particular policy areas see in particular: Armstrong and Bulmer (1998) on the Single European Market; Levitt and Lord (2000) and Dosenrode (2002) on EMU; Grant (1997) and Ackrill (2000) on agriculture; Cini and McGowan (1998) on competition policy; Peterson and Sharp (1998) on technology policy; McCormick (2001) on environmental policy; Ginsberg (2001), Hill and Smith (2005), and Bretherton and Vogler (2006) on external policies; and Holland (2002) on development policy.

Amongst the many useful sources in the growing literature on Europeanisation and the impact of the EU on member states are Goetz and Hix (2001), Héritier *et al.* (2001), Green Cowles *et al.* (2001), Kassim *et al.* (2000), and Grabbe (2005).

On enlargement see Baun (2000), Brimmer and Fröhlich (2005), and Nugent (2004).

The member states and the EU

There is a rapidly developing literature on the member states and the EU, some of which is comparative in nature and some of which consists of single state studies. A good place to start is Bulmer and Lequesne (2005), which combines both comparative and single state approaches and also contains very useful reading lists.

Conceptualising and theorising

Books providing an overview of European integration theory include Chryssochoou (2001), Rosamond (2000), and Wiener and Diez (2004).

Books examining European integration through particular theoretical lenses include Moravcsik (1998) via a liberal intergovernmentalist perspective and Beach (2005) via a more (though qualified) supranationalist perspective.

Much of the debate on integration theory has been conducted through articles in academic journals. Readers that bring together key writings include O'Neill (1996), Nelsen and Stubb (2003), and Nugent (1997a).

Hix (2005) examines the nature of the EU as a political system.

Books focusing on particular conceptualisations and theoretical approaches to analysing policy processes include, Chryssochoou (1998) on consociationalism, Hooghe (1996) and Hooghe and Marks (2001) on multi-level governance, Peterson and Bomberg (1999) on policy networks, and Schneider and Aspinwall (2001) and Pollack (2003) on new institutionalism.

Bibliography and References

Ackrill, R. (2000) *The Common Agricultural Policy* (Sheffield: Sheffield Academic Press).

Allen, D. and Smith, M. (1998) 'External Policy Developments', in G. Edwards and G. Wiessala (eds), *The European Union 1997: Annual Review of Activities* (Oxford: Blackwell): 69–91.

Alter, K. J. (1996) 'The European Court's Political Power', *West European Politics*, 19(3): 458–87.

Anderson, J. F. (2005) 'Germany and Europe: Centrality in the EU', in S. Bulmer and C. Lequesne (2005b), *op. cit.*: 77–96.

Archer, C. (2000) *The European Community: Structure and Process*, 3rd edn (London: Continuum).

Archer, C. and Nugent, N. (2002) (eds) *Special Edition of Current Politics and Economics of Europe: Small States and the European Union*, 11(1).

Armstrong, K. and Bulmer, S. (1998) *The Governance of the Single European Market* (Manchester: Manchester University Press).

Arnull, A. (1999) *The European Union and its Court of Justice* (Oxford: Oxford University Press).

Arter, D. (1993) *The Politics of European Integration in the Twentieth Century* (Aldershot: Dartmouth).

Avery, G. and Cameron, F. (1999) *The Enlargement of the European Union* (Sheffield: Sheffield Academic Press).

Baun, M. (2000) *A Wider Europe: The Process and Politics of European Union Enlargement* (Oxford: Rowman & Littlefield).

Beach, D. (2005) *The Dynamics of European Integration: Why and When EU Institutions Matter* (Basingstoke: Palgrave Macmillan).

Beatty, A. (2005) 'A Military Pygmy or a Sleeping Giant?', *European Voice*, 17–23 November.

Begg, I. (2005) *Funding the European Union* (London: Federal Trust).

Bellier, I. (1997) 'The Commission as an Actor: An Anthropologist's Views', in H. Wallace and A. R. Young, *op. cit.*

Bond, M. and Feus, K. (2001) (eds) *The Treaty of Nice Explained* (London: The Federal Trust).

Bostock, D. (2002) 'Coreper Revisited', *Journal of Common Market Studies*, 40(2): 215–34.

Bretherton, C. and Vogler, J. (1999) *The European Union as a Global Actor* (London: Routledge).

Bretherton, C. and Vogler, J. (2006) *The European Union as a Global Actor*, 2nd edn (London: Routledge).

Brimmer, E. and Fröhlich, S. (2005) *The Strategic Implications of European Union Enlargement* (Washington: Center for Transatlantic Relations).

Bulletin of the European Union (monthly) (Luxembourg: EUR-OP).

605

Bulmer, S. (1983) 'Domestic Politics and European Community Policy-Making', *Journal of Common Market Studies*, XXI: 349–63.

Bulmer, S. (1994) 'The Governance of the European Union: A New Institutionalist Approach', *Journal of Public Policy*, 13(4): 351–80.

Bulmer, S. (1998) 'New Institutionalism and the Governance of the Single European Market', *Journal of European Public Policy*, 5(3): 365–86.

Bulmer, S. and Burch, M. (1998) 'Organising for Europe: Whitehall, the British State and European Union', *Public Administration*, 76(4): 601–28.

Bulmer, S. and Lequesne, C. (2005a) 'The European Union and its Member States: An Overview', in S. Bulmer and C. Lequesne (2005b), *op. cit.*: 1–20.

Bulmer, S. and Lequesne, C. (2005b) *The Member States of the European Union* (Oxford: Oxford University Press).

Burley, A. M. and Mattli, W. (1993) 'Europe Before the Court: A Political Theory of Legal Integration', *International Organization*, 47(1): 41–76.

Caporaso, J. (1996) 'The European Union and Forms of State: Westphalian, Regulatory or Post-Modern?', *Journal of Common Market Studies*, 34(1): 29–52.

Chryssochoou, D. N. (1994) 'Democracy and Symbiosis in the European Union: Towards a Confederal Consortium?', *West European Politics*, 18: 118–36.

Chryssochoou, D. N. (1995) 'European Union and Dynamics of Confederal Consociation: Problems and Prospects for a Democratic Future', *Journal of European Integration*, XVIII(2–3): 279–305.

Chryssochoou, D. N. (1998) *Democracy in the European Union* (London: Tauris Academic Studies).

Chryssochoou, D. N. (2001) *Theorizing European Integration* (London: Sage).

Church, C. and Phinnemore, D. (1994) *European Union and European Community: A Handbook and Commentary on the Post-Maastricht Treaties* (London: Harvester Wheatsheaf).

Church, C. and Phinnemore, D. (2002) *The Penguin Guide to the European Treaties: From Rome to Maastricht, Amsterdam, Nice and Beyond* (London: Penguin).

Church, C. and Phinnemore, D. (2005) *Understanding the European Constitution: An Introduction to the EU Constitutional Treaty* (London: Routledge).

Cini, M. (2000) 'Administrative Culture in the European Commission: The Cases of Competition and Environment', in N. Nugent, *op. cit.*: 73–90.

Cini, M. (2003) *European Union Politics* (Oxford: Oxford University Press).

Cini, M. and McGowan, L. (1998) *Competition Policy in the European Union* (Basingstoke: Macmillan – now Palgrave Macmillan).

Clark, J. R. A. and Jones, A. (1999) 'From Policy Insider to Policy Outcast? Comité des Organisations Professionales Agricoles, EU Policymaking, and the EU's Agri-environment Regulation', *Environment and Planning C: Government and Policy*, 17.

Committee of Independent Experts (1999a) *First Report on Allegations Regarding Fraud, Mismanagement and Nepotism in the European Commission* (Brussels: European Parliament), 15 March.

Committee of Independent Experts (1999b) *Second Report on Reform of the Commission: Analysis of Current Practice and Proposals for Tackling*

Mismanagement, Irregularities and Fraud (2 vols) (Brussels: European Commission), 10 September.

Corbett, R. (1993) *The Treaty of Maastricht: From Conception to Ratification* (London: Longman).

Corbett, R. (1998) *The European Parliament's Role in Closer EU Integration* (Basingstoke: Macmillan – now Palgrave Macmillan).

Corbett, R. (2000) 'Academic Modelling of the Codecision Procedure: A Practitioner's Puzzled Reaction', *European Union Politics*, 1(3): 373–81.

Corbett, R. (2001) 'A Response to a Reply to a Reaction', *European Union Politics*, 2(3): 361–6.

Corbett, R., Jacobs, F. and Shackleton, M. (2005) *The European Parliament*, 6th edn (London: John Harper).

Costa, O. and Magnette, P. (2003) 'The European Union as a Consociation: A Methodological Assessment', *West European Politics*, 23: (3): 1–18.

Council of the European Union (2005) *Note from the Presidency to the European Council: Financial Perspectives 2007–13* (Brussels: Council of the European Union, 19 December, available on Europa website).

Cram, L., Dinan, D. and Nugent, N. (1999) *Developments in the European Union* (Basingstoke: Macmillan – now Palgrave Macmillan).

Dehousse, F. (1999) *Amsterdam: The Making of a Treaty* (London: Kogan Page).

Dehousse, R. (1998) *The European Court of Justice* (Basingstoke: Macmillan – now Palgrave Macmillan).

Dimitrakopoulos, D. G. (2004) *The Changing European Commission* (Manchester: Manchester University Press).

Dinan, D. (2004) *Europe Recast: A History of European Union* (Basingstoke: Palgrave Macmillan).

Dinan, D. (2005) *Ever Closer Union. An Introduction to the European Union*, 3rd edn (Basingstoke: Palgrave Macmillan).

Dosenrode, S. (2002) (ed.) *Political Aspects of the Economic and Monetary Union* (Abingdon: Ashgate).

Dowding, K. (2000) 'Institutionalist Research on the European Union: A Critical Review', *European Union Politics*, 1(1): 125–44.

Duff, A. (1997) (ed.) *The Treaty of Amsterdam: Text and Commentary* (London: Sweet & Maxwell).

Duff, A., Pinder, J. and Pryce, R. (1994) *Maastricht and Beyond: Building the European Union* (London: Routledge).

Ersbøll, N. (1997) 'The Amsterdam Treaty – II', *CFPS Review*, Autumn 1997: 7–12.

Eurobarometer (2001) *Special Eurobarometer: 'Europeans and Languages'*, Eurobarometer Report 54, 15 February (Luxembourg: Office for Official Publications of the European Communities).

European Central Bank (1999) *Organisation of the European System of Central Banks (ESCB)*, < http://www.ecb.int/about/absorg.htm > .

European Commission (1985) *Completing the Internal Market: White Paper from the Commission to the European Council*, Com. (85) 310 final.

European Commission (1992) *From the Single Act to Maastricht and Beyond: The Means to Match Our Ambitions*, Com. (92) 2000 final.

European Commission (1997a) *Agenda 2000: For a Stronger and Wider Union*, Com. (97) 2000 final. Also available in *Bulletin of the European Union*, supplement 5/97 (Luxembourg: EUR-OP).

European Commission (1997b) *Communication from the Commission. Towards a New Shipbuilding Policy*, Com. (97) 470 final.

European Commission (2000) *Reforming the Commission – A White Paper* (1 March) (Brussels: European Commission).

European Commission (2001) *Memorandum to the Members of the Commission: Summary of the Treaty of Nice*, Sec (2001) 99, 18 January.

European Commission (2002a) *Enlargement and Agriculture: Successfully Integrating the New Member States into the CAP – Issues Paper*, 1P/02/176, 30 January.

European Commission (2002b) *General Report on the Activities of the European Union: 2001* (Luxembourg: EUR-OP).

European Commission (2002c) *General Budget of the European Union for the Financial Year 2002* (Brussels: EUR-OP).

European Commission (2002d) *Communication from the Commission: The Reform of the Common Fisheries Policy*, Com (2002) 181 final, 28 May.

European Commission (2002e) *Communication from the Commission to the Council and the European Parliament: Mid-Term Review of the Common Agricultural Policy*, Com (2002) 394, 10 July.

European Commission (2003) *Communication from the Commission to the Council and the European Parliament. Wider Europe Neighbourhood: A New Framework For Relations With Our Eastern and Southern Neighbours*, Com (2003) 104 final, 11 March.

European Commission (2004) *Communication from the Commission to the Council and the European Parliament: Building Our Common Future Policy Challenges and Budgetary Means of the Enlarged European Union 2007–2013*, Com (2004) 101 final.

European Commission (2005a) *Report from the Commission on the Working of Committees During 2004*, Com (2005) 554 final, 10 November.

European Commission (2005b) *General Report on the Activities of the European Union: 2004* (Luxembourg: EUR-OP).

European Commission (2005c) *Communication from the Commission to the Council, the European Parliament, the European Economic and Social Committee and the Committee of the Regions: i2010 A European Information Society for Growth and Employment*, Com (2005) 229 final, 1 June.

European Commission (2005d) *Doing More With Less: Green Paper on Energy Efficiency*, Com (2005) 265 final, 22 June.

European Commission (2005e) *Communication to the Spring European Council. Working Together For Growth and Jobs A New Start For the Lisbon Strategy*, Com (2005) 24, 2 February.

European Commission (2005f) *White Paper: Financial Services Policy 2005–2010*, Sec (2005) 1574, 1 December.

European Commission (2005g) *Key Facts and Figures About Europe and Europeans* (Luxembourg: OOPEC).

European Commission (2006) *General Budget of the European Union For the Financial Year 2006* (Luxembourg: OOPEC).

European Communities (1987) 'Interinstitutional Agreement on Budgetary Discipline', *Official Journal*, L185/33, 15 July.

European Council (1992) *Conclusions of the Presidency*, Lisbon, 26–27 June (Brussels: General Secretariat of the Council).

European Council (1993) *Conclusions of the Presidency*, Copenhagen, 21–22 June (Brussels: General Secretariat of the Council).

European Council (1994) *Presidency Conclusions*, Corfu, 24–25 June (Brussels: General Secretariat of the Council).

European Council (1997a) *Presidency Conclusions*, Amsterdam, 16–17 June (Brussels: General Secretariat of the Council).

European Council (1997b) *Presidency Conclusions*, Luxembourg, 12–13 December, Europa website.

European Council (1998) *Presidency Conclusions*, Cardiff, 15–16 June, Europa website.

European Council (1999a) *Presidency Conclusions*, Berlin, 24–25 March, Europa website.

European Council (1999b) *Presidency Conclusions*, Cologne, 3–4 June, Europa website.

European Council (1999c) *Presidency Conclusions*, Tampere, 15–16 October, Europa website.

European Council (1999d) *Presidency Conclusions*, Helsinki, 10–11 December, Europa website.

European Council (2000a) *Presidency Conclusions*, Santa Maria Da Feira, 19–20 June, Europa website.

European Council (2000b) *Presidency Conclusions*, Lisbon, 23–24 March, Europa website.

European Council (2000c) *Presidency Conclusions*, Nice, 7–9 December, Europa website.

European Council (2001) *Presidency Conclusions*, Laeken, 14–15 December, Europa website.

European Council (2002a) *Presidency Conclusions*, Seville, 21–22 June, Europa website.

European Council (2002b) *Presidency Conclusions*, Copenhagen, 12–13 December, Europa website.

European Council (2003) *A Secure Europe in a Better World: European Security Strategy*, Brussels, 12 December, Europa website.

European Council (2005a) *Presidency Conclusions, Brussels*, 22–23 March, Europa website.

European Council (2005b) *Presidency Conclusions*, Brussels, 15–16 December, Europa website.

European Court of Justice (2005) *Statistics Concerning the Judicial Activity of the Court of Justice and the Court of First Instance*, accessed from the Court of Justice's web pages on the Europa website.

European Investment Bank (2005) *Financing Europe's Future*, EIB web pages on Europa website.

European Parliament (2001) *Draft Treaty of Nice (Initial Analysis)* (Brussels: Directorate General for Committees and Delegations).

European Parliament (2005) *Rules of Procedure*, Europa website.

Featherstone, K. and Radaelli, C. (2003) (eds) *The Politics of Europeanization*, (Oxford: Oxford University Press).

Forster, A. (1998) 'Britain and the Negotiation of the Maastricht Treaty: A Critique of Liberal Intergovernmentalism', *Journal of Common Market Studies*, 36(3): 347–68.

Forster, A. and Blair, A. (2002) *The Making of Britain's European Foreign Policy* (London: Longman).

Forster, A. and Wallace, W. (2000) 'Common Foreign and Security Policy', in H. Wallace and W Wallace, *op. cit.*: 461–91.

Galloway, D. (2001) *The Treaty of Nice and Beyond: Realities and Illusions of Power in the EU* (Sheffield: Sheffield Academic Press).

Garrett, G. (1992) 'International Cooperation and Institutional Choice: The European Community's Internal Market', *International Organization*, 49: 533–60.

Garrett, G. (1993) 'The Politics of Maastricht', *Economics and Politics*, 5(2): 105–24.

Garrett, G. and Tsebelis, G. (1996) 'An Institutionalist Critique of Intergovernmentalism', *International Organization*, 50(2): 269–99.

Garzon, I. (2006) *Paradigm Shift in the Common Agricultural Policy* (Basingstoke: Palgrave Macmillan).

George, S. (1994) 'Supranational Actors and Domestic Politics: Integration Theory Reconsidered in the Light of the Single European Act and Maastricht', *Sheffield Papers in International Studies*, no. 22 (Department of Politics, University of Sheffield). Also published in Nugent (1997a): 387–408.

George, S. and Bache, I. (2001) *Politics in the European Union* (Oxford: Oxford University Press).

Ginsberg, R. H. (1999) 'Conceptualising the European Union as an International Actor: Narrowing the Theoretical Capability-Expectations Gap', *Journal of Common Market Studies*, 37(3): 424–54.

Ginsberg, R. H. (2001) *The European Union in International Politics: Baptism by Fire* (Boulder, CO: Rowman & Littlefield).

Giustino, D. de (1996) *A Reader in European Integration* (London: Longman).

Goetz, K. and Hix, S. (2001) *Europeanised Political European Integration and National Political Systems* (London: Frank Cass).

Grabbe, H (2005) *The EU's Transformative Power: Europeanization Through Conditionality in Central and Eastern Europe* (Basingstoke: Palgrave Macmillan).

Grant, W. (1997) *The Common Agricultural Policy* (Basingstoke: Macmillan – now Palgrave Macmillan).

Green Cowles, M. and Dinan, D. (2004) *Developments in the European Union 2*, (Basingstoke: Palgrave Macmillan).

Green Cowles, M., Caporaso, J. and Risse, T. (2001) (eds) *Transforming Europe: Europeanization and Domestic Change* (Ithaca: Cornell University Press).

Greer, A (2005) *Agricultural Policy in Europe* (Manchester: Manchester University Press).

Greenwood, J. (2003) *Interest Representation in the European Union* (Basingstoke: Macmillan – now Palgrave Macmillan).

Grieco, J. M. (1995) 'The Maastricht Treaty, Economic and Monetary Union and the Neo-realist Research Programme', *Review of International Studies*, 2: 21–40.

Haas, E. B. (1958) *The Uniting of Europe: Political, Social and Economic Forces 1950–57* (Stanford, CA: Stanford University Press).

Hall, P. A. and Taylor, R. C. R. (1996) 'Political Science and the Three New Institutionalisms', *Political Studies*, 44(5): 936–57.

Hallstein, W (1972) *Europe in the Making* (London: Allen & Unwin).

Hanlon, J. (1998) *European Community Law* (London: Sweet & Maxwell).

Harryvan, A. G. and van der Harst, J. (1997) (eds) *Documents on European Union* (Basingstoke: Macmillan – now Palgrave Macmillan).

Hartley, T. C. (2003) *The Foundations of European Community Law*, 5th edn (Oxford: Clarendon Press).

Hayes-Renshaw, F. and Wallace, H. (2006) *The Council of Ministers*, 2nd edn., (Basingstoke: Palgrave Macmillan).

Héritier, A. *et al.* (2001) *Differential Europe: The European Union Impact on National Policymakers* (Lanham: Rowman & Littlefield).

Hill, C. and Smith, M. (2005) *International Relations and the European Union* (Oxford: Oxford University Press).

Hix, S. (1994) 'The Study of the European Community: The Challenge to Comparative Politics', *West European Politics*, 17(1): 1–30.

Hix, S. (1998) 'The Study of the European Union II: The New Governance Agenda and its Rival', *Journal of European Public Policy*, 5(1): 38–65.

Hix, S. (2002) 'What Role for the European Parliament in a More Democratic European Union?', *One Europe or Several? – Newsletter*, 7 (Brighton: University of Sussex).

Hix, S. (2005) *The Political System of the European Union*, 2nd edn (Basingstoke: Macmillan – now Palgrave Macmillan).

Hix, S. and Lord, C. (1997) *Political Parties in the European Union* (Basingstoke: Macmillan – now Palgrave Macmillan).

Hodson, D. and Maher, I. (2001) 'The Open Method as a New Mode of Governance: The Case of Soft Economic Policy Co-ordination', *Journal of Common Market Studies*, 39(4): 719–46.

Hoffmann, S. (1966) 'Obstinate or Obsolete: The Fate of the Nation State and the Case of Western Europe', *Daedelus*, 95: 862–915.

Hoffmann, S. (1982) 'Reflection on the Nation State in Western Europe Today', *Journal of Common Market Studies*, 21(1–2): 21–37.

Holland, M. (2002) *The European Union and the Third World* (Basingstoke: Palgrave – now Palgrave Macmillan).

Hooghe, L. (1996) *Cohesion Policy and European Integration: Building Multi-Level Governance* (Oxford: Oxford University Press).

Hooghe, L. (2001) *The European Commission and the Integration of Europe: Images of Governance* (Cambridge: Cambridge University Press).

Hooghe, L. and Marks, G. (2001) (eds) *Multi-Level Governance and European Integration* (Oxford: Rowman & Littlefield).

Howe, P. (1995) 'A Community of Europeans: The Requisite Underpinnings', *Journal of Common Market Studies*, 33(1): 27–46.

Jacqué, J. P. (2004) *Droit Institutionnel de L'Union Europénne*, Paris: Dalloz.

Jeffery, C. (2002) 'Social and Regional Interests: The ESC and Committee of the Regions', in J. Peterson and M. Shackleton, *op. cit.*: 326–46.

Joint Statement by the Council and Representatives of the Governments Meeting Within the Council, the European Parliament and the Commission (2005) *The European Consensus on Development*, Europa website.

Judge, D. and Earnshaw, D. (2003) *The European Parliament* (Basingstoke: Palgrave Macmillan).

Kassim, H. (1994) 'Policy Networks, Networks and European Union Policy Making: A Sceptical View', *West European Politics*, 17(4): 15–27.

Kassim, H., Peters, B. G. and Wright, V. (2000) (eds) *The National Coordination of EU Policy: The Domestic Level* (Oxford: Oxford University Press).

Keohane, R. O. and Hoffman, S. (1991) *The New European Community* (Oxford: Westview Press).

Keohane, R. and Nye, J. (1977) *Power and Interdependence: World Politics in Transition* (Boston, MA: Little, Brown).

Kohler-Koch, B. and Eising, R. (1999) (eds) *Transformation of Governance in the European Union* (London: Routledge).

Kok, W. (2004) *Facing the Challenge: The Lisbon Strategy for Growth and Employment Report From the High Level Working Group Chaired by Wim Kok*, November, Europa website.

Koslowski, R. (1999) 'A Constructivist Approach to Understanding the European Union as a Federal Polity', *Journal of European Public Policy*, 6(4): 561–78.

Kreppel, A. (2000) 'Rules and Ideology and Coalition Formation in the European Parliament: Past, Present and Future', *European Union Politics*, 1(3): 340–62.

Kreppel, A. and Tsebelis, G. (1999) 'Coalition Formation in the European Parliament', *Comparative Political Studies*, 38(2): 933–66.

Kuasmanen, A. (1998) 'Decision-Making in the Council of the European Union', in L. Goetschel (ed.), *Small States Inside and Outside the European Union* (London: Kluwer): 65–78.

Laffan, B. (2002) 'Financial Control: The Court of Auditors and OLAF', in J. Peterson and M. Shackleton, *op. cit.*: 231–53.

Langenberg, P. (2004) 'The Role of the Member States in the European Union', in P. W. Meerts and F. Cede (eds), *op. cit.*, 51–70.

Laursen, F. (2006) *The Treaty of Nice: Actor Preferences, Bargaining and Institutional Choice* (Leiden: Martinus Niijhoff)

Lenaerts, K. (1991) 'Some Reflections on the Separation of Powers in the EU', *Common Market Law Review*, 28: 11–35.

Levitt, M. and Lord, C. (2000) *The Political Economy of Monetary Union* (Basingstoke: Macmillan – now Palgrave Macmillan).

Lijphart, A. (1969) 'Consociational Democracy', *World Politics*, 21(2): 207–25.

Lindberg, L. N. (1963) *The Political Dynamics of European Economic Integration* (Oxford: Oxford University Press).

Lowi, T. J. (1964) 'American Business, Public Policy, Case-Studies and Political Theory', *World Politics*, 16(4): 677–715.

Macmullen, A. (2000) 'European Commissioners: National Routes to a European Elite', in N. Nugent, *op. cit.*: 28–50.

Magnette, P. (2005) *What is the European Union: Nature and Prospects* (Basingstoke: Palgrave Macmillan).

Majone, G. (1992) 'Regulatory Federalism in the European Community', *Environment and Planning C: Government and Policy*, 10(3): 299–316.

Majone, G. (1994) 'The Rise of the Regulatory State in Europe', *West European Politics*, 17(3): 77–101.

Majone, G. (1996) *Regulating Europe* (London: Routledge).

Marjolin, R. (1989) *Memoirs 1911–1986* (London: Weidenfeld & Nicolson).

Marks, G., Hooghe, L. and Black, K. (1996) 'European Integration from the 1980s: State Centric v Multi-level Governance', *Journal of Common Market Studies*, 34(3): 341–78.

Mathijsen, P. S. R. F. (2004) *A Guide to European Community Law*, 8th edn (London: Sweet & Maxwell).

Matlary, J. H. (1993) 'Beyond Intergovernmentalism: The Quest for a Comprehensive Framework for the Study of Integration', *Cooperation and Conflict*, 28(2): 181–210.

Mattila, M. and Lane, J.-E. (2001) 'Why Unanimity in the Council? A Roll Call Analysis of Council Voting', *European Union Politics*, 2(1): 31–52.

McCormick, J. (2001) *Environmental Policy in the European Union* (Basingstoke: Palgrave – now Palgrave Macmillan).

McCormick, J. (2005) *Understanding the European Union: A Concise Introduction*, 3rd edn (Basingstoke: Palgrave – now Palgrave Macmillan).

McNamara, K. (2002) 'Managing the Euro: The European Central Bank', in J. Peterson and M. Shackleton, *op. cit.*: 164–85.

Meerts, P.W. and Cede, F. (2004) *Negotiating European Union* (Basingstoke: Palgrave Macmillan).

Meunier, S. and Nicolaidis, K. (2001) 'Trade Competence in the Nice Treaty', *ECSA Review*, 14(2): 7–8.

Miles, L. (2005) (ed.) *Journal of Common Market Studies: The European Union Annual Review 2004/2005* (Oxford: Blackwell).

Milward, A. S. (1984) *The Reconstruction of Western Europe 1945–51* (London: Methuen).

Milward, A. S. (2000) *The European Rescue of the Nation-State*, 2nd edn (London: Routledge).

Monar, J. (2002) 'Institutionalising Freedom, Security, and Justice', in J. Peterson and M. Shackleton, *op. cit.*: 186–209.

Monar, J. (2005) 'Justice and Home Affairs', in L. Miles *op cit*: 13–46.

Monar, J. and Wessels, W. (2001) *The European Union After the Amsterdam Treaty* (London: Continuum).

Monnet, J. (1978) *Memoirs* (London: Collins).

Moravcsik, A. (1991) 'Negotiating the Single European Act: National Interests and Conventional Statecraft in the European Community', *International Organization*, 45(1): 19–56.

Moravcsik, A. (1993) 'Preferences and Power in the European Community: A Liberal Intergovernmentalist Approach', *Journal of Common Market Studies*, 31(4): 473–524.

Moravcsik, A. (1995) 'Liberal Intergovernmentalism and Integration: A Rejoinder', *Journal of Common Market Studies*, 33(4): 611–28.

Moravcsik, A. (1998) *The Choice for Europe: Social Purpose and State Power from Messina to Maastricht* (Ithaca, NY: Cornell University Press).

Nelsen, B. and Stubb, A. C.-G. (2003) *The European Union: Readings on the Theory and Practice of European Integration*, 3rd edn (Basingstoke: Macmillan – now Palgrave Macmillan).

Nicoll, W. and Salmon, T. C. (2001) *Understanding the European Union* (London: Harvester Wheatsheaf).

Norman, P. (2003) *The Accidental Constitution: The Story of the European Convention* (Brussels: Eurocomment).

Nugent, N. (1997a) (ed.) *The European Union. Volume I: Perspectives and Theoretical Interpretations* (Aldershot: Dartmouth).

Nugent, N. (1997b) (ed.) *The European Union. Volume II: Policy Processes* (Aldershot: Dartmouth).

Nugent, N. (2000) (ed.) *At the Heart of the Union: Studies of the European Commission*, 2nd edn (Basingstoke: Macmillan – now Palgrave Macmillan).

Nugent, N. (2001) *The European Commission* (Basingstoke: Palgrave – now Palgrave Macmillan).

Nugent, N. (2004) (ed.) *European Union Enlargement* (Basingstoke: Palgrave Macmillan).

Nugent, N. and Saurugger, S. (2002) 'Organisational Structuring: The Case of the European Commission and its External Relations Responsibilities', *Journal of European Public Policy*, 9(3): 345–64.

Official Journal of the European Union (various issues) (Luxembourg: EUR-OP, published most working days).

Olsen, J. (2002) 'The Many Faces of Europeanization', *Journal of Common Market Studies*, 40(5): 921–52.

O'Neill, M. (1996) *The Politics of European Integration: A Reader* (London: Routledge).

O'Neill, M. (2000) 'Theorising the European Union: Towards a Post-Foundational Disclosure', *Current Politics and Economics of Europe*, 9(2): 121–45.

Page, E. C. (1997) *People Who Run Europe* (Oxford: Clarendon Press).

Peters, B. G. and Wright, V. (2001) 'The National Co-ordination of European Policy-Making', in J. Richardson, *op. cit.*: 155–78.

Peterson, J. (1995) 'Decision-Making in the EU: Towards a Framework for Analysis', *Journal of European Public Policy*, 2(1): 69–93.

Peterson, J. and Bomberg, E. (1999) *Decision-Making in the European Union* (Basingstoke: Macmillan – now Palgrave Macmillan).

Peterson, J. and Shackleton, M. (2002) (eds) *The Institutions of the European Union* (Oxford: Oxford University Press).

Peterson, J. and Shackleton, M. (2006) (eds) *The Institutions of the European Union*, 2nd edn (Oxford: Oxford University Press).

Peterson, J. and Sharp, M. (1998) *Technology Policy in the European Union* (Basingstoke: Macmillan – now Palgrave Macmillan).

Phinnemore, D. (2004) *Treaty Establishing a Constitution for Europe: An Overview* (London: Royal Institute of International Affairs).

Piening, C. (1997) *Global Europe: The European Union in World Affairs* (London: Lynne Rienner).

Pierson, P. (1996) 'The Path to European Integration: A Historical Institutionalist Analysis', *Comparative Political Studies*, 29(2): 123–63.

Pierson, P. (1998) 'The Path to European Integration: A Historical Institutionalist Analysis', in W. Sandholtz and A. Stone Sweet, *op. cit.*: 27–58.

Pollack, M. (1994) 'Creeping Competence: The Expanding Agenda of the European Community', *Journal of Public Policy*, 14(2): 95–145.

Pollack, M. (1998) 'The Engines of Integration? Supranational Autonomy and Influence in the European Union', in W. Sandholtz and A. Stone Sweet, *op. cit.*: 217–49.

Pollack, M. A. (2000) 'The End of Creeping Competence? EU Policy-Making since Maastricht', *Journal of Common Market Studies*, 38(3): 519–38.

Pollack, M. A. (2003) *The Engines of European Integration: Delegation, Agency and Agenda-Setting in the EU* (Oxford; Oxford University Press).

Pollack, M. A. (2004) 'The New Institutionalisms and European Integration' in A. Wiener and T. Diez (eds) *op cit*, 137–56.

Pollack, M. A. (2005) 'Theorising EU Policy-Making', in H. Wallace *et al.*, *op. cit.*: 13–48.

Pollard, S. (1981) *The Integration of the European Economy since 1815* (London: George Allen & Unwin).

Preston, C. (1995) 'Obstacles to EU Enlargement: The Classical Community Method and the Prospects for a Wider Europe', *Journal of Common Market Studies*, 33(3): 451–63.

Putnam, R. D. (1988) 'Diplomacy and Domestic Politics: The Logic of Two-Level Games', *International Organization*, 42(3): 427–60.

Rees, N. and Holmes, M. (2002) 'Capacity, Perceptions and Principles: Ireland's Changing Place in Europe', *Current Politics and Economics of Europe*, 11(1): 49–60.

Regelsberger, E., de Schoutheete de Tervarent, P. and Wessels, W. (eds) (1997) *Foreign Policy of the European Union: From EPC to CFSP and Beyond* (Boulder, CO: Lynne Rienner).

Rhodes, R. A. W., Bache, I. and George, S. (1996) 'Policy Networks and Policy-Making in the European Union: A Critical Appraisal', in L. Hooghe, *op. cit.*

Richardson, J. (ed.) (2001) *European Union: Power and Policy-Making*, 2nd edn (London: Routledge).

Richardson, J. (ed.) (2006) *European Union: Power and Policy-Making*, 3rd edn (London: Routledge).

Robertson, A. H. (1961) *The Council of Europe: Its Structure, Functions and Achievements* (London: Stevens).

Rometsch, D. and Wessels, W. (1996) *The European Union and Member States: Towards Institutional Fusion?* (Manchester: Manchester University Press).

Rosamond, B. (1995) 'Understanding European Unity: The Limits of Nation-State-Centric Integration Theory', *The European Legacy*, 1: 291–7.

Rosamond, B. (2000) *Theories of European Integration* (Basingstoke: Macmillan – now Palgrave Macmillan).

Ross, G. (2001) 'France's European Tour of Duty, or Caution – One Presidency May Hide Another', *ECSA Review*, 14(2): 4–6.

Salmon, T. and Nicoll, W. (1997) *Building European Union: A Documentary History and Analysis* (Manchester: Manchester University Press).

Sandholtz, W. (1996) 'Membership Matters: Limits of the Functional Approach to European Institutions', *Journal of Common Market Studies*, 34(3): 403–29.

Sandholtz, W. and Stone Sweet, A. (eds) (1998) *European Integration and Supranational Governance* (Oxford: Oxford University Press).

Sbragia, A. (1992) 'Thinking About the European Future: The Uses of Comparison', in A. Sbragia (ed.), *Euro-Politics: Institutions and Policymaking in the 'New' European Community* (Washington, DC: Brookings Institution).

Schimmelfennig, F. (2001) 'The Community Trap: Liberal Norms, Rhetorical Action, and the Eastern Enlargement of the European Union', *International Organization*, 55 (1): 47–80.

Schimmelfennig, F. (2002) 'Liberal Community and Enlargement: An Event History Analysis', *Journal of European Public Policy*, 9(4): 598–626.

Schmitter, P. (2004) 'Neo-Neofunctionalism', in A. Wiener and T. Diez (eds), *op. cit.*: 45–74.

Schneider, G. and Aspinwall, M. (2001) (eds) *The Rules of Integration: Institutional Approaches to the Study of Europe* (Manchester: Manchester University Press).

Schneider, V., Dang-Nguyen, G. and Werle, R. (1994) 'Corporate Actor Networks in European Policy-Making: Harmonizing Telecommunications Policy', *Journal of Common Market Studies*, 32(4): 473–98.

Sedelmeier, U. (2000) 'Eastern Enlargement: Risk, Rationality, and Role-Compliance', in M. Green Cowles and M. Smith (eds), *The State of the European Union: Volume 5 – Risks, Reform, Resistance, and Revival* (Oxford: Oxford University Press): 164–185.

Session News: The Week, Brussels: European Parliament Directorate for Press and Audiovisual Services (weekly).

Shackleton, M. (2002) 'The European Parliament', in J. Peterson and M. Shackleton, *op. cit.*: 95–117.

Sherrington, P. (2000) *The Council of Ministers: Political Authority in the European Union* (London: Pinter).

Sjursen, H. (2002) 'Why Expand? The Question of Legitimacy and Justification in the EU's Enlargement Policy', *Journal of Common Market Studies*, 40(3): 491–513.

Smith, A. C. (1992) 'National Identity and the Idea of European Unity', *International Affairs*, 68(1): 55–76.

Spinelli, A. (1986) 'Foreword', in J. Lodge (ed.), *European Union: The European Community in Search of a Future* (London: Macmillan – now Basingstoke: Palgrave Macmillan): xiii–xviii.

Steiner, J., Woods, L. and Twigg-Flesner, C. (2003) *Textbook on EU Law*, 8th edn (London: Blackstone Press).

Stevens, A. and Stevens, H. (2001) *Brussels Bureaucrats? The Administration of the European Union* (Basingstoke: Palgrave – now Palgrave Macmillan).

Stirk, P. M. R. (1996) *A History of European Integration since 1914* (London: Pinter).

Stirk, P. and Weigall, D. (eds) (1999) *The Origins and Development of European Integration: A Reader and Commentary* (London: Pinter).

Stone Sweet, A. and Sandholtz, W. (1997) 'European Integration and Supranational Governance', *Journal of European Public Policy*, 4(3): 297–317.

Taylor, P. (1991) 'The European Community and the State: Assumptions, Theories and Propositions', *Review of International Studies*, 17: 109–25.

Taylor, P. (1996) *The European Union in the 1990s* (Oxford: Oxford University Press).

Teasdale, A. (1995) 'The Luxembourg Compromise', in M. Westlake, *The Council of the European Union* (London: Cartermill): 104–10.

Thorhallsson, B. (2000) *The Role of Small States in the European Union* (Aldershot: Ashgate).

Tranholm-Mikkelsen, J. (1991) 'Neo-functionalism: Obstinate of Obsolete? A Reappraisal in the Light of the New Dynamism of the EC', *Millennium: Journal of International Studies*, 20: 1–22.

'Treaty Establishing a Constitution for Europe' (2004), Europa website.

'Treaty Establishing the European Community: Consolidated Version' (1997), in *Official Journal of the European Communities*, C340, 10 November; also in *European Union Consolidated Treaties* (Luxembourg: EUR-OP).

'Treaty of Amsterdam, Amending the Treaty on European Union, the Treaties Establishing the European Communities and Certain Related Acts' (1997), in *Official Journal of the European Communities*, C340, 10 November.

'Treaty of Nice, Amending the Treaty on European Union, the Treaties Establishing the European Communities and Certain Related Acts' (2001), in *Official Journal of the European Communities*, C80, 10 March 2001.

'Treaty on European Union, Together with the Complete Text of the Treaty Establishing the European Community' (1992), in *Official Journal of the European Communities*, C244, 31 August.

'Treaty on European Union: Consolidated Version' (1997), in *Official Journal of the European Communities*, C340, 10 November; also in *European Union Consolidated Treaties* (Luxembourg: EUR-OP).

Tsebelis, G. and Garrett, G. (1997) 'Agenda Setting, Vetoes and the European Union's Co-Decision Procedure', *Journal of Legislative Studies*, 3(1): 74–92.

Tsebelis, G. and Garrett, G. (2001) 'The Institutionalist Foundations of Intergovernmentalism and Supranationalism in the European Union', *International Organization*, 55(2): 357–90.

Urwin, D. W (1995) *The Community of Europe: A History of European Integration since 1945*, 2nd edn (London: Longman).

Van Schendelen, M. P. C. M. (1996) 'The Council Decides: Does the Council Decide?', *Journal of Common Market Studies*, 34(4): 531–48.

Wallace, H. and Wallace, W. (2000) *Policy-Making in the European Union*, 4th edn (Oxford: Oxford University Press).

Wallace, H. and Young, A. R. (1997) *Participation and Policy-Making in the European Union* (Oxford: Clarendon Press).

Wallace, H., Wallace, W. and Pollack, M. (2005) *Policy-Making in the European Union*, 5th edn (Oxford: Oxford University Press).

Warleigh, A. (1998) 'Better the Devil You Know? Synthetic and Confederal Understandings of European Integration', *West European Politics*, 21(3): 1–18.

Warleigh, A. (2000) 'History Repeating? Framework Theory and Europe's Multi-Level Confederation', *Journal of European Integration*, 22: 173–200.

Warleigh, A. (2002) *Understanding European Union Institutions* (London: Routledge).

Webb, C. (1983) 'Theoretical Perspectives and Problems', in H. Wallace, W. Wallace and C. Webb (eds), *Policy Making in the European Community* (London: John Wiley): 1–41.

Wessels, W. (2001) 'Nice Results: The Millennium IGC in the EU's Evolution', *Journal of Common Market Studies*, 39(2): 197–219.

Wessels, W., Maurer, A. and Mittag, J. (2001) (eds) *Fifteen into One? The European Union and its Member States* (Manchester: Manchester University Press).

Westlake, M. (1997) 'Keynote Article: Mad Cows and Englishmen. The Institutional Consequences of the BSE Crisis', in N. Nugent (ed.), *The European Union 1996: Annual Review of Activities* (Oxford: Blackwell): 11–36.

Westlake, M. (1999) *The Council of the European Union*, rev. edn (London: John Harper).

Wiener, A. and Diez, T. (2004) (eds) *European Integration Theory*, (Oxford: Oxford University Press).

Wincott, D. (1995) 'Institutional Interaction and European Integration: Towards an Everyday Critique of Liberal Intergovernmentalism', *Journal of Common Market Studies*, 33(4): 597–609.

Wincott, D. (1999) 'The Court of Justice and the Legal System', in L. Cram *et al.*, *op. cit.*: 84–104.

Wood, D. and Yesilada, B. (2002) *The Emerging European Union*, 2nd edn (London: Longman).

Index